AF594575

HEBREWS

COMMENTARIES FOR CHRISTIAN FORMATION

Stephen E. Fowl, Jennie Grillo, and Robert W. Wall
Series editors

The **Commentaries for Christian Formation** (CCF) series serves a central purpose of the Word of God for the people of God: faith formation. Some series focus on exegesis, some on preaching, some on teaching, and some on application. This new series integrates all these aims, serving the church by showing how sound theological exegesis can underwrite preaching and teaching, which in turn form believers in the faith.

Uniting these volumes is a shared conviction that interpreting Scripture is not an end in itself. Faithful belief, prayer, and practice, deeper love of God and neighbor: these are ends of scriptural interpretation for Christians. The volumes in Commentaries for Christian Formation interpret Scripture in ways aimed at ordering readers' lives and worship in imitation of Christ, informing their understanding of God, and animating their participation in the church's global mission with a deepened sense of calling.

HEBREWS

Amy Peeler

William B. Eerdmans Publishing Company
Grand Rapids, Michigan

Wm. B. Eerdmans Publishing Co.
4035 Park East Court SE, Grand Rapids, Michigan 49546
www.eerdmans.com

Published 2024
Printed in the United States of America

30 29 28 27 26 25 24 1 2 3 4 5 6 7

ISBN 978-0-8028-7738-3

Library of Congress Cataloging-in-Publication Data

A catalog record for this book is available from the Library of Congress.

CONTENTS

SERIES INTRODUCTION

The **Commentaries for Christian Formation** series serves a central purpose of the Word of God for the people of God: faith formation. Some series focus on exegesis, some on preaching, some on teaching, and some on application. This new series integrates all these aims, serving the church by showing how sound theological exegesis can underwrite preaching and teaching, which in turn forms believers in the faith.

Although we encourage all believers to pick up Scripture and read it, we do not assume that the work of Scripture happens easily or well without the guidance of others. The basis of this guidance is the Holy Spirit, who leads believers into all truth (John 16:13) and calls to mind the words and deeds of Jesus (John 13:26). One way the Spirit accomplishes this work is through the work of dedicated commentators. Along with the Ethiopian eunuch in Acts 8, we recognize that it is often hard to understand Scripture without someone to teach us. Thus, these commentaries play the role of Philip in Acts, explaining texts in ways that make the church's gospel manifest to expectant readers. Each volume aims to help its readers enter into conversation with the church's canonical heritage, especially its two-testament Scripture and the ecumenical creeds. Further, a theological commentary must consider the various ways in which Scripture performs in worship, catechesis, mission, and devotion to cultivate theological understanding and holy living within and for readers' cultural settings. If a commentary cannot help Christians negotiate a faithful path through life and deepen their love for God and all their neighbors, it is not clear that it is truly a theological commentary.

Given these commitments, we take both parts of the term "theological commentary" seriously. The authors of these commentaries strive to keep theological concerns and ecclesial practices, broadly conceived, in the forefront of their interpretive work, paying attention to the ways Scripture shapes and is shaped by theology. Many recent commentaries distinguish historically informed exegetical work from the theological, moral, and pastoral concerns that animate the imaginations of most commentary readers. This bifurcation reflects a pattern typically found in today's seminaries, where Scripture is taught separately from the theological disciplines. We are eager to avoid the modern tendency to compartmentalize the tasks of exegesis and theological reflection. Theology is not the result of exegesis; nor is it one discrete element that is separable from exegesis carried on by other means. Rather, *exegesis is itself a way of doing theology*.

Thinking this way does not limit the questions and concerns believers might bring to scriptural interpretation: we do not require or expect a specified interpretive method from the commentators in this series. What unites these volumes is a shared conviction that interpreting Scripture is not an end in itself. Faithful belief, prayer, and practice, deeper love of God and neighbor: these are ends of scriptural interpretation for Christians. The volumes in **Commentaries for Christian Formation** interpret Scripture in ways aimed at ordering readers' lives and worship in imitation of Christ, informing their understanding of God, and animating their participation in the church's global mission with a deepened sense of calling.

PREFACE

The Baptist church in which I grew up and the faithful witness and encouragement of my parents inspired me to be a regular reader of Scripture. I am sure I had read Hebrews before, but the first time I remember being captured by it was in high school, when I came to this verse: "For if we continue in sin willingly after receiving the knowledge of the truth, there no longer remains a sacrifice concerning sins but a certain fearful expectation of judgment and a zeal of fire that is about to devour the adversaries" (Heb 10:26–27). I had gossiped when I knew I should not, watched a PG-13 movie that transgressed my conscience, and committed other sins about which I had the knowledge of the truth but did anyway. What did this mean for my salvation?! A wise teacher at my Christian high school encouraged me not to despair but to keep reading. Not only did I find that the sin under discussion in this passage was apostasy, not succumbing to peer pressure (see 10:29), but I also discovered some of the most assuring passages in all the New Testament, and they too were in Hebrews. A key verse in that early encounter was Heb 10:14: "For by one offering he has perfected forever those who are being sanctified." Hebrews taught me that God knows our finitude and propensity to succumb to temptation. Therefore, God has made continual access to perfection possible through the priesthood of Jesus the Messiah so that we can continually grow in sanctification. It was a basic lesson, but I desperately needed to learn it: Christians will take actions we know we should not—we will sin—and we can ask forgiveness through Christ.

My appreciation for Hebrews continued throughout my education, and as it came time to declare my particular path within biblical studies, I knowingly selected to become a Hebrews scholar. As someone who wanted to teach undergraduate students, I knew this epistle would keep me tethered to both testaments with its many citations of Israel's Scriptures and resonances with other New Testament books, aiding my ability to keep before them the grand narrative of God's salvation. Admittedly, some of my reasons were less spiritual and more practical. While I was energized by the letters of Paul, that field was quite full. The field of Hebrews, at the time, was only beginning to flower again as a vibrant community, so it seemed spacious enough for a young scholar to find her voice. The community was erudite and also welcoming. The first session on Hebrews I attended at the Society of Biblical Literature (SBL) featured several young female scholars (among them Pamela Eisenbaum and Gabriella Gelardini). As the tagline for Logia proclaims, I could be who I could see. I could see myself as a part of this group. The first time I presented at SBL, Eric Mason and George Guthrie took time to get to know me and George even introduced me to publishers. I had found my community.

As I had opportunity to keep researching, presenting, and teaching on Hebrews, I realized that many readers, myself included, needed guidance to begin to see how this author's complex argument creates a powerful picture of the beauty of God's faithfulness. When the invitation was presented to write this commentary, I knew it would give me the opportunity to seek out this guidance and then contribute some of my own. Unlike writing a dissertation on a focused thesis or a chapter on a particular theme in Hebrews, in this work I could take up the discipline of persistent and thorough study in an effort to understand the whole. Not everyone was drawn to this book as I was; some, in fact, were repelled by it. I could draw from the appreciation I had for this sermon and my experience in its interpretive community to invite others to hear the voice of God speaking therein. Like a docent in a museum, I imagined I could provide some orientation and encouragement to see the art of this letter; my goal was to propel readers not to hang on my words but to linger longer with the piece.

When I was first approached by my series editors, Rob Wall and Stephen Fowl, to formally present the invitation to write a theological commentary on Hebrews, one of my initial questions was this: how would one write a nontheological commentary on Hebrews? That question indicates something about the time and places in which I've come through the academy. It has been the norm for me from undergrad to PhD to ask, "What do these texts reveal about God and about the world in relationship with God?" Theological interpretation has always been the air that I've breathed. Commentaries for Christian Formation hit the bullseye of the kind of interpretation I wanted to do, as one called to teach in the church and in the Christian academy, the central goal being to discover afresh the Lord in Hebrews in order to deepen the faith of teachers, whether they be small group leaders, professors, clergy, spritiual directors, mentors, or parents, so that they could, in turn, deepen the faith of those they taught.

One can imagine, then, that the writing of a theological commentary plays to my natural inclinations but has also invited me and sometimes has demanded of me that I recognize, describe, and press more deeply into that previously unquestioned process of breathing. That process has not been easy, but it has made me, I hope, a better theological interpreter.

To achieve a vision of the whole, as coherently and deeply as possible, my primary method was to read through Hebrews slowly, and do that multiple times. First, I sketched out my ideas of what the text was saying about God and, in turn, the world. Then I read interpreters from the past and wrote my way through, again expanding the commentary. Next I sought out the most recent scholarship to see what ideas I had not noticed and then wrote through again. It was important to me to learn from the influential giants in the field as well as those insightful interpreters whose voices take more effort to discover. It was as I sent in these installments that my editor, Rob Wall, provided me thorough responses, sometimes at the level of formatting and mechanics. For example, I knew the importance of consulting the wisdom of other generations, especially in the genre of theological commentary, and did so not because I had to but because I benefited from it. But they had so many good things to say that my commentary became splattered with tidbits from a wide variety of previous interpreters. In my desire to include them, not only did I lose my own voice, but I also wasn't really reading them, but instead prooftexting from them. Appropriately, I was encouraged to read a few consistently and well instead of many in a poor way.

This is one of the greatest gifts Hebrews offers believers. Because of its complexity, it propels readers to study in community. This begins with its interconnectedness to the canonical community of authors. Students of Hebrews are inspired to go and read the stories of Israel that the author is discussing, and then also to compare with other New Testament books and their treatment of

God's faithfulness in Christ. The connection continues into church history as Hebrews provides the affirmations that led to key doctrines. Neither separated from what comes before it nor unrelated to what follows after, Hebrews never stands alone, and it is best studied with others who can provide insight to see connections that a single reader might not notice.

For the fourth round of writing, I sought to incorporate all the comments of my editor for each chapter, to smooth out the edges of a long and multilayered project into a coherent work. When I submitted that fourth version of chapter 1, my editor offered insightful, but I must admit gut-wrenching, feedback. "You've captured the 'what,'" he noted, "what this text says about God, but you've not yet pressed into the 'whys' and the 'so-what's.'" Related to this issue, he noted that I consistently used adjectives, sometimes artful ones, but did not define them. For example, about Heb 1:1, I had written, "In the stream of tradition in which this author stands, the communication of God—the fact that God spoke—remains a consistent and vital feature of the divine identity." He prodded: "What is vital about this feature?" I think he was saying that I was describing theology but not doing it.

That was hard to hear because I thought I was near the end, and yet it seemed I had not even begun the task of meaningful theological commentary. Although it was hard to swallow initially, I eventually concluded that he was exactly correct. I have recognized a propensity in my own writing style to collect data dutifully and sometimes even beautifully, but I needed honest assessment from wise readers to turn that data into something of value, something worth consulting.

In my effort to answer the whys and the so-whats it was quite natural to expand into other New Testament authors. As theological commentary engages both human and divine authors, it is fitting to consult what the divine author has expressed through other humans in the same sacred collection.

Through this long process of writing theological commentary, I have discovered a few principles. First, I do not believe the writing of a theological commentary can be rushed. I sense this is the case because this kind of writing is not formulaic. It is not the case, it seems to me, that one can proceed verse by verse, do the word studies and syntax analysis, research any historical/contextual issues, consult major interpreters, package all the data, and then move on to the next verse. That work is necessarily in the background, but it is preparatory, not the work itself. I believe there is a dynamism of the text because its author is living, both the human author within the mystery of being absent from the Body and present with the Lord and also the divine author, who has this frustrating tendency to move more slowly than I often desire. I own that maybe I'm coming up with theological excuses for my own ineptitude. But it does seem to me that, even for those blessed authors among us who don't need five or six drafts to get it right as I have, good writing, especially good writing about God, takes time; to write about the God who created time demands patience, fortitude, maturity. This has certainly been the case in my other writing. I needed to become the person who could write the book. There is no shortcut through this process. It simply takes time.

Second, a theological commentary within our faith traditions is by necessity a communal endeavor. It was not wrong for me to start with my own reading, for I too have something to contribute. I don't think, however, it would have been a faithful theological commentary if I had stopped there. God is so majestic and the word of God given to us is so rich that no one person can ever see its entirety. We need the voices of many interpreters from different times, places, and perspectives. Because this word is vast, there is still more that God desires to reveal through thoughtful engagement with these texts. We become both beneficiaries of and contributors to the chorus of interpreters. Theological commentary, focused on the inexhaustible depths of God's revelation, allows for many expressions because there can never be one final definitive interpretation.

That leads to a third point: the richness of the text allows a theological interpretation to press into ever deeper levels of meaning. My editor was precisely right to continue to urge me to press deeper into the whys and the so-whats. On the other hand, there is also a comfort in knowing that one can never get to the bottom of the depths of its meaning. I could always write more, but because I am not capable of providing the final word on this text, I also have the freedom to stop, to bring the work to a close even though more could be said.

Living with Hebrews has shaped the formation of my Christian life in countless ways, but it is possible to highlight a few particularly deep and persistent ways this has been true. First, it has provided a continual encouragement to prayer. Knowing that God already perceives what is in my heart better than I do, knowing that Jesus's one-time sacrifice grants me access, I can heed the encouragement to draw near with boldness to the throne of grace (Heb 4:16). Because of God's sovereignty over all things and compassion toward humanity, I rest assured that I will find precisely the mercy and grace I need at that moment. If my prayers are inadequate or if it is impossible to pray at all, I also remain confident that Jesus is praying on my behalf (Heb 7:25). This is the second feature that has shaped my formation and has deepened my sense of awareness of God's goodness. Whenever I go for prayer alone or with others, I know that our human words are joining into a conversation already in progress. God has ensured an intercessor within the very divine life of God in the person of the Son. His prayers are fully wise and fully beneficial. He intercedes at God's right hand, victoriously resurrected. Through Hebrews and particularly David Moffitt's insights into it, the ascension of our Lord has become an appropriately major feature of my Christology.

As the Son of God's prayers are wise and beneficial, so, too, are God's actions. Third and finally, Hebrews has continually reminded me that whatever I experience—especially difficulties that arise out of my confession of Christ (which have never even come close to what persecuted brothers and sisters across time and across the world have experienced)—these experiences are not a sign of God's absence or God's lack of compassionate awareness of my situation but are, instead, a sign of God's presence and estimation of my potential to grow in maturity. This assurance has aided my ability to heed Jesus's command to "rejoice and be glad when you are persecuted" (Matt 5:12). The race of faith is not easy, but it is good. God has a benevolent plan for the process and has already assured the final result. As the temptation toward comfort looms large for all believers, this truth that we should go outside the gate because Jesus is present there (Heb 13:13) allows us to choose the arduous and straight path as we follow our Lord, Savior, and brother Jesus the Messiah, who has already walked it and made it possible for us to do the same. As we stayed anchored to him we will arrive on the celebratory mountain of God with all the saints.

I am incredibly grateful to the many students who have journeyed through Hebrews with me at Wheaton, Nashotah House, and Northern Seminary and at many churches, including my own, St. Mark's Episcopal, where many members have delighted in Hebrews with me. Their questions and insights have never ceased to propel me more deeply into the exhortative beauty of this sermon. Research assistants have provided invaluable work along the way, especially the group who selflessly helped me the week the manuscript was due, including Megan Stidham, Becky Miller, Laura Howard, Belle Bryant, Josh McQuaid, and Addison Ream. Andy Iversen's careful research over the past several years into such topics as supercessionism and covenant has made my reading of Hebrews more coherent and careful, and, at the end of this writing process, Kevin Johnson's incisive eye has improved the clarity of this commentary a hundredfold.

I am in debt to the many interpreters of Hebrews cited throughout the commentary, the design of which allowed me to cite only a fraction of their influence on me. Although readers encounter her name several times, I am especially thankful for Dana Harris's careful work with the Greek text. In addition to the written word of scholars, I benefited numerous times from the verbally communicated insights and prayers of the commentary writing group hosted by Jeannine Brown.

Going through the process with Eerdmans has been a wonderful experience throughout. In addition to Rob Wall and Stephen Fowl, Trevor Thompson continually offered his oversight and support, and the good humor (and firm hand) of James Ernest and Shane White helped me see I could do more than what I thought possible when it came time to bring this to completion. Collaborating with Ryan Davis in the copyediting process, one that I had feared, turned out to be a delight, and I could not be more grateful for the graciousness and care exercised by Laurel Draper with the page proofs.

The constants in my life continued throughout this process, making it possible for me to do the work of listening to and learning from the early preacher who composed Hebrews. Thank you to everyone at FTXCrossFit, especially Joe Willmann, whose gift of John W. Kleinig's Leviticus and Hebrews commentaries greatly improved my ecumenical perspective. To my community at Wheaton, to my many friends, and also to my family, especially my mom, Pam, as well as my children, Kate, Maxson, and Kindred, I am incredibly grateful for the light you bring to my life and thought. Lance, thank you for being my very best friend and greatest cheerleader and for pulling several late nights with me the last week of this project.

From the time I was invited to do this commentary in 2017 until its completion in late 2023, as the Lord led me over several mountaintops and through a few pretty harrowing wilderness experiences (sometimes simultaneously!), the Epistle to the Hebrews was instrumental in helping me make sense of it all under the banner of God's trustworthy faithfulness. I pray that readers will find the resources I have collected here from so many of the wise and faithful before me an aid for their own race of faith.

The Feast of All Saints
2023

ABBREVIATIONS

AB	Anchor Bible
ACCS 10	Heen, Erik M., and Philip D. W. Krey, eds. *Hebrews*. Ancient Christian Commentary on Scripture, New Testament 10. Downers Grove, IL: InterVarsity Press, 2005.
2 Bar.	2 Baruch
BCP (1979)	Episcopal Church. *The Book of Common Prayer and Administration of the Sacraments and Other Rites and Ceremonies of the Church: Together with the Psalter or Psalms of David according to the Use of the Episcopal Church.* New York: Seabury, 1979.
BDAG	Danker, Frederick W., Walter Bauer, William F. Arndt, and F. Wilbur Gingrich. *Greek-English Lexicon of the New Testament and Other Early Christian Literature*. 3rd ed. Chicago: University of Chicago Press, 1999.
CBQ	*Catholic Biblical Quarterly*
1 Clem.	1 Clement
1 En.	1 Enoch
2 En.	2 Enoch
Herm. Mand.	Shepherd of Hermas, Mandates
Herm. Sim.	Shepherd of Hermas, Similitudes
JBL	*Journal of Biblical Literature*
Jub.	Jubilees
LNTS	Library of New Testament Studies
LSJ	Liddell, Henry George, Robert Scott, Henry Stuart Jones. *A Greek-*

	English Lexicon. 9th ed. with revised supplement. Oxford: Clarendon, 1996.
LW	*Luther's Works*
NA[28]	*Novum Testamentum Graece*, Nestle-Aland, 28th ed.
NETS	*A New English Translation of the Septuagint.* Edited by Albert Pietersma and Benjamin G. Wright. New York: Oxford University Press, 2007.
NICNT	New International Commentary on the New Testament
NovTSup	Supplements to Novum Testamentum
NPNF[1]	*Nicene and Post-Nicene Fathers*, Series 1
NPNF[2]	*Nicene and Post-Nicene Fathers*, Series 2
Odes Sol.	Odes of Solomon
RBS	Resources for Biblical Study
RCS 13	Rittgers, Ronald K., ed. *Hebrews, James.* Reformation Commentary on Scripture, New Testament 13. Downers Grove, IL: IVP Academic, 2017.
SNTSMS	Society for New Testament Studies Monograph Series
WA	*D. Martin Luthers Werke: kritische Gesammtausgabe* (*Weimarer Ausgabe*)
WBC	Word Biblical Commentary
WUNT	Wissenschaftliche Untersuchungen zum Neuen Testament

Introduction

This commentary arises out of a fundamental commitment that shapes the whole of my life: the belief that the Bible is God's good word. The documents included in the Bible are complicated, thoroughly human documents, both in their creation and in their assembly, a complexity the story of Hebrews demonstrates with particular intensity. It is through these very documents that followers of Jesus Christ have heard the voice of God. I share this seemingly paradoxical belief, that God chose to give divine revelation through a human collection. This is how God so often chooses to work, with and through humanity, from the stewarding of creation, to the administration of the law, to the word and work of the prophets, and chiefly in becoming human himself. We should not be surprised that the sacred text arrives through the same method.

The document that has long been referred to as the Epistle to the Hebrews is one piece of God's human-composed holy Scripture.[1] Although many questions remain unanswered, it is clear that Hebrews was written by a confessor of Jesus to a community who shared the same faith. This author builds on that confession of Christ to press his addressees on to more maturity. The document the church calls the Epistle to the Hebrews provides the same invitation for any believer in Jesus who takes it up and reads. It is a sermon for those who have heard God speak and accepted the message, for those who want to know God deeper and trust God more fully. It is written for those who need to be equipped to face whatever

1. A mention of a sermon "to the Hebrews" is first attested by Tertullian in *Modesty* 20.2, written at the beginning of the third century. See Erik A. de Boer, "Tertullian on 'Barnabas' Letter to the Hebrews' in *De pudicitia* 20.1–5," *Vigiliae Christianae* 68.3 (2014): 243–63.

challenges come against the radical confession of faith they have made, that the eternal Son of God is Jesus of Nazareth, crucified and risen, who advocates at God's right hand for all those who are following him to dwell with God forever.

That means that whenever anyone devotes themselves to studying this early sermon, they will hear God's voice with more richness as they pay attention to the human situation out of which this extended teaching arose. At the same time, God's communication through this text is not circumscribed by that original situation even though it arises from it. God is not inhibited by the fact that most subsequent readers are unaware of the details of this work's background. Since this is God's communication through human words, God can take those words and multiply their impact to inexhaustible ends in each and every new setting. Readers can trust that when they take up this book they will always hear God speaking and also that the speech will be for their good. The words will admonish or encourage as the Holy Spirit knows is needed by each reader. This particularized work can draw from both types of speech—that which provides challenge and that which offers comfort—because the spread of that spectrum appears readily in Hebrews. Readers will also discover that God's communication is not monodirectional but instead invites a response, as Hebrews itself displays when the audience voices their prayer to God near the end of the sermon (13:6). In addition to reading on our own, as Hebrews itself states, we need other believers to tune our ears to God's word (3:13). A commentary is one way to have a communal conversation. I have listened to this letter as well as other interpreters who have immersed themselves in it for most of my adult life. I share my slice of the conversation here, hoping that those who take up this commentary will find it beneficial for the dialogue they are having in prayer as well as the ongoing conversation about this ancient yet living sermon in which they participate with other believers. May we all be drawn to worship more fully the God who was willing to be our helper (13:6) as we study this sermon that extols God's faithfulness manifest through the enduring high priesthood of God's eternal Son.

THEOLOGY OF HEBREWS

Despite the fact that many things about Hebrews are mysterious, it is nevertheless clear that the author of Hebrews wishes to instill within his community this truth, that God is trustworthy, or, stated in his words, that the one who promised is faithful (10:23; 11:11). Given the difficulties of their present circumstances, in order to motivate them to trust God for their future, the author recalls for them God's fulfilled promises in the past. He highlights God's faithfulness to the people of Israel, including significant reflection on Abraham and his family (esp. 2:16; 6:13–16; 11:8–22), and chiefly he proclaims God's fulfilled promises to the Son, Jesus, their Lord. It is a move that is resonant with the one made by Paul, in which he demonstrates that gentiles can trust God's promises in Jesus Christ only to the degree that God has shown faithfulness to the covenant promises to Israel. Similarly, the author of Hebrews shows the consistency of God in fulfilling the covenant through the realization of the new covenant with the people of Israel (8:1–10:18), the seed of Abraham (2:14). The eternal Son, Jesus, who died on the cross and was raised from the dead, reveals divine trustworthiness with unparalleled power.

Christology

Jesus the Jewish Messiah is the focus of the sermon. As the radiance of God, he reveals with utmost clarity the trustworthiness of God. As explained further below, the textual anonymity of Hebrews was no barrier for the power of its Christology. From the sermon's beginning, the author lays out the two natures of the Son, his eternal relation with God as creator and sovereign in ch. 1 paired with his comprehensive taking of a human body and human experience in ch. 2, and this is only the majestic beginning. Then the author explains that it is the eternal Son who is called into the very human job of priesthood (5:1–5), on which the author spends the majority of his time in the center of the letter. Finally, at the close it is Jesus who is the one who has been the same from eternity past and will be the same to eternity future (13:8). Christology formed in response to the New Testament documents could have come to exist without Hebrews, given that this author's statements are coherent with those of other authors of the New Testament, but Christology would lack clarity and significant verve were this author's voice not part of the conversation.

This author's contribution of seeds that resulted in two-natures Christology is communicated in a distinct way. In a previous work I called attention to the distinctives of Jesus's sonship in this sermon.[2] By learning from other inter-

2. Amy L. B. Peeler, *You Are My Son: The Family of God in the Epistle to the Hebrews*, LNTS 486 (London: Bloomsbury T&T Clark, 2014).

preters, I have adjusted some of my perspectives since that publication, but I remain committed to the insight that the author of Hebrews casts God's speech as filial; in other words, after the revelation of Jesus, the author can see all of God's communication as "son-shaped," and that provides the tones in which the reader should hear the identity of God (as Father) as well as their own identity (as children in God's family). It is vital to Christian faithfulness to know we are in relationship with a God whose eternal relationship is fittingly described as familial, and who chose to be revealed through the instruction of the Holy Spirit as Father and Son. The God who is Judge (12:23) and Lord is, most intimately and by great grace, our Father. Hence, the eternally begotten one who became human to redeem humanity entered a particular nation (2:16), a particular tribe (7:14), a particular family as part of his experience of empathy so that he might open the way for all those who share in flesh and blood to become part of God's family. The sermon's exhortations to have assurance and to grow in maturity ring out with greatest clarity and power when heard within the familial framework. While Hebrews contributes powerfully to the understanding of Jesus as Son of God and the theology that radiates from that point, the author of Hebrews is in line with all other authors of the New Testament who also emphasize Jesus's sonship. Throughout the commentary I will call attention to those resonances as well as the valuable distinct contribution Hebrews adds to the affirmation that God's self-revelation is as Father, Son, and Holy Spirit.

With respect to the other major christological pole of the sermon, Christ's high priesthood, the author is quite distinct among the voices in the New Testament. Other authors hint at this priestly role. For example, Paul gestures toward the cult occasionally (e.g., Rom 3:25), and interpreters have seen priestly themes in the Gospels.[3] Hebrews, nonetheless, is the only text to say explicitly that the God-man is High Priest, mediator between God and humanity in a way that no other human priestly mediator has ever been or will ever replicate. This author argues extensively that this priest, who is taken from among humans, as are all priests (Heb 5:4), is not just proximate to God, or someone who simply serves as God's representative, but is himself God in the flesh. His mediation is unparalleled not only in his person but also, because of his unique being, in the actions he takes. All priests make sacrifices, but he is the only one who sacrifices himself (9:14). Because of this, he makes

3. For example, Nicholas Perrin, *Jesus the Priest* (Grand Rapids: Baker Academic, 2018).

the sacrifice not frequently but once (9:26), for if a human person is going to sacrifice themselves completely to the point of death, and everyone knows humans can die only once, as the author of Hebrews states (9:27), then this can only be a one-time offering. Moreover, he performs his priestly ministry not in the tabernacle made with hands (9:11, 24) but before the very throne of God (8:1). Jewish sacrifices offered before his sacrifice graciously maintained the presence of a holy God amid an impure people and pointed the way to the unique and final offering of the Son that was to come.

This once-for-all sacrifice for sin, the defeat of death itself (2:14), as described in Hebrews, has resulted in an interpretive debate within Hebrews scholarship that has become quite lively in the past decade. Scholars have turned attention to the place this offering occurs and the effects it achieves. David Moffitt's revised dissertation, *Atonement and the Logic of Resurrection in the Epistle to the Hebrews*, has created renewed interest in the soteriology of this letter.[4] Readers of my commentary will notice that I have found his arguments generative. To be clear, I assert that the cross is central in Hebrews. This is where the death of the Son of God incarnate takes place (12:2). It is the culmination of his suffering and the place where he completes the death necessary for his sacrifice. At the same time, the cross is *not* salvifically sufficient on its own. The author also knows of Jesus's resurrection (13:20) and places Jesus's self-presentation to God his Father in heaven (e.g., 9:24). Since he goes to heaven after his resurrection and after his ascension, this heavenly presentation is best interpreted as the completion of his self-sacrifice. The author of Hebrews is not as explicit as Paul concerning the connection between sin and death (Rom 5:12–21), but it seems to me that the same connection underlies the logic from which the author of Hebrews is working, which should not be surprising for someone who gives evidence of being acquainted with Paul. It is the death of the Son that brings forgiveness and release from the captivity of death. That being said, it is also clear that before the resurrection, while he was still in the tomb, he was in no position to release anyone else from death. Only when he had come through death, and in so doing defeated it, then and only then could he instigate the fulfillment of God's promise for the eternal sovereignty of humanity over creation (Ps 8/Heb 2). In the schema of this au-

4. David M. Moffitt, *Atonement and the Logic of Resurrection in the Epistle to the Hebrews*, NovTSup 141 (Boston: Brill, 2011).

thor, as informed by the sacrificial system of Israel, Jesus must *die and defeat death* in order to present the final and solely sufficient offering for sins and sin's consequences. His bodily presence before God is a perpetual reminder of his final, sufficient sacrifice, and in the crucified and resurrected body he makes continual intercession for his siblings who are on the way to realize the full benefits of his incarnate priestly work (7:25).

Attention to this Christology allows even more precision on the nature of the fundamental theological aims of the sermon. The author is not encouraging a general trust in God's ability to keep promises but instead is specifically seeking to inculcate the necessity of trusting that God is the God who has the power to raise the dead. This is the shape of Christian faith, the belief in the power of the living God, even in the face of death. The resurrection thread runs throughout the sermon—more explicit in some places and more implicit in others—but is present nonetheless in all the descriptions of faith. The faith the author is encouraging his readers to maintain is a faith in their resurrected High Priest.

Israel's Scriptures

This theological aim results in the author's thoroughgoing incorporation of Israel's Scriptures into his own word of encouragement. Readers will notice that I seek to do two things in the commentary with regard to the quotations and allusions to Israel's Scriptures. First and foremost, I elucidate the author's work with those passages. He makes choices about what to include and draws the attention of his readers to those inclusions in particular ways. He is a preacher and therefore incorporates those texts into his preaching in service of a particular goal. My primary concern is that readers of my commentary will hear his sermon, including his incorporation of sacred texts.

At the same time, Hebrews is not the only book in the Christian canon but one of a collection, including all the books from which the author cites. Consequently, my second aim as I attend to these texts is to turn the attention of the reader to the whole context of the passage cited or alluded to in Hebrews. I have been trained to notice the evocations of Israel's Scriptures in the New Testament and then to investigate the wider account from which those evocations come.[5] I have found this training to be beneficial in many ways. In the

5. Richard Hays's *Echoes of Scripture in the Letters of Paul* (New Haven: Yale University Press,

commentary, I invite readers to consider the stories in their original context. I call attention to elements of those accounts that resonate with the text of the author of Hebrews. I do so to aid canonical readers' trust in the superintendent divine author who speaks throughout all these texts composed by different human authors by providing resources to imagine points of connection for spiritual benefit and edification in teaching. In short, it is my conviction and experience that to hear the passages in conversation—both the author of Hebrews' sermon and his sources—serves the aim of Christian formation.

Relation with Jewish Faith

As is clear from this discussion and any reading of this sermon, the author could not preach his sermon without the Law and the Prophets and the Writings.[6] That being said, he makes a few statements about God's law that seem quite disparaging, chiefly Hebrews 7:18–19, "For on one hand there is a removal of the earlier commandment because of its weakness and uselessness—for the law perfected nothing," and Hebrews 8:13, "In saying 'new' God made the first old, and that which is old and gray is near disappearing."

Hebrews is one of the texts of the New Testament that have been used to serve the abuse and persecution of the Jewish people.[7] Some have seen in texts

1993) was incredibly influential in the formation of my own hermeneutic, especially through the relational and pedagogical connection with J. Ross Wagner, his student and my doctoral advisor.

6. Monographs that give attention to the author's citation methods include Susan E. Docherty, *The Use of the Old Testament in Hebrews: A Case Study in Early Jewish Bible Interpretation*, WUNT II.260 (Tübingen: Mohr Siebeck, 2009); Madison N. Pierce, *Divine Discourse in the Epistle to the Hebrews: The Recontextualization of Spoken Quotations in Scripture*, SNTSMS 178 (Cambridge: Cambridge University Press, 2020); Georg Walser, *Old Testament Quotations in Hebrews: Studies in Their Textual and Contextual Background*, WUNT II.356 (Tübingen: Mohr Siebeck, 2013); Radu Gheorghita, *The Role of the Septuagint in Hebrews: An Investigation of Its Influence with Special Consideration to the Use of Hab 2:3–4 in Heb 10:37–38*, WUNT II.160 (Tübingen: Mohr Siebeck, 2003); Gert Jacobus Steyn, *A Quest for the Assumed LXX Vorlage of the Explicit Quotations in Hebrews*, Forschungen zur Religion und Literatur des Alten und Neuen Testaments 235 (Göttingen: Vandenhoeck & Ruprecht, 2011).

7. Jesper M. Svartvik, "A Dangerous Book: Reading Hebrews without Supersessionism," *Christian Century* 138.19 (2021): 34–36. Svartvik states it this way: "One New Testament text has done more than any other to cement the notion that Judaism and Christianity are two separate covenants, that the newer covenant is better, and that this is fundamental to Christian faith:

like Hebrews evidence that God has given up on the Jews and transferred the blessings to the Christian church, but nothing could be further from the truth of an informed reading of these New Testament texts. If this were true, if God had given up on the Jews, then God would cease to be trustworthy but would instead be a capricious god. There would be no guarantee, given that track record, that God would not someday do the same to the readers of Hebrews.

Despite the implausibility of such an anti-Jewish reading, interpreters must respond to the ways in which certain statements in Hebrews have served ill motives and horrific actions. Often this conversation takes place under the banner of supersessionism, a term that has been highly debated.[8] My understanding of the author of Hebrews is this: He, like all other early believers in Jesus, would describe himself as a Jew. He is a follower of the Jewish Messiah, who was revealed to be the man Jesus of Nazareth, the one crucified by the Romans and raised from the dead by God. The author believes in God's gracious election of and participation with the people of Israel as revealed through Israel's Scriptures. These texts and the actions they prescribe preview what was on the way when the eternal Son of God took on flesh. Those who experienced Jesus could not have understood him and his work if God had not already communicated—revealed the truth of God's character and way of working—in Israel's sacred texts. The author would have sawed off the branch on which he was standing and fallen miserably into incoherence had he disparaged and cut himself off from Israel, both the texts and the people. Hence it is fitting to state that the author does not see Jesus superseding and replacing but rather fulfilling God's promises to the people of Abraham.[9]

Hebrews. This is not surprising. Hebrews includes 14 of the New Testament's 33 uses of the Greek word *diathêkê* ('covenant') and 13 of its 19 uses of *kreittôn* ('better')" (34). See discussions in Andreas-Christian Heidel, *Das glaubende Gottesvolk: der Hebräerbrief in israeltheologischer Perspektive*, WUNT II.540 (Tübingen: Mohr Siebeck, 2020); Craig A. Evans and Donald Alfred Hagner, eds., *Anti-Semitism and Early Christianity: Issues of Polemic and Faith* (Minneapolis: Fortress, 1993); Lillian C. Freudmann, *Antisemitism in the New Testament* (Lanham, MD: University Press of America, 1994); Alan C. Mitchell, "'A Sacrifice of Praise': Does Hebrews Promote Supersessionism?," in *Reading the Epistle to the Hebrews: A Resource for Students*, ed. Eric F. Mason and Kevin B. McCruden, RBS 66 (Atlanta: Society of Biblical Literature, 2011), 251–68. I am grateful to Andy Iversen's work on this topic which aided my collection of literature.

8. Lloyd Kim, *Polemic in the Book of Hebrews: Anti-Semitism, Anti-Judaism, Supersessionism?*, Princeton Theological Monograph Series 64 (Eugene, OR: Pickwick, 2006).

9. Richard Hays ("'Here We Have No Lasting City': New Covenantalism in Hebrews," in *The Epistle to the Hebrews and Christian Theology*, ed. Richard Bauckham et al. [Grand Rapids:

On the other hand, it would be disingenuous not to acknowledge that if the author of Hebrews encountered a Jewish person who had *not* come to believe in Jesus the Judahite as Messiah, a Jew who desired to practice the law and the sacrifices (if they were still available in the temple) instead of depending on Jesus's sacrifice for relationship with God, he would not accept their religious practice as salvifically viable. He, like Paul, might allow the possibility that the Jewish people could greet the promises of God through Christ from a distance[10] and come to submission to Christ eschatologically (as one way of interpreting Rom 11:26), but he would not grant that a Jewish person could remain in God's family after actively choosing against Jesus as Messiah. He would say to them, as he does in this sermon, that the only sacrifice they needed to trust was that which had already been offered, accepted, and made effective when presented to God the Father by Jesus the Son—his self-sacrifice of his body and blood before the very throne of God. Jesus had not superseded and replaced Judaism, but by fulfilling the promises made within Israel's Scriptures, he had superseded and replaced some key practices of the law. This sermon holds the scandal of exclusive salvation found in Jesus, the Jewish Messiah.[11] In sum, this author would never let go of God's promises to the people of Israel, nor would he compromise on the sole sufficiency of the offering of Jesus Christ. To read this text well today in a post-Holocaust world demands humble and honest conversation between Jewish and Christian interpreters of this text, which must take place in communities of mutual respect and deference before the sovereignty and wisdom of the God that all desire to serve faithfully.

HEBREWS' PLACE IN THE CANON

Hebrews' presence within the documents of Christian Scripture should not be taken for granted. Early interpreters were not ignorant of its anonymity, and its

Eerdmans, 2009], 151–73) provided me the language for this statement (155). He proposes that Hebrews both "carries forward the heritage of Israel" and "transforms Israel's identity." Or put differently, "[Hebrews] confirms Israel's story as truly revelatory, even though incomplete" (167).

10. Hays, "'Here We Have No Lasting City,'" 167–68.

11. See a similar conclusion in Oskar Skarsaune, "Does the Letter to the Hebrews Articulate a Supersessionist Theology? A Response to Richard Hays," in Bauckham et al., *Epistle to the Hebrews and Christian Theology*, 181.

perceived rigidity with regard to repentance raised concerns for many Christ followers. Two factors, however, one external and one internal, prevented these strikes against it from being fatal to its inclusion. First, Hebrews was regularly included within the Pauline orbit, even if sometimes on the edge. As will be clear in the commentary, when I draw attention to multiple resonances with the Pauline letters, I agree that this association is warranted. Second, Hebrews earned its place on the merits of its own theological power. When doctrinal controversy arose, it was recognized for its inestimable riches that contribute to a robust view of the eternal divinity of the Son, and hence contribute to Christian confession that God is Triune. Even without a name and without a context to make sense of its intense warnings, it has persistently been included within Scripture because of its carefully crafted and awe-inspiring depiction of God and concomitant roadmap of costly faithfulness to that God.

The earliest evidence of Hebrews' existence appears in the letter of 1 Clement, dated to the end of the first century.[12] In his reflections on Jesus written to the Christians at Rome, Clement includes descriptions distinctive to Hebrews: that Jesus is High Priest, a helper of human weakness who possesses a radiance and name superior to the angels. In addition, Clement also cites three of the passages from the catena in Hebrews 1 (1 Clem. 36.1–5). His knowledge of Hebrews seems clear.

About one hundred years later, Hebrews appears in P^{46}, the earliest extant collection of Paul's letters, slotted by length after Romans. This is an affirmation that Hebrews was included under the umbrella of the authoritative voice of Paul, and this inclusion was vital in securing Hebrews' place as one of the authoritative Christian documents.

Portions of Hebrews appear in several papyri as well as all the major uncials. Sinaiticus and Alexandrinus include the full text, and significant portions appear in Vaticanus, Ephraemi Respecritus, and Claromontanus. Finally, it appears in the translations of Old Latin, Copic, and Syriac.[13]

Early interpreters persistently valued the themes in Hebrews, including the motif that faithfulness is a journey as well as Hebrews' discussion of the priest-

12. See esp. 1 Clem. 36 and also 1 Clem. 9, 12, 19, 21. While many have dated 1 Clement to the 90s, Jonathan Bernier argues that it should be dated to the 60s (*Rethinking the Dates of the New Testament* [Grand Rapids: Baker Academic, 2022], 239–51). This is possible if Hebrews is also dated to the 60s, a suggestion I find plausible. See the following discussion on the date of Hebrews.

13. See discussion in Luke Timothy Johnson, *Hebrews: A Commentary*, New Testament Library (Louisville: Westminster John Knox, 2006), 3.

hood of Christ. Theologians such as Clement of Alexandria and Origen cited from Hebrews frequently, but they knew that the lack of typical authorial identification did not sound like Paul. Hence, they surmised that Paul had remained anonymous out of humility or a desire to avoid contentiousness in writing to Jews since his calling was to the gentiles (Rom 11:13). Even more, they saw that the language was different from that in his other letters, so they suggested that this document was translated from Paul's Hebrew into Greek, either by Luke or Clement.[14] In sum, even for those who found great value in the insights of the sermon, the anonymity of the letter presented an issue to be addressed.

For others, the difficulty with Hebrews resided in the content, particularly the sections that seemed to indicate that repentance after grievous sin was impossible (2:1–4; 6:4–6; 10:26–31; 12:15–17). The Shepherd of Hermas, a document associated with Rome and written over a period of time in the mid-second century, seems to be in disagreement with a rigorist interpretation of Hebrews' warning passages. Throughout the long text, the author wrestles with the issue of repentance. Ultimately, this author remains open to repentance after baptism, available until the arrival of the eschaton (Herm. Mand. 4.3.1–7; Herm. Sim. 9.26.5–6). Conversely, Montanists, a liminal Christian group often viewed with suspicion, found their belief in the impossibility of repentance confirmed by their interpretations of Hebrews. Tertullian, who identified with this group for a time, stated plainly that no repentance was possible for things like adultery and apostasy (*Modesty* 20). Hebrews' resonance with a dissident group did not aid its reception. Even more significant, during the Decian persecution (249–250) the Christian bishop Novatian used Hebrews to prohibit the rehabilitation of those who had denied Christ under threat. Cyprian, bishop of Carthage, disagreed and argued that hope remained for the lapsed, but that they had to demonstrate their recommitment through a period of penance.[15] Hebrews, because of its statements on repentance, was caught up in these battles, leading some like Cyprian not to cite it or some like anti-Montanist Roman elder Gaius to speak against its authoritative authorship.[16]

14. Comments of Clement of Alexandria and Origen are retained in Eusebius (*Ecclesiastical History* 6.14.2–4; 6.25.11–14).

15. Cyprian, "Epistle to Cornelius," in *Saint Cyprian, Letters 1–81*, trans. Sister Rose Bernard Donna, Fathers of the Church 51 (Washington, DC: Catholic University of America Press, 1964), 171–93.

16. For discussion of these debates see Craig R. Koester, *Hebrews: A New Translation with Introduction and Commentary*, AB 36 (New York: Doubleday, 2001), 23.

Its absence from the Muratorian Fragment has also been interpreted as possible evidence that Hebrews was rejected by whoever compiled that list.[17]

Questions about the authorship or rigor of Hebrews became less pressing when Arius began citing from Hebrews in the mid-300s. He zeroed in on the begottenness of the Son that was said to occur on a certain day (Heb 1:5) as well as the author's statement that God "made him" (a wooden translation of 3:2). Arius appealed to these texts to support the assertion that the Son was the first of God's creations. Instead of turning away from Hebrews, Athanasius found in it the unassailable eternal connection between the Father and the Son (1:3; 13:8). While Arius could prooftext from Hebrews, the whole of its complex argument so powerfully supported the two natures of the one eternal Son that it became indispensable in the formation of central Christian doctrines like the Trinity and two-natures Christology. The radiance of its christological light made the sections on repentance appear less glaring. Ambrose suggested that the author in these sections was only prohibiting a second baptism, not the chance for any repentance (*Concerning Repentance* 2.2), a solution that persisted for many years. At the same time the emphasis on priesthood in Hebrews became a valuable resource for the formation of the concepts of ordained ministry and the presentation of the Eucharist as a sacrifice.[18]

Athanasius, Augustine, and Jerome considered Hebrews inspired Scripture, sometimes within the writings of Paul and sometimes on the edge of them.[19] It is present in Athanasius's *Festal Letter* 39, an early example of the list of texts that Christians came to call the New Testament. Its inclusion was reflected again in the list of inspired documents agreed upon at the Council of Carthage in 397. By this point Hebrews' place in Christian Scripture was assured.

That security does not mean that it has always been well received. Calvin surmised the work of the enemy in the disputes that arose over its authority, and concluded, "Let us not therefore suffer the Church of God nor ourselves to

17. Clare Rothschild notes that this is an argument from silence, given that the Muratorian Fragment does not explicitly reject Hebrews as it does several other letters. See *Hebrews as Pseudepigraphon: The History and Significance of the Pauline Attribution of Hebrews*, WUNT 235 (Tübingen: Mohr Siebeck, 2009), 21–24.

18. For a more robust discussion and sources, see Koester, *Hebrews*, 24–25; Johnson, *Hebrews*, 6.

19. Athanasius, *Festal Letters* 39.4–5; Augustine, *Guilt and Remission of Sins* 1.50; Jerome, *Letters* 59.3.3.

be deprived of so great a benefit [Hebrews], but firmly defend the possession of it."[20] Luther, on the other hand, who acknowledged that it was marvelous, was also so troubled by its seeming resistance to repentance to the degree that he classified it as "deuterocanonical."[21]

The shifting reception of Hebrews provides an instructive account for how people of faith approach all of what has been recognized as God's word. Some portions of Scripture are confusing, and at times interpretations arise that do damage. Other sections seem unimportant, overly mundane, without the ability to impact readers beyond the initial audience. Over time, the Spirit of truth is faithful to correct misinterpretation or to shed light where there was opacity. Given shifts of theological need and cultural pressure, passages that seemed inert become vital. God has provided a trustworthy revelation in these texts, and only careful attention as well as patience over time allows interpreters to discover the riches often hidden in plain sight.

Hebrews' marginality has been a consistent feature since its inception. It sits on an edge within the canon. On one side, it is in conversation with Paul's soteriology in the letters that precede it. To these epistles it adds the dimension of sacrifice to understand the coming of God's Messiah, a category pervasive within the religious schema of the ancient world but comparatively minimal in Paul. On the other side of its canonical location, Hebrews introduces many of the themes that appear in the epistles that follow it, including suffering as a mark of Christian faithfulness as well as exalting Christ as the one who intercedes.[22] Its marginal position facilitates a canonical conversation between the two collections on either side of it.[23] Its marginality is also apparent in the honor afforded to it. While its place in canonical Scripture has not shifted since the late fourth century and its popularity has waxed and waned, it has never held pride of place alongside the theological giants like Luke, John, or

20. John Calvin, *The Epistle of Paul the Apostle to the Hebrews; and the First and Second Epistles of St. Peter*, trans. William B. Johnston, ed. David W. Torrance and Thomas F. Torrance, Calvin's New Testament Commentaries 12 (Grand Rapids: Eerdmans, 1963), 19.

21. John Kleinig, *Hebrews*, Concordia Commentary (Saint Louis: Concordia, 2017), 33.

22. Karen H. Jobes, *Letters to the Church: A Survey of Hebrews and the General Epistles* (Grand Rapids: Zondervan, 2011), 3–6.

23. Robert W. Wall and Eugene E. Lemcio, *The New Testament as Canon: A Reader in Canonical Criticism*, JSNTSS 76 (Sheffield: Bloomsbury, 1992), 178; Elizabeth Rundle Charles, *Within the Veil: Studies in the Epistle to the Hebrews* (London: SPCK, 1888), 9.

certainly Paul. Few Christians have considered Hebrews the most prominent New Testament letter, but I hope that time with it through reading this commentary will reveal why it has long been considered a vital necessity for the formation of Christian theology and integral for receiving the encouragement needed to endure the Christian life faithfully until the end.

I am grateful for the freedom afforded by this series, which allows me to draw these canonical connections. Chiefly, I will call attention to connections with Israel's Scriptures with which Hebrews is continually in dialogue. The connections will also range widely into other New Testament voices as well. A commitment to the belief that all these texts share a common divine author, one who is trustworthy and good, presents an invitation for readers to contemplate the connections I will draw and discover other resonances on their own.

SETTING

Hebrews' lack of explicit ownership by any named author is the seed from which every other unknown about Hebrews grows. It is not clear from where or to where this anonymous author is writing or when. Even the genre is up for debate, given the sermonic start and epistolary close. The vacuum of uncertainty has been filled with multiple suggestions, some more plausible than others.

Authorship

The most active field of conjecture has been that of authorship. As noted, Christians in the East, like Clement of Alexandria and Origen, often associated the letter with Paul, although some commentators noted the differences between Hebrews and other Pauline letters and provided explanations for them, including the possibility of Lukan translation. In the West, Tertullian, who favored the teaching of Hebrews, ascribed it to Barnabas, who, in his view, was passing along apostolic ideas.[24] Those who rejected its rigorist language believed it could not have been written by Paul.[25] Once Hebrews was accepted,

24. Tertullian, *Modesty* 20.2.

25. Gaius the Roman elder made this statement as found in Eusebius, *Ecclesiastical History* 6.20.3.

it remained within the Pauline orbit, even when authors acknowledged this ascription had its dissenters.[26]

I find direct Pauline authorship implausible, as have many interpreters through the ages. Certainly, there are differences in style and vocabulary. These stylistic differences between Paul and Hebrews do create a different reading experience—but this is an insufficient argument to make when the corpora of New Testament documents remain relatively small. Most persuasive for me are two points. First, the documents use different methods of scriptural citation. Paul describes Israel's Scriptures as those that are written, whereas this author refers to them as speech, dominantly God's speech. These alternative descriptions are not diametrically opposed to one another, but they are noticeably different. The second point carries more weight in my interpretation: I reject Pauline authorship chiefly because I do not think that Paul would so easily relinquish his experience with the risen Lord. The author casually acknowledges that he did *not* hear the gospel from the Lord, but from those who had heard it from the Lord (Heb 2:3), and does so when it is not the main point being made. In other words, it is rhetorically noticeable that this statement is uncontroversial for the author. I grant that Paul also acknowledges that he receives testimony about Jesus (1 Cor 15:3), but this statement in Hebrews suggests that this author is one step removed from the incarnate Jesus. It is difficult for me to imagine Paul *not* mentioning his encounter with Jesus on the road to Damascus or his spiritual instruction in Arabia (Gal 1:11–17) as well as his experience in the third heaven (2 Cor 12:1–5) in such a nonchalant way. Paul spent a significant amount of his ministry defending the fact that he heard the gospel from God (Gal 1:1). His qualifications of apostleship are different from the Twelve's, but he still claims to be an apostle. The author of Hebrews does not share the same concern for proving this kind of proximity to Jesus. Given the frequent resonance between this author and the writings of Paul, including such teachings as an exalted Christology (Heb 1; 13:8; Phil 2; Col 1), a concern with the consistency of God's promises through the covenant (Heb 8–10; Gal 3; Rom 4), and an emphasis on rigorous faithful endurance

26. For example, Eusebius in *Ecclesiastical History* 3.3.3. Koester collects the early Christians who associated this epistle with Paul directly, or on the margins of his literature (*Hebrews*, 26–27). See also David Young, *The Concept of Canon in the Reception of the Epistle to the Hebrews*, LNTS 658 (London: T&T Clark, 2022).

(Heb 12:1–13; 1 Cor 9:24–27), it seems best to imagine this author not *as* Paul but as someone in conversation with him.[27] In my estimation, this sermon is written by a member of the broad Pauline network of gospel ministers.

The suggestion that this document was written by a friend of Paul has been part of the conversation about Hebrews from the beginning. As mentioned, Luke, Clement, and Barnabas were early suggestions. Silas is a possibility as well because he could explain a connection with Timothy (mentioned in Heb 13:23; see also Acts 17:14–15; 18:5; 2 Cor 1:19; 1 Thess 1:1; 2 Thess 1:1) as well as the fact that he could explain the similarities between Hebrews and 1 Peter, with which he was also involved (1 Pet 5:12).

Given this Pauline connection as well as the author's anonymity, some scholars have posited female authorship, focusing on Prisca/Priscilla, one of Paul's fellow workers in gospel proclamation and instruction (Acts 18:2, 18, 26; Rom 16:3; 1 Cor 16:19; 2 Tim 4:19). At the turn of the twentieth century, Adolf von Harnack suggested that she might have written the sermon along with her husband, Aquila, which would explain the authorial "we" as distinct from the audience (Heb 6:9; 13:18).[28] Almost a hundred years later, Ruth Hoppin argued for Priscilla's authorship, noting the presence of women in the list of the faithful (Heb 11:11, 23, 31, 35), the familial themes, and the pathos of the letter.[29] Given that there was a shame associated with women in philosophical circles[30] and Christian texts that seemingly prohibit women from teaching (e.g., 1 Tim 2:12), Priscilla would have had good reason to remain anonymous. This suggestion finds support in the reality that anonymity was a common pathway for female authors throughout Christian history.[31] If only God

27. See a list of similarities in Kenneth Schenck, *Understanding the Book of Hebrews: The Story Behind the Sermon* (Louisville: Westminster John Knox, 2003), 90. Rothschild also amasses an extensive list of connections between Pauline texts and Hebrews, especially ch. 13 (*Hebrews as Pseudepigraphon*, 63–118).

28. Adolf von Harnack, "The Authorship of the Epistle to the Hebrews," *Lutheran Church Review* 19 (1900): 448–71.

29. Ruth Hoppin, *Priscilla's Letter: Finding the Author of the Epistle to the Hebrews* (Fort Bragg, CA: Lost Coast, 2009).

30. See discussion of this reality in Lynn H. Cohick, *Women in the World of the Earliest Christians: Illuminating Ancient Ways of Life* (Grand Rapids: Baker Academic, 2009), 243–46.

31. Cynthia Briggs Kittredge, "Hebrews," in *A Feminist Commentary*, vol. 2 of *Searching the Scriptures*, ed. Elisabeth Schüssler Fiorenza (New York: Crossroad, 1994), 428–54, at 433.

knows who wrote this sermon, as Origen famously averred,[32] then Priscilla, like any other thoughtful and inspired follower of Jesus, could be a candidate for this role.[33]

Seemingly, it was Luther who first suggested Apollos as a potential author.[34] His profile in Acts 18 corresponds with the characteristics one might intuit about its author from reading Hebrews. He is Jewish and from Alexandria, where he might have been conversant with Jewish interpreters who emphasized the heavenly realm (as in Heb 8:5). He knew the Scriptures of Israel well, and he was rhetorically adept. In conversation with fellow Jews, he demonstrated that Jesus was the Messiah by arguing powerfully from the Jewish Scriptures (Acts 18:24–28). He traveled to the same places as Paul, functioning as an instructor in the faith (1 Cor 1:12; 3:4–22; 4:1–6; 16:12).[35] Of the persons known from the documents of the New Testament, Apollos appears to have the qualities that set him apart as the best option for the unknown author. If that is the case, then the fact that he was instructed by Priscilla and Aquila in the faith (Acts 18:26) means that her influence is present in this letter even if the words are not her teaching but the production of her student. Because I find some of the arguments in favor of Priscilla's authorship entangled with feminine stereotypes that I firmly reject (not all women are especially focused on emotion, and men care about familial issues as well) and because of the internal connections with Apollos's description, I will follow the masculine participle in Hebrews 11:32 and refer to this author as male. Given the points I raised for female anonymity, I respect those interpreters who conclude differently. If, in the kingdom of God, Priscilla herself corrects me, I will with great delight admit my error in judgment.

It could be that this author was known to the community to whom he was writing, but whose identity faded from even the earliest Christian record. That

---

Joy A. Schroeder and Marion Ann Taylor, *Voices Long Silenced: Women Biblical Interpreters through the Centuries* (Louisville: Westminster John Knox, 2022), xii–xiii, 10–12.

32. Origen made this statement as reported by Eusebius, *Ecclesiastical History* 6.25.14, but in many instances he supports Paul as the author of this sermon. See Matthew J. Thomas, "Origen on Paul's Authorship of Hebrews," *New Testament Studies* 65.4 (2019): 598–609.

33. Kittredge holds space for this possibility more so than most other modern commentators ("Hebrews," 433).

34. Luther, *Commentary on Genesis* 1545, *WA* 45:349.

35. For discussion of Apollos's authorship, see Johnson, *Hebrews*, 42–44.

is, another plausible conclusion is that this writing is truly unattributable to any known early Christ follower. I have often puzzled over my lack of "connection" to this author. Having closely studied this sermon for over a decade, I feel little sense of camaraderie with the person who wrote it. That could be an individual deficiency on my part, but in comparison with the letters of Paul, on which I have not spent as much time, the difference is striking. I feel that I know Paul and cannot wait to have particular discussions with him in the kingdom of God. Conversely, the author of Hebrews remains largely a blank slate, an unknowable mystery. Instead of frustration with this person's demureness, I am impressed with the way in which he has so thoroughly drawn his listeners' attention to God. I may feel little to no connection with whoever this may be, but I do love—deeply—what this author has written. This provides one viable and impressive path of ministerial leadership to truly, in the words of John the Baptist, decrease so that Christ may increase (John 3:30). Our communication of God's word depends not on our person but on the content itself. Fame and following have always tempted Christian leaders, and if this is Apollos, they were particularly tempting for him given his rhetorical finesse (1 Cor 1:12; 3:4), so the author of Hebrews provides an example of someone whose personal legacy died with the community who knew him, but whose immeasurable impact for the kingdom of God has continued to endure and grow. I will attend to the very few things revealed about the author and discuss the elements we can know about the community and his commitment to their endurance, but I will attempt to do what he seems to have desired: keep our focus on the word of God.

Genre

It is clear that whoever this author is, he is writing to fellow Christ confessors from whom he is currently separated. What exactly he is writing is also a point of debate. Throughout the commentary, I will refer to this document with two primary descriptors: sermon and letter. Both are fitting and both aid interpreters in the act of hearing the author well. This book of the New Testament is a piece intended as transformative oratory brimming with concern for the community who will hear it, a concern heightened by personal absence.

Readers do well to remember that this text is meant to be heard. It begins not with typical epistolary greetings but with a powerful and rhetorically beautiful paragraph-long sentence extolling the communicative God. Throughout, it utilizes rhetorical form and technique to persuade the hearers to endure.[36] Repetition of themes is beneficial for any teaching but especially for a listening audience. The author himself describes this as a *word* of exhortation (Heb 13:22), indicating that he wants them to hear the word of God by hearing the words he has selected and constructed. A caution with this terminology is necessary. I am convinced that sermons in this time period did not look the same as they do in many Christian spaces in later eras. To be clear, what scholars can uncover of synagogue practices does not indicate a forty-five-minute monologue but instead a community dialogue about sacred texts through the vehicle of prophetic sharing.[37] If this is the case, then the reading out of Hebrews was intended to elicit conversation. For an author so committed to communal support of faith, it is not surprising that he would want them to learn together as they converse after hearing his word of exhortation.

Because he was separated from them (13:19), he could not deliver this teaching himself but had to send it as a letter. This reality explains the typical epistolary features at the end, including travel plans (13:19, 23) and greetings (13:24). Reading this as a letter, as early interpreters so designated it, illuminates the fact that he sent this missive rather than waiting to deliver it himself and therefore underscores the urgent concern he had for this community. They needed to hear the assurance of God's good faithfulness as soon as possible. This author knows this community, their past as well as their present, and he is writing this sermon and sending it to them, not willing to wait until he can personally share the content with them (13:19). He does so to support the movement of their faith into the future. He would have asked someone else to deliver the document, possibly read the sermon, and be ready to answer questions about its content, much as Paul does when he sends Romans with Phoebe (Rom 16:1–2). This author trusted that God could use many servants,

36. See Daniel J. Treier, "Speech Acts, Hearing Hearts, and Other Senses: The Doctrine of Scripture Practiced in Hebrews," in Bauckham et al., *Epistle to the Hebrews and Christian Theology*, 337–50, and David A. deSilva, *Perseverance in Gratitude: A Socio-rhetorical Commentary on the Epistle "to the Hebrews"* (Grand Rapids: Eerdmans, 2000), 35–39.

37. See Carl Mosser, "Torah Instruction, Discussion, and Prophecy in First-Century Synagogues," in *Christian Origins and Hellenistic Judaism: Social and Literary Contexts for the New Testament*, ed. Stanley E. Porter and Andrew Pitts, Texts and Editions for New Testament Study 10 (Boston: Brill, 2012), 523–51.

his own composition as well as another person's voice and knowledge, to get the message across. He planted, someone else would water, and God would bring the increase (1 Cor 3:6–8).

One final point about the genre of Hebrews is necessary. This was originally written not as an evangelistic but as a discipleship text. The author is writing to people who have already made a confession of Christ (Heb 3:1; 4:14; 10:23; 13:15). They agree on Christ's majesty and on his humanity. It is Christ's priesthood that is the newer truth, and therefore they need more instruction on it. Hence, the author devotes the bulk of the word to this theme. He makes all these affirmations about their Lord Jesus in order to shore up their trust in God, who has promised to carry them through their difficulties until the end. God can use anything to draw people to salvation, and so its original aim does not prohibit Hebrews' use for initial gospel conversion. Therefore, I seek not to draw the lines too sharply between texts that are meant to convert to faith and texts that are meant to develop existing faith. Nevertheless, readers might be less befuddled at Hebrews' complexity when we remember that the audience had existed as believers in Jesus for some time (Heb 5:12), demonstrated the reality of their faith (6:10; 10:32–34), and were therefore ready to receive this challenging word as they progressed deeper into maturity. As I share my comments on the text, I assume a similar audience: believers who have a desire to know more of God so that they can go deeper in faithful and fruitful trust.

Audience

The ethnic makeup and previous cultural background of these believers in Jesus have not been clear, despite the name—first attested by Tertullian in the second century—that this author is writing to a group of Hebrews.[38] Previous interpretations assumed he was warning them not to return to Judaism now that Jesus had fulfilled the covenant promises and ended the need for sacrifice. More recent scholarship has noted that the author never actually issues this admonition.[39] The robust reflections on Jewish Scripture would be vital for

38. *Hebraioi* was a term favored by the people of Israel for themselves (Joshua D. Garroway, "Ioudaios," in *The Jewish Annotated New Testament*, ed. Amy-Jill Levine and Mark Z. Brettler [Oxford: Oxford University Press, 2011]), as in 2 Cor 11:22; Phil 3:5.

39. See Kenneth L. Schenck, *Cosmology and Eschatology in Hebrews: The Settings of the*

anyone incorporated into the Jesus movement no matter their background. Note, for instance, Paul's frequent and deep appeals to Israel's Scriptures in his letters to gentile communities (1 Cor 10; Gal 3–4).

In recent scholarship, the ethnicity question has narrowed to the list of "basics" in Hebrews 6:1–2. Several interpreters have noted that these sound like things gentiles would need to be instructed in but are concepts that a Jewish person would have known since birth.[40] A recent challenge to that interpretation has called into question the meaning of the foundation metaphor in 6:1. Marcus Mininger argues that foundations were not the same as basic things, not the same image as "milk" that a learner should progress past, but the permanent part of a structure that should remain. Hence, Mininger argues that the author is urging them not to build a structure on the things of the old covenant: continual repentance, faith in God (note that the author does not say faith *in Christ*), and washings, which would seem to suggest that they were Jewish and should not seek to return to that foundation that lacks Jesus as the Messiah.[41] The interpreter coming to Hebrews for formation might entertain both options, gentile and Jewish background, to test out the potential fruit of each reading.

As the gospel of Jesus Christ broke into the Hellenized Jewish world and spread to the Roman Empire, whose distinct localities held varying responses to the Jewish faith, one's ethnic and religious background had a major impact on how one received and lived out the gospel. Consequently, positing the ethnic identity of the recipients has direct bearing on imagining the situation that motivated the author to write in the first place. Despite substantive differences in interpretation over potential situations that might be testing a Jewish or gentile audience, those temptations lead to a similar end: the temptation to turn away from the persecution that comes from confessing Christ. The

Sacrifice, SNTSMS 143 (Cambridge: Cambridge University Press, 2008), 26–41; Eric Mason, "The Epistle (Not Necessarily) to the Hebrews," in *The Letter to the Hebrews: Critical Readings*, ed. Scott D. Mackie, T&T Clark Critical Readings in Biblical Studies (London: Bloomsbury T&T Clark, 2018), 389–403.

40. Kenneth Schenck, *A New Perspective on Hebrews: Rethinking the Parting of the Ways* (Lanham, MD: Lexington Books/Fortress Academic, 2019), 31–41.

41. Marcus Mininger, *Impossible to Be Restored? Temptation and Warning in the Message of Hebrews*, New Studies in Biblical Theology (Downers Grove, IL: InterVarsity Press, forthcoming).

clearest statements concerning the situation of the addressees appear in the latter sections of the letter:

> But remember the earlier days in which, having been enlightened, you endured a great contest of sufferings. This, on the one hand, as those who were publicly exposed to both insults and tribulations. Also, on the other, as those who became partners with those whose who were treated in that way. For you also suffered with prisoners, and you received the seizure of your possessions with joy, knowing that you yourselves have a better and abiding possession. Therefore, do not cast away your boldness, which has a great reward. (10:32–35)

> As those who fight against sin, you have not yet resisted to the point of blood. (12:4)

> Remember prisoners as fellow prisoners and those who have suffered evil as also you yourselves are in a body. (13:3)

The addressees have found themselves in difficult situations because of their faith. On the other hand, the correction in ch. 5 might sound like they are simply immature:

> For you ought to be teachers because of the time. Again, you have need that someone teach you certain basic things about the beginning of the words of God, and you have become those who have need of milk and not solid food. For everyone who shares of milk is untested with respect to the word of righteousness because that person is an infant. (5:12–13)

The lack of growth in their faith, I posit, is not due to languishing in comfort, however, but because they have faced persecution and are continuing to do so. They are experiencing things that are full of grief (12:11), which the author wants them to interpret as God's disicipline. Members of their community were previously imprisoned (10:34), and some of them are still there (13:3). The author's continual calls to endurance are not simply because they are lazy but because they are weary from the fight. He is worried that they are not responding to the intense training God is allowing them to experience in the resistance they face. The sin with which they struggle (12:4) is the sin to give up.

He goes on to say,

> But solid food is for the mature, those who have senses that have been trained; because of maturity they discern between good and also evil. (5:14)

The author makes a deep investment of time and energy extolling the faithfulness of God as revealed in the sole sufficiency of the crucified, resurrected, and exalted Messiah. He proclaims how good this word is, so no one would want to ignore it, even if persecuting forces are tempting them to do so (10:32–39; 12:3–11). In other words, his admonitions are not aimed at a disaffected group, whose confession is being crowded out by other distractions, but to a group under fire, who are weighing whether holding fast to the confession of Christ is worth the cost. He extols Christ's majesty and urges their attention to it so that the option of acquiescing to persecution might pale in comparison. A return to either the worship of the gods or the worship of the God of Israel, save the embarrassing confession of a crucified messiah, would alleviate the pressure they are facing.

The situation of Christians who read Hebrews is more diverse than was true for its original audience. Some may be facing intense persecution or shaming because of their confession of Christ, but other readers may not. This word of exhortation, by the power of the Holy Spirit who communicates divine speech, continues to issue a call to consistent faithfulness and increasing maturity, no matter what situation surrounds the reader. The evil one who has lost hold of the world by virtue of Christ's defeat of death (Heb 2:14–15) continues to wreak havoc and tempt confessors to question the goodness of God, not unlike the initial inquiry from the serpent that stimulated doubt (Gen 3:1). My commentary endeavors to bring out, chiefly, the majesty of God so that no matter what pressures are tempting a reader away, the glory of God's goodness present in Hebrews might shine more brightly to make those things that only seem to glimmer reveal their worthlessness.

Date

A decision concerning the people to whom the author is writing and the situations they are facing that led to this sermon bears on the imagined date of composition. As is often true in New Testament studies, the hinge point is the destruction of the Jewish temple in AD 70 by the Romans, a devastating moment for Jews that would have made an impact on those who followed Jesus as the Jewish Messiah, no matter their ethnic or religious background. While this date affects the interpretation of several New Testament books, its impact is especially strong in Hebrews since the sermon spends significant energy reflecting on the rituals that would have taken place within the temple. It must be acknowledged immediately that the author never uses temple terminology but refers to the structure of the meeting place with God only as the tabernacle (8:2, 5; 9:2–3, 6, 8, 11, 21; 11:9; 13:10) as he attends to the scriptural descriptions of it. Nevertheless, this sermon would have sounded differently if the Jewish temple were still standing and functioning (pre-70) than if the temple had been decimated and ceased its atoning work. Other authors give evidence that Jewish discourse could continue to speak of the functioning of the temple in the present tense even after its destruction.[42] The author of Hebrews possibly felt no need to speak of an event about which everyone was painfully aware, so as not to rub salt in the open wound of defeat.[43] I find the silence on this event of destruction slightly more persuasive for a pre-70 date. Especially in sections where he speaks of the old covenant as near its end (8:13), it seems odd that he would not say it has already ended if he is writing post-70. Whether Hebrews was composed in a time of tumult in Israel or shocked grief, its teachings can meet the challenge of either situation. The session of the Messiah (the fact that he is seated at God's right hand) reveals both God's sovereignty over the storm and God's victory in the face of loss.

Location

The only explicit tether to a geographical location appears in 13:24: "Those from Italy greet you." Whether the author is writing from Italy, to Italy with some expats, or from and to an entirely different location with people who hail from Italy cannot be determined. Some authors have seen the mentions of Jerusalem and being outside the camp as an indication that he is writing to Christians in Roman Palestine,[44] but the first citations of Hebrews in 1 Clem-

42. Josephus, *Antiquities* 3.224–57.

43. Ken Schenck, *Explanatory Notes on the Sermon of Hebrews* (Eugene, OR: Cascade, 2023), 5–6.

44. George Wesley Buchanan, *The Book of Hebrews: Its Challenge from Zion*, Intertextual Bible Commentary (Eugene, OR: Wipf & Stock, 2006), 469–77; Carl Mosser, "No Lasting City: Rome, Jerusalem and the Place of Hebrews in the History of Earliest 'Christianity'" (University

ent, connected to Rome, as well as urban themes in the letter,[45] has made a Roman destination a prominent suggestion. The call to bear Christ's shame outside the camp calls readers in any location outside the comfortable center of their community to embrace the liminality of the radical way of Jesus.

The Benefits of Hebrews' Mysteries

Some readers may feel frustrated with the lack of certainties concerning the setting of Hebrews. In my years of studying the text, I have never experienced this as a barrier to fruitful exegesis and spiritual benefit. This word originates from a specific person to a particular community at a unique moment in time to address a pressing need. At the same time, this fruitful word is not bound to that first sprout from a particular historical soil. Readers in all times and places can partake of the fruit without fully understanding the root system. Received by the church as God's word, it is indeed living and active (4:12). My hope is that my rather agnostic conclusions on these questions will not be a distraction, either to those who wish my decisions on the background were more self-assured or to those who are frustrated that I have landed, if quite tentatively, on the opposite side from them. The words of Hebrews have proven their worth, even though their origin story has been unclear for as long as the historical record has existed. The Holy Spirit need not wait for conclusive decisions about background before the work of exhortation through this sermon can begin.

HEBREWS FOR CHRISTIAN FORMATION

This commentary series serves a singular aim: faith formation. Hebrews offers ample riches to serve this goal. Its text is complicated and demands patient

---

of St. Andrews, PhD diss., 2005). For an abbreviated version of part of this argument, see Carl Mosser, "Rahab Outside the Camp," in Bauckham et al., *Epistle to the Hebrews and Christian Theology*, 383–404.

45. Jason A. Whitlark, "'Here We Do Not Have a City That Remains': A Figured Critique of Roman Imperial Propaganda in Hebrews 13:14," *JBL* 131.1 (2012): 161–79. For material-culture support of Roman provenance from early Christianity, see Jason A. Whitlark, "Funerary Anchors of Hope and Hebrews: A Reappraisal of the Origins of the Anchor Iconography in the Catacombs of Rome," *Perspectives in Religious Studies* 48.3 (2021): 219–41.

consideration. It is a sermon meant to be heard and preached again and again because it contains a word meant to be obeyed. It is my prayer that my love for and study of this sermon—decades distilled into the words of this commentary—might come alongside those who are hearing God's voice in this letter. Every verse of Hebrews serves this end, but a few distinctive themes that serve faith formation necessitate explication at the beginning.

Access to God

Because the way from death to life has been opened, the veil entered by the human who has gone into the throne room of God serving as a pioneer for the rest of humanity (2:10; 6:19; 10:19–20), access to God is the dominant note of Hebrews' formation for the Christian reader. This access, coming boldly to the very throne of God (4:16), is open for all by virtue of what Christ has done. It is striking that in a highly cultic book there is invitation for all to function in ways that evoke the actions of priests, to approach God's holy place and to minister (9:14; 12:28), following the order of their High Priest. Without using the phrase, as Peter does (1 Pet 2:9), Hebrews aligns with an affirmation of the priesthood of all believers. If there is one sole sufficient High Priest, and we are all sharers of him, then the blessing of access is open to all.

The when and the how of that access is more complicated. The author seems to assume that those who are listening to the sermon of Hebrews can go to God now, and this encouragement seems to me to point to an act of prayer. At the same time, the journey motif throughout the letter, whether through the lens of the wilderness generation (Heb 3–4) or through the metaphor of a race (Heb 12), assumes that they have not yet arrived at their destination with God. There remains an eschatological hope of access. The author of Hebrews is certainly not alone in working within a modality typically referred to as an "already/not yet" schema. This is not evidence of a confused set of beliefs; rather, his statements are coherent within the sermon as a whole, especially in light of the early Christian belief in bodily resurrection. Through the eyes of faith, which can trust in the things not seen (11:1), his listeners know that Jesus is seated at the right hand of God advocating for them (7:25), and therefore can approach God in whatever situation of need they find themselves, moment by moment (4:15–16). They are proximate to God's celebratory heavenly kingdom as those who stand at the base of a mountain and gaze up at its crest

(12:22–24), and yet even more so because while the top of a mountain may seem vastly far away for those who are beginning a climb, this community hears the voice of God from this mountain directly in the person of the Son (1:2), and in the words of the Holy Spirit, who communicates God's scriptural revelation to them anew every day they listen. This word of faith, as Paul might say quoting Deuteronomy, is not distant from them but instead is as near as their own hearts and lips (Rom 10:8). When they gather in community and praise the Father of their brother Jesus, repeat God's name as he taught them (Heb 2:11–12), and sense the encouragement of the saints who have gone before them (11:39–12:2), God is near enough to them so that they have everything they need to endure, whatever contest of faith or wrestling with sin or shame that they might face in the present.

On the other hand, Jesus has trod the path to eternal dwelling with God and has done so by being raised from the dead in his body. The same will be true for them when they defeat death as he has—better said, when they defeat death *because* he has. At that point, they will dwell embodied with God forever. The presence of God in their midst now does not mean they do not also have this resurrection hope to which they look forward. God's presence does not mean they have no need of faith to trust that the unshakable kingdom is to come (12:26–28). With faithful hope, they move forward with God's help in the journey toward the permanent rest with God.

The journey motif and the conversations concerning maturity in chs. 5 and 12 make clear that faith in Hebrews does not stop with sentiment but is a trust expressed in action. Discipleship in Hebrews is active and costly. The addressees have been and will be shamed by those external to their group when they continue to meet together to confess the name of Jesus as Messiah and God (10:32–34; 13:13). It will not be easy but instead challenging (12:5–11) to refrain from the immorality of lust and greed around them as they support those in need and those who are persecuted for their faith (13:1–5). With sufficient access to the presence of God now and hope for eternal embodied dwelling with God in the future, all readers can continue to run the race of faith with endurance (12:1–2).

The Warning Passages

One more word on discipleship in Hebrews is necessary. I was first attracted to this New Testament book, or maybe it's better to say I was *captured* by it, because of its warning passages, those heavy statements that suggest one can turn away from God's grace (2:1–4; 3:6, 14; 4:11; 6:4–6; 10:26–31; 12:15–17). For millennia, the church has wondered whether the author meant that if a Christ follower turns away in apostasy, there is no chance to return again. These statements in Hebrews have at times been heard as a harshness dissonant with the teachings of Jesus, who describes God as a Father eager to receive back the rebellious son (Luke 15:11–32) and who himself receives back Peter, his dearest friend and most vehement denier (Mark 14:53–65/Matt 26:57–68/ Luke 22:54–71; John 18:13–27; 21:1–14).

At this point in my study of Hebrews, I have reached two hard-won conclusions about these passages, though I am confident that I will continue to learn more, given their complexity. First, Hebrews is adamant about the necessity of community for endurance in faith. It is not as if church attendance equals salvation for this author, but he does teach that a confession of Christ cannot be nurtured on one's own. To be protected from the deceitfulness of one's own heart, each Christ confessor must be among members of the gathering of Christ, those who are also on the journey to God's presence. This means that Christian formation requires being in vulnerable community, where one knows others and is open to being known. This is a type of community where a person is open to accountability, open to the possibility of someone pointing out the first sprouts of bitterness that need to be plucked (Heb 12:15).

To encourage the steadfastness of each heart in the community, the author several times paints a picture of the horrific consequences of turning away from God's salvation procured by Jesus the High Priest. He sketches a picture of an alternative universe, describing what could be if they were to do the unthinkable—namely, to reject the redeemed life they are already experiencing by virtue of their confession of Christ. The question that naturally arises from later readers of these texts is some version of "What if someone turns away and wants to come back?" A vital aid in interpreting these texts is to acknowledge that this is simply *not* the question at stake for this author. Every time he describes the situation of apostasy, he in effect says to his listeners, "This has not happened to you" (6:9–10; 10:32–34; 12:22–24). Hence, the second conclusion I have reached is that these are *warnings* to this community, not yet realities. Members of his community have not walked away, and he uses this alternative-reality approach as one more tool to help them understand and actively embrace the majestic sole sufficiency of Jesus Christ the mediator.

In writing to a group who has not yet walked away, the author of Hebrews asserts that it would be impossible to have repentance restoring one back to God. Given the logic of the sermon, it is clear he makes these bold statements because the work of Christ that the apostate rejected can never be redone. All these passages in Hebrews speak of impossibility: How will we escape if we neglect so great a salvation (2:3)? It is impossible to restore again to repentance (6:4). There no longer remains a sacrifice for sins, but a certain fearful expectation of judgment (10:26–27). Esau could not find a place for repentance even though he sought it with tears (12:15–17). Passion cannot produce the impossible. My exegesis has led me to conclude that those passages speak to the unrepeatability of the sacrifice of Christ. If it is rejected, his work will not be redone, because once death has been defeated, it cannot be entered into again.

On the other hand, it is up to God to decide what to do with the one who walks away and then wants to return *to Christ*. Hebrews does not address this situation. Other passages in Scripture speak of God holding out open arms to disobedient people all day long (Rom 10:21 citing Isa 65:2 LXX), and God consigning all to disobedience in order to show mercy to all (Rom 11:32). Hence, the canonical conclusion is that it is very difficult to imagine God rejecting the repentant person who desires to be restored to the family of God through Christ. The interpreter then has to use this tool of warning from the author of Hebrews with the greatest of wisdom and care. A sensitive soul who is already attentive to the weight of sin and desires relationship with God needs to be comforted with the assurance of Hebrews' emphasis on Jesus's completely efficient finished work. Alternatively, a person who imagines the grace of God as that which gives license to be faithful *or not*, to come in and out of confession without any respect for the holiness of God as revealed in the costly work of the Son, needs to hear the message of warning: do not presume on the grace of God. There is no salvation outside that offered in Christ, and if one turns away from him, it is within God's justice to allow the apostate to experience the consequences of rejecting the only pathway to salvation. Given that judgment comes after human death (9:27) and that Christ will soon consummate salvation (9:28), taking a break from faithfulness may put one into that territory of consequences and time may run out. The author of Hebrews leaves those consequences in the hands of God. His call, and therefore all future interpreters' task, is to communicate the message that God has provided salvation in the death and resurrection of Jesus Christ. To willfully reject this offer, to cut oneself off from any relationship with Christ and fellow Christ confessors, is to put oneself in the space where God deals with sin outside the salvific sacrifice of Christ.

Hebrews provides resources for both needed comfort and appropriate warning. Elizabeth Rundle Charles, a nineteenth-century female interpreter of Hebrews, drew these cords of the sermon together in this way: "[Hebrews] is a continuation of the Gospel-story of the Incarnation, Passion, Death, Resurrection and Ascension into the world 'within the veil.' It is, indeed, an Epistle full of the intensest and most real human sympathy with the actual difficulties and dangers, trials and endurances, of those addressed, never chilling into an impersonal treatise, but always tenderly attracting, and as tenderly warning, sweeping them on by call and rebuke and encouragement; the tempted [called] to Him the great High Priest, who also was tempted, the many chastened sons to the Son who 'was made perfect through sufferings.'"[46] My hope is that all readers will find the resources needed for each pastoral situation in the wealth that Hebrews offers.

CONCLUSION

Hebrews comes to us as one unknown, as it has from almost its earliest days, and so provokes an existential encounter. It is the word we hear, not the personality of the author, not the identities of the first recipients, but the God who speaks therein. Through this ancient sermon, God speaks to the time and situation in which all readers find themselves, the day called today, before all things are shaken and only the unshakable kingdom remains (12:26–28). This is the day in which the Holy Spirit's communication of God's speech through the Son prompts a response of faith. This faith trusts and lives out of that trust, no matter how costly that response might be. We find camaraderie with generations of interpreters who notice and then build their lives on the same faithfulness of God, as revealed in the eternal Son, who became human, died, and rose again, and serves as our living High Priest. Moreover, we find comfort that the questions that we have about Hebrews are not new. Have we heard

46. Charles, *Within the Veil*, 6–7.

rightly the fervor of this author's concern for his community or fallen into the precipice that imagines God as a cold judge, hiding behind and mocking the face of the compassionate Savior? Or have we tilted to the other side where God is nonchalant and does not really mean what he says, communicating judgment only with a wink and a nod? Neither are palpable readings of Hebrews, and so we endeavor to stay on the straight path, holding together in our hearts both the fear of God and a deep confidence in that same God, the judge of all who has elected to become our Father through Jesus Christ.

Given that the human heart is deceitful above all things (Jer 17:9), to hold together these truths about our God often necessitates the insight of other believers who can see aspects of God from either pole that we might tend to diminish on our own. Because this series is meant to assist those who are studying the Bible, whether this commentary on Hebrews deepens your study for personal edification or aids your preparation for teaching a class or preaching a sermon, I encourage you to discuss what you are learning with others in such a way that they can dialogue with you. The best way to study this early Christian sermon that puts such emphasis on the mutual support necessary for the Christian journey is to do so *with others*. When this occurs, we can all listen more perceptively and see more clearly and therefore rest more confidently assured in this: the one seated on the throne, the reflection of God who is our great pioneer, invites us to approach because he has made the way of approach possible. His opening of the way is the best evidence that God who makes promises is indeed faithful.

Commentary

HEBREWS 1:1–14

THE EXALTATION OF THE SON

Commanding attention with its first words, the sermon known as one delivered to the "Hebrews" eloquently articulates the work—and therefore the character—of God. The author does so in an artfully complicated first sentence that stretches over four verses. Writing to an audience he knows and loves, he assumes shared knowledge, theological commitment, and even familial relation with them. They agree on God, which is of utmost importance. Out of this common belief, they consider the same text (Israel's Scriptures) and the same life (Jesus, from the line of Judah; 7:14) as the revelation of the one God. The audience has confessed Jesus as Son of God and therefore would concur with the statements with which the author begins. By starting here, he calls attention to a reservoir of agreement from which he can draw later in the sermon when he urges them to endure in valuing the majesty of what God has done and is still doing for them.

This opening sentence, however, not only rehashes what they know but also signals the grand presentation of the Son's vocation of priesthood, a topic that is unchartered terrain for this audience and also distinct within the documents of the New Testament. In other words, while it assumes a shared theology, the sermon is written to a community who needs a bold reminder that God is faithful, particularly that God is faithful to the promises given in the Scriptures. For this author, Jesus's priesthood is the prime example of God's faithfulness.

The bedrock of this opening sentence is the simple statement "God spoke" (1:1), but like the filigrees of an ornate design, multiple rich phrases encircle this foundation. After he presents a brief reminder of God's communication in the past (1:1), the author introduces the Son in v. 2, and after that point every phrase in this long sentence describes this one who is God's communication. The author represents the comprehensiveness of the filial speech of God in seven descriptions, a number that exhibits completion (1:2–4). The rich sentence proclaims that the God of Israel is not silent, and that the definitive expression of divine speech has arrived in the person of the eternal Son who has entered time. In this, the author has introduced two of the core themes of the sermon: the communicative divine identity and the complex nature of the title "Son." What is preserved in this sentence reflects what early Christians had confessed about the God of Israel as now understood through the purifying work of the eternal and recently embodied Son, and therefore these few words played a key role in forming the church's very understanding of God, what came to be known as the doctrines of the Trinity and Christology.[1] With these opening words, the author has crafted enough beauty for centuries of contemplation. He begins here, however, not only to *contemplate* theological intricacy but also because he wants his readers to live out of the assurance that salvation depends on the Son's achievement and their continued trust in it.

After the first extensive sentence in which the author artfully exalts God's revelation in the majesty of the Son, in the next section (1:5–14) the author yields the floor to God's voice communicating through the texts of Israel's Scriptures. The Father whom he was talking about is now doing the talking. This catena of Scriptures supports the author's initial descriptions of the Son even as they add nuance and color. Here too, as was true for the phrases about the Son, the author chooses to have seven, an affirmation in form as well as in content of the Son's *complete* majesty.

As a group, these Scriptures work to compare the Son to the angels. In this section, they serve as an extended example, similar to the opening comparison with the prophets, of the author's use of *synkrisis.* A common rhetorical device, this allows a rhetor to compare two things, arguing for the superiority of one of them. In Hebrews these comparisons are never made with the rubric of negative versus positive, but instead according to the structure of something good and God-given in comparison with some*one* even better. The author will show many similarities between Jesus and the angels, all of whom fulfill God's plan, but his overarching aim is to show, without ambiguity, the Son's superiority over them.

1. See introduction, pp. 5–6, 14.

Some contemporary readers may be surprised at that choice of comparison and wonder at the angels' persistent and prominent placement in this opening chapter, as angels are not often evoked in certain sectors of contemporary theology or piety. For the author of Hebrews, however, at least in the first chapter, the angels are the fulcrum around which he turns the portrayal of the Son. Because of the attention given to the theme, the Son's position over the angels must be a vital point for him to make. Multiple suggestions for these beings' presence seem plausible. The author will show the superiority of the covenant the Son enacts over the covenant communicated by angels (2:2). The angels are ephemeral spirits (1:7), while the Son has taken on flesh (2:14).[2] The angels mark out the edge of the created terrain; if the Son is superior to them, the only place he can exist is on the divine side of the line.[3] Any suggestion that finds support in the developing argument of Hebrews aids interpretation of this section and the letter as a whole. By offering these Scriptures as the voice of God, the author asserts that God speaks and does things for the Son that God does not with the angels. Chapter 2 states clearly that when the Son took on flesh, the Son was—for a time—below the angels, but now, after the purification for sins (1:3), he sits above them. The catena proclaims in the voice of God through Israel's Scriptures that the eternal Son ever has been and the incarnate Son is now exalted above the angels and therefore above *all created things*. His exaltation is the cornerstone of the argument that will unfold over the next twelve chapters. As God's Son he is worthy of worship because he created all things and will rule forever. The heights of his glory leave his confessors in awe of his humble incarnate mediation on their behalf and confident in his authority over their future. He is the ultimate example of the word of God's trustworthiness and the guarantee that they will reach their goal of dwelling with God as has their brother (2:11–12), who is their Lord (2:3; 7:14).

1:1–4 · GOD'S SON-SPEECH

[1]In many and various ways, long ago God spoke to the ancestors by the prophets; [2]in these days of the end God spoke to us by a Son,

2. Moffitt, *Atonement*, 45–53.

3. Bauckham, "Divinity of Jesus Christ," 23.

whom the Father appointed as heir of all things,
through whom also God made the ages,
[3]*who is the radiance of God's glory and the impress of God's being,*
and he is the one who bears all things by his powerful word;
after he made purification for sins, he sat down at the right hand of the majesty on high,
[4]*becoming better than the angels as he has inherited a more excellent name than theirs.*

In the stream of tradition in which this author stands, the communication of God—the fact that *God spoke*—remains a consistent and vital feature of the divine identity. The God of Israel, who is the God of the universe, spoke creation into existence (Gen 1:4–26), called Abraham into the covenant (Gen 12:1–3), and proclaimed and wrote the law (Exod 31:18). Life is possible because of God's word. From ages past, *long ago*, God has frequently employed a variety of methods—articulated here with the alliterative playfulness of the terms *polymerōs* and *polytropōs*, "*in many and various ways.*" Both terms indicate variety as opposed to singularity to convey the many ways God spoke. Then the author narrows the focus to God's speech to the covenant people. The ancestors heard God's word through the vehicle of *the prophets*, whose personalities met the situations in which they found themselves to produce great variety of divine speech. The variety is multiplied because the author of the sermon has granted the prophetic mantle to the writers of poetry and recorders of wisdom, whose writings he will quote. They are all prophetic in the sense that they are speaking the words God desires to communicate with the covenant people, who are called into their very existence by God's word. The prophets, shaped by their time, culture, and personal makeup, communicate God's message in their own voice, a clear demonstration of divine revelation coming through very human means. God met the people where they were with what they needed to hear. Hence, for the author to name God's speech with the rhetorical finesse of alliteration encompasses the incredible breadth of divine words given through divinely commissioned human speech. The plenitude reveals a propensity in God, evident also in nature, for the beauty of variety. At the same time, since this variety has one source in God, it is coherent. Although the author will next emphasize the singularity of God's speech in the one Son, his faithful and compassionate statements and acts discussed throughout Hebrews display the same beautiful variety and attentive meeting of particular needs proceeding from one divine person.

The audience of Hebrews stands in the same listening community as those previous generations who heard from the prophets. Long ago God spoke *to the ancestors*, a kinship term that suggests the addressees are part of the same family.[4] Because they live after the Son has been revealed, their time is *these days of the end*.[5] The arrival and work of the Son has begun a process that will culminate in all things being put under his feet (Ps 110:1, first cited in Heb 1:13). This community lives in the interim between these events, his arrival and his comprehensive reign. While this community can—and *will* through this very address and its many evocations of Israel's sacred texts—benefit from the polyphony of the prophets, that symphony has now been caught up into a single melody. They are so very privileged to live in a time when they hear God speak in the simplicity of One, *by* the person of the *Son*. Because the author will show how the speech of the prophets lines up with the revelation of God's Son-speech, this is evidence of God's intention to speak in the Son from the beginning. This filial speech, speech in a person who is God's begotten, is not a response to a failure of communication in the prophetic mode but the goal for which all the other communication was preparing.

Before attending to the power and beauty of that speech, it is worth asking why this author begins in the way that he does. This is categorized as the *Epistle* to the Hebrews, but it begins unlike any other epistle in the New Testament and most other epistles in the ancient world. The author offers no information about himself or his addressees, where any of them are located, or the nature of their relationship. Possibly the first leaf fell away from the letter so early that it left no textual memory. Alternatively, the author intended the absence of those normal features on account of both logistics and theology. Logistically, given the emphasis on listening throughout the sermon, it seems most plausible that this work is primarily intended as a spoken word, which, because the author was separated from this community (13:18–19), was by necessity written and

4. As several scribes assumed with their addition of the pronoun, *hēmōn*, "our." I have chosen an inclusive translation of *patrasin*, which would be more woodenly translated "fathers," because the author makes clear that God communicates with women as well (11:11, 23, 31, 35).

5. A similar phrase appears in Israel's Scriptures to speak of the end (Gen 49:1; Num 24:14; Deut 4:30; 31:29; Josh 24:27; Hos 3:5; Mic 4:1; Jer 23:20; 37:24 LXX; Ezek 38:16; Dan 2:28–29, 45; 10:14; 11:20.

then mailed. This epistolary quality could have been one reason why the most complete early manuscript of Hebrews, preserved in P[46], sits alongside the epistles of Paul. Theologically, the absence of the author's authorial identity at the beginning serves to emphasize the presence of God's. From the very first sentence, the author steps back so that divine speech takes prominence. It is the author, of course, who writes the words that get his readers to listen to God's voice and makes the choice concerning which scriptural texts he conveys for them to hear. He is committed to giving them clear instruction, and yet he displays a deference to God's voice above his own, a sobering example for any who bear the mantle of Christian teaching. He wants this community to know and hear that God has been and will always be a speaking God.

Now, in the time in which they and all subsequent readers of Hebrews live, God has spoken in a Son. The author's first use of that incredibly important title, son, lacks a definite article. Although the rest of the sentence reveals that *the* Son is the focus, it is most fitting to translate this phrase as *spoke to us in **a** Son*. While God's care is revealed in deciding to communicate rather than to be silent and to communicate through the great variety of prophetic speech to meet the various needs of the people, something more intimate is revealed in Son-shaped speech. The anarthrous noun points to the *quality* of speech God is now giving. As the author will specify in the descriptions of the Son, those who hear God speaking through him can hear and see God. The prophets faithfully revealed God's character which the Son confirms but the Son reveals the identity of God in an unparalleled way.

In the eloquent phrases of 1:2b–4 the Son is heir, creator, radiant image, sustainer, purifier, sovereign, and heir again. Both in their individual parts and in the grouping as a whole, the author conveys truth about this Son. He is divine communication, and so he is divine *revelation*. When one hears Son-speech, one is listening to God. If this community, or any who read this work, are struggling with God's trustworthiness, they can look to the sovereign and eternal Son, who has now, in these days of the end, been made known. That faith-building listening begins with attending to the descriptions of the Son.

Out of a desire for clear theological organization, a temptation might arise to divide the seven phrases into the different natures of the Son. It is certainly the case that several of the phrases more fittingly point toward either his divine nature or his human nature, but from the viewpoint of Hebrews there is no separation between them since they are unified in one person. In the days after the Son has become incarnate, all humanity can know the divine—all God has said and done—through the lens of his human life. A unified understanding of the Son in this sentence is fitting both grammatically and theologically. The descriptions of the Son reveal that this one has a past, a present, and a future, but the subject, whether acting, being, or being acted on, is the same throughout. The Son has always been so intimately related to God and working with God as to be God's mode of expression. It is only the last days, however, that have brought the ability of God's people to perceive the divine communication through the eternal Son of God who willed to take on flesh.

That one title, *Son*, encompasses all the author wishes to affirm.[6] It aptly communicates Israel's royal tradition that he fulfills along with the unparalleled intimate eternal relationship he has with God. Moreover, the Son discloses the character of the God who chose to give divine revelation preeminently through a Son and therefore to be known as Father. Inviting his audience to view God as their Father is one of the author's chief methods of encouraging their enduring trust.

The Son's status as *heir of all things* provides the first piece of evidence for his filial relationship with God. In Hebrews' time and culture, heirs were the children of the testator, either by birth or adoption. That God the Father *appointed* the Son to this position demonstrates the giving nature of God: what belonged to God, God promises to give to the Son. As the sentence continues, however, it becomes clear that such giving is not an act of unmerited grace. God does not give to one who was unqualified to receive such an inheritance. The Son, made evident by all the other things that are said about him, was already sovereign over all things, and yet God appointed him, or placed him (*tithēmi*), in this role of heir. Early interpreters were well aware of the potential for confusion; seventh-century theologian Photius cautions, "Yet in order that you would not dare to interpret 'heir' as according to grace or favor, rather than according to birth and nature, he adds, who is the reflection of [God's] glory."[7]

6. Theodore of Mopsuestia, writing in the late fourth and early fifth century, says it this way: "First of all, [the author of Hebrews] signifies the true Son, and by true Son I mean the one who possesses sonship by his natural birth. In the second place, he also includes in this designation the one who shares truly in the dignity of sonship because of his union with God" (*Fragments on the Treatise on the Incarnation* 12.1 [ACCS 10:10]).

7. Photius, *Fragments on the Epistle to the Hebrews* 1.2–3 (ACCS 10:9).

The author's use of an aorist verb, God *appointed*, suggests that the Son's being set in this place is an event in time. However, because this paragraph will move on to speak about things outside time, this appointment could be an eternal one, before even time itself was made. God promised to the Son all things even before any created thing existed. To be an heir has within it an anticipation of the future because an heir is one who, by definition, is looking forward to an inheritance. Being appointed heir before creation, the Son was anticipating the creation he would fashion and inherit.

On the other hand, because this sentence will also point to the Son's work in his incarnate life, it is fitting to see this phrase explaining what God did for the eternal-become-incarnate Son. God appointed him *in his humanity* to the position he always enjoyed as eternal Son.[8] In a way very different from how inheritance usually works, he was promised this inheritance not when his father died but when he did. Hence, as the author will further describe the Son, it is clear that ever since all things existed, they have always belonged to him by virtue of his creating and sustaining them, both of which are based in his being in inexorable relationship with God as the Son of God. In short, God appointed the eternal Son heir of all things before creation. It is also true that God the Father appointed the incarnate Son heir of that which was already his. God has promised to give to the incarnate Son what he already sustained. With the first description, the author is stating very complex dual realities about this one called Son. It is an early indication that this Son's relationship with God includes aspects of both things eternal and things new. The Son this audience has recently heard and seen installed (2:8–9) is the same Son who was reigning over them even before they realized it.

The second affirmation, conversely, is the easiest to mark with regard to time because it takes place before time itself begins. This Son is the same

8. Chrysostom saw this statement as bringing his flesh into the same sovereignty as was held by his eternal relationship with God (*Hebrews* 1.2 [*NPNF*[1] 14:367]). Similarly, Aquinas argued that in his divine nature Christ is "not constituted heir, but He is the natural heir." His human nature, however, "was constituted as heir of the universe," but only as "the true Son of the Father" (Thomas Aquinas, *Commentary on the Letter of Saint Paul to the Hebrews*, ed. John Mortensen and Enrique Alarcón, trans. Fabian R. Larcher, Latin/English Edition of the Works of St. Thomas Aquinas 41 [Lander, WY: Aquinas Institute for the Study of Sacred Doctrine, 2012], 1.1.20, p. 14).

one *through whom also God made the ages*. *Aiōnas* is most often a temporal term, noting ages of time.[9] The Son existed before any age and was the means through which all ages came to be. This indicates that this Son was with God before time itself began. Verse **2c** is one of the classic texts that, to use Kavin Rowe's phrase, "exerted pressure" toward the Christian tradition's affirmation that the Son is eternal.[10] Theodore of Mopsuestia notes that this phrase indicates that the Son is "eternal," which differentiates him as "the cause of all ages that have a beginning."[11]

The term can also include all things within time.[12] Because the Son was involved in the making of all things, all things bear the imprint of the Son's handiwork. Creation does not have two sets of fingerprints, however, but only one, for to see evidence of the Son of God is to see evidence of God. The Father of the Son speaks, and the mode of this filial speech is to create through the Son. In line with the following description of his divine glory, it is fitting to say that in the act of creation, the Son is the expression of the Father, the one *through* whom God creates. Resonant with the wisdom tradition, the personal Son stands as God's agent in ways similar to Jewish authors' descriptions of God's wisdom or word.[13] Importantly, the author emphasizes that it is the *Son* through whom God creates, the familial term indicating that he is not an ethereal emanation out of God but a person in relation with God. Being the one through whom God creates in no way makes the Son inferior to the Father, for later in the scriptural catena the Father will name the Son as full creator (1:10). Chrysostom states it eloquently: for God the Father "to create by him" indicates that God "begat him a Creator."[14] The Son as the active means of creation confirms not the inferior nature of the Son but his emanation from

9. "*'Aiōn*," LSJ, 45.

10. C. Kavin Rowe, "Biblical Pressure and Trinitarian Hermeneutics," *Pro Ecclesia* 11 (2002): 295–312.

11. *Fragments on the Epistle to the Hebrews* 1.2–3 (ACCS 10:8). So too Calvin: "That is the proof of the eternity of Christ; He must have existed before the world was created by Him" (*Hebrews*, 6).

12. "*'Aiōn, -ōnos*," BDAG, def. 3, 33.

13. Prov 8:27. See Harold W. Attridge, *The Epistle to the Hebrews: A Commentary on the Epistle to the Hebrews*, ed. Helmut Koester, Hermeneia (Philadelphia: Fortress, 1989), 40–41.

14. Chrysostom, *Hebrews* 2.2 (*NPNF*[1] 14:371).

the Father. As Richard Bauckham says with clarity, "Jesus cannot function as God without being God."[15] The unity of the Father and the Son finds further confirmation in the next statement.

The third description of the Son stands not only formally at the center of the list but also as the locus of the Son's identity. God acts for and through the Son in v. 2, and in the remainder of vv. 3–4 the Son will act. Here, however, the Son simply *is*. The participle describing him (*ōn*) is neither object nor action verb, but a verb of being. The Son is the one *who is*, and his being is defined in relationship to God.

Such a statement does a great deal to elevate the Son. He is the very image of God, conveyed here not by the term *eikōn* (icon/image) as in the Pauline Epistles (Rom 8:29; 1 Cor 15:49; 2 Cor 4:4; Col 1:15) but instead by *radiance* (*apaugasma*) and *impress* (*charaktēr*). As the radiance, the Son is the dazzling display of God's glory. As the impress or imprint, the Son is the exact reflection of God. In fact, if the language of numismatics is allowed to inform translation, the Son is the one who has the authority to demonstrate God. He is the "authenticating mark."[16]

The terms used to point to God, *glory* (*doxa*) and *being* (*hypostasis*), indicate that the Son reveals not just one or two attributes of God but fundamentally who God is. Glory is the evidence of God's presence (Exod 24:16–17; see also Exod 33:18; 40:34; Num 12:8; Ps 24). Similarly, with the theologically weighty term *hypostasis*, which means foundation or grounding, the author names the being or nature of God. This statement confirms what the author has been saying about God the Father from the beginning. God does not remain hidden, but God has chosen to communicate with creation by creating, by giving the prophetic word, and by speaking through the Son. To add to this auditory revelation, both phrases at the beginning of v. **3** affirm that the Son is the visual revelation of God. God's glory radiates out in him, and God's being appears in the one who is God the Father's imprint. To experience the Son is to experience the God of Israel. Just as God is not silent, so also God is not imperceptible. In the Son, God is radiantly and truly seen.

15. Bauckham, "The Divinity of Jesus Christ in the Epistle to the Hebrews," in Bauckham et al., *Epistle to the Hebrews and Christian Theology*, 17.

16. Michael P. Theophilos, "The Numismatic Background of χαρακτήρ in Hebrews 1:3," *Australian Biblical Review* 64 (2016): 69–80.

As was true of the author's assertion of the Son's role in creation, the phrases employed here to describe the Son also appear in Jewish literature of which the author was likely aware. Like God's wisdom or God's word, the Son participates in creating and maintaining the world because the Son truly reflects God.[17] It is worth emphasizing again that by utilizing the personal and relational term "Son" as the heading for all that is said, the author distinguishes the Son from the impersonal "aspects of God" connotation possible in the terms "wisdom" and "word." As John Webster says, "Because God's speaking ἐν υἱῷ [*en huiō*] is God speaking in person, it requires us somehow to conceive of a repetition or differentiation within the being of God himself."[18]

For early interpreters endeavoring to speak truly of God, this verse was invaluable. It affirmed the eternal relationship between God and the Son. One does not exist without the other: "For as soon as the lamp appears the light that comes from it shines out simultaneously. . . . In this place [Heb 1:3] . . . the Son is of the Father, and . . . the Father is never without the Son, for it is impossible that glory should be without radiance."[19] It also affirmed the Son's faithful and trustworthy revelation of the Father. Theodore of Mopsuestia states, "For he says that Christ preserves an accurate representation of God's nature, so that whatever you would think God's nature to be, so you must also think Christ's nature to be, inasmuch as Christ's nature bears the accurate representation of God's nature since Christ's nature does not differ from God's in the least."[20] In addition to true revelation, in these descriptions of light and imprint lies distinction. There are not two glories but glory and its radiance; not two *hypostaseis* but God's being and the Son's impress of it. With that distinction there is no difference in degree. It would be inappropriate to speak of lesser and greater since the Son fully and truly reveals the Father.

The Son reflects God in divine actions as well. Like the Father, the Son speaks, and *his word*, his *rhēma*, is *powerful*. Powerful enough, in fact, to *bear*

17. See Prov 8:26–30; Wis 7:21, 25–26; 8:6c; 9:2, 4, 10; Philo, *On the Special Laws* 1.81; *On Planting* 8–9, 18; *On Flight and Finding* 10.10.

18. John Webster, "One Who Is Son: Theological Reflections on the Exordium to the Epistle to the Hebrews," in Bauckham et al., *Epistle to the Hebrews and Christian Theology*, 80. See discussion in Peeler, *You Are My Son*, 21–29.

19. Gregory of Nyssa, *On the Faith* (*NPNF*^{2} 5:338). See also Gregory of Nyssa, *Against Eunomius* 8.5 (*NPNF*^{2} 5:206).

20. Theodore of Mopsuestia, *Fragments on the Epistle to the Hebrews* 1.2–3 (ACCS 10:10).

all things. This phrase reflects the Jewish belief that their God was both creator *and sustainer*. Psalm 103 LXX, from which the author will soon quote (Heb 1:7), is an excellent example of this belief about God: "He founded the earth on its foundation; it will not tip forever. . . . The one who sends out water springs in the chasm; in the middle of the hills, the water flows giving drink to every wild animal of the field. . . . The one who causes grass to spring up for the animals, and plants for the service of people, to bring forth bread from the earth, and wine to make glad the human heart, oil to gladden the face, and bread to strengthen the human heart." God remains intimately involved with creation. Now that God has revealed the Son by speaking through him, it is clear that the Son has always been present with God in that act of sustaining. The mutuality between Father and Son is apparent again in this phrase. The Son upholds all things *by his* power, but the masculine pronoun could refer either to the Father or to the Son. In this instance again, the reader is granted a vision of the Son who, in his activity, reveals the activity of God; the difference between the power of the two is imperceptible because it is the same divine power. It is the heretics, Chrysostom notes, who say that "the Father . . . commanded, and the Son obeyed," because both creating and upholding are "indeed great and wonderful, and a certain proof of exceeding power."[21] At the same time, this mutual, exceedingly strong power is manifest through attentive care. Luther observes that the divine action here "expresses a certain tender and, so to speak, motherly care for things that he created and which should be cherished."[22] Certainly, both fathers and mothers can be tender. The interesting point about Luther's observation is *the way* in which divine paternal and filial power is defined—not through divine fiat that steps away after the action is accomplished but through a powerful word that upholds, a powerful word expressed through care and sustenance. Hence it is not inappropriate for Luther to think of the actions of a *nursing* mother in this intimate preservation. To see the particular expression of the Son's power is to see the shape of the action of the Father, a power expressed in divine attentive care.

In the next line the author moves from the pre- or supratemporal statements about the Son's relation with the Father to an event that happened in time: *after he made purification for sins*. Such purity is the hope of the psalm-

21. Chrysostom, *Hebrews* 2.2 (*NPNF*[1] 14:372).

22. Luther, *Lectures on Hebrews*, 1:3 (*LW* 29:112).

ist (Ps 18:13; 50:4 LXX), the desire of God for the covenant people (Isa 53:10; Jer 40:8), the prize of the martyr (4 Macc 17:21), and, most often in the Scriptures, the effect of priestly work (e.g., Exod 29:36; 30:10; 34:7; Lev 12:8; 14:19, 31; 16:30; Job 1:5). This is the first indication in the sermon of the author's soon-to-unfold deep reflections on the Son's priestly ministry. The work of the Son for purity coheres with the law God graciously gave to maintain divine holiness among the people. It should be no surprise, given the extensive focus of God's law to deal with the problem of sin, that the Son of God continues this work. With this statement the author of Hebrews tantalizes his readers for what is to come, but at this point in the address he offers no specifics as to the manner of purification. The brevity of his statement serves to emphasize the Son's achievement. In whatever way he did so, it is done. He has *completed* the purification for sins.

With his work completed, the Son now takes his seat. The final line of v. 3, *he sat down*, includes the only appearance of a finite verb (*ekathisen*) employed to describe the Son's actions. This grammatically most simple statement about him in the list of seven appears rather mundane. The act of sitting rarely elicits excitement. As is always true, context matters. In this instance, sitting reiterates the finality of his work. He has nothing left to do with regard to the cleansing of sin. His being seated is a sign of neither laziness nor normality but of incredible achievement and powerful sufficiency.

It is also a sign of power. He takes his seat *at the right hand of the majesty on high*. The "Most High" is not a common divine epithet in Israel's Scriptures, although readers are left with no question as to whom the author refers. None are as exalted as God, nor is anyone else as great. This description of God occurs with most frequency in the narrative of Melchizedek's meeting with Abraham, certainly a story that interests this author.[23]

That the Son sits at the right hand associates him with God's power. "Right hand" is the language used for describing strength (Ps 110:1 is, for the author, the most influential example; see also Exod 15:6; Ps 17:35 LXX). To be at the right hand distinguishes the Son from the majesty on high, but it in no way communicates the Son's inferiority to the Father. Chrysostom states, "He at-

23. Other Jewish interpreters, including the authors of Daniel, Sirach, and Jubilees, utilized this epithet for God to make connections to the Melchizedekian priesthood. See Perrin, *Jesus the Priest*, 162.

tained even unto the very throne of the Father: as therefore the Father is on high, so also is He. For the 'sitting together' implies nothing else than equal dignity. . . . For had he intended to signify inferiority, he would not have said 'on the right hand,' but on the left hand."[24] It is also true that Jewish writings affirmed belief in only one throne.[25] The implication is that the Son inhabits the same throne in the position of divine power and does so as the acting force, the hand, of God. Once again, the author emphasizes that to see the powerful work of the Son is to see the powerful work of God. The revelation of the Son is trustworthy and assuring, especially for those listening to this sermon who have (Heb 10:32–34) or are experiencing injustice.

When he is exalted at this point in his life, the Son does not take a seat that has never been his.[26] As the eternal eminence of God, as creator, and as sustainer, the Son does not experience reigning on the divine throne as a new reality. That being acknowledged, it is also true that the circumstances have changed. He now reigns after he has accomplished the task of purification, and as the sermon will disclose, to do so he took on flesh. He has returned to his rightful place, but now with a body.

In the first description of these seven statements, the Son inherits everything (v. 3). God places him over everything, as superior to everything, indicated by the fact that he will possess everything. In the final description, the Son is again heir, but the author focuses on his superiority over only one class of created things—namely, *the angels*. The author does not describe the Son as *being* better than the angels, as previously "being" characterized the Son's reflective relationship with God. Here the Son "becomes" (*genomenos*) better than the angels. The aorist of *ginomai* can denote a change, especially when this participle is related to a verbal description of a past event, indicated by the phrases "he sat down" and "he has inherited." He becomes better than the angels when he takes his seat of divine power after the purification of sins. It is clear that he has always been superior to the angels, for they are created beings (as the citation of Ps 103:4 in v. 7 will confirm) and he is the creator. As

24. Chrysostom, *Hebrews* 2.2 (*NPNF*[1] 14:373).

25. "The cosmic throne of God was a central symbol for the Jewish understanding of the one God and his relation to all reality." Bauckham, "Divinity of Jesus Christ," 32.

26. Note Cyril of Jerusalem's comment: "He did not gain his throne by way of advancement, but from the time that he is—and he is eternally begotten—he sits with the Father" (*Catechetical Lectures* 14.27 [ACCS 10:17]).

the glory and imprint of God, he proceeded from God in a way the angels did not. Hence, just as was true with his session on the throne, in his becoming superior to the angels something becomes true of him that was always true of him. To be precise, after he made purification for sins, he became better than the angels, though he was always better than the angels. This is the kind of exegetical tension the church came to articulate as the Christology of two natures in one person. The Son, who was eternally superior to the angels, became better than the angels *in his flesh*.

The author relates this new superiority over the angels to the inheritance of a name, *as he has inherited a more excellent name than theirs*.[27] Similar to the Son's session on the throne and place above the angels, it is true yet again that something new has happened. When he is seated after making purification, this one inherits the *title* "Son of God"—that is, the honorific title often given to the human anointed one, the Messiah, in Jewish literature.[28] The newness he has achieved, however, is not new *for him*. This person has always been so intimately related to God as to be fittingly named "Son." He shares God's glory, eternity, and actions, because he shares God's being, but now an additional meaning of the title "Son of God" has been bestowed on him in time because of his effective dealing with sins. God the Father's eternal reflection (the Son) is now also the reigning Messiah (the Son).[29]

The Son is now exalted above all. He has taken his place as sovereign over everything in time that he has ever possessed outside time. With this final description of the Son, the author is giving evidence of both a consistency and a change. The Son as Son does the work of his Father and so has revealed an eternal relational quality in God, and the Son has done that revelatory work as a human

27. The pronoun I have translated as "theirs" would be translated woodenly as "them," since this is an accusative and not a genitive. The preposition *para* takes an accusative case, but because the pronoun refers to the angels and not only their name, it points to the comprehensive difference between the Son and the angels.

28. For the messianic sense of this phrase, see discussion in Matthew V. Novenson, *The Grammar of Messianism: An Ancient Jewish Political Idiom and Its Users* (New York: Oxford University Press, 2017), 68, 82–91.

29. I am grateful for Robert Jamieson's insightful reading, which has corrected shortfalls in my own previous interpretations of this text. See R. B. Jamieson, *The Paradox of Sonship: Christology in the Epistle to the Hebrews*, Studies in Christian Doctrine and Scripture (Downers Grove, IL: IVP Academic, 2021), 16–17.

person. With this sentence the author plants the seeds of a story of God's filial revelation that will take thirteen chapters to cultivate and millennia to harvest.

Readers of this commentary will need to investigate the development of these ideas in the rest of the sermon, but it is important to name, at this point, the nature of the divine revelation beginning to be disclosed here. As is often true in good poetry, the next phrase invites a reconsideration of the others that precede it. The fifth description of the Son found in v. 3 states, *after he made purification for sins.* Because the Son revealed in these last days allows perception of God, the *mode* of his revelation matters. The divinely revelatory Son is the same Son who purified sins in a shocking way. Hence, the beauty, power, and very being of God have been disclosed in the human body of one who was willing to die in shame on a cross (12:2) and was then mightily restored to everlasting life (13:20). To repeat what I said earlier, God is radiantly and truly seen in *this Son* and the entirety of *his* story. God is as radiantly and truly seen in the Son's pretemporal creating and eternal living reign as in his cries in the face of death (5:7) and his hanging on a cross (12:2). Like Paul's surprising assertion of slave status for one in the form of God (Phil 2:6–7), or John's arresting turn that the eternal Logos took on flesh (John 1:14), or Mark's most powerful portrayal of the King who dies on the cross (Mark 15:18–39), the author of Hebrews asserts that creation hears the voice and sees the image of God in the man willing to die in order to purify sin. Given the author's felicity with Jewish texts and themes, it is not a new thing for this community to know that God speaks to them, but there is evidence they have lost the assurance of God's presence with them (5:11–14; 12:5–11). God's filial revelation who joins with them in suffering, death, even death on a cross, and then is victorious over these foes, revives them to the knowledge of a God who knows, cares, and has dealt with the dire difficulties they face. This is a God to whom they can listen because their God has been preparing for and has now spoken definitively in the life of *this Son.*

1:5–14 · GOD'S SPEECHES TO THE SON

5 *For to which of the angels did God ever say, "You are my Son. I have begotten you today"?*

And again, "I will be to him as a Father, and he will be to me as a Son"?

6 *And again, whenever God leads the firstborn into the world, God says,*

> *Let all the angels of God worship him.*

[7]*And gesturing toward the angels, God says,*

> *The one who makes his messengers spirits and his ministers flames of fire.*

[8]*But to the Son,*

> *Your throne, O God, is forever and ever,*
> *and the scepter of righteousness is the scepter of your kingdom.*
> [9]*You have loved righteousness and abhorred lawlessness.*
> *Because of this, God, your God, has anointed you with the oil of rejoicing*
> *beyond your companions.*

[10]*And,*

> *You at the beginning, Lord, founded the earth,*
> *and the heavens are the works of your hands.*
> [11]*They will perish but you remain,*
> *and all will grow old as a garment*
> [12]*and like a cloak you will roll them up*
> *and as a garment they will be changed,*
> *but you are the same and your years will not end.*

[13]*And to which of the angels has God ever said, "Sit at my right hand until I place your enemies under your feet"?*

[14]*Are they not all ministering spirits that are sent to serve for the sake of those who are about to inherit salvation?*

With a question that expects a negative response, the author queries if any of the angels has ever heard such an address from God: *For to which of the angels did God ever say.* Psalm 2:7 provides the first of the many divinely spoken texts from Israel's Scriptures throughout Hebrews, and as is true more often than not in this sermon, God the Father speaks the word. In this instance, the divine speech is directed to God's Son. The royal psalm asserts God's intimate relationship with the addressee. Because he is God's Son, his name is superior to the angels.

The previous statement in v. 4 (*Becoming better than the angels as he has inherited a more excellent name than theirs*) asserted that the Son's elevation over the angels was due to his inheritance of a superior name. The introduction to the citation in v. **5** includes the connective *gar* (*for*) indicating that the spoken text is related to that assessment of his superiority. This first quote from the psalm, *You are my Son*, suggests that the name in question that elevates him above the angels is *huios* (son). Because the Son has dealt with the problem that plagued humanity, namely by purifying their sin, he is now exalted to reign at God's right hand above the angels as an exalted king who has defeated the forces opposed to God. In this way it is fitting that at his exaltation he inherits the anointed messianic name "Son of God." This interpretation honors the fact that the first two citations are drawn from texts that refer to the king of Israel. Psalm 2 speaks of the Lord's anointed and God's establishment of his kingdom. The second citation comes from Nathan's speech to David, where God promises to establish a house—meaning a line of descendants—for David.[30] Other Second Temple Jewish groups reflected on these texts together, as evidenced, for instance, by the Dead Sea Scrolls (4QFlor and 4QTestim),[31] so it seems likely that the author is drawing on a shared hope for the reestablishment of the just kingdom of Israel through the installment of God's anointed.

On the other hand, the interpretation that the name he inherits is "Son" includes some difficulties. For one, since Israel's Scriptures do refer to the angels as sons of God (Gen 6:2–4; Ps 29:1), the term *huios* (son) would not in itself be sufficient to distinguish him from them.[32] Moreover, while some Jewish texts reflect a belief in angelic worship of exalted humans,[33] this is not a common theme in Jewish messianic texts. Finally, the text that Hebrews chooses to cite in v. **6** (Deut 32:43) was originally spoken to encourage the worship of God.

For these reasons and others, a group of interpreters have argued that the divine name is the *only* name that would differentiate him from the angelic

30. This conversation appears in both 2 Sam 7:14 and 1 Chr 17:13, the other possible location for this citation.

31. Attridge, *Hebrews*, 50.

32. Amy Peeler, "Sons of God," in *Son, Sacrifice, and Great Shepherd: Studies on the Epistle to the Hebrews*, ed. David M. Moffitt and Eric F. Mason, WUNT II.510 (Tübingen: Mohr Siebeck, 2020), 1–12.

33. David Moffitt discusses texts like *The Life of Adam and Eve* and *The Cave of Treasures* (*Atonement*, 133–44).

sons of God, placing him firmly above the angelic host and establishing that he is worthy of their worship.[34] Since two of the following citations have God addressing the Son with the names of God, *theos* (1:8) and *kyrios* (1:10), that God's Son inherits the divine name seems an interpretation fitting to the chapter as a whole.

This suggestion, despite its benefits, raises other difficulties. If the Son was already intimately joined with the identity of God before creation, as the first four verses clearly state, then the divine name could not be inherited at the point of his exaltation. His relationship with God, as Hebrews has already asserted, has not arisen in time. One who, as God, created time with God could not then inherit the name of God on a specific day. Moreover, the citations in which God addresses the Son with divine names speak of his eternality, in time future (1:8) and time past (1:10), not a change in identity that occurs after his purification of sins.

For these reasons, I have become persuaded that the title "Son" is the *onoma* (name) the eternal Son inherits when he, embodied and resurrected, takes his seat at God's right hand and becomes better than the angels. Having accomplished his work, he takes on the messianic title "Son of God." He receives that title in his embodied, resurrected, and exalted humanity, but it is a name that, by virtue of his *eternal* relation with God, has been his eternally. At the moment of exaltation, when God says, *You are my Son*, this eternal filial relationship is reiterated, as it was common for kings to name their relation to their fathers at the point of their inaugurations.[35] It is also proclaimed anew by virtue of what the Son *as human* had accomplished in the purification of sins. In Robert Jamieson's words, "the Son became Son."[36] He receives this ruling title of "Son" in a different key than any anointed leader before him. This one who has always been begotten of God is now graced with the title "Son of God" when he rests from the work that will fully and finally defeat God's enemies. The rest of the citations make clear that what was always true of the

34. Richard Bauckham, *Jesus and the God of Israel: "God Crucified" and Other Studies on the New Testament's Christology of Divine Identity* (Grand Rapids: Eerdmans, 2009), 199–200; Peeler, *You Are My Son*, 51–61. See discussion in Jamieson, *Paradox of Sonship*, 109–10.

35. Peeler, *You Are My Son*, 44–46. While sonship is reiterated at inaugurations, divinity is not. Therefore, I no longer believe that the divine name is in any way "inherited" at the exaltation.

36. Jamieson, *Paradox of Sonship*, 108.

divine eternal Son—one who is worthy of worship (1:6), sovereign forever as God (1:8), and the Lord who creates all things (1:10)—God proclaims to be true of the human-enthroned-as-Messiah-Son. The one who was always Lord God, Son of God, is now Messiah Son of God. With a singular *onoma* (name/title) the author evokes two realities: the Son inherits the messianic title "Son of God" because of the work only he as the eternal Son of God could do, work possible only for one who by virtue of his relation to God has always borne the divine name. This wealth is evoked when the author cites God saying, not to the angels but to the Son, *You are my Son.*

The duality of his nature serves as fundamental encouragement for the readers of this letter. The hoped-for King has come from among the Jewish people as God has promised. He has defeated not temporary political enemies but the baseline problem for all creation, sin, and its result, death. He has opened the way into the throne room of God's presence so that other humans can follow (6:19–20; 10:19–20). In an unexpected way the revelation of this royal Son has also been a revelation of God, for the Davidic Son is one and the same as the eternal Son. It is God himself who has inhabited the human drama and changed it.

Much discussion of the first statement in the catena is necessary because the christological assertions about it illumine the rest of the citations. The voice of God in speaking Psalm 2:7 continues with *I have begotten you today*. Since the filial title "Son" points toward the fact that he is the bearer of the divine name, the one who was with God in eternity could not become related to God on a specific day. *Sēmeron* (*today*) can be a comprehensive term in Hebrews, as in chs. 3 and 4 where "today" is the whole era in which God is speaking (3:7, 13, 15; 4:7). Similarly in this instance, *today* could be a reference to the eternal relation of divine begottenness the Son enjoys with the Father outside time. As Luther notes, St. Augustine understood it as referring to the divine birth. Therefore, he explains that *today* means "in eternity."[37] Similarly Aquinas says, "This generation is not temporal but eternal . . . 'today,' that is, in eternity. . . . This generation is always, and is perfect."[38] Because "Son" also affirms that he has performed a vocation specified by the messianic title "Son," begottenness on a particular day aligns with the bestowal of the name Son at the exaltation

37. Citing *Enarrations on the Psalms* 2.6 in *LW* 29:113.

38. Aquinas, *Hebrews* 1.3.49.

of the human Messiah. The Son was "begotten" on that day into the particular role of reigning Messiah.

As the unfolding argument of Hebrews will make clear, he could not be inaugurated as the reigning King who had dealt with sins if he had not taken on a body to do so. These statements assume the reality of the incarnation, that God's will was accomplished through the willing offering of the one from whom the Son took his human body—namely, Mary his mother.[39] Luther saw the word *sēmeron* also in this way: "One may understand the words "today I have begotten thee" to refer to both births of Christ. . . . It is not improper to understand it as referring to the human birth."[40] The one who is eternally related to God as Son, hence eternally begotten, was birthed into creation and was then, after his death and resurrection, begotten/installed into his role as Messiah.

The author joins a second quote from another of the well-known royal texts,[41] with the phrase *and again* maintaining the power of presenting these citations in the very voice of God. Here the citation is set within a conversation between Nathan and David that displays the closeness of relationship between God and the one to whom God is speaking. *I will be to him as a Father, and he will be to me as a Son.* They share a familial relationship. Two distinct persons share a commonality of resemblance and authority, qualities that assert the place of the Son as distinct from and superior to the angelic host. Temporally the citation asserts a futurity to the relationship. *I will be* and *he will be*. When this text is first spoken to David by the prophet Nathan about his son Solomon, it describes what will be true when Solomon becomes king. In Hebrews' context, in light of the pronouncement that the relationship has already been established (1:2–3), the name already inherited, the quote declares that what has always existed and is true now will continue forever. Because the following citations proclaim the unending reign of this King, readers can rest assured that this relationship, which has only recently been revealed to them, will continue without end (as it has existed forever in the past). The one who came on their behalf and serves as the first human to dwell in God's presence will always be there in intimate relationship with God. This is the assertion that supports

39. Amy Peeler, *Women and the Gender of God* (Grand Rapids: Eerdmans, 2022), see esp. 118–51.

40. *LW* 29:113.

41. 2 Sam 7:14, repeated in 1 Chr 17:13.

the author's comforting reminder that their Savior lives to make intercession for them (7:25). Moreover, since the author will soon name them as children of God the Father (1:14; 2:10), he sets the template for their enduring relationship with God in the person of the Son.

The author continues God's speech to the Son for the second time with the phrase *and again* for the second time. In this next verse (v. 6), the citation evokes the Song of Moses (Deut 32),[42] and introducing it, the author gives to the Son a different familial title, that of *firstborn*, *prōtotokos*. This term connects to his Davidic heritage. He is the firstborn heir of which royal Psalm 89:28 speaks. Readers familiar with the New Testament might also call to mind when the Son of God is born in Luke as Mary's *prōtotokos* (Luke 2:7), and the angels praise God for his arrival. This title also establishes him in a position of relation to both God and humanity. He is born (*tiktō*), which relates him to his just previously named divine Father. While conceiving of the Son of God as born could prove confusing, the dual meaning of "son" disclosed throughout this chapter aids interpretation here as well. Being born is simply a way of speaking of his filial relationship with God. Since Hebrews has established that this relationship existed eternally, this birth is not in time but an eternal one. At the same time, he is the firstborn human who has defeated death and is now seated incarnate in God's presence. He is both eternally born, humanly born, and newly "born" into his messianic reign.

All of his "births" are integral for the Son to take his seat at God's right hand, but if the timing of the statements in Hebrews stays consistent, then the moment and location of *whenever God leads the firstborn into the world* correspond best, not to the Son's eternal begottenness or his birth in Bethlehem, but to the Son's enthronement. God's "leading in" of him here connects to God's leading of him as the pioneer of salvation in 2:10. This divine leading to the seat of exaltation finds confirmation in the author's other use of "world," *oikoumenē*. The author says in ch. 2 that he has been speaking of the coming world (2:5), over which Christ, the exalted human, is reigning and will reign. While Hebrews' use of *oikoumenē* (realm) is more expansive than a reference to the earth alone, which is the typical use of *oikoumenē* (Ps 9:9; 17:16; 18:5;

42. The citation is not exact, but given the author's citation from Deut 32 in 10:30, this is likely the location from which he is drawing. For a discussion of the complexities, see Pierce, *Divine Discourse*, 53–54n121.

23:1; 32:8; 48:2; 49:12; 71:8; 76:19 LXX), the author is not describing a separate spiritual world but the realm of God that exerts influence over the tangible universe. Hebrews does not advocate escape from the presently perceptible creation but anticipates God's redemptive transformation of it when the Son will reign over all things, the earth included, without resistance.

He is not only the one born (*tiktō*) but also the one born first (*prōtos*), which shows his connection to other children of God, who will soon appear in the discussion of Hebrews (as early as 1:14). The Son of God sets the template for others. God is also leading them on a journey into God's own presence (2:10; 4:9; 6:18–20; 10:19; 12:1). At the same time, as firstborn Son he is distinguished from the other children. In the original setting of this speech in Deuteronomy, God is not speaking but being spoken about. Moses calls forth the worship and respect of the heavenly hosts to be given to God. Here in Hebrews, God calls for the angels to worship the firstborn. Several of the citations in this list are royal, referring to the heir of David, but this is not true of Deuteronomy 32:43, where God reveals that the praise Moses directed toward God is appropriately directed toward God the Son. Reformation pastor Veit Dietrich notes, "The apostle inserts these words . . . : 'Worship Him all you gods and angels.' Now Scripture clearly says, 'You should worship God the Lord and serve him only.' If one should worship Christ . . . , then it certainly follows that he is God."[43] The firstborn receives something at the enthronement that no other child of God will ever receive, and yet, as the firstborn of many, his receiving worship will have implications for other humans; they will have a share in the kingdom over which he reigns (Heb 12:28).

Although it serves the overall comparison between the Son and the angels, the citation of Psalm 103:4 also provides several points of contrast with the other verses in this collection. I titled this section "God's Speeches to the Son," but this citation is not. It is the exception that proves the rule. Unlike God's speech to the Son, in this quote God only speaks *about* the angels. Hence, I suggest the translation, *And gesturing toward the angels, God says.* (By comparison, all the statements to the Son save one, Heb 1:6, come in the form of direct address.) In addition to the form of address, here the psalm says that God is the *one who makes* (*poiōn*) the angels, whereas God made *through* the Son (1:2). This difference suggests a distinction: the angels are created and the

43. Veit Dietrich, *Summary of the Epistle to the Hebrews* 1:6 (RCS 13:23).

Son is not.[44] The psalm reflects on God's utilization of the elements of nature for divine purpose. The author of Hebrews emphasizes that theme by specifying that the angelic beings are created things, both *pneuma* and flames of fire. *Pneuma*, whether translated as "winds" or "spirits," emphasizes their ephemeral, disembodied nature.[45] They may blow wherever God directs them, even taking on an embodied appearance (13:2), but they, unlike the Son, have never taken on flesh (2:14). As *flames of fire* they advertise God's presence (12:18, 29) and can participate in the enactment of God's judgment (10:27). The angels are God's ministers doing God's bidding in both communication and service, either with the gentleness of a breeze or the intensity of a flame. The author will evoke the psalmist's language in 1:14, where he refers to them as "ministering spirits," a combination of each phrase cited here. This citation provides one point of unity between the Son and the angels: both are *ministers* on behalf of humanity. God will use any means necessary for the sake of humanity's good. The angels are sent out to serve those who are about to inherit salvation (1:14), and the Son has a ministry of atonement and advocacy in God's true tent (8:2, 6). The angels do so, however, as part of creation that is, whether in the appearance of spirit or fire, decidedly not human.

Only the Son, however, who has become human, performs his ongoing ministry seated on a throne. In the next verse, drawn from Psalm 44:6–7 LXX—another royal psalm praising the king of Israel—God speaks to the Son about his *throne*. As mentioned in the discussion of the inherited name, many interpreters understand the first instance of the word for God, *theos*, as a vocative. God is addressing the Son as "*O God*." In its original setting the psalmist is praising the king and using a term of highest honor as God's representative (although Israel resisted the divination of their kings).[46] In Hebrews, if God is speaking this text to the same one who has been in relationship with God eternally, the title is both honorific *and* true. The divine meaning of the title is

44. See discussion of 3:2 where God *makes* the Son, but in the sense of appointing him to a particular role.

45. The translation of "winds" more closely aligns with the nature focus of the psalm, but "spirits" facilitates more easily an imagination of how these messengers can interact helpfully with humans (1:14; 13:2).

46. L. D. Hurst, "The Christology of Hebrews 1 and 2," in *The Glory of Christ in the New Testament: Studies in Christology in Memory of George Bradford Caird*, ed. L. D. Hurst and N. T. Wright (Oxford: Clarendon, 1987), 161.

confirmed by the next statement. This one's throne will last *forever and ever*. The psalmist would have hoped (and confidently so, on the basis of God's promise to the king's sons) that his throne would last forever because his sons would continue to reign on it successively. In this instance, however, since the Son will never die again (a point the audience already knows and trusts), he and he alone can remain on this throne forever.

If human rulership through the ages is any indication, a throne without term limits raises concerns. Thankfully, this one who rules radiates the just God's very being, so there is no danger of a misuse of eternal sovereign power. The language of the psalm itself assures that his reign will be above reproach. The *scepter* was the king's symbol of implementation, and for this king he implements his decisions for his kingdom with *righteousness*. It is his desire to rule in this way because it arises out of his *love* for righteousness. Conversely, he *abhors* lawlessness. For those in any time or place who suffer under unjust rule, the assurance of the one who really sits on the ultimate throne, loving what is good and hating what is evil, and who will be there forever, offers deep comfort and strength to endure.

In addition to the granting of the throne to the ascended Son, in response to his righteousness (*because of* this) God performs another act to demonstrate the Son's kingship: anointing. This is the first instance of the word group that grants Jesus's honorific title as the anointed one, the Christ (first appearing in this letter at 3:6). Church historian Eusebius of Caesarea was well aware that anointing was practiced for both kings and priests and sometimes prophets, and so he sees in this phrase an allusion to Jesus's roles in Hebrews, the Son-King and High Priest sent from God to speak God's words.[47] As in the first line of the psalm, there is the possibility that the first *theos* in the phrase is functioning as a vocative: *God, your God*, has anointed you, a fruitful duplication within one *theos* for an author who has claimed personal relations within the being of God.

What is applied to the Son in this instance is the *oil of rejoicing*. Because this particular phrase never appears anywhere else in Israel's Scriptures—an absence that indicates this was not a common way of speaking about the anointing of priests or kings—some interpreters saw in the word for "rejoicing" allusion to the person of God who brings gladness—namely, the Holy

47. Eusebius, *Ecclesiastical History* 1.3 (ACCS 10:25).

Spirit—as supported in the parallelism of Psalm 50:14 LXX: "Restore to me the joy [*agalliasin*] of your deliverance, and with a leading spirit support me." Reformation interpreter Lucas Osiander states, "He is anointed with the oil of gladness, that is, God the Holy Spirit, conferring his own gifts abundantly and without measure on the Son of Man."[48] Even if the allusion to the Spirit is not prominent, "rejoicing" indicates the celebratory nature of the enthronement. The purification of sins having been secured, there is certainly reason to celebrate. When the author describes God's holy city in ch. 12, it is a place of celebration (12:22).

The celebration helps inform the interpretation of the final phrase of v. **9**. The psalm states that he has been anointed in a way that goes *beyond* (*para*) his companions. In light of the consistent comparison with angels, those other sons of God, this statement is another way of asserting his supremacy over them. Even though both do the will of God, he is enthroned as King in a way the angels are not. Moreover, both the Son and the angels may minister to humanity, but only the Son does so as anointed human King and Priest. Throughout the rest of Hebrews, however, the word for *companions* (*metochos*) refers to those humans who have cast their lot with Jesus the Messiah (3:1, 14; 6:4; 12:8). The fact that they can become his companions gives him joy (12:2). When he is anointed, they are not all in his midst, not in an embodied way anyhow, so he is anointed not alongside them but beyond them.[49] Hence, his anointing takes primacy over any reception of the Holy Spirit or vocational anointing his human followers may receive. This is true because he is first chronologically, the first human to reign with God. He is also beyond them because he is superior to them. Although his companions will also inherit a kingdom (12:28), he is the King. Although they will perform priestly acts (12:28; 13:15), he alone bears the designation of High Priest. It is his superiority both temporally and qualitatively that makes their embrace of the kingdom and service to God possible. For any beleaguered readers, hemmed in by either threat of mortal death or the weight of any emotional or spiritual battle, an unending, righteous, and even joyful King offers an assurance of his control over all things and a promise that dwelling in his kingdom is their ultimate end.

48. RCS 13:25.

49. *Para* with an accusative typically conveys a comparison. Dana M. Harris, *Hebrews*, Exegetical Guide to the Greek New Testament (Nashville: B&H Academic, 2019), 29.

From eternity future to eternity past, with the use of Psalm 101:26–28 LXX in vv. **10–12** the author presents the voice of God to say that the Son's participation in creation first mentioned in 1:2 happened by actively creating. In the psalm, a weary and oppressed person cries out to the Lord in trust. The unchangeability of God provides a bulwark against the persistent instability of life. In vv. 26–28 the psalmist continues the refrain in direct address to God. As was true with the citation of Deuteronomy 32:43 in v. 6, the author transforms a statement of praise from a human to God into a statement of proclamation from God to the eternal and now embodied Son. *And, "You at the beginning, Lord."* The vocative of *kyrios* aligns with the vocative of *theos* in the previous verse. God the Father asserts that the enthroned Son is the same one who is also and always has been fittingly addressed with the divine name. He is the LORD.

The temporal focus of this statement affirms his divine being. Before creation had a beginning, he was there. The King who will reign forever over the entirety of creation (v. 8) is the same one who *laid the foundations of the earth.* God can also say to the Son, *The heavens are the works of your hands.* It is fitting to say that as a master builder (see discussion of 3:4) the Son with his Father founded the earth and formed the heavens with his fingers. As was true in 1:3, the author affirms that the comprehensive universe bears his imprint.

That which bears his mark, however, is not eternal as he is. The created things *will perish; all will grow old as a garment . . . and as a garment they will be changed.* Created things come and go, grow old and are changed as is clothing. Science shows this process even in the human body, as our cells are replaced on a regular basis. The Son plays an active role in this. God can say, *Like a cloak you will roll them up.*

With such phrases from the psalm the author is not saying that creation itself will pass away. Instead, in Hebrews this psalm functions as evidence of the Son's sustaining power. This puts the author of Hebrews at odds with any idea that creation itself is eternal in nature. As stated earlier, all things are upheld by the word of his power (1:3). As elements of creation pass away, he ensures that more arise.

In addition to a statement of regular renewal, this psalm in Hebrews does not point to his destruction of all material, especially not a destruction that could take place outside the divine will. Creation may perish, but it too will be resurrected. The Son's own embodied experience provides the template for all creation, not just humanity. As Hebrews 12:26–27 affirms, there will be a great shaking, but that which is unshakable will remain and be sustained by him. The continual changing of the guard of creation and its final purification serve as evidence of his unchanging and gracious nature toward nature.

Juxtaposed with created things that pass away, the psalm says of the Son, *But you remain* and *but you are the same and your years will not end.* Resonant with the assertion in Hebrews 13:8, "Jesus the Messiah is the same yesterday and today and forever," the psalm proclaims his steadfast and powerful existence. Surprisingly, the author just affirmed that this one, the Son, *has* undergone a change. In these days of the end, he has made purification for sin and then sat down at the right hand of God. He has inherited an honorific title, Son of God, in a way distinct from his eternal being as Son of God. The coherent chapter affirms that he has remained unchanged in his relation to God, and in line with that eternal divine relationship he has willingly fulfilled the divine will he shares, undergone a new experience, and even been given the messianic title. He is now the embodied sovereign over all things that have ever been his possession by the divine right of creating. If readers, like the psalmist, have concern because of the instabilities that threaten their lives, they too can look to the Lord, their redeemer Jesus, who eternally has all things in control.

The culminating citation (from Ps 109:1 LXX) stands in this place in the catena for several possible reasons. First, Psalm 110 arises out of the Jesus tradition (Matt 22:44/Mark 12:36/Luke 20:42) and gets repeated by several other early Christian authors (e.g., Acts 2:34; 1 Cor 15:25). Citing this passage would be to proclaim a shared belief among the community or to articulate a confession that already binds them together. The author continues to cite or allude to this text throughout the sermon (e.g., Heb 8:1; 10:12; see discussion at 8:1). Christians affirm that the Son whom they confess is the heir of David for whom many Jews had been hoping.

Second, this citation reiterates the position of Christ's sovereignty the author has been asserting throughout the chapter. Highlighting the connection with 1:3, Veit Dietrich comments, "To sit at God's right hand means to have the same authority as God, that is, to rule and govern over all things."[50] Chrysostom beautifully states, "This again belongs to Sovereignty, to Equal Dignity, to Honor and not weakness, that the Father should be angry for the

50. RCS 13:26.

things done to the Son."[51] God will avenge the Son, and those forces opposed to God's embodied Son are opposed to all humanity. Ultimate victory and freedom from any form of bondage is guaranteed.

The author introduces this citation with a reminder about the Son's position vis-à-vis the angels: *And to which of the angels has God ever said.* With consistency, the author asserts the Son's sovereignty by comparing him with God's heavenly hosts. They serve God around the throne and do God's bidding on earth (v. **14**; 2:2), and yet they have never been invited by God directly to sit on the seat of power. The embodied Son is given the gracious command by God to *sit*, now that purification of sins has been accomplished, at the place of power where he eternally reigned, at God's *right hand.*

Finally, Psalm 109:1 LXX introduces an element of promise that will become a focus of the next chapter. The Son is seated, but enemies remain. He is invited to sit *until I place your enemies under your feet.* God has guaranteed their obeisance to the Son. This promise resonates with God's assurance to humanity in Psalm 8:7 cited in 2:8. The Son as human now has feet—scarred ones, John suggests (John 20:27)—under which God will place the enemies. That event, however, remains in the future. Everything belongs to the Son, by virtue of being God's heir eternally, by virtue of creating and sustaining all things, by virtue of dealing with the problem of sin and winning creation back (see comments on 2:14–15). Though the enemies' defeat is guaranteed by his work, they continue to wreak havoc, as will become clear when the author speaks of the audience's struggle with faithfulness (Heb 3–4), persecution (10:32–34), and death (12:3–4). The Son is awaiting the day in which the inheritance that is his is free from the wounds inflicted by these enemy forces. This is the promise that remains. *How* to live in such a situation of the Son's guaranteed but unrealized sovereignty becomes the driving question for much of this pastor's exhortation.

The closing question of the section, *Are they not all ministering spirits that are sent to serve for the sake of those who are about to inherit salvation?*, again puts the attention on the angels and, in so doing, the Son's superiority to them. The superiority becomes most apparent when the description of the angels stands next to that of the Son point by point. As mentioned, the Son also ministers on behalf of humans (8:2, 6), and the Son is sent by God to humans (3:1).

51. Chrysostom, *Hebrews* 3.4 (*NPNF*[1] 14:376).

The author never explicitly describes the earthly service of the Son, as do other Christian traditions like Mark (Mark 10:45) or John (John 13), but his once-for-all and ongoing priestly work certainly counts as service rendered. The comparison with the angels who are ministering spirits leaves only two differences. First, many angels exist, but there is only one Son. Second, the angels are spirits, and the Son, as the next chapter will show, is embodied. Only he, whose ministry with respect to sin is now done, can sit on the very throne of God, and only the Son, as God and Messiah, has all the qualifications that fit him to do so. The angels do not.

That they are inferior to the exalted Son does not mean that the author paints them negatively. They play a vital role in the salvation of God's people. The sermon will soon discuss their role in passing on God's law (2:2). Here at the end of ch. 1, the author notes that they serve those *who are about to inherit salvation*. By speaking of salvation in this way, as an inheritance, the author highlights his persistent project of connecting humanity with the Son. As the Son has been appointed heir (1:2), humans are heirs as well. Humanity needs the service of God's messengers so that they might persist toward what lies ahead, their inheritance of salvation. Because the enemies of the Son have not yet been put under his feet, the angelic host serve those who are afflicted. The author has consistently compared the value of the angels, and their role in the economy of salvation, with the supremacy of the Son, but does so in such a way that it is clear they are not the Son's opponents. They and the Son are on the same team, doing God's will for the benefit of creation.

The majestic elevation of the Son in this chapter through scriptural allusion and God's very voice, although it is rich in complexity, is not an example of academic theology. Instead, it is the example par excellence of God's communication to the people God desires to redeem, having accomplished the work necessary to do so. Whatever a reader may be facing, the divine posture of power for good provides a firm foundation on which to build the calls for endurance that follow.

HEBREWS 2:1–18

THE HUMILITY OF THE SON

The author opened this message with an example of theological art at its finest. He put the majesty and grace of God on display through God's revelatory speech in the eternal Son who became the exalted messianic Son. Humanity was certainly not absent from this reflection, but the focus remained steadfastly on the work of God. At the beginning of ch. 2, the attention shifts to those who are listening to God, specifically the author and the community to whom he is writing. The first verse clearly indicates both a new focus and a connection to what has come before. For the first of many times, the author offers an exhortation to his listeners (and includes himself within it): they must pay attention to what they have heard. All that he has said in ch. 1 provides his reason for believing this exhortation is necessary. Because they have heard from God ("God spoke to us"), and because God has spoken in the most excellent Son (1:2), the necessity of listening to God's communication is greater than it ever has been. The author illustrates this "even more" quality by describing the previous communication from God in comparison with the current communication from God. He describes the current communication as both Triune—a faithful description by virtue of the mention of the Lord (2:3), God (2:4), and the Holy Spirit (2:4)—and embodied, given the reference to the human participants in this communication not only as recipients (2:4) but also as messengers (2:3).

Having described the salvation that has been manifest among them in the past, the author turns to the implications of that salvation in the future as well as in the present. God's intent, expressed in Psalm 8 (portions of which are cited in 2:5–7), is that humans gloriously reign over all creation. That intent has not been realized, and the author blames death and sin as the cause for that sad reality (1:3; 2:9, 14–15, 17).

God's sending of Jesus solves those related problems. The author reads the psalm about humanity as a fitting description of Jesus in particular. The comprehensive reign over all things is his after he suffered death (2:8–10). The author focuses first on the familial relationship Jesus shares with humanity, articulated in the Son's speaking of Scripture (2:12–13). Then the author proclaims clearly that the Son took on flesh and blood, and therefore experienced both temptation and mortality, but allowed neither sin nor death to defeat him. He instead overpowers them both (2:14–15). In so doing, he can safely lead his siblings, the members of God's covenant family (2:16), through their struggles with sin and death to God's realm of glory. For the first of many times in the letter, the author describes this movement and leading by the Son as his high priestly role (2:17–18).

2:1–4 · ATTENTION

[1]Because of this it is even more necessary for us to attend carefully to the things we have heard, lest we drift away. [2]For if the word spoken through angels was binding and every transgression and disobedience received a just retribution, [3]how will we escape if we ignore so great a salvation, which, at the beginning was spoken by the Lord, was then confirmed to us by those who heard, [4]being testified by God with both signs and wonders and various powers and distributions of the Holy Spirit according to God's will?

Establishing a strong link with what has come before, the author begins this sentence with *Because of this*. The "this" is God's speech to them in the Son, which revealed that the God who has been in communicative relationship with humanity since creating all things is the same God revealed personally in the Son. This revelation has assured the comprehensive and lasting victory to which the ancient communication was pointing. It was always necessary to listen to God, but now that sin has been purified and the enemies are awaiting their certain defeat, listening is *even more necessary*. If someone does not heed God's message in the Son, there is no other access to this victory.

The author ties the link directly to the previous statement in two ways. First, both the first and the second chapter share an assertion that God has sent aid to the covenant people. God sends the angelic ministration to those who are about to inherit salvation (1:14). As they await that salvation and experience testing, God sends (*apostolos*, 3:1) the aid of the Son who was tested (2:18). These brackets of divine aid demonstrate the consistency of God's benevolence, through angelic beings and now also in the Son. The statements also indicate that the Son's superiority over the angels does not mean that they are his competitors; instead, they are his co-laborers in God's work. That being the case, while the aid of the angels is a vital blessing, it can never match the aid of one who has fully entered into the human condition.

A second connection between the first two chapters is implied by the statement in 1:14. Along with the good news that God has promised an inheritance of salvation and that angels are serving those who are waiting for it, the author includes the sober assertion that salvation has not yet been inherited. It remains in the future. The connection is that both the Son and his followers are waiting for the consummation of what he has begun, the placement of his enemies under his feet (1:13) and their salvation (1:14). While those who have been promised salvation are receiving the ministration of angels, they will also need to exercise their own will to endure until that future arrives. Hence, they need to *attend carefully to the things we have heard* (v. **1**). This kind of attention is recommended in situations where one needs to watch out in order to avoid something negative (Matt 16:6/Luke 12:1), but also when one should devote attention to something good (Acts 8:6; 16:14). In this instance, what they have heard is very good. The author's point is that this message deserves their focus. Here, in this first exhortation, he tells them what to do ("pay attention to what you have heard"); in the following exhortation of ch. 3, he will tell them *how* to do it.

To reiterate his instruction for attentiveness, he also names the consequence if there is a failure to listen. If they do not pay attention during this interim, they might perform the opposite of holding fast and, regrettably and at great cost, *drift away* (*pararyōmen*). The author has chosen a unique term, at least as far as the New Testament literature is concerned. It is built on the verb for "flow" (*rheō*), as in "flowing water" (John 7:38; Isa 44:4 LXX). It appears in Proverbs 3, a chapter from which the author will cite in ch. 12, but there the form is active: "My son, do not break away [*pararryēs*] but keep my counsel and insight" (Prov 3:21). Here the form is a passive subjunctive: *lest we* (be made to) *drift away*. They may not actively choose to turn away from what they have heard, but if they do not focus on it, all that swirls around them may in fact *carry* them away. The author's language strongly suggests that one cannot be neutral or stagnant in faith; a person is either intentionally attentive or being carried backward. This statement can serve as a jolt to consider the status of one's faith, but lest that wake-up call become a source of counterproductive guilt, it is necessary to hear again the good and powerful speech about the Son from ch. 1. That is the message to which the faithful must remain attentive. It is so good that no one would want to ignore it, even if persecuting forces (Heb 10:32–39; 12:3–11; 13:3) are tempting them to do so. In other words, the author's warning is aimed at a group whose confession is being threatened by other demands, a group under fire, who are weighing whether holding fast to the confession of Christ is worth the cost. Because they have not yet inherited salvation, they must hold fast to what they have heard. He extols Christ's majesty and urges their attention to it, so that the option of acquiescing to persecution might pale in comparison.

The human condition, however, is often mysteriously self-defeating. Consequently, the author must say more, and he does so by adding a comparative term in this verse, *even more*. The things they have heard about the Son to which they need to hold fast are weightier than the messages God gave in the past. The reference to hearing connects this comparison to the first statement in the letter. God's speech given through prophets was necessary and good, but the prophetic word alone cannot compare with the statements of the prophets in light of the filial divine speech. God's communication through the person of the Son teaches them how to hear God's other communication. Because the Son participates in God's being as radiance and imprint (1:3), and therefore he is eternal creator and sustainer (1:2, 3, 8–12), filial speech reveals God more fully. The prophetic words are not obliterated, however, but necessarily retained. In addition to the fact that they prepared humanity to understand the revelation of the Son, these prophetic words remain necessary and beneficial now as they are interpreted through God's speech in the life of the Son. The author illustrates this comparison between past and present divine speech in the next verse.

They need to hold fast *even more* because turning away from the filial divine speech will have deeper consequences than disobeying the angelically conveyed divine speech. With this sentence, one of the angelic undercurrents of the letter becomes explicit. God often communicated to humanity through angelic messengers, and so *the word spoken through angels* is another way to articulate the word of God spoken through the prophets (1:1). A particular manifestation of that communication mediated through angels is the law God gave to Moses on

Mount Sinai (Exod 20–35), or at least, according to several interpreters of the time, this law was given through angels (Paul refers to this in Gal 3:19, as does Acts 7:30, 38, 53).[1] They served as the mediators of God's word.

This word *was confirmed* in that it was upheld as authoritative and consequential. In any instance when someone disobeyed the word, they *received a just retribution*. Israel tests the seriousness of the law almost immediately when they disobey the first command against the worship of idols (Exod 20:4) with the creation of the golden calf (Exod 32). The author elaborates the kind of disobedience they committed by describing it with two terms, *parabasis* and *parakoē*, *every transgression* and *disobedience*. In the New Testament *parabasis* is always associated with law. When a line is drawn in the sand, to transgress is to step over that line. The Israelites were given the law with clarity and then disobeyed it. The second term highlights the importance of listening, a theme that runs throughout the first part of the sermon (Heb 2:1, 3; 3:7, 15–16; 4:2, 7). *Parakouō* is to hear but not obey. The punishment they received for this first action of disobedience was intense. They were made to taste of their creation (Exod 32:20), three thousand died (Exod 32:28), and the Lord struck the people (Exod 32:35). The author of Hebrews sees this punishment as a *just* one. To reject the God of redemption and life exposes one to the ravages of death. The consequences of turning from God are grave.

If outright disobedient transgression—doing precisely what God said not to do—against the angelically communicated word resulted in such consequences, it is obvious to the author that an even less serious action against God's definitive communication in the Son would also justify punishment.

	Angelic	***Filial***
Communication	word	so great a salvation
Infraction	transgress and disobey	ignore

The author describes both the communication and the infraction against God's Son-speech in different terms than in the example from Israel's past. Whereas the Israelites crossed the line and disobeyed, the option on the table for this community is to *ignore*. This is a more passive response, to "walk

1. Jubilees as well as some rabbinic texts also reflects this tradition. See Attridge, *Hebrews*, 65n28.

away" (Matt 22:5) or fail to pay enough attention (1 Tim 4:14). Even God ignores when God disregards the Israelites after they fail to keep the covenant (Heb 8:9/Jer 38:32 LXX). The rhetorical impact of "to ignore" is less serious than "to actively disobey," but given the majesty of the message they would be ignoring, if they do not pay close attention to what they have heard (2:1), they are committing a more serious infraction. If they ignore what they have heard in God's Son, they will be neglecting *so great a salvation*. This is the salvation that those whom the angels serve look forward to inheriting, an inheritance from the God who keeps promises (1:14). It is rightly described as great because it includes purification from sin (1:3) and inclusion in the kingdom of the Son that will never end and will someday have no threat from enemies (1:13). If they *ignore* this, the consequences are obvious. The author poses the conclusion as a question: *How will we escape*? He will use the language of escape again in his admonition in ch. 12 when he speaks again of the generation who received the law from Sinai (12:25). If that generation did not escape punishment, without a doubt those who ignore the great salvation of the Son will not either.

To further emphasize the greatness of this salvation, the author spends more time on the persons who communicate it. Whereas the word came to Moses through angels, the great salvation comes to this audience through a threefold divine witness.

First, the author says that *at the beginning* this salvation *was spoken by the Lord*. In ch. 1 the author proclaimed that God is now speaking through the one who is eternal, who is creator, the one who is king, who is God's radiance and reflection. Now he says that the same one is he who first communicated the arrival of this great salvation. Here the author refers to the Son as the Lord, as was true in the citation from Psalm 101 in Hebrews 1:10. The author will use this honorific for the Son again in 7:14, referring to his descent from Judah, and in 13:20 to refer to his resurrection. The author will also cite texts from Israel's Scriptures in which *kyrios* indicates God the Father of the Son (7:21; 8:8–11; 10:16, 30; 12:5–6). In this instance, it seems clear that he refers to the Son during his human life when he shared the good news of God's salvation with those around him. This is the first instance in which the author indicates his knowledge of the traditions about Jesus recorded by the four evangelists, although he refers to those traditions here in a general way.

That word was then spread by those who heard the Lord speak. As he says, it *was confirmed to us by those who heard*. This salvation was *confirmed* (*bebaioō*) just as the word of the law was confirmed (v. **2**), and it became confirmed to the author and his listeners by those Christ sent out to share the news of salvation. The message was communicated by those whose lives had been transformed by it; they provided the tangible proof of the salvific good news the Lord preached to them. Scholars have debated whether "those who heard" heard the message about the Lord[2] or heard from the Lord himself;[3] the sequence of the statements suggests the latter as the stronger reading. One thinks of people like Peter, who had been restored after denial (John 18:25–27; 21); Mary Magdalene, who had been healed from the demonic (Luke 8:2; John 20:17), or James the brother of Jesus, who had been transformed out of disbelief (John 7:5; 1 Cor 15:7). Whereas the angels passed on the divine word to Moses, the Son's human messengers passed on the salvific word to this community. The integrity of the message, however, is maintained if the degree of separation between this community and Jesus is only one or a few. This great salvation coheres with the communication of God for millennia and, as the following statement will show, was confirmed to them by divine testimony in their midst. Hence, it is fitting to see these human messengers as connected to the Lord, for they form a witness of the salvation he brings.

God confirms the respect due to their message by corroborating. God willed to bless this community with supernatural manifestations as testimony to this salvific message. The salvation was *testified by God with both signs and wonders and various powers and distributions of the Holy Spirit according to God's will.* The triad of signs, wonders, and powers appears three times in the Pauline corpus as well (Rom 15:19; 2 Cor 12:12; 2 Thess 2:9), demonstrating that this is not a unique grouping but one that could communicate the gracious divine power of God's gift. As is true in the accounts preserved in Acts and in other epistles, the revelation and acceptance of the message of salvation through the Son is no quiet and hidden event. God's work becomes manifest in powerful and unmistakably divine ways.

The last divine gift in the group, *distributions of the Holy Spirit*, is that which makes possible all the rest. Hebrews highlights the work of the Spirit in communicating to God's people (3:7; 9:8; 10:15). So also here, the Spirit is one

2. Attridge, *Hebrews*, 59.

3. Gareth Lee Cockerill, *The Epistle to the Hebrews*, NICNT (Grand Rapids: Eerdmans, 2012), 122.

way God testifies of the great salvation. Because the phrase is in the genitive case in this sentence, the author might be indicating that the divisions given are gifts *from* the Holy Spirit. It is also fitting to see God apportioning *the Holy Spirit* to those who have received the great salvation. This reading aligns with the evidence preserved in Acts, where, beginning with Pentecost, the early church experiences signs and wonders when the Spirit comes upon them (Acts 2:18–19, 38–43) and when the Spirit is present with them throughout their ministry (Acts 4:30; 5:12; 6:8; 14:3; 15:12). This latter interpretation also aligns well with the author's assertions of the community's participation in the Spirit. His comments on the work of God's Spirit may be few, but they form a powerful infrastructure to the life of the community. In Hebrews the Spirit provides the way in which people can participate in the salvation of God. It is the Spirit who facilitates the salvific self-offering of the Son to the Father (Heb 9:14). Consequently, it is not surprising that one of the indications of repentance is to share in the Holy Spirit (6:4) and that to turn away from the Son is to outrage the Spirit of grace (10:29). In line with other New Testament authors (classic texts include Rom 8; Acts 2; John 14; 1 Pet 1), the author of Hebrews envisions human participation in the life of God as possible through the gift of God's Holy Spirit.

The author discloses God's graciousness and desire for relationship in the final phrase. The great salvation has been revealed to them by these multiple forms of witness all *according to God's will.* In ch. 10 the author will return to the theme of God's will, when through Psalm 40 he shows that the Son came to fulfill the divine will (10:7, 9). There the sanctification of humanity defines God's will (10:10). When humans are made holy, they can behold the Lord (12:14). Having become sanctified, humans can now do God's will (10:36; 13:21). God could choose to remain separate from the humanity that has become separated from holiness, but God has not willed to do so. Instead, God has provided everything necessary for their restoration into relationship with God, and this restoration is their salvation.

Borrowing language from the later tradition, it is fitting to say that this first brief exhortation paints God's salvation as both Triune and embodied. The Son, the Father, and the Spirit communicate this great salvation in such a way that the audience receives it from other humans and sees it manifest in word and action among the members of their own community, events explicable only by the holy presence of God. If they turn away from all this testimony, there will be no escaping what befalls those who are *not* waiting to inherit salvation (1:14). The author leaves them wondering why they would ever want to turn away from a God who communicates salvation to them and whose salvation had already accomplished so much among them. Unlike the forceful voices who might be telling them to turn away from this divine speech, the author is knitting them even more tightly into the community where God communicates. It is good, right, and even joyful to continue to pay attention to the salvation given through the Son.

2:5–18 · FOR US AND FOR OUR SALVATION

[5]For it was not to angels that God subjected the world to come, concerning which we speak. [6]And someone testifies somewhere saying,

> *What is a human that you remember him*
> *or the son of a human that you care for him?*
> *[7]You made him a little lower than the angels;*
> *you crowned him with glory and honor;*
> *[8]you subjected everything under his feet.*

For in subjecting everything to him, God left nothing unsubjected to him. But now we do not yet see everything that has been subjected to him, [9]but we see Jesus, the one who has been made a little lower than the angels through the suffering of death, the one who has been crowned with glory and honor, so that by the grace of God he might taste death for all.

[10]For it was fitting for God, for whom are all things and through whom are all things, in leading many sons to glory, to perfect the author of their salvation through sufferings. [11]For both the one who sanctifies and the ones who are sanctified are all from one. For this reason, he is not ashamed to call them brothers and sisters, [12]saying,

> *I will proclaim your name to my brothers and sisters;*
> *in the midst of the assembly I will praise you.*

[13]And again,

> *I will be one who has trusted upon him.*

And again,

> *Behold, I and the children whom God gave to me.*

[14]Therefore, since the children have shared of blood and flesh, also he likewise shared of the same things, in order that through death he might destroy the one who has the power of death—that is, the devil—[15]and might rescue those who through the fear of death throughout the whole of their lives were ones who were subject to slavery. [16]For it is clear he did not take hold of angels but took hold of the seed of Abraham. [17]Whence, he ought to be made like his brothers and sisters according to all things in order that he might become a merciful and faithful High Priest with respect to the things aimed at God for the purpose of pardoning the sins of the people. [18]For because he has suffered when tested, he is able to aid those who are being tested.

The angels, as communicators of the divine law, held impressive authority in the past, as the author has just described. When the law they passed on was transgressed, punishment justly followed. Now in these last days (1:2) with the age to come approaching, God has installed a human over the position of the angels. Hence, the author begins the next sentence with *For it was not to angels that God subjected the world to come, concerning which we speak.*

The author uses the term *oikoumenē* to name this realm. In the New Testament, this *world* appears as a description of the whole world/the earth and the people in it (Matt 24:14; Luke 21:26; Rev 12:9) or the section of the world that matters to a particular people group (Luke 2:1; Acts 11:28). The use of this term hinders a purely "spiritual" reading of the world over which the Son reigns. The author casts a vision of the Son's reign that certainly includes the material world as they know it.

The author also says this is the world about which *we speak*, meaning that he has been discussing this world already. The use of *oikoumenē* in v. **5** and 1:6 is mutually informing. The world in question is the world that the one God (Father and Son) created (1:2, 10) and the world over which the embodied and exalted Son now reigns as he sits at God's right hand (1:3, 6, 8–9). This world also has a future element to it: it is the *world to come*. When the audience reads this letter, the Son is already seated at God's right hand and sovereign over the world. This adjectival phrase "to come" asserts that there is something yet to be realized about this world over which the Son reigns. That futurity aligns with the Father's invitation to the Son to wait for the subjection of the enemies (1:13). Lack of realization does not raise doubts that this subjection will happen, however.

To articulate this reality of subjection to the Son but not to the angels, the author cites a psalm that praises God for the enviable position of humanity, Psalm 8. The indeterminacy with which the author introduces the citation (*And someone testifies somewhere saying*) suggests that this could be a familiar text to the readers. Even with the few verses evoked the audience would know its location.[4] The author's rhetorical skill shines here. He gives a compliment to the listeners by assuming they share the knowledge of this psalm with him. By introducing it as testimony, he highlights the solemnity and verifiability of the statement. Moreover, the lack of focus on a human speaker allows the attention of the hearer to focus more fully on the action of God the psalmist describes.

The psalm begins with praise to the Lord whose majesty was lifted above the heavens (Ps 8:2 LXX). That the majesty of the Lord "was raised" (passive of *epairō*) resonates with the claims of the author who has just named the Son as Lord (Heb 1:10) and who will describe the Son as the Lord ascending above the heavens later in the letter (4:14; 7:26). Though the first few verses of the psalm may provide a connection to a larger christological theme of the sermon, the author chooses to cite from the middle of the psalm where the psalmist—in a state of wonder—marvels that the God who formed the heavens also takes note of humans. (Ps 8:4 LXX shares several verbal similarities—heavens, works, fingers/hands, founded—with Ps 101:26 LXX, which the author quoted in ch. 1.) God notices humans by remembering (*mimnēskomai*) and caring (*episkeptomai*) for them. The psalmist asks in v. **6**, *What is a human that you remember him?* Humans need reminders of certain pieces of information because the human mind cannot retain all things. This limitation does not apply to God, certainly the God who is actively sustaining all things (Heb 1:3). When authors speak of God's remembering, it is a way of speaking of God's turning toward humanity to show them mercy (Luke 1:54, 72; 23:42).[5] Here both the psalmist and Hebrews assert that by remembering God actively gives attention to humanity. Hence, the parallel line emphasizes that God *cares*

4. Chrysostom, *Hebrews* 4.2 (*NPNF*[1] 14:383).

5. At times it is God's act of forgetting that demonstrates mercy. Later in the sermon, the author of Hebrews will twice cite Jer 31, where God chooses *not* to remember sins (8:12; 10:17).

for humanity. This is an attentiveness that not only notices the entity but takes steps to do good for the thing being noticed (Matt 25:36; Luke 1:68; Acts 15:36; Jas 1:27). This line from the psalm affirms specifically for humanity what is true of God's gracious sustenance of all creation, which the author proclaimed at the beginning (Heb 1:3).

In short, the focus here in the psalm and Hebrews is on humanity. The psalmist is in awe of God's attention to a person. This citation and the author of Hebrews' discussion of it is one of the most interesting and challenging sections for New Testament translation, particularly with regard to gendered language. In the Greek version, the psalmist asks about the nature of a singular *anthrōpos* and then the son (*huios*) of an *anthrōpos*. The singular pronouns at the end of each line are then grammatically aligned with their antecedent. They, too, are masculine.[6] As is often the case in ancient languages, the masculine singular can represent all humans, and so the translation could be a wooden one ("What is man that you remember him or the son of man that you care for him?") into which women would need to assume their presence. I have chosen against that option in my translation for several reasons. First, the psalm and Hebrews are written to men and women. In light of the assertion of the *imago Dei* in both men *and women* at creation (Gen 1:26–27), Israel's faith is not meant for men alone. Moreover, in modern parlance, "man" is no longer heard as inclusive by all listeners. Choosing to translate the first *anthrōpos* as "human" is a grammatically appropriate way to translate this term that gives voice to the inclusion of all in the *imago Dei* in more fitting language for my time and social location. On the other hand, I also opted against a fully inclusive translation ("What is humanity that you remember them or the children of humanity that you care for them?"). The masculine terms ("son" and "him") are retained because the author will use this psalm as a way of speaking of Jesus, *his* experience and *his* representational nature. Because God remembers and cares for *him*, all humans are embraced into God's redemptive care and can inherit God's glorious intention for human creation. The christological lens leads to the translation "son of a human" for the second line. This translation allows for a resonance with the "Son of Man" title attested for Jesus in the Gospels, but also leaves space for an affirmation of the birth

6. This is also true in the Hebrew text of the psalm, which includes both *ʾenosh* (humanity) and *ben ʾadam* (son of humanity).

narratives of Matthew and Luke, where it is clear that Jesus is decidedly *not* the son of a man but the son of a woman, Mary.

The psalmist then asserts that God has placed humanity in a state of honor just below that of the angels. The psalm uses a phrase, *brachy ti*, that denotes a small quantity. In the psalm this smallness is a positive thing indicating the close proximity humans share with respect to angels. This is a status in which God crowns each human with glory and honor. Save the angels, God has subjected all created things under their feet.

So says the psalm. The author of Hebrews multiplies its meaning with both emphasis and silence. First, he emphasizes the final phrase he has quoted. He reiterates subjection (*hypotassō*) twice and everything (*ta panta*) twice, once positively (*For in subjecting everything to him*) and once negatively (*God left nothing unsubjected to him*). The obvious conclusion is that truly nothing is outside the realm of his sovereignty. The emphasis on comprehensiveness illuminates the verses of the psalm the author chose *not* to cite. He chose not to include Psalm 8:6a LXX, "And you set him over the works of your hands," which is specified as various animals in vv. 7–8, because that list would not be sufficient for the kind of sovereignty for which he is arguing for the Son. The Son does not just reign over animals and plants, as was true of Adam and Eve (Gen 1:28–30), but truly over everything: all humans and all angelic beings. Nothing is outside his reign as he sits as the enthroned Son of God.

While this sovereignty is assured, at present it is not yet visible. *But now we do not yet see everything that has been subjected to him.* By this point in the sermon, the pieces are in place to wrestle with the Son's sovereignty over this world. The author here claims that everything has been subjected to the Son (v. **8**), but that the subjection is not yet evident. One could interpret v. 8 alone to mean that the Son reigns over all things, but it is not yet possible to *see* the world's subjection. This verse alone could suggest that the *revelation* of the world's position with reference to the Son is what is *coming*.

In light of the citation of Psalm 110:1 in Hebrews 1:13 that the enemies are not yet under the Son's feet (1:13) and also the description of the world as one *to come* (2:5), however, that "subjected-but-presently-hidden" reading falls short. In those places the author suggests that *not* everything has been subjected to the Son. The pressing question is this: Are the enemies subjected or not?

A way through the conundrum is to attend to the importance of God's speech for Hebrews. By proclaiming subjection, as recorded in these psalms, it is guaranteed. All things, including enemies, will be put under the feet of the Son—nothing is left unsubjected to him (v. 8). Currently, however, that subjection is not evident because it has not yet fully taken place. Enemies still wreak havoc. This interpretation has the advantage of not devaluing current suffering as a mirage. What the readers of Hebrews, then and now, experience is real. They cannot see the world to come in which Christ fully reigns because all things have not yet been fully subjected to the Son. At the same time, because God has promised that all will be subjected to him, his uncontested reign is guaranteed. It is only a matter of time before the world is fully and also clearly subjected to him.

Given the brokenness of life around them, the author and his audience do not see the subjection of all things to humans, particularly their Lord, the Son. They are, nevertheless, privy to something—or, better said, someone: *but we see Jesus.* Then, in a condensed fashion, the author tells the story of that subjection with the artfully arranged phrases of v. **9**. By repeating phrases from the psalm, the author applies the laudable human condition described there to Jesus (*the one who has been made a little lower than the angels . . . , the one who has been crowned with glory and honor*).

When applied to Jesus, however, the psalm does not proclaim his static position, the honorable place he holds in creation with respect to both angels and animals; instead, the author uses it to tell his dynamic story. The author transforms the psalm (not utilizing the aorist verbs of the psalm but employing perfect participles) into the narrative of the Son. Verse 9 begins with his lowering from his reign with God to becoming human on earth. Jesus, the Son about whom the author has been writing, was not always below the angels, as ch. 1 clearly portrayed. His position above them is obvious because he created them (1:2, 7). When he came to make purification for sins, he was willing to be below the angels. What is true of humans always was true of the Son only for a little while (drawing on the temporal meaning of *brachy ti*).[7] In his incarnate life he stepped into the place of humanity, which is below the angels. This, however, is not the end of his story. Having taken his seat at the right hand of God, he is now crowned with glory and honor above the angels (1:4–5).

At the center of these descriptions is the author's assertion *we see Jesus*. This is the first mention of his given name in the sermon (3:1; 4:14; 6:20; 7:22; 10:10,

7. "*Braxus, eia, u,*" BDAG, 183.

19; 12:2, 24; 13:8, 12, 20–21), an affirmation of his particular humanity, that he is a Jewish man. The way in which the author has proclaimed his excellency throughout the sermon thus far should jolt the reader, reminding them that all those majestic and divine assertions are true of the man named Jesus who lived, taught, and died in first-century Roman Palestine. He, as creator and sustainer with the Father, is the same one who entered in humility as a human even to the point of a shameful death. The other phrase in the center, *through the suffering of death*, serves as the lynchpin explaining both his being made lower than the angels and his being crowned with glory and honor. His excruciating death offered incontrovertible proof of his human mortality, and it was also the path through which he became crowned. *Through the suffering of death* serves as more explanation of how he made purification for sins (1:3).

He is the same one who is now crowned in his exalted state at God's right hand. The author can say that he and his community now *see* Jesus in line with his consistent appeals to terms of vision (2:8–9; 3:9, 12, 19; 8:5; 9:28; 10:25; 11:1, 3, 5, 7, 13, 23, 27; 12:14, 25; 13:23).[8] This use aligns most closely with his instruction in ch. 12 that they should look to Jesus as they run the race of faith (12:2). He indicates a thoughtful contemplation of Jesus, but this is not an embodied vision because they are still looking forward to his appearance when he comes to bring salvation (9:28). Without seeing him physically, the eyes of faith—which see what is unseen (11:1–2)—can give them the visionary encouragement they need to hold fast to this great salvation he has brought. This is true for both the first audience of Hebrews and all subsequent listeners. The faithful could have a sense of Jesus's exaltation through their participation in worship and prayer, or through visionary experiences attested in Scripture and throughout Christian history. They know to direct their vision to his reign because they have received and agreed with the divine word about him, the salvation communicated to them (2:1–4) in coherence with the divine speech given through the prophets. The eternal Son, who had become the human Son, is crowned in a way distinct from any other human. As mentioned, the sovereignty of this man extends beyond the animal creation on earth to include truly all things, even the angels. He comes to take that unparalleled position of sovereignty *through the suffering of death.*

In the final phrase of v. 9, the author asserts that this death superseded the event of mortality experienced by any other human in that his experience

8. Treier, "Speech Acts," 337–52.

made an impact on everyone else. The author states that he undergoes this suffering so that *he might taste death for all.* At times tasting, *geuomai*, can indicate the consumption of a small amount (Matt 27:34; John 2:9), but it is also used metaphorically for experiencing something in full (interestingly, it is used in this way for the experience of death in Matt 16:28/Mark 9:1/Luke 9:27; John 8:52). The sermon will make clear the author has no doubts that Jesus fully died, and yet the term "taste" also conveys that he was not dead for long.[9] This is the first explicit indication in the sermon that Jesus's death impacts people other than himself, not only in that they mourn him, but in that his experience of death is *for all.* This is a comprehensive statement in which the Son represents all and impacts all, the details and implications of which will gain clarity as the sermon continues.

The author also asserts that this death was by the *grace of God.*[10] Because the noun is in the dative, it could be a dative of association in that when he tastes death he has the grace of God with him, but it is more likely the common dative of means, indicating the instrument by which the Son tastes death. This aligns with the way the author uses "grace" in association with God. It describes not a *thing* God gives distinct from God, but instead describes God's graciousness in entities intimately associated with God—namely, God's throne (4:16), God's Spirit (10:29), and God's goal for the covenant people (12:15). It was by the grace of God—in other words, under the auspices of God's graciousness—that Jesus experienced death. It was, shockingly, the good and giving character of God that allowed this suffering and death to occur. This statement is an important benchmark for the author's further description of the Son's suffering (5:7–9) and his followers' suffering (12:5–11). It is God's

9. Chrysostom, *Hebrews* 4.3 (*NPNF*[1] 14:383–84)

10. Although *chōris theou*, "apart from God," is a reading known to several early interpreters including Origen, Jerome, and Ambrose, and it is resonant with the author's citation of Ps 22 in 2:12, I follow the better-supported reading not only for text-critical reasons but, more substantively, for theological ones. It would be dissonant with Hebrews to say that Jesus suffered and died apart from God, because it is God who lowered and crowned him (2:7, 9), who made him like his mortal siblings (2:17), who called him to the priesthood in which he offered himself (5:5), and who willed that he sanctify through the offering of his body (10:10). Moreover, if Jesus the Son suffered and died apart from God, the author would have no point of connection to make with the audience in their suffering. Instead, he directly connects them to the sovereign presence of their Father God in the midst of their suffering (12:4–11).

grace, not capriciousness or disdain, that allows the Son to die for all. The rest of the chapter explains how the proclamations of Psalm 8 can be realized for all humans because Jesus has already and is currently living out the story of the psalm.

In the author's reading of Psalm 8, Jesus is the glorified human whose suffering of death made an impact on all. An emphasis on comprehensiveness continues in the next verse (v. **10**) when the author describes God as the one *for whom are* ***all things*** *and through whom are* ***all things***. God is the aim (*di' hon*, *dia* with the accusative) and agent (*di' hou*, *dia* with the genitive) of *all things*.[11] God caused everything to exist and did so for God's own pleasure and glory. Hebrews asserts that it was the will of God to create and to reconcile all things under divine authority.

The vastness of God's concern in no way inhibits, however, God's intimate care for particular humans. The same God who created all is in the business of *leading many sons to glory* on the arduous path of salvation. This assertion is in line with Psalm 8, a text that speaks of both the general and the specific: the sovereign creator God is the same God who cares about humanity, including individual humans. The author says that God is leading many *sons* to glory. This is the first time in the letter that humans (other than Jesus) in relationship with God are all called sons. This relationship is hinted at when the author asserts that those who are being served by angels are *inheritors* of salvation (1:14), but here the connection between the Son of God and other sons becomes explicit. These humans being led to glory are *sons*, the same relational term used to name the one who now communicates God's salvation; this name unites their relational identity with God to the message of salvation they have heard and confessed. I have chosen to retain the exclusive masculine term to highlight this christological connection. The filial term does not exclude the women of this faith community but unites them—along with their male confessors—with the firstborn Son.[12]

God's action with this group of sons—namely, of *leading*—also evokes family relationship. God leads humans four times in this sermon: 1:6; 2:10;

11. Paul evokes the nature of God through prepositional phrases as well in Rom 11:36.

12. This act of uniting is wondrous for men, who are naturally sons, and even more of a grace for women, who are naturally daughters. See Amy Peeler, "'Leading Many Sons to Glory': Historical Implications of Exclusive Language in the Epistle to the Hebrews," *Religions* 12 (2021): 844–57.

8:9; 13:20. Twice God is leading the firstborn Son, into the inhabited realm (1:6) and up from the dead (13:20). In ch. 8, Jeremiah's prophecy recalls when God led the people of Israel out of Egypt by the hand. The picture is intimate, caring, and even familial since this is Israel, God's son, who is being led out of Egypt (Hos 11:1). Hence the picture of God leading sons here in Hebrews 2:10 suggests an image of God as a Father.

God is leading these sons *to glory*. Within this section, the aim of God's guidance is the same as the hope of the psalm (Heb 2:7; Ps 8:6 LXX). God is leading them into God's goal for humanity, which is to be crowned with glory. The reflections on God and the Son in ch. 1 reveal that God's goal for humanity is to come to share in God's own presence, for God is glorious (1:3). The eternal Son has always been the emanation of that glory, and now also as human has stepped into the glory planned for all humanity. God is leading them, as a good Father, on the path pioneered by the Son to arrive where the Son already is, in the glorious presence of God.

The author takes this opportunity to remind them of the pathway the Son took. He directly connects God's leading of many sons with God's work *to perfect the author of their salvation*. This is the first of three instances in the letter in which the Son, the very reflection of God's being, *becomes* perfect (see also 5:9 and 7:28). It cannot be the case that the Son is imperfect, because he is the very radiance of God (1:3). His fellow humans, however, certainly fall short of the goal God intended for them all (as communicated in Ps 8)—namely, honorable glory as they reign over creation. If he was to be their leader or author, the one who both plans and executes their salvation, the one who makes it possible, then he had to complete the process of being perfected. He had to become perfect, meaning he had to fulfill all things to become the effective leader of humanity. This was possible only by perfecting/completing his work *through suffering*.

To redeem them out of the situation in which they do not inhabit the glory God had planned for them, they need to be saved. Hence, their author the Son is the cause and leader of *their salvation*. Salvation implies being saved both from something and for something. The author has indicated that the Son brings purification from sin (1:3), deals with death (2:9), and opens the path to glory (2:10).

God and the Son did this work *through sufferings*. It was not a simple and quick process nor an example of divine fiat, even for the God who speaks creation into being. Salvation was achieved through the Son's suffering, even the suffering of death (2:9). The author opens this sentence by stating that this shared work of the Father and Son was *fitting*. This process fit the situation in which humanity found itself. Because Jesus tasted death, because he suffered, because he became the perfect Savior, many others can take God's hand on the path to glory.

Next, the author portrays this path of salvation to glory as the path of holiness by naming the Son and his followers in this way: *the one who sanctifies and the ones who are sanctified*. The author of their salvation, Jesus, is now the sanctifier and the sons are now those who are being sanctified. Holiness is a vital concept in Hebrews. It characterizes God's Spirit and God's realm (e.g., 2:4; 3:4; 6:4; 8:2; 9:2–3; 10:19) and is a gift that has been given to those who confess the Son (6:10; 10:10, 14; 13:12), including the addressees of this letter (3:1). It is a quality they will need in order to see and dwell with God (12:14). While the author certainly discusses the need for growth and maturity (5:11–14; 12:5–11), he assumes a growth in sanctification that has been granted by the work and will of God. The eternal Son's sharing humanity with them means that he also shares sanctification with the humans who confess him.

The sanctifier and the sanctified are *all from one* source. Because the ideas previous to this verse have focused on the common lot Jesus shares with humanity, as seen in Psalm 8, it is fitting to see Adam or humanity in general as a likely reference. Jesus shares a human ancestry with the other sons and daughters of God through his mother Mary. It is possible that the author also imagines God as their common source, since he has just painted God as creator here (through whom and because of whom are all things; 2:10). God created all things, including the human condition the Son Jesus shares with them. The dominant picture of God thus far, however, is God as Father, self-named as such in 1:5 and evoked through the complementary relation of "son." Jesus and the others are all human, and they are all human by virtue of God's creation, but now because of the coming of the Son they know God the creator to be their Father. The singular reference to "one" shows the connection they share with Jesus, beginning with their humanity up through their relationship with God as creator, who now through the Son is revealed as *their* Father. The singular term "one" can include all these relationships.

For this reason, he is not ashamed to call them brothers and sisters.[13] The shared participation in the human condition as well as in the family of God results in the Son's proclamation of the sibling relationship he shares with them, a proclamation he makes without shame. One might imagine that the Son could experience shame in this connection to humanity because, in order to achieve it, he had to be lowered from his position above the angels to one below them, at least for a time (1:5–13; 2:5–9). His lack of shame can be viewed from two angles. First, he is not ashamed because this family was achieved by the divine will. God's grace allowed his suffering and death (2:9–10), and this was his plan as well, as one who participates in the glory, actions, and name of God. It was the united will and action of the Triune God that accomplished salvation. Hence, he had no shame in the achievement of the very plan he willed. Second, he has no reason to be ashamed of his human siblings because they are on their way to promised glory. Their perfection and rule over creation is guaranteed. He boldly proclaims humanity created by God—and now, because of his work, made holy—as his brothers and sisters. Although they still have much of the path to tread, Jesus sees them for who they will be as promised by the sovereign divine will. The reigning Lord's lack of shame in being associated with humanity is a powerful encouragement to any who struggle with self-loathing.

As their leader, Jesus now speaks to God. God captures much of the focus of Jesus's scriptural speech in vv. **12–13**: it is God who is proclaimed, God who is praised, God who is trusted, and God who gives the children to him. Only the first line comes as direct speech to God, but the theological focus propels many commentators to cast this as a conversation.[14]

Just as God the Father did in ch. 1, Jesus speaks Israel's Scriptures. He begins with Psalm 21:23 LXX: *I will proclaim your name to my brothers and sisters.* There are other texts, even in the Psalms, where the speaker refers to

13. I have chosen to include "sisters" here in my translation even though the Greek is the masculine *adelphous*. I did not switch to a neuter "sibling" because the author will use a neuter term in vv. 13 and 14, and I wanted to make the distinction clear. "Brother" is not as clear a christological title as "Son," and so the connection with Christ does not necessitate the use of the masculine term alone. Moreover, since these verses are about corporate worship and Christians retain their embodied distinctiveness in those settings, it seemed important to name both in my translation.

14. Pierce, *Divine Discourse*, 98–113.

"brothers" (Ps 121:8 LXX), but this text offers the example of that naming with the added benefit of being a valued text in the gospel tradition. According to Matthew (27:46) and Mark (15:34), Jesus cried out with the words of this psalm from the cross, and all the Synoptics describe Psalms 22's casting of lots for Jesus's clothing (Ps 21:19 LXX; Matt. 27:35; Mark 15:24; Luke 23:34). This psalm evokes the cross, the suffering and death of which the author has been speaking (Heb 2:9–10). Coming from the latter part of the psalm, these words also evoke the psalmist's hope in God's deliverance. When the psalmist cries to God, God listens (Ps 21:25 LXX), a direct verbal connection with the Son's cries being heard by God (Heb 5:7). The psalmist knows that those who seek and praise the Lord will have hearts that live forever (Ps 21:27 LXX). Hence, this psalm does double duty of evoking both the cross *and* the resurrection. Finally, the psalm affirms God's sovereignty, reigning as king with people falling in worship before him (Ps 21:29–30 LXX), precisely the position in which Jesus the Son now sits at God's right hand. The psalmist's praise expands the family of God (Ps 21:28, 30, 31 LXX). For those who might know the entirety of the psalm, the author of Hebrews has made a rich selection indeed.

Jesus is saying to God what he will say to his siblings. The Son does what is the job of the angels with whom he has been compared. He, too, passes on a message (*apangellō*), as he is *saying, "I will proclaim your name to my brothers."* As the angels communicated the word of the law (2:2), the Son communicates *God's name*. If the granting of the superior name in 1:4 evokes the divine name, then Jesus is proclaiming the name of God that is his own. As in the gospel accounts, Jesus's disclosure of his own identity and God's identity are always intertwined, as one would expect for the Son who is the radiance of God's glory and imprint of God's being (1:3).

The psalm expresses Jesus's proclamation as song: *I will praise you*. The act of singing casts Jesus's speech as joyful, precisely the same emotion the author will invoke when discussing the cross in ch. 12: "for the sake of the joy that lay before him, [he] endured a cross" (12:2). He sings to God and in so doing proclaims God's name.

Through the double-line poetry of the psalm, the siblings are then specified as the *assembly*. The psalm on the lips of Jesus asserts that he is *in* their *midst*. He was present among those who first heard his message (2:3), and now that he is seated at God's right hand, his presence is still manifest among his followers but in a different way. Used frequently in Acts and the Epistles, *ekklēsia* appears only twice in Hebrews, here in the psalm text and near the end when the author describes the group gathered on the heavenly Mount Zion (12:23). The connection between the two texts presses the question of the relationship between the community gathered on the mountain and those who receive the letter. The following discussion of *the timing* of Jesus's speech suggests multiple meanings for the identity of the assembly.

With the phrase *and again* the author introduces two more statements of Jesus. While the first, *I will be one who has trusted upon him*, is short enough that it could come from at least two scriptural locations, Isaiah 8:17 or 2 Samuel 22:3, the Isaian location seems most likely because the next statement also comes from Isaiah 8. This chapter, like Psalm 21 LXX, is cited by other New Testament authors (Rom 9:32–33; 1 Pet 2:8; 3:14–15), yet the author of Hebrews cites from a portion that no one else does. Isaiah 8:17 introduces a person who chooses to trust in God even in the midst of God's punishment of the nations and even of Israel. The children born to this person during this time are evidence of God's sovereignty, the Lord Sabaoth who dwells on Mount Zion. The themes of trust displayed and a family established in the midst of suffering align perfectly with the themes the author of Hebrews has been developing through this section. By separating the verses with the phrase *and again*, the author highlights the relation of the statements but also their distinction. It is the trust of the Son that then allows God's giving of the children.

Trust is a powerful way of demonstrating the Son's humanity. Every other place this word appears in Hebrews (6:9; 13:17–18), it describes a human response. The Son Jesus trusts in God *as a human*, even a human in the midst of suffering and death. In this statement we hear the Son's verbal response to the fact that the Father allows his process of perfecting to take place through the suffering of death (2:9). He demonstrates that this kind of trust is possible for other humans who are in the midst of suffering or even those who are facing death, an important reminder for the audience who has faced and will face hardship (10:32–35; 12:4). Even more important than his example, it is his trust that makes this faithful action *possible* for others. Because he has trusted God in suffering and death, others are named as members of God's family and are being sanctified as they walk the path toward glory in trust.

Because he trusted God even through death, he is able to proclaim his association with the children of God entrusted to him (*Behold I and the children*). With the use of the term *children*, the author is foreshadowing the house image he will employ in 3:6, where the Son reigns over the household of God. *Paidion* often denotes small children, but the term is not meant to belittle Christ's confessors. The smallness associated with the term does serve to emphasize the grandness of the Son who reigns. In his light, they are insufficient and need to depend on him. Moreover, the use of the grammatically neuter *paidion* shows the author's ability and willingness to communicate in gender-inclusive language. It is a confirmation that previous "sonship" language is intended to include women fully as well.

When, though, does the author imagine this speech of the Son happening? The incarnate life of the Son provides the clearest setting. In his communication about salvation from God (2:3), the Son reported God's name and gave God praise. He trusted in God and with thanksgiving identified with those of whom he could say *God gave [them] to me* (the resonance with Johannine language, as in John 17:6, is strong in Heb 2:13b). The appearance of Psalm 21 LXX in the crucifixion narratives gives an even more precise incarnational moment for this whole speech. In death, Jesus trusted God, and as he was lifted up, by God's grace he gathered many to himself.

The community of this letter, by the author's own description in 2:3, however, was not privy to those events, so if the author is imagining this speech in the incarnate life of Jesus alone, that would leave the audience at a distance from this conversation. In addition to what Jesus said on earth, it is also possible to imagine that Jesus continues to have this conversation with God as he is on the throne at God's right hand. As mentioned, just as Psalm 21 LXX is associated with the crucifixion, it also evokes resurrection with its reference to perpetually living hearts (Ps 21:27 LXX). As the one who has died, but now is living, Jesus continues to praise God among the assembly of the firstborn enrolled in heaven (the only other use of the term *ekklēsia* in the letter, 12:23). This community who lives on earth, as they are included with those in heaven (see also 11:39–12:1), is privileged to hear his speech to God. Because the Son is the medium of God's speech to them now (1:2), he proclaims God's name to them, and they can hear his praise to God. They see his continued trust in God as the faithful High Priest awaiting God's act to put all things under his feet. In addition to the people who followed Jesus at the beginning, likely decades before the writing of this letter, this community who first received this sermon also can identify as his siblings and as the children God has granted to Jesus. The conversation of honor and trust between the Father and the Son is ongoing and catches Jesus's first followers as well as Hebrews' congregation up into it. As believers throughout time continue to affirm that Jesus is seated in sovereignty, they affirm that his speech continues and all generations henceforth who confess him can hear the proclamation that they are included in his familial embrace.

God's gift of these children to the Son occurs at a deeply intimate level. They are given to him because he has been given to them, by willingly participating in the human condition. The next paragraph builds on the words of Jesus: *Therefore, since the children* (the author uses *paidion* here in repetition of Isaiah's language just cited) *have shared of blood and flesh, also he likewise shared of the same things*. Because they are participants in blood and flesh, Jesus becomes a participant in flesh and blood. The joining of these two terms, *haima* and *sarx*, blood and flesh, is a way of speaking about the human condition (Matt 16:17; 1 Cor 15:50; Gal 1:16; Eph 6:12). Hence these children God gives are not foreign objects to be possessed but his siblings because he was willing to become human like them.

His embrace of human embodiment includes his willingness to go to the extremity of the human condition, not just birth and life but also *death*. The author makes a bold statement in the remainder of this complicated sentence concerning the impact of Jesus's death.

Initially he focuses on the impact made against the powers opposed to God: *in order that through death he might destroy the one who has the power of death—that is, the devil.* While the author of Hebrews has nothing else to say about this figure, other New Testament authors use the term "devil" to describe God's enemy. This figure brings temptation to Jesus (Matt 4:1–11/Luke 4:2–13) and trickery, sickness, lies, murder, hate, and oppression to all God's people (Matt 13:39; 25:41; Luke 8:12; John 6:70; 8:44; 13:2; Acts 10:38; 13:10; Eph 4:27; 6:11; 1 Tim 3:6–7; 2 Tim 2:26; Jas 4:7; 1 Pet 5:8; 1 John 3:8, 10; Jude 9; Rev 2:10; 12:9, 12; 20:2, 10). The author of Hebrews focuses on the power the devil has with regard to death, a common association for others of his time.[15] As creator and sovereign king, the one who sustains life (1:3), God has the ultimate power over life *and* death,[16] and so the author clarifies the extent of

15. Attridge notes many examples in Jewish and early Christian writings, including Gen 3:1; Exod 12:23; Wis 2:24; 1 Cor 5:5; John 8:44 (*Hebrews*, 92).

16. A point Aquinas recognizes, citing 1 Kgs 2:6 and Deut 32:39. Thomas Aquinas, *Hebrews* 2.4.141, p. 69.

the devil's power with regard to death. The devil's deathly power is fear. When the author introduces the impact of Christ's death on humans, he describes them as *those who through the fear of death throughout the whole of their lives were ones who were subject to slavery.*[17] For the extent of their lives, humans are enslaved to this fear of death. The devil is able to inhibit the freedom of humanity because they live in fear of the inevitable. They will die, but when? Before that time, will they get to live a full life or not? And how will they die? In pain or terror? What will it be like to pass through death itself? Although it manifests in different ways in different times and cultures, all humanity lives in response to the fear of their mortality. This fearful life lived under the shadow of death is the power of the devil.

The theme of deliverance from this fear was incredibly tangible in the life of John Jea, an enslaved African who was converted to Christianity. When he faced beatings from his enslaver for preaching the gospel, he quoted Hebrews 2:15. Lisa Bowens notes that he interpreted "fear as part of death's ability to keep people in bondage. But Jea, refusing to be afraid of death, triumph[ed] over it."[18] What a powerful application of the truth proclaimed in Hebrews. The good news from the author of Hebrews is that the devil, and therefore his power, has been *destroyed* by Jesus's death. The devil, then, is an enemy who has already been defeated and therefore will be placed under Jesus's feet (1:13). Clearly for the original hearers as well as contemporary ones, this fear of death is not eliminated, but it cannot ever win the upper hand for those who are members of Jesus's life. Calvin encourages, "Even if the devil still thrives, and works hard for our ruin, nevertheless his power to harm us is abolished or blunted. It is a great encouragement for us to know that we have to deal with an adversary who has no power against us."[19]

Moreover, in defeating the devil, Jesus is also able to *rescue those* who were enslaved. He has changed their situation, removing them from the slavery of fear and moving them into freedom. They no longer need to fear death because the Lord they have confessed has defeated it. Chrysostom has a powerful illus-

17. A common trope in the Greek and Roman writings. See Patrick Gray, *Godly Fear: The Epistle to the Hebrews and Greco-Roman Critiques of Superstition* (Atlanta: Society of Biblical Literature, 2003).

18. Lisa Bowens, *African American Readings of Paul: Reception, Resistance, and Transformation* (Grand Rapids: Eerdmans, 2020), 63.

19. Calvin, *Hebrews*, 31.

tration on this point. Although this community suffers, they have the superior lot because they do not fear death. Others may have an easy life, but the fear of death poisons even their pleasures. He asks which position is preferable: "those who are fed in the prison-house while every day looking for their sentence, or those who contend much and labor willingly, that they may crown themselves with the diadem of the kingdom?"[20] The answer is obvious.

The shocking thing is that Jesus destroyed the power of the devil by succumbing to it. Aquinas states that because Jesus was sinless, death had no power over him. When the devil exercised that power over Jesus, in this act "he deserved to lose his power."[21] Yet this seems to assume that the devil had the power of death, and not just the power of the *fear* of death. I wonder if this grants too much power to the devil that the theology of the text does not justify. Hebrews does not speak of the overreach of the devil; the sermon says only that through death Jesus destroys the devil and his power and, consequently, is able to rescue all those who were enslaved to the devil's fear. As Hebrews will describe in ch. 5, Jesus was willing to experience the emotions that accompany certain death (5:7–8). By dying and rising again, he shows that for those who confess him, death is nothing to fear. The community will continue to face death (12:4), but they need not fear its lasting effects. Jesus obliterates the power of the enemy, the slavish fear of death, so that he can remove humans from the enemies' control. For their God, as revealed in the communicative life, death, and resurrection of the Son, death is no barrier to eternal relationship. The presentation of Jesus's humanity begun with the citation of Psalm 8 has been focused on his death *and* on his defeat of death. By taking on flesh, by being transformed into the fearful human condition, contending with death and defeating it, he can transform his siblings out of the devil's grip.

On the basis of the author's discussion thus far, it should be obvious to his audience that the Son came to help those who *could* die and therefore feared death. Hence, he says, *For it is clear he did not take hold of angels*. The term often translated as "help" here, *epilambanomai*, is most often employed when the action involves physical embrace, for good (Matt 14:31; Mark 8:23; Luke 9:47; 14:4). Jesus takes *hold of* humanity, not angels, by becoming human. Because

20. Chrysostom, *Hebrews* 4.6 (*NPNF*[1] 14:85).
21. Aquinas, *Hebrews* 2.4.142 (*NPNF*[1] 14:69).

he came to "help" mortal humans, not angels, he took on flesh. It is humanity who is enveloped in the Son's embrace.

Equally obvious to them is the fact that he *took hold of the seed of Abraham*, which means that Jesus became a member of the covenant of Abraham. The author makes a similar statement in 7:14, stating that *clearly* Jesus arose from the tribe of Judah. This is an affirmation of his ethnicity.[22] His particular embodiment as a Jew is the way in which he extends aid to all humanity. He is the fulfillment of the promise to Abraham that through *his seed* all nations would be blessed (Gen 12:3). The author focuses this ancient blessing in a priestly way. *Whence, he ought to be made like his brothers and sisters according to all things in order that he might become a merciful and faithful High Priest.*

Verse **17** begins with the connective term *hothen*. Interpreters are correct to see a logical connection between all the author has said previously and this summative statement, just as the author uses this term several other times (3:1; 7:25; 8:3; 9:18). The locative meaning of the term, *whence*, should not be dismissed. Since Jesus locates himself within the people of Abraham by embracing them, it is from this human position, as a particular human with a particular family history, that he is able to be like all humanity.

He became human to serve as High Priest. God the Father's action is invoked here with the passive infinitive *to be made like*, reiterating the grace and perfecting of God mentioned in 2:9–10. God made him like his human siblings in all ways, and because the Son is God and shares this plan for creation, this was not forced on him but was God the Father's employment of the shared divine decision.

The way in which he is made like his siblings—in *all things*—is, clearly, comprehensive, including body and emotions. The author has already named the body—blood and flesh—as well as the will of Jesus, exercised in trusting God (2:13). The body and faith of the Son set up the functions of his high priesthood, exercised in mercy and faithfulness. For the author, mercy is associated with God's throne (4:16). Mercy is definitive for the character of the God of Israel (Exod 20:6; 34:6; Deut 5:10; Ps 20:8 LXX, as only one of the

22. Ethnicity is an incredibly complicated reality (for its integration in biblical studies, see Janette Ok, *Constructing Ethnic Identity in 1 Peter: Who You Are No Longer* [London: T&T Clark, 2021]), but the point the author seems to affirm here is that Jesus's particular embodiment came from a family (best said, from a woman within a particular family) who identified their ancestry and culture as Jewish.

nearly 150 expressions in the Psalms), and so it is no surprise that the one who radiates God's presence (Heb 1:3) demonstrates mercy too. As the author will show throughout the sermon, the Son exhibits incredible understanding and grace—in other words, mercy—toward those whom he represents as High Priest. Second, the author says that the Son's priestly work endures. He is *faithful* in it, trusting God in taking on flesh, in death, in resurrection, in enthronement, and as he waits for the submission of his enemies. His faithfulness toward God means that his confessors can trust him to be trustworthy with their needs.

The author then names these needs when he articulates the aim of Christ's priesthood. He is merciful and faithful as High Priest *with respect to the things aimed at God for the purpose of pardoning the sins of the people.* The structure of the sentence shows the Son's mediatorial role.[23] He is positioned toward God in his high priestly work, and at the same time he does this work because of a problem of the people—namely, sins—which establishes a verbal connection with the early assertion that the Son has made purification for sins (1:3). As the embodied High Priest, he turned toward God to pardon or make atonement (*hilaskomai*) for these sins of the people. Although this term has been debated in theological interpretation, with the dominant camps arguing for either removal or appeasement,[24] the author of Hebrews' only other use of the word group connects the action with a specific place, the lid of the ark of the covenant (9:5). I question the benefits of embracing one trajectory over another (removal or appeasement). This is an early statement in his letter, and the author will develop at length the way in which the Son's high priestly work deals with sin. The author's statement is clear enough at this point in the presentation. Without giving the specific mechanics, the author asserts that the Son Jesus *deals* with the problem of sin as an expression of God's consistent and trustworthy mercy.

A connection between sin and death also surfaces in this statement. The author has not yet articulated an answer to the pressing question of why human mortality as well as the shared fear of it exists. The answer begins to

23. Harris notes that this phrase, *ta pros ton theon*, is associated with priesthood in, for example, Exod 4:16 and 18:19 (*Hebrews*, 65).

24. Paul Ellingworth, *The Epistle to the Hebrews*, New International Greek Testament Commentary (Grand Rapids: Eerdmans, 1993), 188–90.

appear here with the mention of pardoning sins. If the Son destroys death by going through death and his priesthood makes atonement for sins, then there must be a relation between the two. Death is associated directly with sin in several intriguing places in Israel's Scriptures, including the exodus narrative (Exod 10:17), the law of Deuteronomy 21:22, a fruitful theological text for Paul (Gal 3:13), the suffering servant passage (Isa 53:12), and the prophet Ezekiel (Ezek 33:14). The author has not yet shown the stitching connecting them, but he brings them together here. Because death and sin are entwined for humanity, the Son's priestly atoning work is to defeat death through dying and rising again.

It is in this connection that Hebrews demonstrates resonance with other New Testament authors. Twice, James asserts a connection between sin and death—namely, that the end of sin is death (Jas 1:15; 5:20). This concept is most fully developed in the canon in the Pauline corpus, especially in Romans where Paul presents a clear progression from sin to death (Rom 5:12, 21; 6:16, 23; 7:5, 13; see also 1 Cor 15:56). The mechanics are not stated here in Hebrews, but this statement is not dissonant with Paul's vision of the relationship between the two. Hebrews' cosmic presentation of the realities of death and sin, while distinct, is at home in the New Testament canon.

As a merciful High Priest who has trusted in God, the Son *has suffered* (a reiteration of the author's interpretation of the psalm in 2:9) by *being tested* (*peirastheis*). The sovereignty of God the Father over the incarnate life, death, and resurrection of the Son, paralleled by the sovereignty of God over this community's suffering (12:5–11), suggests that "testing" in the sense of disciplining, maturing, or perfecting is a fitting translation of *peirastheis*. That being said, God's allowance of tests includes the exposure to the temptations of sins, although, as James comments (Jas 1:13), it is not God who is holding out the temptation to sin. James situates the site of temptation within the human person (this is the same passage where he links sin and death). The author of Hebrews acknowledges the internal danger when he speaks of the evil heart (3:12), but here, given what has come before, he emphasizes God's allowance of the experience of temptation in a world where God's enemies are not yet defeated. This testing surely includes the testing of suffering and dying, but it includes more than those things that happen at the end of the Son's mortal life. In 4:15 his testing in all ways allows him to be sympathetic with human weakness. Hence, by virtue of the verbal connection between the passages in

Hebrews, his suffering in testing mentioned here in v. **18** is comprehensive of the human condition, although the focus on death in this section, and human lifelong fear of it, allows that test given at the end to radiate back to all parts of life. The comprehensiveness of his testing supplies a correlative wideness to his mercy. *Because* of it, *he is able to aid those who are being tested*, no matter what the specific manifestation of their test may be. No situation exists that he cannot or will not help them through.[25] His priestly ministry of purifying sins is joined with a pastoral ministry of compassionate aid.

In these last two verses of ch. 2, the author speaks of the Son's mercy and help surrounding the assertions of Jesus's faithfulness and work with sin through suffering and death. His priestly sacrifice costs him something—namely, his human life—and in the act of offering it, not only does he secure freedom for humanity as well as win reconciliation between God and God's people, but he also achieves the ability to be empathetic toward those people.

Hebrews 2:5–18 offers a sustained argument. This entire section explains how humanity can reign in glory. To do so, they must defeat death and sin. Christ became human to do just this *for them*. Since he now reigns, they can trust that as they are tethered to him, so too will they reign. He is able to give them sympathetic and effective aid as they continue on this salvific path to glory.

25. This is an important point to keep in mind because it aids interpretation of those intense passages in Hebrews that warn against turning away from him. If one rejects the High Priest who mercifully offers help in all situations, one is in a dire state indeed, without the aid of the only one who can fully help with the problems of sin and death.

HEBREWS 3:1–4:13

THE WILDERNESS

The author of this sermon boldly crafts his words so that his listening congregation can hear the words of God, first by hearing of the magnificence of the eternal Son in ch. 1 and then by hearing the incarnate Son himself proclaim his solidarity with and redemption of humanity (2:12–13). After his exposition of Jesus's speech in ch. 2, which gives voice to the Son's fulfillment of the divine plan for humanity as described in Psalm 8, the author turns to another exhortation. Similar to the way that he followed the speech of God in ch. 1 with an exhortation to listen (2:1–4), at this juncture of the sermon he follows the speech of the Son with an exhortation to trust. Instead of asking the audience to attend to the message they heard, as he did in 2:1–4, in 3:1–6 he asks them to turn their attention to the Lord of that message. To show the greatness of Jesus, the apostle and High Priest, he compares Jesus with Moses and highlights their similarity as honored members of God's family and also the distinctions of their positions in that household.

The author supports his exhortation to hold fast to their boldness and hopeful boast in Christ with a citation from the word of God. In 3:8–11 he says that the Holy Spirit speaks Psalm 95, a psalm in which God speaks. From 3:7 to 4:13 the author cites verses from Psalm 95 five times, as well as Genesis 2:2. From these texts he makes applications to his listeners. The first and longest citation (3:7b–11) compels him to urge attention to personal and communal spiritual health. The second (3:15), where Psalm 95:7b–8 is repeated, draws his focus to urge rejection of the intertwined sins of disbelief and disobedience. The third (4:3) and fourth (4:5) citations repeat Psalm 95:11 and, joined with Genesis 2:2 in Hebrews 4:4, highlight the existence and desirability of

God's rest. Finally, the author cites Psalm 95:7 once more (4:7), noting the time in which these words were written by David. His conclusion is that God's rest remains available; therefore he and his listeners should hasten to enter it (4:11).

The author's appeal to the psalm's recounting of and admonition from this event in Israel's history places him and his listeners "in the wilderness" in ways similar to the ancient generation. Moses led the people into and through the wilderness, and Christ does the same (see 2:10; 12:2; 13:13), but whereas Moses and the elder generation of Israelites were not able to enter God's restful land, the author has better hopes for those following Jesus, who has already entered his rest and can assuredly bring his followers to do the same. This section aligns with the author's frequent exhortations throughout the letter that urge forward movement.[1] He casts a generative vision in which believers can acknowledge both the hope that lies before them and the challenges in the present path, challenges that necessitate continued faith in the one who has already redeemed them and who can bring them to the end where he already resides.

Unsurprisingly, after presenting the voice of God through the Spirit so often, the section closes with a portrayal of the awe-full power of God's word. The warning to listen, coupled with the fearful example of those who did not, prepares the congregation to see their need for Jesus the High Priest. The focus on belief and God's rest remains prominent throughout this section.

3:1–6 · SON OVER THE HOUSE

[1]Therefore, holy brothers and sisters, sharers of a heavenly calling, consider the apostle and High Priest of our confession, Jesus, [2]who is faithful to the one who appointed him as also Moses was in the whole of God's house.

[3]For this one is considered worthy of more glory than Moses, just as the one who builds the house has more honor than the house. [4]For every house is built by

1. The children of God are those who are being led (2:10). In contrast to the inefficient meanderings of the wilderness generation, the author calls his readers to show their status as children by going in (4:3, 6, 10, 11) or approaching (4:16; 7:25; 10:1, 22; 11:6; 12:22). More urgently, he describes them as those who are fleeing to grasp the hope that lies before them (6:18).

someone, but God is the one who builds everything. [5]*On the one hand, Moses was faithful in his whole house as a servant as testimony of the things which would be spoken,* [6]*but on the other, Christ [was faithful] as a son over his house, whose house we are, if we hold fast to the boldness and boast of hope.*

Throughout this sermon, the author does not line up various subjects in a list as distinct items. Instead, he connects the ideas together. This chapter begins with *therefore*. In light of the claims he has made about Jesus the Son, eternal God and exalted human, he asks his listeners to respond. To ground that response, first he reminds them of who they are. Thus far in the letter, the only identity he has granted them is "recipients of God's message," a title assumed when he proclaims that God has spoken to them (1:2; 2:1, 3–4). Here, however, he names them directly for the first time, and he gives them three weighty identities.

First, they are siblings, *brothers and sisters*.[2] They are those to whom Jesus is unashamed to speak (2:11–13); they are the sons God is leading to glory (2:10), the children awaiting their inheritance (1:14). Second, they are the recipients of God's sanctifying work; they are *holy* ones. This address is an assurance that they are included in the group of those who are being sanctified by the sanctifier (2:11). Finally, they are *sharers*, a term he uses to describe them as confessors of Christ again in 3:14. Sharers (*metochoi*), a term that appears with some regularity in Hebrews (1:9; 3:1, 14; 6:4; 12:8) but only once in the New Testament outside this letter (Luke 5:7), signifies those who join together, participate together, or partner in something. By addressing them with this title, the author assures them that by confessing Christ they are given a stake *of a heavenly calling*. The location (heaven) and the vocal nature (a calling) point to the fact that this calling is an invitation coming to them as God's speech (1:2) shaped by the Son who resides in heaven (Heb 1:3). With the assurance of this identity—that family belonging, holiness, and participation in the revelation from heaven are all true of them—the author demonstrates that they are connected to Jesus. He is their brother, their sanctifier, and the one who gives God's speech to them from God's very right hand, inviting them into

2. Note the discussion at 2:10, where I posit that masculine language not only is assuming the inclusion of women, as was typical at the time, but also invites them into the rights and responsibilities of male members of society.

participation with God. If they are facing threats to their faith, such as persecution and their own weariness, it is vital that he remind them of the powerful identity they have by virtue of their confessional faith.

The author's exhortation follows seamlessly from this assertion of the community's identity. Because of their connection with Jesus, it makes sense that *he* should capture the focus of their vision. This is especially true because the author has just named him as the one who is able to aid them with all their trials (2:17–18). Directing their attention anywhere else would make it impossible to receive this empathetic help. *Consider* (*katanoeō*), the author instructs, using a term that includes both perception and reflection. They do see Jesus (2:9), and so they need to think about him. The author aids their ability to do so by providing two titles for Jesus. First, Jesus is the *apostle*. As the noun related to the verb *apostellō*, which indicates the act of sending, *apostolos* refers to the one who is sent. The term is built on a relationship between the sent and the sender and also implies a task: the sender sends the sent one for a particular reason. The Gospels describe Jesus as appointing and sending apostles (Matt 10:1–5; Mark 3:13–19; Luke 6:12–16), and Paul names himself as an apostle numerous times (1 Cor 1:1; 4:9; 9:1–2, 5; 15:9; 2 Cor 1:1; Gal 1:1, 17; Eph 1:1; Col 1:1; 1 Thess 2:7; 1 Tim 1:1; 2:7; 2 Tim 1:1, 11; Titus 1:1). Although Hebrews is the only New Testament document to do so, this is a fitting term for Jesus himself because he was sent from God (Heb 10:7). This term serves as confirmation that the author views the eternal Son (1:2, 8, 10–12) who shared in flesh and blood (2:14) as one who has come from God. He is both the message (1:2) and the messenger (2:3) who proclaimed the salvation he brought to fruition (2:10). As the one sent, he is also *High Priest*, the one who deals with the deep problem of humans' sins and helps them in their testing (2:17–18). The author's grammar emphasizes the unity of these roles,[3] which apply to one and the same person who came to mediate between humanity and God.

He is the focus of, the author says, *our confession*. The apostle and High Priest is not separate from this pastor and his listening community. This admonition builds on the one given at 2:1–4. There, they needed to hold fast to the word they had heard and received. Here in ch. 3 they give a word. They

3. The Granville Sharp Rule is "Two nouns connected by *kai* and governed by a single preposition usually imply conceptual unity." David Alan Black, *Learn to Read New Testament Greek*, 3rd ed. (Nashville: Broadman & Holman, 2009), 182.

have heard and then affirmed what they heard by confessing or speaking in agreement with what God, the Triune God (2:3–4), has testified about the Son. They confess that he is the one who has come from God and taken on the high priestly role. By articulating his given name, *Jesus*, the author emphasizes his humanity alongside his eternity past (as apostle, one sent from God) and his eternity future (as enduring High Priest; see 7:28). The author wants them to focus on the mediatorial role that Jesus, the one who took on flesh and blood from the tribe of Judah (7:14), plays on their behalf. From this truth, they can focus on how they have already taken on a new identity because they heard of him and his work and confessed it as true.

As the author wants them to remain steadfast in their faith toward God by considering Jesus, he reminds them that Jesus *is faithful* to God. In the previous paragraph, the author emphasized Jesus's faithfulness toward God in his high priestly work (2:17). The same vocational focus remains here, evident in the way the author describes God, a description worthy of some reflection. God is the *one who appointed* (*poieō*) *him* (Jesus). While the term *poieō* on its own could convey that the Son was created by God, and therefore was used as support by the Arians,[4] in the context of Hebrews two other meanings are more likely. First, with this term the author points to the fact that God appointed Jesus into his role of High Priest. He has just named him as High Priest in the last breath, has just reflected on his qualifications as High Priest in the previous paragraph (2:17–18), and in ch. 5 will make it clear that God must be the one who calls a person into that role (5:4–5). Second, God's appointing of him could also refer to God's installing him into the royal role as the heir of all things (1:2), seating him at the right hand of the Majesty on high, the role upon which ch. 1 focused, especially 1:13. The "making" has to do with his vocation as messianic heir and High Priest, not the creation of his being.

The vocational appointing seems the best interpretation of the "making" language. By using the word *appointed*, however, I do not mean only his work or job or career, something partial; instead, I intend to connect to the deeper meaning of that vocation language. A response to God's call (in Latin, *vocale*) reorients one's entire life. Moses is called by God from the burning bush and

4. See Khaled Anatolios, "The Epistle to the Hebrews in Patristic Doctrine," in *So Great a Salvation: A Dialogue on the Atonement in Hebrews*, ed. Jon Laansma, George H. Guthrie, and Cynthia Long Westfall, LNTS 516 (London: T&T Clark, 2019), 88–90.

everything changes, not only what he does during his day, but his destiny as well. It is not correct to say that God's call to the Son issues a *change* in the Son's being or his plans (10:5–10), but it is a fulfillment of an eternal divine plan, an embrace of what was anticipated but not realized before the incarnation. Since God's making of his vocation is wholistic, Jesus's followers can anticipate that the call, appointment, and equipping God will do for them will be equally comprehensive.

In addition to the vocational meaning of the term, the utilitarian nature of the word cannot be ignored. *Poieō* is to do or to make. Authors use it to describe action aimed at the formation of things—in other words, bringing things that are not into existence. In addition to appointing him, God also made Jesus—or, better said, God made his flesh—the same flesh and blood the author has been discussing in the previous section as that which qualifies him for the role of High Priest. Worth noting is the fact that the author uses his name as a first-century Jewish man, Jesus, and not his eternal relational divine identity of Son. It was *Jesus* who was faithful to the God who made him, to the God who made him *human*, who created his flesh and blood from the willing body of Mary of Nazareth (Luke 1:26–38).

The human focus is appropriate in light of the following comparison with Moses. Jesus was faithful *as also Moses was in the whole of God's house.* Just as Moses the Jewish leader was faithful in God's household, so too is Jesus the Jewish mediator faithful in God's household. *House* often denotes a particular family (Exod 19:3; Lev 10:6) but can expand to include a whole people—namely, the people of Israel. The word *whole* is textually conflicted, with readings supporting both its inclusion and its exclusion,[5] but I have chosen to include it because it emphasizes the contrast even more. If out of the whole house of Israel Moses was considered worthy of honor, then Jesus's greater glory is all that more astounding. By mentioning the house, the author is alluding to Numbers 12:7, where God speaks of "my house," a citation the author will bring forward in v. 5. In so doing, he also taps into the familial theme he develops throughout the sermon.

The similarity between Jesus and Moses provides a starting point for a contrast. *For this one is considered worthy of more glory than Moses.* Although

5. Bruce M. Metzger, *A Textual Commentary on the Greek New Testament*, 2nd ed. (Stuttgart: Deutsche Bibelgesellschaft/United Bible Societies, 1998), 594–95.

they are both faithful, Jesus is worthy of more glory. Obviously so, for it is *just as the one who builds the house has more honor than the house.* Jesus's glory in comparison with Moses's is similar to the situation in which the builder of the house has more honor than that which is built. The author is not really concerned with the details of structures. Instead, houses provide a textually resonant example for him. He can state the clear fact that *every house is built by someone*, as this is the fitting structure to name because his interest lies with the household/people of God. He started there, showing that both Jesus and Moses are faithful in this household, and he will end there, showing that Jesus is over this household (3:6).

In v. **4** the author casts his ultimate vision as broad as possible: *God is the one who builds everything.* Drawing up the threads from the second chapter, in which he asserts the Son's comprehensive sovereignty when he is crowned (2:7–8), and the first chapter, where the Son participates in the creation of all things (1:3), he asserts a glory for Jesus that *far* surpasses that of Moses. They are both worthy of glory because of their faithfulness, but Jesus is more so because of his position of leadership in the household (soon to be discussed in 3:6). Even more, the human Jesus whom God made is one and the same with the Son who shares the ultimate glory of God because he, the Son, participated with God in the construction of *all things.* Jesus is worthy of more honor because he builds everything with God, and he does so because of his identity as the eternal Son of God. Simply put, Jesus is worthy of more glory than Moses, the creature, because he, the Son, is the creator.

Moses's particular service in the house clarifies the comparison as it points to the greater honor of the Son. With a citation of Numbers 12:7, a section of Scripture that emphasizes Moses's unique leadership, the author asserts that *Moses was faithful in his whole house as a servant* to God. This sentence comes from an event in which Moses's siblings, Aaron and Miriam, speak against him for taking a wife from Ethiopia. No other information is given about this situation, but God's response to them highlights not only Moses's faithfulness but, more importantly, God's intimate communication with Moses. God speaks to him "mouth to mouth" (Num 12:8) in a form Moses can see, so that he sees the glory of the Lord. This statement can align with other passages in which God says to Moses that no one can see God and live (Exod 33:20). Numbers indicates that God revealed the divine identity to Moses in such a way that conversation could happen. This is a true revelation of God, but not a full one of God's entire being, a revelation no human eye could handle.[6] One might wonder if the form God chose to manifest to Moses was a vision of the to-be-incarnate Son, not yet enfleshed but an image of that which was to come, as he is the image of the invisible God (Col 1:15), whose face reflects God's glory (2 Cor 4:6). Whatever form the appearance took, to have an encounter with God is an incredibly high honor for Moses. His role as a servant of God, then, was to be a witness of the things he saw and heard. This aligns well with his respected role as the authorial personality behind the Torah.[7] The author casts his *testimony* as that which points forward. He testifies *of the things which would be spoken*. His life of service was recorded in Israel's Scriptures, and his words were recorded and then reiterated by the prophets. Words of his were now being repeated by this author to this community. Within the framework of the comparison between Moses and Jesus, Moses's testimony throughout the centuries was one of the prophetic witnesses that pointed to Jesus the Son. If Moses is venerated, the Son to whom his testimony points deserves even more. While Moses hears God, the Son is that word (1:2).While Moses sees the glory of God, the Son is that radiance (1:3).

Instead of focusing only on Moses as God's servant, the hearers of this address also need to consider *Christ*, who is the Messiah. For the first time in the letter, the author uses the title *Christos*, Messiah, for the Son Jesus. Without any explanatory introduction, it seems this was a title accepted by this community, as they heard the message of salvation from previous believers in Jesus.

The anointed ruler (as named in the citation of Ps 44 LXX in 1:9) is faithful not as a servant but *was faithful as a son*, not just in the house of God but *over his house*. The author reiterates Jesus the Son's position of ultimate sovereignty in comparison with Moses. Both are of the people of Israel, so this house, this family, is theirs. At the same time, because God has elected this family, redeemed and preserved it, it ultimately belongs to God. Since the Son with the Father created all things, he is sovereign over this family. In addition to creating, it is the Son who took hold of this family to give them aid (2:16), so he has embraced this house as his own. By virtue of his nature as human and

6. Gordon J. Wenham, *Numbers*, Tyndale Old Testament Commentaries (Downers Grove, IL: InterVarsity Press, 1981), 113.

7. John H. Walton and D. Brent Sandy, *The Lost World of Scripture: Ancient Literary Culture and Biblical Authority* (Downers Grove, IL: IVP Academic, 2013), 60–70.

as God, this house belongs to him. A son has rights of inheritance over the house that a servant will never have, and the author already asserted that God appointed the Son as heir of all things (1:2). It is fitting to see the possessive pronoun *his* as referring to both God the Father and God the Son as sovereign over this household.[8]

As this congregation listens to Christ, they are his household. The author can speak of himself and his listeners in reference to Christ, *whose house we are*. They are members of the group he created and rescued. This assertion supports the earlier statement of their identity as sons (2:10). One might imagine that they could be members of the Son's household as servants, as Moses was. Their position, however, is even more elevated (as it seems Moses's is as well: as one of the faithful [11:24–29], he is now among the "firstborn" who dwell on God's mountain [12:23]); they are all children within God's household, where Jesus the anointed Son reigns.

The author joins a conditional to this great assurance: *if we hold fast to the boldness and boast of hope*. Readers may find this "if" statement threatening, especially when viewed in light of the warning passages throughout this sermon. This "if," however, is built not on the strength (or lack thereof) of human faith but on the strong foundation of Christ's faithfulness. It is not wrong to be frustrated or weary, nor to take honest questions and laments to God, all of which this community under fire was likely engaged in. The opposite of holding fast is to deliberately walk away.[9] It makes good sense that they will remain members of this household only as they stay under the authority of the firstborn Son. Staying tethered to him by listening to the message of salvation he brought (2:1–3) and considering him (3:1) gives them *boldness*, for he is sovereign over all things, and gives them the *boast of hope*, because all things will be subjected to him (1:13). Put simply, they do not have to conjure the boldness and the hope on their own. Instead, they hold fast *to him* (as the author urges again in 3:14 and 10:23), and he gives them the reason to be bold and hopeful.

8. As is always the case in my approach to theological language, it is the incarnational lens—through the person of the Son—that both justifies and interprets masculine pronoun use for God the Father.

9. Even in these cases of departure, one must investigate what the person is walking away from. Is it a true or distorted picture of Christ? If it is the true picture of Christ from which someone chooses to depart, it is the property of the Christian God to have mercy on those who return. See discussion of warning passages in 6:4–8, 10:26–31, and 12:15–17.

Blessedly, this encouragement is not only for the original readers of Hebrews. Anyone who has heard the salvific word about the Messiah Jesus and confessed it can also hold on to him and his sovereignty. All who do so find a sense of belonging, identity, and hope. The following extended exegetical section provides all generations with an example to avoid as they continue to hold fast to Christ.

3:7–4:13 · DISTRUST

7 *Therefore, just as the Holy Spirit says,*

> *Today if you hear his voice,*
> 8 *do not harden your hearts as in the rebellion*
> *on the day of testing in the wilderness,*
> 9 *where your fathers tried [God] with a test*
> *and they saw my works for forty years.*
> 10 *Therefore, I was angry with that generation*
> *and I said, "They are always deceived in the heart*
> *and they did not know my ways,"*
> 11 *so I swore in my anger,*
> *"They will not enter into my rest."*

12 *Be on the alert, brothers and sisters, lest there be in a certain one of you an evil*
heart of unbelief that apostatizes from the living God, 13 *but encourage one another*
each day, while it is called "today," in order that a certain one from among you may
not be hardened by the deceitfulness of sin. 14 *For we have become sharers of Christ*
if we hold fast to the beginning of the foundation firm until the end.
15 *As it is said,*

> *Today if you hear his voice,*
> *do not harden your hearts as in the rebellion.*

16 *For who, after hearing, rebelled? Was it not all those who went out from Egypt*
through Moses? 17 *And again, with whom was God angry for forty years? Was it not*

those who sinned whose bodies fell in the wilderness? [18]And against whom did God swear that they would not go into his rest except those who disobeyed? [19]And we see that they were not able to go in because of disbelief.

[4:1]Therefore, let us fear lest someone from among you should be found to have fallen short of the remaining promise to go into his rest. [2]For even we are those who have been evangelized just as also those were, but the word of hearing did not benefit those who had not joined in faith with those who heard. [3]For we who believe go into the rest, just as he said,

> *So I swore in my wrath*
> *they will not go into my rest*

even though "the works" were finished from the foundation of the world. [4]For he has said somewhere concerning the seventh thus,

> *And God rested on the seventh day from all his works.*

[5]And on this again,

> *Surely, they will not go into my rest.*

[6]Therefore, since it remains for some to go into it, and those who were gospeled earlier did not go in because of disobedience, [7]again God sets a certain day, "today," by David saying after such a long time, just as God said earlier,

> *Today if you hear his voice,*
> *do not harden your hearts.*

[8]For if Joshua had given them rest, God would not have spoken of another [day] after these days. [9]Therefore, there remains a sabbath rest for the people of God. [10]For the one who goes into his rest, even he rests from his works just as God [rests] from his own. [11]Therefore, let us hasten to enter into that rest, in order that someone may not fall by the same example of disobedience.

[12]For the word of God is living and active and sharper than every two-edged sword piercing to the division of soul and spirit and joints and marrow and judging

the desires and intentions of the heart. [13]*And no created thing is hidden before him, but all things are naked and bare-necked before his eyes, concerning whom is the word for us.*

The author exhorts his listeners to hold on to the boldness and boast they have in the knowledge of the Son's identity, and the author's first assertion about the Son is that he is God's word to them (1:2). By virtue of that christological reality, the author connects what has come before to what follows with *therefore* (*dio* appears here for the first of several times; see also 6:1; 10:5; 11:12, 16; 12:12, 28; 13:12) as he turns to a psalm that extols listening to God's voice. The wilderness generation provides a counter example of how *not* to respond when God is speaking.

The Holy Spirit speaks the next Scripture. The introduction asserts, *Just as the Holy Spirit says.* It is striking that the dramatis personae have included God the Father, then the Son, and now the Holy Spirit.[10] A mysterious "someone" appears between the Father and the Son as the speaker of Psalm 8 (Heb 2:6), and so the number and order are not as neat as a systematic Trinitarian theology. Nevertheless, the Holy Spirit acts here in a personal way, performing the act of speaking. No other author of the New Testament gives the Spirit such a vocal role. Paul says that people can speak by the Holy Spirit (1 Cor 12:3), and Luke portrays the sound of the rushing wind as the Holy Spirit arrives (Acts 2:2), but in no other place is the Holy Spirit introduced to speak the Scriptures to a listening audience. In the Scriptures of Israel, the Spirit speaks through people, but speaks directly only to Ezekiel (Ezek 3:24; 11:5). As the speech of the psalm unfolds here in Hebrews, it transforms almost imperceptibly from the speech of the Holy Spirit about God to the speech of God directly. The author has both united and differentiated the Lord who is holy and the divinely holy Spirit.[11] The seeds of Nicaea ("We believe in the Holy Spirit . . . who has spoken through the prophets") are here.

The Holy Spirit speaks from the last section of Psalm 95 (94 LXX), a psalm that lauds the sovereignty of God over creation with an attitude of wondrous

10. See Pierce, *Divine Discourse.*

11. Ken Schenck notes, "The author thinks of God and the Holy Spirit as the same speaker, albeit with a slightly difference nuance. The Holy Spirit speaking is God speaking (or perhaps breathing) through the text in the present time." "God Has Spoken: Hebrews' Theology of the Scriptures," in Bauckham et al., *Epistle to the Hebrews and Christian Theology*, 334–35.

thanksgiving that this God took Israel to be the divinely elected people. Higher than the mountains and deeper than the seas, this same mighty God intimately knew and loved these people as a shepherd knows and loves sheep. The section of exhortation from which the author cites arises out of this sense of gratefulness. Similar to the psalm, the author of Hebrews has just extolled the greatness of Jesus the Son as far superior to Moses (3:1–4) because he is reigning and has always reigned with God as God. The author has also articulated this exalted Son's intimacy with this congregation, having taken on humanity to redeem those who are now members of his own household.

Both in the psalm and in Hebrews, the greatness of God and the grace of God's election set the stage for the exhortation from which the author quotes. In light of all that God is and all that God has done, the failure of some among Israel to know, trust, and obey God appears all the more egregious. Because the author is casting himself and his community in ways resonant with that generation of God's people, he is preparing them to reflect on the dangerous potential of unfaithfulness in their own hearts and community. God's one-time gracious redemption of the people does not eliminate the necessity for continued cultivation of faithfulness.

Their connection with God is apparent in the first line of the citation: *Today if you hear his voice*. The "if" might seem ill-fitting in the context of this letter. The author has already stated emphatically that God, as the speaking God, has been speaking *to them*, through the prophets and now in the Son (1:2). There is no doubt that they have had the opportunity to hear God speaking. The only question in the mind of the author is how they will respond. This is an indication of how closely the author joins hearing with action.

The psalm describes the generation of God's people who wandered in the wilderness as an example to avoid when it commands listeners, *Do not harden your hearts as in the rebellion on the day of testing in the wilderness*. The negative terms throughout the citation attest to an ongoing issue with this generation. Although rebelling against or embittering God applies to other generations addressed by the prophets (e.g., Hos 10:5; Jer 51:3; Ezek 2:3), several psalms, in addition to the one cited here, highlight the frequency with which this particular generation provoked God in this way (Ps 77 and 105 LXX). On the cusp of his death, Moses exclaimed that those whom he had been leading were generally "rebellious" (*parapikrainō*, Deut 31:27). As an example, Israel did test God soon after they were redeemed out of Egypt when they longed for water. Their complaints were born out of a theological problem: they wondered if the Lord was among them or not (Exod 17:7). The term translated as *rebellion*, *parapikrasmos*, is related to the word for bitterness (*pikros*). This generation put a bad taste in God's mouth, as it were. The psalm is echoing a statement in Deuteronomy 6, when Moses speaks to the generation about to go into the promised land and commands them *not* to test the Lord God as they previously did (Deut 6:16).

While these terms might allow a general focus on this generation's continual murmuring and rebellion, the author builds on this propensity with his citation of Psalm 95 to put a particular moment in the life of this generation in focus. The day *of testing in the wilderness* revealed their hardheartedness. The psalm invites a specific moment to take center stage when that generation *tried God with a test*. The citation of the psalm focuses on a pivotal moment in their journey—namely, when they did not trust God to lead them into the land of promise (Num 14:20–25). The land was good but its occupants were mighty, and the people did not trust that God could deal with those forces and bring them into the land God had promised their ancestors. While they frequently tested God with their bitter complaining, this moment on the cusp of entering the land was distinct. Lest the readers conclude that this generation was especially bad in ways that they would never replicate, the author sets up this generation as the example his readers need to be careful *not* to emulate. All humans have the potential to embitter God.

The author adds his own focus on the events surrounding this rebellion by the way in which he cites the psalm. Extant versions of the psalm do not include the linking word in v. **10** that he does. In the psalm, "they saw my works" is the last phrase of v. 9, and the next verse begins, "For forty years I was angry with that generation." The forty years are clearly a time of God's wrath. With the presence of *therefore*, the author separates the forty years from the wrath and, consequently, presents the forty years as the length of time this generation saw God at work: *and they saw my works for forty years*. This applies to God's work of compassion to see their suffering and respond to it by means of the miraculous plagues leading to the exodus (Exod 3:7–10) and, even before that, to God's works that sustained them in the midst of their enslavement. Forty years' worth of God's works means that God was with them in their darkest hours, a reminder that the community of this epistle needs to hear as well (Heb 12:5–11).[12]

12. Alternatively, even with the insertion of *dio*, it is also possible to see these works as

Even though they had seen God at work, they hardened their heart against God, and so God responds: *Therefore, I was angry with that generation*. God's anger with that generation arose out of the fact that God had revealed much to them, and still they did not trust. Some readers might be unsettled by an expression of divine anger (*orgē*), but this is a way of articulating God's holy response to sin (see also Lev 26:30) in line with the holy fire of God described later in the letter (Heb 12:29). A God who does not react to wrongdoing, including rebellious lack of trust, is a God who is apathetic and uncaring. A God without this kind of anger cannot be the God of justice or real, costly love.

This generation's chief problem was that, as God says in the psalm, *they are always deceived in the heart*. They had seen God's work evident in their own deliverance and sustenance. Despite all that they had seen, they had not allowed those revelations to change their internal posture. Experiencing deception is part of the human condition, as the author notes (5:2). This generation allowed the report of the ten spies and the stature of the people of the land to trick them into thinking that God was smaller than the inhabitants (Num 13:28, 32–34). To further explain the point, the psalm also includes God saying, *And they did not know my ways*, meaning that they did not really know the identity and power of God. For a sermon intent on God's leading of the people on a particular path (Heb 2:10; 12:1–2, 12–14) and even the precise way of God made possible by the Son (9:8; 10:20), it is a matter of life and death to know the ways of God.

Because that generation did not know the way to follow God by trusting the previous pattern of God's behavior, they did not get to dwell in the place God had prepared for them. God responds, *So I swore in my anger, "They will not enter into my rest."* God decreed that those who failed to trust would not get to enter the land. As the first instance of the term "swear," which will become important in the author's reflections on the Son's priesthood (6:13, 16; 7:21), the psalm underlines the gravity of God's punishment. God's word is valid as the word *of God*, and so when God deigns to add an oath to it, God contributes this unnecessary addition to show the intensity of the statement. The readers can trust that God will keep this promise.

God's works of judgment enacted on this generation as they were made to wander in the wilderness after they would not enter the land. This is the way in which the author reads these lines of the psalm in 3:17. They put God to the test by not going into the land, and then saw the works of judgment. For a clear articulation of this reading, see Cockerill, *Hebrews*, 180–81.

It is beneficial to inquire what made this act of distrust and rebellion different from the several times of mistrust they expressed before. By hardening their hearts, they set themselves as similar to the one who had enslaved them, their enemy and God's—namely, Pharaoh (Exod 4:21; 7:3, 22; 8:19; 9:12; 9:35–10:1; 10:20, 27; 11:10; 13:15; 14:4, 8, 17). They did so not as part of the sovereign plan of God but through their own act of rebellion. As they are poised before the land, they lift up their own voice (Num 14:1), evidence of the downward spiral of mob mentality, rather than attending to the voice of God. Moses and Aaron interpret their act of digging in their heels and not proceeding into the land (Num 13:31) as an act of apostasy from the Lord (Num 14:9), the same thing the author will warn his congregation against in Hebrews 3:12. This aligns with the author's idea that stopping in the journey of faith is comparable to turning in the wrong direction. God says that this is the tenth time of testing (Num 14:22), and since it focuses on the end goal of the exodus, entrance into the land (Exod 3:8), their failure to trust at *this* moment results in serious consequences. God does not obliterate them all right away, but God does allow the adults who failed to trust eventually to die and prohibits them from ever taking possession of this land while they live. In failing to draw from what God had done in the past to trust what God could do in the future, the generation who wandered in the wilderness rejected who God is and therefore could not reside with God.

This is a story of ancient events, but the author of Hebrews has chosen to incorporate the version of it that appears in Psalm 95 into his sermon, thereby making this story speak *directly* to its addressees. As the Holy Spirit speaks to them, the Spirit is concerned with *your hearts* and tells the story of *your fathers*. The word is made fresh because it is spoken *today*. The author introduces this key moment in the life of Israel as an object lesson for his congregation. As was true with Israel, God has not immediately obliterated them for their shortfallings (see 5:11–14), but if they fail to know and trust God and God's ways, and therefore depart from God, they too will reap the consequence of failing to enter God's presence. The psalm recalls the *rest* offered by God to the people in the land of Canaan. This term, especially as the author will interpret it in his following paragraphs, opens up space for a nonliteral, nongeographical application because even though the psalm recalls the wilderness narrative from Numbers, the psalm itself does not speak of dwelling in a particular place but entering a space defined by the presence and activity (or is that lack of activity?) of God. This is resonant with an earlier verse in the psalm that invites worshipers into God's presence (Ps 94:6 LXX).

For the audience of Hebrews to avoid the same mistake as the generation freed from Egypt, they must know who God really is. Hence, the necessity for the extensive theological and christological exposition of the previous two chapters becomes even more clear. The author wants them to have a rich picture of God's identity so that they will have a posture of awe rather than doubt that can lead to rebellion. Although the content of ch. 3 might seem a new section, its exhortation is directly connected to theology of the Father and Son that has come before.

Moreover, the audience of Hebrews includes, by God's gracious providence, all those who have taken up and read this sermon subsequent to this unknown original community. As those living the last days when the Holy Spirit's communication of God's word has been revealed ultimately in the Son (1:2), as those who anticipate the second coming of the Messiah (9:28), all Christians are "in the wilderness." All stand in need of deep and rich exposition of God's identity and work. Until the establishment of God's unshakable kingdom (12:26–28), theological catechesis remains the foundation for faithful Christian living. Knowing God's ways, having eyes of faith to see God's works, provides the safeguards to stay on the path to dwell in God's rest.

Directly after the citation, the author commands them to *be on the alert*. He has put the failure of this generation forward for his community's consideration. He does not want the same consequence to come to them, and so he asks them as *brothers and sisters* to pay attention. He established the familial identity of this group with Jesus's action of boldly calling them siblings (2:11–12), a term he uses because he has joined in the human family (2:17). Here for the first time in the letter, the author addresses them directly with this terminology. If they are not on watch, someone from among them, *a certain one of you*—note that his concern is communal by virtue of being attentive to the individuals *in* the community—may fall into the same deception of heart as was true for the wilderness generation (3:10). In one sense, he is asking them to assess the state of their own hearts, but at the same time he is encouraging them to be on watch for each other, for signs that a brother or sister is regressing in trust and obedience. The stakes are high. What they need to watch out for is the *heart of unbelief* (*apistia*), which, in light of the psalm and the event in the wilderness it evokes, indicates a lack of trust in who God is and what God can do. This heart posture is plainly *evil*, he says.

It equates, in fact, to that which *apostatizes* (*apostēnai*) *from the living God*, a word choice that evokes the narrative of disobedience in Numbers 14 (*apostatēs*, 14:9). The Scriptures of Israel describe God as the living one on several occasions, but it is the appearance in Joshua 3 that is closest to the subject matter of this passage. On this occasion, Joshua is leading the children of those who had failed to trust God, finally bringing them into the land. Then he proclaims God as living: "Draw near here and hear the word of the Lord your God. By this you shall know that a living God is among you" (Josh 3:9–10). The proof of God's presence among them will be the defeat of their enemies, precisely what their parents did not trust that God could do. Soon the author of Hebrews will say that Joshua did not lead the people into full and final rest (4:8), and so the allusion to the living God of Joshua may evoke this entrance, but the verb (*zaō*) that appears here first in Hebrews becomes most closely associated in the sermon with the living Son and the life he gives (7:8, 25; 10:20). The author's aim is that his listeners will trust in the identity of God as communicated in the Son, that they will rely on the *living* God, whose glory is the resurrected Savior. Joshua's story points to Jesus's.

The remedy for an individual who might be tempted to turn away from the living God is to press into the hedging embrace of the community. This does not indicate simple attendance of group meetings but entering into deeper relationship by sharing in worship together. The strong contrast, *but* (*alla*), to the potential for departure from God is to *encourage one another*. Encouragement (*parakaleō*) has a communicative dimension. They are to "speak/call" (*kaleō*) to one another with earnestness for the good of the other, which may demand saying positive and encouraging things as well as honest and difficult things. They are to do this *each day*. This would have been necessary for a community facing shame and persecution, but the same urgency is fitting for believers no matter their situation. The temptation to doubt God remains, and so the necessity of having access to the accountability of other believers daily remains an ideal to seek.

This encouragement should happen *while it is* still *called "today."* The author's use of the term for *today* connects with the first word of the psalm, ***Today*** *if you hear his voice* (Heb 3:7). The author has made it clear that the invitation of the psalm was not limited to only one day in history but extends through an age, the age in which God is speaking. There will come a time, he indicates, when it will no longer be called "today." This is connected to the time described in ch. 12, after the great shaking (12:27–28). Then all things will be settled and no chance for response to God's voice will be on offer because those who have already responded will be with God forever.

This sermon's listeners still remain within this age/day when God is speaking and inviting, however, and so they can encourage one another to listen to God's address more attentively. If they do, the result will be that *a certain one from among you may not be hardened*, the posture warned against in the psalm (Heb 3:8). The author recasts this warning three times in this section (3:8, 15; 4:7). He does not want any of them to be stubborn, unmoved by good argument from their Christ-family members because they have already been persuaded by the deceitful lure *of sin*. *Deceitfulness* is often linked with things that *seem* good—wealth (Matt 13:22/Mark 4:19), lust (Eph 4:22), debate (Eph 5:6; Col 2:8), power (1 Tim 2:14)—but are not only empty but also destructive. The community members may be tempted to listen to voices that are seeking to draw them away with such things, and so the author does not want their hearts to become numb to the insurmountable good of staying with and obediently responding to the living God, whose pathway ends in glory but, on the way, wades through suffering.

In vv. **12–13** the author has laid out a dangerous path. Sin deceives with its offers of (false) success. The one who considers this offer becomes increasingly hard-hearted. In listening to that which is promising more, they become less, less pliable and less open to respond to God. Eventually the hard heart of that person is evil, not trusting God and finally turning away from the source of life.

The way out of this dangerous path sits at the center of his description of it.

v. 12: lest there be in a certain one of you an evil heart of unbelief that apostatizes from the living God,
v. 13a: *but encourage one another each day, while it is called "today,"*
v. 13b: in order that a certain one from among you may not be hardened by the deceitfulness of sin.

His exhortation for fending off this cataclysmic possibility, *encourage one another each day*, is equally radical as the things he is warning against, even though it may not at first appear so. I was invited to speak to a local women's group who had chosen this phrase in 3:13 as their year verse. One could view this as an egregious example of prooftexting—a snippet of a verse chosen to warm the hearts of those who gathered over casseroles to discuss upcoming service projects. As I discussed the context with them, I pointed out that the author has surrounded this phrase with the intense realities of things like evil, apostasy, and the end of the world as we know it. By observing their kindness, commitment, honest conversation, and friendship, I came to see that if I harbored any dismissive assumptions about the group, they would be unfounded. In all the apparent weakness of their far-from-the-center-of-attention activities, they were actually living into the central intent of this passage, practicing real, honest, and effective Christian community. The early church, too, seemed to be made up of weak and unimportant people, and yet they kept turning the world upside down (Acts 17:6). The solution to the danger is incredibly communal. The individual is easily self-deceived. Sin weaves its fairy tale of lies about the power of those in the land (as was true for the wilderness generation, the community of Hebrews, and believers today, be that power terrifying or alluring) and the untrustworthiness of God. Followers of Jesus are in need of voices outside their own heads to correct when doubt starts to win the upper hand. Members of these groups have to know each other; hence they must be proximate to one another; in some way they need to *gather* in order to speak to each other. When the author told his congregation to *encourage one another each day*, he was asking them to implore one another with costly regularity until the end of time, when the unshakable kingdom of God will stand glorious in the midst of the rubble of that which will need to be removed. The way to avoid apostasy before this time might just be to gather over casseroles.

The author roots this admonition in their identity. He declares for the second time (previously 3:1) what becomes a prominent way of describing himself and his community: he says, *we have become sharers* (*metochoi*) *of Christ*. Utilizing the same title he employed for the Son when he named his community as Christ's house (3:6), here he is stating that he and they have shared and participated in the anointed one, the Messiah, the King. This is a term that evokes both his sovereignty and God's faithfulness to establish it. It is a title of honor that invites them to see what God has done for him and, therefore, to continue to trust in God. Proof that they can do so is evident in the fact that they have already responded to that revelation and have become participants in this divine family.

Seemingly, however, the author takes away just what he has given in the next phrase: ***if*** *we hold fast*. We have shared in Christ, but we could lose it, he seems to say. The flicker of the flaming warning passages that follow (6:4–8; 10:26–31; 12:15–17) ignites once again as it did in 2:1. The communal lens of this entire passage illuminates a vital aspect of this warning. If this verse focused only on the individual, the impetus for endurance would hang on a person's power to hold on. If, however, *metochoi* as a plural noun conveys working with Christ in the work of building up the community, they remain his partner only as they remain in the community whose members are encouraging each other daily. Moreover, they are instructed to *hold fast to the beginning of the foundation*. The inauguration of their faith was when they heard the gospel, responded, and as a group experienced God's miracles (2:3–4). They are instructed to hold fast *firm until the end*. The end will come when it is no longer "today," when they no longer need to listen to prevent a hard heart because they will have reached their destination when they will be with God forever. When all the pieces are put together, it becomes clear that this verse is not a warning to individuals to try harder. Instead, it aligns with the verses previous. They can only stay tethered to Christ as they stay tethered to his community. It is not as much about feelings as it is about fellowship.

Some words of clarification are necessary. Admittedly, I am seeking to redress an imbalance toward individualism and scrupulousness over the strength of one's own faith inherent in some receptions of the tradition. I do not mean to imply, however, that a pro forma act of attending church is the silver bullet. Instead, both individual faith and communal participation are necessary for Christian endurance. The author is attentive to the hearts of individuals; he singles out "a certain one from among you" twice (3:12, 13). The section of the psalm from which he quotes mentions hearts twice (3:8, 10), and he replicates those mentions two more times in this section (3:15; 4:7). Moreover, in his own commentary he focuses on individual hearts twice (3:12; 4:12). The interior focus appears again—twice—in his quote from Jeremiah 38 LXX (8:10; 10:16), a citation that bears significant weight in his sermon. Having a healthy interior life, purified and strengthened by grace, is necessary for the journey of faith as he conceives it (10:22; 13:9). Faith for Hebrews is manifest in persons who are steadfastly dependent on God in an intimate way. This author would resonate with the famous words of John Wesley: sharers of Jesus are those who have hearts that have been strangely warmed.[13] In this way he is in good company

13. John Wesley, *The Journal of the Rev. John Wesley . . . Enlarged from Original MSS., with*

with Paul, who, similarly instructed from Israel's Scriptures, sees the heart as the location for receiving God's grace and for living out one's faith (Rom 5:5; 6:17; 10:8; 2 Cor 1:22; 4:6; Gal 4:6; Phil 4:7), as well as James, who issues similar warnings about a wayward heart (Jas 1:26; 3:14; 4:8; 5:5, 8). It is not only necessary but also good to cultivate one's own relationship with God.

At the same time, the passage, in alignment with the entire canon and Christian tradition, asserts that this faith cannot be done on one's own. Those with faithful hearts are the kind of believers, as experience teaches us, who can encourage others and receive encouragement from others when they are in need. There exists a strong symbiosis between vibrant individuals and vibrant community life. God has designed humans to need one another. While attending communal worship is vital, for true protection against deception it must be joined with honest fellowship, a vulnerability to know and be known by other believers. This applies, of course, only to healthy and not abusive communities. If someone is without healthy Christian community, this is a prayer God desires to answer, either by providing something new or opening one's eyes to support what is already available in unexpected places.

Then the author repeats the first part of his citation again (Ps 95:7–8): *As it is said, "Today if you hear his voice."* The time for response is now. They are living in the time of *today*. The author has disclosed to them that they hear God's singular Son-speech (1:2) in many and various ways. God is speaking to them by the Holy Spirit through the Scripture and through each other (3:13). God has not left them with silence. By listening they can remain responsive to God's communication and follow the command: *Do not harden your hearts as in the rebellion.* Unlike the majority of the wilderness generation, their speech to each other can encourage trust and obedience and not, as happened in the rebellion, stir one another up toward hard hearts determined to disobey. Communities can bring about good, but they can also work ill. Groupthink, as history shockingly discloses, can move in positive or atrocious directions. The story of the negative trajectory of the wilderness generation is evoked with this second citation of the psalm. They stayed together as a coherent community, but this was unfortunate because most of them were united in choosing to listen to the testimony of those who doubted God rather than those who

---

Notes from Unpublished Diaries, Annotations, Maps, and Illustrations, ed. Nehemiah Curnock and John Telford, 8 vols. (London: Epworth, 1938), 24 May 1738.

trusted God. This cautionary tale connects to the author's later warnings to watch out for and even purge those who could spread trouble in and among the community (Heb 12:15). Community is necessary, but being a member of one takes discernment.

In the next several sentences in which the author invites reflection on the event in which the wilderness generation's trust failed, he underlines the stark contrast between God's action and that generation's inaction by failing to follow God into the land. *For who*, he pointedly queries, *after hearing, rebelled?* He answers his own question with another that demands a positive response: *Was it not all those who went out from Egypt through Moses?* They were redeemed miraculously through the persistent plagues facilitated by God's work through Moses and Aaron, needed again and again because of Pharaoh's intransigence. The similarities with the audience are chilling. They, too, have been redeemed from a particular kind of slavery (2:15), have seen God's miracles (2:4), and have heard God speaking (1:2). If this previous generation experienced all those things and still, out of a lack of trust in God, put God to the test, the community hearing this sermon must be aware of this possibility and resist it.

In v. **17** he adds a slight shift of meaning in comparison with his previous citation, where he focused on their witnessing of God's works for forty years. Now he points to the reality that God was angry with that generation for forty years by asking, *And again, with whom was God angry for forty years?* This difference from the citation (which included a "therefore" that shifted the meaning) and the explication indicates that he saw both realities at play. They saw God's sustaining power through provision during the exodus and before, and they witnessed the presence of God's judgment for forty years. This judgment was evidence of God's anger for those many decades. During a time when life conditions made a young mortality age the norm, this forty-year divine anger could last someone's entire life. Such was the case for the generation who wandered in the desert.

The idea of God's anger needs comment. It could convey God as petty and capricious. Attributing emotional expression to God, however, demonstrates instead God's care. Were God unresponsive to the doubt and disobedience of the people whom God had called, redeemed, and cared for, that would display God as cold and uninterested. The anger of God gives evidence of the covenant relationship. In other words, anger *can* manifest inappropriately, but in other situations it might be the only *appropriate* reaction. The classic theological assertion of the impassibility of God does not deny the emotions that Scripture attributes to God but affirms that God expresses them not in a reactionary dependence on creation but as a free response to God's freely given love for creation.[14]

This divine and righteous anger had brought about serious consequences. The author renames what they did to receive those consequences when he asks, *Was it not those who sinned . . . ?* Because of their sin of disbelief,[15] they paid with their mortal lives. They were those *whose bodies fell in the wilderness.* Their bodies collapsed as sojourners in the desert rather than being laid to rest in a verdant home. They did not, however, die immediately. God continued to provide for them as they wandered in the wilderness so that their children might survive and eventually come into the land. Even in God's judgment of death, there were grace and provision and sustenance of the life of the covenant people.

The barrage of questions continues as the author repeats the language of the psalm, naming another consequence of their behavior. *And against whom did God swear that they would not go into his rest except those who disobeyed?* Because of their lack of trust that led to disobedience,[16] they did not enter the land promised to their people, and so they did not get to dwell in the rest of God. The frequent lack of trust, climaxing in their unwillingness to follow God into the land, resulted in God's wrath and administration of consequences. Painfully, they never arrived where God desired for them to go, but died outside the land of promise.

The author asked his audience to pay attention, to be on the alert (*blepete*, 3:12). Now that he has told the story of this generation and their failures, he can say, *And we see* (*blepomen*) the reality clearly: *they were not able to go in because of disbelief.* Their lack of faith had devastating consequences. It is theologically weighty that the author ends on this point. Although God metes out the consequences, God does so in response to *their* disbelief. Had they remained faithful in trust, the result would have been different. In other words, for their death in the wilderness they have no one to blame but themselves. God had pro-

14. See Paul L. Gavrilyuk, *The Suffering of the Impassible God: The Dialectics of Patristic Thought*, Oxford Early Christian Studies (Oxford: Oxford University Press, 2004).

15. As the Alexandrinus scribe adds this term explicitly (NA[28], 661).

16. Here P[46] has *apistēsasin*, "distrust," where most manuscripts have *apeithēsasin*, "disobedience." The alternation between distrust and disbelief in the manuscript tradition continues throughout this section, demonstrating the close association between the two terms.

vided abundantly to cultivate their trust through the assurance of miraculous and powerful divine action. How much more is this true for the audience of Hebrews, who not only knows the account of the exodus and wilderness provision but has now experienced the power of God as revealed in the Son! The maintenance of faith is a necessity, and God has provided everything possible for that maintenance. The author has told the wilderness story in hopes of a different result for his community's own journey following God's lead (2:10).

When I was teaching Hebrews one semester, a student commented that in her first attempt to read through the letter, it was halfway through ch. 4 when she gave up; she found it difficult to follow the author's argument. It was a good reminder for me, and any others who love this sermon, that it *is* a complex word that has to be borne (13:22). Hopefully, a brief summary will provide orientation for a detailed study of the complex but powerful richness of this section.

In the first half of ch. 4, the author asserts that God has been resting since the seventh day of creation. That does not mean that God is completely inactive, but instead that God has established a place of rest through resting. God desires that humans enter this place of rest and dwell with him. The invitation had been given to the wilderness generation to join God's rest, but they, through lack of faith, did not. Joshua's subsequent conquering of the land of Canaan shows that the land was not the ultimate rest. Therefore, the psalm shows that God's invitation still stands for any who would trust God and desire to enter the eternal and ultimate rest.

The first verse of ch. 4 includes another connecting word, *therefore*. In view of the warnings the author has issued throughout ch. 3, his admonition *let us fear* is the appropriate response. The author has urged the practices of paying attention (2:1) and holding fast (3:6, 14), and now for the first and only time in the sermon, he urges that they all should fear. He includes himself in these admonitions, recognizing that, even as their guide, he needs to hear the very message that he is preaching.

Fear appears in two registers in Hebrews, the fear of enemies, to which the people need not succumb (2:15; 11:23, 27; 13:6), and the fearful actions of God, which are worthy of reverent fear (4:1; 10:27, 31; 12:21). The holy God issues consequences for sin, and this fact should not be forgotten. The author does not advocate here for fearing *God* (notice that *theos* is not the object of the verb *phobeō*) but instead encourages fear of the *consequences* if one sins *against* God. The distinction is important for a healthy understanding of God. Reverence for the sovereign and holy God is fitting, but the clarity of what should be feared may prevent an unhealthy cowering under and desire to avoid God, the precise opposite of what the author wants.

At base in this contrast is the distinction between trusting in God and not trusting in God. In this section, the author has been asking that his audience pay attention to the examples of those who chose that path of distrust, the path that led to a turning away from God. Alternatively, when members of a community trust in God, they are appropriately fearful of the consequences of disobedience. In other words, they are afraid *not* to draw near to God. If those same members do not trust in God, however, they fall into the various manifestations of unhealthy fear. Either they fear that their enemies are more powerful than God, or they fear that God is neither capable nor good enough to fulfill divine promises. This is based on a view of God as either weak or capricious. No one wants to approach a God of whom one is embarrassed or a God of whom one is terrified. On the other hand, approach is desired when a person knows God's inextricable power and goodness, a theological portrait the author of Hebrews builds in this section through appeal to God's holy presence with the people of Israel. This psalm has been incorporated as an option for daily morning prayer, so countless Christians have heard this text issue the call for listening "today."[17]

Here the author urges fear of a particular consequence—namely, that *someone from among you should be found to have fallen short*. The word for *fallen short* indicates lack or failing to reach a goal. The goal is to enter God's rest, because the author says that the *promise to go into his rest* is *remaining*. The author interprets Psalm 95 as a promise to him and his community. The psalm itself makes no explicit assertion that the promise of God remains open. It ends after telling the failure of faith and sad result of that generation who left Egypt. The author interprets the psalm's lifting up of the possibility of hearing God's voice and responding correctly (Heb 3:7–8/Ps 94:7–8 LXX) as evidence that the rest remains. If God is still speaking to humanity, God must still be inviting humanity into divine rest. The author's support for viewing the psalm as divine promise appears in the remaining parts of ch. 4. At this point, he has not yet defined what God's rest means for him and his community. That also is to come. Readers might be surprised by the assertion that the rest remains *for them* since, in the psalm and his comments on it so far, rest was equated with the promised land. This, too, he will need to explain.

17. *BCP* (1979), 146.

Before that explanation, the author is intent to portray his listeners and himself as those who are poised at a point of decision, much like the generation who was offered entrance to Canaan. The promise to go into God's rest remains an open one for them. If they fear their enemies more than the consequences of not trusting God, as the wilderness generation did, some from among the group may be found to fall short of God's rest. The author could have simply said that some might fall short of God's rest, but the inclusion of the term he utilizes for *be found* (*dokeō*) is translated as "seem" in several versions. This translation holds out hope that such a shortfall may only be an appearance but not a reality. This is not to say that the warning does not speak to actual consequences (the wilderness generation demonstrates that it *is* possible to fall short); nevertheless, this translation illuminates that this is still a warning and not a foregone conclusion. The author's emphasis remains on the promise to go in, which is open for them all. The door is not yet closed.

While it is important to emphasize that this is a warning and not yet a reality, I have chosen to translate *dokeō* as *be found* because that highlights the consequences at risk. Eventually, the internal evil heart will manifest externally, and the distrust will be evident to all when that one does not enter into God's rest. This is a warning, but if any ignore it, the consequences will be undeniable.

The author draws the comparison between the wilderness generation and his community even closer to justify his point: *For even we are those who have been evangelized just as also those were*. The *kai* that begins the verse makes better sense as an intensive, ***even** we*. He says to them, God has given us good news just as God gave them good news. So also that good news was communicated by God's messengers: Joshua and Caleb for the wilderness generation, and for this community, those who heard about salvation from the Lord (2:3). The particularity of the good news differs, of course, but here the focus is on the shared experience of hearing a message from the speaking God. This was also the case in the first sentence of the sermon; both the ancestors and this community have heard God's revelation, and God's revelation is good news. I have chosen to translate *euēngelismenoi* with *evangelized* to stress the points of connection. God is the giver of ultimately good news, and the invitation to the good of resting in the land of promise points to the ultimate good of following Christ faithfully into the place of dwelling with God forever.

With his next phrase the two communities part ways, or, at least, the author hopes they will. The wilderness generation heard the word. God spoke it to them and they listened, but *the word of hearing did not benefit*; in other words, it did no good for them because they were *those who had not joined in faith with those who heard.* The wilderness generation did not benefit from the word they heard because they did not join in faith with those who heard and were ready to obey—namely, Joshua and Caleb, the only ones who responded faithfully. All the others did not (Num 13:30–34; 14:6–9). Since Joshua will be mentioned a few verses later (4:8), this reference to "those who heard" indicates that he might already be on the mind of the author. Since the people joined with the ten spies, and not the two, the word of good news about the land did not benefit them.[18] The emphasis remains on faith. This is fitting since this is the first verse where the word *pistis* appears. It is not enough to hear the good news; God's audience must also respond faithfully to it.

The author has established that *we* are those who have been evangelized, and now he reminds them that *we* are those who believed: *For we who believe go into the rest.* The participle for belief is in the aorist tense, and the reference to the past seems fitting here. He is reminding them of the confession they have already made (3:1). Given the hearing and the response, he can claim that *we*, as those who have heard and have responded, are going into the rest. Two uncials, Alexandrinus and Claromontanus, have the subjunctive here (*let us* go in), which makes good sense since they have not yet entered the rest. The weight of the evidence for the indicative, however, is stronger. The verb for "entrance" (*eiserchomai*) as an indicative is a statement of fact, and it is also in the present tense. This term indicates that entering God's rest is not only something to which they are looking forward; it is also something they are already in the process of doing. Already being on the road, being led by God (2:10), is part of the encouragement to them to keep going into the full and final rest.

Then the author quotes the psalm again with the introductory phrase *just as he said.* The psalm makes clear that this is God speaking, indicated by the shift to first-person speech in 3:9, and yet the author of Hebrews attributes the citation to the Holy Spirit (3:7). If all of God's speech is now in the Son, there is a triplicate to the subject of the "he" with this introduction: God, Son, and Holy Spirit.

18. The alternative textual tradition, communicated with the participle *synkekerasmenous* agreeing with "word" rather than "them," would indicate that the word of hearing was not joined with faith by those who heard and so it did not benefit them. The author would be focusing on the majority of the unfaithful and their failure to both hear and trust. The reading discussed above has better textual support, but in either instance the emphasis on faith remains dominant.

The quotation this time, the third time the psalm appears, is from the last line of the original citation (Heb 3:11/Ps 94:11 LXX): *So I swore in my wrath they will not go into my rest*. If he and his listeners are entering in because they believe, then he reminds them that the wilderness generation did not get to go in because they did not respond to God's word with faith. The reiteration of God's oath taken in wrath and the consequences they faced act as a sober reminder, but also bring a sense of relief. Since he and his listeners *have* joined their hearing with faith, they are *not* part of this group. Hearing plus faith equals entrance. They have the hearing and the faith, and they are already entering. On the other hand, because they have not yet fully entered, they need to hear this warning to be reminded of the necessity of continuing to respond faithfully to God.

The author states next, *Even though "the works" were finished from the foundation of the world*. In so doing, he ties back to the works the people of Israel saw in God's redemption and in God's punishment (3:9). Now he asserts that they had access to God's work from the dawn of time. All of creation should have convinced them of God's power and ability to be faithful to the promise. At the same time, this phrase highlights the cessation of God's works. The reason why the wilderness generation did not enter God's rest is *not* that it did not exist yet.[19] When God pronounces that the wilderness generation will not enter his rest, the author of Hebrews understands the psalm to be referring to a rest that has existed since the time of creation. The land of the promise pointed toward something more, a rest with the God who created all things. It is *that* rest into which the audience of Hebrews are already entering.

For support of this definition of rest, the author appeals to one who has spoken and does so in a rather nondescript way: *For he has said somewhere concerning the seventh thus*. Unlike the reference in 2:6, at least the speaker is more clearly defined here, likely still the Holy Spirit who spoke the first citation of the psalm (3:7). The location of the citation, however, is explicitly unspecified (*somewhere*). Even the most freshly initiated reader would likely know, however, that this comes from the beginning of the Bible. In line with the rhetorical possibility in 2:6, the author might be offering a subtle encouragement to his listeners that they share with him a familiarity with God's word.

19. F. F. Bruce, *The Epistle to the Hebrews*, rev. ed., NICNT (Grand Rapids: Eerdmans, 1990), 106.

The author cites the Greek translation of Genesis 2:2 closely, the only difference being that he supplies *theos* where the part of the sentence he cites has, instead, a masculine pronoun: *And God rested on the seventh day from all his works.* The citation gives textual support for his previous assertion. God's rest has existed, and God's works have been evident because God completed those works and rested from them on the seventh day of creation until the present. In Genesis 2:2, "all the works" refers clearly to God's work of creation. It is not that God ceases from all activity, but the making of the created realm is completed from that time. This provides both insights into creation and the Creator. Creation, unlike God, is not eternal, a fact that highlights the eternality of the Son who took on flesh (Heb 1:3; 2:14). Moreover, while creation will experience change at God's hand (1:10–12; 12:26–27), God will never create all things again. That work is completed. As for the Creator and the action of resting, the shift in the meaning of "rest" is rather ingenious here. In Psalm 95, God owns the *place* of rest. In Genesis, God is doing the resting. The author has expanded the meaning of rest not only as something eternal but also as something in which God participates. The community of this letter are in the process of entering into the place where God is at rest.

The chilling thing is that the Israelites were in that process too, but they fell short of reaching it. The author renames this point by saying *and on this again* as he returns to the psalm for the fourth time and this particular line of the psalm for the third: *Surely, they will not go into my rest.* The line of the psalm gives both warning and hope. The first ones who heard the good news did not go in because of a lack of trust. The same could happen to any of this author's community if they also fail to trust and obey God. At the same time, the psalm points to the continued reality of God's rest and the continued offer of God's invitation into it. The author asserts, *Therefore, since it remains*—the "it" being both the rest and the invitation—and concludes from its existence that it remains *for some to go into it.* He is asserting a great consistency in God. He assumes that if God invited humanity into the place of divine rest in the past, God will continue to offer that invitation. God could have given up on humanity after this failure of the wilderness generation when *those who were gospeled earlier did not go in because of disobedience.* God had no need of fellowship with humanity, because God remained full and complete in the divine communion of Father, Son, and Holy Spirit. But God's desire for, in Willie

Jennings's words, "joining" remains.[20] The author knows this because of the Holy Spirit's speech in the psalm. Because of this psalm, the author can proclaim that *again God sets a certain day, "today," by David saying after such a long time, just as God said earlier, "Today if you hear his voice do not harden your hearts."* Generally, God called out to the Israelites to be faithful and obedient, to have pliable hearts. Moses interprets the story of God's invitation into the land in this way when he retells it in Numbers 32 (see 32:9), but God does not say to them explicitly in the narrative as they are about to enter the land, "Do not harden your hearts." In the psalm God makes this statement only once. Hence, the repetition of this statement must not be when God uttered it to the wilderness generation and then in the writing of the psalm, but the repetition comes between when God first spoke the psalm and now again when God is speaking it to the audience of Hebrews. Through the psalm spoken originally by David and now by the pen of the author of Hebrews—all under the purview of the Holy Spirit—after the wilderness generation had been given the offer and failed to step into it, the invitation came to a new generation who was given the opportunity to hear the account of the disobedience in the psalm to prevent the hardening of their hearts.[21]

In other words, the power of the psalm did not end with David. Now the Holy Spirit is speaking again just as he spoke through David at an earlier time. Now the Holy Spirit is saying to *this* community, in the fifth quotation of the psalm, uttering this specific line for the third and final time in this sermon, *Today if you hear his voice, do not harden your hearts*. The author does not need to repeat the reference to the early generation again by including the phrase "as in the rebellion," because the focus is squarely on those who are listening *today*. What the author knows from the psalm, as spoken by God's Holy Spirit, is that God has planned for a certain day to exist, and this is a day that is not limited to one twenty-four-hour period. Anytime this text is heard, it is "today." Through the psalm and the Genesis narrative, the author asserts that God rests and invites the faithful into that rest. God did not give up on the

20. This is prominent in Willie James Jennings, *Acts*, Belief: A Theological Commentary on the Bible (Louisville: Westminster John Knox, 2017).

21. Richard Hays calls this "the argument from sequence," in which the author displays "an alertness to the *narrative* order of Israel's Scripture and a conviction that God's purpose has a sequential, linear logic to it" ("'Here We Have No Lasting City,'" 165).

enterprise of sharing rest with humanity when the wilderness generation was unfaithful; the Holy Spirit issued the call again through David and yet again through this author. The Holy Spirit has continued to issue the call to any and all who hear this text. Any who hear God's voice are encouraged to prevent a hard heart, trust in God's power and goodness, and enter into God's rest.

The standing invitation into eternal divine rest raises a question about those who eventually did make it into the land of the promise. The author now mentions Joshua in v. **8**: *For if Joshua had given them rest.* His is surely a name that caused the audience to smile. "For if *Iēsous* had given them rest . . ." Jesus and Joshua are transliterated the same way in Greek. The Israelites *did* go into the land of rest under Iēsous's leadership (Josh 22:4). So, too, this community is following a Iēsous through the wilderness into God's rest.[22] Both Iēsouses are faithful to God in the midst of challenge.

These similarities in which Joshua is a type of Jesus allow the differences to shine out with more power. First, a difference exists in the way they lead. While Joshua was with the people in the wilderness, Jesus is already in the place of rest. He has surely gone through the wilderness of the human condition, facing suffering, temptation, persecution, even death. So his session does not remove him from the struggles of the people in the wilderness because of his journey through it. He does, however, offer the realized and embodied guarantee of entry that Joshua, on the road with them, could not. Moreover, his bodily absence emphasizes the importance of listening to God's Holy Spirit.

Second, the destination of their leading is different. The author surmises that the rest into which Joshua led the people of Israel was not the ultimate rest of which the psalm speaks, a confirmation of his earlier argument that this rest is an eternally existing rest with God, not simply a particular section of the land. If it was the case that under the leadership of that Iēsous the people fully entered into God's rest, then the Holy Spirit *would not have spoken of another [day] after these days* of Joshua. The psalm, written after the time of Joshua in which God issues the call to embrace faith, is proof for the author that whatever rest Joshua gave to the people, it was not the ultimate rest. Although Hebrews is referring to the period of the conquests—sections of

22. For a thorough development of this connection, see Bryan J. Whitfield, *Joshua Traditions and the Arguments of Hebrews 3 and 4* (Boston: de Gruyter, 2013).

Scripture fraught with exegetical and ethical difficulties[23]—he mentions them only to say a certain territory is *not* the concern of this community. They are encouraged to endure the violence enacted against them (10:32–34; 12:1–11), not wield it against others.[24]

The divinely spoken psalm text causes the author to conclude, *Therefore, there remains a sabbath rest*. The author utilizes the same word used in v. 6: *Therefore, since it* ***remains*** *for some to go into it*. Fascinatingly, the psalm does not say explicitly that the rest remains and that God is calling others into it. Instead, the psalm includes the assertion from God that God possesses rest (v. 11) and the call to avoid the posture that prevented the wilderness generation from going in. The author has combined the existence of the rest with the warning against hard-heartedness to determine the good news that the rest is still on offer.

The rest remains for a particular group, *the people of God*. Other than the first and last references in the letter (2:17 and 13:12), the author uses *laos*, people, to refer to the covenant people of Israel (5:3; 7:5, 11, 27; 8:10; 9:7, 19; 10:30; 11:25). The author's lack of any explicit discussion of gentile inclusion leads readers to conclude that since the covenant blessings to Abraham were intended to go to all people (Gen 12:3), this sabbath rest is also available to the people of Israel and, through them, all besides.

As a *hapax legomenon*, the term *sabbatismos*, *sabbath rest*, has caused no small amount of debate. The author has ruled out the option that this rest is equated with entry into a land secured through conquest. He has stated that God rested since the seventh day from the act of creation, but God, as Hebrews itself has proclaimed, has been very active since then—speaking, sustaining, procuring purification. This *sabbatismos*, if patterned after God's rest, is not

23. See John H. Walton and J. Harvey Walton, *The Lost World of the Israelite Conquest: Covenant, Retribution, and the Fate of the Canaanites* (Downers Grove, IL: IVP Academic, 2017); Matt Lynch, *Flood and Fury: Old Testament Violence and the Shalom of God* (Downers Grove, IL: IVP Academic, 2023); John J. Collins, *Does the Bible Justify Violence?* (Minneapolis: Augsburg Fortress, 2005); Charlie Trimm, *The Destruction of the Canaanites: God, Genocide, and Biblical Interpretation* (Grand Rapids: Eerdmans, 2022).

24. The admonitions to endure violence raise different ethical concerns—namely, a worry about reinforcing patterns of abuse. See discussions about passivity especially in the commentary on 12:4–11.

the cessation of all activity but, as the verb *sabbatizō* indicates, the cessation of mundane work so that one can participate in "festive worship and praise."[25] This sabbath rest is not the state of doing nothing but, instead, joining with God in restful enjoyment of the good creation as God intended it to be. This concept of sabbath aligns with the idea present in ch. 12 that the created realms will be shaken and transformed but not obliterated. Instead, God will bring them into alignment with God's eternal purposes. Humans will get to join God in the celebration of that good and enduring work.

Since this *sabbatismos* remains, it is possible for the people of God to enter it, and v. **10** provides an example of someone who does so. *For the one who goes into his rest.* The use of masculine pronouns here can become confusing. Into whose rest is the "one" entering, his own or God's? Either is possible, although God's rest seems most likely since that has been the focus of the author's discussion in this section. Moreover, the next statement focuses on human rest, and a double reference to that would be repetitive (for the one who enters into his human rest, even he rests). The second masculine pronoun does refer to the human: *even he rests from his works just as God [rests] from his own.* Read anthropologically, v. 10 is an example of a person from among the people of God entering into the available rest of God. That is not the only way to read the verse, however; it may also be read christologically. Jesus the Messiah is one who has entered into his rest and has rested from all his works when he took his seat at God's right hand (1:13). This reading reiterates Jesus's role as the *archēgos* (2:10), the trailblazer, who makes entering God's rest possible. An interpreter need not choose between the two, necessarily, for Christ's entrance into rest makes it possible for others to do the same, but the christological reading is why I have opted for masculine language here.

The author's presentation of his belief that God's rest remains available for access leads to a hortatory conclusion: *Therefore, let us.* The author closes the reflection on rest with this first-person-plural admonition, denoting that they should join together in an action. He communicates this with a playfulness of words: *let us hasten to enter into that rest.* Simply put: let us rush to rest. He uses the term *hasten* to communicate commitment, intensity, and even speed. I've chosen to highlight not only the commitment (let us "make every effort,"

25. Jon Laansma, *"I Will Give You Rest": The "Rest" Motif in the New Testament with Special Reference to Mt 11 and Heb 3–4*, WUNT II.98 (Tübingen: Mohr Siebeck, 1997), 276.

so the NRSV) but also the contrast with rest by highlighting the urgency, supported by the use of this word in 6:11 as well as the race metaphor in ch. 12.

Interpreters have wrestled with the question of the nature of this rest, whether it is future or present or some mix of both. The future aspect is clear. The members of this community have not yet entered into the very presence of God, nor have they ceased from their daily work and activity. At the same time, the author has asserted that they are in the process of entering—they are "on the way." As believers they are entering into it (4:3). The author seems to believe that being on the path offers some of the benefits of God's rest (seen especially in the verse about approaching God's throne, 4:16), even if they are not yet there fully. These benefits can include regular days or seasons of rest patterned after what God is doing.

The future aspect of the rest is confirmed by the reason for his admonition. He wishes them to show urgent zeal to enter the rest *in order that someone may not fall by the same example of disobedience.* The potential of following not the faithful Son but instead the unfaithful forebears remains a worry for him. As the bodies of the unfaithful "fell" (*piptō*, 3:17) in the wilderness, so too does he not want any member of this community to fall and then die in a state of disobedience to God.

In Hebrews obedience is a holistic reality. It is built on faithfulness to the confession of the God of Israel's revelation of the Son, Jesus, who took on flesh, died on the cross, rose again, and ascended to the right hand of his Father (3:1; 4:14). Jon Laansma notes that "though the author of Hebrews does not mention the name of Jesus anywhere in this passage, all of this magnifies the glory and honor of the one who promises, who is the promise, who keeps the promises, and in whom is all that that promise offers. The one who brings and who is that resting place and its sabbath is the one whom God [calls Son]."[26] This confession of him manifests in faithfulness in the decisions of life, following God's leading and encouraging fellow followers on the way. In short, for Hebrews belief is both doctrinal and active.[27] This is not unusual; Paul, James, and all other theologians in the canon affirm the same. Any temptation to

26. Jon Laansma, *The Letter to the Hebrews: A Commentary for Preaching, Teaching, and Bible Study* (Eugene, OR: Cascade, 2017), 111.

27. See Matthew Bates's work on this topic: *Salvation by Allegiance Alone: Rethinking Faith, Works, and the Gospel of Jesus the King* (Grand Rapids: Baker Academic, 2017), and *Gospel Allegiance: What Faith in Jesus Misses for Salvation in Christ* (Grand Rapids: Brazos, 2019).

embrace only one or the other, privileging doctrine over works or works over doctrine, finds no shelter in the documents of Christian Scriptures, Hebrews prominently included.

One of Hebrews' best-known verses comes next. *For the word of God is living and active* (v. **12**). The temptation to lift it out of its context and apply it generally to any doctrine of Scripture looms large, and this is not a wholly inappropriate move. As testified by many throughout time, God's word in the Scriptures continues to prove itself living and active. In this section, the author has repeatedly emphasized the enduring power of the scriptural text. God *is speaking* these words as long as it remains today, as long as the world as we know it continues to exist. This powerful and redemptive work of the word communicated through the Spirit's inspiration of the words of the Scriptures is a temporary manifestation. The investigation of a person's deepest recesses is necessary while it is still "today." In these days of the end, it is a gift that the word of God does this work.

This wide application to the inscripturated word should not be the only one, however. When maintained within their context, the words of this verse speak of the psalm on which the author has been preaching. This sentence is joined to what has come before by the connecting term *gar* (*for*). In v. 12 the author provides the clarification to his admonition *let us hasten*. The threat of following the example of the wilderness generation evokes Psalm 95 yet again, and so the statement about the word of God has as its primary referent God's speech as introduced in the psalm, *Today if you hear his voice*. The Holy Spirit urges responsive and obedient listening to the voice of God. The other proof that this verse focuses on the speech of God as discussed in Psalm 95 appears in its reference to the heart. The word's ability to judge the thoughts and intentions of the *heart* connects to the psalm's emphasis on the hearts of the wilderness generation (3:10). Hearing God's voice is manifest in the actions that come out of one's heart. The author's statements in v. 12 align with the call issued throughout this section of the sermon where the author has encouraged an openness to hear and respond to God's word. He makes those connections to the psalm in a vivid and intense way, and thereby he makes the point about responsive hearing yet again in v. 12, but in a different key. Whereas his reflections on the psalm put the emphasis on his community's need to hear and respond in faith, captured succinctly in his previous admonition, *Let us hasten to enter into that rest*, verse 12 shifts the focus to *God's* action.

The word of God is *living and active*, he says, with the term for "living" given pride of place as the first word of the sentence. It is not surprising that the word is *living*, because it comes from the living God (3:12). The word of the living God is also *active* or effective. Used only here in Hebrews, this word describes things that are put into practice, demonstrated when Paul hopes for this enactment for his own ministry (1 Cor 16:9) and for Philemon's faith (Phlm 6). The author of Hebrews provides imagery for that enactment in the following verses. God's word is *sharper than every two-edged sword*, a metaphor that allows the author to portray its ability to cut through the innermost parts of the person.[28] The word of God is not just as sharp as that kind of sword but possesses a penetrating quality that supersedes all such swords. Its *piercing to the division of soul and spirit* evokes a common pairing. Soul and spirit often appear together in the New Testament as similar things that nevertheless are not synonymous. In the metaphor here, the focus is not so much the distinct nuances of the two as the internality they both convey. Whatever joins together the hidden realities of soul and spirit, even there the word of God can penetrate. Both terms appear as ways of speaking about the enlivening aspect of the person that makes them a living rather than a dead being. The living word of the living God can pierce to the source of a person's life.

The next pair, *joints and marrow*, are bodily terms. These, too, are hidden, so the seeing word's ability to go internal—to be active among hidden things—is again emphasized. Both that which enlivens a person and that which holds a person together—the energizing aspects of their life and the structures of their bodies—are cleaved by the word so that the *desires* (*enthymēsis*, one's thoughts or internal script unavailable to others) and *intentions* (or plans, *ennoia*) of the heart are laid bare. The author does not know the state of this congregation's hearts, if they are deceived (3:10, 15) or evil (3:12), and so he must warn them with this extended exhortation, but the living and speaking God does and therefore can judge these undisclosed things justly. This aligns with the author's later statement that God is the judge of all (12:23).

He adds intensity to this truth in v. **13**: *And no created thing is hidden before him*. All of creation is exposed before the word. Not one aspect of creation remains hidden (*aphanēs*). If there was a question about the applicability of this section to the people of Israel or to a broader group, now the question is

28. Wisdom of Solomon also depicts the word of God with a sword (18:15–16).

settled. The word's vision apprehends all created things. *All things are naked and bare-necked before his eyes.* The image is meant to evoke either the wrestling ring with an opponent pinning another for the win or, more persuasive in light of the topic that follows, the sacrificial cult, with the animal poised for slaughter.

In this position of exposure, not only should the audience of Hebrews listen, but some interpreters have argued that they will also have to speak, or return their own word (*logos*) to the word. Often this phrase is translated "to whom [we owe] our word." Put differently, they must give an account of themselves to the one who, having done surgery to open the person, sees all.

In my view, the imagery of the verse resists this interpretation. If they are caught in a wrestling match or, as seems more likely, poised as a sacrifice, and if their sinfulness renders them without any defense, they would be unable to offer any word. This text resonates with the conclusion of the catena in Romans 3, when Paul has laid the charges of sinfulness to all and deafening silence is the only response (3:19–20). Consequently, a superior translation is *concerning whom is the word for us.*[29] The author's focus is on the all-seeing word of God. This word of God is the one concerning whom he has been writing. The author then refers to his own act of writing and here as in other places (2:5; 5:11; 6:9) uses a first-person plural to refer to that process. Moreover, by including himself in the dative *for us*, he emphasizes that he does not stand outside the insightful address of God's word. It comes to him, and then he reflects on it for this congregation. He has been talking about God's word, and this word is a direct address for him and his congregation.

The comfort to them all is that if they were nervous about any dark evil hidden in their hearts, even to themselves, they can rest assured that the word of God will bring it to light. Conversely, a serious warning comes to any of them who imagined they could hide their lack of trust in God from the others. There is no doubt that the word of God will discover it. The word of God, for their comfort or their judgment, is for them.

While the word in question is certainly connected to the divinely spoken psalm, and God's speech in Scripture more generally, it also becomes vividly personal here. In light of the author's previous connections between the Spirit

29. See the argument laid out in Jonathan I. Griffiths, *Hebrews and Divine Speech*, LNTS 507 (London: Bloomsbury, 2014), 85–88.

and the Son and God's speech, seeing the activity of either (or all) here seems fitting. The author asks the listeners to imagine themselves as the sacrifice poised with its neck to be sliced, and God is there with the implement that will expose that which is inside. It is especially appropriate to image the invisible God as Jesus the Priest. The necessity of trusting that High Priest in such a moment is paramount. Hence, the author turns next to extol exactly what kind of High Priest he is.

In the *Book of Common Prayer*, the eucharistic service begins with the Collect for Purity. All present are invited to collect their prayers together with these words:

> Almighty God, to you all hearts are open, all desires known, and from you no secrets are hid: Cleanse the thoughts of our hearts by the inspiration of your Holy Spirit, that we may perfectly love you, and worthily magnify your holy Name; through Christ our Lord. *Amen.*[30]

The echoes with Hebrews 4 are unmistakable. As I pray this week by week, while it is still "today," I'm struck by how multivalent it can be. At times I'm comforted that God knows me, especially when I feel like a mystery to myself. God will unearth and convict if there is a sin that remains in ignorance. At others, I'm repentant for the ugly things I know of that should not be present in my heart, but even then it is comforting that I do not have to pretend to be better than I truly am. Pretense is not necessary because it is not possible. Though this passage in Hebrews has focused on the internality of the individual person, these are people in community, so at other times I find comfort in thinking about how this prayer will play out in others' lives. If I am at odds with someone or find it difficult to trust another, I can rest in the fact that God knows them, and I am not required to figure them out. If they are in the wrong, God will convict, but if I am the one in error, God will let me know. Hence, I return to the comfort of the all-seeing word. To find oneself bested in a match or, even more intense, prepared for the slaughter leaves one desperately hoping that the one who stands over you is both good and just, or, in Hebrews' language, merciful and faithful (2:17). Thankfully, when the word of God does the exposing, when Jesus is the priest, this hope

30. *BCP* (1979), 355.

is fulfilled. Many who pray this prayer have discovered that the act of being exposed to God, week by week, is less terrifying than one might imagine. It would be more horrible for the person and uncaring of God to allow ignorance of one's hidden sins to persist. Though the image of Hebrews 4:13 has us bound by the word of God, that consistently proves to be a posture of incredible freedom.

HEBREWS 4:14–5:10

THE GREAT HIGH PRIEST

The imagery of an exposed neck in 4:13 could evoke a vision of a sacrifice and the presence of a priest. Being poised in such a way elicits a strong hope for a just and merciful one. The encouragement of v. 14 follows directly from this sobering image and shows forth the power of the statement about God's living and active word when interpreted in the midst of that context.

Verse 14 begins the author's first extended treatment of priests. In the opening sentences of his foray into that subject, he extols the greatness and compassion of his community's great High Priest, Jesus. He builds on that encouragement in order to offer one more exhortation in line with those of chs. 3 and 4. As he urged them to zealously and urgently go into God's rest (4:11), here he encourages them to draw near to God's throne (4:16).

Having named Jesus as a *great* High Priest, he then lays out what is true of all high priests according to the law of Israel (5:1–4). They display respectable and admirable qualities as they carry out the functions of God's call, within the limitations of their own humanity. This paragraph serves as a control against which Jesus's priesthood is measured. When the author turns to Jesus's priesthood in particular in v. 5, he begins with Jesus's call from God his Father and proceeds to Jesus's prayer to God, maintaining the focus on divine dialogue established in the first two chapters. Since God the Father has the power of life, the request of the Son was fulfilled, but only through a demanding path. The story of Jesus's suffering prepares for the next section of the sermon, where the author reminds the audience that they need to follow Jesus down the challenging path to maturity (5:11–14). In addition to this preparatory work for the immediately following section, in this last statement of this passage (5:10) the author names for the first time the next major subject that will follow the exhortation of 5:11–6:20—namely, the priesthood of Melchizedek, which takes center stage in ch. 7.

4:14–16 · APPROACH

[14]Therefore, because we have a great High Priest who has passed through the heavens, Jesus the Son of God, let us hold fast to the confession. [15]For we do not have a High Priest who is not able to sympathize with our weaknesses, but one who has been tempted similar to every way we are, yet without sin. [16]Therefore, let us draw near with boldness to the throne of grace in order that we might receive mercy and we might find grace as well-timed help.

The intensity of the sacrificial picture in v. 13 sets the next statements into even sharper relief. The author has painted a picture of himself and his community exposed before the word of God. Vulnerability is never comfortable, and so in such a situation one might be tempted to run away. This seems like it has presented itself as a legitimate option for the community members because of the author's continual insistence that they *do not* turn away (2:1; 3:1, 6, 14; 4:11). A less extreme option would be to stay put in the presence of this all-seeing word, but to remain silent. What defense could one offer to the one who can pierce into all the crevices of one's innermost being? I posited that the author focuses on the word coming to them in v. 13. Now that Jesus's identity has been named in the first part of v. 14, the author will not allow them to remain silent. Instead, he urges them all: *let us hold fast to the confession*, to stay tethered to their High Priest and give a word to God's Word. This is the first time the author has used the verb *krateō*, "to grasp" (he will do so again in ch. 6 when he urges them to grasp the hope that lies before them [6:18]), but its tangible connotations—it speaks of the work of the hands to hold on to something—align with the previous admonitions to hold fast (*katechō*, 3:6, 14).

In this instance, though, they are grasping onto a verbal response, their word of agreement, their *confession*. On the basis of the other times he uses this word, this confession centers on the divine identity as revealed in the person and work of Jesus (3:1; 13:15). It is agreement with the story of him being sent from God (3:1; 10:5–10) and now advocating for them before God (7:25), a story that gives them hope (10:23). Grounded in him who sits at God's right hand, their confession need not put confidence in any political system of leadership, much like their forebears who knew their "outsider" status (11:13). With five appearances throughout the sermon (3:1; 4:14; 10:23; 11:13; 13:15), two of which are present in key summaries (4:14; 10:23), confession is a key point the author wishes to emphasize. Their confession objectively gives them access to God because they agree with the way God has provided access through the death, resurrection, and session of the Son. This reality gives them confidence to approach God because they know they have been prepared to do so through Jesus Christ (see more in the commentary on 10:23). Here in ch. 4, retaining a grip on their confession allows them to approach God's throne of grace. The emphasis in this section remains on the incredible grace of that invitation to approach, given their vulnerable exposure before God. God knows who they are and *still* invites them in. The only way they can do so is through the merciful High Priest the Triune God has granted humanity to confess. By confessing him, they are confessing who they truly are, who God is, and how they can approach. This is vitally important for those who find themselves in the midst of the wilderness where the author has positioned his readers. A wayward heart remains a temptation (3:12), and so holding fast to their confession is how the author is encouraging them to endure in the wilderness, holding to the High Priest who has gone before them, so that, as they remain trusting, they will enter God's rest.

The church owes a debt of gratitude to the many faithful who, in the early centuries of our faith, honored the revelation of God in Jesus Christ as attested in the inspired Scriptures by distilling those sacred texts into the creeds. These are human words with a complex history and afterlife, and yet they have been proven by the test of time in which they have allowed generations of believers to hold fast to the faith. I grew up knowing the Apostles' Creed through Rich Mullins's hammer dulcimer–accompanied rendition. Not only did I learn the tenets, but I also inscribed the truth in my mind and in my heart that "I did not make it, but it is making me."[1] Now I am part of a tradition that communally confesses either the Apostles' or Nicene Creed each week. With my mouth I voice these words, and with my ears I hear these words voiced by others. Repetition has not dampened but only deepened my joyful ties to this confession.

1. Rich Mullins, "Creed," track 5 on *A Liturgy, a Legacy and a Ragamuffin Band*, Reunion 49233, 1993, compact disc.

Each week it reminds me who God is, sovereign and inestimably gracious. I find my identity in a story wider and deeper than my own, which catches my finite life up into eternity. Recitation of the creed is also the space for communal unity. I may have different opinions on any number of issues from fellow congregants, but when we confess the same Triune God, we remind ourselves that we are fellow pilgrims on the journey to the same rest. I acknowledge that different Christian groups have different ways of expressing these connections, but some kind of regular return to the simple yet profound faith long held by the saints offers an important means of endurance for individuals and congregations, just as the author of Hebrews suggested it would.

When all their desires and intentions are laid bare, the only fitting recourse for the congregation is to confess—to stand in agreement with—the one who died to purify their sins. The truth of who Jesus is has become their confession (3:1). The author reminds them with all sincerity that they have no other place to turn to deal with the potential for evil in their own hearts than him.

It makes sense, then, that they can hold on to this confession of his identity *because* he is their *great High Priest.* As the High Priest would slaughter the sacrificial goat for Yom Kippur (Lev 16:18), it is fitting to see Jesus the High Priest standing over them with their necks laid bare. Yet, in a startling turn, it is the Priest who is slain. It is as if he takes the knife poised above the victim and turns it on himself. The author's way of describing Jesus here points to this reversal of expectations. First, he is the *great* High Priest. While this adjective praises his majesty and prepares for the comparison with other priests, the use of these terms together in Israel's Scriptures is unusual enough that it is fruitful to consider their Old Testament context.[2]

The high priest is more commonly referred to as the "great priest." In the first instance of that phrase, Leviticus 21, the great priest is held to a higher standard. Whereas other priests may be defiled by a dead body in the case of a relative, the great priest may not go near any dead body. He may not defile himself for any person (Lev 21:10–11). The great High Priest Jesus, however, has not only gone near death; he has gone into it himself and come out the other side.

2. In the Septuagint, "great High Priest" appears only as a description of Simon in the Maccabean literature (1 Macc 13:42; 14:27). This is likely true because even "High Priest" is an unusual collocation outside this later literature, appearing only three times outside of Esdras and the Maccabean texts (Lev 4:3; Josh 22:13; 24:33).

Israel's law also has an example of the restorative death of the high priest. When innocent blood has been shed, the one who did the slaying must reside in the city of refuge until the great priest dies. At that point the slayer may return home (Num 35:28). In this instance, the death of the high priest has dealt with the problem of death.[3] So, too, the death of the Son of God, the great High Priest, frees the fearful from their imprisonment (2:14) so that they can dwell with God forever.

With this language, the author casts a cultic mantle over the entirety of Jesus's life. He became human so that he could be chosen as a priest from among humanity (see 5:1). He suffered so that he could be a sympathetic High Priest (2:17–18; 4:15). He died and rose to defeat death (2:14–15), and ascended to offer himself for sins before God the Father. He continues this priestly ministry advocating at God's right hand (7:25). His priestly ministry touches all parts of his incarnate life.

The author goes on to say that he is the great High Priest *who has passed through the heavens*. His passage through the heavens aligns with the author's assertions of Jesus's session at God's right hand. He has passed through the realms of creation (1:10) to sit where God dwells (8:1). In the story of Hebrews, this movement takes place *after* his death and resurrection, so he enters this realm as the one who has already died and defeated death. Then the author makes explicit what they already know. The congregation's great High Priest is none other than *Jesus*. Jesus is the apostle, the one sent from God (3:1), the one who was made lower than the angels by becoming incarnate, who in his flesh and blood died for all. Jesus is the one they see crowned with glory and honor *because* he suffered death (2:9). Their living High Priest is the one who lived, died, and has been raised.

The one who became and remains incarnate is *the Son of God*, just as he was first introduced in the sermon (1:2). This title evokes both his sovereignty and his faithfulness to the mission of redeeming humans from sin and the fear of death. Hence, since he faced and fully experienced death, that which causes

3. "But the banishment itself was not construed as making atonement for the dead man's blood. Atonement for manslaughter came through the death of the high priest. . . . [Crimes] have caused the death of another man, and only the death of a man can atone for the killing" (Wenham, *Numbers*, 238). He also cites the Mishnah, which states, "It is not exile that expiates, but the death of the high priest" (Makkoth 11b). See also Philip J. Budd, *Numbers*, WBC 5 (Waco: Word, 1984), 82.

fear and bondage, he is the High Priest who sympathizes. The majesty of his position as eternal Son of God who reigns on the right hand of the throne of God in the heavens could emphasize his distance, but the author states his point with clarity by putting it into the negative: *For we do not have a High Priest who is not able to sympathize*. He suffers our struggles as humans because he has faced death and all the fear it brings (see his honest and emotional reaction in the face of death in 5:7). The author applies the perfect participle of *peirazō* (one who has been tempted) to Jesus. Its semantic range can include both testing and temptation, but the latter seems most fitting here since the author joins this word to sin when he says that Jesus was *tempted similar to every way we are, yet without sin*.

In addition to willingly embracing the weakness of death, Jesus also was willing to face the experience of temptation. He does so in an act of grace to experience full humanity so that he can serve not only as a priest who deals with the problem of death but also as one who, with experiential understanding, advocates before the gracious Father to aid humans' endurance in their own journeys of faith, where they must fight against sin. To be clear, the Father does not need to be persuaded, for it was the unified will of God that led to the coming of the Son to effect redemption. At the same time, only the Son became incarnate and experienced the human condition, and so only he can advocate for his brothers and sisters as one who has walked the road they are walking. As a first-century Jewish man, Jesus was not offered the exact same temptations as all other humans throughout history, but the core deceptions of those differently manifested temptations are the same. At the center of those deceptions for the author of Hebrews would be the temptation toward faithlessness,[4] as he emphasized in the extended exhortation of chs. 3 and 4. Importantly, the connection between Jesus and us is similar (*homoiotēta*, 4:15) but not the same, because his temptation never resulted in sin. Therefore, he can serve as both a completely understanding and a completely pure High Priest. He walked the road of temptation, but never succumbed to it, so is both compassionate enough to understand and powerful enough to redeem.

Because he is their High Priest, the author invites his listeners to *draw near with boldness to the throne of grace*. This is the first instance of what will become a repeated and vital theme in the letter, that of approaching (7:25; 10:1,

4. Cockerill, *Hebrews*, 226.

22; 11:6; 12:18, 22). "Drawing near" (*proserchomai*) builds on the exhortation of chs. 3 and 4 where the author urged them to "go in" (*eiserchomai*, 4:1, 3, 6, 10, 11) and encapsulates the author's call for forward movement. In the vision he casts for them, they are all on their way to dwelling with God and can experience God's peace while they journey forward.

They can proceed on this path with *boldness*. "Boldness" appears in two warnings in the letter (3:6; 10:35) and two exhortations (4:16; 10:19). It is both something they already possess and something they should not lose. Their boldness resides firmly in the character of their High Priest and his effective priestly work, an effectiveness drawn from the Son's natures. On one hand, they can be bold in light of his effective ministry because he is exalted. *Their* High Priest is resident with God. On the other, their boldness arises from his sympathy. He understands them, as their Creator, as the Word who sees inside them, *and* as one who himself has experienced the human condition. With him as their advocate, they can approach without pretense and with assurance that they will not be turned away.

In this instance, the particular place they are approaching is *the throne of grace*. So far in the letter the only throne mentioned is that of the Son, where, in the citation of Psalm 45, God the Father proclaims that the Son's throne is eternal (1:8). In the other references in the sermon, the throne is God's (8:1; 12:2), and the Son sits to the right. The throne language applied to both the Son and the Father points to the shared sovereignty of the Triune God.

In addition to divine power, the throne of this God is a throne of grace. God's grace ensured the death of the Son that opened the path of approach for the other children of God (2:10). The Spirit of grace inaugurated their relationship with God (10:29), and grace is also the goal toward which they are going (12:15). In addition to that which began their salvific journey and will be its end, grace is something they can experience now (13:9, 25) as they approach this throne.

The present availability of grace becomes clear in the next phrase. The author urges drawing near so that they might *receive mercy* and *find grace as well-timed help*. It should not be surprising that one would find grace at the throne of grace, but their approach is not simply a fact-finding mission, one in which they discover that grace does actually reside there. Even more, there is an exchange at this throne. Mercy is given by God and then received by them. They stand in need of mercy because when they are exposed before the all-seeing word (4:13), their imperfections become known. The author has prepared them to anticipate the reception of this mercy when he asserted that their brother, the Son of God, is a merciful High Priest (2:17) because he has experienced the full human condition and allows them to receive divine mercy for that condition.

It is the final phrase that confirms that this reception of mercy is not limited to the future. The *help* they receive will be *well-timed.* In other words, it will come right when they need it. In addition to the general sense of aid, this help includes the assistance from their High Priest enthroned with God, who because of his experience of temptation knows what aid to offer (2:18). Because they have received this help at all the right moments, they can, when the author gives them voice to speak Scripture at the end, refer to the Lord as their helper (13:6).

We have this great High Priest, the author proclaims. That should cause holy fear because, as God's speech and as God's High Priest, he knows everything about us and is poised over us. This should also cause gratefulness because in knowing everything about us, he has chosen to be our sacrifice and advocate.

This section might remind readers of the parable of the sinner and the publican (Luke 18:9–14). The only threat at this throne is if one approaches with false pretenses, pretending *not* to need the grace available. But if one comes boldly, ready to be exposed and cognizant of weaknesses, that person will receive everything needed from the God who created, and also experienced, the human condition.

5:1–10 · PRIESTLY COMPARISONS

[1]*For every high priest taken from humanity is appointed for the sake of humans in reference to the things aimed at God, in order that he might offer both gifts and sacrifices for sins;* [2]*being able to regulate emotion toward the ignorant and deceived, since he is also beset with weakness.* [3]*Because of this he ought to present an offering concerning sins, just as he does for the people, so also for himself.* [4]*And no one takes this honor for oneself but is called by God just as Aaron was.* [5]*So also Christ did not glorify himself to become High Priest, but the one who said to him, "You are my Son. Today I have begotten you,"* [6]*similarly also in another place says, "You are priest*

forever according to the order of Melchizedek." [7]*Who, in the days of his flesh offered both prayers and supplications with great cries and tears to the one who is able to save him from death, and he was heard because of his reverence.* [8]*Even though he was the Son, he learned obedience from what things he suffered,* [9]*and, having been made perfect, he became to all who obey him the cause of eternal salvation,* [10]*having been designated by God as High Priest according to the order of Melchizedek.*

The opening statement of this chapter seems to be a truism: *every high priest* is *taken from humanity*. It is not as if God determined the human to be the best option for priesthood as opposed to a member of the animal or plant kingdom, but this rather obvious statement takes on weight given the care with which the author established the humanity of the Son. Of course, high priests are humans, but it is no negligible fact that Jesus the great High Priest is also human. Because of the Son's sharing in flesh and blood (2:14), he, as human like the high priests before him, can, like them, be appointed for the sake of his fellow humans.

The passive forms of the verbs *taken* and *appointed* assume the activity of God in the work of selecting and establishing the high priest, but the author does not name that divine activity until v. 4. The focus remains on the job the high priests are selected to do. God appoints these human high priests for the task of dealing with the *things aimed at God*. The author's language conveys the mediatorial positioning of the high priest. As the high priest is turned toward the things of God (*pros to theon*, which is a directional preposition), at the same time the high priest is representing humanity. One can imagine the high priest who is taken from among humanity as standing in front of them. With God before him and other humans behind him, the high priest is in the middle. That being the case, all the high priests before Jesus found their identity fully on only one side of their mediation. The previous high priests were fully *and only* human. Jesus, however, as the first few chapters of the sermon have made clear, is a mediator not only in function but also in identity. He, too, is fully human, but also, as eternal Son, is fully God.

The author does not linger on that christological point but moves on to specify what precisely are *the things* aimed at God. The high priest is appointed to this middle position so that he might offer *gifts and sacrifices for sins*. "Gift" and "sacrifice" are overlapping terms in Israel's Scriptures (e.g., Lev 2:1; 21:21; Num 7:13; Job 20:6), both conveying the sense of cost for the one who gives the gift or sacrifice. The use of multiple terms also conveys their frequency. God prescribed that the high priest offer more than once and that he offer multiple gifts and sacrifices (Lev 21:21). In distinction, the author will show that Jesus offers only one sacrifice (Heb 10:12, but see 9:23 where the *sacrifices* purify the heavenlies).

The other high priests and Jesus share another similarity. They are all making offering *for sins*. The author states that the Son made purification for sins in the opening sentence (1:3); hence it is clear that for this author sin is something that makes one impure. Sins need to be atoned for (see discussion of 2:17); they cause a rift between God and God's people. Moreover, sins deceive (3:13). Within the thought world of Hebrews, the reality of sin and the need to do something about it is a given.

Thankfully, in such a broken reality, priests are able to exercise a graciousness toward those who are deceived. They are *able to regulate emotion* (*metriopatheō*). The word here is not sympathy (*sympatheō*) as in 4:15, which the author used to describe the activity of Jesus. In such short succession, the author's employment of these similar but not exact words suggests a contrast.[5] The priest is able to moderate his frustration *toward the ignorant and deceived*. Ignorance indicates that these sinners did not know that they were doing wrong (see Acts 17:30), a category of sin the law names and for which the law outlines sacrifice (Lev 4:13; 5:18; 22:14). By also using deception language the author employs a term related to the act of wandering (Heb 11:38), a fitting image for a sermon focused on forward movement. People in sin are led to wander away as the Israelites did (3:10). While ignorance covers unintentional sins, to be deceived is to be on the receiving end of malicious intent, but it carries more of a sense of agency. If one allows oneself to be deceived into disobedience especially in choosing to stray from the path God has set (Deut 11:28), then there is some culpability. These are the sins for which the priest makes offering.

The human high priest can moderate his frustration with others *since he is also beset with weakness*. In other words, he cannot get too upset with others if at times he falls into the same mistakes. One would imagine that a shared experience would produce true sympathy rather than a less compassionate

5. Attridge notes, "The ordinary high priest controls his anger; Christ actively sympathizes" (*Hebrews*, 144).

moderation. One effect of the weakness of the priest, however, might be the inability to be fully compassionate to others because he is beset by his own sinfulness. Conversely, Jesus not only knew temptation but, unlike any other human, knew what it was to resist temptation (4:15). This allows him an unparalleled ability to be fully compassionate, uninhibited by any selfishness.

Because of this sinfulness in the other high priests, the author names the fact that the high priest *ought to present an offering concerning sins, just as he does for the people, so also for himself.* This process appears in Leviticus: "And Moses said to Aaron, 'Approach toward the altar, and make the one for your sin, even your whole burnt offering, and make atonement for yourself and your house'" (Lev 9:7). This could be another major difference between Jesus and all other high priests (see Heb 7:27). He does not have to sacrifice for his own sin because he has never sinned.

On the other hand, in conversation with the christological discussion concerning the kind of flesh the Son assumes (fallen or unfallen),[6] Justin Duff has argued that this verse can apply to Jesus as well. He is not morally sinful, but by taking on "somatic sin" by assuming fallen flesh, he, too, would make an offering for his own body.[7] In a paragraph in which the author is making points of connection between Jesus and the other high priests, this seems plausible. More importantly, it captures the depths of the Son's willingness to enter into the condition of humanity as it exists after the fall. The grace of his embrace is profound.[8]

Finally, the author says that *no one takes this honor for oneself* (*lambanō*). This is set in contrast to v. 1 where God took (*lambanō*) the high priest. Instead of grasping the office for oneself, the person accepts the role as a response to God's elective call. The high priests are *called by God just as Aaron was.* The divine initiation of this office began at its instantiation with Aaron. Having

6. For a clear discussion of the issues in conversation with Hebrews, see Marc Cortez, "'He Has Spoken': Revelation, Fallenness, and the Humanity of Christ," in *ReSourcing Theological Anthropology: A Constructive Account of Humanity in Light of Christ* (Grand Rapids: Zondervan, 2017), 130–66.

7. Justin Duff, "'With Loud Cries and Tears': Sin and the Consecration of the Incarnate Son in the Epistle to the Hebrews" (PhD diss., University of St. Andrews, 2019).

8. Cortez, in response primarily to Hebrews but also the Gospels, concludes, "The most natural interpretation of the evidence would be that Christ has a fallen nature like our own" ("'He Has Spoken,'" 165).

been chosen by God as Moses's mouthpiece (Exod 4), he was also appointed by God as the first high priest (Exod 28), as were his descendants (Exod 28:39).

In a first-century context, readers might remember the more recent past in which Jason and then Menelaus bribed Antiochus Epiphanes for the role of high priest of Israel, the precise opposite of what should happen as indicated by the author here. Even if that is not on the radar of the first recipients of this letter, the point is clear. It is God who initiates a person into the priesthood, not that person's own desires. This call for the Israelites was not individualized as it is for clergy today, but happened to a particular subset of a family. Beginning with Aaron's sons, the descendants were called by virtue of their ancestor Aaron's initial call. The author will contemplate the genealogical distinctives of the line in which Jesus stands in 7:3. In a parallel way, those who are allowed into holy spaces by virtue of being sharers of Jesus get to minister to God because of their connection to the elder brother of their household, who does refer to them as children in his possession (2:13). No priest, Aaronic or those who follow after Christ, makes this choice; it is chosen for them on the basis of the family to which they belong.

In sum, Hebrews 5:1–4 is applicable to Christ, but not in all the same ways as other priests. He is taken from among humanity and appointed to represent fellow humans before God, but not as merely human. He does offer a gift and sacrifice, but not the same kind the priests offer. The author of Hebrews might have viewed him as making an offering for himself, but only because he willingly chose to embrace the weakness of the fallen human nature, not because he sinned. Like the others, he did not take this honor but was called by God, but he also has an unparalleled relationship with God, which is the focus of the following citations.

Verse **5** starts with *So also Christ*. Just as was true with Aaron and his sons, Jesus the Messiah *did not glorify himself to become High Priest*. Several things are at play in the way the author has put the statement. It is worth noting what name the author uses for his Lord at any particular point in the sermon: Son, Jesus, or, as the case is here, Messiah or anointed one. In Israel's Scriptures, both priests and kings are "anointed ones" (Lev 21:10; Ps 2:2), and the Son has been chosen by God for both roles. The combination of royal and cultic offices here will ultimately lead to the analysis of the ancient priest-king Melchizedek.

Before the author moves to that discussion, he asserts a truth about the Messiah. Like other faithful high priests, the Messiah did not decide on his own to be High Priest but received that calling from God. Unlike the unfaithful high priests during Greek rule, he did not seize that honor by bribery or force. In addition, Christ did not become High Priest to glorify himself. As the author will lay out, his becoming High Priest necessitated things that are the opposite of glorious—namely, suffering, shame, and death. He did come into glory as High Priest, at his ascension, but not through glorifying himself but because God glorified him through the arduous process of suffering and death and through vindicating him via resurrection and ascension. He came into glory as he served as the inaugural representative of humanity, whom God had intended to reign (2:7, 9). This mention of glory recalls the early statement in the sermon that God the Father is the source of the glory (1:3) that the Son himself radiates (1:3). (An assumption of that eternal glory also appears in 3:3 and 13:21.) God glorified his humanity as High Priest, granting to his incarnate self what was always his eternally.

Since God the Father glorifies the Son, the author presents the glorifying call in God's own words. To feature the Father's verbal appointment of the Messiah to the high priesthood, the author will cite from Psalm 110 (in v. **6**). Before he does so, however, he reminds his listeners what he has already allowed them to hear from the Father's speech to the Son: *You are my Son. Today I have begotten you*, the citation of Psalm 2:7 quoted previously in 1:5. The author evokes again the Father-Son relationship before he shows the divinely spoken establishment of the God-Priest relationship. Hence, Son and Priest are not sequential roles that serve different ends, but realities that inhere in the same person. It is the Son of God who becomes High Priest. All that the author has established by naming that divine relationship at the beginning of the sermon, including the Son's status as eternal, glorified creator and heir (see discussion of the divine and human connotations of his inheritance in the commentary on 1:2), applies to this same one who is appointed Priest. The next several chapters lay out the superiority of his priesthood, but this is a vital first step of the argument. Because of his unparalleled relationship with God as Son, he can become the ultimate and final High Priest. To be clear, I seek not to emphasize his eternal nature alone with this statement. This High Priest is the eternal Son who proceeded from the Father as the radiance of God's glory and who then came to humanity as a human. Within the divine will for reconciliation, the divine Son became human, lived and died so that he could serve as the ultimate and final High Priest.

In other words, his status as Son of God means that his divinity makes his priesthood superior, but that is not the only reality evoked here. His existence as Son of God also includes his becoming human and taking his place as the rightful human heir of all things at the right hand of God (as named in 1:2 and then argued in ch. 2). In ch. 1 the author has set this statement of God, "You are my Son. I have begotten you today," at the time of the exaltation, spoken to the resurrected divine-human Son. By presenting it here again in ch. 5, he is less concerned about its timing and more interested to show two things. First, he indicates that the Messiah's relationship with God makes his high priesthood superior. Second, the author makes clear that his relationship with humanity makes his high priesthood possible.

Grounding the Son's priesthood in his unique relationship with God provides the correct image of the God who accepts his priestly work. Elizabeth Rundle Charles states that Jesus is "the Priest and the Sacrifice, but always first the Son; lest the sacrifice should be mistaken . . . to be a victim to an estranged and offended power instead of the gift of reconciling love; lest the priest should be misrepresented as wringing pardon from a reluctant Deity, instead of sent from the bosom of the Father to win reluctant bewildered wanderers and prodigal sons back to the Father they had lost."[9]

The same God, his Father, who spoke Psalm 2:7 to him speaks in another place from the same collection of writings, this time from Psalm 110. The author appeals to direct divine speech to the Messiah in both instances. New Testament authors appeal to Psalm 110:1 to a significant degree.[10] What differentiates Hebrews' appeal to the psalm is that this author is the only one to keep reading, or at least the only one who gives explicit evidence that he keeps reading past v. 1. He finds in v. 4 of the psalm another fruitful text for understanding the person and work of the Messiah: *You are a priest forever according to the order of Melchizedek.* God the Father has also appointed the Son as a priest forever in the order of Melchizedek. Just as his throne is a forever throne (Heb 1:8), his priesthood is a forever priesthood, and he will serve in this eternal priesthood according to the order of Melchizedek.

9. Charles, *Within the Veil*, 13.

10. Matt 22:44; 26:64; Mark 12:36; 14:62; 16:19; Luke 20:42; 22:69; Acts 2:34; Rom 8:34; 1 Cor 15:25; Eph 1:20. Jared Compton, *Psalm 110 and the Logic of Hebrews*, LNTS 537 (London: T&T Clark, 2015), 6; David M. Hay, *Glory at the Right Hand: Psalm 110 in Early Christianity*, SBLMS 18 (Nashville: Abingdon, 1973).

This is the first mention of the enigmatic priest-king in the letter, who will not become the center of the author's focus until ch. 7. There the author will draw from Genesis 14 to explicate the dynamics of this order. Here the author demonstrates with this psalm text that Jesus may have done his priestly acts in these last days (1:2), but the plan for this vocation goes back at least to the time of David's penning of the psalm. But just as this sonship is proclaimed recently at the ascension but is based on a previous reality, so also God's declaration through David that he will be a priest could be a repetition of a plan that is even older. It will be clear in ch. 7 that the Son's priesthood is actually the template for Melchizedek, who was present in the time of Abraham. All that to say, Jesus's serving as Priest is not a new idea asserted by the author but a divine plan existing at least at the time of the establishment of the Abrahamic covenant itself. It should be noted as well that the author has been asserting that Jesus is High Priest (2:17; 3:1; 4:14–15), but this text asserts only that the addressee will be *priest.* As indicated in the rest of the letter (in which he uses both titles, priest and High Priest, for Jesus), the author sees God's appointment of the Son to an eternal priesthood as an appointment to the role of the eternal High Priest (5:10).

This promise of an eternal priesthood spoken of in the Psalms and planned before that did not come to fruition, however, until the incarnation of the Son. Having established the call from the Father, the author opens the curtain of the audience's mental stage to a scene in the life of Jesus. This is their High Priest who *in the days of his flesh offered* not sacrifices of grain or animals but his own voice and tears through the vehicle of *prayers and supplications.* The author uses a common word for prayer in the New Testament (*deēsis*) as well as the only appearance in the New Testament literature of *hiketēria*, a word for supplication. Multiple terms convey the intensity of the scene. Interpreters have wondered what scene in the life of Jesus this is meant to evoke. Common suggestions include the garden of Gethsemane as well as the cross; even the temptation narrative seems a possibility. Since the terms of description are plurals (*prayers*, *supplications*, *cries*, *tears*), that suggests that multiple instances in the life of Jesus displayed this intensity. Intense prayer was a repeated feature of Jesus's life in the flesh.[11] On more than one occasion he cried out to

11. For example, Matt 14:23; 26:36–44/Mark 14:32–39/Luke 22:41–46; Mark 1:35; 6:46; Luke 5:16; 6:12; 9:18, 28–29; 11:1; John 17.

the one who was able to save him from death—namely, his eternal Father. Having willingly entered the realm where the devil had the enslaving power of the fear of death (2:14), the priestly Son never forgot that it was his own Father who held the superimposing power of life over death, and so to God he cried in prayer.

His Father listened. *He was heard because of his reverence.* Interpreters have debated if this last phrase of v. 7 could be translated "he was heard (and delivered) from his fear (of death)."[12] This seems incorrect in two respects. First, by entering fully into the human condition, he willingly entered into the condition of imprisonment under the fear of death. Hence, death was not easy for him. To the contrary, these expressions display excruciating emotions as he sought deliverance from death. He grieved and even displayed fear in the face of death. Second, he nevertheless reverently feared God more. As one who perfectly depended on and trusted his Father, he knew that death is ultimately nothing to fear in view of the sovereignty of God. Hence, an interpretation that sees this phrase as a deliverance from death is also incorrect because he was delivered not away from death by avoiding it, but out of death by proceeding fully through it and coming out the other side because of the resurrection. His trust in God as the God of life allowed him to proceed all the way through death.

The author of Hebrews asserts that through this process *he learned.* This resonates canonically with Luke's comment that Jesus grew in wisdom (Luke 2:52). Whatever process of learning or growth this included was not through a process of trial and error, or at least not *sinful* error for the author states with the utmost clarity that Jesus never acted in sin (Heb 4:15). The following object clarifies the type of learning the author intends to name: *he learned obedience.* The Son applied his willingness to accomplish the divine plan of rescue through the experience of suffering exhibited in obedience (2:14; see discussion of his willingness also in 10:7). In so doing, *he learned* what it was like to complete his incarnate obedience. The plural relative pronoun *hōn*, *from what things*, confirms that this act of obedience was not a one-time experience but included many experiences throughout life. This confirms the multiplicity of the author's description of the Son's prayers and cries to his Father. Many times throughout his life, though it was not easy, he chose to obey, and

12. Ellingworth, *Hebrews*, 289.

in so doing formed his character through the habit of obedience so that he was ready to obey even at the very end, even in the face of the cross. The habitual choosing of the right is a virtue the author wants his congregation to develop (5:13–14), and here he shows that Jesus provides the example for them.

It is the normal role of sons to learn obedience, as the author will discuss in 12:5–11 by appealing to a common and widespread tradition evoked in his citation of Proverbs 3:11–12. Because he became human, the Son was willing to go through what all children of humanity experience—namely, the process of experiential learning, even and especially through suffering.

Here, however, with the first phrase of v. **8**, the author reminds his readers that this Son is different. He begins this sentence with *Even though he was the Son*. Everything said about him in ch. 1 still applies. He stands to inherit everything; he is eternal, creator, and worshiped because he is the manifestation of God. As such, he is God. This is the heart of the tension in this text. As God, he is above all things (1:2–3); therefore, the concept of *learning* is dissonant with the being of God. Moreover, it is discordant to state that God the Son could learn *obedience*, for the shared will of the Father and the eternal Son disallows one to obey the other.[13] Finally, it seems false to say that God could learn obedience *through suffering and dying*, for these are acts impossible for a holy and living God. This powerful, condensed paragraph is one of the places in the New Testament documents that gifts to the church contributions for the doctrine of Christology. Even though God the sovereign creator cannot learn, and certainly cannot learn obedience through suffering death, the Son of God did so. It is true that the author begins by saying that this happens *in the days of his flesh* (v. 7), but the *even though* at the beginning of v. 8 asserts the singular person of the eternal-then-incarnate Son asserted throughout ch. 1. The Son did not cease to be God, *that kind of Son*, when he took on flesh. He incorporated experiential knowledge of being human into the being of God. Even though he was the divine and eternal Son, he chose to learn obedience through suffering because as God he did not have that knowledge. Hence, the author needs to assert that even though he was such a Son, a Son who was God and had reigned with God before he created the ages, even as *this Son*

13. Amy Peeler, "What Does 'Father' Mean? Trinity without Tiers in the Epistle to the Hebrews," in *Trinity without Hierarchy: Reclaiming Nicene Orthodoxy in Evangelical Theology*, ed. Michael Bird and Scott Harrower (Grand Rapids: Kregel Academic, 2019), 57–84.

he was willing to learn obedience from the things he suffered. To take on this learning was an incredible act of grace. That the sovereign God who lacked nothing was willing to learn presents the graciousness of his descent on humanity's behalf with brilliant power.

This section, recall, has flowed from the author's assertion that Jesus is the sympathetic High Priest who dwells in the heavens. He is sympathetic because he has gone through and completed the process of learning obedience. If another human (and only human) had done so, that would serve as an encouraging example, but because the eternal Son of God has become sympathetic through this experience, he reveals that true sympathy—suffering with—is the desire of the Triune God. Through the human life of the eternal Son, the readers can approach the throne of grace with boldness because they know that God as God desired to understand and transform the human condition *from the inside*. They know they approach the Father and Source of the Son with the aid of the divine High Priest, who, as one of them, has revealed the holy, humble, gracious, and inviting nature of God. This is the gracious God all followers of Jesus profess and approach.

His process of learning clarifies what kind of perfecting can be truly spoken of the Son (v. **9**), how the author can say that he has *been made perfect*. It is not the process of moving out of imperfection but the process of completing what was intended. In the days of his flesh, he accomplished what he was willing to do. In being obedient until the end, he became perfect: the perfect High Priest, who has dealt with sins, and the perfect heir, who has won back his inheritance from the slavery of death (2:14–15). As this perfected Priest and King, he dwells in the presence of God. He did not need to do this for his own sake, for he, as God, was already with God forever, but he did this learning for the sake of others, to open the way of dwelling with God for them.

The author specifies those others as *all who obey him*. Those who are obedient (*hypakouō*) to him just as he practiced obedience (*hypakoē*, 5:8) will join him. As they do, he becomes *the cause of eternal salvation* for them. Those who follow his path into the dwelling place with God will enter the space where salvation is enjoyed forever. In other words, he both makes salvation (dwelling with God) possible and provides the template for how to arrive at that end. He made the way possible because he agreed to make an offering to purify sins forever (1:3). He fulfilled the call to be the *High Priest according to the order of Melchizedek*. The author will soon explicate the majesty of this order, but in this section he has focused on the process by which the Son of God is able to serve in it—namely, his suffering and learning. To be a priest in this order is to be sympathetic to the ones the priest represents. If the author is aiming to keep his listeners faithfully enduring while they are in the wilderness, he has shown that Jesus, in becoming priest, has gone through his own wilderness of temptation. Unlike the generation freed from Egypt, he, in every instance, even in the face of death, chose to trust the God who had the power of life over death. The author has been showing that Jesus does what priests do—make offerings and pray to God—and even more that he fulfills his distinct priesthood in a completely effective and distinctly compassionate way. The explanation of the complex power of such a priestly order will have to wait until after the author pauses for one more exhortation, in which he builds on Jesus's learning through suffering and encourages this congregation to follow him in this way.

HEBREWS 5:11–6:20

THE STEADFAST ANCHOR

Like a cliffhanger at the end of a book chapter or television episode, Hebrews abruptly stops building an argument about priesthood, specifically Jesus's priesthood in the order of Melchizedek (5:10), to take up the second extended exhortation (5:11–6:20). The author has a great deal to say about Melchizedek (Heb 7), but the listeners are not ready. He does not give up on them, however. Instead, he plainly names their problem—immaturity (5:11–12)—and gives them a vision of where they should be headed, a maturity that manifests in discernment because it is rooted in trust (5:14; 6:15), precisely the virtue he's been cultivating through his exhortation beginning in 3:7. Hence vv. 11–14 of ch. 5 are related to reflections on the priesthood in the first ten verses of the chapter, because the listeners need to hear and accept this admonition before they can understand Jesus's priesthood correctly.

To get them moving in that direction, the author first reminds them from where they have come. Chapter 6 is highly debated territory, and that debate begins at the very beginning of the chapter. The list of basics in vv. 1–2 may be Jewish, Christian, or simply generally religious, but the message of endurance in faith remains the same no matter what the presenting temptation in this community might be. After naming the list of seemingly faithful actions and events, he describes, in chilling terms, the consequences of turning away from God's revelation in Christ (6:4–8). The sin of rejection is egregious in light of the gifts God gives through the Son. It is impossible to find another path of salvation. The nature metaphor at the end of this warning reminds readers that all things are in the hands of God (6:7–8).

Given the intensity of the warning, the addressees must surely be listening closely at this point, and so next the author gives them a warm encouragement

(6:9–10). Addressing them with terms of endearment, he names their loving actions as evidence of their salvation. They have not crossed the line into God's judgment. In light of that good news, they should be all the more serious about their current problem of immaturity and move out of it into deep faith as exemplified by someone like Abraham (6:11–12).

Abraham's life as told in Genesis serves as evidence of the faithful virtues they need to cultivate in their growth toward maturity (6:13–15). God's graciousness toward him becomes both an example and the means of God's graciousness toward all the heirs of the promise. God employs oaths with Abraham and other members of his family to demonstrate the unassailable divine will (6:16–17).

The closing tone of this section, which earlier included such a sharp warning, ends with a hope almost too powerful for words (6:18–20). The author attempts to describe it with the odd image of a mobile anchor (6:19), but eventually names plainly the tether of their hope, who is Jesus, the one who has gone before them and now serves as High Priest (6:20).

Like a faithful educator, this author has both humbled and encouraged his listeners through this exhortative section so that they are now ready to learn the ancient promises that are fulfilled in Jesus's distinct priesthood.

5:11–6:3 · MATURE FAITH

11Concerning this, for us the word is great and difficult to speak, since you have
become sluggish with regard to hearing. 12For you ought to be teachers because of
the time. Again, you have need that someone teach you certain basic things about
the beginning of the words of God, and you have become those who have need of
milk and not solid food. 13For everyone who shares of milk is untested with respect
to the word of righteousness because that person is an infant. 14But solid food is for
the mature, those who have senses that have been trained; because of maturity they
discern between good and also evil. 6:1Therefore, leaving the beginning of the word
of Christ, let us take on maturity, not laying again a foundation of repentance from
dead works and faith in God, 2teaching of baptisms and laying on of hands, of res-
urrection of the dead and eternal judgment. 3And this we will do, if God allows.

The phrase that begins v. **11** does not clarify to what the author refers. It could be translated "concerning which" or rather "concerning whom" (the relative pronoun in the prepositional phrase *peri hou* could be either masculine or neuter). Is it the subject at hand—namely, priesthood—or the person Melchizedek or Jesus specifically? Pinning it down may be impossible, as all are, at this point in the sermon, various foci of the same subject. Hence, I have chosen the translation *concerning this.* The word the author will speak about the subject of the Melchizedekian priesthood in which Jesus ministers, he says, both *great and difficult to speak* about *for us*. It is both weighty and challenging for him to speak and weighty and challenging for this congregation to hear. The subject matter itself is significant and hard to understand, as his following treatment of the Genesis 14 passage will show, but this is not the only reason for the challenge.

The difficulty of communication also arises because the listening community is not really listening. The word is difficult to speak *since*, he says, *you have become sluggish with regard to hearing*. This is the first direct critique of the community in the letter. Previously he spoke warnings in language of a possible concern, communicated with the word "lest": "lest we drift away" (2:1) and "lest there be in a certain one of you an evil heart of unbelief" (3:12). Here, however, he speaks bluntly. The problem he names is already a reality. They have become dull of hearing. What a damning charge coming on the heels of two chapters' worth of admonition about the importance of listening, emphasized with the scriptural phrase "Today if you hear his voice" (3:7, 15; 4:7)! Nevertheless, the author leaves a space for hope. They are currently sluggish with regard to hearing (see the connotation of laziness for this term in Prov 22:29; Sir. 4:29; 11:12) but not yet completely deaf. He still finds it worth his effort to send this word of exhortation to them. He will end this exhortative section with the same word, "sluggish," in 6:12 where he says with a bit more encouragement that he is hopeful that they will *not* become sluggish in their deeds. Ultimately, he sees a way out of the current sluggishness of their hearing.

Given the contrast with 6:12, several interpreters have seen the statement of their sluggishness in 5:11 as a rhetorical device. The slight against the hearers is intended to put them on the defensive and demonstrate that the opposite is true. Because the author writes several sentences that describe what is true of them in contrast to what he wishes were true, I do not see this statement as this kind of device. The author is naming real challenges he sees in the community, but he does state them to elicit a response. After all, he does not consider them so inept that he ends the sermon at this point.

Their sluggishness is made apparent in their lack of progress. *Because of the time* as confessors of Christ, they *ought to be teachers*. This is a fascinating indication of the spiritual age of this community. They had heard the gospel from Jesus's followers (2:3) long enough ago in the past that by the time of the writing of this letter they should have progressed to the level of instructors. The Christian community addressed in the letter of Timothy is also encouraged to acknowledge that those who teach should not be new converts, although no specific timeline is given (1 Tim 3:6). Here in Hebrews the ability to teach does not seem to be limited to a specific office for only some in the community but is the hope and expectation for all addressed. Given the time since their conversion, they should by now all be teachers.

Instead of being ready to teach, they still *have need that someone teach* them. To describe the content they lack, the author piles on descriptive words: they need to be taught *certain basic things about the beginning of the words of God*. Then he employs a common picture to emphasize what neophytes they are. They have *become those who have need of milk and not solid food*. He uses the word for "need" twice, emphasizing their dependency. Moreover, through the use of the verb "become," he further emphasizes the passage of time. By not listening, they are far behind where they should be. He then connects the metaphor with the previous statement to specify what *basic things* he has in focus. *Everyone who shares of milk is untested with respect to the word of righteousness*. Hence, the beginning of the words of God, about which they still need to know the basics, is the word concerning righteousness. He will soon translate Melchizedek's name as "king of righteousness" (7:2). If they are inexperienced with this quality, they are not yet ready to learn about this person and the Priest-King who is appointed in his order, whose rule is characterized by righteousness (1:9). Because he will cite Habakkuk, who connects righteousness with faith (10:38; see the continuation of the connection in his recounting of Abel, Noah, and others in 11:4, 7, 33), their lack of experience with righteousness is another way of saying that they need to grow in faith. They will grow into more righteousness as they correctly perceive that the suffering they are experiencing is taking place within the sovereignty and goodness of God (12:11). This critique of the community's lack of righteousness in faith aligns with the author's previous exhortation to be on the watch to endure in faithfulness (Heb 3–4).

Being *untested* with regard to righteousness/faith indicates a lack of experience. The word of righteousness is something they should listen to but also *live* into. The person who does not listen well to this word cannot then respond correctly, and therefore this person is *an infant.* Neither in the ancient world nor today is this a compliment.

The other end of the maturity spectrum gives even more clarity to what virtues the author's listeners lack. In distinction from milk, *solid food is for*, not babies, but *the mature*. The mature are those who have *senses that have been trained; because of maturity they discern between good and also evil.* He wishes for his listeners to gain the same maturity; *because of maturity* is a fitting translation of the phrase *dia tēn hexin*, which indicates the result of training instead of the practice that gets the result (older translations often opted for "habit" for this phrase).[1] The author is worried that their immaturity may not allow them to discern the evil from the good. Like those in the wilderness generation, they might not be able to discern the false report of the ten spies, motivated by fear, from the true report of the two, motivated by faith. Righteousness is to live rightly, and for the author of Hebrews that kind of right living is born out of trust in God's character, as the faithful of the past have shown (10:38; 11:4, 7, 33; 12:11, 23). This explicit warning connects with the concern in ch. 3 that they might be tempted to follow an example of an evil path of immature unbelief because they lack trust in God. The wisest pedagogical decision (which the author chooses) is not to leave them bearing the guilt of their immaturity but to attempt to address its root cause by leading them deeper into trust in God. It is a model for all discipleship: without ignoring the presenting issue, leaders can press into the underlying cause, which is more often than not related to a skewed picture of God.

Depending on the translation accessed, an initial reading of the beginning of ch. 6 sounds dissonant with the conclusion of ch. 5. The author has stated that they have need of the beginning teachings. Moreover, they are only ready for milk (5:12). Does he then suggest the opposite, that they should leave behind the beginning of the word of Christ? I conclude that *aphiēmi* here is better viewed in the sense of "leave intact" or "allow to remain." He wants this foundation of righteous trust to remain and be strengthened. Only then can they move on to maturity.[2] His recommendation is that they leave intact *the beginning*

1. Harris, *Hebrews*, 130.

2. See also Ellingworth, *Hebrews*, 311: "*Aphiēmi* here means not 'abandon' . . . but 'go on to something else.'"

of the word of Christ. In the previous paragraph, the word was "of God" (5:12) and "of righteousness" (5:13). The parallelism shows the similarity, yet again, between God and the Messiah. The one word is related to both. It also shows the connection between the Messiah and the community. They are members of the house where the Messiah reigns (3:6) and have partaken of him (3:14). The word of God revealing the Messiah is a word they have already heard and accepted (2:3). They do not need to hear and accept it again, but they do need to pay attention to what they have heard (2:1) and to hold fast to their agreement with it (3:1, 14; 4:14). The time is now ripe for them to build on this foundation and *take on maturity.* Standing on the foundation and building up to more difficult topics captures the admonitions for both steadfastness and progress articulated throughout the sermon. I imagine a weightlifter with a solid stance, who can then add on more and more weight to her lift. The solid foundation allows her to progress. The term for *maturity* here, *teleiotēs*, has been interpreted as moving on only in the understanding of Christian doctrine, but this seems limited in light of the knowledge *and action* admonitions of Hebrews. Maturity includes correct and deep knowledge as well as faithful response. I would also resist the translation of "completeness," given that the author envisions them on a long journey of the Christian life in which they always have ways to deepen their life with God. The specific term appears only here and in Colossians 3:14, where it is brought into a close comparison with love. Rightly responding to God and to others is evidence of well-developed faith. In contrast with babes, he is asking them to become more advanced in their faith, their knowledge, their action—in short, their love of God, neighbor, and self.

He asks them not to lay again *a foundation*. The author recounts the scope of this foundation with three pairs, which, from a certain perspective, follow one another sequentially. At the beginning was *repentance from dead works and faith in God.* The notion of repentance is to turn from one thing to another. The works/faith pairing evokes Pauline literature and has led commentators to wonder if these are gentile converts to Christianity because of the doubt that this author would call Jewish works dead.[3] Then he mentions *teaching of baptisms and laying on of hands.* These are things that often happen after initial repentance and faith, as the expression of them. The plural here of "baptism" is curious. Christianity embraced a singular baptism as participation in the

3. Schenck, *New Perspective on Hebrews*, 39–41.

one-time event of Christ's death and resurrection. The laying on of hands evokes images of healing but also anointing for ministry (Acts 13:3; 1 Tim 5:22). Finally, the author lists eschatological matters, *resurrection of the dead and eternal judgment.*

The description of the foundation could specify *the beginning of the word of Christ*, and so would be referring to christological teaching. The word concerning Christ aligns with the confession of Christ that they have already made (3:1; 4:14). Repentance and faith make sense as the beginning of their confession in Christ. With the plural of "baptism," the author could mean the singular baptism of many people. Together, resurrection of the dead and eternal judgment are one of the important data points that show this author's alignment with other Christians—an affirmation of bodily resurrection and the judgment that will follow, establishing one's place in eternity (e.g., 1 Cor 15; Rom 8; Matt 25). A vital part of the Christian faith is its future. If this list describes things taught and experienced as one adopts the Christian faith, then the author is encouraging them that their foundation already exists and that it needs to be maintained and strengthened, but he states that these foundational things are not the only teachings they should dwell on.

At the same time, it is important to recognize that these are not topics that are meant to be assented to once and then put aside. An initial confession still demands a perpetual faith. An initial repentance still demands a continual rejection of sin. These are both one-time events and continual realities. Baptism and laying on of hands are the kinds of events that happen at key moments in the Christian life. These are events that will happen only once (baptism), or at least infrequently (healing or ordination), but they are events that need perpetual remembrance. Each time a new congregant is baptized or ordained, those who have participated in this transformative ritual are admonished to remember their own. The final pair of terms connect to their faith as well. When they signed on to this confession in the Messiah, they knew him to be one who had defeated death, and so they were freed from its power (2:14–15). They also knew they would stand before God's judgment, but by confessing Christ they had a merciful High Priest when they were exposed before God (see 4:12–14). They hold on to this hope of his merciful priesthood as they move closer to final resurrection and judgment.

On the other hand, while these features make sense in a Christian context, nothing in this list is clearly and explicitly Christ-centered (in contrast to the list in vv. 4–5), and some things sit at odds with Christian practice. For example, multiple baptisms is not a Christian teaching. When the author refers to multiple washings in 9:10, they are connected with the Levitical priestly system. In addition, the author associates hands with things that are "hand-made," which contrast with the sanctuary of the new covenant priest (9:11, 24). Given these connections and the lack of specific Christian features, some interpreters have wondered if the author is referring to Jewish ideas with this list. Because foundations are meant to be permanent, the author would be saying that they should not lay *another* foundation—namely, a Jewish-without-Jesus one—after they have made a confession of Jesus as the Son of Israel's God.[4]

Because so much of the foundation of Jewish and Christian faith is shared—because Jesus is the Jewish Messiah—it is difficult to make a definitive decision between these options: either the author is urging the audience not to become non-Jesus-confessing Jews or he is urging them not to dwell only on the beginning points of their faith. Either alternative offers insight for those who interpret Hebrews after its original recipients. On one hand, for some who have joined Christian movements, there may be a temptation to let go of their Christian confession and return to the dominant religion of one's culture, whether that be another organized religion or an indefinable spirituality. It might be tempting to diminish the specific and exclusive claims of Jesus the Messiah. On the other hand, there may be a temptation toward immaturity. Congregations are not well served by a perpetual reminder of the necessity of conversion and initial faith. It is necessary to progress to the complexities of maturing discipleship in order to have growth rather than boredom and stagnation. Hence, whatever the particular background issue in Hebrews, this passage can speak to multiple situations experienced by readers after that time.

Without ignoring their immaturity, the author will not allow his readers to remain in it. His desire for them is that they hold on to their confession of Jesus as Messiah, and so he asks them to keep listening to his teaching in hopes that they will remain faithful and become mature. He wants them to grow into those who are ready to teach (5:12). His teaching itself serves as a conduit of God's righteous word to them, a word about the Messiah. His job as a teacher is first and foremost to bring them along to a deeper encounter with God. That,

4. Mininger, *Impossible to Be Restored?*

in fact, is the ultimate job of all Christian teachers. This Christian teacher will bring his students along *if God will allow*. Thankfully, God's clear desire is for their increasing maturity, for their ability to know God's righteousness and choose to live in line with it. This is why God has not given up on speaking to them either.

6:4–8 · IMPOSSIBLE

4For it is impossible for those who have once been enlightened and tasted of the heav-
enly gift and become sharers of the Holy Spirit 5and tasted of the good word of God
and of the powers of the coming age, 6if they fall away, to renew again to repentance,
because this would be crucifying again for themselves the Son of God and exposing
him to public shame. 7For the land that drinks the rain which comes upon it often
and bears fitting produce for those for whose sake it is cultivated receives a blessing
from God. 8But the land that spews forth thorns and thistles is useless and near a
curse, whose end is burning.

Maturity is necessary for engaging such a passage as this, yet it is frequently the young in faith who encounter it and react in fear, worried that through some sin they have fallen away and, therefore, can never return to God. If someone is heartbroken that they may have fallen away from the faith, that concern over one's relationship with God is evidence that they have *not* fallen away. Alternatively, another form of immaturity could be manifest in the tendency to ignore or dismiss this text. Because this is part of divine revelation to the church, it is necessary neither to ignore nor to soften the full impact of this difficult sentence in the letter.

This passage first identifies a group of people by using four participial phrases. First, they are *those who have once been enlightened*. Light language recalls the assertion about the Son in the first sentence of the sermon, that he is the radiance of God's glory, the divine light (1:3). Those who have been enlightened have come to see who Jesus really is, and that enlightenment has happened to the readers of this letter (10:32). Second, he describes them as those who have *tasted of the heavenly gift*. While the author describes the gifts the priests offer several times (*dōron*, 5:1; 8:3–4; 9:9), this is a related but distinct word, *dōrea*, that authors employ to indicate bounteous or great gifts (1 Esd 3:5;

Wis 7:14; 16:25; Dan 2:48; 11:39). In the New Testament literature, this term is used only to name gifts that come from God (John 4:10; Acts 2:38; 8:20; 10:45; 11:17; Rom 5:15, 17; 2 Cor 9:15; Eph 3:7; 4:7). Here in Hebrews as well, this gift comes from God's dwelling realm of heaven (11:16; 12:22). This gift giving is reminiscent of what happened within this community when God granted signs, powers, and divisions of the Holy Spirit (2:4). Hence, to taste of the heavenly gift suggests not a small sampling but a full participation, just as Jesus fully participated in death by tasting it (2:9). Third, they have *become sharers of the Holy Spirit.* To be a sharer is to be a companion or participant, to join together. The author has used this term to describe this community several times (3:1, 14). Moreover, they have heard from the Holy Spirit (3:7) and been granted the Spirit from God (2:4). Finally, the author describes them as people who have *tasted of the good word of God and of the powers of the coming age.* The participatory language continues with the second reference to tasting. In this instance they taste of God's good word, the word that sustains all things (1:3). As recipients of God's communication through the Son (1:2), the recipients are those who have heard God's word to them in their present time (3:7–4:10). These are also people who have tasted of the *powers* of the coming age. Specifically, it is God's word of *power* that sustains all things (1:3), and power that God gave to this community (2:4). This power is the inbreaking of the age to come already made manifest in the reign of the Son, though not fully realized (2:6).

As the specifications of the list demonstrates, with each term it becomes clear that the group described is not some distant community. These are all descriptions fitting to the listeners themselves. The author sets up this situation with a hypothetical third-person *those who*, but the presuppositions apply to the community. They have been the beneficiaries of God's light, gift, Spirit, word, and power. That means that the author considers them at risk for the warning that follows.[5] He lays out for them the consequences if they choose to reject Christ.

The sin under discussion here is "falling away." Absent in the other texts of the New Testament, the term for "falling away" is most prominent in the book

5. Those who believe that rejection of salvation is possible see the warning applying to everyone in the community, and those who believe it is impossible to lose the salvation God has given see the pastor speaking to a mixed community, some of whom may not be true believers. See Herbert W. Bateman, ed., *Four Views of the Warning Passages in Hebrews* (Grand Rapids: Kregel, 2007).

of Ezekiel, and there it is a very negative thing—namely, to transgress God's command (Ezek 14:13; 15:8; 18:24; 20:27; 22:4). This word does not describe an accident but a choice, a connotation supported by this section and others in the letter, where the concern is over a grave sin such as "turning away" (Heb 3:12) or "shrinking back" (10:38–39).[6] This grave sin is to turn away from what God has provided in Christ. It is to cease to trust (3:19). This does not mean that doubt constitutes this grave sin. Presenting honest spiritual questions and struggle before God who already knows all (4:12–13), as the man did who asked Jesus for help with his unbelief (Mark 9:24), can be a vital part of spiritual life. The type of distrust discussed here includes an active cessation, after an adoption of gospel truth, of both mental and lived faith in God among God's people. It is the sin of apostasy.[7]

If recipients of God's gifts in the Son turn away, then, the author says, *it is impossible . . . to renew them again to repentance.* To highlight the weight of what he is saying, the author begins this section with the word *impossible.* If he is warning them against turning to the old-covenant practices without Jesus, then he is also saying that it would be impossible (as v. 4 says) to renew to effective repentance through the tools of the old covenant alone after the arrival of the new through Jesus. Since the old-covenant practices in his estimation all point forward to Christ, to return to them would be in effect to return to the preparatory time in which one was waiting for Christ to die and rise again. If they are tempted to turn toward Greek or Roman religion to avoid persecution, nothing there could lead them to a saving relationship with the God of Israel.

To be renewed again to repentance would necessitate *crucifying again for themselves the Son of God and exposing him to public shame.* If they reject the Son, it is as if they would ask God to redo the work of salvation, to allow the Son to taste death for all (2:9) again, to ask him to defeat the one who has the power of death (2:14) once more. To do so would be to ask him to die his publicly shameful death all over again. The Son of God, as the sermon has made clear, is the eternal one who has taken on flesh and died. God has heard the Son and rescued him out of death (5:7). He is now resurrected from the dead and sitting

6. DeSilva, *Perseverance in Gratitude*, 225.

7. Johnson says it well, describing apostasy as "making a deliberate choice not to participate in the gift once given" (*Hebrews*, 161).

at the right hand of God as the eternal priest. This Son, now resurrected and ascended, immortal in his human body as he is eternal in his divine person, cannot die again. This is what is *impossible*. If one chooses against the Son, no other path of salvation to God's glory exists because he is immortal and, therefore, cannot die to open the path of salvation again. As intense and fearful as this warning is, it aligns perfectly with the consistent message of Hebrews that proclaims the singularity of the salvific work of Jesus Christ, Son of God. In short, it is impossible that the one who has died and been raised could die again. Moreover, *exposing him to public shame* also emphasizes the public nature of this turning away for the community. Because they have made a public confession, which has come at great cost (10:32–35), ceasing to associate with the community of this Son would also have communal repercussions.

The author then pivots to nature imagery as further support for his statement of impossibility. Those who turn from Christ's singularly sufficient salvation face judgment. Similar to Jesus's parable of the seeds (Matt 13/Mark 4/Luke 8), the author describes land that brings forth different kinds of plants. Before the appearance of the crops, the land *drinks the rain which comes upon it often*. Very little activity is required of the land in this step. As land, it can do nothing other than soak up the rain that falls. The coming of the rain is similar to the gifts of God described in vv. 4–5. What matters is what one does with the gifts God has given.

One kind of land *bears fitting produce*. The word for bearing here is *tiktō*, the word used for the bearing of children. Authors can use it metaphorically (as James does in 1:15), but even metaphorically it connotes the production of life. This land gives birth to vegetation that serves a purpose for *those for whose sake it is cultivated*. This land births produce that is useful, whether for eating or building. This productive land *receives a blessing from God*. God has already blessed with rain, so this is describing a second blessing. That might indicate that this land continues to receive God's favor in the form of rain and other nourishment, so that it continues to produce useful plants. It might also point to God's provision in the fruit itself. As Deuteronomy teaches, those who obey God receive the blessing of fruit (Deut 30:2–16). Good land yields good produce. This picture aligns with the author's sense of progress. Growth in mature faith results in more growth.

The alternative is *land that spews forth thorns and thistles*. Here the term for production is *ekpherō*, which has the sense of "carrying out." Whereas *tiktō* evokes a sense of connection between the bearer and the born, *ekpherō* has the connotation of distancing: something is removed from the presence of something else. Whatever the land produces in this instance is in dissonance with the land because it is not what the land is meant to produce. In this instance the land produces *thorns and thistles*. This is language from the curse after Adam and Eve's disobedience (Gen 3:18), which appears as well in the prophet Hosea as a sign of desolation (Hos 10:8). This produce *is useless*, the opposite of what one would want to receive from land. Hence, this production is *not* fitting. It does not yield what one would hope nature would produce, but instead it yields failures and frustrations. The land that produces these things is the opposite of blessed; it is cursed. Strikingly, however, the author says that it is only *near a curse*. The presence of *near* here is unexpected for two reasons. First, it breaks the parallel established between blessing and cursing from v. 7 to v. 8. Second, if the land is producing the fruit of the curse (Gen 3:17–18), the fact that it is only *near* a curse is surprising. The danger of being near that curse is certainly profound, for the cursed land that spews forth thorns and thistles ends in *burning*. Burning is eschatological imagery of God's judgment (Dan 7:11; 2 Pet 3:10–12). On one hand, vv. 7–8 continue the intensity of the author's warning. If anyone turns away from God's gifts in the Son, God's consuming judgment awaits them (see the warning in 10:27 where fire consumes God's enemies). It makes perfect sense within the thought world of Hebrews (and the New Testament as a whole) that salvation is found only by participation in the Son; outside of participation in the Son is judgment that comes against those who have no merciful priest to atone for their sins.

On the other hand, the language of the author leaves space for a different interpretation. This text has proven so unsettling, not because it proclaims the exclusivity of salvation in Christ, but because it has led people to doubt the possibility of return if someone turns away from Christ. The issue of return—and this recognition is vital—is *not* the question of the author and his community (see discussion of the following paragraph, 6:9–12). The question of return has nevertheless been the question of many generations who have read this text. We should not be surprised if the text, as God's living word, makes allowance for that question (and provides an answer to it) even if that is beyond the purview of the human author.

The land that produces thorns and thistles is *near* a curse but not yet cursed. One might imagine that the production of the useless plants would automatically result in the curse, but that is not what the passage says. If the equivalent of the thorns and thistles is the disobedient falling away from Christ (6:6), then repentance from that is impossible in the sense that Christ cannot go through the process of defeating death and winning salvation again. Hence, restoration to a fresh repentance in light of a new work of Christ is impossible because that new work cannot take place.

If, however, the land wants to get rid of those thorns and thistles and exchange them for useful produce, because the land is only near a curse but not yet under it, that seems to be a possibility the verses leave open. If one turns toward Christ after having turned away, there might be time to avoid the full consequences of the curse. I wager that, if asked, this author would support repentance back toward the solely effective work of Christ. This is the faith to which he has been directing the community throughout the letter thus far—to hold on to their trust in God as revealed in the person of the Son, their High Priest. Conversely, the author would not believe it possible to have effective repentance to God *without* the work of Christ.

Restoration to the previously accomplished work of Christ also seems plausible in the reference to burning. The end of the curse is burning, but if the metaphor is consistent, to burn thorns and thistles is not to destroy the land; it is instead to cleanse it so that fresh things can grow. God employed such purgative burning for the people of Israel (Isa 4:4), and Paul speaks of judgment in this way in 1 Corinthians 3:13. Even if they experience God's fire, God's purgative judgment, this could be a divine act of cleansing so that the thorns and thistles of rejection are removed.

Teachers of this portion of the letter must exercise great care. The impact of the warning must not be dulled. To turn away from Christ is to turn from God's blessing and into God's judgment. This is a space in which one would not want to live and would certainly not want to die or meet Christ at his return (9:28). It may seem freeing for a time to extricate oneself from the lordship of Christ, but the end is sure and certain destruction.

On the other hand, the text itself allows for the one who has turned away to return to the work Christ has already done (as opposed to asking Christ to do the work again). The fires of God could cleanse the disobedience before the curse is fully and finally realized. This reading resonates with the patience of God displayed in the parable of the fruitless fig tree in Luke 13:6–9. Multiple chances are given, and time is allowed before the final end. In this way, even this intense warning in Hebrews sits in coherence with the rest of the New Testament, which allows repentance from even the rejection of Christ and God's family (blasphemy against the Son [Matt 12:32/Luke 12:10], the prodigal son [Luke 15:11–32], Peter's denial and restoration in the Gospels [Mark 14:53–65/Matt 26:57–68/Luke 22:54–71; John 18:13–27; 21:1–14]). By utilizing a nature metaphor, the author puts the emphasis on the action of God. It is God who gives the rain (see also Matt 5:45), God who blesses, and God who decides when it is time to curse. The author of Hebrews stands in the role of the farmer (as one of their leaders, he is one who enjoys the fruit of the land that is cultivated), and it is his job to help his land avoid the thorns and thistles. He does so with this warning, but the ultimate fate of the land is in the hands of God.[8]

6:9–12 · BETTER THINGS

[9]But we are convinced concerning you, beloved, of better things, even that you have salvation, even though we are speaking in this way. [10]For God is not unjust to neglect your work and the love that you demonstrated in God's name, having served the saints and still serving. [11]And we desire that each of you demonstrate the same haste toward the fullness of hope until the end, [12]in order that you may not be sluggish ones but imitators of the heirs of the promises, who inherited through faith and patience.

With the following sentence (v. **9**), it becomes clear that although the author has used terms in vv. 4–5 that refer to their experience, this is a *warning* for his congregation, not a foregone conclusion. His listeners have not fallen away yet. In the following statements, he and those who are with him (possibly those from Italy, 13:24) demonstrate their confidence about the members of this congregation. They are able to say, *We are convinced concerning you.* To utilize this verb for confidence aligns this action with the action of the Son, who places his confidence in the Father (2:13). The author makes his assessment of them on the basis of what he believes to be true about them. By recounting the proof

8. See David deSilva, "Exchanging Favor for Wrath: Apostasy in Hebrews and Patron-Client Relationships," *JBL* 115 (1996): 91–116.

of their faith and continuing to teach them, he demonstrates his trust that they are brothers and sisters in Christ who are able to learn more.

He first demonstrates this trust by the name he calls them. For the only time in the sermon, he addresses them as *beloved*.[9] He is expressing a personal tenderness after a heavy section of the sermon and in so doing reminds them that they are the recipients of God's love (1:9; 12:6). The warm confidence about them concerns *better things*. Specifically, he is confident that they *have salvation*. They have not yet neglected God, and so they are on the pathway toward salvation (1:14; 2:3). *Even though we are speaking in this way*, he says, he does not doubt where they currently stand in their relationship with God by having confessed Christ. The rhetorical aim of such intensity in the previous verses is to prevent them from going down the pathway of departure from God. Had they already taken this step or were too far gone toward it, there would be no need for any warning at all. By comparison, it is clear that he has corrected them for immaturity (5:11–12), but he is only warning them (though harshly) about apostasy.

To demonstrate his confidence in them even more tangibly, he looks to the past. They did *work*. Clearly these things are different from the dead works from which they repented (6:1). The author specifies this work as *love . . . demonstrated in God's name* manifest as *serv[ing] the saints*. This is similar to the writings of John (e.g., 1 John 2:5; 4:7): love of the other is the marker of being a member of God's family, those on the way to eternal salvation. As they have been loved by God, they have in turn loved others. Moreover, because they have heard the revealed worship-worthy name of the Son (Heb 1:5), who proclaimed to creation the name of his Father (2:12), they have worked for the glory of his name by loving the others who have been made holy by God (2:11). How wide the circle of saints might reach is not clear, but it would surely include those who had experienced persecution for their faith (10:32–34).

The past, however, is not the only proof of their salvation for the author. This work of love in God's name continues because, he says, they are *still serving* the saints in the present. By ministering to others, they are doing the same work as God's heavenly host (1:14). This comparison demonstrates the honor given to humble service in the Christian community. To serve is to do angelic work. Importantly, though, their work would not matter if God did not pay

9. This term of endearment is better attested in the manuscripts than the familial form of address, *adelphoi*.

attention to it. Therefore, before he names the good *they* have done and are doing, he assures them that *God is not unjust*. God will not *neglect* what they have done. Just as God is attentive to their current and potential failures, God also has paid close attention to their past and present successes.

The concern of the author and his companions is that the congregation keep going. Employing a word that conveys passion, he lays out the following as his *desire*. Much like he did in the warnings of chs. 3 and 4, he pinpoints the individuals of the congregation. This desire is for *each of you*. Just as they have demonstrated love, they also need to continue to *demonstrate the same haste*. As he called them to hasten to go into God's rest (4:11), now he calls them to show haste toward *the fullness of hope until the end*. It is not as though he wants them to rush carelessly, but he wants an intensity from them as they move forward. This approach will correct the immaturity he has called out in them (5:11–13). In this instance when he encourages progress, he describes them as moving forward toward the *fullness of hope*. Hope is a vital concept for the author (3:6; 6:11, 18; 7:19; 10:23; 11:1). Here it is clear that he imagines that they can grow in hope. They can pursue deeper and deeper depths of it until they reach *the end* goal, when their hope is finally realized and they dwell in glory with God (2:10).

The intense pace he desires is made clear by that which he wants them to avoid in v. **12**. They should demonstrate haste so that they *may not be sluggish ones*. He had already stated that they have become sluggish with regard to their hearing (5:11). The intense warning hopefully quickened their ears so that they can move out of sluggishness into attentiveness and action.

By enclosing the intense warning with the frame of sluggishness, the author suggests a connection. If they remain immature, the risk of falling away completely is great. Alternatively, if they, with intensity, move toward maturity, that risk of apostasy diminishes. This encouraging and instructional paragraph puts the warning into the right light. For those who have loved ones about whom they are worried concerning the state of their relationship with God, the author demonstrates a way forward. Look for the evidence of godly fruit in their lives, in the past and the present. Then call attention to that fruit to suggest ways to pursue deeper relationship with God. As students often rise to the high expectations of their teachers, those dull in their faith might very well do the same if friends or mentors assume it possible that they, too, can grow in maturity with God.

To prod them forward, he wants them to be *imitators of the heirs of the promises*. The promises surely include the inheritance of salvation (1:14) or, put differently, the promise of entering God's rest (4:1). These heirs obtained those promises *through faith and patience*. Faith is not just necessary at the beginning (6:1) but is needed throughout the journey toward God's rest. It is the foundation that should ever remain strong. Since that journey lasts one's entire life, and life is not as it should be (2:8), the journey also demands patience. Abraham serves, for the author, as a good example of both.

6:13–15 · ABRAHAM'S FAITHFUL PATIENCE

[13]*For when God made a promise to Abraham, since God had no one greater by which to swear, God swore by Godself,* [14]*saying, "Surely blessing, I will bless you, and multiplying, I will multiply you,"* [15]*and, thus, after being patient, Abraham obtained the promise.*

While there are many to whom God made promises (6:12), as the author will catalogue in ch. 11 (11:13, 33, 39), the time *when God made a promise to Abraham* provides an important example (true also for Paul; see Gal 3:18; Rom 4:21), one the author of Hebrews appeals to early and often. God displays the divine quality of promise-maker to Abraham. (Note that he is named by his covenant name, not his original name, Abram. The transition happens in Gen 17:5.) "Promise keeper" is one of the key assertions of God's identity throughout the letter (Heb 6:17; 8:6; 10:23; 11:11; 12:26). The audience has already been the recipient of this divine quality as those for whom the promise to go into God's rest remains (4:1). Looking forward to this promised inheritance shapes their ongoing relationship with God (6:17; 9:15; 10:36). In the sermon, Abraham and Sarah provide the most frequently cited example of divine promise-obtainers (6:13, 15; 7:6; 11:9, 11, 17); even Abraham's identifying phrase can be "the one who has the promises" (7:6). They knew God to be trustworthy in light of their own experiences (11:11), and this is the character of God to whom the audience should hold fast as well (10:23). The frequency and integral role of the promise motif indicates the author's desire that this community relate with God as one who is trustworthy. They can rest assured that God will do what God has promised. The author demonstrates that if that is true for Abraham, they can trust that it will be true for them.

To emphasize the divine trustworthiness with Abraham, *God swore*. The discussion here may set off concerns when connected with Jesus's statements in the Sermon on the Mount that no one should swear (Matt 5:33–37; the same word for swearing appears in both). Actually, however, the two discourses affirm the same point: only God has the character and power to back up promises given. Hebrews has already cited a place where God swears. It occurs when God promises not to let the faithless generation into the land of rest (Ps 95:11/Heb 3:11, 18; 4:3). Here the author turns to a more positive example. *God swore by Godself* when making a promise to Abraham *since God had no one greater by which to swear*. Chrysostom notes the discomfort readers might feel about God swearing: "But since the race of humanity is hard of belief, [God] condescends to communicate on our level. So then for our sake, he swears, even though it be unworthy of him that he should not be believed."[10] Because of graciousness God sought to encourage trust by adding a personal oath to the divine promise, though it was unnecessary in light of God's being and actions.

In this instance, God promises and swears to Abraham, *Surely blessing, I will bless you, and multiplying, I will multiply you*. The author is quoting here from Genesis 22, both in the introduction to the verse (Heb 6:13/Gen 22:16) and in the citation itself (Heb 6:14/Gen 22:17). This is the pivotal moment in Abraham's life of faith. He has just shown his willingness to offer his son, Isaac, the son of the promise, to God. The angel the Lord called out to stay his hand from the slaughter (Gen 22:11–12), and, in this citation, the angel of the Lord gives voice to the first-person speech of God. This instance of promise is a reiteration of what had come before. God had promised blessing to Abraham at the first encounter, along with multiplication of his progeny, which was expressed in the promise to make Abraham a great nation (Gen 12:2). So also in Genesis 15 God promised that a child of Abraham's own body would result in descendants as numerous as the stars (Gen 15:5). The promise is repeated yet another time in the conversation in Genesis 17:1–21, and also by the divine visitors in Genesis 18:10, 14. Only here in Gen 22 does God add an oath to the reiteration of the promise, and only here does God speak of the descendants as numerous as the sand on the shore (Gen 22:17; evoked in Heb 11:12). When speaking the promise this time, God affirms that the multiplication will happen through this miraculous child.

10. Chrysostom, *Hebrews* 11.2 (*NPNF*[1] 14:419).

This is not the only example of trust that Abraham displays. Jubilees gives evidence of a Jewish opinion that Abraham walked through ten tests with God, the sacrifice of Isaac being the last one (Jub. 17:17). When the author of Hebrews treats Abraham's life rather extensively in ch. 11, he also includes more instances of faith than simply the sacrifice of Isaac, including going out of his homeland, living as a foreigner, and trusting God for a child and an enduring homeland (11:8–16).

In ch. 6, however, the sacrifice of Isaac is the moment on which the author focuses. He first attends to Abraham's posture and particular virtue, saying, *And, thus, after being patient*. The author's assessment of Abraham is that he displays one of the hallmark qualities of God, patience (Exod 34:6; Num 14:18; Neh 9:17; Ps 86:15 LXX; 103:8 LXX; Joel 2:13; Jonah 4:2; Wis 15:1), a quality that is never explicitly attributed to Abraham in Israel's Scriptures. Because he was willing to be trained by God through this incredibly difficult act, he took on God's qualities (Heb 12:11).

After being patient, Abraham got that promise for which he was waiting. Several options exist for the particular promise the author has in mind when he says that Abraham *obtained the promise.* In the immediate context of Genesis 22, Abraham does receive his son, Isaac, as the author will discuss (Heb 11:17–19). He was ready to give him wholly to God, but then received him, the child of the promise, back from the threat of death. Isaac, however, cannot be the only referent for several reasons. First, while Isaac is a vehicle of blessing and multiplying, he is not the realization of those promises in full. One child is a poor fulfillment of a guarantee of innumerable descendants. Second, the author indicates that Abraham showed patience *after* he had received this promise. In Genesis 22 he already had Isaac, after waiting for his birth and also receiving him back after being willing to offer him. When the promise is given by the angel of the Lord, Abraham has nothing else to be patient about concerning Isaac. Therefore, the promise must include the fulfillment of the promise of blessing and multiplying, a promise Abraham did not obtain even by the end of his life. He had a few other children (Gen 25:1–6), though not within the line of covenant blessing, and had also lived to see the birth of Jacob and Esau. Even these grandchildren are hardly equal to descendants as numerous as the stars or the sand, through whom all nations of the earth are blessed (Gen 22:17–18, the continuation of the statement from which the author cites in v. 14). Because the blessing here is for multiple children, it seems that Abraham never obtains this promise during his life. If Abraham was patient until he obtained this promise, it would be a postmortem attainment, precisely the kind to which the author alludes in 11:39 and 12:22–24. As a member of the faithful witnesses, he would be able to see the countless descendants to whom the Son gives aid (2:16). Hence, the patience he needed to display was a lifelong patience and also a patience after death as he waited for the time of perfection (11:39). If God's oath-supported promise allowed him that long-suffering virtue, God's promise can surely support this community in whatever patience they need to display.

6:16–20 · THE ANCHOR

[16]*For humans swear according to something greater, and an oath given as assurance puts an end to every dispute among people.* [17]*Because God willed even more to show to the heirs of the promise the unchangeableness of his will, God interceded with an oath,* [18]*in order that through two unchangeable things, in which it is impossible for God to lie, we can have this strong encouragement, those who are fleeing to grasp the hope that lies before us,* [19]*which we have as a steadfast and certain anchor of the soul, which goes inside the veil* [20]*where the forerunner has gone in for us, Jesus, who became High Priest forever according to the order of Melchizedek.*

To make the theological point with even more clarity, the author draws from common life again. *Humans swear according to something greater* than themselves. The tone of the New Testament on this topic of swearing is negative, at least where humans are concerned. Both Jesus and James instruct against swearing oaths (Matt 5:34; 23:16–22; Jas 5:12). Herod does it to his regret, and to John's death (Matt 14:7–9/Mark 6:23–26); Peter does it in duress (Matt 26:72–74); and the Jewish exorcists do so ineffectively (Acts 19:13). There is no example of a human swearing for good. God, on the other hand, swears to Abraham and David (Luke 1:73; Acts 2:30), and, as Hebrews records more than any other text, God swears to the wilderness generation (Heb 3:11, 18; 4:3), to Abraham (6:13), to Jesus (7:20, 21, 28), and to his followers (6:17). In Israel's Scriptures, swearing is much more common and accepted, and even can be used for good (Gen 21:23; Exod 22:8), as is true in Philo (*On Dreams* 1.12).[11] The author of

11. Attridge, *Hebrews*, 180.

Hebrews is not explicitly recommending this practice; he only acknowledges that it happens. Moreover, he notes that in human dealings it can be beneficial. *An oath given as assurance puts an end to every dispute among people.* The author's point is that with oaths, matters are settled. Humans, who are finite and fallible, have to invoke something greater than themselves to show that they mean to keep their word. If they fail to do so, the oath acts as a legal guarantee, much as a signed contract would function in contemporary society. If this works for humans, how much more does a divine oath grant assurance that the promise will be realized when God is doing the swearing. Since God is swearing on God's own character, a character that is both sovereign and righteous, nothing can fail about the promise.

In v. **17** the author pivots from God's interaction with Abraham so that he can broaden the practice of divine oath making to others. He invokes the previous discussion by saying, *When God interceded with an oath* (I've opted for a fulsome translation to make explicit the meaning of the prepositional phrase *en hō*). Given the immediate context, it seems likely that the focal event is God's conversation with Abraham, although this statement could apply to God's oath to the wilderness generation. In making the oath, God has in view not only the direct addressee but also those who will hear this oath-speech in Scripture. *God willed even more to show.* God has plans over and above those plans for the ones to whom God is speaking. God's intention, by interceding with an oath, is to display *the unchangeableness of his will.* The authors dual use of "will" (*God willed* and *his will*) emphasizes God's power. God willed to show the divine will. Because God is God, what God wills comes to fruition. That indicates a beautiful theological truth. There is a simplicity in God—not hope and then action but a divine plan that is the guarantee of the realization of the plan. No poor planning nor inability can interrupt God's will from coming to be. Even more encouraging is the second assertion that God willed to disclose the divine will. God could have elected to act and kept that hidden from humanity, but in this instance God not only willed but also willed to reveal that will. The revelation of God's will increases the ability of humanity to know and trust God.

In a society in which humans use oaths to helpful ends, God has performed the revelation of the unchangeable will by *interceding with an oath*—in other words, by adding *an oath* into the mix. This is the first time in the letter the author uses this word group for mediation henceforth employed as a title for

Jesus, the mediator (8:6; 9:15; 12:24). The choice seems deliberate. God fills the space between Creator and human creation with a practice that makes sense to them—namely, oath making. This mediatorial act is a preview of God himself coming to mediate.

The way the author describes the recipients of God's oath is also illuminative of God's character. God chooses to display the unchangeableness of God's will to those who are waiting on something, to *the heirs of the promise*. As heirs, God's addressees do not have their inheritance yet, and so they need to know that what God has promised will come to be. This phrase could connect with the statement in 1:14 that God's people are those who are about to inherit salvation, the promise of God's rest (4:1). So near the story of Abraham and Isaac, the phrase takes on another meaning as well. As heirs, the recipients of God's mediated oath stand in a family system. They are children of God, but they also count Abraham as their father (1:2; 2:16). This way of describing them reveals a beautiful connection to the promise God made to Abraham, which was for descendants and blessing. As heirs in this covenant family, they are part of the fulfillment of God's promise to Abraham. They help make up the innumerable descendants. Their very existence within God's covenant family is evidence of God's trustworthiness. In addition to being fulfillment for Abraham's promise, they are also looking forward to it. With Abraham, they, too, anticipate the fulfillment of the second part of the promise, the blessing to all. This is a promise that remains to be fulfilled.

To cultivate trust until the fulfillment of that promise arrives in full, God discloses these *two unchangeable things*. Interpreters have offered different suggestions for what these two things might be, but within the passage God's will (as named in v. 17) and God's oath, which is based on God himself, seem the most coherent option. God's character is such that these things are unchangeable; therefore, *it is impossible for God to lie*. The encouragement the author offers is stunning. If God has made a promise to them, they will, without a doubt, receive it. Although their current struggles may cause them to doubt God's presence (12:4–11), the author offers this assurance to which they can hold fast. Hence he can say, *We can have this strong encouragement*, although *strong* seems even too feeble a word for what he has described. Their encouragement is based in the very being of God. Moreover, the encouragement is for *them*. He has been talking about Abraham and the third-person "heirs," but here his encouragement becomes personalized for this community.

In v. **18** he describes himself and his listeners as *those who are fleeing.* This phrase conveys the sense of forward movement so common in the letter, as well as the sense of urgency he has been cultivating. To flee is to escape something, be it the imprisonment they experienced under the control of the devil (2:14) or their former persecutors (10:32–34). Whatever is behind them, they are moving to something sure in front of them. They will be able *to grasp* it. While this term can be used metaphorically (Col 2:19; 2 Thess 2:15), that he chooses to use a term associated with touch conveys the firmness of that to which they are fleeing (as made clear in the following statements). What they will attain is the *hope that lies before* them. Hope is a frequent and vital refrain in the letter (Heb 3:6; 6:11, 18; 7:19; 10:23; 11:1), but hope is not really a thing in and of itself but the vehicle that gets a person to a desired end. Readers might wonder how one can grasp something as intangible as hope.

It makes sense, then, that the author has more to say about hope. In v. **19** he names it as something very tangible and very strong—namely, an *anchor*, an anchor whose strength he emphasizes by describing it as both *steadfast and certain.* The Greek word for *steadfast* (*asphalē*) becomes in English the cognate "asphalt." In addition, he has just used the term for "certain" to describe the nature of the assurance given by an oath (v. 16, *bebaiōsin*). This immovable hope anchors *the soul.* As the inmost part of the person, which God can see (4:12), this is the very part that could begin to waver in faith but can instead hold fast to this stalwart hope.

It is odd, then, that something which should be immovable, an anchor, moves forward in the very next phrase. The anchor *goes in.* Previously this term for "going in" appeared eleven times as the author described entering God's rest (3:11, 16; 3:18–4:1; 4:3, 5–6, 10–11). Now, the hope-anchor enters into a cultic space, *inside the veil.* This is an insular place separated by a curtain. For readers of Israel's Scriptures this phrase clearly describes the holy of holies in the tabernacle (Exod 26:33; Lev 16:2). Throughout the sermon thus far, then, the author has used different terms, rest and the inside of the veil, to describe one concept—namely, the holy presence of God. This is where the hope of their souls has gone.

In v. **20** the identity of this firm but mobile hope is revealed as *the forerunner*, the one who *has gone in.* He is *Jesus.* Although the author had utilized strong words and images to describe the hope, hope in and of itself remains an ephemeral concept. If one's hope rests in a person, however, that hope is potentially graspable. It can, as John says, be touched and handled (1 John 1:1). Jesus is the object of their hope. He is the one who has gone ahead. He is the human being who has already entered into God's rest, dwelling in God's presence, as he is seated at God's right hand. He has entered into this holy space *for us*. With this phrase, the author continues the personal connection to himself and his congregation of fellow Christ confessors. Jesus's representative entering in has at least two dimensions. First, as the representative human who reigns (2:7–8), he shows other humans that such entrance, and the reigning that comes with it, is possible. Second, as the advocating human who represents us to the Father (4:14–15), his entrance aids the humans who are following him as they journey to his location.

That being asserted, hearers might counter that they cannot physically grasp Jesus because he is removed, seated on a throne at the right hand of the Father. The tension between the Savior's presence with God and his absence from the saved runs throughout the New Testament. Initially, it is helpful to recognize that the author does assert that they are fleeing forward to grasp, not that they have already done so. They are on the path to dwell in resurrected bodies with Jesus but are not there yet. Nevertheless, the author is aiming to give them the absolute assurance that as they continue on this path, they *will* arrive there. Much like he does in his treatment on faith, he is granting them assurance for what lies ahead by reminding them of what has come before. God has been faithful to their forebears, such as Abraham (6:13–15), and God has been faithful in the life of the Son, as other believers have told them (2:3).

In addition to this future dimension, it is true that they can hold on to Jesus now, even if not physically. With the imagery of an anchor of the soul, Jesus the forerunner serves not just as an example of possibility, nor only as a sympathetic and effective but distant representative, but as one to whom they remain deeply connected. They are tethered to him as a boat is connected to its anchor. Although it is not mentioned explicitly here, in light of other New Testament documents, the church will come to understand that intimate connection between Jesus and his people as the work of the Spirit. Christians may not be able to touch his resurrected body, but by the gracious power of the Spirit we are truly connected to him. Moreover, that connection is manifest in the tangible realities of baptism, Eucharist, fellowship, and service.

As Jesus is the representative of and advocate for humans to God, it is not surprising that at this point the author rearticulates Jesus's role as a priest.

When he entered into this holy space, Jesus the forerunner *became High Priest forever according to the order of Melchizedek.* Having woken them up to their lethargy (5:11–6:12) and then given them unassailable hope, the author is now ready to turn to the great and difficult word concerning the priestly order of Melchizedek.

HEBREWS 7:1–28

THE ORDER OF MELCHIZEDEK

In this chapter the author returns to the thread he first mentioned through a citation of Psalm 110:4 in 5:6 and alluded to in 6:20—namely, his exposition of the story of Melchizedek. Although this figure might be unfamiliar to some contemporary readers, he is in no way ancillary to the author of Hebrews. From the first sentence this author has claimed sacerdotal activities for Christ (purification of sins, 1:3), and the christological foundation of chs. 1 and 2 culminates in naming his high priesthood explicitly (2:17). Now that the author has delineated the features of priesthood—Jesus's specifically (4:14–5:10)—he can focus on the figure who gives the scriptural image of the unique and powerful realities of Christ's priesthood. Melchizedek is rather minor in Israel's Scriptures, both quantitatively and qualitatively, but for the author of Hebrews his story provides a hermeneutic for seeing God's providential consistency at work in Jesus's priesthood.

The author begins by citing several phrases from the Genesis 14 narrative (7:1–2), and then comments on all but one (Abraham's defeat of the kings). The identity of Melchizedek is the focus of vv. 2–3 and 8b, the tithe in vv. 4–6 and 8–10, and the blessing in v. 7. Attention to the details of the story, those stated and left unstated, lays the exegetical groundwork for the return to the nature of Christ's priesthood in the rest of the chapter.

The author focuses on Christ's priesthood through an extended engagement with Psalm 110:4, which provides the scriptural inertia for his argument. In 7:11–21 he shows how God's oath-backed statement and fulfillment of a priestly call for one from the tribe of Judah invites a reinterpretation of the law. Given God's statements, the author surmises that the law must have lacked perfection and was never meant to be permanent. These striking statements against the law receive clarity in the closing sentences of the chapter, in which the author extols the living and perpetual priesthood of Jesus, to which the law always pointed. Christ alone can offer Hebrews' audience the hope of full salvation and the assurance to bring them into it.

By proclaiming the good that comes to them in the priesthood of Jesus, the author prepares the way for his introduction of the new covenant. By virtue of this priest's life, stemming from the unparalleled relationship he has with God, only Jesus can bring the long-hoped-for enduring covenant.

7:1–3 · MELCHIZEDEK

[1]For this Melchizedek, king of Salem, priest of God Most High, who met Abraham when he returned from the defeat of the kings and blessed him, [2]to whom also Abraham divided a tenth from all things; first, his name is translated "king of righteousness," and then also King of Salem, which is "king of peace"; [3]without father, without mother, without genealogy, having neither beginning of days nor end of life, and having been made like the Son of God, he remains a priest forever.

Having mentioned him three times (5:6, 10; 6:20), the author is now ready to turn his attention fully to Melchizedek. He quoted from and alluded to the mention of his name in Psalm 110:4, but at the beginning of ch. 7 he cites from the only other passage where this person appears in the Scriptures of Israel, Genesis 14:17–20. He quotes several phrases from the passage, but not all of them and not all in the same order as laid out in Genesis.

Hebrews 7:1–2

For this *Melchizedek, king of Salem, priest of God Most High, who met Abraham when he returned from the defeat of the kings and blessed him, to whom also Abraham* divided a *tenth from all things.* First his name is translated "king of righteousness," and then also *king of Salem,* which is "king of peace."

Genesis 14:17–20

And the king of Sodom went out to meet him after he returned from *the defeat* of Chodollogomor and *the kings* with them into the valley of Shaveh (this was the plain of a king).

And *Melchizedek king of Salem* brought out bread and wine; and he was *priest of God Most High.*

And *he blessed* Abram and said,

Hebrews 7:1–2	*Genesis 14:17–20*
	"Blessed be Abram to God Most High, who created the heaven and the earth, and blessed be God Most High, who has delivered your enemies subjected to you!" And he gave to him *one tenth from everything.*

In the narrative of Abraham's life, this brief encounter serves the primary goal of showing God's continual blessing to the man with whom God is making a covenant. The author of Hebrews takes an admittedly small scene to make a vital point for his argument in support of Jesus's priesthood. Like other Second Temple Jewish interpreters, he is drawn to the sudden entrance of this unexpected figure, and he makes his story serve his christological argument in distinct ways.[1] The author recounts six things from the encounter in Genesis 14 explicitly: his name, his royal title, his relationship with God (priest of the Most High God), the setting of the encounter (when Abraham returned from the battle between kingdoms), his blessing of Abraham, and Abraham's paying of a tithe to Melchizedek.[2] Hebrews' shortened summary calls attention to a person in Israel's story who holds both the title of a king and the title of a priest. Some kings in Israel do priestly actions (1 Chr 16:2), but no one other than the figure in Psalm 109 LXX shares this dual designation. With overtones of his royalty at God's right hand (Ps 109:1 LXX) and his priesthood (Ps 109:4 LXX), the addressee of Psalm 109 LXX has both vocations in common with Melchizedek.

Another striking realization is that this person, Melchizedek, serves God Most High at the time that God has called Abraham to begin the covenant.

1. For citations and an overview of Jewish mention of Melchizedek, see Eric F. Mason, "Cosmology, Messianism, and Melchizedek: Apocalyptic Jewish Traditions and Hebrews," in *Reading the Epistle to the Hebrews*, ed. Eric F. Mason and Kevin B. McCruden, RBS 66 (Atlanta: Society of Biblical Literature, 2011), 68–76. Ps 110 was also used by the Hasmonean line to give support for their embrace of both royal and cultic leadership. See Perrin, *Jesus as Priest*, 151n40.

2. The pronouns do not give clarity to which "he" is intended in the exchange—does Abraham tithe to Melchizedek or the opposite?—but nearly all have interpreted Abraham as the tithe giver. Mason, "Cosmology, Messianism, and Melchizedek," 69.

Although his backstory is not told as it is with Abraham, the biblical text is suggesting that God has established a relationship with Melchizedek as well. Because the Genesis text describes God as the *Most High*, the citation connects with the author's description of Jesus taking his seat at the right hand of the majesty *on high* (Heb 1:3).

The author of Hebrews recounts the story. Melchizedek *met Abraham when he returned from the defeat of the kings*. He continues to employ the covenant name of Abraham (as he did in ch. 6), even though he is recounting a story from Genesis 14 and the patriarch's name will not be changed in the narrative until Genesis 17:5. At this point in Genesis, Abraham has graciously chosen to become entangled in a regional conflict. King Chedorlaomer and his allies have had two victories (Gen 14:5, 10–11). When Abraham gets involved to help his nephew Lot, he defeats Chedorlaomer, the king who was holding Lot captive. This demonstrates the power of Abraham, who is able to run the armies away from the land of promise.[3] *Defeat* seems a better translation than "slaughter" here because Abram does what Chedolaomer has done to others (Gen 14:5, 7). Because they are able to run away from Abram (Gen 14:15), that means they are not all dead. This is the only element of the story the author mentions but does not comment on. On the heels of discussing God's promise of blessing to Abraham (Heb 6:14), this story is an example of that blessing playing out during his life, in his ability to be successful against strong foes as he seeks to bring blessing to his extended family.

Then the author notes that Abraham *divided a tenth from all things* he had recovered in the rescue mission. He does not use the word that appears in the extant versions of the Greek texts of Genesis (*edōken*) but instead utilizes the cognate of a word (*emerisen*) that the author had used for God's divisions of gifts (*merismos*, Heb 2:4), a word choice that more closely aligns Abraham's action with the work of God.

After mentioning these contours of the story, the author then builds an argument on most of them. He begins by citing the Genesis text with the name of this figure. He transliterates the Hebrew into Greek, as the Greek translation of Genesis does, by stating the name as *Melchizedek* in v. 1. Then, referring to that name in v. **2**, he says that it is *translated "king of righteousness."* He then rearticulates Melchizedek's title *king of Salem* and provides its

3. Gordon J. Wenham, *Genesis 1–15*, WBC 1 (Waco: Word, 1987), 301–7.

translation, *which is "king of peace."* In other books of the New Testament, such explanatory translations are taken as an indication of gentile readership. As that possibility has become accepted by some interpreters of Hebrews, this verse could support an audience's need to understand the Hebrew. Disconnect with the Hebrew language might also be true of a diaspora community of Jews. Whatever their ethnic and linguistic background, naming the qualities of his identifiers connects Melchizedek with the way the author describes God and God's people in the sermon. Righteousness is what the royal Son loves (1:9) and what the audience needs to grow in (5:13) so that they can be like the faithful members of God's family (10:38; 11:4, 7; 12:11, 23). Similarly, God is defined by peace (13:20), and so readers should aspire to it (12:11, 14). Melchizedek may be an enigmatic character from the distant past in some sense, but in another he displays familiar qualities with those who are part of God's household.

After translating his name and royal title, the author spends more time reflecting on Melchizedek's priesthood. It is striking that he is the first priest mentioned in Israel's narrative, and not surprising that he would grab the attention of this author who is well versed in the Scriptures of Israel and quite interested in priests. After remaining so close to the text of Genesis in vv. 1–2, in v. **3** the author then departs from the text, at least according to modern sensibilities. Better said, he ceases to read the peaks of the account but instead focuses on the valleys. He reads the gaps rather than the affirmations, a move not uncommon for Jewish readers.[4] He notices that Genesis 14 has nothing to say about Melchizedek's ancestry. He is *without father, without mother, without genealogy*. In the account, there is no mention of a father, a mother, or any extended genealogy, although this is odd for one who is a priest, given the concerns for the particular descents of Israel's cultic leaders (Exod 28:43; Ezra 2:62; Neh 7:64). On the other hand, the narrative role of Melchizedek serves the patriarchal narrative as an outsider who affirms God's blessing on Abraham.[5] For such a small role, the lack of a genealogy may not be an oddity. It is the author of Hebrews who lifts up this silence for his listeners' attention. In his reading, the absence communicates that Melchizedek has no *beginning of days*. At the other end of the life spectrum, the author notices that neither does the

4. Attridge mentions examples in both Philo and Rabbinic literature (*Hebrews*, 190). See also Compton, *Psalm 110 and Hebrews*, 78–79.

5. Wenham, *Genesis 1–15*, 315–22.

Genesis story indicate Melchizedek's death. He states it this way: Melchizedek does not have an *end of life*. Hence, in the narrative Melchizedek is *made* to look *like the Son of God*, who, as the author has argued early in the sermon, has neither beginning of days, since he existed with his Father before the creation of the ages (1:3), nor end of life, since his throne is forever and he has defeated death (1:8; 2:14–15). Without an account of Melchizedek's death, the narrative leaves open the possibility that Melchizedek *remains a priest forever.*

This has proven to be a confusing statement. Some early interpreters argued that Melchizedek was an appearance of God the Son in history. If this is a Christophany, then the similarities between Melchizedek and the Son make perfect sense, for it is actually the Son himself who appeared as a king of righteousness and who remains a priest of God. Several difficulties are present within this interpretation, however. First, it might introduce the idea of a bodily appearance of the Son before the incarnation, but the author of Hebrews is committed to the idea of the appearance of the Son in human flesh, that happened recently in the author's own time (1:2; 2:3). Second, it is difficult to see how the Son could be made like himself (v. 3). The author seems to be working with two distinct beings that can be compared.[6]

More recent discoveries that disclose how other Jews considered Melchizedek as a heavenly figure have opened new interpretive options. In congruence with the Jewish literature preserved in the Dead Sea Scrolls, some have suggested that the author of Hebrews views Melchizedek as a heavenly angel.[7] Since the angels are messengers and ministers of God (1:14), the angelic Melchizedek could remain a priest while Jesus is the High Priest. If the author does imagine Melchizedek as an angelic figure, he would be stating that he has no fleshly, human beginning. Another interpretation posits that Melchizedek was a human in history, and because his end is not narrated, he could have joined the ranks of those humans who dwell with God forever (12:24) and serve as priests (12:28; 13:15). Both of these suggestions, however, present a conflict with the phrase *having [no] beginning of days*, because both humans and angels are created, and, of course, humans do have genealogies.

6. Epiphanius of Salamis, *Panarion* 4, *Against Melchizedekians* 7.3 (ACCS 10:100).

7. Eric F. Mason, "Hebrews 7:3 and the Relationship between Melchizedek and Jesus," *Biblical Research* 50 (2005): 41–62. See also Mason, *"You Are a Priest Forever": Second Temple Jewish Messianism and the Priestly Christology of the Epistle to the Hebrews*, Studies on the Texts of the Desert of Judah 74 (Leiden: Brill, 2008).

The literary interpretation of Melchizedek remains another option.[8] The way that the words about Melchizedek run in Genesis remind readers of what is true of the Son of God. The author of Hebrews is reading Melchizedek figurally, as a type of some things that are true about Christ. The Son of God is both priest and king, one who displays righteousness and peace. As God, the Son has no beginning and no death. Instead of the Son having an *end of life*, his priesthood comes about through the power of an indestructible life (7:16). Without death his priesthood is perpetual (see 7:23). In all these ways, the narrative sets up Melchizedek as similar to the Son of God. This is not to say the author believes this story to be a literary fiction, but instead, as God has spoken through the prophets and narrated mysterious encounters in the life of Abraham, those accounts in Genesis are meant to prepare the way for the understanding of God's communication in the Son.

The author retells Melchizedek's encounter with Abraham, but his story is not the ultimate interest in Hebrews. The author brings this priest-king forth so that he can show how Melchizedek's story informs the interpretation of Jesus's. He is making the argument in his sermon that the combination of these roles uniquely inheres in the person of Jesus. He agrees with other early Christ confessors that Jesus bears the title of Messiah, Son of God (as presented in the first chapter). To that shared conversation, he has contributed a focus on Jesus's priesthood. What is without debate is that the author has been claiming Jesus as the sole efficient and eternal High Priest, and so Melchizedek is certainly not his rival but his signpost.

7:4–10 · ENCOUNTER WITH ABRAHAM

4 *And see how great this one is, to whom Abraham, the patriarch, gave a tenth from*
the spoils. 5 *And on the one hand, those who descended from the sons of Levi who*
receive the office of priest have a commandment to tithe from the people according to
the law—that is, from their siblings—even though they have gone out from the loins
of Abraham. 6 *But on the other, the one who has no genealogy from them has received*
a tithe from Abraham and blessed the one who has the promises. 7 *And outside of*
every disagreement, the lesser is blessed by the greater. 8 *And here, on the one hand,*

8. See also Cockerill, *Hebrews*, 302–3.

dying men receive tithes, but there, on the other, he is one about whom it is testified that he lives. [9]*It is almost as if one could speak the statement that through Abraham even Levi, the one who receives tithes, has given a tithe,* [10]*because he was still in the loins of his father when Melchizedek met him.*

The pastor wants his congregation to *see how great this one is*. To do so, he moves to the end of the Genesis pericope where it was Abraham who gave a tithe to Melchizedek. This is the author's way of clarifying the ambiguous Hebrew grammar, anyhow, which could support the tithe going from Abraham to Melchizedek or vice versa. By clarifying the roles and using "Abraham" instead of "Abram," the author's aim is to show the relationship between Melchizedek and the patriarch of the covenant family. His covenant name grants Abraham more standing and, therefore, Melchizedek greater standing as his superior.

The author also specifies from what Abraham takes the tithe, not just from "all things" (Gen 14:20/Heb 7:2) but *from the spoils*, a term that does not appear in the Greek text of Genesis. Moreover, he denotes Abraham as *the patriarch*, a specific title for Abraham that appears only in later literature (4 Macc 7:19; 16:25). These are both indications that he is retelling this account in his own terms, as influenced by ways he might have heard the story. It is not that he disrespects the scriptural story, but like any good preacher he shapes the retelling of the story in his own words for people of his own time to serve his homiletical end. In line with the passage, however, he takes up the verb *didōmi*, *gave*, from the Genesis text in distinction to his use of *merizō*, *divide*, in v. 2. With his retelling, he gets the main point across: even the esteemed father of the faith, the covenant partner of God, Abraham, tithed to Melchizedek. That fact indicates something powerful about the priest-king's greatness. The sermonic goal, however, is not only to elevate Melchizedek but ultimately to tell his story so that its contours illuminate that which is more pertinent for the congregation—namely, the priesthood of Jesus.

To prove Melchizedek's greatness to serve the ultimate christological end, he recalls the practice of tithing among the people of Israel. Melchizedek's receiving of tithes is similar to the reception of tithes by *those who descended from the sons of Levi*[9] who receive the office of priest (Josh 18:7). They *have*

9. This is a derivative genitive (Harris, *Hebrews*, 162).

a commandment to tithe from the people. They do not take this honor for themselves; it is given *according to the law* (Deut 26:12; Num 18:21), a point the author reiterates with three terms, *receive, commandment*, and *law*.

The author mentions this so that he can highlight a difference between the Levites and Melchizedek. The Levites needed the law to clarify the system of tithing among equals. They collect a tithe from people who are *their siblings*. They are siblings with the members of the other tribes because they all descend from Abraham. They have all *gone out from the loins of Abraham*. This is a biologically frank way to say that they share the same ancestry.

On the other hand, Melchizedek and Abraham are not brothers. They are not equals by descent, because Melchizedek, according to the author of Hebrews' attention to and highlighting of the gaps in the narrative, does not have one. At least the Genesis narrative gives no indication that he shares a family relationship with Abraham. He is the *one who has no genealogy from them*. He is not a Levite. Said more clearly, if the readers are tempted to think that the Levites are just as good as Melchizedek because they all receive tithes, they are wrong. The Genesis 14 narrative indicates that he is superior to them in two respects. First, he *has received a tithe from Abraham*. He does not get tithes from the children but from the father, the patriarch himself. Second, the Levites receive tithes from the descendants of Abraham who are their familial equals. It is the law's instruction for priesthood, including tithing, that creates their distinction above their sibling Israelites. Melchizedek receives tithes from one who is not his brother because his genealogy is distinct. He is in a different category than Abraham even before the giving of the tithe.

In addition to receiving a tithe, Melchizedek has *blessed* Abraham, the *one who has the promises*. Abraham is the one with whom God chose to establish the covenant relationship and promised him blessing, as the author discussed in ch. 6. If Melchizedek can bless such an honored one, that again indicates something powerful about him with respect to Abraham. That the author chooses to communicate the tithe and the blessing with perfect verbs suggests the enduring impact of this exchange.

It is a nonnegotiable for the author that *the lesser is blessed by the greater*. In fact, as he states, this is *outside any dispute*. Readers knowledgeable of Israel's Scriptures might counter that humans can bless God (Noah is the first to do so in Gen 9:26, but it is a frequent refrain in the Psalms: 16:7; 26:12; 34:1; 63:4; 66:8; 96:2; 103–104; 113:2; 115:18; 134:1; 134:2; 135:19; 145), which is a reversal of what the author claims is true. This kind of blessing from humans to God, however, is only one offered *in return*. Similar to Paul's citation of Job 41:3 in Romans 11:35, no one can give first to God; one can only return what God has already given. This resonates with the moment in some services, when, to prepare for the time of offering, the pastor proclaims 1 Chronicles 29:14, "All things come of thee, O Lord, and of thine own have we given thee." In Melchizedek's place, however, by blessing Abraham he acts toward Abraham similarly to the way God has acted toward Abraham. God gave the promise to Abraham, and Melchizedek gave a blessing. Melchizedek, however, does not bless Abraham himself, but as revealed in the full narrative, Melchizedek's blessing to Abraham is actually to proclaim the state of blessing that Abraham has with God (Gen 14:19) and then to bless God in return (Gen 14:20). Both God and Melchizedek give good to Abraham, showing Melchizedek's similarity to God's work, confirmed by the fact that Melchizedek's blessing points to the blessing of God.

In v. **8** the author brings to light another dimension of the story. *And here*, he says, with the Levites, you have a situation in which *dying men receive tithes*. To describe them in this way highlights the human mortality of the Levites (see also 9:27) as those who are under the enslaving fear of death (2:14–15). They are, like all humans, from the very moment of their conception moving toward death. Alternatively, *there* in Genesis, with Melchizedek, is *one about whom it is testified that he lives*. With no death recounted in the narrative, he appears as the very opposite of the Levites.

Naming this difference in their respective ends prompts the author to pivot back to the other side of life, its beginning. He notices that Levi himself has a connection to this event in Genesis 14. *It is almost as if one could speak the statement that through Abraham even Levi, the one who receives tithes, has given a tithe, because he was still in the loins of his father when Melchizedek met him.* As it did in v. 5, familial descent connects Levi solidly with Abraham, resulting in an ironic twist. Levi, the tithe receiver, is first the tithe giver. The author recognizes that Levi exercises no personal agency in this exchange, but there is no doubt with whom he is associated (Abraham) and in what position he stands (the lesser).

The author's attentive reading of Genesis has established the point he made in 7:1: Melchizedek is great. He receives the tithe from none less than Abraham, and he, like God, blesses Abraham. The equation between Abraham and

Melchizedek is clear. In this interaction, Melchizedek is the superior one (thus: Melchizedek > Abraham).

The exegetical and homiletical skill of the author of Hebrews shines here. A read through the Genesis narrative might very well pass quickly over Melchizedek, or at most pause to puzzle over him, but not for long. In the grand sweep of the story, he plays a minor role, whose actions serve to highlight the importance of the primary protagonist, Abraham. It is not that the author of Hebrews invents things about him, but by paying very close attention to the details of the text, both the statements and the gaps, he lifts up Melchizedek for his listeners' consideration in order to serve his sermonic goal.

By noticing the relationship between Melchizedek and Abraham in this encounter, he is able to point out where the Levites stand in this equation. Because he is their ancestor, they are with Abraham and therefore inferior to Melchizedek (thus: Melchizedek > Abraham/Levites).

Retelling the story in this way allows the author to complete the comparison with the Levites. It is Jesus who stands in the line of Melchizedek because God, as recorded in Psalm 109:4 LXX, says so (thus: Melchizedek/Jesus > Abraham/Levites).

Consequently, the author brings forth in this brief account in Genesis the exegetical confirmation for the argument he is seeking to make. Jesus is a priest, and his priesthood is superior to the Levitical priesthood, even though the Levitical priesthood was established by God in the law. The Melchizedekian priesthood of Jesus is not superior because it is brand-new, a replacement for the Levitical. It gives no evidence that God is changing course. Quite the opposite. The author discovers in Genesis 14 that this superior priesthood has existed even before Levi was born. Levi and those in his line were always meant to serve in deference to, by pointing the way to, another priesthood.

7:11–28 · THE CULTIC LAW

[11]*Therefore, if completion was through the Levitical priesthood—for the people received the law through it—what need would still exist for a different priest to be raised up according to the order of Melchizedek and not to be spoken according to the order of Aaron?* [12]*For a change of the priesthood by necessity also becomes a change in the law.* [13]*For these things are spoken about one who has participated in another tribe,*

from whom no one has paid attention to the altar. 14*For it is clear that our Lord has arisen from Judah, about which tribe Moses said nothing with regard to the priesthood.* 15*And it is even more clear, if another priest arises according to the likeness of Melchizedek,* 16*he comes not according to the law of the fleshly commandment but according to the power of an indestructible life. For it is testified, "You are a priest forever according to the order of Melchizedek."* 18*For on one hand, there is a removal of the earlier commandment because of its weakness and uselessness—*19*for the law perfected nothing—but on the other, the introduction of a better hope, a hope through which we draw near to God.*

20*And since this was not without an oathtaking—for there are those who have become priests without oathtaking—*21*but he [became priest] with oathtaking, through the one who said to him,*

> *The Lord swore and will not change his mind;*
> *you are a priest forever.*

22*According to this, he has become security for a better covenant.* 23*There are many who have become priests because they were prevented from remaining by death,* 24*but he has an unchanging priesthood because he remains forever.* 25*Whence, he is able to save to the fullest extent those who are approaching God through him, because he is always living to petition for them.*

26*Such a High Priest was fitting for us, holy, innocent, and undefiled, one who has been separated from sinners, and one who has become higher than the heavens,* 27*who does not have need each day—as the high priests—to first offer sacrifices for his own sins, then for those of the people. This he did once for all, offering up himself.* 28*The law appointed men who have weakness as high priests, but the word of the oath, which comes after the law, appoints a son who has been perfected forever.*

Melchizedek's interaction with Abraham would simply be an interesting one if Israel's Scriptures said nothing else about him. But because a psalm claims that Melchizedek is not simply a priest but also has an order, and because the psalm provides a divinely given promise that one would stand in his order forever, his story has lasting implications beyond himself. *Therefore*, the author joins his appearance in Genesis to the other mention of him in Israel's Scriptures. In the next paragraph, the author returns to that other text that mentions Melchizedek, Psalm 109:4 LXX (after last citing it in 5:6). God's speaking about another priest in the order of Melchizedek *after* the establishment of the Levitical priesthood is an indication after the fact (whereas the Genesis interaction is an indication before the fact) that the Levitical priesthood was not the ultimate one. Hence, *completion*, rather than "perfection," is the best sense of *teleiōsis* here in v. **11** because even though the author will discuss the lack of internal cleansing through the Levitical cult, here the focus is on the endurance of each priesthood's effects. *If completion was through the Levitical priesthood . . . what need would still exist for a different priest to be raised up according to the order of Melchizedek and not to be spoken according to the order of Aaron?* The author makes the answer to the rhetorical question clear with the use of an unreal condition.[10] The passive infinitives ("to be raised" and "to be spoken") assume the action of God. Because God did speak about another order in the psalm, that meant that the first order had not completed the aim of the sacrificial task.

The comparison between the orders would be quite balanced if the author had used the same word on both sides of the equation: God *spoke* about the order of Aaron; God *spoke* about the order of Melchizedek. This is not how he chooses to articulate the comparison. God did not speak about another priest according to the order of Aaron, but here he says a priest is *raised up* (*anistasthai*) from the order of Melchizedek. The word choice appears too striking and too distinct to be a thoughtless variation. It aligns well with a nod toward the resurrection (13:20) and foreshadows what the author will say about the power of an indestructible life (7:16).

In the midst of this comparison, the author also introduces the fact of the law's connection to the priesthood. *For the people received the law through it*—namely, the Levitical priesthood. Particularly in the time of the tabernacle, the people's experience with much of the law was often aimed at the tabernacle and facilitated through the priests (Exod 19–40). Since priests are so connected to the law, *a change of the priesthood by necessity also becomes a change in the law.*[11] The author has set up an alternating pattern to show the connection between priesthood and law even with his rhetorical structure.

10. Harris, *Hebrews*, 169.

11. Mary Schmitt, "Restructuring Views on Law in Hebrews 7:12," *JBL* 128 (2009): 189–201.

Lack of completion with the Levitical *priesthood*
　　Those who gave the people the *law*
Need for the raising of another *priest*
　　This necessitates a change in the *law*

Whereas the term *metatithēmi* can indicate removal or change, the kind of change the author has in mind is not fully clarified until the following section.

It *is* clear at this point that the author has Psalm 110:4 in mind because he says, *For these things* (namely, the things in the psalm about the order of Melchizedek) *are spoken about one who has participated* (the word for "participating" here, *metechō*, connects to the author's affirmation that the Son shared in flesh and blood like God's other children [2:14]) *in another tribe*, a tribe *from whom no one has paid attention to the altar.*

It is also *clear* to the author and his audience that *our Lord has arisen from Judah*, David's tribe. This author shares the common Christian confession of Jesus as a Davidide along with the Gospels (Matt 1:1; 9:27; 12:3, 23; 15:22; 20:30; 21:9; Mark 10:48; 11:10; Luke 1:32; 18:38; John 7:42) and Paul (Rom 1:3; 2 Tim 2:8). The choice of *arise* or "spring up" from the tribe of Judah is an interesting one, connecting with the earlier "arises" to denote upward movement and acts as another affirmation of the resurrection/ascension theme. The author reiterates that *Moses* the lawgiver *said nothing* about this tribe *with regard to the priesthood.* One might recall some exceptions to this statement when David constructs and serves at altars (2 Sam 24:25; 1 Chr 16:2), but the author is making a legislative point, a vital one for him given the sermon's focus on the high priest's work in the Yom Kippur ritual. Only one tribe was singled out for priestly service (Exod 28–29; Lev 8–9), and Judah was not it. Since there is no doubt Jesus was from Judah, that leaves him outside the circle of the Levitical priesthood.

An allusion to the resurrection with the author's language choices is likely because he goes on to state a fact that *is even more clear* (he uses a different term for "clear" here, *katadēlon*, as distinct from *prodēlon* in v. 14, possibly as a way to further emphasize the point of increased clarity): *if another priest arises according to the likeness of Melchizedek, he comes not according to the law of the fleshly commandment but according to the power of an indestructible life.* His standing in the line of Judah would not be enough to qualify him for the order of Melchizedek, even though Jews often interpreted God's promises in Psalm 109 LXX as spoken to an heir of David.[12] The only way he could be a priest *forever* is if he had an indestructible life. Jesus qualifies for this because he is the Son who is eternal, as the beginning section of the sermon proclaimed (esp. 1:2, 3, 8, 11–12). At the same time, the author has established that priests must be taken from among humanity to represent humanity (5:1). Being the eternal Son who became human, died, and rose again is the only way he could fulfill this promise. He can be a priest forever in the order of Melchizedek only through incarnation and the resurrection from the dead. In the narrative, Melchizedek figurally represents this because the narrative makes no comment about either his beginning or end of life, and so his story points to the one who would come in his order. As the eternal Son who has no beginning and as the incarnate Son who, after the resurrection, will never die, he is the only one who truly has no beginning or end (see also 13:8). It has now become clear what *is testified* in the psalm: *You are a priest forever according to the order of Melchizedek*. The one who is everlasting God came in the line of David, rose in defeat of death, to be priest eternally.

With the installation of this priest, there are both a removal and also an introduction. The *removal* that takes place is *of the earlier commandment*. The author has just stated that their Lord did not come according to the fleshly commandment. His installation as eternal High Priest showed that that command was no longer in effect. The commandment that priests had to be a part of the tribe of Levi was not followed in his instance, and because he is now High Priest and serves in this role forever, there is no longer a need for this command. To say that the earlier command has been "removed" (*athetēsis*) is a stronger statement than the one in v. 12, where the law was "changed" (*metathesis*). He has already stated that there has been a change in the law, and the statements about Aaron's priesthood are included in the law. A change in the law, though, could suggest that God is prone to mind-changing, which would make it difficult to trust God. To suggest a different priesthood could introduce doubt toward God, and so the author will have to address that issue (see comments on v. 21). It should be noted, however, that it is not the *law* that is removed, but the earlier *commandment*. The non-application of one of

12. Novenson, *Grammar of Messianism*, 90.

the commands aligns with a change in the law. In other words, by removing a command, the law has changed but not been obliterated.

The most challenging aspect of v. 18 comes with the causal phrase. The author adds that the commandment was removed ***because of*** *its weakness and uselessness*, a statement that could easily lend itself to the defamation of the Jewish law and, by implication, the Jewish people. This is compounded when the author adds the explanatory phrase *for the law perfected nothing*. The immediate context, however, prevents such a sweeping dismissal of the God-given Jewish law. In fact, were the law not from God, the author would have much less work to do. He could dismiss it outright. Instead, he has to show God's consistency both in giving the law *and* in the coming of the Son. The focus of this section is on *indestructible life*. The commandment for a Levitical priesthood was weak and useless *in this respect*. By its very nature, a commandment based on descent assumed death (as the author will state explicitly in v. 23). Because one generation died, those priests would have to be replaced by others. God's calling of Aaron and his Levitical sons to the priesthood did not grant them unending life. That priestly call, as valuable and important as it was, did not defeat the power of death. Therefore, it is in this respect that the author can say that the law perfected nothing. This is a statement that shows the possibility of this author's awareness of Paul's teaching on this subject (Rom 3:20–21; 8:3; 10:4; Gal 2:16). The law, even the commandment pertaining to the priesthood, was good for the people of Israel, chiefly in that it maintained God's presence among the people. However, it did not solve the problem of death, but instead had to work within death's continuing dominance.

Positively, when a new priest is installed and the old command is removed, that opens the door for *the introduction of a better hope*, a hope *through which*, the author can say to his readers, *we draw near to God*. Because of their High Priest, they have the sure hope that as they follow him, they are on the way to dwelling with God (2:10; 6:18–20). Since he dwells with God in the state of indestructible life, and they share in him, they have the same hope of resurrected dwelling with God. Jesus has opened a way to God that was previously impossible through participation in the law. Everyone listening can now draw near because they participate in the one who is perfected and makes their perfection possible.

The author returns to his discussion of oaths, which last appeared at the end of ch. 6 (vv. 13–20). The priesthood of Jesus about which he has been speaking did not lack this process: *And since this was not without an oathtaking.* He uses *horkōmosia* here as opposed to *horkos*, which he used in ch. 6 (vv. 13, 16, 17). The extended term, which is a combination of the noun *horkos* and the verb for swearing, *omnuō*, gives the oath discussed here in ch. 7 a heightened emphasis over that of ch. 6. God's oath to Abraham provided an important example, but the oath God gives to Jesus is something of even more weight.

Unlike Jesus, *there are those who have become priests without oathtaking.* God did call Aaron and his descendants to be priests (Exod 28:1). It is even written that they would have the priesthood perpetually (Exod 29:9, 28), yet God did not swear (*omnuō*) when installing Aaron as priest. The Melchizedekian priesthood, on the other hand, does have this weighty addition. *But he* became a priest *with oathtaking, through the one who said to him, "The Lord swore and will not change his mind; you are a priest forever."* The author has not yet mentioned God explicitly in ch. 7. Instead, he has been evoking God's presence through the mention of the oathtaking, but now the audience hears the voice of the Lord. For the third time in the sermon, the author cites Psalm 109:4 LXX, which he has been preparing to discuss since 5:6. Situated within the often-cited psalm, this statement comes to the same one whom God invited to sit at the right hand, the same one to whom God promised total sovereignty (Heb 1:13), the one who is the Son of God (5:5–6). To *this* one God swears the priesthood and will not regret it nor change course from the installment (see these meanings for the term for "change" in 2 Cor 7:8 or Matt 21:29, 32; 27:3).

The format of God's oath is similar to the example of Abraham. There God issued both a promise and an oath (6:13–14). Here, in this text, God's call and oath recall the two unchangeable things on which the listeners' sure hope is built (6:18). God's declarative pronouncement would be sufficient (*you are a priest forever*), but with the addition of the oath (*the Lord swore*) it is *even more* assuring that God will not alter this decision to install the Son of God as High Priest forever.

The author's statements about the change in the law and the removal of the command (7:12, 18), especially in light of the scriptural assertions of the perpetual priesthood of Aaron (Exod 29:9, 28), present a difficulty that demands attention. One would be excused for wondering if God made a promise that was then revoked. It could be this worry that motivates the author to emphasize the distinction between the priesthoods with regard to oaths. For Jesus,

God made an oath; for Aaron, God did not. That reason alone, however, seems a bit cheap. Is an oath added as a way to negate a former promise? The flow of the text indicates, instead, that the author sets up the argument differently than simply the "trumping" factor of the oath.

More coherent interpretations of the difficulty exist. Exodus 40 indicates, "And you shall bring Aaron and his sons near . . . and they shall serve me as priests, and it shall be so that their anointing for priesthood is forever for their generations" (40:12, 15). The perpetuity of that priesthood would continue throughout *their* generations, but now that the last days have arrived (Heb 1:2) and the coming world has broken in (1:6; 2:5), their generations have ceased. It is also true that the author speaks in the present tense when he speaks of the men who are appointed as priests (7:28). Since he imagines sharers in Jesus doing priestly activities (serving, 12:28; offering sacrifice of praise, 13:15), those in the line of Levi and Aaron could be priests forever, no longer providing daily abeyance of the infecting power of sin, but if they are members of the faithful who looked ahead to the promises of God (11:29), they could be serving under the leadership of the perpetual High Priest, Jesus. Hence it could be that their priesthood is not "replaced" by that of Jesus but enveloped within it.

Most importantly, the author has clarified his meaning of the terms for change and removal by asserting that while it was beneficial for maintaining the covenant, the Levitical priesthood never defeated death and so, even before its establishment, God foreshadowed that Levitical priesthood culminating in the living priesthood with Melchizedek. God has not "changed his mind" or negated a promise with an oath; rather, from the beginning of the covenant, God disclosed the intent for a perpetual priesthood in an order distinct from the line of Abraham/Levi. Within that intent God called the Levites to demonstrate the truths of priesthood—namely, God's desire to dwell among an unholy people. Then, when the end of the ages had arrived, God allowed the demonstrative priesthood to reach its fulfillment in the living priesthood of Christ. The priesthood lasts because its demonstrative quality is caught up into Jesus's priestly ministry. The priesthood of Christ was always the only perpetual one, for whom and with whom others serve.

In v. **22**, to articulate the aim of quoting this trustworthy statement from God, the author completes the thought begun in v. 20. *According to this, he has become security for a better covenant.* This is the first explicit introduction of the term *covenant* in the letter. Much like he introduced the name of Melchizedek some time before he treated his story, the author does not immediately describe this better covenant, but he introduces the concept in order to prepare his hearers for it. The "betterness" of the covenant connects it most recently with the better hope, by which they draw near to God (7:19). Since covenants establish and maintain relationships, and this covenant is related to that hope of drawing near, it seems a safe conclusion that this covenant will allow access to God. In other words, this covenant is the "better things" the author had in mind for his audience (6:9). Jesus functions here as their *security* of this covenant. Much like the imagery at the end of ch. 6, the embodied Lord, about whom they heard and who is now seated at God's right hand, is the tangible reality to which they can hold concerning their future hope. He is the anchor of what is to come. He is the guarantee of what this covenant promises.

Before the author turns to the subject of the covenant as his main focus, he first brings out another point of contrast between Jesus and the other priests. The introduction of covenant followed by a return to the priesthood demonstrates that these concepts are connected for the author, as his following argument will make clear. In v. **23** he states that in the Levitical system, *there are many who have become priests because they were prevented from remaining by death*. Two contrasts are at play here. First, Jesus is singular and the Levitical priests are many. Second, they die and Jesus lives. This is the weakness and uselessness of the commandment that installed them. It did not allow them to defeat death. In the Levitical system, the office of the priesthood continued even though the people serving the office changed, because they died and needed to be replaced. The Scriptures of Israel did not mourn this fact, so the author is making a new and quite radical point. He is showing his readers that death is not something that they should accept but something from which they should long to be redeemed.

On the other hand, Jesus, the singular priest, *has an unchanging priesthood because he remains forever*, as God has sworn in the psalm and fulfilled with the incarnation and resurrection. His priesthood will not be broken, nor will he turn away from it. (The descriptive term *unchanging, aparabatos*, appears only here in the New Testament, but its opposite, *parabatos*, appears in Matt 15:2–3 and Acts 1:25, indicating a break or departure.) This statement aligns with the presentation in ch. 1 that God installed Jesus into this priestly order when he died and then was resurrected, after which he was no longer subject to death in his humanity. Only then could it be said that Jesus, taken from among humans, could never cease to live.

A lack of trust in the Jewish priesthood could be under the surface here. No one could bribe God, as happened in the time of the Hasmoneans, in order to change this priesthood. If the letter is post-70, this assurance would add another needed reminder. No one could destroy Jesus's priesthood because no one could kill him or raid and burn the heavenly tabernacle where he serves. Frustration with the instability or cessation of the Jewish priesthood makes this point about his perpetual priesthood incredibly meaningful for a first-century community. Although the exigencies are different, Christians throughout time who have reason to doubt their spiritual authorities, who should be in line with and appropriately represent Jesus the High Priest (see 13:17), can nevertheless trust in Jesus's authority when leaders do not live up to his standards.

Because he remains forever, *he is able to save to the fullest extent those who are approaching God through him.* The good of his priesthood, however, is not just that he is one consistent person. The good of his priesthood is that, by virtue of his unchanging person, he brings salvation. As the author states, *he is able to save.* Salvation is something in which the audience is already included, and they are journeying toward the fullness of it (1:14; 2:3, 10; 5:9; 6:9; 9:28). But as a verb in Hebrews, saving is something only God and Jesus do. God is able to save Jesus out of death (5:7), and Jesus is able to save others (7:25). Jesus is doing the same action as God because, as God and as a human who has defeated death, he has the power to do so.

In 5:9 Jesus became the cause of eternal salvation for a particular group—namely, those who obey him. Here, with a similar claim, the author states that Jesus has the power to save a particular group—namely, *those who are approaching God.* Approaching is an action to which the author has already called himself and his audience (4:16, as he will do again in 10:22). They do not have to approach God on their own, but they approach *through him.* Jesus is the one in whom they participate (3:1, 14), their forerunner (2:10; 6:20), as well as their priestly representative and advocate. Drawing near to God is a priestly act (Lev 9, 21; Num 16), and he gives them access to the very throne of God in heaven (Heb 4:16). Their High Priest allows them to follow him in priestly entrance.

The author describes his salvific act as that which is *to the fullest extent.* His saving act is able to go the distance, to bring them to the end of their journey, a vital encouragement for those who still have a way to go before they reach God's rest (4:11; 12:2). Moreover, the nature of his salvation is comprehensive. His perpetual resurrected life indicates that they will share in the same. Any contemporary bifurcation between the soul and the body, in which the salvation of the soul alone is the extent of the Christian hope, would fall short of what Hebrews describes here. The sermon suggests that as they follow the pattern of Jesus, they will inherit a salvation of the body as well. Moreover, his saving act is communal and cosmic; it will install all of those who are approaching God as sovereigns over God's creation (Ps 8/Heb 2:8). This salvation is so much more than the preservation of an individual ephemeral soul. Instead, it is a robust and full-orbed saving act for all God's creation.

This complete salvation is possible because Jesus is always living to petition for them. Because death can never defeat him, it is possible for him to be a priestly advocate forever. Priests offer sacrifices for sins, and Jesus did that once and for all when he offered his resurrected self to God. At the same time, his mediating work before God is not done. Priests also represent people to God and in that way plead their case for forgiveness and continued divine presence.[13] Julian of Norwich connects the salvific effect of Jesus's blood with his ascended body, seemingly in response to this passage in Hebrews: "The precious plenty of his beloved blood ascended up into heaven . . . and is in him there, bleeding and praying for us to the Father—and is and shall be for as long as it is needed."[14] Jesus's perpetual life serves the purpose of petitioning for those who are approaching God through him. To petition is fittingly associated with prayer since it describes crying out to God (Rom 11:2; 1 En. 9:3).[15] This particular word (*entynchanō*) is not used to describe the activity of priests in Israel's Scriptures. However, since its basic meaning points toward being present with,[16] this is an especially apt term to describe the activity of Jesus, who is not praying to God from a distance but sitting enthroned at God's right hand. This is the same term Paul uses for Jesus's and the Spirit's petitioning before

13. See Nehemiah Polen, "Leviticus and Hebrews . . . and Leviticus," in Bauckham et al., *Epistle to the Hebrews and Christian Theology*, 216.

14. Julian of Norwich, *Revelations of Divine Love*, trans. Barry Windeatt (Oxford: Oxford University Press, 2015), 57–58. The explanatory notes suggest a connection with Heb 7:25, 9:14, and 12:24 (184).

15. Koester, *Hebrews*, 366.

16. "*Entynchanō*," LSJ, 578.

God the Father (Rom 8:27, 34), giving evidence of a common understanding of divine advocacy in early Christian circles. Moreover, Jesus's priesthood is a living one, in which his defeat of death allows him to pray for his followers to overcome their own deaths as well. He petitions God to aid their endurance, the very plan God desires and is already playing out (Heb 2:10; 12:5–11). Jesus need not win over the recalcitrant Father with his pleading; rather, he asks for that which is already in line with the divine will, and does so in person with God in heaven. If God the Father and God the Son are for this Christian community, who can stand against them (as the author will say in 13:6, as does Paul in Rom 8:31)? If the author is gravely worried about the possibility that they may not endure in faith, he is even more confident in God's ability to ensure that very same endurance.

The perpetual life of the Son raises the question about the possibility of his eternal petitioning. Once those who are approaching God arrive at God's rest, would there be any need for him to continue to plead their case? No longer will sin or death be a problem, but this statement does open the door to the possibility of continued growth in eternity, and a Son who always advocates for it.

For the second time in the letter, in v. **26** the author utilizes an argument from fittingness. *Such a High Priest was fitting for us*. It is not the case that they *deserve* such a High Priest. They were slaves to death (2:14), are prone to evil (3:12), and are currently immature (5:11–12). The fittingness arises because the human condition is such that they *need* one who can petition for them at the right hand of God and save them to the fullest extent. The author uses five words and phrases to describe their High Priest. He first describes him as *holy*. This specific term for holiness appears in Hebrews only in this verse but is used by authors of the New Testament literature to indicate one who is devout or set apart (1 Tim 2:8; Titus 1:8); it is also used to describe Jesus and God (Acts 2:37; 13:35/Ps 15:10 LXX; Rev 15:5; 16:4). *Innocent* is also a unique word in Hebrews, clearly delineating a freedom from evil. This could describe an untested simplicity, which opens one up to deception (Rom 16:18), but in Hebrews this kind of innocence is evidence of maturity as the goal of training, which is to discern evil and then avoid it (Heb 5:14). Their High Priest has always made the right choice in this regard. Finally, their representative before God is *undefiled*. He is not tainted with anything bad but is full of what is good in God's sight (Heb 13:4; Jas 1:27; 1 Pet 1:4). The first three terms, *holy*, *innocent*, and *undefiled*, focus on his sinlessness, as asserted in 4:15. The fourth does as well, but it also acts as a transition to the next idea. He is *one who has been separated from sinners*, thus emphasizing his distinct holiness from all other humans while also pointing to his change in location, stated clearly in the final descriptor. He is finally *one who has become higher than the heavens*. The term *heavens* is often plural in Hebrews, in which it denotes the holy layers of the upper and divine regions, as was common in Judaism.[17] Their High Priest can move through them all into the very realm of God (see also 9:24), and that is where he dwells in his resurrected state.

Having emphasized his holiness and his location, the author returns to Jesus's sinlessness with another comparison to other high priests. He *does not have need each day—as the high priests—to first offer sacrifices for his own sins, then for those of the people*. This dual procedure, for themselves and for others, is the process for the high priest on the Day of Atonement (Lev 16:6), but this was not a daily but a yearly sacrifice, which the author of Hebrews clearly knows (Heb 9:7, 25; 10:1, 3). It was possible that the priest could sin unintentionally (Lev 4:1–12) and need to offer for himself, which could occur at any time. Moreover, the ordination sacrifices are interpreted as an offering for the sin of the priest (Lev 9:8). Within the framework of the weakness of the priests, the author is not saying that they offered daily sacrifices for themselves, but the need to do so, because they were caught up in human sin and mortality, was ever present.

Differently, their High Priest did this *once for all, offering up himself*. The distinction is twofold. First, he does not need to offer for the people repeatedly, because his singular offering was sufficient once and for all. Second, he does not offer *for* himself, because he is sinless (4:15).[18] Instead he offers himself. If the author did in fact use the preposition *ana* with the verb for "offer," as many manuscripts have it, the word has an upward connotation and so aligns with the imagery of the Son presenting himself as the living offering at the ascension.

17. 2 Cor 12:2; 2 En. 1–20; Ascen. Isa. 7–9

18. I appreciate the argument of Justin Duff ("'With Loud Cries and Tears'") that if Christ had sinful flesh, he would have needed to make an offering for the flesh he willingly took on. Because the author has so thoroughly emphasized Jesus's sinlessness in this paragraph, it seems he is saying that Jesus did not have to make two offerings, one for himself and one for others, but only one *of himself* for others who were sinful.

Finally, the author includes one final contrast between priests, which summarizes his argument in ch. 7. *The law appointed men who have weakness as high priests, but the word of the oath, which comes after the law, appoints a son who has been perfected forever.* First, he reiterates the earlier argument about oaths. According to his previous treatment (6:13–18 and 7:20–21), an oath is more powerful than the law alone. Moreover, the statement of the oath *after the law* shows that the law was not permanent. In addition, because the oath concerns Melchizedek, a pre-law figure, the oath indicates that the law was never in existence without the order of Melchizedek present in the plan of God. Second, the author evokes the shared call that Jesus has with other priests—both are appointed—but the identity of the appointees is distinct. Distinguishing *son* versus *men* highlights the connection Jesus has with God, which is unparalleled by any other (1:5; 5:5).

Finally, the men have *weakness*, but the Son *has been perfected forever*. Weakness is a human condition (4:15; 5:2), indicating that humans are entangled in sin and subject to death. For all other humans save Jesus, these have been an inescapable reality. Hence, the other high priests can offer little help to humans because they find themselves similarly entrapped. The Son, however, is the only one who has been fully perfected. He has always been perfect with regard to sin, both as the eternal, divine Son of God and as the sinless human, but now he has also been perfected with regard to death. Hence, he has been perfected *forever*. He is mature, has completed the task to which God has called him (see 10:5–14), and dwells in a resurrected body in the realm of perfection with God. Jesus is a priest separated from the listeners' situation. He is not sinful, nor mortal, nor on earth. These distinctions do not, however, make him distant. Instead, they are the aspects that make him an effective priest, so that as he prays for them, he can make a true difference in their future and in their journey toward it.

Although Christians have been familiar with the idea of Jesus's priesthood for millennia, the ingenuity of the author of Hebrews should not be missed. He is committed to the belief that the Son is eternal God, and that this truth has been revealed in the life, death, and resurrection of Jesus Christ. From that commitment, he reads the Scriptures of Israel to develop a priestly Christology.

If the listeners are wondering if God will change the priesthood again as happened from the line of Levi to Jesus, they have two guarantees that this will not happen. First, God swears to Jesus and did not swear to Aaron. Second, and even more assuring concerning the trustworthiness of God's character, God had planned for this priesthood even before Levi's birth and even before Aaron's call. The priesthood of Melchizedek was always meant to be the permanent one, and the priesthood of the Levites pointed the way to its own fulfillment.

HEBREWS 8:1–10:18

THE NEW COVENANT

Enclosed within the dual citation of Jeremiah's new-covenant prophecy (Heb 8:8–12 and 10:16–17), this central section of Hebrews presents the need for and the effects of Christ's priesthood. It is central in the sense that it lies near the middle of the sermon, and also in that it is where the author invests the most to support his distinct argument that Jesus is both Son of God and High Priest. Although this section of the commentary is lengthy, it is ideal to keep the pieces of it tethered together to see the relationship among the passages and the flow of the argument more clearly.

The rather succinct summary at the beginning of ch. 8 draws together the points of the sermon given thus far. This community has an exalted High Priest who is a servant. The *place* of his service takes prominence in vv. 1–5. He could not have served on earth, in the tent that replicated the heavenly, but serves instead in the true tent built by the Lord. With the introduction to the citation of Jeremiah (vv. 6–7), the *nature* of his service takes precedence: it is a better ministry. His superior priestly service is to mediate a superior covenant.

In vv. 8–12 the author cites from Jeremiah 38:31–34 LXX, the longest citation of Israel's Scriptures among the New Testament texts. Here the voice of the Lord delineates the shortfall of the covenant God made with the house of Israel and Judah after the exodus—namely, that the people did not remain in it. God's faithfulness to this people issues forth in the promise of a new covenant, which will implant God's laws within the people, leading to a renewal of the depth and breadth of their relationship with God along with God's merciful forgetting of their sins. The author shares his interpretation of the prophecy in v. 13: when God said "new" through Jeremiah, the first became old, and old things are on their way out.

Having introduced the words of God that compare and contrast the covenants, in ch. 9 the author will do the same. He first focuses on the holy tent and the objects in each section of it (vv. 1–5). He readily admits that he does not go into the detail that Israel's Scriptures do with these descriptions, but he gives enough to grant a basic picture—a map—in the minds of his listeners.

He creates this mental picture in order to describe the activity that happens therein (9:1–10). The daily work of the priests and the yearly work of the high priest do not facilitate entry into the true heavenly sanctuary because that priestly work attends to the flesh and not the conscience. It was not intended to last forever, but only until the time of restoration.

The next set of verses (vv. 11–15) continues the comparison between covenantal practices and utilizes them to highlight Christ's priestly work—namely, where he offers, what he offers, and its effects. The author speaks again of the amazing results of the new covenant (v. 15) and then compares it to two other covenants in which death is involved, human wills (vv. 16–17) and the first covenant (vv. 18–22). That prepares him to focus on Christ's work again, the purification of heaven itself when Christ appears before God (vv. 23–25). Christ's singular entry and enduring appearance are set in contrast with the repetitive offering of the high priests. Because Jesus is offering himself, and does so through the process of death, as would be true for any human, this offering can happen only once (vv. 26–27). Verse 28 summarizes what the author has proclaimed throughout this paragraph—namely, the suffering death of Christ and his living appearance before God—adding his eagerly anticipated return.

In ch. 10 the author balances the goodness of God's law in the first covenant with its insufficiency. The frequent offerings only served to remind the worshipers and God of the persistent reality of sin. The author then presents a portion of Psalm 39 LXX on the lips of the Son of God as he is coming into the world (vv. 5–7). The psalmist, in line with many of the prophets, sees that God's desire is not first and foremost for sacrifice but for obedience. Because the Greek text asserts that God prepares a body for the speaker, this psalm serves as an affirmation of the incarnation and how that act is the beginning of the process that accomplishes God's will. The author repeats the psalm, gathering up the negative assessments of the sacrifices and juxtaposing them not only with the Son's *hope* to do God's will (as is true in the psalm) but also with the Son's assurance of accomplishing it (vv. 8–10). Finally, he clarifies the result of God's will—namely, sanctification.

The author then returns for the final time in this long section to a comparison between the former system of sacrifice and that of Christ. Naming six points of contrast (vv. 11–12), he joins Christ's sacrificial work to his session, alluding to Psalm 110:1 yet another time (v. 13). With the work of Christ presented, and their understanding of it deepened, his listeners are now ready to hear the Holy Spirit speak the prophecy of Jeremiah *to them*, and the author adjusts the citation to that end (vv. 15–17). His final statement is a simple one: where there is a release of sins, there is no longer an offering for them. The author's in-depth analysis of the sacrificial system in light of Christ—his most distinct contribution to the New Testament literature—is now complete.

8:1–13 · JEREMIAH'S PROPHECY

[1]And the headline of the things said is this: We have such a High Priest, who sat down
at the right hand of the throne of the majesty in the heavens, [2]a minister of the holy
place, even the true tent, which the Lord built, not a human. [3]For every high priest is
appointed to offer both gifts and sacrifices; whence it was necessary also for this one
to have something that he might offer. [4]Therefore, if he was on earth, he would not
have been a priest, being one of those who offer gifts according to the law, [5]who serve
an example and shadow of the heavenly, just as it was revealed to Moses when he was
about to complete the tent, for God said, "See that you make everything according
to the type showed to you on the mountain." [6]But now he has obtained a superior
ministry inasmuch as he is a mediator of a better covenant, which is legislated on
better promises.

[7]For if that first [covenant] was blameless, a place would not have been sought
for a second. [8]For finding fault with them, God says,

> *Behold, days are coming, says the Lord, and I will complete with the house of*
> *Israel and with the house of Judah a new covenant, [9]not according to the covenant*
> *that I made with their fathers in a day when I took them by their hand to lead*
> *them from the land of Egypt, because they did not continue in my covenant, and*
> *I neglected them, says the Lord.*
>
> *[10]This is the covenant that I will covenant with the house of Israel after those*
> *days, says the Lord, giving my laws into their mind, and I will write them on their*
> *hearts, and I will be their God and they will be my people, [11]and each will not*

teach his fellow citizen and each his sibling, saying, "Know the Lord," because all will know me from the least to the greatest of them [12]*because I will be merciful with their instances of unrighteousness and their sins I will not still remember.*

[13]*In saying "new" God made the first old, and that which is old and gray is near disappearing.*

At this important transition point, the author uses the term *kephalaion*. It is a cognate to the multidimensional word *kephalē*, meaning, at base, "head," so *headline* seems an appropriate English translation. The headline will act as the sum *of the things said*. These things certainly include the focus on priesthood, which began at 4:14, but since mentions of Jesus's priestly service appear before then (1:3; 2:9, 17; 3:1), it is not wrong to see this as summing up the whole of the sermon. In v. **1** readers hear the compilation of all the author has discussed put into a succinct statement. The large, boldfaced headline is this: *We have such a High Priest*. What follows is the author's reiteration of what he has asserted about the *kind* of High Priest they are privileged to have.

Utilizing Psalm 110:1 as the first point of summary, the author suggests that this High Priest is one who has finished his work, indicated by the fact that he is one *who sat down*. Session indicates accomplishment (see also a royal example in 2 Sam 5:9). He takes his seat at the place of greatest power conceivable, God's right hand, drawn out with the poetic and respectful-of-the-divine elocution: *the right hand of the throne of the majesty in the heavens*. This is the third of six times the author refers to the right hand of God, all grounded in Psalm 110:1, cited first in 1:13, which is the most basic: "Sit at my right." This example in ch. 8 is the most drawn out with three descriptors of the right hand, in comparison with the other allusions, which include only two descriptors.

Ps 110:1/Heb 1:13	sit at my	right				
Heb 1:3	sat	right of			majesty	heights
Heb 8:1	sat	right of	throne		majesty	heavens
Heb 10:12	sat	right of		God		
Heb 12:2	sat	right of	throne	God		

As this is the sum total of the things he is speaking about, it makes sense that this citation in 8:1 is the most fulsome description.

A throne certainly indicates God's power, and the *right hand of the throne* is a place of respect and strength (see commentary on 1:13). Since God the Father did declare that the Son has an eternal throne himself (1:8), the statement that he is at the right hand of God's throne does not indicate a place beside God as less important than God the Father, but points to the shared power the Son has with the Father. *Right hand of the throne* aligns with other descriptions of the Son as fully God (as God's radiance and imprint, 1:3), who, like a hand from a body, enacts the divine power. It is a common throne Father and Son share as God to which the faithful can approach (4:16).[1] Here the author describes that throne as the throne of *majesty*, a frequently named quality of God proclaimed in response to God's acts of mercy and power (Deut 32:3; 1 Chr 29:11; Ps 78:11; 144:3, 6). Finally, the author says to his community that their High Priest has taken his seat at a location that is in *the heavens*. He has stated this fact about Christ's priesthood twice already (4:14; 7:26), but by doing so here, he is preparing for the focused discussion of the locale of Jesus's ministry.

Verse **2** repeats and enriches the assertions of v. 1. Although Christ is seated and his work of offering is completed forever (9:27), he is still working as a *minister*. Their High Priest, who could be exalted no higher than the very throne of the sovereign God, is also a servant. As a basic word for service of any kind, in Israel's Scriptures *leitourgos* becomes associated with cultic activities (Ezra 7:24; Neh 10:39; Isa 61:6). The author of Hebrews applies it to angels (1:7, 14), Jesus (8:2, 6), and the cult of Israel (9:21, 10:11). The one who reveals God does so as king and priestly minister.

The author uses two phrases for what the High Priest serves, the holies and the true tent. The plural of *hagios* in Hebrews is most often used to denote the sacred space of the tabernacle, *the holy place* (9:2, 3, 8, 12, 24, 25; 10:19; 13:11). The second phrase, then, clarifies *which* holy space the author has in mind. This is *the true tent, which the Lord built, not a human.* As the one who is Lord (1:10), he is serving in the place that he, as God, built. This is the first of two times that the author describes the tabernacle in this way (see also 9:24). It is not a statement that the comparative tabernacle, the one on earth, is false, since it was commissioned by God. Instead, the author uses "true" in the sense of being the template. The true tent sets the standard on which the earthly is patterned (8:5).

1. Bauckham, *Jesus and the God of Israel*, 250n38.

To further explain this divinely built tent, the author draws another comparison. Since *every high priest is appointed to offer both gifts and sacrifices,* and the Son is a High Priest, *it was necessary also for this one to have something that he might offer.* As he stated in ch. 5, priests are appointed to offer both gifts and sacrifices (5:1). The author mentions both terms that often appear in Israel's Scriptures, not to point to two different things, but to explain each other (a gift *is* a sacrifice; Lev 2; 3:1, 6; 6:20; 7; 21:6, 21; Num 5:15; 7; 15:4; Job 20:6 LXX; Isa 66:20). Later in v. 4 he simply refers to the things offered as gifts. The double terminology here reminds readers that giving to God was costly. A theological insight is present as well. With the eternal High Priest, God has not moved away from the system previously established; in both, priests make offerings. There has been, however, a modulation. The High Priest still offers, and it was a costly process to make that offering. The differences are that his offering is personally costly in a way no other Levitical sacrifice has been and that his offering is not made on earth.

Therefore if he was on earth, he would not have been a priest, being one of those who offer gifts according to the law. The author does not state the reasons for Jesus's lack of earthly cultic vocation again, but he has previously named two. First, this High Priest is not of the correct tribe to offer in alignment with the law. He is not a Levite but a Judahite (7:14). Second, he makes his offering according to God's oath (in Ps 110:4), not according to the law (7:28). Hence, he would not meet the qualifications for gift-offering to be a priest on earth. This is not an embarrassment the author has to explain but an advantage he will soon explicate.

The priests on earth lawfully offer their sacrificial gifts in a location where they *serve an example and shadow of the heavenly.* There is a true holy place that the Lord built in heaven, and an example of it on earth. Examples are helpful things. They give a picture of a reality so that those who observe the examples can better understand and respond to the reality. This author knows how to understand the impact of Christ's death and resurrection because he has had the example of the tabernacle to study. *Shadow* is also not a negative assessment of the tent on earth. Shadows can indicate bad or good; it all depends on the object to which the shadow is attached (for example, the New Testament mentions the shadow of death [Matt 4:16; Luke 1:79], but also Peter's shadow that brings healing [Acts 5:15]). A shadow, like an example, gives evidence of another reality.

The author has a clear text from Scripture for his assertion of the type of relationship that exists between the heavenly and the earthly tents. It is *just as it was revealed to Moses when he was about to complete the tent, for God said, "See that you make everything according to the type showed to you on the mountain."* God showed Moses a tabernacle in heaven, and Moses was to copy it in all respects with the tent and its instruments on earth. In Exodus 25, God states this process of following a pattern to Moses twice (25:9, 40); in both instances God does so before specifying many details. The tabernacle on earth is not a cheap knockoff. It is a precise replica of what God revealed to Moses. The author's goal with this comparison, it seems, is not to say how poor the tent on earth was. On the contrary, that example gave humans the picture by which they could understand God's holy heavenly space and, ultimately, the final sacrifice the Messiah offered within it.

Just because that ministry in the earthly tent was good, however, does not mean that it was equal to its heavenly pattern. Shadows can be positive, but when compared with the object casting the shadow, substance is to be preferred over shadow (see the use of this argument in Col 2:17). The other priests had a divinely ordained ministry, *but now he has obtained a superior ministry*, even over theirs. He has taken hold of a service that is even better than theirs was, because he serves in the heavenly reality rather than the earthly shadow.

At v. **6** the author pivots from the *place* of service to the *impact* of the service. Their High Priest's service is superior *inasmuch as he is a mediator of a better covenant.* His service and the covenant within which he serves are intimately related.

In ch. 7, when the term "covenant" first appeared, the author asserted that Jesus is the surety of a better covenant (7:22). It is now clear that he is the guarantee of this covenant because his service is to be the mediator of it, bridging the relationship between God and humanity that is possible within this superior covenant. With a clear sense of his superior ministry—effective, perpetual, living, and heavenly—the author is now ready to attend to the covenant within which he serves, mentioned but as yet undeveloped at 7:22.

This better covenant *is legislated on better promises.* The author of Hebrews does not place law on one side with the old covenant and promise on the other side with the better covenant. Instead, both the old and the new covenants have laws, and both have promises. God made a promise to Abraham (6:13) in the first covenant. With the better covenant, God made a promise to Jesus that he would be priest forever (Ps 110:4/Heb 5:6; 7:17, 21). The author has already shown the superiority of God's promise to Jesus, a promise of perpetual life. In the first covenant, through Abraham's descendants the Levites, the people experienced the law (7:11). In the better covenant, the people will also experience God's law (see 8:10 and 10:16).

As faithful and beneficial as the first covenant was, it was not blameless. The author deduces that since there is a new covenant mentioned by God in Israel's Scriptures, that means the old was not flawless. God decided to establish a new one. With a contrary to fact condition, the author reveals his logic: *For if that first [covenant] was blameless, a place would not have been sought for a second.* The author does not name specifically that he is speaking of a first and second *covenant*, but because he has just mentioned a better covenant (8:6) and because the citation will speak of a new covenant (8:8), this seems a likely inference. The passive verb *ezēteito*, "have been sought," suggests that it is God who is doing the seeking, confirmed by the citation where God does the speaking/establishing of the covenant. The author uses *place* metaphorically here, as he does in 12:17, and so "opportunity" would be a fitting translation for that which God was seeking. Nevertheless, because the citation does emphasize the internal location of the covenant, a word that has locative connotations (*place*) prepares for that point.

The author introduces the citation as God's words proclaimed in alignment with God's fault finding. Something was wrong, and so God spoke to change it. A textual variant leaves translators curious about whether it is best to render the text as God found fault with them (*autous*) or as God spoke to them (*autois*). Even if the dative pronoun ("to them") is to be preferred—and the majority of commentators do *not* take this position—it still leaves open the option of the fault residing in the people. For, finding fault (assumed: in the people), God spoke to them. As the following citation will make clear, the people committed errors. They were faithless in ways the author has already warned against (Heb 3–4). God did find fault *with them.*

On the other hand, vv. 7 and 8a place culpability in both the covenant and the people. God makes *this* covenant with *this* people, and so they are intertwined. God sees the fault in the whole system and so speaks to the people who participate in it. Striking in consistency as well as grace, when the people do not abide by the covenant, God does not give up on the people, nor the laws specified in the covenant, but on the modality of the covenant itself. God proclaims such a radical change that the author can describe these instantiations as a first and second covenant.

Throughout the sermon, the author has asserted his belief in God's sovereignty and holiness, so in asserting that God found fault, the author is not describing a moment in which God slaps his hand on his forehead in frustration over an error. I suggest instead that God's creation of the first covenant with these fault lines included therein was the pathway to the second covenant. The old had everything *perfectly* in order to point to the new. It was a covenant set up to point forward beyond itself.

After this negative introduction, the author cites from Jeremiah 38:31–34 LXX, the longest citation of Israel's Scriptures in the New Testament. Jeremiah 38 LXX is also set in a wilderness, but the prophet is not speaking to the same generation the author of Hebrews had discussed earlier in the sermon with his allusions to Numbers and the citations of Psalm 94 LXX (Heb 3–4). Jeremiah speaks to the people of Israel whose *ancestors* went into the land of promise with Joshua, settled, built kingdoms, and then, because of unfaithfulness to God, were forced away from the land and back into the wilderness of exile. Jeremiah recounts a wilderness situation in which the people, because of God's purgative work among them, have prayed and sought God in repentance (Jer 36:11–12 LXX). They are asking to return to God's place of blessing. Jeremiah describes an incredible act of graciousness where God *goes out* to the wilderness to bring the wounded and enslaved children home.

Beginning with this portion of Jeremiah 38 LXX is attractive to this author for multiple reasons:

- *Behold, days are coming.* God's statement is forward-looking. It points toward a particular set of days, days that are future for Jeremiah but that align with the last days, the time of the author of Hebrews and his congregation (Heb 1:2).
- *Says the Lord.* This passage is the direct speech of the Lord, the type of text the author most often cites.[2] He does so to highlight God as the one who speaks.
- *And I will complete.* The passage speaks of completion or perfection, a consistent and important theme in the sermon. The only other time

2. Pierce, *Divine Discourse*; Docherty, *Old Testament in Hebrews*, 157.

the author uses this particular word (*synteleō*) is for the completion of the ages (9:26) brought about by the work of Christ. As he will show in this section, the completion of the new covenant as well is made possible by the work of Jesus. Most extant manuscripts of the Greek translations of the Hebrew instead use the verb *diathēkē* here, suggesting the author used a different term (*synteleō*), which conveys the same idea but in such a way that it fits in with the key theme of perfection in his sermon.[3]

- *With the house of Israel and with the house of Judah.* The passage shows God's faithfulness to the covenant people. God is making a new covenant but with the same people, who multiple times over had rebelled against God. This confirms God's propensity to grant mercy. In fact, in the verse after the author's citation, God assures that even if creation changes, God will not reject the people of Israel (Jer 38:35 LXX). Because the citation uses the descriptor "house," it reiterates what the author said about him and his people making up the house of God, the seed of Abraham (Heb 2:16; 3:6; see also 10:21).

Readers familiar with the whole New Testament will hear the echoes of "new covenant" in Paul and Luke. While Matthew and Mark have Jesus describe the cup as his "blood of the covenant" (a phrase Hebrews quotes from Exod 24 in 9:20), only Luke portrays him saying, "This cup is the new covenant in my blood" (Luke 22:20), a clear allusion to Jeremiah. Paul includes precisely the same phrase in 1 Corinthians 11:25 when he recounts the supper of the Lord. Both of them make the connection between Jesus's death and the new covenant explicit and immediate, but without a broader appeal to Jeremiah. The author of Hebrews takes the opposite approach. He spends significant time in Jeremiah before making several connections to Jesus's blood (9:12, 14, 25; 10:19, 29; 12:24; 13:12, 20) and the role it plays in his priesthood. It is as if the author of Hebrews takes the statement of Jesus and draws out its richness, in both its background meaning and its effects.[4]

3. See discussion of this variant in Pierce, *Divine Discourse*, 79–81.

4. Note also that Paul mentions his own ministry as being under the new covenant (2 Cor 3:6). For a treatment of this theme in the New Testament, see Scot McKnight, "Covenant and Spirit: The Origins of the New Covenant Hermeneutic," in *The Holy Spirit and*

To further these aspects of both continuity and change, the prophet differentiates this *new covenant* from another. It is *not according to the covenant that I made with their fathers.* To describe that covenant the prophet recalls the definitive event of the exodus, when, *in the day*, like a good parent, God says, *I took them by their hand to lead them from the land of Egypt.* Once they were delivered from slavery, Moses led the people to the mountain (Exod 19). This is when God made a covenant with them, but that covenant did not produce the endurance of faith. As God states, *They did not continue in my covenant.* The people not only created the golden calf shortly after agreeing to the covenant (Exod 32), but they also lacked trust in God throughout the journey into the land of promise. They did not continue to perform the promises they made in the covenant, because, most fundamentally, they did not continue to trust God. That lack of trust resulted in consequences. These lines of Jeremiah recall the author's lengthy treatment of the wilderness generation in chs. 3 and 4, but Jeremiah's context also includes those future generations who, once in the land, failed to continue in the covenant as well.

The prophet Jeremiah interjects again that it is the Lord who is speaking—*and I neglected them, says the Lord*—which serves to highlight God's frustration with the people. God's statement, *and I neglected them*, is ironic. God did not cease to pay attention to the people of Israel, and this is true in two respects. First, God was attentive to that generation, allowing the consequences to result from their decision not to act in trust. God turned away from them in the sense that God did not force them into the land when they lacked faith nor supported their desire to enter the land without God's support (Num 14:40–45). A separation developed between them and God, but this is not total abandonment on God's part but instead the gracious divine allowance of freedom and the consequences that flow from that freedom. "Neglect" carries a sense of irony for a second reason as well. In the next phrase God declares the establishment of a new covenant *with the same people*, the people of Israel. God has certainly not disregarded this group and left them alone. God has not neglected the house of Israel forever. God's neglect, meaning God's non-dwelling with the people, is in response to their actions (and inactions) that arose out of a lack of faith in God.

Christian Origins: Essays in Honor of James D. G. Dunn, ed. Stephen C. Barton et al. (Grand Rapids: Eerdmans, 2004).

In addition to highlighting God's grief over the course this generation chose to take, the repetition of *says the Lord* highlights the divine action in the giving of the new covenant. In Hebrews 8:10/Jeremiah 38:33 LXX, the voice of God pivots from recalling the previous covenant to describing the new one. Similar to v. 8, here in v. **10** God proclaims his action of making a covenant with the people of Israel that will take place in a future time. The ideas are the same, but the words and structure are slightly different. In this instance it is not called the new covenant again (as in Jer 38:31/Heb 8:8) but referred to with the phrase *this is the covenant.* Instead of completing (*syntelesō*) a covenant, this is a covenant, God says, *that I will covenant.* The prophet uses the verbal form of the noun *diathēkē* here to show the resonance between God's action and the thing God's action created. In this verse God's covenant is *with the house of Israel* rather than with the house of Israel and Judah. The lack of the mention of Judah does not exclude them but includes them in the more ancient name, that given to Jacob by God (Gen 32:28). Whereas the first announcement *starts* with the framing of the time, this proclamation *ends* with a temporal reference. This action will take place *after those days.* Listeners to Hebrews rightly wonder if God's promises for this new covenant are now coming to fruition in their time, since it is the last days (Heb 1:2). For the third time the prophet interjects that this is God's speech, by ending with *says the Lord*, maintaining direct focus on God's presence, voice, and action in this prophecy from Jeremiah.

In this covenant, what the acting God will do is named as *giving my laws into their minds and writ[ing] them on their hearts.* God acts graciously, freely giving to the people of Israel. This lines up with the character of God when the Son of God says that God gave children to him (2:13). In this instance, God gives *my laws.* The good that God laid out in the law, which was intended for the flourishing of creation, has not been abandoned and replaced with this new covenant but instead is retained within it. The laws themselves cannot bring perfection (7:19), especially the perfection of indestructible life. The laws are working within the repetitive reality of death but do not break the cycle of it as the death and resurrection of the incarnate Son of God does (2:14–15). That being the case, because the laws are designed by God the creator who desires good for creation, they can bring good. Hence, they remain integral to the lives of God's people, even within the perfected life that will continue forever.

In fact, the laws become more intimate to the people than was true previously. Joshua instructed the people of Israel to do the laws and serve God with their minds (Josh 22:5), and Deuteronomy instructs the people to have the law on their hearts (Deut 6:6; 10:16; 11:18; 30:2, 10, 14), but in this new covenant *God* places the laws internally (Deut 30:6 is resonant in that God's purging of the people's hearts prepares them to love God and live). The part of themselves that is prone to a lack of trust (Heb 3–4)—their hearts—is the very place where God inscribes the laws. The word for "inscription" is used for signs, coins, and monuments (Matt 22:20; Mark 12:16; 15:26; Luke 20:24; 23:38; Acts 17:23), and it conveys something more intentional and permanent than simple writing with ink. The laws will be impressed within them deeply.

With that internal work, there is confirmation of what God intended from the beginning. When God made covenant with the people of Israel, God established the relationship and gave the law (Exod 19:4–6). Earlier in the prophecy of Jeremiah, God says,

> Ephraim is my beloved son,
> a child to delight in;
> because, since my words are in him,
> I will remember him with remembrance.
> Therefore, I hurried for him;
> in having mercy I will have mercy on him,
> quoth the Lord. (Jer 38:20 LXX NETS)

This new covenant confirms the statement *I will be their God and they will be my people*, which was proclaimed to the people at the exodus (Exod 6:7) and also with the giving of the law (Lev 26:12; Deut 29:13). The people then sang this idea in praise to God (Ps 94:7; 99:3). After the unfaithfulness and the consequence, the new covenant promises the restoration of relationship.[5]

God's work of restoration will be with all Israel. *Each will not teach his fellow citizen and each his sibling, saying, "Know the Lord," because all will know me.* In a letter full of instruction, Jeremiah's claim may be hard to believe. The context of Jeremiah illuminates the meaning of this statement. Jeremiah is not speaking of doctrine here, that members of the new covenant will have all theological knowledge. Instead, he is speaking about the *experience* of God's

5. Christopher Wright, *The Message of Jeremiah: Against Wind and Tide* (Downers Grove, IL: InterVarsity Press, 2014), 323–39.

deliverance. They will know that God is the one who sought them out in the wilderness (Jer 38:2–3 LXX), healed and restored them, brought them home and built them up. They will all know God because God's acts will not come to them as some distant story concerning ancestors in the past but will be their own experience of deliverance. A person does not need instruction on what they have lived.

The prophecy notes the comprehensiveness of this knowledge. The "all" is made up of those *from the least to the greatest of them.* God is no respecter of persons. The restoration of the people of Israel is not only for the elite or the royal leaders but also for the lowly and common.

In Jeremiah the evidence of the restoration God emphasizes is forgiveness. God is evident to them—they all experientially know God *because*, God says, *I will be merciful with their instances of unrighteousness and their sins I will not still remember.* Throughout Jeremiah, unrighteousness and sin often appear together to describe the pursuit of other gods (e.g., Jer 3:13; 11:10) and the broken human relationships that result (see Jer 5; 8). The new-covenant people will know God because they will know that God has dealt with their sins.

The author ends his citation with v. 34. The next line of Jeremiah's prophecy speaks of God's constancy with Israel even in the face of the demise of creation (Jer 38:35 LXX). This idea resonates with the author's reflections on God's shaking of all things together with the endurance of the kingdom given to the author and his listeners (Heb 12:26–27). By ending with this phrase about God's forgetting of sins, however, the emphasis in Hebrews remains on forgiveness. The later decision to split Jeremiah 38:34 LXX into two verses (Heb 8:11 and 8:12) puts even more focus on the distinction of the forgiveness of sins, precisely the issue on which the author spends a great deal of time in the next chapters.

For Abraham's descendants listening to this prophecy from Jeremiah, these words offered incredible hope. With the concluding comment, the author of Hebrews begins to reveal what this promise means for *his* addressees. All the way back in the time of Jeremiah, God, *in saying "new," made the first old.* The end of the first covenant is not due to a corrupt priesthood nor the working of the Romans but is God's doing, heralded by God back in the time of the prophets. In other words, the author can comfort his readers that God is not surprised by the tumult of the 60s or the destruction of the 70s, whatever the temporal setting of this sermon might be. God's plan for the end of the old and the beginning of a new covenant with Israel has been promised for a very long time and is not caused by crises on the political stage but is God's decision to act in these last days. God's statements given through Jeremiah also mean that the proclamation of a better covenant by the author of Hebrews is not his own novel idea. Since the time of the prophet, there has been a hope that in some future time renewed relationship with God through forgiveness and the internal transformation of the people of Israel would arrive.

Given that God's pronouncement of "new" makes the first "old," the author and his listeners know from life observation that *that which is old and gray is near disappearing.* If the proclamation happened in the time of Jeremiah, then that which is old and gray has been near disappearing for a long time. Before turning to a reading of Jeremiah as a word for the community of those who hear Hebrews (originally and up to the present), the issue of supersessionism must be addressed. The *Oxford English Dictionary* defines supersessionism as "the belief that the New Testament covenant supersedes the Mosaic covenant of the Hebrew Bible, and that the Christian Church has displaced Israel as God's chosen people." It is immediately clear how prominent the language of Hebrews is implicated in this definition, but I suggest that the author of Hebrews has presented a logic that does *not* align with this term. It is the case that the author has described the Mosaic covenant as old and another covenant promised by God as new, but both covenants are presented in the Hebrew Bible, the new one from the prophet Jeremiah himself. The New Testament can never cut itself off from Israel's Scriptures, because so much of this testament includes and aligns with texts of the Hebrew Bible. Even more important in this instance, it is a portion of the Hebrew Bible itself that differentiates a new and a previous covenant. The author of Hebrews is only stating what is proclaimed by God's speech preserved there. Proclaiming "new" by virtue of comparison makes the other covenant "old." Most importantly, Hebrews is not a supersessionist text because it does not claim that "the Christian church has displaced Israel." This new covenant is promised to the house of Israel and the house of Judah (8:8, 10), and the author sees himself and his community within this group, not distinct from it (1:1; 2:16; 3:6, 9). They are joined together with the faithful of Israel who lived under the first covenant. The author states that this first covenant and the ways it adjudicated relationship with God are disappearing—ch. 8 makes clear that the better hope of 7:19 is realized in the better covenant (7:22; 8:6)—and so it is the first that is disappearing, but not the people with whom God establishes *both covenants.*

That is my position on Hebrews, which I hope my exegesis here supports. At the same time, Christians must acknowledge the horrific history of Christian aggression against Jewish people that has arisen, in part, from this belief in supersessionism, which has been shaped by New Testament texts, including Hebrews. Christian teachers, whatever their setting—the classroom, the church, or the public square—must present passages like these with care, emphasizing God's continued covenantal faithfulness to the house of Israel. Hebrews is claiming that the temporary and insufficient nature of the first covenant has been fulfilled in the new covenant made possible by Jesus of Nazareth, whom this author claims to be the Son of God and the Jewish Messiah. Christians may hold to God's everlasting faithfulness to the house of Israel even as they affirm that confession of Jesus as the Christ who is the only way to live within God's everlasting faithfulness forever. I do not think it is fitting to say that the faith taught by Hebrews is supersessionist, but it is correct to acknowledge that it is exclusive. Maintaining God's faithfulness to Israel and the necessity of faith in Jesus Christ leads one to the exclamation penned by Paul in Romans that we cannot know the depths of the wisdom of God (Rom 11:33–35). Hopefully there is space under that shared confession of God's glory (Rom 11:36) for Jewish and Christian scholars and neighbors to gather in lament over what has occurred in the past and in hope for the learning and community action that can take place through conversation together, conversation rooted in conviction and grace.

With the lens of this interpretive statement in v. 13, I suggest that readers revisit the new-covenant promises and, when they do, notice that every point of the promise has come to fruition among this community. The author of Hebrews asserts that for his listeners the new covenant is a reality. They have the assurance of forgiveness through Christ's work that Jeremiah's addressees did not. With this final phrase of Hebrews 8, the author states his conviction that the promises of the new covenant have now arrived for those who live in the last days (1:2). Jesus is the guarantee of this better covenant (7:22) and has a ministry that mediates this better covenant (8:6). The full disclosure of this conviction will unfold over the next several chapters. Jeremiah quotes God to say that the new covenant will entail *giving my laws into their minds* and *writ[ing] them on their hearts.* The thoughts of their hearts are exposed before God's word (4:12, which resonates with both mind and hearts of the

Jeremiah citation). The communication of God to them in the Son is well fit to do the work in inscribing (8:10) since he is the seal of God (1:3). Through Israel's Scriptures catalyzed by the teaching of this pastor and the encouragement of fellow believers, their hearts can be transformed from the hardness of distrustful sin (3:12–13). God said, *I will be their God and they will be my people.* They are in relationship with God through the Son as his household (3:6) and his siblings (2:11–12), making them the children of God (1:14; 2:10–13). *Each will not teach his fellow citizen and each his sibling, saying, "Know the Lord," because all will know me.* As was true for Jeremiah's audience, the audience of Hebrews need not be taught about God, because they experientially know him. They, too, have experienced God's miraculous deliverance and restoration (2:3). They all know God and what God has done. This applies *from the least to the greatest of them*, which could include an economic and social diversity as it does in most early Christian communities, but "least and greatest" could also apply to ages, both the elderly and the young, as well as the mature and the less-than-mature. All have been given this innate and experiential knowledge of God. This is a particular comfort for an audience that has been exposed for immaturity (5:11–14).

God's dealing with sin is a weighty promise for the author of Hebrews. *I will be merciful with their instances of unrighteousness and their sins I will not still remember.* This is a comforting word for the audience of Hebrews because they are guilty of less righteousness than they should have (5:13), and so will find God's promise of mercy assuring. Because of their merciful High Priest, God is merciful to the ways in which they have not demonstrated righteousness (4:16). God's decision not to remember their sins does not indicate that God is ignorant of the wrong they have done or could do. God is aware of their potential unrighteousness and sins because God gives instruction through this letter so that they can avoid falling prey to them. It is still possible that sin will deceive them (3:13). By declaring that God does not remember their sins, however, the author is asserting that God chooses not to pay those sins any attention (a similar use of *mimnēskomai* as "attention" appears in 2:6). This is true because, as the author has said multiple times, Jesus has dealt with their sins (1:3; 2:17; 4:15; 5:1; 7:27), and so even this promise applies to them.

At the same time, I do not negate the fact that there are still vitally important things in the future for the community of Hebrews: the Son yet still has enemies, humans do not reign peacefully as God planned (2:8–9), and death snatches the mortal lives of all. In these ways, then, this community lives in hope as Jeremiah's did, as they are still waiting for all things to be put under the feet of their royal High Priest. The author is proclaiming that God's mercy and forgiveness are present for them in Christ, but he also acknowledges the continuing reality of sin. This leads to the conclusion that they live in a time in which the new covenant is mediated to them, but they need encouragement to continue to trust in it. *This* is what the author is aiming to provide with his lengthy citation and exposition.

The need remains for all future readers of Hebrews as well. Christians are blessed to live in the time in which, by the power of the indwelling Spirit, God gives discernment in line with God's law. All believers are privileged to know God through intimate relationship. As proclaimed in Scripture and liturgy and song, in Christ sins are mercifully forgotten. In light of confusion, disunity, and the failures of sin, the reality of the new covenant is difficult to trust at times. Consequently, the words of Jeremiah as communicated by the author of Hebrews remain just as necessary for contemporary readers as they were in the first century. We all need to hear the proclamation "The new has arrived."

The beginning of the eighth chapter of the sermon focused on the place of Jesus's priesthood. Now with the citation of the prophet Jeremiah, the nature of it is more evident. Jesus's priestly service is to mediate this new covenant, to bring its promises into the lives of God's people. While they experience its benefits, their reception of his mediation of it is a process that will demand patience and faith, exactly the virtues the author encouraged in ch. 6 (6:15).

9:1–5 · THE FIRST TENT

[1]Therefore, on the one hand, the first [covenant] had regulations for ministry and the holy place on earth. [2]For the first tent was prepared in which was a lampstand, and the table and the offering of loaves, which is called holy. [3]And after the second veil a tent that is called most holy, [4]having a golden altar of incense and the ark of the covenant, which is surrounded everywhere with gold, in which is a golden jar having the manna and the rod of Aaron that bloomed and the plates of the covenant, [5]and above it cherubim of glory overshadowing the mercy seat, concerning which things it is not possible now to speak in detail.

Although the first covenant had been declared as "old" since the time of Jeremiah's prophecy when God spoke of something "new" (Heb 8:13), and even though the Son of God has entered the world and made the new possible, the author still takes time to describe the place and practices within the old covenant. This is a clear indication that his assessment of its "oldness" is not derogatory or dismissive but simply a view from the chronology of God's plan as revealed in the divine communication of the Son. *Therefore* indicates that this section is connected to the long quotation that has come before. To prepare for a discussion of the new covenant's realities, which are consistent with yet different from the first, he sketches out the sacred space of the old covenant. He builds on the scriptural descriptions of two covenants in Jeremiah to present his own summary of things involved in the first.

The sentence continues with the term *the first*—the best manuscripts have no other noun here. Several minuscules and manuscripts of the Vulgate supply "tent," and because the author will describe two tents, this makes good sense. Alternatively, *first* may refer back to the first covenant named in 8:13 and discussed throughout ch. 8. Because the things said about the first in v. **1** apply to both inner and outer tents, "covenant" seems the best option. This first covenant *had regulations*—literally righteous things (*dikaiōmata*)—*for ministry* as well as a place to apply them, *the holy place on earth*. The use of the imperfect here (*eichen*, "had") conveys that the tabernacle is no longer in use but served the people of Israel for an extended period of time. The author's language is laudatory. This space was orderly and just. God made the statutes clear so that by keeping the regulations there could be a space ready to receive God's holiness. How gracious it was of the holy God to give instructions so that the divine presence might dwell in the midst of an unholy people!

The author then focuses on the tent, or tabernacle, that functioned as the center of divine connection in the first covenant. In this paragraph he describes the concentric tents. *The first tent was prepared* by human hands following God's instructions, and although very positive, this term *prepared* points toward human action, which differentiates this tent from the heavenly one built by God (8:2). *In* this tent *was a lampstand*. In Exodus 25:30–39, this is described as an intricate golden lampstand with seven lamps. It provides both beauty and brightness. Although the next item, *the table*, is described earlier in the chapter of Exodus (Exod 25:22–28), the author of Hebrews mentions the table after the lamp, which is also golden and intricately crafted. Tables convey a sense of provision, and, to heighten that image, God instructs that *an offering of loaves* should always be present on the table (Exod 25:30). The people provide the loaves and build the table and lampstand, but only because God has granted the vision to Moses of how this space should be constructed (Exod 25:9, 40). This elegant yet inviting atmosphere is a location where God and the representatives of the people will meet.[6]

All of this is called holy, including that which is *after the second veil*, a tent called holy. *How* holy is contested since the manuscripts are divided here in vv. **2–3** between several different options. While Exodus calls the outer tent the holy one and the inner tent the holy of holies, Attridge presents a compelling case that the designations could be switched on account of the author's reading of Numbers and Leviticus.[7] This insight propels the loose translation I have adopted here: *which is holy. And after the second veil a tent that is called most holy.* The textual difficulties, however, do not seriously impede interpretation. Because the author has described what is in these sections, it is clear he is indicating the two sections of the tent, even if the precise term he uses to refer to each of them is not clear.

This is not the only textual difficulty between Hebrews and the descriptions of this space in Israel's Scriptures. The author of Hebrews indicates that the space behind the second veil had *a golden altar of incense.* Exodus and Leviticus could indicate that this incense altar is located within the first tent, but again, Attridge presents a compelling case for a reader of Israel's Scriptures to determine that it is located within the second tent.[8] Wherever it is located, the incense altar communicates the perpetuity of the sacrifices before God, since God commands it to be "incense of continuity always before the Lord" (Exod 30:8 LXX).

6. Desmond Alexander highlights this theme frequently in *Face to Face with God: A Biblical Theology of Christ as Priest and Mediator* (Downers Grove, IL: IVP Academic, 2022).

7. After a close reading of Numbers, Attridge concludes, "A reading of the LXX of Numbers . . . provides adequate grounds for the reversal of the ordinary designation of inner and outer sanctuaries" (*Hebrews*, 238). I agree with Ellingworth (*Hebrews*, 423) that Attridge is on less solid ground by arguing for "holies" in v. 3, and hence there is good reason to see "holy of holies" as the best reading in both v. 2 and v. 3. The difficulty is that this would eliminate a verbal contrast between the sections. In other words, it would not make good sense for the author to refer to both sections, inner and outer, by the same name. I've adopted what seems to me to be the least problematic translation.

8. Attridge, *Hebrews*, 234–35.

The next part of the description is not contentious. All manuscripts agree that the author of Hebrews says that the inner tent includes an *ark of the covenant . . . surrounded everywhere with gold.* The initial instructions for construction appear in Exodus 25, and the ark features in Israel's sacrificial liturgy only on the Day of Atonement when the high priest enters the inner tent (Lev 16). Since the author of Hebrews will spend time on this ritual, it is important to him to mention the ark. In the New Testament, the authors of Hebrews and Revelation are the only ones to refer to this important piece of Israel's worship (Rev 11:19).

The author then specifies what is in the ark: *a golden jar having the manna,* a testament to God's deliverance and provision for the generation whom God freed from Egypt (Exod 16:33); *the rod of Aaron that bloomed,* which specifies the rod that indicated God's choice of the Levites for priestly service (Num 17:8, 10); *and the plates of the covenant,* which display the Ten Commandments given to Moses after the rebellion of the people with the golden calf (Exod 32). The description closes with what is above this ark. There stand *cherubim of glory overshadowing the mercy seat.* This is the place from which God said, "I will be known to you from there, and I will speak to you from above the mercy seat" (Exod 25:22 LXX).

This brief list is all the author allows himself, acknowledging that *concerning [these] things it is not possible now to speak in detail.* He neither comments on nor explains the list, but with it he has included everything within the two tents and in the ark. He does even more, differentiating the bread from the table and naming objects of memorial (the manna and the staff) that are within the ark, as do some other early Jewish interpreters.[9] He does not give extensive detail about each, but he does provide a thorough picture of this space.[10] While some of his statements do not align easily with Exodus, a good case can be made that the careful attention he gives to Israel's Scriptures throughout the sermon continues here.

9. Lane, *Hebrews 9–13*, 221.

10. Eyal Regev sees such focus on detail as evidence that this author is not superseding and disregarding the law of sacrifice in Torah. If that were the case, "the author would hardly need to review the Levitical system in such detail. His use of the high priesthood and sacrifices offered for sin as well as their rationale and practices all acknowledge the integrity and power of the Temple cult, showing great respect for the priestly system." *The Temple in Early Christianity: Experiencing the Sacred* (New Haven: Yale University Press, 2019), 279.

By naming everything within these tabernacle spaces, he has recalled beautiful objects, whose gold and glory point to God's majesty. Their existence indicates God's gracious dealings with Israel, including the ways in which God has invited Israel to respond in worshipful fellowship with their God. He presents this full but brief sketch of items of the tabernacle to move to a larger point—namely, that there are two distinct concentric tents, where different acts of ministry take place.

9:6–10 · THE SERVICE IN THE TENT

[6]*And when these things were prepared in this way, the priests enter into the first tent*
continually to complete their ministry, [7]*and into the second, one time of the year,*
only the High Priest [enters] not without blood that he offers for himself and for the
people's instances of ignorance; [8]*the Holy Spirit showing this: that the way of the*
holies has not yet been revealed while the first tent has standing [9]*(which is a parable*
for the time of its standing). According to the first [covenant] both gifts and sacrifices
are being offered that are not able to perfect the conscience of the ones who minister,
[10]*but [are] only for food and drink and various washings, righteous ordinances for*
the flesh applied until the time of restoration.

And when these things were prepared in this way—by humans, but at God's command. The verbally constructed tabernacle sets the stage for the author to focus on the ministry that takes place in these tents. He begins with *the priests* who *enter into the first tent.* They do so *continually to complete their ministry.* This ministry includes the perpetual maintenance of the oil in the lamps (Exod 27:20–21) as well as the weekly placement of the loaves that are to be before the Lord continually (Exod 25:30). The descendants of Aaron attend to the items in the outer tent, doing everything God instructed. By selecting a word from the terms meaning "fulfillment" or "perfection" (*teleō, to complete*), the author indicates that the lack in this system still exists even when the priests completely fulfill the tasks assigned to them.

Many priests doing perpetual service with bread and oil is then contrasted with one High Priest manipulating blood only once a year. *And into the second, one time of the year, only the high priest [enters] not without blood that he offers for himself.* In Leviticus's description of the Day of Atonement (Lev 16), the high priest slaughters a bull for himself as a sin offering. He burns incense on the incense altar and then sprinkles the blood on the mercy seat of the ark. He also slaughters a goat as a sin offering for the people and brings its blood to be sprinkled on and in front of the mercy seat (Lev 16:6–16). The text is very clear that only the high priest can enter in and do this work (Lev 16:17). Exodus also mentions a once-a-year rite of atonement on the horns of the incense altar with the "blood of the atoning sin offering" (Exod 30:9–10). To make this offering is the job of Aaron and then his descendants who step into his role of high priest. Putting these texts together paints a picture of the high priest applying blood both to the horns of the incense altar and to the mercy seat. Hebrews' description is thus far in clear alignment with this event.

What demands more explanation is the description of the communal offering. The high priest also offers *for the people's instances of ignorance* (*agnoēmatōn*). Some have wondered if Hebrews has imported a distinction between unintentional sins (*akousiōs*, Lev 4; Num 15:24–29) and high-handed sins (Num 15:30–31),[11] but because Hebrews does not employ the term found in Numbers, that interpretation is not assured. While the phrase *instances of ignorance* does not appear in cultic texts of Israel's Scriptures (only in the Joseph narrative [Gen 43:12], where the word describes an "oversight"), it does resonate with Hebrews' theme of the importance of *knowing* God. The wilderness generation rebelled because they did not know God (Heb 3:10/Ps 94:10 LXX), and the promise of the new covenant is that all Israel will have a knowledge of God (Heb 8:11/Jer 38:34 LXX). Both the Exodus and Leviticus texts speak without distinction about "sins" (Exod 30:10) and even "all sins" (Lev 16:30) being atoned in the yearly Day of Atonement offering. Hebrews appears to be working with the grain of these texts. If sin is at base a lack of trusting knowledge of God's character, which is what Hebrews has been arguing, then the yearly atonement ritual performed an annual reset of that foundational human problem. This atonement would certainly include the thoughtless mistakes of "unintentional" sins, but also instances that are more thoughtful and could be traced back to a lack of trust in God.[12]

11. Attridge, *Hebrews*, 239.

12. Although he is not dealing with it in this section, my assumption is that the author would see the high-handed sin of Num 30 in line with the final instance of the wilderness rebellion and the sin of apostasy (Heb 6:4–6), both of which exclude the offender from the community and presence of God.

The author has sketched the outer and inner tent as well as the actions performed in them to call attention to a divine lesson. *The Holy Spirit* is *showing*. Readers may wonder *how* the Holy Spirit is doing this work of demonstration. Because the author has appealed to Israel's Scriptures to construct his map of the tent in vv. 1–5, and because the Holy Spirit twice communicates Scripture in Hebrews (3:7 and 10:15), it seems likely that the Holy Spirit's demonstration happens within God's word to Israel. The Holy Spirit indicates *this*: that *the way of the holies has not yet been revealed while the first tent has standing*. Based on his description of tabernacle functions in vv. 6–7, the author points out that the pathway of the high priest into the inner tent is not revealed, either to him or the people, while the outer tent is performing its function. On every other day of the year, when the priests are doing the work in the outer tent, the way into the inner tent is closed. On Yom Kippur, the opposite is true. No one can be in the outer tent when the high priest goes in to make the blood offering for sins (Lev 16:17). The functions in the two sections of the tent are mutually exclusive. When one is open, the other is closed.

This structure *is a parable for the time of its standing*. Again, the author uses a form of *histēmi*, suggesting a connection with the phrase at the end of v. 8, *has standing*. The comparison between the first and second tent sets up a comparison between the first and second covenant. While the first tent was being utilized, the revelation of the important work of yearly offering for sins by the high priest in the second tent was not put before the attention of the people of Israel. Similarly, while the first covenant had standing, the way into the holy space of God in heaven was not revealed. Because the author has used the phrase "the holies" to describe the place where Christ serves at God's right hand (8:2), and "the way" refers to the path made open by the work of Jesus (10:20), it is likely that the phrase *the way of the holies* does double duty, both as a reference to the inner section of the tabernacle and as a description of God's heavenly presence. The *parable* of the sections of the tabernacle points to the reality of the eras of covenant time. The covenant and its practices had been proclaimed "old" by the Lord through Jeremiah, but it was still in existence until the Son of God came, performed his faithful work, and opened the way to God's presence forever. The time in which the first section of the tabernacle was used demonstrated the time in which the first covenant was the way of relating to God. When the author of Hebrews is writing, neither have standing any longer. The tabernacle is no longer used, and the first covenant is now old.

In the remainder of vv. 9–10, he names again the positives and the shortfalls of the first covenant system. *According to the first [covenant] both gifts and sacrifices are offered.* The language of gift and sacrifice aligns with the descriptions of offerings *God* prescribes. The words are often paired as one thing (as in Lev 2:1, 4), or appear together when sacrifice describes the particular gift (as in Lev 2:5, 7, 13; 3:1), or are set in the same place in parallel statements (Lev 21:21; Job 20:6 LXX). The terms highlight the selfless nature of the giver. As the author reminds the readers that they *are offered*, he connects them not only to the continual important work of the priests but most closely with the offering of the high priest, whose work the author named in the previous use of the verb (v. 7). In that event, once a year the high priest addresses the fundamental problem of sin, rooted in a malformed knowledge of God.

Despite all the import this system has for the relationship between God Most Holy and the people of Israel, the author also states its insufficiencies. The offered gifts and sacrifices *are not able to perfect the conscience of the ones who minister*. In that system in which the priests are obeying God's instructions, the conscience remains imperfect. This assertion indicates that the author of Hebrews is reading the yearly blood ritual as that which does not cleanse the internal aspect of those involved. Although he does not use the same terminology as appears in chs. 3–4 (hearts) and 8 (hearts and minds), *conscience* indicates an awareness that involves a person's mind and actions, and in the New Testament literature focuses on one's self-awareness before God (Acts 23:1; 24:16; Rom 2:15; 9:1; 1 Cor 8; 2 Tim 1:3; 1 Pet 3:21). Put differently, this first system was unable to do the inner heart work anticipated in the new covenant. Although the ministry was fulfilled (*epiteleō*, 9:6), it could not perfect (*teleioō*) the internal sense of even those who served within the system. If the leaders remained imperfect, the people certainly stood in the same position.

The author states that the service of the priests deals *only* with *food* (both bread and meat, Exod 29:32) *and drink* (the drink offering, Exod 29:4). To prepare for their service they are anointed with water (Exod 29:4; 30:19; Lev 8:6), or one could say they participate in *various washings*. These are *righteous ordinances*—another reiteration that this system is good and has value, both for those who are utilizing it and for those in the future who can look back to see its teaching. Nevertheless, these ordinances are only *for the flesh*. They apply externally but not internally. The work of the high priest keeps the place of divine meeting in the presence of an unclean people (Lev 16:16). This is vital work. At the same time, this blood offering, according to Hebrews' reading of Jeremiah, does not address the heart issues as named in Psalm 95 and Jeremiah 31. These sin offerings may atone for acts against God over the course of the year, but they do not change the ones who commit that action, the very problem the new covenant seeks to address.

Moreover, these offerings were signposts pointing to another reality. They *applied* to God's people *until the time of restoration*, until things could be made right. "Restoration" is a hope of both Isaiah and Jeremiah (Isa 16:5; 62:7; Jer 7:3, 5). This restoration as described by Hebrews is as God intended when hearts *and* bodies are made pure (see 10:22). In making this comparison between the flesh and the conscience, the author would reject any pendulum swing from one direction or another—namely, a rejection of the flesh for a sole focus on the spirit—for his letter shows a deep concern for the flesh, chiefly in the body of Jesus. Instead, he is setting up a contrast in which Jesus's offering does cleanse the body and more; it also applies to the inner aspect of the human being, the conscience or the heart.

9:11–14 · CHRIST'S PRIESTLY SERVICE

[11]But Christ, who came as High Priest of the good things that came through the greater and more perfect tent not handmade—that is, not of this creation—[12]neither through the blood of goats and calves but through his own blood, he entered in once for all into the holies, finding eternal redemption. [13]For if the blood of goats and bulls and the sprinkling ashes of a heifer sanctify those who participate for the purification of the flesh, [14]how much more will the blood of the Messiah, who through the eternal Spirit offered himself blameless to God, purify our conscience from works of death to minister to the living God!

Everything in the first ten verses of this chapter focuses on the first covenant: the setting, the priests, their actions, and the impacts of those actions. At v. **11** the author turns, as indicated by *but*, to discuss the priestly work of *Christ*. The author has referred to Jesus the Son of God as Messiah (*Christos*) four times previously in the letter (3:6, 14; 5:5; 6:1). This term evokes the Son's anointing as sovereign (3:6), who is filially related to God (3:6; 5:5). This is a basic affirmation this community shares with other Jesus-as-Christ confessors. By joining *Christ* with *High*

Priest, this verse is similar to 5:5 where his sonship is united to his priesthood. The hoped-for anointed one is now their representative before God. No other New Testament author makes this ingenious combination so explicitly.

If the other priests entered into the first tent, the outer and the inner sections respectively, Christ made a movement as well. He *came* or appeared (*paraginomai* is a verb of movement, arrival from one place to another). His arrival, as the rest of the verse indicates, is in the presence of God. Before the author describes the location, he names the Messiah's role. He came *as High Priest.* While the author will also refer to Christ as simply "priest," these are most often in association with the citation of Psalm 109:4 LXX (5:6; 7:11, 15, 17, 21). *High Priest* seems to be the author's preferred title, and it makes especially good sense here after a contrast between the work of priests in the outer tent and the singular role of the high priest in the inner tent. Jesus the Messiah is the superior High Priest *of the good things that came*—at least that is the verb tense of the best manuscripts. The good things that came could refer to the offerings that come with Christ into God's presence—namely, his own blood (v. 14). Alternatively, the good things could refer to the results of his offering, the redemption he finds and pure consciences that result for his followers (9:12, 14). By naming these results of Christ's work, the author specifies the good things hoped for by Jeremiah's prophecy of the new covenant. On the other hand, a number of manuscripts, including some important uncials, describe Christ as High Priest of good things *which will come*, unsurprising in light of the uses of *mellō* earlier and later in the letter (a verb that indicates actions that are to come; 2:5; 6:5; 10:1). If the good things refer to the results, both a past and a future verb form are true. This author and his audience already have good things in their present relationship with God (namely, the internal forgiving work of God with whom they are related—in short, the new covenant), and they will have more good things in the future (namely, an unshakable kingdom [12:26–28] where everything will be under the feet of the Son [1:13; 2:8]), so the balance of the manuscripts between these readings makes good sense.[13]

Having named Christ's high priesthood and its goodness, the author first reiterates his priestly location. He comes *through the greater and more perfect*

13. It is difficult to determine what the author wrote, but scribes saw either a present or a future tense as a coherent reading. It is likely that *tōn mellontōn agathōn* in 10:1 influenced the scribes (Metzger, *Textual Commentary*, 598).

tent. This is a tent with superiority in authority and age, being the template from which the other was built. That the tent is *more perfect* is striking. Within certain definitions of perfection, one might imagine that perfection could not be improved on. With this description, the author of Hebrews affirms the goodness of the first tent. It was made according to God's specifications, and priests brought their work to completion in it (9:6). The standard of perfection in one realm, however, is not the same as in another. This tent into which Christ enters is even more perfect by comparison because of its maker. To recall the discussion of buildings in ch. 3 (especially 3:4), a divine maker would construct an even more perfect tent than a human builder. Hence, the author says next that this tent is *not handmade—that is, not of this creation.* This statement is a reiteration of 8:2, that the tent where their High Priest ministers is built by the Lord and not a human. In addition, its superior perfection is due to its endurance. Unlike the tabernacle, or even the temple that Herod made so great, the more perfect, heavenly tent will endure.

The author then contrasts the offering presented in the earthly and heavenly spaces. Jesus came as High Priest *neither through the blood of goats and calves but through his own blood.* Goats appear in the initial offerings at the tabernacle as described in Numbers 7, and God instructs Moses to prepare a sacrifice of sheep and calves soon after giving the Ten Commandments (Exod 20:24). These animals represent inaugural moments of the first covenant. Moreover, when the high priest offers the sin offering for himself and for the people, he is to have the blood of a calf (Lev 4:3, 14) as is true in the Yom Kippur offering (Lev 16:3). In both offerings, goats are also present, but the texts use slightly different terms for the animal (*chimaros*, Lev 4:23–24 and Lev 16:5–10 rather than *moschōn*). By naming these two animals, the author is also pointing back to the ceremonies he has described in the first part of the chapter.

In contrast to the blood of another being—an animal rather than a human being—Christ arrives *through his own blood.* Having his own blood implies his death, but the fact that *he goes in* with it suggests that he is alive to carry it in. That the author chooses the preposition *dia* (*through*) indicates the way in which blood allows for entry into God's presence.[14] As the Torah describes, without blood the high priests could not pass through the veil into the inner sanctuary to make the offering for the sins. The instrumentality of blood co-

14. This is the instrument that allows his entry (Harris, *Hebrews*, 223).

heres with the author's recognition of its importance, which he will state later in 9:22 ("And almost everything is purified by blood according to the law, and apart from the shedding of blood there is not release").

Next the author compares the timing. Whereas the other high priests enter in once a year (*hapax*), Christ the High Priest *entered in once for all* (*ephapax*), a more intensive form of singularity that shows his unparalleled distinction. The once-for-allness of his death is an idea articulated by other Christian authors as well (Rom 6:10; 1 Pet 3:18), and it plays an important role in the author's intense warnings against turning away from it (Heb 6:4–6; 10:26, 29; 12:15–17).

Then the author mentions location again. Christ goes *into the holies*. The articular plural (*ta hagia*) aligns with the heavenly meaning of the word I suggested in 9:8, as well as the author's description of the place Jesus entered in 8:2, 9:24, and 10:19. This one-time offering happens before the very throne of God.

Finally, the author names one result that comes from Christ's ministry, his *finding eternal redemption*. This is a theme that appears not frequently but widely among New Testament authors (Matt 20:28; Mark 10:45; Luke 1:68; 2:38; 24:21; Acts 7:35; Titus 2:14; Heb 9:12; 1 Pet 1:18), and it conveys the idea of moving a person from a negative to a positive sphere. In the Septuagint, redemption is associated with God's deliverance of the people of Israel from Egypt (e.g., Exod 6:6; 15:13; Mic 6:4), God's deliverance from the exile (Mic 4:10), and the redemption of firstborn sons from God's service by the setting apart of the Levites (Exod 13:13–15). It is not, noticeably, a promise given in the cultic system, indicating that Jesus's offering does something the first did not do—namely, redeem from death. This is the case in Hebrews, where a reference to redemption recalls the imprisonment to death under which humanity found itself (2:14–15).[15]

This redemption into which the Messiah moves people exists forever. It is *eternal*. Because the offering Christ brings defeats death and allows God's merciful and permanent forgetting of sins, it will never need to be replaced with another redemption. (See also the commentary on 5:9 and 9:15 where the author describes this reality as eternal *salvation* and eternal *inheritance*).

15. Jon Laansma notes concerning redemption language, "This is not terminology used with the Day of Atonement in the LXX, but once the latter is seen as the means of arrival at the goal of salvation the conflation of images is natural" (*Letter to the Hebrews*, 209).

In vv. **13–14** the author focuses again on the offerings and their results. He mentions three animals: *For if the blood of goats and bulls and the sprinkling ashes of a heifer sanctify*. As mentioned, goats appear in the inaugural offering in Numbers 7. Heifers appear there too, as well as in the first description of a sacrifice for the covenant between God and Abram (Gen 15). Both bulls and goats are offered in 1 Esdras when the people return from exile (1 Esd 8:63). Bulls and goats also appear together in critiques of sacrifice (Isa 1:11; Ps 49:13 LXX). In sum, these are animals associated with sacrifice, including important inaugural sacrifices. Mentioning them is a way of evoking the whole sacrificial system.

The *ashes* of a heifer refers to a more precise event. It appears only in the sacrifice of the red heifer described in Numbers 19:9. Similar to the author's claim in v. 10 that the sacrifices are righteous ordinances "for the flesh," here he states that these sacrifices *sanctify those who participate* in them. They are done *for the purification of the flesh*. Numbers 19 is a clear example. The ashes of the heifer are for purification (Num 19:9 LXX). In the law of Israel, given by God, cleansing of the flesh is real and important. It is the means by which a holy God dwells in the midst of an unclean people. It is an outward sign of God's election of them (beginning with Abraham) and deliverance of them, both from Egypt and from exile. By making the blood and the ashes the active agents—they are not sprinkled (passive participle) but *sprinkling* (active participle)—the author highlights the effective action of the system ordained by God.

The goodness of this divinely given system allows the superlative contrast. *How much more will the blood of the Messiah . . . purify . . . ?* If the other sacrifices purified the flesh, the Messiah's blood will do the same *and more*. His blood is *human* blood, a sacrifice that God's law outlawed (Lev 18:21; Deut 12:31; 18:10), although the personal cost was revealed in the account of God's command that Abraham be willing to sacrifice Isaac (Gen 22). What the Triune God would not allow to happen to others, God allowed for himself—willingly—in the person of the Son. Because blood signifies the human condition (Heb 2:14), mentioning his blood connects to his particular life. His is the blood *of the Messiah*. That is, on the basis of the scriptural catena in ch. 1, his blood is anointed blood, royal blood that God has intended to reign over all things. His blood is precious blood indeed by virtue of his being human, one made in the image of God, and also by the fact that he is a very respected human, the Messiah. Moreover, readers know that his human blood flowed in the veins of a perfect human, untainted by sin (4:15). For all these reasons, it is not surprising that this blood has different and superior effects.

The author says more about the singular sacrifice of Christ than he did about the numerous other sacrifices (other than the phrase "the ashes of the heifer," the loose allusions via a handful of animals leave interpreters unsure to what sacrifices he refers). Possibly this is intentional. He gestures generally to sacrifice but now focuses more precisely on the means and effects of Christ's work through offering his own very particular life/blood.

Whereas the priests remained absent from v. 13 and the blood and ashes did the work, in this phrase of the comparison Christ is active. He *offered himself.* Five times previous to this point, the author has named the fact that priests make offerings (5:1; 8:3, 4; 9:9, 13) and in three he specifies that they have to do so for themselves before they can offer for others (5:3; 7:27; 9:7). In preparation for his offering, Jesus offered prayers and supplications (5:7), but not the blood of an animal. Then in this sacrifice he offered *himself blameless to God.* Although he entered into the state of humanity, a state that was tainted by sin, this is a distinction between him and other priests. They need to be sanctified first by the blood of an animal to be inaugurated as priests (Exod 29:29; Lev 8:30). Then, when they sacrifice, they sacrifice *for* their sinfulness first. Jesus has no need to offer and be sanctified for his own sins. He can offer his blameless self and meet the requirement for sacrifice mentioned over fifty times in Israel's Scriptures (when the sacrifices are described as "without blemish" throughout Exodus, Leviticus, Numbers, and Ezekiel). By naming both the blood of the Messiah and his self-offering, the author portrays an image of Christ carrying his own blood into God's presence. He is performing a similar action as the priests who carry the blood of the animal into the tent of meeting (as in Lev 4:5). He does so, however, as the resurrected Jesus who presents himself and his living blood. In whatever way the author intends it, it is clear that human, messianic, sinless blood is involved and that Jesus is an active agent in this process.[16]

Jesus, though, is not the only one. He makes this offering *through the eternal Spirit.* While several manuscripts have "Holy Spirit" instead, *eternal* is

16. David Moffitt presents the logic for this interpretation in *Atonement and the Logic of Resurrection in the Epistle to the Hebrews* and *Rethinking the Atonement: New Perspectives on Jesus's Death, Resurrection, and Ascension* (Grand Rapids: Baker Academic, 2022).

supported by earlier witnesses and is the harder reading as this is the only occurrence of the phrase, whereas "Holy Spirit" appears five times in Hebrews (2:4; 3:7; 6:4; 9:8; 10:15). While the Spirit associated with God is most often called holy, it is also the Spirit of grace in this letter (10:29), an indication that the author can use flexible terminology for God's Spirit. These scribal decisions to have "holy" instead of "eternal" indicate that early readers were seeing in this phrase the work of a third entity involved in the effective offering, facilitating the work of the Messiah aimed at God the Father.[17] This is a fitting interpretation of the preposition *dia* with a genitive as an indication of personal agency.[18] That the spirit is *eternal* associates the spirit with God, who created the ages and will outlast them (1:2, 12), and also with the eternal priesthood of Christ (5:6; 7:25) that secures eternal redemption (5:9) and salvation (9:12).

The result of the work of Christ is that he purifies *our conscience*. With the use of *conscience*, the author's focus is on the soul of the community: *our* (plural) *conscience* (singular), highlighting the communal status of reconciliation with God. Conscience in the New Testament refers to moral actions and, in light of that, confidence (or lack thereof) in how one assesses one's status before God (Acts 23:1; 24:16; Rom 2:15; 9:1; 13:5; 1 Cor 8:7, 10, 12; 10:25, 27–29; 2 Cor 1:12; 4:2; 5:11; 1 Tim 1:5, 19; 3:9; 2 Tim 1:3; 1 Pet 3:16, 21). In other words, it indicates not just where one stands, but how one feels about that standing. This aligns with the experiential knowledge of God and God's forgiveness promised in the new covenant (Heb 8:11–12). His sacrifice purifies the conscience (what the community knows about themselves before God) with only one eternal offering so that people are freed to serve the God who knows hearts—namely, the living God (3:12 and 9:14). Through his self-offering, Jesus mediates this new covenant that brings God's forgetfulness of sins (8:12). They are free to forget their sins as God does. This is a freeing word for humans in any time and place. When God offers forgiveness in Christ, confessors of him are forgiven indeed.

Here in 9:14 the author is making a comparison between the external work of the animal sacrifices (9:10) and the internal work of Christ's offering. A key

17. For example, Chrysostom reads and comments on this as the Holy Spirit (*Hebrews* 15.5 [*NPNF*[1] 14:440]).

18. Daniel B. Wallace, *Greek Grammar beyond the Basics: An Exegetical Syntax of the New Testament with Scripture, Subject, and Greek Word Indexes* (Grand Rapids: Zondervan, 1996), 166.

text concerning blood in Leviticus, however, states that blood sacrifices make atonement/reconciliation "for your souls" (Lev 17:11). "Soul" in Leviticus is a way of speaking of the whole person; it seems not to present a division between body and heart. Hence, the author's comparison may include a difference between the internal and the external, but may not be limited to that difference alone. If animal blood makes life with God possible for the whole person in Leviticus, then the blood of Christ does so in a superior way. In ch. 10 the author will reflect on the repetition of the animal sacrifices to clarify an experiential difference between the sacrifices of the old and new covenants (10:3).

Finally, Jesus's sacrifice, in distinction from the previous ones, affects life and death. He purifies their conscience *from works of death*. His offering will do what the previous offerings could not (9:9). This could be the author's way of describing the sins in his community's past from which they have been forgiven, indicating the transition from their previous way of life ("dead works," 6:1) to being a participant in Christ. It could also be more comprehensive. He purifies their conscience from works of death, which include any activity done in a system that will still result in the death of the participants, no matter what purification or atonement they experience through it. For the author of Hebrews, works are a good thing, done by God (1:10; 3:9; 4:3, 4) and by the community (6:10; 10:24). Works of death may not be sins from which they need to be forgiven, but any activity that exposes them to the reality of death. Much like in the law of Israel, encounters with dead bodies, a good act of care, also demanded purification (Num 19). Christ purifies their conscience not only from their sins but also from the overwhelming and comprehensive experience of the reality of and fear of death (Heb 2:15). In the author of Hebrews' logic, it is Christ's work that fulfills the Jewish trust in God's faithfulness even in the face of death, which resulted in a belief in bodily resurrection among many Second Temple Jews.[19]

When freed from this, they are able *to minister to the living God*. In the previous system, even those facilitating the sacrifices, the priests, were not perfected (9:9). In Christ's system, everyone is invited to minister and can do so because of what Christ's offering has done for them (although there remains

19. For discussion of these interrelated beliefs, see Kevin J. Madigan and Jon D. Levenson, *Resurrection: The Power of God for Christians and Jews* (New Haven: Yale University Press, 2008).

a category of "leaders" [13:17] who have the call to oversee the congregation). That the author chooses to describe God as *living* here suggests the contrast is between the end of life and its continuation. Only Christ's sacrifice makes a difference in this equation. This is the second time the author has named God as living (also 3:12), and the discussion of Christ's priesthood has emphasized his living and perpetual priesthood. Only his offering can free them from death so that they can serve the eternal God perpetually, and the only way this is possible is if they experience eternal life the way Christ does. Consequently, "ministering to the living God" suggests a resurrected service, as they follow in the footsteps of their resurrected High Priest.

By laying out this comparison between previous priests and Jesus, the author shows that God did not give up on blood and sacrifice. The structure of this way of relating with God continued but within a different system. Appreciation for the God-given sacrificial system and what it achieved allows the author to draw from it to describe the life and work of Christ rather than posit Jesus the Messiah as radically different from and opposed to this system.[20] The affirmation allows the proclamation: Christ the High Priest who sacrificially offered himself, his blood, in a different sanctuary has achieved a strikingly different result, fulfilling the hopes long held among God's covenant people.

9:15–22 · COVENANTS

[15]And because of this he is mediator of the new covenant, so that those who have been called might receive the promise of the eternal inheritance because a death happened as a release of the transgressions under the first covenant. [16]For where there is a covenant there is a necessity that the death of the testator be offered. [17]For a covenant is established upon death, since it is never strong when the testator lives. [18]Whence neither was the first inaugurated without blood. [19]For after every commandment was spoken according to the law by Moses to all the people, taking the blood of calves with water and scarlet wool and hyssop, he cast blood on both the book itself and all the people, [20]saying, "This is the blood of the covenant that God commanded to you."

20. Early interpreters of Hebrews did the same. First Clement continues appreciation for the detailed instruction of offerings in Israel's law (1 Clem. 40–41; see Regev, *Temple in Early Christianity*, 292–93).

[21]And the tent and also all the vessels of ministry similarly he sprinkled with blood.
[22]And almost everything is purified by blood according to the law, and apart from the shedding of blood there is not release.

The features of the new covenant have echoed throughout the previous section, but now the author names it explicitly. *Because of this*—the self-offering of the Son who is Messiah and his offering's effects—*he is mediator of the new covenant.* As a bookend to the statement the author made before presenting the prophecy of Jeremiah (8:6), the author repeats Christ's mediating role, in which he opens the way for the covenant to move from God to the people. Here, however, the author aligns his previous language of a "better" covenant (8:6) to match Jeremiah's language of a "new" covenant (8:8). The hopes of this covenant for *enduring* internal change, intimate relationship for all, and mercy are now possibilities because of Christ's mediation.

The author succinctly names those possibilities with this phrase: *so that those who have been called might receive the promise of the eternal inheritance.* The called ones, in 2:11, are the siblings of Jesus. The suggestion that the author is evoking familial imagery here finds confirmation when these called ones receive the *inheritance*, that which is given to designated descendants. This inheritance is *eternal.* Unlike perishable materials, this inheritance will last. This is precisely the distinguishing feature of the new covenant, endurability. The way the new covenant grants that eternal inheritance is a radical fulfillment of Israel's resurrection faith. In other words, even if that which is inherited does last, say, in the case of land, the inheritor will not. Death will prevent the heir from enjoying the inheritance forever. If this is an eternal inheritance, yet again, that demands their enduring life as heirs. As mediator Christ has fully and finally dealt with the problem of sin as well as the reality of death. In addition, this inheritance is one that is connected to a *promise*. The sermon has now shown how Christ has brought the new covenant. The promise to Jeremiah has been fulfilled to them.

Along with that promised covenant is the promised inheritance of salvation (1:14). That is not an inheritance the members of the new covenant receive right away. As is true with a typical inheritance, it is hoped for before it is granted. They have received the promise of the new covenant, but have not yet received the promise of dwelling with God (2:10) or salvation in God's rest (4:1). This element of futurity prepares the way for the author's discussion of human covenants that follows. The author spent considerable time on God's promise to Abraham (6:12–18), God's promise to Jesus (5:10; ch. 7), and now God's fulfilled new-covenant promise to them (ch. 8) so that his audience could have examples on which to base their trust in God's yet unfulfilled promises. As Abraham inherited the promise (6:12), they are promised the inheritance. The interchangeability of the terms highlights both the fulfilled and the future aspect of God's promises to all.

The author also includes a phrase explaining how those called are able to receive the promises both now and in the future: *because a death happened as a release of the transgressions under the first covenant.* While the author has been focusing on the active work of Christ who presents himself to God (thus assuming his active resurrected life), here he focuses on Christ as the recipient of death—*a death happened* to him. If he had not first experienced death, then his offering would not accomplish the goal of redemption.

Because the author is again considering the enduring nature of the effects of Christ's mediation (an eternal inheritance, 9:15), it is not surprising that he returns to the concept of redemption/release (*lytroō*), since he said that Christ's offering allowed him to discover eternal redemption, *lytrōsis* (9:12). Although redemption is not a term in the literature describing the sacrificial system, it is used extensively in Israel's Scriptures to convey release from slavery or the purchase of something out of the hands of another. With the people of Israel as his template, the author of Hebrews affirms a redemption from slavery, whose catalyst was the death of the Passover lamb (Exod 12). Because the redemption Christ secured is accomplished by death, it resonates with the earlier statement that Jesus releases humanity from its slavery to the fear of death *through dying* (2:14–15). The effect is connected to the mechanism. Redemption was made possible because *a death happened.* In other words, as stated in ch. 2, through death he destroyed the one who has the power of death, and he redeemed those who were caught. Redemption always includes a before and an after, redemption *from* as well as redemption *for.* With the story of Israel providing the imagery, the association of both redemption and inheritance casts those who are so redeemed into the wilderness. They follow the one who has redeemed them as he leads them from slavery to God's promised eternal presence.

That being said, in this verse the redemption is not from death explicitly but from *transgressions*, those "line crossings" that happened *under the first covenant.* Transgressions that occurred during the first covenant, the one given to Moses through angels (2:2), came at a cost. Those transgressions received a fitting and just reward (2:2). Transgression is often followed by death. The golden calf transgression (Exod 32; Deut 9) resulted in the deaths of some of the Israelites (Exod 32:28). Leviticus 26:14–39 lays out the deathly consequences of disobedience, and in Joshua 23:12–13 the consequences of transgression include perishing. If the death of Jesus has paid the price for these transgressions, that means that he has taken this result upon himself. He died the death that resulted when the first covenant was transgressed.

The application of this redemption includes two groups pertinent to Hebrews. First, it suggests that all those who lived before this audience, who transgressed the commands of the first covenant, now have the offer of redemption through Christ. The full stories of those mentioned in the catalogue of Israel's faithful confirms that those who were not perfect, who transgressed the law at times, found a place in God's eternal family (chs. 11–12). Although the author names the first covenant here, he speaks of precovenant history as a time in which transgression, specifically murder, could happen (11:4), and also says that if the Messiah suffered often, it would have had to happen from the foundation of the world (9:26); hence the rules of the first covenant could be transgressed even before they were given.[21] In short, the effects of Christ's offering reach back in time. All the repetitive offerings for sins were pointing forward to the final effective offering of Christ.

Second, because those who are listening to this sermon are part of the group called siblings of Jesus (2:11–12; 3:1), the redemption also applies to them. If the laws of the first covenant are still a part of the new covenant (8:10), then transgressions against God's good laws are still possible, and Christ has also paid the price for those. God has already dealt with the possibility of future sin with the one-time offering of God the Son, opening the door to mercy and the forgetting of sins.[22] Even members of the new covenant will struggle with sin, both sin they commit and sin that is committed against them. Just as redemption is *from* slavery, it is also *for* God's plan, and God's plan includes time in the "wilderness," a wilderness in which sin remains a reality. That

21. See Paul's articulation of this in Rom 5:13.

22. If anyone were to depart from Christ and his resurrected offering, then access to the answer to sin and death would be severed (6:4–6), which the author displayed by analogy to the wilderness generation's decision not to trust in God's leading into the land of promise (3:6–4:13; 8:9).

was true for the people of Israel redeemed from slavery in Egypt, as well as the patriarchs and matriarchs who wandered as strangers and aliens looking forward to dwelling with God (11:9, 10, 13–16). This is how the author has cast the lives of his congregation, as those who are journeying in the wilderness on their way to be with God forever. It is redemption that put them in this place of challenge and difficulty, but that is much superior to remaining enslaved. Christ's redemption from transgressions applies to the entirety of these last days, no matter how long they may last. In sum, the once-for-all offering of Christ radiates its effectiveness in both temporal directions. This gives clarity to the distinction between the old and new covenants. It is not as if the problem with the old covenant is that people could not endure in it, and now in the new covenant they can. Instead, the repetitive sacrifices of the first covenant were pointing toward their fulfillment in Christ. God never demanded perfection from recipients of the covenant, only reliance. Now that the Son has been revealed, it is clear that covenant reliance is reliance on the one offering of the Messiah, an offering that secured forgiveness forever.

Death—namely, the death of the Son—plays a key role in this new covenant, but this is not an anomaly. The author proceeds to give two examples of covenants and how death plays a role in them as well. The first example is human covenants, or, better said, human testaments or wills. *Where there is a covenant*, there is also *a necessity that the death of the testator be offered.* The author articulates the common idea that people have to die before their inheritance is distributed and their wills are put into effect. The author could have said, more simply, that it was a necessity for the death of the testator to *happen*, but the passive of *pherō* (offer) links this statement with the offering of Christ (*prospherō*, 9:14), establishing a poetic resonance with the result of his death—namely, that his offering after death resulted in a covenant. In so doing the author shows that the God who made the covenant also experienced death to enact that new covenant. It is startling that in the new covenant the Son makes the sacrifice and sacrifices *himself.* This parallel puts Jesus, who died, on the side of the one who makes the covenant, and therefore is another affirmation of his shared unity with the God of Israel.

In v. **17** the author asserts the presence of death in covenants again with different terminology. *A covenant is established upon death.* In other words, the solidness of the testament is based on death. Just like the works humans do inevitably result in death (9:14), so, too, the importance of handing on one's property and legacy is based on the reality of death. The author then states the necessity of death a third time: *since it is never strong when the testator lives.* His verbal evocation of God's covenant continues as he describes common human situations. By speaking of the firmness (*bebaios*) and strength (*ischyō*) of the human testament, the author evokes words he has used for the confidence and encouragement his community has in Christ, the mediator of the new covenant (3:14; 6:18). Moreover, in his assertion about the necessity of death, he utilizes irony as well. Yes, there has been a death that has established the new covenant, but it is the crucified one who has become, through resurrection, the *living* High Priest. It is he who makes this covenant strong, or, better said, it is he who puts it into force. It bases its strong reality on both his death *and life.*

In v. **18** the author moves to the second example as he names the consistency between human and divine covenants and between God's old and new covenants. If the basis of death is how human testaments work, and the death and resurrection of Jesus has made the new covenant possible, then he wants to show explicitly that *neither was the first inaugurated without blood.* Without a specific noun joined to the word *first*, it could refer to either "covenant" or "tent," both of which he will soon mention (covenant, 9:20; tent, 9:21) and has mentioned previously (covenant, 9:17; tent, 9:11). Since they are intimately related, it is not necessary to choose one or the other. Nevertheless, since the narrative he will recall happens before the erection of the tabernacle, "first covenant" is most likely. When the old covenant was *inaugurated* (*enkainizō*), when it was "new," this inauguration took place with blood. With this statement the author transitions to discuss the covenant ceremony as recorded in Exodus 24.

He begins the story by reminding them of *when every commandment was spoken according to the law by Moses to all the people.* In Exodus 24 the people have been redeemed from Egypt and brought to the wilderness of Sinai. Moses goes to meet God on the mountain and is told that God wants to give a covenant to the people. The people are prepared for the encounter, and Moses goes up again where God gives him the law. When he goes back down, Moses communicates to the people all God's words and statutes.[23] Then all the people

23. In this verse, Exod 24:3, the Greek manuscripts say "words and ordinances" (*dikaiōmata*) of God, but later in Exod 24:12 appear the terms that the author of Hebrews uses here in 9:19, *entolē*, "commandment," and *nomos*, "law." His familiarity with the whole passage could lead to his terminology in this retelling.

answer with one voice, saying, "All the words that the LORD has spoken we will do and heed" (Exod 24:3).

What Hebrews does not recount is Moses's construction of an altar, and the young men who offer sacrifices to the Lord (Exod 24:4–5). The author picks up when Moses, *taking the blood of calves,*[24] *cast blood on both the book itself and all the people.* The setting does not lend itself to imagining Moses's act with the delicate translation of "sprinkling." If all the people are gathered and Moses applies blood to a crowd from a basin, the imagery is more visceral than the treatment of precise and limited drops. Since the author will later use this term to describe the blood of Christ applied for the salvation of the people (Heb 10:22; 12:24; see also 1 Pet 1:2), the word evokes an abundance, not a stinginess on the part of God. They are efficiently covered by this blood.[25]

The author of Hebrews portrays Moses also applying blood to the book of the covenant that he creates (Exod 24:4) and reads to the people (Exod 24:7), even though this application of blood is not explicit in the Exodus account. Nevertheless, in such a creative weaving together of multiple texts and moments in Israel's story, the inclusion makes sense. Since this is in fact the blood of the *covenant*, it is fitting to be associated with the *book* of the covenant. As evidence of this fulsome reading, the author also includes along *with* the blood *water and scarlet wool and hyssop*. Water is present in the cleansing of the priests and the people (Exod 29:4; 30:18–21; 40:12; for instances of bodily impurity, see Lev 14–17), scarlet wool appears only in a contrast between scarlet sins and forgiveness that is white as snow (Isa 1:18), and hyssop, a perennial plant widely known for its medicinal properties, is used for cleansing. It first appears as the instrument by which the Israelites are instructed to smear the blood of the Passover lamb over their lintels (Exod 12:22). The confluence of all three—water, a red cord, and hyssop—occurs in two places. First, in Leviticus 14 the priests are instructed to use the blood of a bird, crimson yarn, hyssop, and water to cleanse after a person or a house has had leprous disease. Second, in Numbers 19 unspecified red material is joined with hyssop and the ashes of the heifer to create the water of purification, used when someone

24. Some manuscripts add "and the goats," but since this is textually questionable and is not present in Exod 24, it seems a scribal addition to put this verse into alignment with 9:12.

25. For a fuller explanation of this argument, see Amy Peeler, "Desiring God: The Blood of the Covenant in Exodus 24," *Bulletin of Biblical Research* 23 (2013): 187–205.

encounters a dead body. That the author conflates the inaugural blood ritual with later instructions for purification from exposure to disease and death evokes the multiple meanings of purification in the covenant. As he sets up the unchanging nature of the way God has worked, he evokes the effects of Christ's sacrifice of himself, which deals with the "disease" of alienation from God.

He has layered different sets of instructions from Israel's law in one sentence, typical of the varied references that appear often in Jewish interpretation. Nevertheless, it is clear that Exodus 24 remains central since he cites from it in the following verse: *This is the blood of the covenant that God commanded to you.* The Greek text of Exodus preserved has "Lord" instead of "God" (Exod 24:8), but these terms for the deity both appear throughout Exodus. Another difference is that Exodus has the Lord setting (*dietheto*) the covenant, whereas Hebrews has God commanding (*entellō*) the covenant, a word the text of Exodus 23–25 also utilizes (Exod 23:15, 22; 25:22). Possibly the author wants to distinguish the setting of the new covenant (Heb 8:10; 10:16) from the commanding of the first. The important point is that God initiated this first covenant and solidified it with blood.

The author's description of Moses's manipulation with blood continues when the tent is prepared for sacrifice. *And the tent and also all the vessels of ministry similarly he sprinkled with blood.* This is recorded in Leviticus 8 when Moses is preparing the space for the work of the priests. There it only mentions that Moses applies blood to the altar. (In Exod 40 he anoints the tent and the vessels, but with oil; since blood is the main emphasis here, the Levitical description is the one more likely evoked.) It is also the case that blood is applied to the vestments of priests (Exod 29) and to the holy veil (Lev 4:6, 17), but most frequently it is applied to the horns or poured out at the base of the altar. This may be what the author refers to by mentioning the tent and its *vessels*, the chief tool of divine encounter being the altar. Doing so serves the author's overarching point: the presence of blood in the covenantal process. He can summarize by saying, *And almost everything is purified by blood according to the law.* Blood is not everything, as he knows, made evident by his mention of the water, hyssop, and red wool, but its presence is persistent and prominent in rituals of purification and atonement. The point is important enough to him that he repeats it in a varied form: *And apart from the shedding of blood there is not release.* While this term for release becomes a word that communicates forgiveness among the authors of the New Testament (Matt

26:28; Mark 1:4; 3:29; Luke 1:77; 3:3; 4:18; 24:47; Acts 2:38; 5:31; 10:43; 13:38; 26:18; Eph 1:7; Col 1:14), it appears in Israel's Scriptures as a description of freedom or return of property, frequently in the Year of Jubilee. The only time this term appears in sacrificial contexts is during the Yom Kippur ritual. The live goat on whom the high priest confesses the sins of the people is sent out for release (Lev 16:21, 26). That goat's blood is not shed, at least within the camp, but that of its companion is (Lev 16:9–11). The message is clear that release does not come about without death, the shedding of blood and a banishment outside the people, both of which the author will say is true of Christ (Heb 9:12, 14; 10:19; 13:12), leading to the new-covenant promises of forgiveness he ushers in (8:12; 10:17).

By retelling aspects of the first covenant, the author displays that it started with blood garnered through the death of the animals. He fast-forwards from this inaugural event of Exodus 24 to the establishment of the tabernacle later in the covenant. There as well, sprinkling of blood occurred. God is consistent. God has purified through the use of blood, which signifies a life given (Lev 17:11). This is in alignment with the reality that human covenants are established upon death. Both types of covenants include the necessity of the passing on of a life in the enactment of covenants, either by the one who made the testament (Heb 9:16–17) or by the animal (9:18–22). The broad statement at the end of v. 22 makes sense not only for the law of Israel but also in human covenants. Testators do not have to literally shed their blood, or die a violent death, but since the term for "shedding of blood" in the cultic space simply signifies the giving of life, the phrase recalls both the slaughtered animal whose blood is brought in to maintain the covenant and the fact that a testator does have to die to put the will/covenant into effect. Without the end of a life, there can be no release of sins (in Israel's cult) or release of an inheritance (in human testaments). To name both is important for the author because both forgiveness and inheritance feature in God's relationship with Israel. Without the giving of a life, God's presence could not forgive the sins and remain with the people of Israel, and the inheritance of the covenant could not be given to its recipients.

The recipients of Hebrews should not be surprised, then, that the wondrous promises of the new covenant are built on the same means. As the willing sacrifice that makes possible God's covenant promises, Jesus their Messiah and High Priest, the Son of God, has brought redemption (9:15) and release (9:22) through his death. He is the one who forgives sin and opens up the floodgates of covenant blessings, the eternal inheritance. He does so, like the animals and like the testator, by dying, by shedding his blood all the way to the point of death. At the same time, between his act and the other covenants there is one startling and radically transformative difference. The blood of the new covenant is presented by the one who does not stay dead.

9:23–28 · CHRIST'S PRIESTLY MINISTRY

[23]Therefore it was necessary for the examples of the things in the heavens to be purified by these and for the heavenly things themselves with better sacrifices than these.
[24]For Christ did not enter into the holy spaces made with hands, the antitypes of the true things, but Christ has entered into heaven itself, now to appear before the face
of God for us, [25]not so that he might offer himself often, as the high priest enters into
the holies year after year with the blood of another; [26]then it would be necessary for
him to suffer often from the foundation of the cosmos, but now he has appeared once at the completion of the ages for removal of sins through the offering of himself. [27]And
just as it is held for humans to die once, and after this judgment, [28]so also Christ,
having been offered once to bear up sins of many, will be seen a second time separate from sin by those who eagerly await him for salvation.

The author mentioned the tent and the vessels of ministry in the first covenant (v. 21) and the purification of them and almost everything else with blood (v. 22). Now he will transition back to his discussion of the elements of the new covenant with the connective term *therefore*. First, he summarizes his recounting of the first covenant communicated by Moses: *it was necessary for the examples of the things in the heavens to be purified by these.* The tangible earthly examples were purified by the blood of animals (Exod 29:36). On the day of atonement, the high priest was to make atonement for the holy tent and the things pertaining to the priests (Lev 16:16, 20). God decided that blood, which conveyed life (Lev 17:11), would be the agent of purification for the sacred space and its instruments. Hence, the author's statement of necessity arises from the revelation of how God chose to maintain relationship with Israel. If God commanded it, it must have been necessary. At the same time, he asserts that the necessity applies to the comparison he is making. If the blood of animals was necessary for the purification of the earthly implements, then it is necessary that *the heavenly things themselves* are purified *with better sacrifices than these.* The author has already made clear that Christ offers a superior sacrifice with his own blood and self (Heb 7:27; 8:3). What is not clear is *why* heaven itself would need to be purified, if that is the verb implied in the second half of the phrase, which would be most likely grammatically. "Purified" could be used here in the sense of inauguration, so that the heavenly tabernacle is not in use until the perfect High Priest comes to serve there and presents his blood. Another approach applies this cleansing to the church. Mary Healy notes that the cleansing of the copies points to greater realities: "the law written on the heart, the redeemed people of God, the true tent that is Christ's glorified humanity, and the new covenant liturgy." These things have "*become* heavenly by Christ's sacrifice in order to participate already in the 'heavenly Jerusalem.'"[26] Finally, it seems possible to me that just as the tabernacle space on earth was infected by human sin, so too could the heavenly space be. The mechanism for this infection arose only because of God's mercy to be in relationship with humanity, first by choosing to dwell with Israel and then by choosing to send the Son to share in the human condition and return to heavenly space to represent humans as a human who had an encounter with death and bore its scars. In both instances, it is God's presence with humanity that sets the stage for the need to cleanse impurity, and then God's setting up of a system using blood sacrifice to deal with that impurity. Moreover, because Christ comes before God *for us* (v. 24), he opened the way of access to God's presence in the present for other impure humans. He provides the once-and-for-all purification for their continual entrance. This explanation could make sense of the odd use of the plural for *sacrifices* in this verse. Jesus only offers himself once, but he presents himself living to make perpetual intercessions for his followers. His sacrifice is invoked frequently as he prays for them and invites them to approach the throne in prayer for timely aid (4:16). His ascension both created the necessity by which heaven stood in need of purification and provided that purification through his own self-offering.

The author then provides specification of that purification process. *For Christ did not enter into the holy spaces made with hands.* He reiterates the

26. Mary Healy, *Hebrews*, Catholic Commentary on Sacred Scripture (Grand Rapids: Baker Academic, 2016), 185–87.

point he made in 9:11 by saying that Christ did not enter into *the antitypes of the true things*. By using another term for "example" he confirms the description of the heavenly type and earthly antitype given in 8:2. Jesus did not live during the time of the tabernacle and could not have entered into the holy spaces of the temple since he was not a Levitical priest. This obvious statement then leads to what could *not* be observed during the earthly life of Jesus. Christ does not enter the ancient tabernacle nor Herod's temple but goes into that which the author can describe as *true*. This is not to say that the other tent that traveled with Israel was "false," because the author has shown many aspects of its goodness. This term emphasizes only that this heavenly tabernacle, and what happens in it, is the one that provided the standard for Israel's places of sacrificial worship. Moreover, it is a space that is true in the sense of being worthy of their trust (see the connection of trust in God's truthfulness in John 17:3; 19:35).

But Christ has entered into heaven itself. Scholars have debated whether the author envisions an actual structure in heaven. The presence of heavenly things (9:23) and the heavenly tent built by God (8:2) and revealed to Moses (8:5) suggests this. This verse confirms that interpretation because Christ, after being raised from the dead (13:20), has gone through the heavens to get there (4:14; 7:26).

Even if the precise nature of the location of Christ's entry remains debated, the clear and vital reality is that Christ is *now to appear before the face of God for us*. The author's description is very tangible, utilizing a term for *appear* that indicates a visual perception. This supports the idea that Jesus the Messiah appears before God embodied. God is personified as well, as having a face before which the Messiah can appear. The author of Hebrews is the only New Testament author to use the collocation "face of God," but he is in alignment with several authors of Israel's Scriptures (e.g., Gen 3:8; 4:16; 32:30; Judg 5:5; 1 Kgs 13:6).

Similar to Jesus going behind the veil *for us* (6:20), here he goes before God *for us*, indicating that this is a different way of saying much the same thing, for as the high priest met the descended presence of God behind the veil, so does Jesus meet the exalted presence of God by passing through the veil when he goes into heaven. He had no need to leave his heavenly throne in the first place but did so out of a desire to rescue his creation that was corrupted by sin and captured by death and the devil. Then he returned to his Father with the effective sacrifice *for us*. This representational appearing before God supports the interpretation that the necessity of cleansing the heavens was because of humanity being ushered into God's presence.

The author has established that Christ offers a better sacrifice in heaven itself, distinct from the animal sacrifices on earth. Now he turns to the difference in frequency between these offerings. Christ entered in *not so that he might offer himself often, as the high priest enters into the holies*[27] *year after year with the blood of another*. Strikingly, the instructions for the Day of Atonement in Leviticus—the only yearly offering with blood carried into the inner sanctuary—emphasize that ritual's *infrequency*. The high priest is cautioned that he cannot go in "every hour," but only on the tenth day of the seventh month (Lev 16:29), only once a year (16:34). Hebrews, alternatively, emphasizes that even an *annual* observance is repetitive; it happens year by year by year.

Moreover, in making this comparison of frequency by assuming (for a moment, in order to show its ridiculousness) that Christ would follow the pattern of other high priests, the author states again the distinction in what is sacrificed. The high priest enters in with the blood of another. Since Jesus offers himself by bringing in blood that he himself shed, and if he had followed this pattern of frequency, *then it would be necessary for him to suffer often from the foundation of the cosmos*. Two aspects of this statement are striking. First, it should not be missed that the author states that Jesus would have had to *suffer* often. On this point the comparison between the sacrifices of the first covenant and Jesus's sacrifice of the new covenant breaks down—or, said differently, this is another point of contrast between the first and new covenant systems. In the offering of animals, suffering was prohibited. The animals needed to be blameless (*amōmos*, as Hebrews describes Christ [9:14], a term used dozens of times to describe the sacrificial animals of Israel), which implied careful attention and preservation of their health. They could not be "beaten up" in preparation for the slaughter.[28] Slitting the throat brings their death as quickly as possible. Conversely, the author is aware that Jesus suffered. Although he portrays Jesus's offering presented when he is living, it is the offering of blood

27. The best manuscripts indicate that the author is using *ta hagia* again for the inner sanctum.

28. John W. Kleinig states, "The animal could not be . . . castrated, injured or maimed; it had to be a healthy specimen." *Leviticus*, Concordia Commentary (St. Louis: Concordia, 2003), 61.

that was shed through suffering. In fact, Jesus's suffering appears four times in the sermon (2:18; 5:8; 9:26; 13:12) as a key aspect of his exemplary and compassionate priestly and familial relationship with those who confess him. The necessary limitation on his suffering here—the assumption that he did *not* suffer from the foundation of the world—points to the fact that his human suffering culminated in his death on a cross, an unrepeatable event.

Second, intriguingly, the author dates this frequent suffering not simply from the time of the incarnation forward but instead *from the foundation of the cosmos*. Founding the cosmos is the same language the author uses for creation (4:3). Two assumptions undergird this assertion. First, a need for offering, thus indicating a break in the relationship between God and humanity, existed from the beginning. The author recounts the first murder (11:4), but this statement indicates his awareness of the entry of sin or impurity from the beginning. This might point toward an echo of the Adam and Eve narrative, the existence of the serpent who tempts them, or the existence of death and impurity even before the fall. This author, in contrast with Paul (Rom 5; 1 Cor 15; 2 Cor 3), has no explicit discussion of Adam and Eve, but instead puts his focus on the needs of all God's creation, dominantly those needs of the covenant family, Israel. Whatever the precise referent, this statement affirms that creation was in need of reconciliation from near the beginning. Second, the statement assumes that Jesus's one-time effectual offering for sin reverberates forward *but also backward*. If the world stood in need of an offering from the beginning, the author has already established that only Christ's would be sufficient. This is further confirmation that his death and living presentation did remove the sins committed under the first covenant (9:15). He has secured eternal redemption for those who came after him as well as those who came before.

If Christ followed the frequency pattern of the other high priests, he would have to suffer and die often so that he could make his offering repeatedly from the time of the world's founding. The author has assumed this frequency in order to show—emphatically—that it is *not* how God has worked. The work of Christ is not, as the author has said several times, repetitive. Instead, it is singular. The author contrasts hypothetical perpetual suffering since the founding of creation with the way things have actually happened. He begins by highlighting the reality of the present time: *but now*. The author has used the word "now" to indicate the time in which he and his readers live (2:8), even the moments in which they are listening to this sermon (9:5). In this time, in which they are blessed to live, Christ *has* truly *appeared.* The perfect tense of the verb communicates the continual effect of the one-time action. This is a different word from the one the author used in 9:24 for "appear," but this one also has a visual connotation. It refers to the entirety of his human appearance. First, this includes the incarnation. They have heard the message of salvation from those who heard and saw him in the flesh (2:3), during the one incarnate life he lived. Second, it includes his ascension. The appearance is also before God and the hosts around God (ch. 1) as he ascended to the right hand and lives to make intercession (7:25). Instead of often, like the high priest on Yom Kippur, he has appeared *once*, once on earth and once now resurrected has entered once into heaven. (Note that the author will soon discuss a second appearance to creation in 9:28.) The high priests may only appear before the altar once a year (9:7), but Christ has appeared truly only once.

He does so not at the foundation of the world but *at the completion of the ages*, a poetic balance to *the founding of the cosmos* as well as an alignment with the phrase "these days of the end" of the sermon's first sentence (1:2). The author believes that all of time has changed with the appearance of the Messiah. Christ's offering of his life before God indicates the completion of an era. With *the completion of the ages*, a phrase used elsewhere in the New Testament only by Matthew (Matt 13:39–40, 49; 24:3; 28:20), the author of Hebrews makes clear that Christ has inaugurated an end to the way things were. He has brought in the days that were future for Jeremiah so that God could complete the new covenant (Heb 8:8) at this end of the ages. Final judgment has not yet been experienced by the author and his audience—they still have some promises yet unfulfilled—but Christ's death has truly inaugurated the final end. This allows him to say, a bit later, that the time of the reception of the kingdom has already begun (12:28). Christ has made this possible *through the offering of himself.* Since the author has made clear that Christ did not bring in the blood of another but his own blood (9:14), the offering of his own blood is in fact a sacrifice of himself. Sacrifices deal with the problem of sin and separation from God, and his sacrifice of himself has dealt with separation—sin and death—once and for all.

That the author intends to connect these comments to the new-covenant passage is clear with the next phrase: he appears *for removal of sins*. He has made possible what the new covenant promised, God's merciful forgetting of sins (8:12). That assurance offers immediate comfort for those plagued by temptation and guilt. Christ allows a setting aside (*athetēsis*) of sin, which permits the author to instruct his readers, similarly, to lay aside (*apotithēmi*) sin (12:1). The connection between what Christ has done and what they need to do indicates that sin is still a reality for them, but it is possible to put it aside because of his sacrifice. As his appearance before God is perpetual as he sits on God's throne and intercedes, so too is God's mercy. In short, when he appears before God, God forgets sins.

For those who have been sinned against, God's forgetfulness might seem an injustice, an inability to attend to the damage done to the victim. I do not believe this is what is intended in Hebrews. The removal of sins is comprehensive. Christ provides healing to the one who has been hurt and the one who has done the hurting, for both are caught in the web of sin and damaged in different ways. All are in need of restoration. The removal of sin does not mean that God ignores the serious problems, but instead restores those damaged by the problem. Longing for the healing of all the victims of sin, even the perpetrators, allows the healing balm of Christ's forgiveness to radiate and restore. God forgets sin by healing it because the perpetually present High Priest has taken the cost of sin into the very life of God and paid it in full. Although Christ's offering is only once and the priests of Israel offered frequently, Christ is ever present before the Father, and hence there is no time in which the removal of sins is not before God's face. If the audience struggles with a singular event (Christ's death on the cross, resurrection, and ascension) that becomes more distant in the past as they move forward in time, the author is showing them that Christ's dealing with sin is an ever-present reality to which they have constant access.

To emphasize the singularity of the Messiah's sacrificial entry before God, the author brings forth a human example. *And just as it is held for humans to die once.* The verb for *held* indicates things stored up or held at the ready, so the sense here is one of waiting. All humans are awaiting death, and this is related to the fear they live under because of anticipating it (2:14). Whether it is natural (7:23) or through punishment (10:28) or through murder (11:4, 37), all humans die, and it happens only once. Death has not been cheated by any human other than Jesus. Death, however, is not the ultimate end, for the author speaks of both death and *after this judgment.* Resonant with other thinkers within Judaism (1 En. 1:7; 5:6; 50:1–5; 53–55; Dan 7:26; 2 Macc 6:26; 7:19, 17),[29]

29. See discussion in Attridge, *Hebrews*, 265; Johnson, *Hebrews*, 245.

including those who wrote the documents of the New Testament (Matt 10:15; 12:36; Luke 10:14; 11:31–32; 2 Pet 2:9; 1 John 4:17), this author assumes that death will be followed by God's judgment, most often imagined as a day of judgment for all humanity.[30]

So also Christ: since all humans die once and Christ is human, he, too, died only once. The singularity of all death, chiefly his, confirms the impossibility of repentance (6:4). If someone rejects his death and resurrection, there is no other option for repentance since Christ the human cannot die again. The language the author uses to describe Christ's death is this: he was *offered once*. In a dramatic portrayal of Christ's offering of himself, the author uses the passive form of the verb. It is Christ who does the offering (9:14, 25), but because he offers himself, it can also be correct to say that he *was* offered. The purpose of his self-offering was *to bear up sins of many.* To bear up sins evokes the sacrificial context with which the author has been engaged, where offering up sacrifices is done because of sins (Lev 4:26; 9:10; 16:25; 2 Chr 29:21). That he bears *up* the sins also conveys a vertical movement, in alignment with the resurrection, ascension, and enthronement of Christ, his movement through and into the heavens where he presents himself as sacrifice.

That being said, although the author has emphasized Christ's entry into heaven, where he presents his offering, this verse focuses on what precedes that living offering—namely, his death on the cross. The first clue is the passive verb. While he does offer himself, in no place is his passivity more evident than when he is dying on the cross. This is also a fitting image of "bearing up," as he is lifted on the cross (resonant with the theological contemplation of John's Gospel concerning the cross and the similarity to Moses's serpent; John 3:14). Moreover, while these two ideas, sins and offering up, appear in the sacrificial contexts, "bearing up sins of many" appears elsewhere only in Isaiah's description of the suffering servant (Isa 53:11, 12). The servant takes the sins of others with pain (Isa 53:11), unlike the sacrificial animals, but similar to the suffering Christ (Heb 9:26). Taking the sins of others is a fitting picture for one who was without sin (4:15). Isaiah's depiction is a text that other early Christians also associated with the cross (Matt 20:28; Mark 10:45; 1 Pet 2:24).

30. See an insightful treatment of human death and judgment in James Beilby, *Postmortem Opportunity: A Biblical and Theological Assessment of Salvation after Death* (Downers Grove, IL: IVP Academic, 2021).

Finally, the author says *he will be seen a second time* by humans. This indicates that humans saw him the first time when he bore up sin. Humanity saw him when he lived and then died the death that makes their salvation possible, and because it was fully efficient, the next time they see him, his appearance will be *separate from sin*. The author has asserted that this removal from sin is true of their High Priest now, that he is separated from sinners (7:26). Because he has fully dealt with sin, he need never address it again. This time, *he will be seen . . . by those who are eagerly awaiting him*. Anticipation is a concept Paul also frequently associates with the return of Christ (Rom 8:19, 23, 25; 1 Cor 1:7; Gal 5:5; Phil 3:20). That they have to wait for Jesus confirms that although Christ's offering occurred at the end of the ages (9:26), all is not finished yet. He will yet still appear *for salvation*. Those who wait for him must be patient for the coming of their salvation that Christ will bring, the fullness of the inheritance that awaits them (1:14). This completely changes how confessors of Christ live in the face of mortality and judgment. Because of their connection with Christ, the judgment that is awaiting them after death is God's pronouncement of salvation.

10:1–3 · THE SHADOW OF THE LAW

[1]*For the law—having a shadow of the good things to come, not the image of the things itself, year by year the same sacrifices being offered continually—was never able to perfect those who approach;* [2] *since, would the things offered not have ceased because those ministering, having been purified once, would not still have one consciousness of sins?* [3]*But with these [sacrifices], there is a reminder of sins year by year.*

Christ's one and sufficient offering returns the author to a reflection on the law, specifically the laws associated with sacrifice. Although this is an appropriate break, and so was determined to begin a new chapter, this section is connected by the term *for*, indicating that what follows will provide another line of argumentation to support the sole sufficiency of Christ's heavenly self-offering. Christ made an offering because the cultic laws, as good as they were, did not fully achieve salvation; they failed to deal with the consciousness of sin and the problem of death. Here the author describes *the law* as *having a shadow of the good things to come*. With the language of shadow and image, many have seen connections between his statements and some form of Platonic thought. This has been fruitful space for reflection on potential connections between the author of Hebrews and Philo, a Second Temple Jewish interpreter influenced by Platonic thought. The goods brought by Christ and the law show the general connections, as most students know from a reading of Plato's allegory of the cave. The way in which the author of the sermon uses the terms, however, shows his creativity rather than a slavishness to a philosophical system.[31] For Hebrews, the good things and the law are not two entirely different systems but are related in that they are both gifts from God. They are not equal, however, because the shadow is intended to point to the image/reality. For the author, the law sets up the system of sacrifice, which is given by God. Moreover, the laws help the people see who they are in relationship with God (9:19). God does not give up on the law wholesale but implants the divine laws into the minds and hearts of the new-covenant people (8:10; 10:16). The law of priesthood is changed with Christ because it did not bring perfection (7:12, 19). Hence, *shadow* language here conveys the same points as were present in 8:5. A shadow is evidence of a reality and grants some sense of the reality, its outline and scope. An approaching shadow could indicate that someone is approaching you, and if this is a good person, their shadow heralds a positive arrival. This is the case for how the author views the law.

The shadow indicates that *the good things are coming*. The law was the shadow of the impending incarnation and work of the Messiah. The author affirms that good things result from the suffering death and living ascension of Christ, as he did in 9:11. Between those two references he has specified that the good things include pure consciences, freedom from death, ministry to God (9:14), a new covenant, redemption of sins, an eternal inheritance (9:15), Jesus's living advocacy before God (9:24), removal of sins (9:26), and the promise of salvation (9:28). These are many good things indeed. At the giving of the law the coming of Christ was in the future, but now it is in the past for the audience who hear this sermon. The good things, however, are not limited to the past. Most other times the author speaks of what is to come, he points to the promises still yet to be realized for the audience. The law pointed not only to the work of Christ accomplished but also to the benefits that result at the full

31. Hebrews, *Attridge*, 269–71; James W. Thompson, *Hebrews*, Paideia (Grand Rapids: Baker Academic, 2008), 194.

completion of the age when he returns to grant salvation (9:28) and bring the unshakable kingdom (12:28).

As good as a shadow may be, it is *not the image of the things itself.* Shadows frequently convey temporality, the fleeting quality of life (1 Chr 29:15; Ps 101:12 LXX; 143:4 LXX; Job 8:9). As opposed to a shadow, an image is solid. It can be seen and touched, terminology that offers a beautiful affirmation that they serve an embodied Savior. In the New Testament, "image" most often refers to Christ, who reveals both God and true humanity (Rom 8:29; 1 Cor 11:7; 15:49; 2 Cor 3:18; 4:4; Col 1:15; 3:10). For Hebrews also, the image of those good things is the embodied Messiah. The laws herald his coming, and he enacts the good things they foreshadow. Here the emphasis is on the good things that *result* from Christ. This community has begun to experience the good things from his ministry in and among themselves (2:3; 8:9–12). The icon tradition in the Eastern church gives an example of this affirmation. Those intricate images painted prayerfully by hand act as a tangible conduit to draw one into worshiping the God of beauty. The good gifts among this community should draw them to reflect on Christ, which leads them to engage in worship of the triune God on the throne.

The author sets up the shadow-icon contrast to return to focus on the practices of the law. *Year by year the same sacrifices* are *offered continually.* The author triply emphasizes the repetitiveness of this system. Because he mentions *year by year*, his primary focus remains on the Yom Kippur sacrifice. He also says these are *the same* sacrifices and that they are *offered continually*, opening up the vision of his listeners to the other sacrifices that happen on a more regular basis. Despite the volume of sacrifice, the law is *never able to perfect those who are approaching.* Even when this system is functioning according to God's commands, from the author of Hebrews' perspective it lacks the ability to achieve perfection. That power simply does not reside within the system. God did not design it with that intent. The procedures for the high priest as laid out in Exodus 29 and Leviticus 8 do emphasize the eternal perfection of the priests, most often of their hands, which will perform the offerings (see also Lev 4:5; Num 3:3). As the author has stated (Heb 9:10) and will soon indicate again, this perfection part of the mortal body is not the full perfection he has in mind. *Those who approach* include both the priests who enter into the tents to do the offering and the people who bring the sacrifices, those whom the priests represent. Everyone in this system is approaching God, and graciously God allows it even though they are not fully perfected through it. The shadow had its place for millennia, but without being able to achieve perfection it was not meant to endure forever. As a shadow it was fleeting and pointed to something else.

The proof that the law lacks the ability to perfect is apparent, for the author, in its very repetitiveness. Of course, this "proof" was not evident to everyone, prominently the Jews who did not view Jesus's death as the end of the cultic practice. In addition to a belief in the effectiveness of Christ's death on the cross, a confession of his resurrection and living intercession before God led this author to see the Jewish cultic practice in this new light. For him, the continual presentation of sacrifices for sins indicated that the sins were still a reality that needed to be cleansed. He asks, *Would the things offered not have ceased because those ministering, having been purified once, would not still have one consciousness of sins?* Presenting in Greek a contrary-to-fact condition,[32] he offers a critique of the processes of sacrifice. If those approaching God through this system had been purified once and for all, they would have ceased to offer the sacrifices because they would have no consciousness of their sin. Hence, the opposite must be true. Because they were aware of their sin, they continued to offer, and that indicated that they had not been purified fully. The author sets the bar high with the word *mēdeis*, "not one." Even consciousness of *one* sin would demand offering. He has in view a complete perfection, which the previous system did not achieve.

The frequency assumes the opposite reality. *But with these [sacrifices], there is a reminder of sins year by year.* It is the case that the sacrificial system given by God was meant to have positive reminders. The implements in the tent, as mentioned by the author (9:2)—specifically the loaves—are intended as a reminder of the everlasting covenant (Lev 24:7–8). In Numbers the sacrifices are a reminder to God, needed to secure deliverance from enemies (Num 10:10). Here, however, the reminder focuses on the Yom Kippur sacrifice, made clear by the *year by year* ascription. Since it deals with "all sins" annually, it is the ritual that collects up all the others. The author sees that the sacrifices of the first covenant remind those involved that the sins need to be dealt with over and over because their effects are not fully eradicated with each offering. They can be done faithfully and still do not perfect the whole person permanently.

32. Harris, *Hebrews*, 253.

The author's logic sees the covenant between a holy God and an unholy people maintained through sacrifice. The people had been atoned through blood, but that blood atonement had to be regularly repeated. On the other hand, Christ's offering is singular; there is not a constant reminder of their sins. Because the effects of Christ's offering abide in a way the previous covenant's did not, there is no need for another atoning sacrifice. Put simply, there is a difference in the *endurance* of the effects between the offerings of animals and the offering of Christ. Jesus's offering, and the meal that commemorates it, confirms that the problem of sin has been dealt with once and for all. The author has opened wide the door to a pressing question: Is it the case that the new covenant brought by the priestly work of Christ *does* completely eradicate the consciousness of sin?

10:4–10 · THE SON'S SPEECH

4*For it is impossible for the blood of bulls and goats to remove sins.* 5*Therefore, en-*
tering into the world, he says,

> *Sacrifice and offering you did not desire,*
> *but a body you prepared for me.*
> 6*Whole burnt offerings and [offerings] for sins you did not desire.*
> 7*Then I said, "Behold I have come—in the scroll of a book it has been written concerning me—to do, O God, your will."*

8*Above saying that*

> *sacrifices and offerings and whole burnt offerings, and [that which is] concerning sins you did not desire nor were you pleased*

which are offered according to the law.
9*Then he has said,*

> *Behold I have come to do your will.*

He takes away the first in order to establish the second, 10*by which will we are*
those who have been sanctified through the offering of the body of Jesus Christ once and for all.

Readers might be wondering about the insufficiency of the first system. If God had instructed this system, why was it not sufficient? The answer for the author involves blood type. He states boldly: *It is impossible for the blood of bulls and goats to remove sins.* As he said earlier in 10:1, the system does not have the power within itself to deal with sins in a complete and enduring way. In a sacrificial context, bulls and goats appear together in only two places, both of which are sections in Israel's Scriptures critiquing sacrifice. In the first Israel is completing the sacrifices (Ps 49:9 LXX), but God reminds them that he already owns all the earth, and so God expresses the ultimate aims of the sacrificial system—namely, praise, dependence, righteousness, and an acceptance of God's discipline. Similarly, in Isaiah 1 the voice of the Lord decries the continuation of sacrifices when evil deeds are present in their souls (Isa 1:11–16). The sacrifices are abhorrent if they are not joined with "cessation from wickedness and learning to do good" (Isa 1:16–17 LXX). The term for "removal" is a bold one. It indicates that the sacrifices cannot "cut off" sin (this is the term used for the removal of the slave's ear in the garden of Gethsemane [Matt 26:51; Mark 14:47; Luke 22:50]; hence it has the sense of separation). The sacrifices of animals, as the prophets attest, do not take away sins.

Having stated plainly the law's insufficiency with regard to the removal of sin, the author focuses in on, not the shadow, but the icon, the Messiah himself. Because this sermon made such a boldly negative pronouncement about the sacrifices commanded *by God*, the author must show *from God's word* that the laws were shadows and not the icon. He supports his case with Scripture, so he introduces one who speaks through Scripture with the introductory phrase *therefore . . . he says.* The scriptural text is spoken this time by one who is *entering into the world.* All the other "entering" terms in Hebrews concern movement into God's space, either by God's people (3:11; 3:18–4:1; 4:3, 5–6, 10–11), the high priest in the first system (9:25), or Jesus himself (6:19–20; 9:12, 24). In this instance alone is someone entering into creation's space. That the Son moves into created space suggests that he comes from God's realm, and it shows his personal agency and intent prior to the incarnation. This is the Son who was with God the Father prior to the creation of all things (1:2) and exercised his decision to come into the world.

Then the author puts Psalm 39 LXX on the lips of the Son. This psalm continues the critique of sacrifice and the desire for faithfulness. It also has themes of endurance (v. 1), deliverance (v. 2), the internality of God's law

(v. 9), and proclamation (vv. 10–11), themes resonant across the sermon. The author cites from vv. 7–9, with a few differences from the Greek text.[33] Two are notable. First, the Hebrew version of the psalm has "ears you have opened for me," suggesting the idea of a person being able to hear God's instructions, but the version quoted by the author follows the older Greek translation that has "a body" instead. This is a clear indication that the author is drawing from the Greek text rather than the Hebrew, because the Hebrew text has "ears." In the psalm, "body" indicates that God's desire is for the whole person, yet this poetic expression could not be more fitting for the author, who has asserted that the eternal Son of God took on flesh and blood (Heb 2:14). He discovers here a declaration of the incarnation in the Scriptures of Israel. By mentioning this body God prepared, the author of Hebrews provides a tantalizing alignment with the traditions' assertion that it was God who prepared the body of the Son from the body of the Virgin Mary. Through God's gracious invitation, she assented to have her body overshadowed so that his body could be prepared from her flesh (Luke 1:26–38). For Hebrews, since human children share in flesh and blood, the Son took it on as well (2:14). It is she who provides the particular flesh and blood in which the Son of God becomes incarnate as Jesus of Nazareth. The second notable difference is that the author eliminates "I desired" from the last line he cites. The infinitive of "to do" then completes "I have come" rather than "I desired"; hence the author of Hebrews has the speaker say, *I have come to do*, rather than "I desired to do." The Son does not only express a desire to do the will of God but in fact comes to complete it.

With these distinctions clear, reading the psalm as the author has presented it reveals an alternation between what God does not want and what God has done instead. The psalmist recognizes that *God did not desire* either *sacrifice or offering*, the precise things the priests are called to offer (Heb 5:1; 8:3; 9:9; 10:1). Psalm 50:18 LXX and Hosea 6:6 LXX state the same idea, that God desires heartfelt and repentant obedience, not sacrifice alone. From the Messiah, God will receive both.

In response to this lack of desire, it is *God* who acts to create that which God *did* desire. The speaker says to God: *but a body you prepared*, using a word

33. Hebrews has *eudokeō*, "well pleased" (Heb 10:6), instead of *aitia*, "request" (Ps 39:7 LXX). *Mou*, "my," does not appear in Hebrews' citation, and *theos*, "God," is moved earlier in the phrase.

(*katartizō*) that indicates care, focus, and time, another fruitful alignment to the miraculous formation of his body from the Virgin Mary. Because this preparation happens *for* the speaker, it shows that he is sentient and communicative *before* he has a body. This also points to the personal existence of the Son before the incarnation. This verb highlights that God did this action for another—namely, for the speaker of the psalm. Hence, he says, the body is prepared *for me.*

The parallel structure of the psalm now names the particular sacrifices, including *whole burnt offerings and [offerings] for sins*, a distinction that appears in several sacrificial texts (Lev 5:7; 6:25; 7:27; 9:2, 7, 22; 12:6, 8; 14:13, 19, 22, 31; 15:15, 30; 16:3, 5; Num 6:6; 8:12; 15:24; Ezra 8:35). The whole burnt offering is to give something entirely in order to please the Lord. The sin offering is given when an error has occurred. These sacrifices are prevalent, occurring as well in places important thus far in the author's engagement with Scripture. God instructs these kinds of sacrifices early when telling Moses what the people will do when they are exonerated from slavery (Exod 10:25); these are offered to God at the covenant-inauguration ceremony (Exod 24:5); it is the offering prescribed for the consecration of the priests (Exod 29:18, 25), and God prescribes these for the Day of Atonement ritual (Lev 16:3, 5).

The psalm makes the clear claim that sacrifice itself does not please God. It is not the only text of Israel to do so. Jeremiah 14:12 LXX also makes this claim about God's lack of pleasure in sacrifice because the sacrifices are coming from people continuing in sin. Psalm 50:18 LXX makes the same critique, but once David humbles himself and does good, then God takes pleasure in whole burnt offerings (Ps 50:20 LXX). Animal sacrifice was prescribed by God, but it was never intended to be the only nor the most important thing that maintained a relationship of blessing between the people and God. It is heartfelt obedience that God desired most of all.

In the stanza of v. 7, after God does the action of preparing a body, it is the entering one who acts first by speaking: *Then I said.* The speaker has heard God's voice and now responds with direct address back to God. He recounts his action: *I have come.* The transition from a future verb to a perfect shows the passage of time. What God promised to prepare has come to be so that the entering one can inhabit that body and make it act according to his will.

With the interjection of the next line, the reader has to wait to hear *what* he has come to do, creating a sense of anticipation. His coming, though personally willed, is not independently invented. *In the scroll of a book it has been written concerning me.* His embodied arrival is in alignment with God's plan already written in Scripture. This is a fortuitous statement for an author who has seen the preview of God's filial revelation throughout the Scriptures of Israel. This statement resonates with the scene in which Luke, too, has Jesus interacting with a scroll to read about himself (Luke 4:17–20).

In the final line of v. 7 the intent of his arrival becomes clear: *to do, O God, your will.* The speaker has seen what God does not desire and, in response, enacts the plan of doing God's will. By ending here rather than including the rest of Psalm 39:9, the author, as mentioned, transforms the psalm text from an expression of desire to do God's will or God's law—even an internal desire that arises from the midst of the psalmist's gut (Ps 39:9b LXX)—to the enactment of it.[34] He ends the citation climactically with the performance of God's will. He will specify that particular will of God in the following section.

To make sure the point is clear, the author repeats portions of the psalm. This allows the statements to be made in the voice of the speaker another time, but in a newly arranged order. *Above saying that "sacrifices and offerings and whole burnt offerings, and [that which is] concerning sins you did not desire nor were you pleased."* He now groups the four sacrifices that are assessed negatively by God and emphasizes their repetitiveness by transforming the two singular nouns (sacrifice and offering) of v. 5 into plural nouns in v. **8**. He states again that God neither desired nor was pleased by them, parallel responses that convey affective reactions before and after the giving of the sacrifice (Ps 50:18 LXX joins these divine reactions together as well). About all of these, the author comments that they are those *which are offered according to the law.* The shadowy law of 10:1 is here specified as the sacrificial law. Even when these are offered correctly, according to the instructions prescribed by God, they are not God's ultimate desire. The author of Hebrews is not innovating against the Scriptures of Israel on this point. This conundrum of God's prescription of something that is not God's desire exists in the Scriptures themselves. The sacrifices are clearly graciously given by God to ameliorate sinfulness and impurity, but even the texts of Israel never describe the offerings as that which God wills (*thelō*). Instead, God sets them up to point to the ultimate divine will, the coming of the Son.

34. Intriguingly, the psalmist's desire to do God's will arises from his belly (*koilia*), the precise location where the Son enters the world to perform God's will (Luke 1:42; 2:21; 11:27).

For the author and his listeners, the Son's proclamation and enactment of God's will is in the past, which the perfect tense in the verse portrays: *Then he has said, "Behold I have come to do your will."* The best manuscripts lack the direct address to God, the vocative of *theos*, as appeared in the first verse of the citation (10:7), but the addressee of the speech is clear. In short succession the author has quoted this portion of the psalm twice. It is his strong desire that his readers hear this statement spoken by the Son to God the Father. The Son, as the one who creates, sustains, and purifies, shares this will about which he speaks (1:2–3).

The author puts forth the words of the Son twice to demonstrate this point: *He takes away the first in order to establish the second.* The shadow is no longer necessary once the reality arrives. The word choice here for "take away" is rather intense; it is a term typically used to describe death. This is appropriate if Jesus's death made sacrificial animal death unnecessary. What the blood of bulls and goats could not do (10:4), he did—namely, take away the need to deal with sin repeatedly. "Establishment" works well with the shadow/icon statements in that it portrays what is brought by Christ with a term that conveys firmness. "First" and "second" language evokes the covenants and the tents that are employed within them. The author will soon cite the new covenant passage again, evidence that this entire section is a reflection on that theme. The Messiah's drastic removal of the first confirms the author's statement that since the time of Jeremiah the first was growing old and was *near* disappearing. Now the Son has taken away the need for the first by introducing the promises of the second.

To fill out the implications he now specifies, *by which will.* God's ultimate will was not for repeated animal sacrifices but, as has been stated several times, for the Son to become incarnate, to die for all (2:9), to defeat death (2:14–15), to offer himself to God to remove sins, and, because of that, to distribute the Holy Spirit (2:3). By this divine will, the author can say, *we are those who have been sanctified.* This is the realization of the promise given to Moses at the outset of the first covenant (Exod 19:6) and reiterated throughout the law; sanctification is the result of keeping it (Exod 22:31; 31:13; Lev 11:44–45; 19:2; 20:7, 8, 26). Sanctification is a blessing of God that applied specifically to the priest (Lev 21) and the first fruits, including the firstborn who were marked for redemption (Exod 13:13–15; Num 18:15–17) and in Numbers redeemed by the Levites (Num 3:11–13; 8:16–18). Now sanctification applies to this community who has confessed Jesus as Messiah. This gift of God's Holy Spirit means that they have been made holy. The incarnate one has taken away the system of consecration in the first covenant and replaced it with his offering. This is now how consecration happens. What the law aimed to do and did for some bodies is now done for all externally *and internally* forever by Christ.

Recalling 2:11, where the sanctifier and the sanctified all share a common source, here it is God's will that unites the ones made holy with Jesus, for sanctification comes to them *through the offering of the body of Jesus Christ once and for all.* Twice the author has said that Jesus offers himself (9:14, 25), but in light of the psalm's attention to a body, now he specifies that *body* as the object of Christ's self-offering. The author has not spoken the name of Jesus since the first mention of covenant in 7:22, but with the naming of his body, it is appropriate to evoke his particular identity as the Jewish man. He is, at the same time, the anointed one, the Christ/Messiah. In other words, the ruling one is the same one who was willing to offer himself and serve as a priest. By this point in the sermon, it is important that the author had laid the groundwork for the unification of these roles in the scriptural person of Melchizedek (7:1).

Then, for the third time (also 7:27; 9:12), the sermon states that Jesus's offering is a one-time offering. Having become incarnate only once (2:14), having died and defeated death only once (2:15; 7:25, 27), his is a once-for-all offering (9:12). He cannot be born again, since he has already taken on flesh and blood from Mary. He cannot die again, because he is human (9:27) and, even more powerfully, because he has defeated death (2:14). He cannot be enthroned again, because God has given him supremacy forever (1:8). This is the logical unrepeatability that undergirds the warnings of Hebrews. If anyone turns away from what God has done once and for all in Christ, it cannot be done again. Because of his nature and faithfulness, this singular offering of his body is completely efficient, and it completely sanctifies.

In sum, God's will, articulated in the Psalms (which indicates that this plan is not new), is that the body of Jesus the Messiah be offered once. This includes his being lifted up on the cross and also presenting his resurrected body in heaven to God, so that the author and his entire listening community (original and ever thereafter) can be made holy. They have all moved into the category that will qualify them to see the Lord (12:14). They are all now like the priests who were prepared to come into God's sacred space. God desired the holiness of creation so that the deep and enduring relationship between

God and creation could exist. The law of sacrifice previewed and prepared for this, and Jesus the Messiah made it possible forever.

The author stated before he introduced this citation that repetitive sacrifice of the first covenant brought a remembrance of sins (10:2). For New Testament authors, "remembrance" (*anamnēsis*) is a weighty word, appearing outside this reference in Hebrews only in Jesus's words of institution (Luke 22:19; 1 Cor 11:24–25). A remembrance recalls another reality. In both the old and the new covenant, sacrifices serve as a reminder of the presence of sins, both for the people and for God. They also serve as a reminder of God's mercy in dealing with sin. The difference between the acts of remembrance in the old and new covenants is that the repeated sacrifices denoted the need to continue to sacrifice, whereas remembering Jesus's self-offering serves to remind participants that God has forgotten their sins (8:12) and that they have been sanctified (10:10). The question lingering at the end of 10:3 now has an answer. Whenever someone approaches the throne of grace with a need for forgiveness, this affirmation of Christ's sanctification should work to ameliorate the consciousness of sin.

10:11–18 · THE NEW COVENANT FOR US

[11]*And on the one hand, every priest stands ministering day by day and offering often the same sacrifices that are never able to remove sins,* [12]*but on the other hand, this one after he offered forever one sacrifice for sins sat down at the right hand of God,* [13]*still waiting until his enemies might be placed under his feet.* [14]*For by one offering he has perfected forever those who are being sanctified.*

[15]*And the Holy Spirit testifies to us, for after, [the Spirit] says,*

> [16]*This is the covenant that I will covenant* with them
> *after those days, says the Lord,*
> *giving my laws upon their hearts*
> *and upon their mind I will write them.*
> [17]*And their sins* and their lawlessnesses *I will never still remember.*

[18]*Where there is release of these, there is no longer an offering for sin.*

The author shifts his vision from the yearly to the daily sacrifice to underline the stark difference in repetition between the old and the new covenant, and this pivot allows him to highlight other differences as well.

> ***Old Covenant (v. 11)***
> every priest
> stands
> ministering day by day and
> offering often
> the same sacrifices
> that are never able to remove sins

The best manuscripts have *priest* instead of "high priest" at the beginning of v. **11**. Along with the mention of daily offerings, the external evidence makes this shorter reading the most coherent for the sentence. There are multiple priests and *every* one of them is involved in the work of sacrifice. That they *stand* (*hestēken*) contrasts with the establishment (*stēsē*) of the second system (10:9) brought about by Christ who sits (1:3; 8:1; 10:12; 12:2). The standing of the cultic servants appears in the Scriptures when the Levites are set apart and brought before Aaron in Numbers (Num 3:6; 8:16). Deuteronomy also describes the service of the Levites as standing and ministering (Deut 10:8). This posture is assumed in the description of the priestly services in which there is neither time nor a place to sit given the work they are doing in the first tent.

The author packs three reminders of repetitiveness into the next phrase, *day by day*, *often*, and *same*. Much as he said in 7:27, these sacrifices happened daily, mercifully maintaining covenant, but at the same time they were reminding the people that sacrifice was necessary because sin was still present. He noted that the same sacrifices were offered in the yearly ritual in 10:1, and now he rhetorically heaps up the lambs offered by referring to the morning and evening sacrifice (Exod 29:38–42; Num 28:3–8). So also he noted the "oftenness" of the annual sacrifice (9:25–26), and now he applies the same principle to the daily sacrifice. If there was any attraction to the idea of a daily offering to maintain relationship with God or the gods, the author is preparing to show how Christ's one-time offering for sins meets that desire and more, as it provides perpetual freedom from sin.

Reiterating what he said in 10:4, the author asserts the inability of these sacrifices to *remove* sins, using another form of the verb *haireō* (take away), this time *periaireō*, a less intense form than in v. 4 (*aphaireō*, "to cut off"), which simply indicates removing something or casting it away. These sacrifices, no matter that they were performed every day, could not purge sins from the midst of the people, a promise the Lord makes to the people of Israel in Zephaniah (3:11, 15), but one that is never claimed in the sacrificial narratives.

Verse **12** offers the other half of the contrast.

Old Covenant (v. 11)	*New Covenant (v. 12)*
every priest	this one
stands	sat down at the right hand of God
ministering day by day and	
offering often	after he offered forever
the same sacrifices	one sacrifice
that are never able to remove sins	for sins

Only *one* priest did this work, and he is the one on whom the author has been focusing, the one who offered his own blood and body. Here the author's offering language is in the aorist tense, *he offered*, indicating the punctiliar nature of his offering as opposed to the continual nature of the priests' offering (*prospherō* is in the present tense in v. 11). The author describes his body here as his *one sacrifice*, the singularity of which is very different from the daily repeated offerings of the priests, and yet his action aligns with what God asked of priests, to offer sacrifices. Whereas the others were not able to remove sins, this one offering is *for sins*, so that sins can be taken away (9:26). As opposed to offering often, he makes this one offering once, but the effects stand *forever*. The phrase for "forever" could modify either "offer" or "sit," but grammatically it is more likely connected to "offer," given that it follows that word.[35] This grammatical connection aligns with what the author has been saying. Jesus's one-time offering is present before God forever because *he* is present before God forever. The continual offering of the animal sacrifices (10:1) was ineffective, but the continual presentation of his one offering is effective, accomplishing God's will for the removal of *sins*. On the other hand,

35. Harris, *Hebrews*, 265.

if *forever* is connected to his being seated, to be sitting forever also evokes his continual presence before God. Although the author can speak of sin in the singular, almost as a power (3:13), here the word is in the plural, capturing the many sins of many people that he and he alone can remove completely. His perpetual presence before God to deal with sins is in alignment with his perpetual intercession (7:25).

The enduring nature of his one-time offering finds confirmation in the last phrase. After offering this one-time sacrifice, he *sat down at the right hand of God*, making his presentation of himself before God perpetual. This is the simplest reference to Psalm 109:1 LXX in the letter (see discussion at 8:1). While I believe that the author's choice of "world" in 10:5 demands that he has the approaching incarnation in mind for the Son's statement of Psalm 39 LXX, a reader could also imagine Jesus saying this same psalm upon his exaltation. "I have come before your face to present my body as an offering for sins, to do your will, O God." Since the author puts ancient Scripture on the lips of the eternally living Son of God, it is plausible that the Son can speak this statement on more than one occasion. Though the previous sacrifices garnered sanctification, at least for the priests, they could not remove sin. Only Christ's sacrifice could take it away completely (although imperfect humanity may need to access his elimination of sin regularly). The fact that he takes his seat indicates that Christ's work with respect to sin is done.

His story, however, is not complete. While he sits, he is *waiting*. The author specifies with an adverbial phrase that he is waiting *still*. This descriptor is confirmation that the completion of the ages (9:26), or these last days (1:1), is not one moment but a period of time in which the necessity of the old has been taken away, the promises of the new granted, but the restful kingdom remains in the future (12:28). For the remainder of these last days, he is in the state of anticipation *until his enemies might be placed under his feet*. The author cites from Psalm 109:1 again, as he did in 1:13, but changes the pronouns to the third person and the verb from active to passive since he is referring to God's speech rather than citing from the psalm directly.[36] This statement posits God the Father as the actor, working to subdue the enemies now that the Son's work of offering is done. That the enemies will be placed in a place of shame under

36. This citation also does not include the particle *an*, "ever," but the futurity of the statement is still communicated through the subjunctive mood.

his feet shows his sovereignty over all things and the control God will exercise over the forces now in opposition to the Son.

This evocation of the psalm shows that Jesus and his people are both waiting (9:28), looking forward to the fulfillment of God's promises, and that Jesus and his siblings' expectations are intertwined. Although his work with sin is done, sin remains a battle for his siblings (12:4) and therefore an enemy of his. Although he has rescued from death, they still have to face it in their mortal bodies (12:4), and so it, too, remains an enemy. The forces of sin and death still exist, but they themselves exist under a death sentence. When the Son's enemies, who are enemies of his siblings, are all subjected, then his siblings will attain the full salvation for which they are waiting (9:28).

In other words, the simultaneous experience of both completion and waiting applies to him and his followers as well. The author connects Jesus Christ's expectant session to the present experiences and future hopes of his followers with the phrase beginning v. **14**, *for by one offering.* For the fifth time now, the author refers to the offering of Christ (also 9:14, 28; 10:10, 12). This time he says that by it *he has perfected.* In contrast to the critique he has raised multiple times that the law of sacrifices did *not* perfect (7:11, 19; 9:9; 10:1), he proclaims that Jesus Christ, who has been made perfect (2:10; 5:9; 7:28) through suffering death and defeating it, can now perfect others. Although perfection is the standard to which God holds the people of Israel (Deut 18:13) and is the prayerful request of Solomon (1 Kgs 8:61),[37] like the experience of full and permanent sanctification, perfection remained one of the hopes of the community.

The author's assertion that through his offering Jesus has perfected those who are sanctified, which includes the addressees (3:1), stands in tension with his charge that they are *not* among the mature (5:14) and need to press on to perfection (6:1). The same difficulty applies to how he names them as *those who are being sanctified.* As a present passive participle, it conveys continuous action or a process of sanctification, but the author has previously said that they are those who *have been* sanctified (10:10).

The key to the riddle, it seems to me, lies in the intervening phrase *forever*, appearing here for the third time in this section. In each instance, it indicates continuous action instead of a static state. The continual multiple offerings

37. A prayer of which he falls short (1 Kgs 11:4; 15:3) but King Asa, at least in his heart, achieves (1 Kgs 15:14)

(10:1) stand in contrast to the singular perpetual offering of Christ (10:12). This occurrence in 10:14 asserts that the perfection that Christ has secured for all time is available continually. This is how to solve the tension between the completion of Christ's work with regard to sin and the continuing battle with sin in the lives of Christ's followers. By this one-time, ever-effective offering, they have access to continual perfection and continual sanctification. As long as confessors stay tethered to him, they can approach God's throne of grace (4:16) to have access to the perfection and holiness he offers.

This readily available perfection and holiness is how the new covenant, long ago promised through Jeremiah, is now possible. Having laid out the argument of Christ's high priesthood and what it has achieved, the author is ready to cite God's speech from Jeremiah again. *And the Holy Spirit testifies to us.* Testimony is the language this author uses for Scripture (7:8, 17; 11:5), and he continues the assertion that the Scriptures are not inert documents but instead living words by which God directly addresses him and his community (4:12). In this instance it is the Holy Spirit who is speaking, completing the action of a personal agent who communicates. There is not a fully developed pneumatology here, but the seeds present in this section of Hebrews resonate with other similar instances of Holy Spirit speech in the New Testament, which early interpreters like Justin appealed to in their formation of doctrine.[38] The Spirit of holiness is aligned with what God is doing but named differently than *theos*, "God." Unity of action and also distinction of person are especially clear in this instance because this Scripture is spoken for the second time. In ch. 10 it is now the Holy Spirit who is communicating the words that the Lord had spoken previously in the sermon. The alterations between citations in chs. 8 and 10 demonstrate the application of text to the congregation in the present by the work of the Spirit.[39]

The author introduces this Scripture with an articular infinitive, *meta to eirēkenai*, *for after, [the Spirit] says. Meta to* indicates subsequent action, usually communicated with the gloss "after." Following several minuscules and later versions, several translations divide the quotation in two. After the Holy Spirit

38. Kyle Hughes, *The Trinitarian Testimony of the Spirit: Prosopological Exegesis and the Development of Pre-Nicene Pneumatology* (Leiden: Brill, 2018), 92–94.

39. See Jack Levison, "The Theology of the Spirit in the Epistle to the Hebrews," *CBQ* 78 (2016): 90–110.

says the text of v. **16** (*This is the covenant that I will covenant* with them *after those days, says the Lord, giving my laws upon their hearts*), then the Spirit speaks the text of v. 17 (*And their sins* and their lawlessnesses *I will never still remember*). This seems a fitting break since this citation of Jeremiah 38 LXX in Hebrews 10 eliminates 38:33–34 ("and I will be their God and they will be my people, and each will not teach his fellow citizen and each his sibling, saying, 'Know the Lord,' because all will know me from the least to the greatest of them") that would come between the text of 10:16 and 10:17 if they were cited here as they were in 8:10–11. The manuscript tradition is an indication that some scribes made sense of the articular infinitive *for after* in this way, by including the phrases "saying earlier" (v. 15) and "later he says" (v. 17). With this division, the promise of the covenant stated earlier is followed by the more recent assurance of forgiveness.

This division, however, is not in the earliest manuscripts, in which the phrase "later he says" is not inserted into the Jeremiah quote in v. 17. Another point against this reading is that *both* parts of the citation are in the future tense. In addition, in its original setting in Jeremiah, this portion is not divided into a "then" and a "now." If the author did not put the division in, in line with a unified Jeremiah text, he might have used the introductory phrase for an alternative meaning: *after* the one offering of Jesus, then the Holy Spirit speaks the Scripture anew *to us*. The citation in ch. 8 concerns the fault God found in the first covenant and how the people made missteps within it. It is focused on the time of Jeremiah. Now that the work of Christ is done, and now that this author has explicated it for his listeners, they are ready to hear this text again in a fresh way. They do not need to hear the story of exiled Israel again, nor be reminded of the relationship and knowledge of God that they have already experienced. They do, however, need to hear the description of the new covenant, how it instills God's law within them, and how it brings forgiveness to them. Consequently, in this citation the author does not refer to the covenant as that which God makes with the house of Israel, as Jeremiah says (38:33 LXX) and as he had quoted in 8:10, but he says that this is the covenant God makes *with them*. The Holy Spirit is speaking the new-covenant passage to them after they have been reminded of and taught about the work of Christ, which took place after God spoke the promise to Jeremiah in the first instance.

The Holy Spirit says, *This is the covenant that I will covenant with them*. Since the Holy Spirit is speaking to them, the Spirit says that the covenant is with them, rather than mentioning Israel and Judah as in 8:8. This community, whoever they may be, is not replacing the house of Israel (8:10), since Christ gives aid to the seed of Abraham (2:14) and the addressees of the prophets are their ancestors (1:1). They are caught up in the covenant promise to the people of God, but the Holy Spirit specifies that this is not just for their forebears in the past, but it is addressed *to them.*

If the Holy Spirit is speaking to them in the present, the inclusion of the phrase *after those days* suggests again that the full arrival of the new covenant for which Jeremiah had hoped has come true for them. The days in which they live are the last days (1:2), and the author asserts that they can still respond to God's call (it is still called today, 3:13). The new covenant is available for them. The author's choice to include the phrase *says the Lord* shows the alignment between the voice of the Lord and the testimony of the Holy Spirit. These words, which are largely the same words, overlap, but there are two different agents speaking.

When God establishes the covenant with them, this will include *giving my laws upon their hearts.* The first citation of this verse from Jeremiah stayed in line with the prophet's order, but this time the author of Hebrews switches *hearts* and *mind.* I do not see that this changes the meaning of this text since both lines still appear. That God "gives" shows the graciousness of God, initiating this covenant and giving what is necessary for it to continue. That the laws are God-given suggests that, although the author has shown the temporal nature of the cultic laws, this statement affirms that the entirety of God's law has not been abrogated. The author has consistently argued that the law of priesthood and sacrifices has been changed (7:12), but also that they have not been eliminated. There is still a High Priest who has offered a sacrifice. On the other hand, the law organizing the repetitive first-covenant sacrificial system cannot bring perfection (7:19; 10:1), but God can. God can bring perfection—and has (10:14)—*through* the laws' instructions. Now that people will have purified consciousness freeing them to serve God (9:14), God can give the divine laws on their hearts. The plural of hearts is attentive to the individuals within this covenant. God will place good laws on just that instrument prone to hardening and lack of trust (3:8, 10, 12, 15; 4:7).

And upon their mind I will write them. In the next line, the parallelism of Hebrew poetry utilizes a different term to capture the internal nature of a person, *the mind*, a term the author uses only in his citation of Jeremiah. In some New Testament literature, the heart and mind are distinct, as in Jesus's repetition of the great commandment (Matt 22:37; Mark 12:30; Luke 10:27), indicating that this term is specifically focused on one's thoughts. God's promise is that their way of thinking will be shaped by the law. Here the singular noun, *mind*, with a plural pronoun, *their*, emphasizes the opposite of the previous line, not the individuals of the community, but the community members' shared mindset. Groupthink can be for good or ill, and here, if it is shaped by God, it will be for encouragement and edification. The Lord is very active here again, portrayed as inscribing the laws into their minds. Contemporary readers might think of the painstaking work of rerouting neural pathways, but an ancient reader would imagine the care of a scribe taking time to write well and clearly, respecting the grains of the papyrus so that the text is as readable as possible. Writing on the mind is intimate divine work, showing again God's graciousness to take the effort to do it.

The author then moves to the last line of his previous citation of Jeremiah's new-covenant prophecy, *And their sins.* Sins are what sacrifices are aimed at but cannot remove. Christ's offering, however, has, as the author said in the first sentence, made purification for sins (1:3) and has atoned for sins (2:14). Being without sin (4:15), he has borne sin (9:28) so that it might be removed (9:26). He never needs to deal with sin again (9:28; 10:12), but sin remains a threat for this community (3:13; 10:26; 12:1, 4), and they can access his aid to deal with it (2:18).

The author then adds another phrase to the citation of Jeremiah 38, although it is language that Jeremiah uses in other places (Jer 2:29; 5:25; 6:13; 16:18; 36:23): *and their lawlessnesses.* What God had given, the good instruction of the law, the people had transgressed. This was an act worthy of death (Heb 10:28). Even so the Lord promises, *I will never still remember.* Changing the aorist subjunctive (8:12) to a future indicative (10:17) in this version of the citation, the vision is clearly aimed at the future. Now that this time has arrived, the Holy Spirit asserts that God will never again remember their failures and shortfalls. The author knows they will still struggle with sin as they continue to grow in the discernment of increasing maturity. Staying tethered to the one who mediates this covenant, they can rest assured that their sins will be perpetually forgotten, justly and with healing, by God.

The author concludes this long and intense section with a statement that begins, *But where there is release of these.* Because of Christ's shed blood, there is forgiveness (9:22), release of sins and lawlessness. These are not retained against the people but let go. Where this is the case, within the new covenant that he is bringing, *there is no longer an offering for sin.* This new covenant means that sins, which were regularly remembered during the time of the first covenant, through the God-ordained practice of regular sacrifices, are now released. They do not have to be remembered, because they are gone. He has made the offering once and for all, and so no sacrifice needs to be offered again. If they succumb to sin, they do not need to make a sacrifice, but appeal to the mercy that comes through the new covenant mediated by Christ. Hence, the divine forgetting of sins will be ever available but has to be accessed by approaching the throne (4:16), by following the one who has gone within the veil (6:20).

The author of Hebrews is making a radical claim. So radical that it is hard to believe in light of the sin we see evident within and around us. This claim makes the author a companion of Paul, who was misunderstood to be saying that "sin should increase so that grace can abound" (Rom 6:1–2). As the following warning section will show (Heb 10:26–31), and as the previous warnings have emphasized (ch. 3 especially), the complete forgiveness of sin because of the offering of Christ is not a license to engage in sin. Nor is it God turning a blind eye to the painful damage wrought by sin. Quite the opposite, the lack of necessity for any more offerings opens the call to complete sanctification of body and mind that is now possible.

At the same time, the radical forgiveness should not be lost in the admonition toward sanctification. Earlier I had posed the question, "Is it the case that the new covenant brought by the priestly work of Christ does eradicate the consciousness of sin?" The precise and passionate argument of the author of Hebrews leads me to say yes. The arrival of the new covenant truly means that sins in one's past and in one's future are already taken care of by Christ. If one sins, forgiveness is freely available because it has already been secured. This should radically impact how one prays to and lives before God. This assurance is what gives access to the throne of God with confidence (as the author asserts in 10:22). This truth should also radically impact how one deals with others. When they sin knowingly or in ignorance, a confessor of Jesus can access the living High Priest's completed work with respect to sin in order to pray for and interact with others. Christ's self-offering that removes sins is the foundation on which one can pray both of the heavy lines of the prayer Jesus taught (Matt 6:12/Luke 11:4):

> Forgive us our trespasses
>   as we forgive those who trespass against us.

HEBREWS 10:19–39

APPROACHING IN FAITH

Now that the author has invested significant energy to present the relationship between the new covenant and Jesus the Messiah's priesthood, he builds on that connection to offer a series of encouragements and admonitions to his listeners. In vv. 19–21 he reminds them of what they have as members of the new covenant: a bold way into the presence of God and a great High Priest who is there in the presence of God for them. Strikingly, as he describes this, it becomes clear that Jesus is both the way and the goal. As they focus on him, they can respond to the three invitations to action the author presents in vv. 22–25: approach, hold fast, and attend to one another.

These three directives lead the author to the next major warning passage, where he shows the mirror opposite of their confidence. He describes what *would* be the case if they ceased to be confessors of Christ, those who fail to approach, hold fast, and attend. He also states again the impossibility of any salvific sacrifice other than that given by Jesus. To paint the consequences of such sinful rejection of God's Son, the author both cites and alludes to examples of failure and punishment under the Mosaic law (vv. 27–28). Then, with three intense phrases (v. 29), he describes what someone who disrespects the gift of God in the Messiah is really doing. Assuming that they will agree that a worse punishment is necessary in such an instance, he cites from Deuteronomy where God judges the people of Israel after they turn away from him. There is no escape from God's holy presence, and therefore they should be appropriately fearful of shaming God's Son.

As he has done with the previous warnings, in the following section the author offers another comfort for his community. In so doing, he presents one of the most extensive insights into their past in the sermon (vv. 32–34). They both suffered personally and aided others who were suffering, demonstrating the virtues of Christ as they trusted in him. Building on their exemplary past, he issues one final warning: they need to keep going. As the prophets proclaimed God's coming justice (vv. 37–38), he assures them of Christ's perfectly timed return and reminds them once more of the consequences of not waiting for him in faith. He is confident, however, that they *are* people of faith, and so he provides for them more examples of it from their family's past. This leads him to the well-known catalogue of the faithful preserved in Hebrews 11.

10:19–25 · THE ONE WHO PROMISED IS FAITHFUL

[19]*Therefore, siblings, having boldness for entrance into the holies by the blood of Jesus,*
[20]*which is a new and living way he inaugurated for us through the veil—that is, his*
flesh, [21]*and having a great Priest over the house of God,* [22]*let us approach with a*
true heart in full assurance of faith as those who have been sprinkled from an evil conscience with respect to the hearts and as those who have been washed with pure
water with respect to the body; [23]*let us hold fast to an unwavering confession of hope,*
for the one who promised is faithful. [24]*And let us attend to one another for strength-*
ening of love and good deeds, [25]*not deserting the gathering of yourselves, just as is the*
habit of some, but encouraging, and all the more as you see the day drawing near.

Because the priestly work of Jesus has perfected them (10:14), sanctified them (10:10), and taken away their sins (8:12), they can go into God's presence, and so the author invites them there: *Therefore, siblings*. He evokes their familial identity as children of God, which appeared with the term "sibling" in the Jeremiah citation (8:11) but not in the author's own voice since 3:14. Now that the sermon has walked through the entirety of the priestly argument, the impact of God's plan to become a human priest and offer a sacrifice so that humanity could be in the family of God, the author's rearticulation of the familial identity is more clear and more powerful. In addition to their familial identity, this verse ascribes to them priestly privileges. They have boldness for *entrance into the holies*.[1] The neuter plural is used again as a way of referring to God's space, as in 9:24. That being the case, their ability to go into this realm allows them

1. The noun *eisodon* (entrance), which has a verbal aspect, is followed by *tōn hagiōn* (the holy place), which is an objective genitive, the object of the verbal aspect of the first noun.

greater access than the priests, who can only enter the outer areas of the tabernacle, and even greater access than the former high priests, who had access to the holiest space *on earth*. They are allowed to enter into the holiest space in heaven, where God dwells. Moreover, they get to enter not with trepidation but with *boldness*, a virtue the author encourages them to embrace here and in 4:14. This is a virtue he also challenges them to hold on to in both 3:6 and 10:35. Clearly, they are entering with confidence not in their own righteousness but in what Jesus has secured for them.

That the way is opened *by him* is made clear by the last phrase: *by the blood of Jesus*. The author last referred to his blood in 9:14, where he designated it as the blood of the *Messiah* that purified their conscience from works of death to serve the living God. Now the phrase emphasizes the humanity of *Jesus*. It is this blood that allows entrance into the space where they can minister to God. Like other priests, they are able to enter in because of the blood of another. For them, it is not blood of a slaughtered animal but the effective blood of the sinless Son of God.

The threefold liturgical "by, with, in" from the eucharistic prayer might be just the kind of fulsome language appropriate to capture the preposition *en* (translated simply as "by" above) in this last phrase of v. 19. As the prayer says, "All this we ask through your Son Jesus Christ: By him, and with him, and in him, in the unity of the Holy Spirit all honor and glory is yours, Almighty Father, now and for ever." Because of what he did by shedding and presenting his blood with his trailblazing leadership going behind the veil, and because they are sharers of him (3:1, 14), it is the blood of Jesus that makes possible the children of God's bold arrival into the holy realm. This entrance is possible by the work of Christ, with the advocacy of Christ, and because they are sharers in Christ.

The antecedent of the relative pronoun *which* that begins v. **20** is "entrance" (*eisodos*). This entrance is *through the veil*. The veil language calls up the imagery of the tabernacle that the author constructed for their mental schema in 9:1–5, and since he mentioned only one veil, on the other side of which is the holiest space (9:3), this is where the audience imagines they can go in. Not the holy space on earth, but as ch. 6 confirms, this is the most holy space in God's realm where Jesus has already gone in (6:19–20). Going through the veil is the same as entering into the holies.

In the next clause, the author describes two features about this entrance: it is new and it is personal. First, he emphasizes its newness. The author describes the entrance as a *new . . . way*, employing a term used for fresh food (Num 6:3) or recent events (Deut 32:17; Ps 80:10 LXX; Eccl 1:9; Sir 9:10). Although this community should be teachers because of the time since their conversion (5:12) when they heard about Jesus from his original followers (2:3), even so the events of his life are not distantly in the past but relatively recent. The way that he has opened has not been there for a long time but is new. Being now two thousand years removed from his earthly life, the way he has opened has not now become old, because it began a new age in which confessors still live. In addition, the author names the action of Christ and emphasizes its close proximity in time by saying that *he inaugurated* this new way. When paired with something new, this term is used for the dedication or consecration of a thing for the action for which it was created. Just as the first covenant was inaugurated with blood (9:18), so too the way to God has been inaugurated by the blood of Jesus.

Having just mentioned blood in v. 19, now the author turns to the body of Jesus. When he does, he highlights the second feature of the way, its personal nature. He does so by describing this way as *living*. The way is not a thing but a person. That it is alive solidly associates this way with God, whom the author frequently describes as living (3:12; 9:14; 10:31; 12:22; as is the word of God, 4:12). Moreover, both the namesake and the fulfillment of the priestly order of Melchizedek are living (7:3, 8, 16, 25). Hence the life of this way prompts the readers to see it not only as a way to God but also as a way *of* God, made possible by the Priest who defeated death as the incarnate God and now lives forever. The author also shows the personal nature of this way by saying that it is *through the veil—that is, his flesh*. With the mention of his blood in v. 19, the readers are reminded that he is recently slain and yet now living, an unmistakable reference to his death and resurrection. That allusion illuminates the author's equation of the entrance with the flesh of Jesus. The way they pass through is a person, specifically his flesh. In other words, if they are going to arrive with God, they will need to pass the way of Jesus's flesh; hence they need to experience resurrection as he did. That resonates with the author's assertion that this inauguration was *for us*. The Son was ever with God but then became human and defeated death *so that* his human brothers and sisters could do the same, dwell with God forever. Now he has made possible what was not possible before, eternal embodied life. Because he lives, this way of following him into eternal embodied life is always available, always a live option.

The author has focused on their pathway to God, how they should enter (with boldness) and the way of their entry (Jesus himself). Then he focuses on

Jesus not as the way but as the goal. As they are moving toward God's realm, they also have *a great Priest* who is already there. An adjective he uses several times for Jesus (4:14; 13:20), *great* need not be in comparative form here ("greater") since the author has already shown multiple times the Son's superiority over other priests. If God is the greatest (6:13), then their priest is the same. No one can be greater. It is striking, then, that in this last reference to Jesus as priest, he is simply *Priest* rather than *High* Priest, the author's preferred term (2:17; 3:1; 4:14, 15; 5:5, 10; 6:20; 7:26, 27, 28; 8:1, 3; 9:11). High priests are, of course, priests, so this title is not in disagreement with the rest, but the author's use of only "priests" here may create a connection back to the Psalm 109:4 LXX citation (first in 5:6), showing his dependence on Scripture for this view of Jesus's vocation. Because they *have* him, they have access to all the blessings he provides.

That their priest is *over the house of God* asserts both his presence with God in the holies behind the veil as well as his sovereignty over all things (1:2, 13), since God is the builder of all (3:4). This statement connects with the opening paragraph of ch. 3, where the author compared Moses as a servant in God's house to Jesus, the Son over God's house. Since the author equated the house of God with himself and his listeners, that Jesus is over this place indicates not that he is distant and removed from them as he dwells with God but that he reigns over their congregation directly even as he is with God. Because the Jeremiah citation also utilized house language three times (8:8 [twice], 10), this phrase also connects them with the house of Israel. Interpreters may disagree over their ethnic identity, but according to the author, whatever their background might be, they are now within God's household, those with whom God chooses, repetitively, to make covenant.

With bold faith in their High Priest, the author invites his listeners, *Let us approach*. Continuing the journey motif, he invites them into forward movement as he did at 4:16 ("let us draw near"). This invitation is also closely related to his description in 7:25 ("those who are approaching"). Since they have a great priest who has opened this way, they can approach. As they do so, they are positioning themselves as those whom he is ultimately able to save to the utmost (7:25a) since they are those for whom he is making intercession (7:25b). This faithful approach will qualify them to please God (11:6) and ascend Mount Zion (12:22).

It is not surprising, then, that the author has criteria for their approach. They should come *with a true heart*. The singular *heart* for a group of people highlights their connection to one another, a preview of what he will soon admonish in 10:25. In distinction from the hearts of the wilderness generation, which were hard (3:8, 15; 4:7) and deceived (3:10), they can reject the evil unbelieving heart (3:12) that he warned them against now that the new covenant has opened the door for God to place the good laws in their hearts (8:10; 10:16). They can approach with *true* hearts, not ones that are duplicitous, and *in full assurance of faith*, a phrase that shows the author is playing off the warning in ch. 3 to show its opposite. Instead of being unfaithful like those who wandered in the wilderness (3:12, 19), they can have the fullness of faith. To have this faith is to trust in the one who is faithful, to trust that God the Son is the glorious revelation of God the Father's faithfulness (2:17; 3:2; 10:23; 11:11). Trust in God's faithfulness, for the author of Hebrews, is a posture toward God that results in action, as it did for Joshua and Caleb (4:2) and Abraham (6:12). He reminds them that they are a community on a journey, trusting God to lead them to the promised end (4:3).

As he urged them to carry the fullness of hope (6:11), here he encourages the fullness of faith, another evidence that he is laying the groundwork for his extensive discussion of faith in the next chapter. That he chooses to employ a term (*plērophoria*) related to the verb *pherō*, "to bear," connects the holding of their assurance to the sacrifice that Jesus carried in (Heb 5:3; 9:14, 25, 28; 10:12).

If the author left the exhortation here, readers might worry about the ability of the original listeners to maintain such a posture given that he has warned them against falling back into the opposite stance toward God—namely, lack of faith. Therefore, he assures them further that they can enter with this kind of faithful heart because they are those *who have been sprinkled from an evil conscience with respect to the hearts.* Precisely that danger which he urged them to be on the watch for—namely, an evil heart (3:12)—has been attended to by this sprinkling. The battle they fight against sin (12:4) begins in the heart. Because he warned about individuals in the community who might have this problem in ch. 3, here he assures with the plural noun *hearts* that each heart is sprinkled. Highlighting the divine consistency in method, they have been sprinkled as the first covenant instructed for inauguration (9:19, 21) and purity (9:13); here, though, the internal aspect of the person receives the sprinkling. That which was not possible with the blood of animals (9:9; 10:2) is now possible with Christ. That which the author looked forward to in 9:14 ("how much more *will* the blood of Christ . . . purify our conscience") he now says has already been applied. Their hearts have already been sprinkled (perfect tense), and so the evil conscience has been removed.

This transformation applies not only to the internal dimension, however. The author also says that they are those *who have been washed with pure water with respect to the body*. The collocation of washing, the body, water, and purification aligns this phrase with the red-heifer ritual described in Numbers 19. As the first covenant had a procedure for purifying bodies that encountered death, so too does Christ. By offering his body (10:5, 10), he has made it possible for the body of this community (the singular noun yet again puts the emphasis on unity) to be purified. That this happens through the medium of water and not blood suggests an allusion to baptism (a similar idea is expressed in Eph 5:26). In fact, the instrument of pure water could apply to both the hearts and the body, a confirmation that Christian baptism affected the whole person (Gal 3; Rom 6). With such activity being done to them, they could ask for no higher degree of confidence as they enter into God's presence. As they are on the path to dwelling with God bodily forever, they can even now boldly approach God's throne in worship and prayer (as stated in Heb 4:14). Hebrews offers meaningful relational engagement with God in the present, as members of Christ who look forward to their future.

At the same time, they must not have fully entered into God's heavenly space, because the author has one more admonition: *Let us hold fast.* He used this particular instruction twice in ch. 3 (vv. 6, 14). There also it was related to God's household. They are God's house as they display the firmness of a building, holding fast (3:6). Similarly, they remain partners of Christ, very sensibly, as they stay tethered to him (3:14). As is so often the case in the sermon, the author urges both approach and steadfastness, forward movement as well as retention of a confession previously made. For the author, these are not in opposition but necessary to each other. They can only move forward toward Jesus, on the pathway that is through him, as they stay connected to him. Therefore, since he asks them to hold fast to *the confession* and in every instance the confession is related to Jesus, then holding fast to him is to hold fast to their word of agreement about who he is and what he has done. In this instance, the content of the confession consists *of hope*, which is a virtue the author encourages often (3:6; 6:11; 11:1). The christological nature of the confession is maintained by describing it as one of hope since the author has drawn such close associations between hope and Jesus's work (6:18; 7:19). Their confession, as is true in the Creeds passed down through generations to Christians today, is not only a proclamation about the past but also concerns what God will do in the future. The movement between past and future is why the author asks that they hold on to this *unwavering* confession. The confession itself is firm because it is based on God's solid and trustworthy work in Christ.[2] It follows from this point that since the confession of what God has done in Christ is unchanging, they can hold on to it, without wavering, an idea that works well with the image of forward movement (without wavering they can stay on the straight path toward God; 12:13). The unwavering confession also works with the admonition to hold fast, or that they should remain steadfast. They will be able to do so because they have already seen what God has done in the past, and so can trust what God will do in the future. Hence, the author is able to say, *For the one who promised is faithful*. God is the one who made a promise to Abraham and Sarah and kept it (6:12, 13, 15; 11:11, 17). God the Father made a promise to Jesus the Son and kept it (8:6). God has made the promise of the new covenant and brought it to fruition. God has made promises to this author and his community (6:17): to enter rest (4:1), to receive an eternal inheritance (9:15), to shake the earth and heaven (12:26). Consequently, they can trust that these promises as well will come to fruition. As those acquainted with the story of Israel, they know the God of Israel to be trustworthy, but through the sermon the author has reminded them of pertinent examples of faithfulness to strengthen their faith. While God, often specified as the Father, has made the promises and so has shown faithfulness, it is the Son who is most often described as faithful, a faithful High Priest (2:17) and faithful to God (3:2). The audience is aware that the Father's promises have been and will be realized by the faithfulness of the Son. The one who promises includes both the Father and the Son, as well as the Holy Spirit who has communicated the promises.

As they hold on to Jesus, approaching him and approaching God's presence through him, they also need to be mindful of one another, and so the author adds the third admonition of this paragraph: *And let us attend to one another*. This is no surprise as his previous admonitions focused on them as

2. Johnson's reading seems correct: "It is a natural temptation to make [this word] translate the unswerving conviction of the believers, as though it were an adverb. Nevertheless, the emphasis here is on the confession itself as steady, as the next clause makes clear: they can hold on, because the one who has made the promise is 'faithful' (*pistos*)" (*Hebrews*, 259).

individuals and as a group. As he urged them earlier to devote their thoughts to Jesus (3:1), now he asks them to turn their minds to the fellow members of their family. The goal of this attention is *for strengthening*. As the only New Testament author to use this term positively, the author has chosen a word that most often indicates some kind of "irritation."[3] It serves as an honest reminder that community life is not always positive and comfortable, but it is often the difficult moments that result in growth, an insight that has to be shared with all pastoral sensitivity. As God disciplines because God loves (12:6), so too community members should be willing to enter into hard situations when necessary out of love. If they are willing to be honest and bold in their attentiveness to one another, their attention will result in the strengthening *of love and good deeds*. They have already demonstrated love through deeds when things were difficult in their community (6:10), and so the author invites them to continue to do so. As was true with what God had done in the past, their past should give them confidence for their future action. By naming both love and work, the author encompasses both the attitude they should have toward one another and what should result from that attitude. He leaves no space for a love that does not act.

They cannot do any of this for one another unless they are meeting together, and so the author states an obvious corollary to his last hortatory subjunctive: *not deserting the gathering of yourselves*. In New Testament literature, the word for "deserting" has a more intense meaning than "forgetting" or "neglecting." It conveys not a sense of being distracted and failing to attend but an active desertion. For example, the word appears on the lips of Jesus in the cry of dereliction from the cross (Matt 27:46; Mark 15:34) and the woeful tale of those who have deserted Paul (2 Tim 4:10, 16). This term evokes the intense warning against falling or turning away (Heb 6:6), which is not surprising given that another warning passage is on the horizon. The author does not want them to reject the closeness of the group who is *gathering*, a term that conveys proximity and intimacy (Matt 23:37; 24:31; Mark 1:33; Luke 12:1; 2 Thess 2:1).

This admonition is necessary because some have neglected this gathering, and so he adds *just as is the habit of some*. The term *habit* indicates that this desertion is neither a singular anomaly nor an irreparable act. It has become customary for some; they have done it several times, but that does not necessarily mean that

3. "*Paroxysmos*," LSJ, 1343.

they cannot change their habits (as the author urged the listeners to do in 5:14) and return. Those who have chosen regularly *not* to gather might be the ones the author names as weary and weak, in need of the strengthening of encouragement (12:12–13). He wants the influence to move in the right direction so that all are gathered in together, rather than have a situation in which those with poor habits draw the faithful into their desertion. The author does not want that to be true for those who are reading his missive. Hence, he urges the opposite of deserting each other when he says *but encouraging*—literally, be near so that you can speak. He does this for them through the sending of this sermon, even when he cannot be present in body (13:19, 22). He urges them to practice the same encouragement for each other (3:13) as they stay together through regular meeting.

He wants them to be about the work of encouragement *all the more as you see the day drawing near*. Given the challenges their community has faced, and potentially could face in the future (12:4), encouragement is vitally important. This need is even more pressing in light of their ability to read the times. They are in the last days (1:2), living while it is still called today, and they hear God's voice (chs. 3 and 4). The day that Christ will return for full salvation (9:28) and their transformed bodies can draw near to God (7:19) is, as Paul says, nearer than when they first believed (Rom 13:11). Until the final end of these last days, they must be in regular, thoughtful, and mutual relationship with other members of the family of God.

Hebrews 10:25 is one of the few instances in which an ethical instruction has a clear prooftext. When asked if Christians should attend church, one can answer, on the basis of this verse, with a solid yes. Real life is complicated, and so there may be times for exceptions to the rule, but the ideal presented here is that believers need one another. They need to be known by one another well enough so that both encouragement and provocation can be given and received with wisdom and mutual understanding. On one hand, attending church alone may not fulfill this admonition, for while learning about and praising God with others is vital, if it is done without real relationship, the singular Christian is left exposed to the deceitfulness of sin because they have no other believers with whom they can dialogue. On the other hand, while Christian friendships can meet the relational need, if they have no tether to a local body of believers, they lack the protection of external accountability. So v. 25 does encourage church attendance, church membership, and church fellowship as a worthy and necessary goal, and some may find themselves in situations where the only thing they can do is to pray for and pursue the realization of this goal.[4]

Within this summative and climactic paragraph (at the close of the new covenant section), the author provides a triad of exhortations: let us approach (10:22), let us hold fast (10:23), and let us attend to one another (10:24). They capture the heart of his entire exhortative sermon. This community, and by extension all believers before Christ appears a second time (9:28), are "in the wilderness." All are called to have our vision set on a final destination, dwelling with God in God's kingdom (12:2, 25–26). This sets any current difficulties into right perspective. When we know that truly "all will be well,"[5] we can have a healthy eschatology that allows honesty about challenges (12:11) but does not afford them more than their actual weight (see also Rom 8:18). Forward motion is only possible when a believer is tethered to the anchor, Christ, who reveals divine faithfulness (6:19). The heart language and accountability themes throughout Hebrews demonstrate that each person will answer for how they trusted God's word. God has provided everything necessary to energize that trust. The admonitions are built on the fact that God, in gracious respect of a human capacity that he created, invites the agency of human response. God also designed humanity not to go through this journey alone. Attending to one another is not a distraction from the personal work of faith but a necessary aspect of it. Not only do individuals benefit from the support of others, but getting outside oneself, demonstrating love and good deeds for another, is to follow the way of God, who did not selfishly hoard the love between the Triune persons but allowed that love to overflow for the good of all creation. Being willing to receive help from others and to take the time to give help to others is not only the best way, but truly it is the only way to approach God and hold fast to Christ.

10:26–31 · SINNING WILLFULLY

[26]*For if we continue in sin willingly after receiving the knowledge of the truth, there no longer remains a sacrifice concerning sins* [27]*but a certain fearful expectation of*

4. See Amy Peeler, "Church," in *Life Questions Every Student Asks*, ed. Gary Burge and David Lauber (Downers Grove, IL: IVP Academic, 2020), 81–96.

5. Julian of Norwich, *Revelations of Divine Love*, 75.

judgment and a zeal of fire that is about to devour the adversaries. [28]*For anyone who disobeys the law of Moses "dies without mercy upon [the testimony of] two or three witnesses."* [29]*How much do you think will the one who tramples the Son of God, regards the blood of the covenant in which they were sanctified as common, and mocks the Spirit of grace be worthy of worse punishment?* [30]*For we know the one who said,*

> *Justice is mine; I will repay.*

And again,

> *The Lord will judge his people.*

[31]*It is a fearful thing to fall into the hands of the living God.*

Just as he previously warned against the deceitfulness of sin and urged the act of encouraging one another to fight it (3:13), so too here does the author build on the recommendation for encouragement of one another to urge them against falling into sin's trap.

The language seems to include the author himself in this warning: *if we continue in sin willfully.* This is an act of rhetorical solidarity expressing that he does not imagine himself as exempt from warning. The first-person plural casts the vision of this sin as broadly as possible. Anyone reading this letter who sins willfully will reap the consequences. To sin *willfully* is to choose to sin rather than be forced into something (Rom 8:20; 1 Cor 9:17; Phlm 14; 1 Pet 5:2); the term is used frequently in the Scriptures of Israel for the *freewill* offering (e.g., Lev 7:16; 23:38; Num 15:3; 29:39; Deut 12:6). The author has warned against the deceitfulness of sin (Heb 3:13), but this instance of sinning indicates clear vision. This is confirmed when he states that this act of sinning willfully would take place *after receiving the knowledge of the truth.* He has just stated that they may approach God's presence with a true heart (10:22), and since their High Priest is mediating the new covenant, they are those who have intimate knowledge of God (8:11). Consequently, they qualify as the group of people who could turn from the experientially good knowledge they have been given and choose this path of intentional sin. Were they to sin in this way, there would *no longer [remain] a sacrifice concerning sins.* Since Christ's offering for sins is singular (10:12) and fully effective, no possibility remains for another one, as the author stated at the end of the previous section (10:18).

Without the sacrifice, all that remains is a *certain fearful expectation of judgment*. The intentional sinner would be cast back into the realm where the fear of death reigned (2:15), where the fear of not resting with God was present (4:1), the fear to which those who do not have the help of the Lord succumb (13:6). The realm outside God's household is a scary one because it is the domain of the evil one (2:14). Instead of looking forward to the salvation that Christ will bring (9:28), those who continue to live in sin willfully will also live in fear of judgment (9:27), a daunting prospect before a God who knows all (4:12–13).

This judgment is something to fear as it includes *a zeal of fire that is about to devour the adversaries*. God's judgment is associated with fire in Israel's Scriptures (Deut 4:24; Ps 78:5; Zeph 1:18; 3:8; Isa 26:11; Ezek 23:25; 38:19), particularly against enemies (Isa 26:11; 64:2; Lam 2:4). These verses have strong resonance with Numbers 15, which juxtaposes unintentional sins (Num 15:24–29 uses the term *akousiōs* for "unintentional" as opposed to the term the author of Hebrews uses, *hekousiōs*) with an act done with a hand of arrogance (Num 15:30), which provokes God (*paroxynei*, same term used in Heb 10:24). That person shall be wholly destroyed from the people, removed from community and eliminated (Num 15:30), and the sin destroyed with the person (Num 15:31). As an example of this, a man who shows intent to violate the Sabbath command is stoned outside the camp (Num 15:32–36), and then God instructs that fringes be put on the people's garments so that the people will *not forget* God's commands (Num 15:37–41). In the following chapter in Numbers, an extended story of rebellion against God's chosen leaders results in God's fire consuming the rebels (Num 16:35). This section of Israel's story demonstrates the intense consequences of disobedience under the Mosaic law. If God has inscribed the law not on the Hebrews community's clothes but on their hearts and minds, they should have even less reason to forget God's instructions and make a plan to sin.

The author is drawing on themes present in Israel's texts, and so in v. **28** it is not surprising that he states explicitly the realities of punishment under the law. He turns to the example with the phrase *for anyone who disobeys the law of Moses*. The author uses a term, *atheteō*, related to a term that he has employed twice before, once to refer to Jesus's priesthood not following the law of fleshly descent (7:18) and again when he speaks of Jesus taking away sin (9:26).

Those usages indicate that the image here is someone setting aside the law or removing its requirements from themselves. Hence, either by commission or omission, this person disobeys what God has communicated through Moses. By naming this as the law of Moses, the author supports the weight of the comparison. If the consequences were so serious for Moses's law, how much more serious will the consequences be for those who disregard the promise as made manifest in the Son, who is worthy of more glory than Moses (3:3)?

The consequences for transgressing the law of Moses are incredibly heavy. That person *dies without mercy upon two or three witnesses.* If the events of Numbers 15 and 16 are in the background, those chapters recount multiple examples of mortal death after disobedience. The particular words used here indicate that the author is citing from Deuteronomy 17:6, which emphasizes that only one witness would be insufficient for capital punishment (as does Num 35:30). The principle applies broadly: with sins such as these it would not make sense for only one person to bring charges against another. This kind of sin would be recognizable to many. Moreover, this citation may also indicate that only one lapse would be insufficient, but after two or three events of sin witnessed, a pattern of continual sin would be hard to deny and would need to result in consequences.

If death is the result in the first covenant, the author asks his community, *How much do you think . . . ?* Think with me, the author says, and then the threefold description in the rest of the verse gives purchase on the meaning of the term *sin* in v. 26, disclosing what type of sin he is discussing.

First, *the one who* commits the sin he is describing *tramples the Son of God.* To trample on the Son of God is to treat him as worthless (Matt 5:13; Luke 8:5). Shusaku Endo's novel *Silence* provides haunting narrative detail to this term, as informed by the painfully true history where Japanese Christians were asked to trample on a *fumi-e*, an image that represented their faith, in the person of Jesus or Mary. When applied to an actual person rather than an image, it is a violent picture—to trample on someone could result in death. This description puts this statement into alignment with the "falling away" in ch. 6, which was to "[crucify] again for themselves the Son of God." That the author chooses to use the title of honor, "Son of God," as described in ch. 1 shows the absurd juxtaposition of his honor and the sinful disrespect in this act.

Second, this type of sin *regards the blood of the covenant in which they were sanctified as common.* To regard the sanctifying blood as common is to consider the blood of Christ and conclude the precise opposite of what is true about it. It is to consider the blood that Christ offered, the most effective sacrifice ever given that resulted in the possibility of sanctification (10:10, 14) and the removal of sin, and then decide that it was commonplace. Even more damning, this blood had done that work of sanctification and removal of sins for the person in question. This is both a theological and a personal affront. It is hard to put into words the heights of disrespect that this act reaches.

Finally, this sin *mocks the Spirit of grace.* An insult is something that is verbal and public. This kind of sin mocks the Spirit who had communicated the good news of the new covenant directly to this community (10:15). The grace that facilitated Jesus's death (2:9) and made access to God's throne possible (4:16) is now being mocked. To insult the Spirit of grace is to return evil for good. In sum, this person's sin has derided the most serious and elevated realities, including the Son, the covenant he inaugurated, and the Spirit who communicates it. The author has clarified the nature of the willful sin. The threefold description shows that this sin is to reject the salvation given in Christ and, in the process, cast shame on it.

With such heavy descriptions the author has set up the question in such a way that it is only possible for his listeners to answer in the affirmative. Certainly, that person would *be worthy of worse punishment.* For an author who often has used comparatives and superlatives for the goodness of Christ, this is the only time he employs a negative comparative term. When someone profanes the one who is worthy of more glory even than Moses (3:3), that person becomes worthy of greater recompense than the person who willfully transgressed the law communicated by Moses.

In light of what precedes and follows, it makes most sense that this kind of sin is related to leaving the community. This is not simply a heart posture or loss of belief, a common assumption in more individualized cultures, although that internal attitude is included. Rather, this sin manifests a particular action. To walk away from the community of Christ confessors is to walk away from Christ because it is impossible to fight sin on one's own and because there is no path to salvation anywhere else other than in God's household over which the Son reigns. With this kind of sin, one has chosen to leave the safety of the household and enter the camp of God's enemies.

To sin in this way leaves one without access to a sacrifice that would deal with the problem of sin. Access to the good is gone. At the same time, while the sinner lives in the realm of fear, that person is not yet finally judged. As was true in the warning in ch. 6, the final result of the sin is anticipated but not yet realized. The judgment is expected, not already given out. That person would be worthy of worse punishment, but the author does not say it has been meted out yet. The zeal of God is *about* to devour the adversaries (v. 27) but has not yet done so.

The author answers his question concerning the worse degree of punishment by appealing to Scripture and allowing God to speak. Just as it should be clear to them that such actions are worthy of extreme punishment, so too is it clear to them that God has spoken about being wronged. The author assumes that he and his listeners *know the one who said.* He cites a chapter (Deut 32) often cited or alluded to by New Testament authors (Paul quotes this particular verse as well in Rom 12:19), and one that the author of Hebrews himself cited in ch. 1 (v. 6), so it is correct to suggest that they already know these texts. Even more, he can be completely confident by virtue of their confession and experience that they know the God who says them.

The author first recounts Deuteronomy 32:35: *Justice is mine; I will repay.* He does not replicate a reference to the *day* of vengeance present in the Greek manuscripts and instead has a first-person pronoun that more closely emphasizes the vengeance as belonging to God, as does Paul (Rom 12:19). The one who insults God, the Son of God, the covenant, and the Spirit of grace will be judged by the one who possesses all justice, who is completely just (as Deut 32:4 states). The term "justice" is related to the judgment God metes out, either for good to those who deserve it (Luke 18:7–8) or for punishment of those who have gone against God's ways (2 Thess 1:8). In this instance, something wrong has been done, and so fittingly and rightly God responds. The evocation of repayment suggests that God returns what was given—in this instance, disrespect and shame. For someone who has been given so much good in Christ, this is an ill-fitting gift to give to God in return (see Deut 32:6). In Deuteronomy, those who sin actively go after other gods (Deut 32:17). God's response in judgment shows both power and care for the people, exposing their need so that they can see that the gods they were serving were false (Deut 32:38). Moses issued these words so that the people would know the consequences of their disobedience before they entered the land (Deut 32:46–47). Similarly, the author of Hebrews issues the warning so that his readers can know an even greater punishment awaits them for disrespectfully sinning against the promise fulfilled in Christ.

Then the author joins the next verse in Deuteronomy (32:36): *The Lord will judge his people.* (He does not cite the other phrases in Deut 32:35, which mention the day of destruction being near, although this idea resonates with the author's phrase in 10:25, that the day is drawing near.) Those who have joined God's people open themselves up to God's judgment when they do wrong; in other words, they are not exempt because they have joined the movement (previewing the theme of divine paternal discipline the author will develop in 12:5–11). The futurity of these two statements (reinforced by the section not cited but alluded to in Deut 32 concerning the day of judgment) emphasizes the warning aspect. As was the case with Israel, God's patience endured until punishment was the most just and caring option. The punishment that would come to someone who turned away from Christ would be worse but, on the basis of this paragraph, may not be immediate. It is not surprising, given the revealed character of God, that God would allow time for return.

Then comes a statement for which this author is well known: *It is a fearful thing to fall into the hands of the living God.* If transgressors of Moses's law lived in fear (10:27), transgressors against the Son of God would experience nothing less. That he uses the language of falling results in an intriguing picture. As was true in ch. 6, he associates these serious sins with falling (6:6). This also recalls the wilderness warnings, where the bodies fell in the wilderness (indicating mortal death, 3:17), providing the example for the admonition that they should not fall into such disobedience (4:11). Here in ch. 10, all these exhortations against falling culminate in a fall that lands one not distant from God but in God's very hands. The words of the psalmist are fitting: "Where could I go from your presence?" (Ps 139:7–12). Even in disobedience against God and turning away from God, one ends up with God. The hands that formed creation (Heb 1:10) and led Israel out of slavery (8:9) are the same hands that render justice. This is not meant to be a comfort, however. The author intends to put a healthy fear of God in his congregation. Just as the living God can fulfill promises past the point of death, so too can the living God mete out punishments past the point of death. If mortality was the recompense for disobeying the law of Moses, a postmortem punishment seems probable in light of the enduring nature of the Son who was rejected. Whatever this intense punishment might be, it is up to God to decide.

This is also the point at which the author reveals the "alternate universe" nature of this warning. Because he and his listeners are confessors of Christ and can approach God with confidence, to fall into the hands of the living God is the goal of their hope, not the object of their fear. This entire paragraph is a description of what is *not* true of them. In a stark way, the author assures their confidence by considering the opposite, by taking the contrary to its logical conclusion. If they have known what it is to live in the fearfulness and hopelessness of a life characterized by guilt and death, they will not desire to return to that life given the gifts they have experienced in Christ. The warning serves to remind them of what they already hold to be true.

Hopefully, careful consideration of this passage accomplishes two things. First, it offers comfort to the anxious. The sin described here is not a one-time transgression, even a willful one, nor doubt about the faith. The multi-phrased definition of this sin reveals that this is a thoughtful choice to leave the Christian community and deride their Lord during and after the exit. If that is comfort to those who greatly desire to stay within the fold even if they are wrestling with sins other than apostasy, at the same time, and hence second, this text comes alive in powerful and sobering ways in an era of public deconversions. Those who have left might only be rejecting false and oppressive versions of Christianity, rather than the Son of God, the covenant, and the Spirit. That should be celebrated and patience exhibited as they sort through the wheat and the chaff of their past experience. Others, however, who might be considering walking away from the paradox of a crucified Savior and issuing a smear campaign as retaliation will do well to hear the pathos of this text. Judgment is up to God who so often shows mercy, but punishment beyond death would not only not be out of line but would be righteous in light of the magnitude of the gift rejected.

10:32–39 · STAYING BOLD

[32]But remember the earlier days in which, having been enlightened, you endured a great contest of sufferings. [33]This, on the one hand, as those who were publicly exposed to both insults and tribulations. Also, on the other, as those who became partners with those who were treated in that way. [34]For you also suffered with those in chains, and you received the seizure of your possessions with joy, knowing that you yourselves have a better and abiding possession. [35]Therefore, do not cast away your boldness, which has a great reward. [36]For you have a need for endurance in order that doing the will of God you might obtain the promise.

[37]*For still*

in a little while
the one who is coming will come and will not delay,
[38]*and my righteous one will live out of faith,*
and if they shrink back, my soul will not be pleased in them.

[39]*But we are not of shrinking to destruction but of faith to the preservation of the soul.*

The author then pivots from warning to encouraging, and to do so he recalls their past (as he will do in the next chapter on faith, where he looks to the past to establish faith in God for the future): *But remember the earlier days.* Since some time has passed since they made their confession of faith (5:12), he needs to call to mind for them their first days as followers of Jesus. Since he is speaking to the group, that suggests that they made their individual confessions of faith around the same time. It is clear he is speaking about the time after their conversion since he mentions *the earlier days* when they had already *been enlightened*, a term he used in the warning of ch. 6 as well (6:4), confirmation that enlightenment is a way he speaks of conversion. This imagery is fitting for the embrace of a confession of Jesus Christ, who is God's radiance (1:3). After they were enlightened, they *endured.* As the first of six instances of the terminology of "endurance" (10:32, 36; 12:1–3, 7), the author introduces a theme that will be pivotal in both this exhortation and that of ch. 12. As he is going to be urging them toward endurance, it is important to remind them that they have already exhibited this virtue previously. What they endured shows their former strength. He first describes it as *a great contest of sufferings.* With the term *contest*, the author introduces athletic imagery (as appears in 2 Tim 2:5), which will continue with the comparisons he employs in ch. 12. Their competition was not a casual one, nor one that would be assessed as victorious by their culture, but instead it was one of sufferings. In every other instance in the letter, suffering is what Jesus does (Heb 2:9–10, 18; 5:8; 9:26; 10:32; 13:12). By asserting that they endured sufferings and a *great* contest of them, the author shows their participation with Christ. Quite the opposite of deriding him, they have joined in his suffering, as the author will urge them to continue to do (13:12–13).

In the next verse the author specifies the nature of this suffering. First, they *were publicly exposed.* The author uses a different term, but one that resonates with the way he described the falling away in ch. 6 as that which publicly exposes Christ (6:6). If the comfort is meant to mirror the warning, this is further confirmation that the sin described earlier in ch. 10 has a public component. What they were exposed to in the past included *both insults and tribulations.* Twice the author associates insults with a confession of Christ (11:26; 13:13). As Jesus himself promised, if persecution came for him, it would come for his followers as well (John 15:20). In addition, tribulations were experienced by those faithful of the past of whom the world was not worthy (11:37). It is clear that because of their confession of Christ and association with God's people, they, too, have suffered tribulations. Shameful things were said about them and done to them. Moreover, they *became partners with those whose who were treated in that way.* They did not shy away from their new siblings who experienced ill treatment, but remained in fellowship with them, bearing their shame and suffering and aiding them in it.

The next verse asserts the same experiences in mirror order, beginning with what they did for others and concluding with what happened to them personally. *For also you suffered with those in chains.* Yet again their suffering joins them with the work of Jesus, not only in suffering but also in sympathy (4:15). They suffered with those who were imprisoned. This happened in their past, but as ch. 13 indicates, it remains the fate of some connected to their community (13:3). While bondage can be metaphorical (Mark 7:35; Luke 13:16), since this context speaks of persecution, it is most likely literal, as was often true in the life of Paul and other Christ confessors (see, e.g., Acts 5:17–42; 12:1–17; Rom 16:7; 2 Cor 6:5; 11:23). By suffering with these prisoners, they not only felt their pain but also provided for their needs as they could, precisely what Jesus had instructed (Matt 25:34–40).

In addition to noting their work for others, the author can say, *You received the seizure of your possessions.* Seizure typically has a negative connotation but always conveys the movement of something from one place to another. In a time in which most people did not have excess, to have one's livelihood stolen away was incredibly serious. If this happened to the whole community, they would have no resources left to aid one another. Even in light of this desperate situation, the author affords them incredible agency with this statement. They would not have chosen to lose their things, but they could choose how to react to that loss. As the author will indicate in ch. 12, such things are not outside the good sovereignty of God, and so they could take even such a negative event as a gift. They chose to accept it, and not begrudgingly but *with joy*. They were able to take circumstances that were painful and *not* joyful (12:11) but respond positively. This is the attitude Jesus had toward the cross (12:2), another indication that they were being like him.

This attitude was possible for them because, he says, they were *knowing that you yourselves have a better and abiding possession*. That they *knew* this shows the degree of faith and trust they exhibited. They were able to look beyond what they could see—their present circumstances—and trust in something different. This is precisely the attitude of faith the author extols in ch. 11. The author juxtaposes their multiple livelihoods with a singular *possession*. This emphasizes the unity of the group, those who joined together in what they share. That he describes it as *better and abiding* associates this possession with their salvation (6:9), hope (7:19), the new covenant (7:22; 8:6), perfection (11:40), and the kingdom (12:28). He will soon say that the faithful looked forward to a better city and a better resurrection (11:16, 35). Similarly, in ch. 13 he contrasts the temporality of the present city around them with the city to come (13:14). All these references associate this possession with their lasting relationship with and dwelling in the presence of God. The author emphasizes that *they themselves* had this possession, even though it was something that would be fully realized only in the future. Since they have their High Priest (4:14–15), they have the guarantee of the good he is and will provide.

In light of their deep and active faith exhibited in the past, he urges them, *Therefore, do not cast away your boldness*. He has just said that they do have boldness by virtue of what Christ has done for them (10:19). Earlier in the sermon as well, he assumed they had this attitude as he instructed them to hold firm to it (3:6) and urged them to activate it as they approached God's throne (4:16). All of these are communal actions, so they possess this boldness as a group, emphasizing the importance of staying with those who share the same posture toward God rooted in an experiential trust in God's goodness. If this kind of faith is something they already possess, all they need to do is resist the temptation to throw it away. As with the warning earlier in this chapter, this word for *cast away* conveys an intentional and drastic action.

If they do retain what they have already been given by Christ, it *has a great reward*. Further emphasizing the future aspect of their possession, as they retain it, they will reap the natural consequence of doing so and be rewarded by God. Although he does not specify the reward in this verse, later he does say that it is greater than the wealth of Egypt (11:26). Interpreters should be careful to note that this author is interested in an unshakable kingdom (12:27); he would have little interest in a transitory thing like economic wealth. The reward's enduring greatness is no surprise since it is associated with the realm of God. The affirmation of a promised reward raises an important point as the author prepares to launch into his discussion of faith. Faith is trust that results in action, and those obedient actions will be met with a reward.

The author has reminded them of what they have: a possession that comes with a reward because they have such a great High Priest. Here he then says *you have* one more thing, *a need for endurance.* In an ironic assertion, the one more thing they have is actually something they lack. They stand in need of endurance. That being said, they have shown endurance in the past (10:32), so he is not asking them to do anything of which they are incapable. He then specifies what they need to endure in doing—namely, *doing the will of God.* It is God who makes possible the enacting of the divine will, which is that humans become holy. Jesus came to achieve this will (10:7 and 10:9), and God the Father restores the readers so that they can do it (13:21). If they accept and receive what God has done and is doing, they will reach the goal of doing God's will. The only thing they need to avoid is resisting God's will at work for, within, and among them. The expression of Christian faithfulness is obedience rooted in a posture of receptiveness to God. Faith results in good works (10:24), and those arise from the God who is already at work in them.

The result of their endurance, the author says, is that *you might obtain the promise.* This is the reward of which he spoke in the previous verse. As a verb in the middle voice, *receive* conveys that God will give what is promised, and they will be ready to receive it. What has been promised to them is the inheritance that lasts (9:15; 12:26), salvific rest with God (1:14; 4:1).

To support his point, the author brings forth a citation made up of phrases from Isaiah and Habbakuk. Without any introductory formula, the citation becomes associated with the promise just mentioned. The phrase "a little while" appears only in the twenty-sixth chapter of Isaiah. This passage contains several intriguing associations with Hebrews, including the assurance of fire consuming God's adversaries (Isa 26:11), the same language the author used in 10:27. It also describes tribulation as God's discipline (Isa 26:16, resonant with Heb 10:33 and 12:5–11). Moreover, it names the hope for resurrection (Isa

26:19), making it a fruitful co-proclaimer with Hebrews. In Isaiah the short amount of time is waiting for the wrath of God. In Hebrews that is not absent, as enemies will be put under the feet of the Son (1:13) but waiting on the Son for the full revelation of salvation is the main focus.

The majority of the citation comes from the prophecy of Habakkuk in which the speaker cries out to God for justice, a sentiment the congregation would have shared when they continued to be treated harshly. They might resonate with the reality that "an ungodly person oppresses the just" (Hab 1:4). It is one thing to endure persecution with the zeal of a fresh faith; it is another to endure it for a long time. In Habakkuk 2, from which the phrases come, the prophet anticipates a vision as response from God. God says that the appointed time for the vision is that which is coming and will not delay, or possibly that the one giving the message (Yahweh) will not delay.[6] Habakkuk 2:4 asserts that God is not pleased with one who draws back from the message. Conversely, the righteous response is to live by God's faithfulness. Because God can be trusted, the righteous can keep going even in the midst of a prolonged experience of injustice, waiting for God's communication to come.

The author of Hebrews uses this scriptural language in a way that is largely coherent with the desire for God's justice, but he does so with more focus on people rather than events, not surprising since he views the Son as God's communication (1:2). Since they have already endured and still need more endurance, he begins with the encouragement that the time will not draw on forever. From the perspective of God's eternity, it will only be a little while. Differently than the available Greek translations of Habakkuk 2:3, the author of Hebrews substantivizes the participle and makes it a personal noun, *the **one** who is coming will come and will not delay*. The author has depicted Jesus moving through the heavens (4:14), into the veil (6:19–20), and into the sanctuary (9:12, 24). He has also referred to his entry into the world (10:5). Here in 10:37 he refers to the approach of Christ with respect to salvation for the second time (also 9:28). The return is guaranteed in light of God's promise. Just as he came to do God's will by living as a human, dying, and then, once he was resurrected, presenting his offering (10:7, 9), he will come again as the agent of God's restorative justice. Although the time may seem long, his return will be at just the right time, with no delay of God's plan.

6. Francis I. Andersen, *Habakkuk*, AB 25 (New York: Doubleday, 2001), 207.

The author focuses on the righteous one who belongs to God: *But my righteous one*. Whereas the personal pronoun "my" follows "faith" in the prophet's communication of God's words ("And the righteous one will live from my faithfulness" [Hab 2:4]), here in Hebrews the personal pronoun *my* appears after *righteous one*. This presents the truth in God's own words that God is sovereign over and intimate with this representative of the community. That righteous one trusts in God (Heb 2:13) and lives because of it (5:7; 13:20). The phrase seems to have a double referent; it refers not only to *the* righteous one, God's Messiah, but also to the righteous ones who are made so by being members of him. While Jesus is associated with righteousness (1:9; 7:2), more often in Hebrews this is the quality granted to God's faithful people (5:13; 11:4, 7, 33; 12:11, 23). Righteous ones are members of the group who, after being perfected, dwell with God (12:23). This community includes people who qualify for this address because they have received God's light (1:3), are part of God's household (3:6), and are experiencing God's training (5:13; 12:11). They have been made right with God by virtue of their confession of Christ and his self-offering. Moreover, as members of the living High Priest (7:25) they are promised life, both in the future and in the present. They are those who are living and who *will live*, and they can do so *out of faith*. The author is beginning to prepare for his great chapter on faith but has already shown bad (4:12) and good examples (6:12) in this regard. The audience members themselves are equipped to live out of faith, given what Christ's offering has done for their bodies and hearts (10:22). They only need to live by virtue of what has already been provided to them.

The last phrase of the citation (Heb 10:38b) cannot be an assertion about Christ and Christ's return, but instead focuses on how others should live in light of it. Clearly this line of the citation cannot apply to the Son of God, because God would not be concerned about the possibility that he, the sinless Messiah (4:15; 7:26) who has accomplished God's will, would then "shrink back." This verse (Hab 2:4/Heb 10:38) does not apply to the coming one.

The author uses Habakkuk's words to reiterate the warning with which this section began. The opposite of living out of faith is to *shrink back*, to fail to complete an action or let go of responsibility. This term from Habakkuk is resonant with Hebrews' reflections on apostasy, the act of turning away from God. In the New Testament, "shrinking back" is used to describe someone who lets down a group (Acts 20:20, 27; Gal 2:12), suggesting, as has been true throughout this section, an anti-communal turn. If someone chooses not to endure in faith but turns back, then God says, *My soul will not be pleased in them*. Soul language shows the comprehensiveness of God expressing displeasure. This kind of displeasure is similar to what was true of God's response to the sacrificial system (10:6, 8). The author discussed the consequences that result in disobedience; now the readers hear how *God* articulates a response to that disobedience.

Canonically, the author's use of Habakkuk 2:4 provides one of the closest connections with Paul. This verse serves as part of the thesis statement for his letter to the Romans (Rom 1:16–17). Paul has never "shrunk back" but continues his boldness in proclaiming the gospel, knowing that it is the power of God and the revelation of God's righteousness. That revelation proceeds down the path of faith, and, for Paul, Habbakuk voices that process. Life comes through faith. All these authors show the necessity of active trust in God for eternal and abundant life with God.

After this warning full of pathos, the author presents one more comfort. With emphasis he says, *We are not of shrinking to destruction*. The author makes clear that God's displeasure results in elimination of God's enemies, either through mortal death or worse. He need not linger on those consequences any longer because he and his listeners are the alternative: we are *of faith to the preservation of the soul*. According to his assessment, they are people of faith and therefore will hold on to God and keep their lives safe. The word for "preserve" here (*peripoieō*) is resonant with the word for *doing* (*poieō*) God's will in v. 36. Jesus keeps their soul secure (6:19), so as they trust in him, they will endure into eternal life, doing that which pleases God (13:16).

Although interpreters have debated—and rightly so—the biblical definition and implications for the weighty theological term *pistis*, which I've chosen to translate as *faith*,[7] this author seems rather sure of the simple yet profound truth he wants his readers to grasp: because faith looks both backward and

7. I concur with the proposal articulated by Matthew Bates, who asserts that the term "allegiance" would be more suitable than "faith" (see Bates, *Salvation by Allegiance Alone* and *Gospel Allegiance*). Nevertheless, in order to align with the prevailing understanding of this chapter, I chose to retain the term "faith." This decision was made with due consideration to the author of Hebrews' explicit clarification that "faith" cannot be reduced to mere intellectual assent to a set of propositions. Rather, the author's conception of faith is grounded in God's initiative and is demonstrated through corresponding action.

forward to God's actions, it *is* a firm foundation. That might seem a difficult concept to grasp for those who picture faith, at best, as an intangible thing or, at worst, wishful thinking. If this dissonance exists for a contemporary reader, that indicates that while the author of Hebrews acknowledges the intangible aspect of faith, he is ultimately employing an understanding of faith that includes active response to observable realities. To encourage them to live out of this confidence he places in them, he proceeds to say much more about the way of life that should shape their lives, the way of faith.

HEBREWS 11:1–40

THE TESTIMONY OF THE FAITHFUL

The author has just proclaimed that he and the congregation he addresses are people of faith, and this faith will preserve their souls from destruction (10:39). It makes sense that he would now define and provide examples of this saving concept. It should not be imagined, however, that "faith" is relegated to only this section of the sermon. Explicitly, in the previous chapter, he urged them to have bold faith in their approach to God (10:22) and before that he urged them to depart from examples of unfaithfulness (4:2) and follow examples of faithfulness (6:12). In addition to those explicit uses, the author has been preparing his audience to hear this extended treatment on faith since the beginning. As he frequently mentions things that await them in the future—their inheritance of salvation or the promise (1:14; 6:17), the subjection of the world to their representative Messiah (2:5–9), dwelling in glory (2:10), entering God's rest (4:1–11), and receiving a reward (10:35)—he has been directing them to embrace a forward-facing vision that trusts in what God has promised. To put it in his words, they must trust that the one who has promised is faithful (10:23).

In the style of an epideictic speech, which lifts up a theme for praise and contemplation, he catalogues instances of their ancestors in the past. He demonstrates that they also trusted that God was faithful, in the face of all circumstances, even death. After poetically defining the term (11:1), he traces that trust through antediluvian history, from Abel to Noah and the deluge itself (vv. 3–7). The faith of Abraham, Sarah, and the first several generations who come after them comprises a large section in vv. 8–22, Moses and the exodus in vv. 23–29, and then a short recounting of the conquest narratives in which he mentions the walls of Jericho and Rahab (vv. 30–31). He recognizes that he does not have the time to recount all that he could, so the prophets and the kings only get mentioned (v. 32) before he names general experiences that could apply to a number of specific eras (vv. 33–38). His conclusion unites all the faithful of the past with this struggling community to whom he is preaching, granting them the encouragement they need to keep running their own race of faith.

This chapter is neither a poetic flourish nor a dry recounting of history that departs from the main christological theme of the sermon (and takes a *long* time to do so!). Instead, it is as intriguingly crafted and life-altering as everything else in this letter. By appealing to examples from their ancestors, the author teaches how to practice that most basic posture in Christianity, to have faith in God. This chapter offers meaningful resources for pastoral counseling, conversations with friends, and personal spiritual growth. Christian faith, as the author of Hebrews discloses, is manifest in both mundane and pivotal moments but is, most importantly, *possible*. Because of what God has already done and graciously revealed, it is possible to trust him and take the actual steps to follow where the pioneer is leading.

The commentary I provide for this chapter aims to equip the interpreter with two things. First, and most important, is a reading of Hebrews 11, which is a series of accounts that support the author's definition of faith, the faith that is living and active (10:39). It is a worthy exercise to contemplate to what stories and personages all of his phrases point. Possibly this is the intent of the author's gestures, so that the mind of the reader might comb through the stories of the faithful, being renewed as they do so. Hence, my second aim of this section of the commentary is to visit the biblical narratives the author mentions with special attention to the ways themes of those narratives connect to the sermon of Hebrews. I am not suggesting that the readings of the stories I propose are in the mind of the author, but I include them to provide resources for a creative reading of a New Testament text along with its Old Testament co-text. I provide these suggestions for the reader who desires to be formed by the canonical Scriptures to hear what the Spirit might be saying through the juxtaposition of these many accounts of faithfulness.

The listener who only hears the phrases of Hebrews' sermon gets the main point—namely, that faith in God allowed victory (keep in mind that the definition of victory becomes more nuanced as the descriptions continue). The reader who investigates the stories behind the phrases gains a greater blessing.

11:1–2 · DEFINING FAITH

[1]And faith is the foundation for the things for which we hope, the proof of those things that we do not see. [2]For by this, those who lived before us were commended.

Christian faith is not blind. The introduction to this famous hymn to faith dances between the tangible and the supernatural, the seen and the unseen. The alacrity of its art demands careful consideration in order to follow the steps. With some movements, the ideas appear to be ephemeral. Faith trusts in the *unseen*, the *communicated* but not visual word of God. The art of the sermon moves through this space but neither begins nor lands there, for the author also asserts that faith looks to that which God caused, the tangible and the seen, and hence can function as something firm, the foundation and the proof.

A definition of faith informed by Hebrews sees faith as a firm *foundation*. It is trust in God, based on divine revelation, that results in tangible expressions of obedience. I base that definition of faith in the words the author chooses to use. Scholars have had many discussions whether the terms here, *hypostasis* (foundation) and *elenchos* (proof), are intended to be objective entities or subjective feelings. The author of Hebrews uses *hypostasis* in both ways, as the basis of God's being (1:3) and as a commitment of confidence (3:14, as does Paul [2 Cor 11:17]). *Elenchos* appears as a noun only here in the New Testament literature, and so direct comparison is impossible, but as a verb its nearly twenty instances convey the ability to charge someone on the basis of *proof*. As the rest of the chapter unfolds, the stories the author tells indicate that the objective connotation plays the primary role. God acted. The faithful saw the action and therefore trusted that God would bring to pass promised future actions. For the author and this community, faith is based on things very tangible. They have heard, seen, and experienced the miraculous and powerful works of God through the revelation of the Son and the distribution of the Spirit (2:3). Countless Christian communities would agree. What God has revealed of the divine character is that which gives confidence that God will bring remaining promises to fruition in the future. Christian faith is neither ignorant nor naive. Faith is to see what God has already tangibly revealed to be true and trust that God will continue to act in line with the revelation of that truth. Faith is to rely on the promises of God given in the revelations of

God. This community can have faith in God because they have seen what God has done. John Chrysostom, an early preacher of this text, urged his readers to apprehend faith along this model: "Christ foretold many things. If those former things did not come to pass, then do not believe them; but if they all came to pass, why doubt concerning those that remain?"[1]

At the same time, the subjective, intangible aspect is not absent. If faith concerned only God's observable acts, this community might be tempted to believe that God's work was limited to the past, to the lives of their forebears and their own past successes. In times of difficulty, the tangible realities seem to work against faith. Consequently, they should observe God's past action, this proof, so that it can support them in the difficult present and drive them forward to the unseen future. The firm foundational nature of faith in what God has done allows them to look ahead confidently to *the things for which we hope*. Without faith, the author and his readers would have no hope for the things they do not yet possess, nor even yet see. Calvin emphasized the importance of patience as an aspect of faith: "Faith can be no more separated from patience than from itself."[2] In its original oration to this first-century community, this definition of faith at the beginning of ch. 11 was right after the admonition for patience at the end of ch. 10. The author is saying to the congregation, "We are those who keep waiting. We are those who continue in faith. We are those who keep hoping." Faith is that which looks backward, and as a result it allows hope that looks forward.

With attention to hope, the author is now articulating with a succinct definition the call he issued to readers twice before: to hold firm to their boast of hope (3:6) and to show haste to possess the full assurance of their hope (6:11). In those previous instances, he was urging them, at base, to have faith. By this point in the letter, the author has already shown them how God has brought bedrock hopes of the people of Israel to fruition. The new covenant has arrived in Christ, and so they have the confident hope of drawing near to God (7:19), as God promised would be true (10:23). In fact, the author has set Jesus as their hope (6:18), the one who has gone into God's presence on their behalf. Trusting in him is how they have firm hope.

1. Chrysostom, *Hebrews* 21.5 (*NPNF*[1] 14:463).

2. Calvin, *Hebrews*, 157.

The next phrase has a similar balance of solid trust and hope for what lies ahead. The author says that faith is *the proof of those things that we do not see.* The rather comprehensive neuter plural "things" was embedded in the neuter participle of the first phrase (*elpizomenōn*, "things for which we hope") but is named here explicitly (*pragmatōn*). The lack of specification of the "things" allows this definition of faith to apply broadly; it is flexible to any circumstance in which a believer in Christ hopes in God. It also connects this definition with earlier passages in the sermon. The author uses this noun twice, first to refer to the unchangeable *things* that point to the impossibility of God lying (6:18), and, second, to refer to the *things* heralded by the shadow that was the law (10:1). What God has promised and sworn and brought to fruition in the priesthood of Christ is the proof of those things they do not yet see, including the world under Christ's reign (2:8). Nevertheless, by seeing Jesus (2:9) they know that they *will* see the realization of the things for which they are hoping.

Both aspects of faith, the objective deeds of God and the subjective stance of hope, patience, and trust affirm that confessors of Jesus have legitimate reason for assurance. If faith has to trust God at his word, then because the word of God has come in the person of the Son, Jesus Christ (1:2), they have everything they need to exercise trust.

That does not mean that faith is easy. Instead, faith sits at the crossroads of Christian paradox. About faith Calvin also said, "We are assured of a happy resurrection, but we are as yet involved in corruption; we are pronounced just, as yet sin dwells in us; we hear that we are happy, but we are as yet in the midst of many miseries; an abundance of good things are promised to us, but still we often hunger and thirst, God proclaims that he will come quickly but he seems deaf when we cry to him."[3] This is the kind of faith the author has been asking of them in the face of sin and death—namely, to trust that Christ's self-offering has removed and defeated the forces working against them. As all who encounter Hebrews hold fast to their confession of Jesus, encouraged by those brothers and sisters who also follow him, they can live out this definition of faith.

As the admonitions indicate, this kind of faith is possible for everyone. To buttress that conviction, the author will present the stories of many from Israel's past. He calls attention to the ways in which they demonstrated active faith in

3. Calvin, *Hebrews*, 221.

God and did not shrink back (10:39). He tells their stories because he believes that he and his listening congregation can have that kind of faith as well.

Most of these persons are revered, to be sure, but all, whose stories are preserved in Scripture and therefore easy to access, also clearly fell far short of perfection. The author's commendation of good moments in their lives does not mean that readers of Hebrews have to imagine that everything about them was exemplary. Reading their stories in full reveals another encouragement: if even *they* could be praised for their faith, it is possible for anyone to trust God with their lives and bear the fruitfulness of faith.

To introduce these stories, the author states that *by this* (faith), *those who lived before us were commended.* Those in previous generations had faith to the degree that it could be observed and then proclaimed. In what follows the author is going to tell that story of the faithful of the past from Abel all the way to the leaders in their present community (13:7). He will commend them by testifying about them. For him to be able to do so, these stories had to be preserved and passed down, so many readers have seen allusion to another commendation, another witness as well—namely, God (hence *emartyrēthēsan*, "commended," is understood as a divine passive here). It is God's voice in the Scriptures that commended the faithful by preserving their stories. How awesome that God would consider humans worthy of commendation for displaying this virtue of faith. Cyril of Jerusalem notes, "Since God is here called faithful, you also in receiving this title receive a great dignity . . . seeing you are to become a partaker of a title of God."[4] The commendation of God preserved in Israel's Scriptures and proclaimed again by the author in this sermon works to encourage readers to aim for a similar commendation, to hear from God, "Well done, my good and faithful servant" (Matt 25:21).

11:3–7 · ANTEDILUVIAN FAITH

[3]By faith we understand that times, spaces, and the things that fill them have been formed by the speech of God, with the result that it is not from perceptible things that the visible has come. [4]By faith Abel offered to God a better sacrifice than Cain; through this sacrifice he was commended as righteous—God commended because

4. Cyril of Jerusalem, *Catechetical Lectures* 5.1–2 (ACCS 10:174).

of his gifts, and through it, even though he died, he still speaks. [5]*By faith Enoch was removed before he saw death, and he could not be found because God changed him. For before the change, it had been proclaimed that he had pleased God.* [6]*For without faith it is impossible to please [God]. For it is necessary for the one who is approaching God to have faith that God is and that God becomes a rewarder for those who are seeking him.* [7]*Having been warned concerning the things he had not yet seen, by faith and in fear Noah built an ark for the salvation of his house; through this faith he condemned the world and became an heir of the righteousness that comes according to faith.*

In the first example of what happens *by faith*, the author names an understanding that he and his readers share. They are all united by a particular perception of the world. *We understand*, he says. He uses a word for understanding that often conveys a perception of what should be obvious (Matt 15:17/Mark 7:18; Matt 16:9, 11/Mark 8:17; Rom 1:20). This is the same kind of faith he described in the previous statement. It makes a decision not out of thin air but on the basis of observation. This faith looks around at the world and consents that God is the ultimate cause of it all. Because God created through speech, *the result* is *that it is not from perceptible things that the visible has come.* Calvin describes this kind of faith by saying, "Though [God] is in himself invisible, he in a manner becomes visible to us in his works."[5] With a play on the same word for "seeing" (*blepō*), the author asserts that what they can see (11:3) points to what they cannot (11:2).

The first particular expression of faith in this lengthy chapter adds a bit more nuance to the previous basic definition. Faith is based on observation, but faith is not the only possible conclusion from such observation. That creation was created by God is the conclusion that Paul hoped all humans would reach when they noticed the world around them, but this was not the most common reaction (Rom 1:18–23). Not everyone in the world believes that all things exist because of God, by virtue of God's speech, and even fewer believe that the observable world arose from the speech of the God of Israel. Others in the time of the original listeners might have agreed that the processes and small parts that made up the world could not be observed, but they had a vastly different cosmology and theology than the congregation addressed by

5. Calvin, *Hebrews*, 224.

this sermon. The esteemed philosopher Heraclitus, ancient author Diogenes Laertius explains, saw the birth of the world as a "downward path": "For fire by contracting turns into moisture, and this condensing turns into water; water again when congealed turns into earth."[6] Leucippus, a disciple of Zeno, the founder of Stoicism, asserted, "The worlds are formed when atoms fall into the void and are entangled with one another; and from their motion as they increase in bulk arises the substance of the stars."[7] A variety of thinkers sit comfortably within the label "atomists," who asserted that "an infinite stock of atoms randomly interacting over infinite space and time was bound at some point to form, quite accidentally, a world like ours."[8] The observation of the world, for these thinkers, led in different directions from those who affirmed the God of Israel as creator.

The understanding about the identity of that Creator that creation has a divine cause may be clear to many, but clarity springs forth from the stance of faith. The word the author uses for understanding (*noeō*) also occurs when explanation is necessary (Eph 3:4; 2 Tim 2:7). For the recipients of this letter, because they were part of a community who interpreted the world through the Scriptures of Israel, they shared faith in God as creator. In the beginning, Genesis says, God made the heavens and the earth (Gen 1:1) and did so by speaking (Gen 1:3). The Greek text and Hebrews use different terms for God's speech (*legō* in Genesis and *rhēma* in Hebrews), but the idea is the same. The Psalms sing of God's fashioning the light (Ps 73:16 LXX) and of God speaking a word to establish the heavens (Ps 32:6 LXX). Jews and early Christians shared this conviction.[9] Just as he did in v. 2 with the affirmation of previous generations' faith, here the author encourages them that this kind of faith is possible by virtue of being tethered to a particular community who share a particular faith commitment. By being a part of the family of God, they understand that all things *have been formed* by God. The word for *formed* conveys a sense of

6. Diogenes Laertius, *Lives of Eminent Philosophers* 9.1.9, trans. R. D. Hicks (Cambridge, MA: Harvard University Press, 1972).

7. Diogenes Laertius, *Lives of Eminent Philosophers* 9.6.30.

8. David Sedley, "Creationism in Antiquity," in *The Cambridge Companion to Ancient Greek and Roman Science*, ed. Liba Taub (Cambridge: Cambridge University Press, 2020), 122.

9. Attridge lists Wis 9:1; 2 Bar. 14.17; Philo, *On the Sacrifices of Cain and Abel* AC 65; John 1:3; 1 Clem. 17.4; Odes Sol. 16.19 (*Hebrews*, 315n117); Johnson adds Sir 42:15 and 2 Pet 3:5 (*Hebrews*, 280).

intentionality and care, an intimacy with which God is involved in the making of creation. The only other time the author uses the word, it is in reference to God's formation of the Son's body (Heb 10:5).

This kind of faith in the careful action of God is so achievable, in fact, that they already have it.[10] In alignment with his frequent encouragements, it should not be missed that the author starts this long catalogue of faithful acts from the past with *their own* faith. They are already employing the kind of trust he is asking them to live into by affirming a particular belief about the origin of the world—namely, that God created through speech. The fact that they have this kind of faith about the past acts as an encouragement that they can have this kind of faith about both their present and their future. Their current struggle seems to be that they can see the actions of God but might not be able to see God or God's word in them. (This is the problem addressed in 12:5–11. They see their suffering but do not know to interpret it as under the gracious maturing action of their loving divine Father.) If they can have this kind of understanding about creation, then they can have this faithful understanding of everything in their lives.

By beginning with *times, spaces, and the things that fill them*, the fulsome translation of *aiōn* I've chosen to adopt,[11] the author shows that it is always God who acts first, who takes the initiative. In this example God decides to create, to make something rather than have nothing. This is the author's way of showing that faith, even from the very beginning of creation, is always a response to what God has done first.

They should take great encouragement that this kind of perception—seeing God's work in the world—is possible because God has spoken to create all things. In Hebrews, this is a christological affirmation. Faith sees in creation the evidence of the spoken word of God, who is the Son (1:2), who upholds all things by the powerful word (1:3 has *rhēma*, as the author uses here in 11:3). It was not possible to see him at the beginning of creation; he has only been revealed in these last days (1:2), yet he was always present with God and acted as the divine word through which God created. Observing creation by faith

10. Jonathan Griffiths notes, "The place of 11.3 within this catalogue of faith is remarkable because here the faith taken as exemplary belongs, not to a biblical figure, but to the contemporary community of faith" (*Hebrews and Divine Speech*, 126).

11. The author most often uses this term for time, but because he will go on to mention the perceptible things, it is more comprehensive here, much like in 1:2.

reveals glimmers of the Son of God who both created it and became part of it (1:3, 10). Even time itself was created by the word of God and bears the fingerprints of the one who will reign *forever* as King and High Priest (1:8; 5:6; 6:5, 20; 7:17, 21, 24, 28; 9:26; 13:8, 21). In other words, faith in God that arises from understanding creation is faith in the God who created and then entered creation as the incarnate Son.

There is a noticeable gap in the author's retelling between the creation of all things and Abel—namely, Abel's parents, Adam and Eve. Because the focus of this section is on faith rather than distrust in God, their absence makes good sense.[12] The author moves to the first human who can exemplify faith. Abel conceivably would have heard the stories of the garden from his parents, but even more personally, he would have seen firsthand the sustaining power of God. His mother had been able to conceive life twice (Gen 4:1–2), and God had provided so that both he and his brother could live off the land. Abel had seen evidence of God, and so he demonstrated that *by faith,* as Hebrews says, *Abel offered to God a better sacrifice than Cain*. That he offered a sacrifice demonstrates that the sacrificial practices of both the Levitical priests and Jesus go back to the near beginning of human history. Neither the author of Hebrews nor the author of Genesis says that this was an offering for sin, but such an interpretation lines up with the author's assertion that if Jesus had to offer himself frequently for sin, it would have needed to begin at the foundation of the world (Heb 9:26).

Jewish and Christian interpreters of Genesis 4—as evidenced by discussion in the Midrash (Genesis Rabbah 22) as well as the writings of Philo (*On the Sacrifices of Cain and Abel* 88) and Josephus (*Jewish Antiquities* 1.54)—have long debated *why* Abel's sacrifice was better. The author of Hebrews does not weigh in on the reason for the superiority of Abel's sacrifice but instead focuses on God's opinion about it. Concerning Abel, the author states that *through this sacrifice he was commended as righteous*. In the next phrase it becomes clear that it is God who gives this commendation. *God* did the commending *because of his gifts*. Genesis 4:4 utilizes this phrase, including the plural "gifts," which could indicate more than one animal or that Abel gave from his flock on more than one occasion. By observing the gifts, God testified that Abel was

12. Ben Witherington III, *Letters and Homilies for Jewish Christians: A Socio-rhetorical Commentary on Hebrews, James and Jude* (Downers Grove, IL: IVP Academic, 2007), 304.

righteous. It is striking that just as faith is based on observation of God's deeds, so too God's declaration of Abel's righteousness is in response to the observation of Abel's faithful giving. God's commendation of Abel is neither blind nor arbitrary, as I argued is true for those who have faith in God. The author's assessment is that God declares to be true of Abel what the author asserted is true of his readers (through his citation of Habbakuk in Heb 10:38), that they are God's righteous ones. They share a kinship with Abel. The Reformers, and several contemporary interpreters who stand in their theological debt,[13] carefully point out that it was not the sacrifices themselves but the motivating faith that caused God to declare Abel as righteous. Luther notices the arrangement of the text closely: "God had regard for Abel"—first because of his faith, not because of his work, for this follows—"and for his offerings. . . . For those who are truly righteous press forward to works through faith and grace."[14] When God speaks to Cain in Genesis, the ominous statement that sin is crouching at the door (Gen 4:7) indicates that something is off about Cain's heart, not his sacrifice.[15] The author of Hebrews does mention the thing given at least twice (better sacrifice and gifts), but the prepositional phrases, *through this* (*di' hēs*) and *through it* (*di' autēs*), could refer either to the sacrifice or to the faith behind it. This verse becomes a classic example of the interpretive temptation to divide what Scripture holds together. God noticed Abel's faith through his sacrifice—not one without the other—and, in noticing it, commended his demonstrated faith as righteousness.

While the readers and Abel share God's declaration of their righteousness, what follows the declaration is strikingly opposite: they will live by it (10:38), but *he died*. Even so, Abel's untimely death at the hand of his brother did not end the proclamation of his faith and his righteousness. The author says that *through it*, referring to his faith as evidenced through his sacrifice, *even though he died, he still speaks*. The speaking one could refer to *God's* ongoing testimony, most evident in the fact that the Scriptures preserve the story of Abel. Early Christians, as evident in the First Epistle of John (3:12), noted that Abel's story and good reputation live on; hence one could say that God's sacred word still "speaks" about him. The "speaking" could also refer to Abel.

13. Bruce, *Hebrews*, 285–86; deSilva, *Perseverance in Gratitude*, 388.

14. Luther, *Lectures on Hebrews*, on 11:4 (*LW* 29:232).

15. Bruce, *Hebrews*, 281.

In the account in Genesis, his blood cries out from the ground after Cain has killed him (Gen 4:10), as remembered by Jesus (Matt 23:35/Luke 11:51). If Jewish interpreters saw the life of the being in the blood, the speech of his blood is, in some way, his speech. Moreover, because Hebrews includes him as one of those commended by God, he is still speaking as a member of the cloud of witnesses (Heb 12:1–2). Because he was declared righteous, he is one of the righteous spirits (12:23) who dwell with God on Mount Zion. It is his speaking blood with which Jesus's is compared in 12:24. Death is no barrier to Abel himself being commended and testifying.

Although Cain the murderer of Abel has a son by the name of Enoch (Gen 4:17), the next person in the list in Hebrews is Enoch who falls seventh after Adam in the line of Seth (Gen 5:19–24). This is the Enoch who lived 365 years and was then removed. Hebrews calls attention to the fact that he *pleased God by faith*, a pattern to which the author calls his congregation twice (12:28; 13:6). He also promises them that it is God who is at work to bring about that which is pleasing (13:21).

Genesis says explicitly that Enoch's life of pleasing God took place after the birth of his son Methuselah, born when Enoch was 165 years old, according to the Greek text (Gen 5:22). He exemplifies the truth that it is never too late to start to live a divinely pleasing life. Jewish tradition noticed this commendation that came later in life and attributed to Enoch the action of repentance (Sir 44:16). Genesis is clear that though his life of pleasing God started later, because of the length of his life he still had two hundred years of faithfulness (Gen 5:22)! Given the life span in the first century (and today), no one will need to demonstrate this kind of pleasing faith for as long as Enoch did.

Enoch had an even better result than Abel. Because of his exercise of faith, God testified about him that he was pleasing (in the Hebrew, he "walked with God," Gen 5:22). Hebrews says, *It had been proclaimed that he had pleased God*. The passive of *martyreō*, "proclaimed," asserts the divine commendation preserved in Scripture that is also present in vv. 2 and 4. Instead of going through death and still being able to speak, *Enoch was removed before he saw death*. The author makes it clear that God took him, preventing him from ever experiencing death, a noticeable departure from the fate of everyone else in the genealogy whose story ends with the stark statement "and he died" (beginning in Gen 5:5). Enoch, however, "lives on" not only in God's testimony in Israel's story but presumably with God (since *he could not be found*). Genesis does not say his location specifically, and so any suggestion must remain at the level of conjecture. The lesson his life teaches, however, is clear. His translation acts as a signpost to a future hope. Through Enoch humans receive "a hope of the destruction of death, and of the overthrow of the devil's tyranny, and that death will be done away."[16]

Knowing that God has honored the faith of those in the past gives proof that God will honor the faith of the community listening to Hebrews, no matter what they face. Both men, Abel and Enoch, point toward the trustworthiness of God in the face of death. Luther comments, "Thus although in Abel the human race saw death, yet in him it saw a better life. Although in Enoch it saw no death, yet in him it saw life."[17]

With such celebrated examples, it would be tempting to assume that some unattainably great faith led to Abel's and Enoch's "living." To the contrary, at the base of the divine commendation of them is their faith *in God*, a faith that the author argues is replicable, or else he would have little reason to recount their stories after affirming that he and his congregation are those who preserve their souls by faith (10:39). In v. **6** he states this point in the negative: *For without faith it is impossible to please [God].* He believes that his addressees have met this criterion. They have demonstrated faith (10:39) and therefore can please God. Then he more precisely defines the affirmations that are entailed within this faith in God. *For it is necessary for the one who is approaching God to have faith that God is and that God becomes a rewarder for those who are seeking him.* He and his listeners are certainly those who are approaching God. The author has invited them into this movement twice (4:14; 10:22) on the assumption that they are already those who are being led by God (2:10), fleeing to grasp the hope in front of them (6:18). For them, then, it is necessary *to have faith* in several things. The first is that God exists, *that God is*, as God revealed himself to Moses as the one who is (Exod 3:14). D. Stephen Long comments, "'That God Is' is first and foremost the divine name revealed to us."[18]

Faith, however, is not the same as assenting to God's existence, an assent that, as James reminds readers, even the demons believe (Jas 2:19). This agree-

16. Chrysostom, *Hebrews* 22.5 (*NPNF*[1] 14:467).

17. Luther, *Lectures on Hebrews*, on 11:5 (*LW* 29:234–35; RCS 13:161).

18. D. Stephen Long, *Hebrews*, Belief: A Theological Commentary on the Bible (Louisville: Westminster John Knox, 2011), 192.

ment is not enough to qualify as faith. The one approaching must also believe *that God becomes a rewarder for those who are seeking him*. The different verbs of "being" employed in this short sentence indicate different moments in life with God. God is who God is (*estin*), but God will become (*ginetai*) a rewarder once the person exercising faith begins approaching. By describing those who are approaching God as those who are *seeking* God, the author has—again—included a sense of journeying, pressing on toward the goal. Seeking conveys both intentionality and trust, that the thing being sought exists and might be possible to attain (Heb 11:14; 12:17; 13:14). Seeking is a display of faith. This kind of faithful seeking trusts that God will be a *rewarder*. The author has invoked this concept of reward in the previous section: their confidence will bring a reward (10:35). Soon, he will say that Moses also looked forward to a reward from God (11:26). As was true with the wilderness generation as well as the readers of Hebrew, the reward is to be *with God*. The one on the journey must trust that God is capable to reward and will be faithful to reward. The incarnate Son dwelling at God's right hand has already demonstrated that it is possible for humans to be with God forever. Because the author has asserted that they are tethered to Christ, they can trust that he will bring them into God's presence. Faith is to live out of the trust that God will continue to be faithful to what has already been revealed through Christ concerning the divine nature and plan for humanity.

If this definition of faith in v. 6 has christological undertones, it is Christ who provides the ultimate example in comparison with both Abel and Enoch. Abel died, but his voice lived on. Enoch did not die but was changed, presumably, in a way that he was removed to be with God. Jesus, like Abel, actually died and, like Enoch, dwells with God. The difference between Enoch and Jesus is that whereas Enoch could not be found, Jesus can be seen enthroned (2:9). Jesus neither skirted the experience of death nor lives as a spirit with God (12:23). Abel's and Enoch's stories are signposts pointing to the hope of victory over death; Jesus, the resurrected Son of God, is that hope. He and he alone has received the reward of eternal embodied life from God. Consequently, he is the only one who grants that those who confess him will, by seeking God through him, receive the same reward.

This kind of faith, which is a trust that God is sovereign, good, and consistent, is certainly hard to muster up at times, especially during seasons of suffering. Hence it is necessary to hear the assertion that faith is not blind.

Often it is true that the crushing weight of current circumstances makes it difficult to exercise faith, but one can look outside oneself to the past, even the beginning of human history, and chiefly to the person and work of Jesus Christ, to see what God has done. This is the way to enable faith that trusts in what God will do, and out of that trust act accordingly.

Noah serves as a pertinent example of the kind of faith the author is advocating, because he is also someone who pleased God (Gen 6:9). In Noah's case, God did not ask him to act on account of his previous experience with floods. Noah had no concept of what a flood entailed; he was *warned concerning the things he had not yet seen*. He did not base his faith on what he had *not* seen concerning floods but on what he *had* seen and experienced—namely, the evidence of God's character. Even before God's instructions to build the ark, the text says that Noah had found favor with God (Gen 6:8) and that he was righteous, pleasing, and perfect (Gen 6:9). He had a solid relationship with God already. Out of that, he responded to God's invitation *in fear*. He might have feared the condition of humanity in his time, and feared God's decision to respond, as the NETS translation suggests, with "ruin" (Gen 6:13). His fear also included reverent obedience to God (like that displayed by Jesus [Heb 5:7]). His fearful faith manifested in trusting actions even in light of this unheard-of situation (Gen 7:1). His faithful obedience (noted several times in the Genesis account [6:22; 7:5]) was much to his advantage. *Noah built an ark*. He mimicked the building work of God (Heb 3:4) and foreshadowed the careful preparation of those who constructed the space for God's presence to dwell among Israel (9:2). His ark, which preserved life, has a connection to the ark of the covenant, which held the instruments of Israel's life with God (9:4). Out of his faith and fear, Noah facilitated *the salvation of his house*, his family and his legacy. Because he was faithful, there was a people with whom God continued the project of restoration, eventually resulting in the audience of Hebrews being named as the house of God (3:6).

In addition to this good result for his family, *through this faith he condemned the world*. Noah's act, and God's blessing of it, stood as a foil to the divine judgment that was playing out against the state of creation at his time. Other people could have had faith as he did, but did not, pursuing evil instead (Gen 6:5). Their choices put them on the outside of the ark, the outside of salvation, and so in the realm of condemnation where God's flood was purging the world God had created of its wickedness.

Noah reaped even more lasting rewards than a legacy. The final thing the author says about Noah is that he *became an heir of the righteousness that comes according to faith.* Like Abel (11:4), Noah, too, is proclaimed as righteous, and the author chooses to reinvoke the language of inheritance with his story (mentioned previously with the promise of eternal inheritance in 9:15). He also stands in right relationship with God and, therefore, dwells on the mountain of Zion (recalling the fact that his ark had landed on a mountain), celebrating with Abel and the angels (12:23). Because of his faith, his house was preserved in the midst of the judgment exercised against the whole world, and he was inaugurated into the house of God with the other children who will inherit right, intimate, and embodied relationship with God forever.

Noah reminds canonical readers of Adam. God gave the world to both of them, the freshly created world and then the freshly purged world. Sadly, the parallels continue. Soon after they receive it, they both choose the path of disobedience. With these similarities, readers can view the movement of vv. 2–7 as proceeding from creation to Abel to Enoch to Noah and back again to (a judged and renewed) creation. Faith in God, in the midst of a broken and sinful world, has been present since almost the beginning. If the listeners look back to the stories of the beginning, their faith will be strengthened. They can renew their trust that God created all things. They see that Abel, Enoch, and Noah believed that God could be trusted. They can even see that Noah, who did wrong and was wronged, becoming drunk and then was shamed by his son (Gen 9:21), still stands as an heir of *righteousness*. They can imitate not every detail of their lives but the faith held even by imperfect people and, in so doing, please God as well. The anchor of the kind of faith that can follow examples from the past is grounded in the person of Christ, the one who will share the reward he has received from God his Father with all those who follow after him.

11:8–22 · THE COVENANT FAMILY

8By faith, when he was called, Abraham obeyed by going out to the place that he would receive as an inheritance, and he went out even though he did not know where he was going. 9By faith he dwelt in the land of the promise as a foreigner, living in tents with Isaac and Jacob, the fellow heirs of the same promise. 10For they were waiting for the city that has foundations, whose builder and designer is God. 11By faith, even though Sarah herself was barren, and Abraham and Sarah were beyond the time of life, he along with Sarah[19] *received power to cast seed, regarding the one who made the promise as faithful.* 12*Therefore, from one dead were born a multitude like the stars of the heavens and an innumerable sum like the sand near the shore of the sea.* 13*According to faith all of these died, without receiving the promises but seeing and greeting them from a distance and confessing that they are foreigners and exiles on the earth.* 14*For those who say these things reveal that they are seeking a fatherland.* 15*Indeed, if they were remembering that [land] from which they had gone out, they would have had opportunity to go back,* 16*but as it is they were desirous of something better—that is, of heaven. Therefore, God was not ashamed to be called their God, for God prepared a city for them.* 17*By faith Abraham had offered Isaac when he was tested; indeed he, the one who had received the promise, was ready to offer the only [son];* 18*to [Abraham] it was spoken, "In Isaac will your seed be called,"* 19*because he considered that God is able even to raise from the dead, whence he received him also with a parable.* 20*By faith Isaac blessed Jacob and Esau concerning the things to come.* 21*By faith Jacob, even when he was dying, blessed each of the sons of Joseph and bowed down, leaning on the top of his staff.* 22*By faith Joseph, when he was nearing his end, recalled the exodus of the sons of Israel and commanded concerning his bones.*

Antediluvian history concluded, the author now moves from Noah through the line of Shem (Gen 11:10) to covenantal history, but the theme of imperfect people having *faith* remains consistent. Abraham (known as Abram at this point in the Genesis story, but the author of Hebrews elects to call him by his covenant name, Abraham, as he does throughout the sermon) also responded correctly in the face of the unseen. He could not have exercised this first example of his faith on account of something visible to him, because *he did not know where he was going*. God said he would go to a land but did not specify which one (Gen 12:1). The only thing Abraham had to respond to was God's call.[20] *By faith, when he was called, Abraham obeyed*. He heard God, had faith in God, and obeyed by *going out*. God was calling him to separate from his

19. See explanation for this unusual translation in the commentary that follows.

20. Raymond Brown comments, "When things seemed against him he looked upwards to a God who had promised to be both his protector and rewarder." *The Message of Hebrews: Christ above All*, The Bible Speaks Today (Downers Grove, IL: InterVarsity Press, 1984), 205.

extended family, to not go back to his place of origin, but to keep moving forward. The author states this action twice with the verb for "go" in this one verse, and it is an action he urges for his readers when he calls them to go out to Jesus (Heb 13:13). He has also been urging them to continue their forward movement, which could also, in some instances, take them away from family of origin and what is comfortable.

The text gives no details of Abraham's previous relationship with God, but his actions give evidence of the existence of it. As one who was called by God, he serves as an example of those whom God calls with the aim of receiving the eternal inheritance (9:15). The connections with that verse are even stronger because next the author says that Abraham was *going out to the place that he would receive as an inheritance.* This obedience took him to a place that God would give him as an inheritance to reward his faith. This inheritance was not from his earthly father because he, Terah, was a stranger in the land where he took his family and then died (Gen 11:31–32). Abraham's earthly father had no legitimate claims on anything in that land that he could pass on to his children, but this inheritance was promised by Abraham's heavenly father, God, who, as Creator (Heb 2:10), owns all things.

The author continues Abraham's story with another example in his life that came *by faith.* After going out to the place of inheritance, he then *dwelt in the land of the promise.* Abraham lived there on the land promised to him by God as that which he and his family would inherit, but he did not own that land. Instead, he lived there *as a foreigner.* He was viewed as distinct, living among people that did not consider him their own. The readers of Hebrews can likely relate to this sense, as they have experienced conflict (10:32–35) and are encouraged to endure shame (12:2–4; 13:13). The author emphasizes Abraham's lack of rootedness by highlighting that he was *living in tents.* This is not a unique form of suffering since there were other nomads in Abraham's time. Instead, the author's point in mentioning the tents is to juxtapose the temporary home with the city God was preparing (11:10, 16). As the sole reference in the sermon to a tent that is not focused on the tabernacle, this mention not only emphasizes the transitory nature of Abraham's life but reinforces the temporary nature of the tabernacle itself. Just like Abraham's situation of living in tents, the tabernacle as the place to meet God was not meant to be permanent.

Living in tents, however, might have seemed like it would go on forever for Abraham's family. The author notes that he is living this way *with Isaac and Ja-*

cob, his son and grandson (the narratives in this section of Genesis frequently mention their tents). By naming Isaac and Jacob before he says more about their stories, the author emphasizes that for *three generations* this family did not see the full realization of what God had promised them. They were in the land but had not inherited it so that they could claim it fully as their own. The propensity for doubt must have been massive. Reformation pastor Heinrich Bullinger comments, "It was a hard and rare deed that, when he arrived at the place that he had anticipated, he discovered nothing solid or firm, from which a certain dissatisfaction could have sprouted."[21] The author knows the difficulty that lack of promise fulfillment raises, and so he set the patriarchs as exemplars for his readers.

Even in the midst of the disappointing circumstances of their living conditions, Isaac and Jacob had to stay tethered to the reality that they were *fellow heirs of the same promise*. God's promise to their father included them and extended to them. Because the readers are also included in the fulfilled promise of assistance given to the seed of Abraham (2:16), they, like Isaac and Jacob, are included in the promises to Abraham.

One might imagine that Abraham, Isaac, and Jacob were focused on a different promise than the readers of Hebrews—namely, the land of Canaan—but the author of Hebrews does not interpret their stories in that way. Next he names the object of their faith: they were not concerned about the land of Canaan but were *waiting for the city that has foundations*. The author has already stated that Jesus is waiting for God to make his enemies a footstool (10:13). Now he asserts that the patriarchs were also practicing the act of anticipation, aimed at a different place to live. That verbal connection with Jesus's trusting expectation suggests their deep trust that God would grant what had been promised. In anticipating a *city*, they were looking forward to something lasting, in contrast to the tents they had to tear down and set up. Later in the sermon the author specifies this city as the city of the living God (12:22) that he and his readers are also anticipating (13:14). This city, the author makes explicit, has *foundations*. In stating what may be an obvious architectural reality, the author reminds them of the previous discussion in which foundations were invoked to indicate what should remain strong and *not* be rebuilt (6:1), as well as the assertion from the psalm in which the Lord is described as the one who lays the foundation for

21. Bullinger, *Commentary on Hebrews*, 11:9–10 120v (RCS 13:163).

creation (1:10). Similarly, in this instance, the foundation layer is God. This city's *builder and designer is God*. The city they were anticipating was not one built by humans, which could succumb to deterioration or destruction, but this city was one whose planner and builder is God, an everlasting city made by an everlasting creator.[22] In resonance with the author's statements that God is the builder of all things (3:4) and the designer and builder of the true tabernacle (8:5; 9:24), here the author describes the creativity and care of God. God is a craftsman who designs and constructs this city. Readers get a glimpse into the handiwork of God, as one who delights in preparing a place for those with whom God has covenanted. This statement about God provides a powerful connection with Jesus's promise that he leaves his disciples to prepare a place for them in the many-roomed house of his Father (John 14:2–3). In the author of Hebrews' homily on their story, the patriarchs did not really care how they were living in Canaan, foreigner or native, in tents or in houses, because they were waiting for the divine city. Pamela Eisenbaum notes how this departs from the way other Jewish exegetes have read Abraham's story, "portray[ing] him as 'at home' when he arrives in Canaan."[23]

This alternative focus reinterprets what the author first said about Abraham. The patriarch did not understand where he was going both because God did not reveal that information (although this had been his father Terah's plan to leave Ur and go to Canaan, but he had only made it as far as Haran [Gen 11:31–32]) and, more importantly, because he was on his way to a city that was not yet prepared. It has its roots in the land of promise but was not exhausted by the land of promise. The authors' statements coalesce with statements about an unshakable kingdom in 12:28. In the framework of a Jewish hope for a renewed earth that they would possess, a heavenly city come down (Jub. 1.29, 4.26, 2 Bar. 4:1–4; 4 Ezra 7:26; 8:52; 10:27; 4Q475; expressed in the New Testament in Rev 21–22 and 2 Pet 3), Abraham would inherit Canaan as God had promised, but it would be a renewed land with a city constructed not by humans but by God, a

22. Koester, *Hebrews*, 484–85. See his discussion of the disdain of tents and the love of cities in the first century (496).

23. Pamela Michelle Eisenbaum, *The Jewish Heroes of Christian History: Hebrews 11 in Literary Context*, SBLDS 156 (Atlanta: Scholars Press, 1997), 157. She includes a salient quote from Philo, who says of Abraham, "He hastened eagerly to obey, not as though he were leaving home for a strange land but rather as returning from amid strangers to his home" (*On the Life of Abraham* 62).

heavenly city come down to a renewed earth—or, maybe better said, a heavenly city that expands to embrace a renewed creation.[24] It was not a problem to live as a foreigner even for three generations because they experienced the down payment of this city in their relationship with God and also because they knew it would not be fully realized until God's renewal was complete, a possibility that might extend past the dates of their own deaths.

From land to heir, the author moves from one promise of the covenant to another. Verse **11** has raised many debates, but the central affirmation is clear and in line with everything that has been said thus far: faith is trust in God who has already revealed faithfulness. The details of how the author gets to that affirmation are as fascinating as they are complicated, but I implore readers not to lose the forest of faith as I focus in on some of the trees.

This verse starts as all the others have, *By faith*, but the confusion arises around *who* is exercising that faith: Abraham or Sarah. It is certainly plausible to read these verses as focused on Abraham all the way down. By faith he *received power to cast seed*. In other literature of the time, this phrase appears as a way of describing the male's role in procreation.[25] Hence, Abraham, as the male, would be the most natural reading of this action. The next phrase reminds readers that the one showing faith was *beyond the time of life*. Abraham was certainly old (Gen 18:11; as Sarah acknowledges, Gen 18:12). He was ninety-nine, actually (Gen 17:1), at the time God promised that he would have a son with Sarah, and he was one hundred when Isaac was born (Gen 17:17; 21:5). Even in the face of these realities, Abraham still regarded God, *who made the promise, as faithful*. Although Hebrews is not replicating any of the precise language from Genesis with these words, the idea that Abraham trusted that God could do what God had said is certainly present (Gen 12:2, 7; particularly 15:4–6; 17:5–9, 16–21; 18:10), whereas there is no explicit mention of Sarah's faith in the Genesis narrative. Therefore, because of his faith in God's faithfulness, from one man, Abraham, who because of his age was as good as *dead*, many descendants *were born, a multitude like the stars of the heavens and an innumerable sum like the sand near the shore of the sea*. This reading echoes Isaiah 51:2, where the prophet calls attention to the time when God called to Abra-

24. Appreciation to a member of our PhD community, Jason Liu, for this insight.

25. Gk. Apoc. Ezra 5:12; Philo, *Creation of the World* 132; Epictetus, *Discourses* 1.13.3; Marcus Aurelius, *Meditations* 4.36.

ham, who was one, and made of him many. This reading that focuses on Abraham also aligns with Paul's comments on Abraham's faith in Romans 4:19–20: "And not being weak in faith he considered his own body as good as dead [*nenekrōmenon*, the same word in Heb 11:12], being about one hundred years old, and he considered the deadness of Sarah's womb. But he did not waver with respect to the promise of God in unbelief but was strengthened in faith, giving glory to God." The support for the Abrahamic reading is strong.

With this reading the phrase that concerns Sarah, *autē Sarra steira*, could function as a Hebraic circumstantial parenthetical: "By faith (*even though Sarah herself was barren*) Abraham received power." It is the case, however, that Hebrews does not tend to use Hebraic constructions.[26] Alternatively, as uncials often lacked the iota that marks the dative, this phrase could be a dative of accompaniment: "By faith he [Abraham] together with barren Sarah received power to beget."[27] This lacks support because there are no manuscripts that have understood the uncials as datives and then written them in.

It is more natural to take Sarah's name, an apparent nominative that stands next to *pistis*, "faith," as the subject, as has been the case in the other examples of Hebrews 11 thus far. Moreover, in the Genesis account, Abraham is not really as good as dead because he has fathered Ishmael and will father six children with Keturah after Sarah dies (Gen 25:1–2). He might be old, but he, unlike Sarah, is certainly capable of procreating. For these reasons, others prefer taking Sarah as the subject of v. 11:[28] "By faith, even though Sarah herself was barren, she received power that resulted in the casting of seed." While that phrase concerning the casting of seed appears in reference to men, theories of conception at the time of the writing of Hebrews were diverse. Some thought that only men cast seed, but others asserted that *both* men and women contributed seed.[29] The author of Hebrews could reflect this view,[30]

26. Ellingworth, *Hebrews*, 587.

27. Both options are discussed in Metzger, *Textual Commentary*, 602.

28. Supported, for example, by Ephrem the Syrian, Augustine, Lucas Osiander, and Johannes Oecolampadius. See discussions in Bruce, *Hebrews*, 294; Johnson, *Hebrews*, 291; Thomas R. Schreiner, *Hebrews*, Evangelical Biblical Theology Commentary (Bellingham, WA: Lexham Academic, 2020), 352.

29. See Alicia Myers, *Blessed Among Women? Mothers and Motherhood in the New Testament* (New York: Oxford University Press, 2017), 51.

30. P. W. van der Horst, "Sarah's Seminal Emission: Hebrews 11:11 in Light of Ancient

even though he would be using this particular phrase in an unexpected way. This might be evidence of the author's desire to include explicit mention of women's faith. Alternatively, the expression might indicate that she received the power to *receive* Abraham's seed.[31] In other words, she received the power so that Abraham's casting of semen could be effective. Early scribes read Sarah as the subject and therefore clarified this reading by providing verbs for procreation and even giving birth in addition to the phrase for casting seed. So the text could read, "She received power to cast seed *with the result to procreate*[32] (D* P 81. 1505 b vg^{ms} (sy^{h})) even though she was beyond the time of life *she bore* (x^2 D^2 K L P, etc.)."

Moreover, Sarah certainly fits the description of one who was *beyond the time of life*, the normal time of life for conceiving children. Not only is she ninety (Gen 17:17), advanced in age (Gen 18:11), but she was also postmenopausal (Gen 18:11). The first thing readers learn about Sarai, Abram's wife, is that she is barren (Gen 11:30), but by this point in their lives, this ever-barren woman is past the point at which *any* woman could have a child. She has more personal obstacles to faith in this particular promise of God than does Abraham. Does she, in fact, overcome those obstacles and trust that the promising God will come through and deliver on the promises? She does laugh when she hears the news (Gen 18:12), noting her track record and Abraham's age, but so had Abraham (Gen 17:17). I will return to the question of whether or not she had faith below.

Another challenge to reading Sarah as the subject of v. 11 is that Abraham seems to be the focus of v. **12**: he is the one from whom the many were born, the one who was as good as dead. It could be that Abraham is the focus of vv. 8–9, Sarah the focus of v. 11, and then Abraham the focus of v. 12. Possibilities exist, however, for seeing a role for Sarah in the phrases of v. 12 as well (the one from whom the many were born, the one who was as good as dead).

Embryology," in *Greeks, Romans and Christians: Essays in Honor of Abraham J. Malherbe*, ed. D. L. Balch, E. Ferguson, and W. A. Meeks (Minneapolis: Fortress, 1990), 287–302.

31. Cockerill, *Hebrews*, 544; Johnson, *Hebrews*, 292. Healy notes, "Sarah stands at the head of a long line of biblical women who suffered the stigma of infertility including Rebekah, Rachel, Hannah, and Elizabeth. Yet in each case God intervened miraculously, enabling the birth of a child who turned out to play a pivotal role in the plan of salvation" (*Hebrews*, 236).

32. Koester notes that this phrase could also be applied to the activity of women or men in procreation (*Hebrews*, 487).

As far as "being dead" is concerned, as I previously stated, that description fits Sarah better than it does Abraham. She has always been barren (Gen 11:30) and is now postmenopausal. Her womb holds absolutely no hope of life. Her body always has been and is now even *more dead* than Abraham's. The problem is that the word for "dead" is either a masculine or a neuter singular participle. It cannot refer to Sarah alone. Moreover, that participle is related to the masculine or neuter noun *henos* in the phrase *from one*. Theodoret of Cyr, a fifth-century Antiochene theologian and churchman, found a way to include her in this phrase: "'From one person' means from Abraham but if we were to take the 'one' to mean both of them [Abraham and Sarah], we would not be wide of the mark: 'the two will be one flesh,' Scripture says."[33] Luke Timothy Johnson agrees that "the phrase 'from one man' does not exclude the role of Sarah's faith. In fact, it is her faith that enables the one man to have so many descendants."[34] Both Sarah and Abraham display features of deadness—she even more so—and she is certainly included with him in the phrase *from one*, especially since the author recognizes the reality of human biology, that the descendants did not come from Abraham alone. This pushes me to think that both the noun *one* and the participle *dead* are neuter and not masculine. It was Abraham's age, but even more so Sarah's barrenness, that was a barrier to the realization of God's promise. It is not just from one man but from one encounter between a husband and his wife that led to the fulfillment of the many descendants.

Alternatively, if the noun *one* and participle *dead* are masculine in v. 12, Abraham might not be the referent for them. One male from whom the many descendants come is also an apt description of Isaac. Although God promises to bless and multiply Ishmael, the *covenant* would continue through Isaac (Gen 21:19–21). Even more clearly, while each of these promises about stars (Gen 15:5) and sand (Gen 13:16) come to Abraham before either boy is born and therefore could apply to either or both, since they both are fathered by Abraham, both promises appear in the text in reference to *Isaac alone* after Abraham was willing to offer him to God (Gen 22:17). Because of Abraham's willingness to sacrifice Isaac, the son of the patriarch could be one described as "good as dead," a story the author will tell in the following verses (Heb

33. Theodoret of Cyr, *Interpretation of Hebrews* 11 (ACCS 10:187).

34. Johnson, *Hebrews*, 292.

11:17–19). God chose to involve Sarah for the multitudinous promise to come to fruition through Isaac. If Isaac is "the one" in focus, Sarah's faith for the conception of him (v. 11) is a natural transition to his story.

The author certainly has in mind God's fulfilled promise to Abraham and Sarah in the birth of Isaac and the people of the covenant who issue from him, but for a letter in which confessors of Christ become children of God, seeing v. 12 as an allusion to Jesus the Messiah as the seed of Abraham offers a final intriguing possibility if *one* and *dead* are masculine. It is Jesus who makes possible the fulfillment of numerous descendants in a way Abraham could never have imagined, and only Jesus is one who was not just as good as dead (metaphorically, partially, or potentially dead) but truly and fully succumbed to death (2:14). The Son, too, does not take on flesh and blood without the faith of women, Mary who bore him as well as Sarah who bore Isaac, his ancestor through his mother Mary. For all these reasons, it is quite plausible to see in vv. 11 and 12 the inclusion of Sarah as a faithful one.

Even if, however, Abraham's faith remains the primary subject, Sarah's is certainly included (hence my fulsome translation): *By faith, even though Sarah herself was barren, and Abraham and Sarah were beyond the time of life, he along with Sarah received power to cast seed, regarding the one who made the promise as faithful. Therefore, from one dead were born a multitude like the stars of the heavens and an innumerable sum like the sand near the shore of the sea.* For Isaac to be born, she, too, responded with active faith to what God had said. In this instance, both of them had to have faith to face not just something unseen but a reality they could clearly see, a reality that appeared hopeless. Barrenness, age, and menopause, conditions opposite to those conducive to life, were the barriers they had to face. The situation was, as the author of Hebrews and Paul put it, necrotic. In light of those realities, God makes a promise that *they* (not just Abraham but Abraham *and Sarah* [Gen 17:15–16]) will have a child. Although they both raise questions and both laugh at the prospect, they must have been trusting enough to give it a try. They both had to be willing to participate in the sexual aspect of marital one-fleshness to open themselves to the possibility of begetting a child. Human experience, sadly and infuriatingly, knows of situations in which a woman participates in the begetting of a child against her will. The Genesis narrative boldly denies that possibility for Abraham and Sarah, for between God's promise that Abraham will father a child *with Sarah* (spoken so that both Abraham [Gen 17:15–16, 19, 21] and

Sarah [Gen 18:9–15] hear it) and the realization of that promise (Gen 21:1–7), the narrative presents the heartbreaking realities of rape (threatened against the angels, Lot's daughters, and Lot [Gen 19:5–9]), incest under the influence of alcohol (Gen 19:30–38), and a situation, because of Abraham's cowardice, in which Sarah herself is almost trafficked (Gen 20:1–7). It is almost as if between the promise and the realization, the narrative says, "Here are all the things this pregnancy *is not*." Sarah is neither forced nor tricked to have this child; she *chooses by faith* to try to do so. Abraham and Sarah are both faithfully involved in the one act that creates the one child whose multitudinous line leads to the one Messiah who makes possible the descendants beyond number. The mutuality of their actions and the double honor of their active faith are clear, no matter the complexity of the grammar written.

In presenting an argument for the inclusion of Sarah's faith, I must not ignore the truly ugly parts of her life. As is true for most of the characters in this list, she can be commended for exercising trust in God without excusing her moral failures. Slavery may have been the unquestioned evil of the time in which she lived, but she trafficked Hagar, abused her (Gen 16:1–6), and then cast her and her son, Ishmael, out (Gen 21:8–10). Wickedness existed alongside faith in her life, a painfully familiar reality in all times and places. God blesses Abraham, and Sarah, *who do not deserve such blessing*. God also sees, meets, provides for, and blesses the woman and child, Hagar and Ishmael, whom Sarah casts out (Gen 21:12–21). It is Hagar who names God as the one who does all this seeing (Gen 16:13).

Now that Abraham's and Sarah's roles have been explored in depth, the amazing fact is clear: innumerable life came from one encounter between two as-good-as-dead people. God's promise of life is simply unstoppable, and faith, even from incredibly imperfect people, can trust in that truth. They both had trusted that *the one who made the promise* was *faithful*. This statement connects to the author's earlier evocation of Abraham's story in which he inherited God's promises because he demonstrated faith (6:15). This truth about God is precisely what the author proclaims to his addressees in the previous chapter as the reality that should ground their hope (10:23). Abraham and Sarah serve as examples, not in all ways, but in how he wants the listeners to live by exercising faith in God.

The cadence of the language changes in v. **13**. Instead of the simple dative of the noun "faith," the author adds a preposition. Hence, the translation is not "by faith" but *according to faith.* Moreover, instead of one individual (or one couple), the author makes a statement about *all of these.* It is rather striking that what all of these did according to faith was *died.* They experienced their own mortality. For those who face death either through old age (9:27) or persecution (12:4), to die according to faith is an important example to follow. The patriarchs and matriarchs reached the end of their earthly lives with faith (it is clear that this verse does not serve as a summation of the entirety of the story of creation told thus far because the statement *all of these died* could not apply to Enoch). This faith allowed them to look past their mortality to the fulfillment of the promises of God that remained for them.[35] They died *without receiving the promises.* Instead, they were *seeing and greeting them from a distance.* Although utilizing a different term for *seeing* (*horaō* here; *blepō* in 11:1), the author puts them forth as an example of his definition of faith, which trusts even in light of what cannot be seen (11:1). They did not see the promises in their possession, but they trusted God would fulfill them and so could see them from a distance. With such trust in the realization of those promises, in addition to seeing them, they *greeted* these promises. By portraying their faith, the author reiterates the theme of hope in the promises of God even in the face of death.

The most immediate promise in view is God's promise of the land, as indicated by the last phrase in v. 13: *confessing that they are foreigners and exiles on the earth.* Their faith was expressed in confessing that this world was not their home. It is upon the occasion of Sarah's death, after God had promised the land several times and after Abraham had great wealth, military success, and respect, that Abraham says that he is only an exile on the land. To show that status, he insists on paying for Sarah's tomb (Gen 23:4), where Abraham will be buried as well (Gen 25:9–10). Their status as foreigners is evidence that they were members of a group the author later tells the congregation to welcome and love (Heb 13:2). This confession of Abraham's, which took place with respect to the land of Canaan (see also Gen 47:4, 9), points to something more comprehensive. The author of Hebrews recalls this statement to indicate that when the covenant mothers and fathers confess their foreigner status, they have more than just Ur of the Chaldeans in mind. They were foreigners in the land of Canaan, rather than natives, but they were not technically exiles, a term that can be used to

35. Harris, *Hebrews*, 319.

indicate people who had been compelled against their will to leave one location for another. They had not been forced to leave Ur; Terah had chosen to do so. Instead, *those who say these things reveal that they are seeking a fatherland.* By emphasizing the spoken vocal nature of their confession, the author aligns their actions with what God does—namely, communicate with words. Their words display a reality that can be observed, just as God's word results in tangible realities that aid faith. What is clear about their confession that they are foreigners and exiles is that *they are seeking a fatherland.* The author has just stated that God rewards those who seek him (11:6), and so their seeking of a fatherland is to say that they are seeking God who has been revealed as Father, chiefly in the coming of the Son (1:5), and that they are seeking a home *with* God. This is an echo of the divine Sabbath rest into which the author has called this congregation (4:8–11). Moreover, as the author notes in v. **15**, *Indeed, if they were remembering that [land] from which they had gone out, they would have had opportunity to go back.* They had ample time to go back to Ur, if they wanted to do so. The author's interpretation of their story is that they were not exiles from Ur, but they were exiles from the place where they dwelt with God. *But as it is they were desirous of something better—that is, of heaven.* They set their sights and their hearts beyond what they could see, to something better, much as this congregation did when they willingly had their goods plundered because they knew they had better possessions (10:34). In their desire to return to be with God, readers might have thought of a version of the Platonic narrative in which souls are exiled into material creation,[36] but the author could also be recalling earlier statements in his sermon about the created place of God's rest (Heb 4). Humanity had been forced to leave this place of life and rest when they came under the control of the devil and death (2:14). As Chrysostom notes, "Did they mean that they were 'strangers' from that land that is in Palestine? By no means: but in respect of the whole world."[37] They were not just foreigners in the land of Canaan but were foreigners on the whole earth—or, put better, foreigners in the world *as it stood.* Their lack of at-homeness in the world showed their dis-ease with how the world currently was, when the enemies were not yet under the feet of God and God's viceroy, humanity (2:8–9). By saying that they "confessed" this status on earth, the author, yet again, casts what they did as an

36. Thompson, *Hebrews*, 238.

37. Chrysostom, *Hebrews* 24.4 (*NPNF*[1] 14:474).

example of what his readers have done and need to continue to hold (3:1; 4:14; 10:23; 13:15). This confession of appropriate disconnect from the land (which all generations of Christians should embrace with respect to whatever nation they inhabit) showed their longing for the heavenly realm where God dwells enthroned in the sanctuary where Jesus serves and reigns. As humans under the realm of death, they had been exiled from the creational ideal of rest with God and longed to return to that state.

During their lives, even though they lived in Canaan, they were looking forward to the place God constructed. They were seeking a land with their Father, who dwells in heaven. This was the vision of their hope, the aim of their faith, and even though they faced their own deaths, they continued to believe that God could fulfill this promise *on the other side of death*. This is a faith, as Ben Witherington notes, that "carries a nuance of faithfulness to the end . . . , as is especially clear when we note the parallels between what is said of faith and what is said of endurance."[38] This kind of faith is both a belief and an action stemming from that belief.

Because of their faithful vision cast on God, *therefore, God was not ashamed to be called their God*. God was in no way ashamed to be associated with them because they had read God rightly.[39] In conversation with Moses, God is willing to take on Abraham, Isaac, and Jacob's names as the way in which to be identified; God names himself as the God of Moses's forefathers (Exod 3:6). Creating a lovely enclosure, the author of Hebrews notes that as God had called to Abraham (Heb 11:8), now God was willing to be called by him and his family. Like the Son (2:11, the only other instance of this verb for gladness), the Father is glad, not ashamed, to be associated with such trusting people.

The patriarchs and matriarchs trusted that God existed and was a rewarder of the faith (11:6)—specifically, that *God prepared a city for them*. Similar to the description of the Sabbath rest, this section affirms again that God, too, was anticipating the time when people would dwell together with Father and Son and Holy Spirit in the divine presence. The idea of preparation indicates attention and care and is a term frequently associated with the work of God to get ready

38. Witherington, *Letters and Homilies*, 295.

39. Interestingly, it is not only Abraham (Gen 13:4; 21:33), Isaac (Gen 26:25), and Jacob (Gen 33:20) whom call God in the narrative, but Hagar as well (Gen 16:13). God is also not ashamed to be called by her, to whom God also makes promises (Gen 16:10; 17:20; 21:13, 18).

the eternal reality for humanity (Matt 3:3; 20:23; 22:4; 25:34, 41; 26:17; Mark 1:3; 10:40; John 14:2–3; 1 Cor 2:9). This is a second mention of the city God is building (Heb 11:10), the same city the author will describe more fulsomely in 12:22–24.

The dwelling place, however, is not the only promise in view, for the author said in v. 13 that they had not yet received the *promises* (plural). Moreover, the author had employed a double description of what they do with regard to these promises: they both see and greet them. It makes sense to see a place but not as much sense to greet a place. It makes better sense to greet a people, as in 13:24 (see also discussion of 11:39).[40] The promise of many descendants remains subtly present in this section (11:13–16) even as it becomes the focus again in the following (11:17–21).

In v. **17** the author shifts attention squarely back to the promise of descendants again. *When he was tested*, as was Jesus (2:18) and as are the listeners (4:15), *by faith* Abraham willingly and without hesitancy *offered Isaac*. In fact, the verb for *offered* (*prosenēnochen*) is given first place in the sentence, right after the repeated linking word, *by faith* (*pistei*). The choice of this verb, which does not appear in Genesis 22 where this account is located, connects Abraham's action with the priestly action of offering sacrifice, mentioned over a dozen times in Hebrews before this occurrence. Depending on how it is interpreted, the perfect tense of that verb might convey the weight of this action; although it happened once, the effect of this kind of faith had lasting impact. Like a Hebrew poet, the author states the truth again with slightly different terminology: *Indeed he was ready to offer the only one*. The author's choice of *monogenē* (*only one*) to describe Isaac evokes a set of intriguing connections. Some Greek texts describe Isaac in that way (Aquila and Symmachus),[41] but others have the voice of God differentiating Isaac by referring to him as the beloved one. *Monogenēs* can be used to refer to one's only child, or one's only child of a particular sex (Luke 7:12; 8:42; 9:38). If readers are familiar with the Abraham narrative, they know that Abraham has more than one son at the time God calls to him, so this recalls again the participation of Sarah. She has only one son, and therefore Isaac is the only begotten of her and Abraham's union. Moreover, at this point in Abraham's story, he has had to send his firstborn son away, along with his mother,

40. Ellingworth, *Hebrews*, 594.

41. Koester, *Hebrews*, 491. Josephus (*Jewish Antiquities* 1.13.1 *par.* 222) also uses this term for Isaac (Attridge, *Hebrews*, 334).

Hagar (Gen 21:12–14). In its canonical setting this word connects Isaac with Jesus, God's only begotten Son (John 1:14, 18; 3:16, 18; 1 John 4:9), one of several allusions the author draws here between Isaac and Jesus.

The author states that Abraham was *ready to offer* the only begotten (*monogenē*)—again the author uses a marked verb tense, this time the imperfect, conveying the process of offering, recalling that long walk up Mount Moriah (Gen 22:6–8). The author marks Abraham as *the one who had received the promise*. The singular noun *promise* here points especially to the promise from God that Abraham would have a descendant with Sarah through whom the covenant would continue (Gen 17:19). Abraham had both received that verbal promise from God and had welcomed into his life the child who began to fulfill that promise. He was willing to offer back up to God the realization of the promise who stood before him, and this must have taken considerable faith.

Then the author gives the promise in the voice of God: *to whom it was spoken, "In Isaac will your seed be called."* He employs a divine passive with his often-used word for speaking to evoke God's promise to Abraham concerning Isaac in Genesis 17:19, even as he cites precisely from Genesis 21:12: "your seed will be called in Isaac." This statement occurs when God distinguishes between Isaac and Ishmael, between the son of the slave, Hagar, and the son of Sarah. In responding to Abraham's concern over his firstborn son, God promises to make him a great nation as well (Gen 21:13). Because Isaac was called the seed of the covenant, others were born from his line and were called into the covenant (Heb 9:15) to the point that their number became innumerable (11:12). Because the blessing of the covenant extends to all people (Gen 12:3), Ishmael's descendants are included as well.

Abraham so trusted in what God had said, and then in the evidence that God provided in this child when he and Sarah could not conceive him of their own power, that he was willing to offer up his son, the one whom he loved, Isaac, the child of the promise. The author explicitly states why: *because he considered that God is able even to raise from the dead.* The author uses a verb for "consideration" that contains the term for speech in it (*logizomai*), drawing a verbal connection with Abraham's trust *in God's word.* This description of God, as being able to raise the dead, connects to Jesus's belief described in Hebrews 5. He prayed to God trusting that God was "able to save him from death" (5:7). Abraham and Jesus share this kind of faith in God. By specifically describing this belief as God's ability to *raise from the dead*, the author shows Abraham as one who shares this shared belief among Jews and Christians (6:2; 11:35), a belief that for Christians is rooted in God's raising up of Jesus from death (13:20). Since God had already revived the necrotic state of his body and the body of his wife, Abraham was not required to believe in something for which he had no evidence. He could look back to his past, see the work of God, and then trust that God could do something similar in the future but on an even more miraculous scale. This is not to say that it was easy for Abraham to offer up his beloved son, to go to the point of taking up the knife (Gen 22:10), but he was able to do so because of that kind of faith, aptly described as resurrection faith.

Abraham's enactment of his faith was parabolic. The author concludes v. 19 and the story of Abraham and his immediate family with this phrase: *whence he received him even with a parable*. With the term *received*, the author connects Abraham with the goal that he just urged for the audience, that they endure so that they may receive what God had promised (10:36). He also sets up a juxtaposition that will demand clarification when he will say that all the faithful did *not* receive what God had promised (11:39; see discussion of that verse for a reconciliation of these two statements).

The author of Hebrews is the only epistle writer in the New Testament to use the term *parable* (here and in 9:9 for the tabernacle), so common in the Gospels. In one way, Abraham received Isaac back not truly from death but from its cusp. His experience pointed tangentially but not directly to resurrection, as parables point "at a slant" to the subject matter at which they are aimed. In another way, Abraham's faith and the rescue of Isaac by the angel of the Lord who stayed the hand of Abraham (Gen 22:11–12) tell a story that points to a greater reality. The application here resonates even with the geometrical application of the related term *parabola*, a line that scoops down and then comes up again. Abraham's faith trusted that even if Isaac was cast down to death, he would be lifted up again. Proto-reformer and pamphleteer Katharina Schütz Zell appealed to Abraham's example of trust in the face of death to encourage the women in Kentzingen in the early 1500s whose husbands had been taken into exile for their Protestant beliefs. They were to take on Abraham's manly courage even as they imagined God's faithfulness to them as maternal commitment.[42]

42. "To the Suffering Women" in *Church Mother*, 51, cited in Schroeder and Taylor, *Voices Long Silenced*, 71–72.

Abraham's receiving of Isaac back from the dead certainly points forward to the resurrection of the Son Jesus from the dead. Several of the early interpreters of Hebrews saw the parable particularly applicable to the ram caught in the thicket (Gen 22:13), as in Augustine: "Note that when Abraham first saw the ram, it was caught by its horns in a thicket of briers. This surely is a symbol of Jesus."[43] Athanasius noted similarly, "When the Lord held him back from sacrificing Isaac, Abraham saw the Messiah in the ram that was ultimately offered as the sacrifice to God."[44] The parabolic connection to Jesus's story could also remind readers not only of his death but also of his ascension. The Father received back at the right hand the Son who became incarnate to complete the divine will. The author's language of Abraham's parable is so vivid, in fact, that as a good storyteller he need not make any further comment but allows the reader to draw the lines of inference themselves. When Abraham received Isaac back from the brink of death, he also received with him a parable, a preview of what God the Father would fully and truly experience with Jesus, the Son of God. By grace (2:9) the Father allowed the death the Son had willed to complete (10:7) and brought him back—fully—from the dead. The author has honored Abraham, Sarah, and Isaac by telling the story of their faith to point to the graciousness and power of God.

In the next sentence (v. **20**), Isaac is not only an adult, but he is also near the end of his life. This is true of the next three patriarchs mentioned. The author focuses in on the moments they bless the continuation of the line of promise as they are facing the imminence of their own mortality. They are looking past even death to the fulfillment of God's promises in and through their family.

In v. 20 the son who existed because of his father and mother's faith, and who experienced his father's faith in his brush with death, now expresses his own faith. *By faith Isaac blessed Jacob . . . concerning the things to come.* Isaac's action recalls the God who blesses (6:7). In the Genesis narrative, Isaac blesses Jacob with an eye to the future. He passes down the blessing that God had given to Abraham, cursing those who curse him and blessing those who bless him (Gen 27:29; Gen 12:3), the promise that Hebrews quotes in the first section on Abraham (Heb 6:14). Isaac adds a blessing of abundance and sovereignty (Gen 27:28–29). Later in the narrative, God confirms Isaac's blessing on Jacob

43. Augustine, *City of God* 16.32 (ACCS 14:191).

44. Athanasius, *Festal Letters* 6.8 (ACCS 14:192).

(Gen 28:13–14). By referring to this future blessing as *things to come*, the author connects Isaac's story with the future realities God is bringing (Heb 1:14; 2:5; 6:5; 10:1, 27; 11:8; 13:14). In the setting of Hebrews, it is right to see his blessing of his progeny as inclusive of both earthly and eschatological realities.

When describing Isaac's faith, the author mentions *Esau* as well. It is of benefit to interpreters of Hebrews to consider his story since he appears again in the intense warning in ch. 12. So much is left *unsaid* in this first mention of his story. Isaac does bless Jacob and Esau concerning the things to come, but the way in which this happens—the order in which this happens, Jacob the younger before Esau the elder—is full of pain and poor choices. In Genesis 27, Isaac, old and blind, does not know when his death may come, and so he desires to eat one more meal caught by his hunter son, Esau. After that meal, he plans to bless him. He sends Esau on the errand, but Rebekah overhears the exchange and encourages Jacob to dress as his brother and secure the blessing for himself. From the beginning each parent had their favorite son (Gen 25:28). As unfair as that may be, in between their birth and this event the narrative has recounted only negative vignettes about Esau. He sold his rights of being the firstborn for a bowl of stew, showing that he despised his place in the family (Gen 25:29–34), a negative example the author of Hebrews calls forth in 12:15–17. Moreover, he had married women who did not get along with his parents (Gen 26:34–35). The reader might wonder if he deserved what he got in the blessing situation, and that is certainly a plausible way to read how the author of Hebrews appeals to him. Even so, the particular story in which Jacob deceives Isaac into giving him the blessing intended for Esau leaves only Jacob and Rebekah playing the villain. The blessing Isaac gives to Jacob promises abundance, sovereignty, and the blessing of those who bless Jacob (Gen 27:28–29); that which is left for Esau offers the opposite: scarcity and servitude, *but not forever*. Isaac promises that Esau will eventually loose Jacob's yoke from his neck (Gen 27:39–40).

As the story continues, Jacob finds himself on the receiving end of deception at the hand of his father-in-law, Laban, but he eventually comes into a place of abundance (Gen 32:5). On his journey away from his father-in-law, the tables between him and Esau are turned. Jacob refers to Esau as lord and calls himself his brother's servant (Gen 32:5, 18). As he is waiting to meet Esau, he wrestles with the angel and receives a blessing, a new name, and a limp (Gen 32:22–32), a further confirmation of God's blessing on him. Right away, when he meets Esau, he bows before his brother. Whereas previously Esau desired to kill him (Gen 27:41), Esau kisses him (Gen 33:4). Jacob takes the blessings God had given to him and shares them with Esau (Gen 33:11), who already had an abundance of his own (Gen 33:9). Although Isaac's "blessing" to Esau sounds rather negative, it is fitting by the end of the story to say that whatever Isaac's words, God blessed them both, because their lives attest to that blessing. Hebrews focuses on Isaac's faith, and his faith is displayed in that he sees what will unfold for them. The inclusion of Esau's name evokes these stories of intrigue, surprising reversal, forgiveness, and restoration. Even so, the blessings Esau receives are not the same as those at stake for this community when they have confessed Christ, and so later the author will focus on the dire consequences that follow Esau's flippant actions (see commentary on 12:15–17).

Jacob, too, showed faith, *even when he was dying* (Gen 47:29; 48:1, 21), in that he *blessed each of the sons of Joseph*. His blessing of the *sons* of Joseph calls forth another instance in which the younger is blessed ahead of the elder (Gen 48:8–20). The author doesn't linger on this point but instead closes this vignette about Jacob with a citation from the chapter before the blessing of Ephraim and Manasseh when he *leans on the top of his staff*. When he does so, he is asking Joseph to swear that he will bury him with his ancestors (Gen 47:29–30). Like Joseph (Heb 11:22), he also desires that his body be buried in the land of the promise. His particular act of leaning (*proskyneō*) indicates his weakness, that he needs a staff on which to rest. At death's doorstep, he looks forward to the line continuing through his grandsons and so blesses them (Gen 48:9–20)—or, maybe better said, passes on God's blessing to them (Gen 48:3–4). Ultimately, he is looking at God, because he knows God and God's promises will continue.

Finally, the author recounts that Joseph exercised faith. *When he was nearing his end* (using a different term for death, *teleutaō*, one that connects to the word group for reaching the end/perfection that appears frequently in the sermon: Heb 2:10; 5:9; 7:19, 28; 9:9; 10:1, 14; 11:40; 12:23), he *recalled the exodus of the sons of Israel*. He remembered God's promise that his family would leave Egypt and go back to the land of promise (Gen 50:24), a promise given to Abraham near the beginning of the covenant story (Gen 15:14). In a lovely turn of phrase, the author states that Joseph remembered the past even as he looked forward to the future. He cannot remember the exodus of the sons of Israel because it has not occurred yet, but he can recall God's promise of return to the land and therefore trust that his descendants will receive that promise. He is so confident of this promise that he also *commanded* them *concerning his bones*, to carry his bones back to the land of promise (Gen 50:25). Because the author mentions the bones going back to a particular place on earth, this suggests that this heavenly city to which they are all looking forward (Heb 11:13–15) has some tether on the current earth.

The consistency among these recollections of their stories is that all were facing death but looked to things past death—the continuation, abundance, and rootedness of their families in the promised land. They could do so because they had heard God's word, had seen evidence of God's power, and, therefore, had faith in God's promises. Their trust in God was firm and therefore active (11:1–2). Their example displays that "soul endurance" the author has urged for his readers (10:39).

11:23–31 · THE EXODUS GENERATION

23By faith Moses, after he was born, was hidden for three months by his parents,
because they saw the child as beautiful and did not fear the commandment of the
king. 24By faith Moses, when he became great, denied being addressed as the son of
the daughter of Pharaoh, 25choosing rather to suffer with the people of God than to
have the pleasures of sin for a time, 26regarding as greater wealth than the treasures
of Egypt the reproach of the Messiah. For he looked forward to the reward. 27By faith
he left Egypt not fearing the wrath of the king. For he was waiting for the unseen one
as if he was seeing. 28By faith he made the Passover and the sprinkling of blood, in
order that the destroyer would not touch their firstborn. 29By faith they crossed the
Red Sea as through dry ground, on which the Egyptians, when they took an attempt,
were drowned. 30By faith the walls of Jericho fell, having been surrounded for seven
days. 31By faith Rahab the prostitute, who received the spies with peace, did not
perish with the untrusting.

The story moves forward in time to Moses, but the first act of faith is done *to* him, not *by* him (this resonates with Stephen's retelling of Moses's story in Acts 7:20). *By faith Moses, after he was born, was hidden for three months by his parents.* His parents were bold in faith to hide him because he was born under the threat of death (Exod 1:16). The reason the author provides for their action is that they—as all parents do—*saw the child as beautiful*, but the word can also indicate their perception of his unusually superior nature.[45] Whether typical or special appreciation, they valued the life of their child over the edict of the pharaoh. The author comments explicitly that they *did not fear the commandment of the king*. Like the midwives in the story before this one (Exod 1:15–21), Moses's parents feared the God who valued all life rather than the ruler who was threatened by the great quantity of Jewish life (Exod 1:7–10). As is so often the case, the bravado of oppressive leadership masks the deep fear that lies underneath. This story of Moses's family is not unlike the unsettledness of Herod (Matt 2:3) and Joseph and Mary's faithful trust in God's steady protection of young Jesus (Matt 2:13–15). No matter what might be motivating leaders who persecute people, to stand against them takes bravery. Moses's parents embrace a boldness the author will later urge for this community, fearing no person because of their trust in God (Heb 13:6). This is a valuable lesson for the audience of Hebrews because they might again need to face authorities without fear (10:32–35; 12:4–5).

Then the author turns attention to Moses when he is grown and has to make his own decisions. At that time, he reveals his solidarity with his own lowly and oppressed people. Some scribes wished for more to be said about Moses. The D uncial and some manuscripts of the Vulgate add that when he became great in his command over the Egyptians, he kept in mind the humble life of his Jewish siblings, an allusion to the account of his killing the Egyptian taskmaster (Exod 2:11–15). Even without this addition, the majority of the manuscripts include the description that *by faith Moses, when he became great, denied being addressed as the son of the daughter of Pharaoh*. In his state of maturity and power (taken from Exod 2:11), he denied his adoptive birthright, his status as the son of the daughter of Pharaoh and all its entailments. He had two families, and he had to choose the one to whom he would practice his allegiance. The community who receives this sermon might also be facing choices of remaining with the family of God rather than pleasing the requests of their non-Christ-confessing family members. Moses's choice included rejecting *the pleasures of sin* and *the treasures of Egypt*. Pleasure is a good thing (see 1 Tim 6:17, where it is provided by God), but this was the false pleasure associated with sin. Moreover, it only lasted *for a*

45. Harris, *Hebrews*, 333.

time. In rejecting these fleeting treasures of Egypt, Moses makes a choice that later Jesus will command—namely, to store up treasures not on earth but in heaven (Matt 6:19–21/Mark 10:21/Luke 12:33–34; 19:21). At the time it might have seemed that Moses made a poor decision: *choosing rather to suffer with the people of God*. Providing an example for what the author will admonish this congregation to do, to suffer with others (Heb 13:3), Moses casts his lot with those who are under the hand of Egypt. In so doing, he joins the people with whom God will make covenant (8:10), the people who are moving toward rest with God (4:9), the people for whom Jesus suffered (13:12). It is a sad reality that the particular group of people whom Moses joins will eventually reject God's invitation into faithful rest (3:16–19), but the author describes Moses as joining not just his generation but the whole people of God. Maria Stewart, the "first American-born woman of *any* race to lecture men and women in public on political themes," appeals to Moses's example in this verse to encourage her fellow African American listeners to turn "their feet from impious ways, rather *choosing to suffer affliction with the people of God rather than to enjoy the pleasures of sin for a season*." She shows that "being in solidarity with those who suffer is integral to the nomenclature of 'God's people.'" She bases her admonition on the fact that her people "belong to God, are loved by God, and called by the God that many whites at the time said did not love them or create them. Stewart affirms her people's worth to the Divine."[46]

Moses does so because he was *regarding as greater wealth . . . the reproach of the Messiah*. It is noticeable that the author does not mention Moses's encounter with God at the burning bush, for there the term "reproach" refers to the sufferings of the people, which God sees and to which God responds by calling Moses (Exod 2:24–25). Hebrews casts Moses's vision toward the theophany of the Son of God who became human, the Messiah. Moses was looking far ahead to the lasting reward that went through the path of reproach borne by his people. Like this community who joyfully accepted the plundering of their own possessions (Heb 10:32–34), Moses was willing to leave what he had and move toward what God had promised (Exod 3:10, 12, 17). Like Moses's acceptance of reproach, the author will ask his listeners to go out and join the shame Jesus bears (Heb 13:12–13). The author grants Moses a far-facing vision, in line with a link between the reproach of the people of God and the

46. Bowens, *African American Readings of Paul*, 124, 128.

Messiah in Psalm 88:51–52 LXX. He looks forward not only to his own people's deliverance but further still to the arrival of God's promised one, the Messiah, a promise that had not yet even been given to David.

By mentioning his parents first in his story, the author introduces the possibility that Moses was able to see so far because he never lost his roots. The kind of faith his parents displayed (Heb 11:23) influenced him. Readers of the exodus narrative note that he would have received this teaching from his parents even from the early moments of being nursed by his mother, through God's miraculous provision and Miriam's ingenuity (Exod 2:9). It could be said of Moses that he knew whence he came. He has the foresight, because of his upbringing, to know what it means to suffer with his people. For a sermon in which membership in the family of God is so vital, this is an important canonical echo.

The author's focus is that Moses could see by faith that those who suffer would be the messianic people. He not only looked forward to the Messiah; he also *looked forward to the reward.* He actually received riches of Egypt when God delivered him and his people (Exod 12:35–36), but this was not the reward to which Moses was giving his attention. In the Scriptures of Israel and now in this sermon, he received the lasting award of a commendation from God. In addition, because he is included in the group who dwell with God (Heb 12:22–23), his reward included even more than the commendation. He, like the audience of Hebrews, was looking forward to a reward that would not fade away because it was provided by God (10:35).

If the author was telling Moses's story chronologically, the departure from Egypt mentioned in v. **27** would be the one in which he fled the land after killing an Egyptian taskmaster (Exod 2:11–15). In that instance, the text explicitly says that Moses was afraid (Exod 2:14, although both Josephus [*Jewish Antiquities* 2.254–57] and Philo [*Allegorical Interpretation* 3.11–14; *On the Life of Moses* 1.49–50)] emphasize his courage in going to Midian).[47] It seems more likely that the author is recounting the miraculous exodus when Moses leads the people out of slavery. *By faith he left Egypt not fearing the wrath of the king.* This sentence radically captures not only his departure from this territory but his willingness, which he had displayed earlier in life, to walk away from its glories. In not fearing the king, Moses follows in the footsteps of his parents'

47. Koester, *Hebrews*, 503.

faith (Heb 11:23) and demonstrates the stance the author desires the listeners to embrace (13:6). In this instance after the Passover, he left boldly. Given all that Moses had experienced in his interaction with Pharaoh, it is sensible that he would not fear the wrath of the leader who could not overcome the will of God, who provided evidence of superior power and grace in the plagues. Through these, God overturned Pharaoh's desire and secured the people's release from slavery. There was evidence that provided the basis for Moses's faith. God had already given sufficient encouragement for his bold action. The author states about Moses, *He was waiting for the unseen one as if he was seeing.* On account of what God had done, Moses had ample evidence to imagine what God had promised—namely, entry of the people into the land of promise, even though he could not see it yet (Exod 13:5). Moreover, as the author has already articulated with Joshua (Heb 4:8) and with Abraham and his family (11:10, 14–16), the land of Canaan is not the ultimate vision before the eyes of Moses that gives him confidence to move forward. He was patient (like Abraham in ch. 6, although the author communicates the virtue with a different term) to wait for the one he could not see. He was acting in a way as if he was seeing him, even as the oppressive weight of the Egyptians was all around him. Connected with the mention of the Messiah in v. 26, it seems plausible that the author casts Moses's vision as a christological one. He was looking forward to the Messiah, and that gave him the faith he needed to lead his people out of slavery and away from the threat of death. He was looking forward to the one who would perform those same actions on behalf of all God's creation (2:14–15).

God invited Moses to participate in the enactment of this deliverance. The author goes back in time a bit, before the exodus, to spend time considering the final event that led to it, the event that became so vital in Israel's annual remembrance. *By faith he made the Passover and the sprinkling of blood, in order that the destroyer may not touch their firstborn.* Moses had to trust to receive God's instructions and then pass them on to the people so that they could be carried out (Exod 12:28). This involved a pouring of blood so that the destroyer might not touch their firstborn. The author clearly refers to the final plague here, but the word for the application of the blood, *proschysis,* in addition to achieving a nice run of alliterative *p* sounds (*pistei pepoiēken to pascha kai tēn proschysin*),[48] appears in the exodus narrative when Moses pours

48. Ellingworth, *Hebrews*, 617.

the blood on the people in the covenant ceremony in Exodus 24, the event to which the author refers in 9:19–20. The pouring of the blood of the Passover is not the beginning of the covenant that will remove the effect of sins; it is to protect from the touch of death. The author has argued that Jesus's blood does both: it removes sins completely and defeats death forever. The firstborn are the ones protected in the exodus narrative, but because the author will name all the faithful as the firstborn (12:23) by virtue of their connection to God's firstborn (1:6), readers will see a prefiguring of their own redemption. This is a fitting mention right after the author described Moses's vision as filled with the Messiah (v. 27).

In between Hebrews' retelling of these events, between the Passover (v. 28) and the Red Sea (v. 29), the people leave Egypt, carrying the bones of Joseph, just as he commanded (Exod 13:19/Heb 11:22). To complete the life of Moses, the author concludes with this: *By faith they crossed the Red Sea as through dry ground.* At this moment, Moses had to trust God's leading, seen in cloud and fire, to allow the people to cross the Red Sea as the Egyptians pressed against them. The author notes that, in addition to Moses, the people had to trust as well. Even though they had expressed fear and frustration (Exod 14:10–12), they exhibited faith by taking the steps into the sea. This is an example of faith even from the generation who would soon choose *not* to trust God, as discussed in Hebrews 3–4. That they were able to demonstrate faith, and then later did not, is a reminder to the listeners that they cannot depend on past faithfulness but must keep their hearts guarded *daily* from the deceptiveness of sin (3:13).

It was through this Red Sea, *which the Egyptians, when they took an attempt, were drowned.* When the Egyptians tested their ability to cross into the sea, they did not survive. The death of the Egyptians demonstrates that Moses and the Israelites had to cross through something that should have killed them as they were being pursued by those who should have killed them, having just been protected from the angel that should have killed them. In all cases, God preserved their lives. Moses had been taught from his first breath that this is who God is—a preserver of life—and so he was able to trust God's word that the lives of all the people he was leading would be preserved. He was able to do so both because he had seen God's redemption from death and because he was looking forward to the as-yet-unseen revelation of God, the Messiah, who would defeat death for all time.

The author quickly moves from the exodus from Egypt to the entry into the land. In between vv. 29 and 30 of his retelling is the time of "unfaith" in the wilderness excoriated by the author in chs. 3 and 4. Neither does he reflect on the giving and receiving of the law, although it appears in many other parts of the sermon. He instead moves to name another collective example of faith. *By faith the walls of Jericho fell, having been surrounded for seven days.* At this time when the people parade around the walls of Jericho for seven days (Josh 6:20), the unfaithful generation is no longer present. The parents who crossed through the Red Sea have perished. It is their children who now have the opportunity to demonstrate faith. Although it is worth noting that neither he nor the people are mentioned by name—*the walls* are the subject that falls—Joshua and the people are doing the work of surrounding. Those with Joshua march persistently for seven days, as a demonstration that they trust what God has said to Joshua (Josh 6:2–5). They are able to have faith in the impossible. Trumpets and marching should not destroy walls. As Chrysostom notes, "Even if one blows for ten thousand years," the walls should not fall, but "faith can do all things."[49] This generation may have some memory from early life of what God had done in Egypt. Moreover, they would have seen the suffering of their parents when they did not trust in God and do not want to replicate the mistake. Similarly, the author has reminded his congregation of God's previous preservation of them, even in the midst of difficulty (Heb 10:32–35). Because they stand in the line of the wilderness generation (3:9), they can choose a different path than those forebears did and, like that generation's direct children, march on the path of bold faith.

The conquest narratives raise necessary and complicated theological questions that are not addressed by the author of Hebrews, but it is of note that he decides that his final vignette in this narration will focus on someone within the walls of the city that fell. *By faith Rahab the prostitute, who received the spies with peace, did not perish with the untrusting.* Rahab's daring reception and protection of the spies (Josh 2:1–21) is an act of faith in response to what she had heard about the God of Israel (Josh 2:9–11). Her reception of them with *peace* makes her an exemplar of the mature child of God (Heb 12:11). It shows a picture of what the audience should do *with everyone*, as she did, extending peace even to her approaching enemies. The author of Hebrews does not shy

49. Chrysostom, *Hebrews* 27.3 (*NPNF*[1] 14:487).

away from including her career of prostitution, not as a commendation, since he later says that God will judge fornication (13:4), but as a testament to her new life when she encountered the God of Israel. It was after her act of faith expressed with the spies that the walls fell and the people of Israel rushed the city. At that point, she and her family were spared the fate of *perish[ing] with the untrusting*, a term that not only indicates those in Jericho but also reminds listeners of those that did not trust God among the people of Israel. God is no respecter of persons; faith is a necessary response from all, as the author indicated early in this chapter (11:6). All the faithful, like Rahab, paid heed to what they had heard from God, and therefore avoided death. It has not escaped notice that the author ends his Faith Hall of Fame with a Canaanite prostitute.[50] Hebrews is not alone in mentioning her. James does as well, as his second example of faith, after Abraham's offering of Isaac (Jas 2:20–26). Faith in the God of Israel knows no boundaries, including ethnicity, gender, or previous career. Anyone can trust in God and, out of that trust, act faithfully.

11:32–38 · FAITHFUL IN SUCCESS AND FAILURE

[32]*And what can I still say? For time fails for me to explain concerning Gideon, Barak, Samson, Jephthah, David, and also Samuel and the prophets—*[33]*those who, through faith, subdued kingdoms, administered justice, obtained promises, shut the mouths of lions,* [34]*quenched the power of fire, escaped the edges of a sword, were empowered out of weakness, and became strong ones in war, causing foreign armies to flee.* [35]*Women received their dead through resurrection. But others were beaten and did not receive release, so that they might obtain a better resurrection.* [36]*And others received a trial of mocking and whipping, and still others a trial of bonds and imprisonment.* [37]*Some were stoned, were sawed, died by the slaughter of the sword, went around in sheepskins, in the skins of goats. They lacked what they needed, were buffeted, suffered evil.* [38]*These were those of whom the world was not worthy, those who wandered in the wilderness and in hills and in caves and in the clefts of the earth.*

At this point in the sermon, and in this extended section on the faithful from the past, the author asks his listeners: *And what can I still say?* Recognizing

50. See esp. Mosser, "Rahab Outside the Camp," 383–404.

that *time fails for me*, he rapidly mentions various names and events in the next paragraph. He is employing a common rhetorical statement signaling that time is slipping away in order to transition to a final portion of a speech.[51] Hebrews would take about forty-five minutes to read out loud, so he might be aware that by this point the audience would be growing weary. Ever attentive to rhetorical dynamics, Chrysostom notes, "For when a person is contending vehemently in argument, if he persists in contending, he wears out the hearer, annoying him when he is already persuaded and gaining the reputation of vain ambitiousness."[52] The author chose not to speak of these stories he mentions in any depth.

This is the first occurrence of a first-person singular verb in the entire sermon, outside the cited scriptural speech of God, a startling reminder so late in the sermon of how little readers hear about the author in the sermon itself.[53] Moreover, this is the place in the sermon that grounds my use of "he" for the author throughout. It is here that the maleness of the author finds the greatest support. This "I" is modified by a masculine pronoun (*diēgoumenon*), leading many interpreters to believe that the author of Hebrews was a man.

In this section in which he begins to pick up the pace, he notes that he cannot *explain concerning Gideon, Barak, Samson, Jephthah, David, and also Samuel and the prophets.* In listing the first four names in this way, he has placed them in the wrong chronological order. Barak should have come first, and Samson should have come last. Possibly the author is reiterating the "younger before the older" theme from the stories of the patriarchs and matriarchs, or it could be simply that he is mentioning their names in a rapid list and order does not matter.

Even more important than the order, the names leave readers wondering what he would have said about these interesting and sometimes revolting characters from the epic narrative of Judges. In what follows, I mention elements of their stories that may prompt connections with the aims of Hebrews.

Famous for asking for signs from the Lord, Gideon displayed humility and honesty (Judg 6:13–15), was faithful to tear down an altar to Baal (Judg 6:25–27), and defeated Israel's oppressors with only three hundred men (Judg 7:8–

51. DeSilva, *Perseverance in Gratitude*, 416.

52. Chrysostom, *Hebrews* 27.4 (*NPNF*[1] 14:488).

53. See discussion of authorship in the introduction.

23). At the same time, his story includes violent deaths and concubinage, and although he says that the Lord should reign over the people (Judg 8:23), he builds a golden ephod that tempts the people to idolatry (Judg 8:27). His story—much like Abraham's and Moses's—displays both faith and failure.

Barak also participated in the deliverance of Israel, from Sisera the Canaanite, and that story does contain violence, but not because Barak has any clear moral failures. His story gains color by virtue of his shared leadership with women. It is the prophetess Deborah who enlists him to serve as commander of the army, and he agrees to do so only when she agrees to go with him (Judg 4:1–8). Then, as she prophesies, it is another woman, Jael, who cunningly eliminates the general Sisera (Judg 4:9, 17–22). In the end, he and Deborah sing God's praises of what God has accomplished through them all (Judg 5).

Jephthah shares a connection with Rahab; he is the son of a prostitute (Judg 11:1), and his half brothers drive him out. Later his people return to him to ask him to be their leader, making his rise to power fit the pattern of an unlikely ruler. He has a good memory of Israel's history, recounting events from the time of the wilderness generation and God's provision for them (Judg 11:14–27). His story ends, however, tragically. He defeats the sons of Ammon but in so doing makes a rash vow that results in the death of his daughter (Judg 11:29–40). Then he engages in a battle with fellow Israelites, the tribe of Ephraim, in which thousands die (Judg 12:1–7). Jephthah had moments of faith but also moments of infuriating and heartbreaking foolishness, which brought about the death of his own kin.

Samson's beginning sounds very familiar to Christian readers. An angel visits a woman to tell her that she will have a son who will deliver Israel (Judg 13:1–6). Differences from the Christian Annunciation are certainly present as well. She is barren—not a virgin—and she is given instructions for her pregnancy so that her child will be a Nazarite. Moreover, she and her husband Manoah have several encounters with the angel of the Lord, as did Gideon (Judg 6:11–23), both examples of entertaining angels unaware (Heb 13:2) as well as avoiding death when witnessing the wondrous presence of the angel of the Lord. One of Samson's first endeavors is to have an encounter with a lion (Judg 14:5–9), and after that he conquers many people out of his vengeful power. His ill treatment of women ends up being his downfall, when his lover Delilah cuts his hair, causing the loss of his strength (Judg 16:14). The Philistines capture and blind him. He exacts a final act of revenge against them and at the same time causes his own death (Judg 16:30). His is an overwhelmingly tragic account.

Then David appears on this list, another younger brother (1 Sam 17:12–14) who rises to prominence when those around him do not expect it. He is the quintessential example of a complicated life, well remembered both for being a man after God's heart (1 Sam 13:14) and for many sins (his acts of violence against Bathsheba and Uriah being a horrific example [2 Sam 11]). It is striking that the preeminent king of Israel gets the same amount of attention in this list as the man who sacrificed his own daughter.

Samuel and the rest of the prophets make up the last pair. Samuel's is yet another story of an auspicious birth to a barren woman (1 Sam 1), who sings praises to the God who upends the unjust system of the world (1 Sam 2). Samuel listens to the Lord and responds in obedience (1 Sam 3), and his entire career is one of honesty and faithfulness before God and with the people Israel. He is the fulcrum between the judges and the kings, as he appoints both Saul and David, and also a key figure in the line of the prophets. Although the rest of the prophets are mentioned only as a large group, their words are evoked throughout the sermon.

Dominantly, the author has chosen to focus on the Pentateuch throughout the letter, and that remains true in ch. 11. Although tempting to wonder at the gaps and the brief mentions, the more sure-footed path is to pay close attention to what the author has chosen to emphasize. After the names, the author mentions a series of nine actions.

These about whom he does not have time to speak with more detail did many strong things *through faith* (the author transitions from the simple dative of *pistis* to a prepositional phrase, further contributing to the changed format of this section). The list that extends from v. 33 to v. 35a, with no connecting words, has similar sounds and balanced syllables that would create a powerful rhetorical effect.[54] The author picks examples of *those who . . . subdued kingdoms*, pointing to success in battles against Israel's enemies, and by using a word built on the term for "contest" (*agōn*), he connects their victorious struggles against flesh and blood with the struggle against sin that he wants this community to win (12:4). Others *administered justice* in doing the good work of judging Israel. This phrase appears in Psalm 14 LXX where the person who

54. Ellingworth, *Hebrews*, 624; Koester, *Hebrews*, 516.

lives rightly can dwell on God's holy mountain and will not be shaken, certainly themes that resonate with the following chapter of Hebrews (12:22–28). As they mature, the community members, too, can become practitioners of justice (5:13; 12:11). Through faith, many in Israel's past *obtained promises* given by God, whether spoken by God, God's prophet, or God's angel. This reception was not in full, as the author will note in v. 39, but during their lives they saw the realization of what God said would happen, as the author stated was true of Abraham (6:15). God did not make them wait for all things but granted fulfillment during their lives as a way to increase their faith. Some even *shut the mouths of lions.* Both Samson and David fight lions, but it is Daniel who is remembered as having the mouths of lions shut (Dan 6:18 LXX; 1 Macc 2:60), indicating that this list has resonance with the six people mentioned in v. 32 but connects with feats not limited to those whom the author has named. If this audience faces the prospect of death for their faith (Heb 12:4), it could come, in the setting of the first century, through battle with animals in the gladiatorial games.[55]

The list continues in v. **34**. The faithful *quenched the power of fire.* Both Jephthah and Samson's first wife are threatened with fire (Judg 12:1; 14:15), and the book of Daniel, previously evoked with the lions, also includes his friends' immersion in fire (Dan 3). Fire is a frequent part of battles, but *quenching* the power of fire appears most often in the words of the prophets who speak of God's wrath against disobedient people (Isa 1:31; 66:24; Jer 4:4; 17:27; 21:12; Ezek 20:47; Amos 5:6). If the people evoked by this phrase did quench the power of fire, that could refer to their bringing the people back to faithfulness to God and avoiding the punishment in line with the author's warning concerning God's fire in both 10:27 and 12:29.

In the midst of these battles, they also *escaped the edges of a sword.* Although I've chosen the word *edges*, the Greek is literally "the mouths (plural) of the sword," which echoes the mouths of the lions in v. 33. The closest echo from Israel's Scriptures occurs when David flees from the mouth of the sword when Absalom is on the attack (2 Sam 15:14), but more generally, winning in battle indicates some clever escape from swords. The plural "mouths" of the one sword also recalls the double-edged sword of ch. 4 (v. 12). God's new-

55. Ingvild Saelid Gilhus, *Animals, Gods, and Humans: Changing Attitudes to Animals in Greek, Roman and Early Christian Thought* (London: Routledge, 2006), 183–87.

covenant people, instead of running away from the swordlike word of God, must *not* flee from God (2:3; 12:25) but must flee toward (6:18) the High Priest who allows them to stand up under God's inspecting word (4:12–13).

The faithful of the past were also *empowered out of weakness.* This next statement is a general one as well, with no exact verbal parallels in Israel's Scriptures. Many in Israel's past had beginnings that did not indicate great promise, including those the author has just mentioned, be that through difficulty of conception (Samson, Samuel), low standing in their family (Gideon, Jephthah, David), or hesitancy in leadership (Barak), but despite this and through the hand of the Lord upon them, they found strength. Weakness, as the author has acknowledged, is part of the human condition (4:15; 5:2; 7:28), and power is the domain of God (1:3; 2:4, 18; 4:15; 5:2, 7; 6:5; 7:25). If his listeners are going to be empowered in situations in which they are weak, it is God who will provide that strength.

For the stories of Israel, the author puts his focus on a military context. They *became strong ones in war, causing foreign armies to flee.* Barak explicitly made Sisera flee (Judg 4:15), as does Gideon to the Midianites (Judg 7:21; see also 8:12). After these militaristic stories, the author closes this list of successes with a tenth statement. *Women received their dead through resurrection.* Yet again he ends a list with a reference to women, as he did with the longer accounts and Rahab (Heb 11:31). With this mention of resurrection, the author may have had in mind the mother whose seven sons are martyred in the Maccabean literature, because one of her sons faces his death by naming his sure hope in the resurrection (2 Macc 7:14). She certainly exhibits the kind of faith the author of Hebrews exhorts, demonstrating courage because she trusts in God as creator and restorer of life (2 Macc 7:20–23). There is a link in this text, as in Hebrews, between God as instrumental in the beginning of life (Heb 11:3, 11–12) and God as the hope of resurrected human life. Even so, she did not receive her sons back, but only *hoped* for them to be resurrected.

The other option for the referent of this phrase is the women whose children had died but were resurrected by the prophets, the widow of Zarephath by Elijah (1 Kgs 17:17–24) or the Shunammite woman by Elisha (2 Kgs 4:17–37). Whoever is intended with this phrase, this is the culmination of good things received by faith,[56] the ultimate picture that weakness and opposition, and

56. Cockerill, *Hebrews*, 590.

even death, were no barriers to God's powerful action, and therefore no reasons *not* to have faith. These women believed concerning God what was basic to faith in the God of Israel (Heb 6:2), what Abraham had trusted was possible (11:19). They demonstrated the same kind of faith in God that Jesus had (5:7) and that this community confesses (13:20), because another group of women were the first to tell the story (Matt 28:1–8/Mark 16:1–8/Luke 24:1–12/John 20:1–18). They all share a resurrection faith.

Then, within v. 35, there is a pivot. The author lifts up everyone before this point for their successes because of faith. The following list is a different group—namely, those who failed, or, maybe better put, those for whom it *looked like* God had failed. God did not show up as they would have desired, but they were still faithful.

First, he mentions that *others were beaten and did not receive release.* In direct contrast to the women who received back their dead, others were tortured (like the seven sons in Maccabees)—the word implies being beaten like a drum. This is an intense image and made even more heartbreaking because they did not receive release from that torture. By saying that they did not receive release, the author suggests that they did not avoid death, nor revive from the dead in this life. Their lack of redemption from death sets them up as those who would be looking forward to the redemption Christ brings from sin, since they had experienced a consequence (unjust death) that flows from sin.

This christological reading is supported by the fact that the author immediately turns to the hope that awaits them. They experienced death *so that they might obtain a better resurrection.* This statement aligns with the New Testament hope of a permanent and bodily resurrection in line with Jesus's own (discussed by Paul powerfully in 1 Cor 15). Because the Messiah has obtained a better ministry within a better covenant (Heb 8:6), he can offer them not only a temporary release from mortal death (a resuscitation) but a full and permanent bodily resurrection.

The list of woes continues after this glimmer of hope: *and others received a trial of mocking and whipping.* Being made fun of was the fate of Samson (Judg 16:25, 27) as well as the Maccabean brothers (2 Macc 7:1, 7, 10). It is the punishment allowed by God for errant people, as spoken by the prophets (Isa 3:4; 33:4; 66:4; Ezek 22:4; Zech 12:3). At the same time, being mocked points to the shame this community is *called* to bear (Heb 10:33; 12:3; 13:13).

Similarly, whipping is what the sons of God should expect as discipline (12:6), a theme played out in the narrative of the Maccabees (2 Macc 3; 7:37; 9:11; 3 Macc 2:21) as well as the Psalms (37:18 LXX; 38:11 LXX; 72:14 LXX; 88:33 LXX) and Psalms of Solomon (7:9; 10:1). The author is setting the stage for how the audience can process the difficulties they face. God was not absent when their faithful forebears of the past went through these horrible things, and neither is God distant from them.

In the next phrase he mentions *still others [who faced] a trial of bonds and imprisonment.* Some of the faithful in the past were imprisoned. Imprisonment plays a prominent part of Samson's story (Judg 16:21, 25) and has affected members of the community of Hebrews (Heb 10:34; 13:3). Moreover, *some were stoned.* A form of punishment in the law (e.g., Deut 13:10; 17:5; 21:21; 22:21, 24), stoning was a threat and reality against David (1 Sam 30:6; 2 Sam 16:6, 13), and Jesus remembers this action against the prophets (Matt 23:37/Luke 13:34) and includes it in his parable of the tenants (Matt 21:35). People want to stone Jesus himself (John 10:31; 11:8) and are successful against Stephen (Acts 7:58) and Paul (Acts 14:19; 2 Cor 11:25). This is a reality in the Christian movement that this community could face in the future. Some were also *sawed.* This next particularly gruesome description, being sawed, finds no example in the Christian experience but appears in a later tradition about Isaiah (Martyrdom and Ascension of Isaiah 5:1–14). In the final reference to violent death, the author lists those who *died by the slaughter of the sword.* In precise opposition to what was true of the successful, who were able to flee from the sword (Heb 11:34), those in this part of the list died by it. For Jeremiah the prophet, this, too, is an example of God's punishment (Jer 11:22; 14:15; 16:4; 21:9), and for Jesus, a sign of the end (Luke 21:24). This reality befell both John the Baptist (Mark 6:27) and the disciple James (Acts 12:2), not as God's punishment, but as the cost of taking a stand with God against the ruling authorities.

The next group of the unsuccessful have stories that are less dramatic. Some of them *went around in sheepskins, in the skins of goats.* This statement recalls those who wore clothing made from sheepskin or goatskin, such as the prophet Elijah (2 Kgs 1:8), for whom this was a demonstration of asceticism.[57] Given the choices they made to follow God radically, *they lacked what they needed.* In sum, they simply did not have enough. This is a reality to which the author's

57. Koester, *Hebrews*, 515.

hearers can relate since they had their own goods taken away (Heb 10:34). In addition, the faithful of the past *were buffeted, suffered evil.* These were frequent experiences of Paul's ministry, as well as those in the community of the Hebrews (10:33; 13:3). Such conditions have afflicted humanity since the beginning. From the time Adam and Eve left the garden, humans have experienced lack and tribulation and have been buffeted by evil. This list continues to preview what the author will speak about in ch. 12. The struggles the audience is facing are not new; their forebears in the faith faced similar things.

Although those mentioned in the latter half of the list often might not have looked "successful" in the eyes of the world's cultures around them, the opposite was actually the truth: *these were those of whom the world was not worthy.* They demonstrated, not their worthlessness, but their worth by living on the outskirts (as the author will tell his readers to do in 13:12–13). In this space they had to wander *in the wilderness and in hills and in caves and in the clefts of the earth.* This language evokes the wilderness generation, but because the author will say that they were all proclaimed as *faithful*, this more likely points to Joshua and Caleb, who had to wander even though they were faithful, as well as Abraham, Hagar, Moses, Gideon, Samson, David, Daniel, and Jesus, who all spent time in the wilderness. Their wandering was not through ignorance or error (as the uses in 3:10 and 5:2 indicate); they wandered because the fallen world did not offer permanent dwelling for them. So many important events happen in the wilderness or mountains or caves for the people in Israel's story, including Abraham (Gen 12:8), Moses (Exod 3:12), and Joshua (Exod 24:15). Here they found both victory and distress. It was often in these places that they met God, on the top of the mountain or in the cleft of the rock (Exod 33:22). God was with them, and so they trusted in God. The addressees of the sermon are also moving through a wilderness toward a mountain to be with God (Heb 12:22). God will, as with their forebears, meet them on the way and continue to direct them forward.

To close with these "failures" invites a reconsideration of the earlier part of the list. It is more than just contemporary sensibilities that cause discomfort with the men and their violent successes named in vv. 32–34. Their stories of *victory* in battle do not resonate with the experience of the initial readers of the letter either. This early Christian community has known shame and struggle, not honor and victory. Neither do these experiences line up with the life of Jesus, who never enacted violence even when violence was done to him (and when his disciple Peter did so, Jesus called him to stop [Matt 26:51–52; Luke 22:50–51; John 18:10–11]). Even the stories of these judges, prophets, and kings—as I have pointed out—included a significant portion of weakness, failure, and opposition. By beginning with violent victories but closing with painful defeats, the author reveals what he might have said about them were he afforded the time. It is true that God granted political and military success to Israel. This allowed Israel to exist distinctly as God's people. On the other hand, God has not granted the same to the followers of Jesus because that which happened in the land of Israel was pointing forward to something better: a better life granted through a better resurrection, which will be lived out in an unshakable kingdom (12:27). The failures made the people long for such an existence, and the victories gave an image of it, *but not in fullness.* Those first mentioned in the list might have had some successes in the world, but the estimation of the world does not count for much. There is another estimation of much greater worth—namely, the commendation of God—granted to the faithful (11:2). Hebrews comforts and challenges its listeners by asserting that it is the weak in the eyes of the world who have greatest success in God's household.

11:39–40 · THE JOINING OF FAITHFUL GENERATIONS

39 *Indeed, when all of these were commended by virtue of their faith, they had not received the promise* 40 *because God was looking ahead to something better concerning us, in order that apart from us they might not be perfected.*

The author is now drawing the section on faith to a close by recalling what he said at the beginning of the encomium, that those who lived before his community had faith and were recognized by God (11:2). *Indeed, when all of these were commended by virtue of their faith.* All these stories were recorded by God in the Scriptures of Israel because of the faith these individuals demonstrated. They were not perfect, and some had more errors than successes, but at some moments in their lives they had faith. They were thankful in their victories, and most importantly, they trusted through their failures. They had faith because, while they looked to the evidence of what God had done and was doing, they also looked forward to the fulfillment of what God had promised.

It is obvious that they had to have faith, because the author asserts that *they had not received the promise*. Several times the author has stated that those in the past did receive the promise, including Abraham (6:15; 11:17, 19) and others (11:33). Here he uses a different verb for reception (*komizō*) that he reserves for future possession (10:36) or Abraham's figurative reception of Isaac (11:17, 19). This statement in v. 39 serves as a bookend to the similar idea in 11:13 that the patriarchs died without obtaining (yet a different verb, *lambanō*) what God promised. This has been a dynamic throughout the sermon. Some promises of God are realized—most importantly, those of the new covenant—but others remain for the future. This is the dynamic of faith the author has been describing in this long chapter: fulfilled promises provide evidence to trust God for what remains unfulfilled.

The logic of promise throughout the sermon points to the scope of the unpossessed promise: namely, they did not live forever at rest in God's land with God's people. At base in this lack of realization is that they did not live (even Enoch and Elijah did not continue life but were taken from it without seeing death). Augustine read the promise in this way: "Now this would be no praise for faith, nor would it be faith at all, if people were believing to follow after rewards that they could see—in other words, if the reward of immortality were bestowed on believers *in this present world*."[58] Nothing in their earthly lives could satisfy the full expectation of the promise. As Heinrich Bullinger puts it, "Thus by 'promise' the apostle does not here mean rest, but rather . . . the resurrection of our bodies," which is dependent on "the coming of Christ."[59] In addition to ongoing life, they did not receive God's intention for Adam and Eve, the promise for all humanity, to reign over, and not be crushed by, God's creation (Ps 8 in Heb 2:6–8).

The lack of attainment was certainly not a surprise to God; God was not unaware of and absent in their struggles. Instead, even *God was looking ahead to something better*. God was not demonstrating faith, because there is nothing greater on which to place trust than God alone (6:16), but even God demonstrates the posture they are instructed to have—namely, a forward-facing vision. God was looking ahead to something better. Based on affirmations through the

58. Augustine, *On the Merits and Forgiveness of Sins and on Infant Baptism* 2.50 (ACCS 14:207).

59. Bullinger, *Commentary on Hebrews*, 11:39–40 126r (RCS 13:169).

sermon, that *something better* seems to be the better resurrection mentioned in v. 35, which is built on the better promises of the new covenant (8:6), brought by the resurrected Son of God, who serves as High Priest forever.

The something better is not only about Christ but also about the author and his readers. He says it is *concerning us.* As he began with their faith in the meaning of creation (11:3), now he reaches the end of this encomium, this praise of faith, with a reminder of their presence in the story. He weaves the thread of their lives into this extensive epideictic section; hence the first part of ch. 12 encourages them to live out their part of the story well.

Their presence in it provides another reason why the forebears did not attain the promise of God fully. That is because God was waiting to give it to them along with the audience of this sermon. God was waiting *in order that apart from us they might not be perfected.* Perfection, which was not unachievable through the law alone (7:19; 9:9; 10:1), had to wait for the Son who became perfect (2:10; 5:9; 7:28), so that he might grant perfection to *all* his siblings. Now that his arrival and work have ushered in the last days (1:2), the generation in which the audience of Hebrews is privileged to live, perfection can be granted for all time (10:14). Now comes the answer to the quandary of how the patriarchs not only saw but also greeted the promises (11:13). God's promise to Abraham's family included innumerable descendants, and now through Christ those many siblings are being brought into the house of God (3:6). The faithful of the past will now be able to greet the people who are the fulfillment of God's promise to Abraham.

This casts the faithful of the past right alongside the present community. Everyone is waiting for the promise, for the better resurrection, when they all, the countless descendants of Abraham, will live together with God in God's eternal city. Beautifully, Chrysostom extends this promise to his congregation several hundred years later, articulating that God as a good father wished for all the siblings to be rewarded together: "For they also wait for the siblings, for, if we are 'all one body,' the pleasure becomes greater to this body when it is crowned altogether and not part by part. For the righteous are also worthy of admiration in this, that they rejoice in the welfare of their siblings, as in their own, and for themselves also, it is according to their wish to be crowned along with their own members. To be glorified all together is a great delight."[60]

60. Chrysostom, *Hebrews* 28.2 (*NPNF*[1] 14:492).

I have frequently chosen to use the descriptor "audience" for those who receive this letter/sermon. By that I mean the first audience, who, under the threat of persecution, desperately needed to hear this word about faith. In addition to them, through the inspiration and preservation of the Scriptures by God's Holy Spirit, all Christian communities are members of this audience. We, too, make up the descendants apart from whom the faithful of the past will not be perfected. The encouragement of being a member of this group granted to those who first heard this sermon comes to readers who have heard it in all times and places thereafter.

Through this beautiful and powerful chapter, the author has cast a vision of faith. Faith looks back to what God has done and finds the mighty God trustworthy. Faith looks forward to what God has promised to do: defeat the power of death and gather all people who trust in the living Son in resurrected bodies to live forever in the heavenly city, which is the center of renewal for the good creation. This is the faith that unites humanity through all generations. This is the faith that allows endurance and righteous action through whatever difficulties any members of this family may face. This is the faith that propels the next reflections in Hebrews, where the author will invite his community to continue running in the race of the faithful.

HEBREWS 12:1–29

RUNNING TO THE MOUNTAIN

Because of the length of the eleventh chapter, interpreters, preachers, or even readers might wish to take a break after its end, but the author won't allow it. After telling the stories of many faithful, he turns his attention to his and his community's faith-in-process. They have not reached the goal, and so they need strong encouragement to remain faithful. After recounting the stories of their forebears, he offers that encouragement in the form of a race metaphor, with Jesus as the victor who should fill their vision (vv. 1–3).

Jesus's suffering path to that victory provides a point of comparison through which the author addresses their current suffering. Using Proverbs as his scriptural anchor, the author invites them to reassess their difficulties in light of God's paternal care (vv. 4–11). The contest they are in is completely under God's benevolent control. With that assurance, he urges them to continue on to the goal that lies before them (vv. 12–14) and avoid the dangers along the way (vv. 14–17). The mention of these dangers culminates in a warning passage that appeals to the life of Esau, introducing the consequences of decisions that even certain forms of repentance cannot undo (vv. 15–17).

The race/journey motif reaches its culmination at the foot of two mountains (vv. 18–24). They have not come to Sinai (vv. 18–21) but to Zion (vv. 22–24). Instead of the command to keep distance, they are being invited up. As they cast their vision to the top of God's heavenly mountain, the author reminds them of how he began this sermon, by asserting that they can hear the voice of God (1:2) and must respond faithfully to it (v. 25). The vocal and visual presence of God will sift all things so that they are left with an unassailable kingdom (vv. 26–29).

Amid the incredible assurance of God's paternal care, the celebratory mountain to which they have access, and the kingdom they are already receiving, the author issues several final warnings against giving up. The end of their story is not yet written, so he employs all facets of pastoral wisdom, from challenge to comfort, to do his best to support their reaching the goal.

12:1–3 · RUNNING TOWARD JESUS

1Therefore since even we ourselves have so great a cloud of witnesses surrounding us, as we lay aside every weight, particularly the entangling sin, let us keep running the contest that lies before us through the act of endurance,
2looking to Jesus, the initiator and perfector of faith, who for the sake of the joy that lay before him endured a cross because he scorned the shame, and he has taken his seat at the right hand of the throne of God.
3Consequently, consider such a person who has endured opposition from sinners against himself, in order that you may not grow weary in your souls and fail.

With a conjunction that appears in the New Testament only here and in 1 Thessalonians 4:8, the author connects the encomium of faith to this exhortation when he begins this section with *therefore* (*toigaroun*). It is as if he is saying, "In light of the faith thus described, *this* is how we should live." He has just articulated a dependence of the previous generations' faithful on the present Christians. They will not be perfected apart "from us" (11:40). Now he names explicitly what has been assumed throughout the whole eleventh chapter: the present Christians should depend on the previous faithful for their witness. *Since we ourselves have so great a cloud of witnesses surrounding us* serves as one of the reasons they can act. The groups, the faithful triumphant and militant, are connected from both directions, and so it is incumbent upon interpreters to join this sentence—although separated by a chapter division—with the previous one.

The foundational image of this complex sentence (which extends through the end of v. 2) is athletic: *let us keep running*. The verb for running appears only here in Hebrews (although more than a dozen times throughout the New Testament), but it joins the chorus of all that the author says about forward movement. The children of God are those who are being led (2:10). In contrast to the inefficient meanderings of the wilderness generation, he calls his readers to show their status as children by going in (4:3, 6, 10, 11) or approaching (4:16; 7:25; 10:1, 22; 11:6; 12:22). More urgently, he describes them as those who are fleeing to grasp the hope that lies before them (6:18). The pace here in ch. 12 is as quick as in ch. 6, but the duration is longer. They must *run*, not walk. That admonition is not so much about speed—he does not imply that they should rush through life—as about discipline. It takes more training to run than to walk. Moreover, they are in this demanding race for the long haul. Consequently, they can run this contest only *through the act of endurance*. In other words, what they face is not a sprint but a marathon.[1] Interpreters need discernment on this point. For some listeners, the experience of a marathon conjures up difficulty but also great joy. For others, however, the image of a marathon appears as an impossibility, unfathomable even to attempt. Consequently, interpreters should not let the homiletic metaphor dissuade listeners from the aim of the passage—namely, the continuation of faith, which, as ch. 11 demonstrated, is achievable for everyone.

The author says that the race of faith is difficult, but not impossible. The author describes what lies ahead of them not as a race (*dromos*) but as an *agōn*. Generally employed as the word for "struggle," the term can also specify an athletic *contest* or game (1 Tim 6:12; 2 Tim 4:7; 2 Macc 4:18). The verb for running used earlier clarifies that he is employing the imagery of a race and not a boxing match in this sentence, but the term *agōn* underlines the difficulty of what they face.[2] Moving forward will not be easy, but he believes that with the right support they can reach the goal.

They will be helped with *the contest that lies before* them (*prokeimenon*) by what lies around them (*perikeimenon*), the *cloud of witnesses* that the author

1. Attridge suggests the same comparison (*Hebrews*, 355). Koester helpfully notes that the marathon was an exceptional race in the ancient world, but even shorter distances required endurance (*Hebrews*, 523).

2. Zoe Hollinger argues that Greco-Roman parallels suggest that the author has in view an intense struggle. See "Rethinking the Translation of Τρέχωμεν τὸν . . . Ἀγῶνα in Hebrews 12.1 in Light of Ancient Graeco-Roman Literature," *Bible Translator* 70.1 (April 2019): 94–111. The author of Hebrews appeals to athletic imagery not to encourage them to train their bodies but to give them imagery with which to envision this struggle. For explication of the visionary power of this section, see Scott D. Mackie, "Visually Oriented Rhetoric and Visionary Experience in Hebrews 12:1–4," *CBQ* 79.3 (July 2017): 476–97.

says is *surrounding us*. As the sentence is structured, before the author gets to what the community must do (run the difficult race), he reminds them of what they *have*. He emphasizes the members of their community at the beginning of the section: *even we*. Things may be hard for them, but they do have each other with whom they can endure. Moreover, they have the community whose stories he has just told. This community support is not something they must seek out (he does not say that they *will* have them in the future), and it is not something—even though most of the people named in ch. 11 are from previous times—that remains in the past. Instead, the encouragement of the witnesses is something they have now and, as they stay aware of it, will continue to have. The present tense of the word for possession (*echontes*, "we have") surely served as a powerful encouragement. The gift of the testimony of the faithful is the reason why this community can run now.

To be clear, what they have is *so great a cloud of witnesses surrounding* them. The author first praises the cloud of witnesses with the adjective *so great*. Employed in 4:7 and 7:22, this term specifies a noun by noting its magnitude. This is not just any group of witnesses, but a great one. Some scribes employed a variant that captures the same idea, *tēlikoutos*, used earlier in the letter to describe the great salvation they have (2:3). Whatever term the author used, the description of greatness makes perfect sense in light of the long and illustrious catalogue of the faithful from the previous chapter. This includes not only those he named explicitly but also the long list of broad groups of people in the latter section (11:32–38). In light of the marathon motif, the author paints a picture in which the stands are bursting with the members of God's kingdom, great because they trusted in a great God.[3] The sermon will return to the image of a celebratory crowd again in 12:22–23, when he mentions the festal gathering on Mount Zion.

Many Christians in liturgical traditions might call up this image every week during the introduction to the Sanctus. My tradition says it this way:

3. The inclusion of women in the list of faithful witnesses at this athletic contest (Sarah, Rahab, the women who received their dead) might strike the interest of ancient readers. Some discussions of the time provide evidence of nervousness at the idea of women being in attendance at sport (see Paul Christesen and Donald G. Kyle, eds., *A Companion to Sport and Spectacle in Greek and Roman Antiquity* [Chichester: Wiley-Blackwell 2014], 487–88). Their inclusion in these "stands" is another indication of the inclusion of men and women in this family of the faithful.

"Therefore we praise you, joining our voices with Angels and Archangels and with all the company of heaven, who for ever sing this hymn."[4] For readers of Hebrews beyond the initial addressees, the stands are even more crowded. Not only do they hold those mentioned and described in ch. 11; they also hold the addressees of Hebrews themselves in addition to all faithful believers henceforth. When we in worship proclaim this company, I sometimes think of congregants or family members recently deceased. If I am studying the works of believers from different eras of the church, I imagine them present. I think of the vast diversity of ethnicities, nations, and ideologies represented. Whatever divided humans on earth ceases to matter before the throne. It is an overwhelmingly great cloud indeed.

The use of *cloud* provides several insights into the nature of the encouragement the author is communicating. As used in classical literature, it is simply a way of saying "many."[5] In addition to the number present, the term *cloud* describes their location. This term, along with *surrounding*, conveys the encircling nature of the witnesses. As one is enveloped in mist, so are the readers of Hebrews hemmed in by the witnesses. Moreover, *cloud* also connects with concepts of the sky/heaven to convey the realm of God (Ps 103:3 LXX; Job 22:14; 40:6). As later sections of the letter will reveal, those who finished their life faithfully now reside with God (Heb 12:22–24). Finally, and importantly, *cloud* communicates the ephemeral nature of the present existence of the previous faithful. They are with God, but they have not yet inherited the unshakable kingdom (12:27). Such a picture agrees with the doctrine of bodily resurrection. They are not yet embodied (again), but they are portrayed as sentient communicators and observers.

The author further describes this surrounding cloud with the term *witnesses*. Witnesses both speak and see. Clearly this group has spoken by the faithfulness of their lives, and so the audience can recall what they have done and said about the faithfulness of God as a way of shoring up their own endurance. The race metaphor, however, adds the dimension of seeing, not just God, but also the Christians presently living and running. Some previous interpreters of Hebrews have raised caution on this point, which is appropriate

4. *BCP* (1979), Holy Eucharist, Rite II, 362.

5. Herodotus, *Histories* 8.109; Homer, *Iliad* 4.274; Vergil, *Aeneid* 7.793; Philo, *On the Embassy to Gaius* 226, as cited in Bruce, *Hebrews*, 333, and Attridge, *Hebrews*, 354.

given the excesses of devotion to the saints in some eras of the church. It is certainly the case that Christians should not practice faithfulness just because "your late grandmother in heaven might see you sinning."[6] This passage does not sanction a voyeurism from the deceased. On the other hand, for much of the history of the church the veil between the living and the dead in Christ has appeared quite thin. As a faithful monk once quipped to me, "I see no reason why all my friends must be alive!" Imagining the faithful of the past cheering on our present endeavors raises the adrenaline and propels one forward, just as cheers from the sidelines effect energy at an athletic event. Such a reminder protects against a temptation toward individualism in faith, which can so easily turn into loneliness and then resignation. Ours is a communal faith, composed not only of our local congregations—as vital as they are, a point Hebrews makes frequently and with force—but also of the global church, and the church triumphant as well. This is a group bound not simply by a love for sport but bound because they are family. Cultures with high respect for previous generations offer insights for Christian interpreters of this text to consider seriously.[7]

As the community runs this long, hard race with this cloud of witnesses around them, they *are* a certain kind of people—namely, those who put away weight and sin: *as we lay aside every weight, particularly the entangling sin*. The verbal form here is a middle participle, and many interpreters have chosen to show its dependence on the main hortatory subjunctive verb, "let us run," by making it imperatival ("let us lay aside").[8] Alternatively, this participle could align with the first participle ("we have") as another affirmation. Just as they already have the cloud of witnesses, they have already put aside various things in order to confess Christ and begin the race. Instead of a command, "Do this!" the author affirms that they already *have* done this. They have not, however, laid aside *every* weight and sin that will appear in their lives, and therefore need to continue. A reading that acknowledges both past action and future continuance agrees with the previous section of the letter (10:32–36) where the

6. Jobes, *Letters to the Church*, 142.

7. HyeRan Kim-Cragg highlights scholars who have studied Asian respect for ancestors and how that might interact with this text's valuing of the saints. Mary Ann Beavis and HyeRan Kim-Cragg, *Hebrews*, ed. Linda M. Maloney and Barbara E. Reid, Wisdom Commentary 54 (Collegeville, MN: Liturgical Press, 2015), 157–60.

8. For example, Ellingworth, *Hebrews*, 638.

author recalls the good they have already done and urges them toward endurance rather than the taking up of new habits. Hence, putting aside these things initially does not mean that one can rest, because the threat of entanglement ever remains. The continual threat leads to the necessity of a *continual* laying aside of entangling realities.

The author names what snares them as *every weight* and *entangling sin*—or, as the NRSV puts it, "the sin that clings so closely." If *weight* is differentiated from sin, it points toward things that are encumbrances but not faults. He draws attention to things in their communal lives that might not be wrong, but that prevent them from running at a good pace. It is an invitation to consider what is both necessary *and* beneficial, both corporately and individually.

More detrimental, and therefore more important to name explicitly, is the *sin* they have put down. It is the "easily entangling" kind. The etymology of the word (*euperistatos*) paints the picture. The sin stands (*histēmi*) around (*peri*) well (*eu*).[9] These are temptations that trip people up easily. Since they accepted the confiscation of their goods with joy (10:34), materialism might be a sin they have previously had success in putting aside. Theodoret of Cyr offers another suggestion, that the burden might be "unnecessary worries."[10] Close attention to the language, however, shows that these are not *sins* that have been put aside but *sin* in the singular, so it might not be correct to determine which *specific* sin is in mind. This community has made a decision regarding sin writ large. They have rejected it in becoming sharers (3:6, 14) and confessors of Christ (3:1; 4:14; 10:23; 13:15). The author sets an encouraging tone here. They have become free; they only need to keep going. Their struggles are issues of continuation, growth, and maturity, but not conversion. Hence, the author describes the kind of running they are doing as happening *through the act of endurance*. Endurance is precisely what they need (10:36).

They can keep going if they keep their vision correctly aligned. In sport, particularly long-distance running, the placement of one's vision makes a considerable difference. Looking at a close point will result in dizziness and imbalance, and looking too far away makes the road seem impossibly long.

9. P[46] has *euperispastos*, "easily distracting." While P[46] is early, the greater evidence supports *euperistatos*, a more negative connotation of constricting or incumbering as opposed to just distracting.

10. Theodoret of Cyr, *Interpretation of Hebrews* 12 (ACCS 10:209).

A midway distance offers the right perspective, and that is easiest to maintain if a runner has a person on whom to set their vision. Often runners are given the mental trick of fixing their sight on a person in that appropriate distance and imagining that they are attached to that person by a rope that pulls them along. That person's momentum becomes one's own.

For the author of Hebrews, that right person is Jesus. In v. **2** he names the object of their vision as they are running: they are *looking to Jesus*. He is both *the initiator and perfector of faith*. By calling him the initiator, the author connects this statement about Jesus with that in 2:10, where he is the pioneer of salvation for the children of God. In that section, the image prepares for the discussion of the wilderness generation whose tribal leaders (*archēgoi*), including Joshua, spied out the land (Num 13:3). In this later section, he envisions his community, those who are in the wilderness as they approach the rest of God (Heb 3–4), as those who are also running toward and into a stadium. In both motifs, Jesus as the leader remains the focus. As the one who has come from God, he blazes the trail before them as he runs and finishes the race before them.

As a balance to this statement of beginning, the author also names Jesus as the *perfector* of faith. Different than in a road race, those who set their eyes on Jesus set their vision on someone who is *not* still running. He is seated (1:3, 13; 8:1; 10:12; 12:2). He has begun the race of faith, plowed the trail, and now has completed it. It is certainly encouraging to have a comrade on the road; it is even better to know that someone has successfully finished the race, to know for certain that such a victory is possible. This is even better news when the finisher is not some random and disconnected person but the Lord in whom one has come to share. As the perfector of faith, it is clear that he reached the goal of his own faithfulness and opened up that destination with God (the telos of faith) to all others. It is important to note that though he has completed his race of faith, his brothers and sisters have not. He remains their pioneer (2:10; 12:2), the anchor that draws them forward (6:19–20). God's desire to be with the many sons and daughters means that Jesus is not seated forever but will return to complete the salvation he has fully secured (9:28). The Lord is so concerned and so connected to those who are still running that his personal completion of the race allows him to be focused on advocacy to aid his siblings in completing their own (7:25). By inaugurating and guaranteeing the possibility of finishing the race of faith, he opens the race for any who will join his "team."

In fact, the author has encouraged his readers to look back to the faithful of the past, look around them to see the witnesses who cheer them on, and look forward to see Jesus's victory, but no matter which direction they turn, the runners are still seeing the faithful work *of Jesus*, in the past, present, and future. Since he is the enactor of faith par excellance, noticing everyone they have been instructed to consider is a way of "looking at Jesus."[11]

Jesus, too, had a point of reference that kept him going, something "before" him that kept him enduring through the race. Next, the author says of Jesus: *who for the sake of the joy that lay before him.* Several realities are motivating that joy. First, Jesus is drawn on by the desire to fulfill the divine will, as he states with the words of Psalm 39 LXX (Heb 10:7). That theological perspective leads to the anthropological one. The divine will is to rescue and sanctify humanity (2:8–15; 10:10), so his joy also includes having many brothers and sisters in his family. It was the divine will for the joyful household that drove Jesus to endure the cross. Near the end of the letter, the author will urge this congregation to live in such a way that they give other members of this household, their earthly leaders, joy as well (13:17).

This joy before him allowed Jesus to *[endure] a cross.* By naming his enduring, the author calls attention to the similarity between Jesus's action in the past and what this community had done in the past (10:32). Moreover, his example will propel them to continue to endure in the future (10:36). Mentioned for the first and only time here in Hebrews, *cross* shows this author's awareness of the historical realities of the life of Jesus of Nazareth. He is also well aware of the meaning of the cross in his context, a device dripping with shame. Jesus knew this as well but did not resist the cross because of it. Instead, he *scorned the shame.* By hating or despising it, by "looking down" on this societal shame, Jesus indicates that it has no hold over him. This does not indicate that he floats above the cross and laughs, as is depicted in some of the noncanonical gospels.[12] He is hanging on it and actually suffering death. Par-

11. Catherine Playoust emphasizes that the author keeps the attention on Jesus rather than the witnesses, who still need the perfecting only he can bring. See "The Location of the Cloud of Witnesses (Heb 12:1): Complexities of Time and Space in Hebrews," *Australian Biblical Review* 64 (2016): 1–13.

12. From the Coptic Apocalypse of Peter: "The Savior said to [Peter], 'He whom you see above the cross, glad and laughing, is the living Jesus. But he into whose hands and feet they are driving the nails is his physical part, which is the substitute. They are putting to shame that

adoxically, he is in a position to look down on this shame not from a vantage point above but one "from below." He scorns the shame from the position of his humility by being willing to stand up underneath it. Whatever acrimony observers hurl at him, these so pale in comparison to his motivating joy that he can disdain their insults. He will not let social pressure dissuade him from the cross and prevent him from obtaining his joy.

Moreover, though the shame includes the cross as well as that which results from the cross—namely, death—he is confident that this shame will not last forever. As this verse proclaims, he moved through and past the cross to take *his seat at the right hand of the throne of God.* The cross, the shame, and the seat point to the three movements of Christ's passion. He endured the cross, then despised the shame of death, before he, having been resurrected and ascended, sat down at the right hand of God. Appearing for the fifth and final time, the allusion to Psalm 109:1 LXX gives the author the language to express Jesus's sovereign victory. Part of his joy is now a reality. He has fulfilled the divine will and dwells in the presence of his Father (Heb 1:3, 13), but he still waits for his many brothers and sisters to join him in his joy.

Although Jesus's victory is secure, the author invites the readers to linger a bit more on his hardship. *Consequently, consider such a person who has endured opposition from sinners against himself.* The disrespect he endured could include both the assaults hurled at him when he hung on the cross (Matt 27:27–31; Mark 15:16–20; Luke 23:35–36; John 19:2–3) and the persistent controversy he faced throughout his adult life from the Roman and Jewish leadership, those with whom he had grown up (Mark 3:21; John 7:3–5), and even his own followers. The one who was set apart from sinners (Heb 7:26) was ridiculed by them. The term chosen for this controversy is especially apt for one who is the communication of God (1:2). It is "contrary words" (*antilogia*) of disagreement that he had to endure, which resulted in his grief. This would have provided a poetic resonance with the first word in this sentence, *consider*, which also includes a form of *logos* in its root (*analogizomai*). Concerning this antagonism, he has already endured it (the participle is in the perfect tense);

which is in his likeness.'" Translation of James Brashler and Roger A. Bullard in *Nag Hammadi Codex VII*, ed. Birger Pearson, Nag Hammadi Studies 30 (Leiden: Brill, 1996), cited in Bart D. Ehrman, *Lost Scriptures: Books That Did Not Make It into the New Testament* (New York: Oxford University Press, 2005), 78.

this approbation is now over. If the perfect tense is to be respected here, that means that the results remain. This might be an indication of the tradition recorded in the Gospels that the scars from the cross remain on the resurrected body (John 20:25). Alternatively, it could point to the resistance that members of Christ's people continue to face. As the resurrected Jesus said to Paul, persecution of the church was persecution of him (Acts 9:4).

If they consider him, all that he endured, and how he came through it to victory, they will not succumb to weakness. The author asks his congregation to consider Jesus *in order that you may not grow weary in your souls and fail.* In some sense they are already weak ones, because they have not advanced in maturity as they should have (5:11–14). All, however, is not lost. They may be weaker than they should be, but they have not failed, fallen down, or completely fainted, as this word is used for those who are hungry to the point of exhaustion (Matt 15:32; Mark 8:3). Hence, the author can warn them against finally "losing their grip" (a translation that highlights the loosening connotation of this word, *ekluō*), a particularly important admonition for a community whom the author has instructed to "hold fast" (Heb 10:23). He is using a term, *fail*, that appears in the citation of Proverbs that will follow (Prov 3:11/Heb 12:5). Failing would be preceded by and accompanied by weariness, which he also wants them to avoid. This is a sickness of the soul, a bone-tiredness (Job 10:1; 17:2 LXX; 4 Macc 3:8). Knowing that Christ has gone through the difficult and endured gives them strength to keep going. As the following section will show, however, often one cannot find the necessary fortitude to endure on one's own. It takes others on the path to assist. Without the hope granted by the steady vision of Christ, however, it would be difficult to the point of impossible for a friend to carry a runner who was unwilling to keep moving.

To prepare for this collective run, the author appeals to Scripture again to put their difficulties into the correct context. In short, the entire next paragraph asserts that difficulty is not the sign of God's absence but is in fact the sign of God's presence.

12:4–17 · GOD'S PATERNAL DISCIPLINE

[4]As those who fight against sin, you have not yet resisted to the point of blood. [5]You have forgotten the encouragement that is spoken to you as sons:

My son, do not devalue the discipline of the Lord;
neither grow weary when you are reproved by him.
[6]For the one whom the Lord loves he disciplines,
and whips every son whom he receives.

[7]Endure as discipline. God is offering this to you as sons. For what son does a
father not discipline? [8]And if you are without discipline, of which all of you have
become sharers, then you are illegitimate ones and not sons. [9]Moreover, we used to
have our fathers of the flesh as disciplíners, and we respected them. Should we not
much more submit to the Father of spirits and live? [10]For our fathers were disciplining
for a little time according to what was seemly to them, but God does so for our benefit
so that we might share in God's holiness. [11]All discipline in the present does not seem
to be joyful but full of grief, but later it yields the peaceful fruit of righteousness for
those who have been trained through it. [12]Therefore, set right the hands that are
drooping and the knees that are paralyzed [13]and make straight paths for your feet
so that the crippled may not be put out of joint but rather be healed. [14]Pursue peace
with all and sanctification, without which no one will see the Lord. [15]Watch out lest
someone come short of the grace of God, lest a certain bitter root that springs up
cause trouble and through it many are defiled, [16]lest there be a certain fornicator
and unholy person as Esau, who for the sake of one meal gave up his own birthright
as the firstborn. [17]For you know that even afterward when he wanted to inherit the
blessing, he was rejected; for he did not find a place for repentance even though he
sought for it with tears.

The author continues his exhortation by reminding them where they stand in relation to sin. He refers to them *as those who fight against sin*. They are involved in an antagonistic struggle. The best manuscripts have the author using the word for "fight" in an intense form, *antagōnizomai* (the other manuscripts have the more basic form, *agōnizomai*, which appears throughout the New Testament). If this longer word is original, then the author of Hebrews is the only New Testament author to use this particular form of the word. In so doing, he emphasizes that they are not just fighting but fighting *against* sin. Since the letter does not include explicit sections that list their errors, except in the mention of their immaturity (5:12), this is likely focused on the more generally applicable *temptation* to sin. Moreover, as the present tense of the verb suggests, they are continuing in this fight: *you have not yet resisted to the point of blood.* For those listening, the fight has not yet resulted in bloodshed. Members of this community have been shamed, have had their property taken (10:33–34), and have been imprisoned (13:3), but there is no indication of martyrdom. That is good news; things have not gotten *that* bad yet. At the same time, it is difficult news in that they need to *keep* fighting sin. The battle might come to that costly point. They need encouragement against weakness because this kind of oppositional relationship with sin should continue, and the consequences of keeping it up may cost them everything. They have just been reminded, however, that those faithful of the past who resisted to the point of losing their lives looked forward to the full and final resurrection from death that God will bring (11:35).

The author paints a very powerful picture by setting up the next Scripture citation in this way. As community members, they are amid this fight, and in that moment someone is speaking encouragement to them, just as a parent would speak to a child. The author implies, with the use of the perfect verb, that they have stopped listening to this voice.[13] *You have forgotten the encouragement that is spoken to you as sons.* They have a cheerleader in their corner, but they have not been paying attention to the voice who propels them to keep going.

By describing this speech as an encouragement, the author invokes again a theme that runs throughout the sermon. God has given them a strong encouragement to keep moving forward (6:18), and this encouragement often comes to them through the vehicle of one another (3:13; 10:25), including the author. In fact, he will describe this entire written speech as an "encouragement" (13:22).

Because this encouragement is spoken to them *as sons*, that suggests that the originator of this message is none other than God the Father. It is God who is cheering them on in their contest, and they have ceased to heed the divine voice.

God's mode of speech here is unique in Hebrews. Whereas God is frequently the speaker of Israel's Scriptures—and it seems to me that modality continues here[14]—the word chosen to introduce the citation (*dialegomai*) ap-

13. Cockerill helpfully states it this way: "Have you truly been living without taking this message from God into account?" (*Hebrews*, 620).

14. Madison Pierce argues that, in light of the fact that God is spoken of in the third person, it is better to see the author/passage from Proverbs as the speaker of the text (*Divine Discourse*, 187–88). The third-person referent to the Lord might indicate that it is the author

pears only here in Hebrews. As one of the cognate forms of *legō*, *dialegomai* appears especially in the context of teaching. This kind of speech is instructive and even invites conversation.[15] The author wants them to listen and obey but recognizes the difficulty of doing so (see v. 11). They have been invited to approach God's throne in the time of need (4:16), and that time can include when they are receiving God's discipline. Hence, a demonstration of God's respect for those being educated begins with this introduction; God is speaking in a thoughtful way to respect children who have reason, an important point to note since the text itself is quite harsh.

The citation is from a Greek version of Proverbs 3:11–12. The tone of the Greek strikes a more ominous note than that of the Hebrew. Rather than closing with an affirmation that God treats the listener as a father who delights in his child (Hebrew version), the Greek states that God *whips* every child whom he receives. When the listeners hear this proverb, the picture of the fight they are involved in morphs. They discover that as they are fighting sin, they are also being buffeted by God. Readers within the faith do well not to pass too quickly over the difficulties of this text. If we ignore the critiques raised against it, we miss the blessings offered in this wrestling match.

One of the boldest critiques appears in the *Women's Bible Commentary* written by Hebrews' scholar Mary Rose D'Angelo. Concerning this theme of God's discipline in ch. 12, she argues, "The abusive connection of punishment and love has endured as a common place of patriarchal education and child rearing from antiquity to this day. Hebrews' counsel puts a divine sanction behind the abuse of women and abusive child rearing, and its focus on obedience can encourage resignations and passivity."[16] Stephen Finlan, a researcher of atonement theories, agrees: "It seems that Hebrews identifies with his abusers and is trapped in the system of abuse, repeating the ideology that punishment is good for us. . . . Jesus is offered as our model."[17] Don Capps argues that such exaltation of punishment has legitimized "authoritarian parenting

---

who is speaking this encouragement to them, but because of the prominence of reminding them that they are children of God, that this is divine address seems more likely to me.

15. "*Dialegomai*," BDAG, 232.

16. Carol A. Newsom, Sharon H. Ringe, and Jacqueline E. Lapsley, eds., *Women's Bible Commentary*, 3rd ed. (Louisville: Westminster John Knox, 2012), 611.

17. Stephen Finlan, *Sacrifice and Atonement: Psychological Motives and Biblical Patterns* (Minneapolis: Fortress, 2016), 111.

orientations." For him, "the major offender in this regard is the letter to the Hebrews," because "the letter to the Hebrews introduces the logic of sacrifice . . . using it as a theological rationale for the punishment of children. . . . The sacrifice of Jesus does not put an end to all divine chastisements, for God now chastises because, through the sacrifice of Jesus, he views us through the eyes of love. The sign of God's love . . . is his chastisements."[18] The logic of these arguments proceeds from Christology to corporal punishment. God the Father abused Jesus, which legitimized God's abuse of the addressees of Hebrews, which resulted in the abuse of many throughout the history of the church.

With appreciation for scholars like these who name the hard things in Scripture and bring to light the abuses wrought by those who have read it (or, as I will argue, *misread* it), I maintain, however, that the intensity of this text should not result in an abandonment of Hebrews nor the God who speaks within it. The whole letter has argued for, and in my reading established, the trustworthiness of the God who is doing the discipline. That divine character should be the primary guide for how to interpret and apply this text. I highlight two ways in which the character of the God of Hebrews shines forth not in spite of but through this intense citation.

First, this citation is addressed to a son. It begins, *My son*. The educational setting of Proverbs assumes a male addressee, particularly clear when both vice and virtue are personified as women with whom the listener could be in relationship (Prov 5:3; 8). The MT, LXX, and Hebrews all portray this statement as addressed to a son, but the particular form of address in Hebrews shares a commonality with the Hebrew text over the Greek, an unusual move for an author who consistently utilizes the Greek text. The author of Hebrews includes a personalization of the vocative, *my* son, rather than the simple address of "son." This more personal form of address could have arisen from his knowledge of the Hebrew *beni*, but that presses the question of why the author does not cite the form of the Hebrew text in the following verse, where the tone is more comforting, as discussed. I have argued that the author employs the more personal form of address, not in adherence to the Hebrew and not simply for emotive effect, but instead as a way of aligning the experience of his readers (women/daughters of God included) to the experience of *the Son*,

18. Donald Capps, *The Child's Song: The Religious Abuse of Children* (Louisville: Westminster John Knox, 1995), 64, 68.

Jesus Christ.[19] By including a personal pronoun, *mou*, the author puts God's address to the audience in line with God the Father's first address to the Son in Hebrews 1:5.[20] In both, God, through this scripture, says, "My son." If the Son who is God actively wills to experience temptation, suffering, and even death so that he might be perfected, other members of the family of God should not be surprised that they are encouraged to embrace the same. Although the author uses the term for *discipline* only in this section (12:5, 7, 8, 11), it lines up with the way in which the Father worked with the Son during his incarnate life (2:9–10; 5:7–9). God's discipline follows a christological pattern, and that means that the audience can look to the example of the Son for empathy and encouragement so that they, too, can endure unto victory.

Second, God's very present paternal hand in their difficulty serves to cast this text positively. The audience is *already* experiencing intense hardship, including shame from their culture, the seizure of their property (10:32–34), and imprisonment (13:3). This citation of Proverbs is not a blanket statement that all suffering is educative but specifies God's knowledge of and power over their particular situation.[21] By portraying God as the one who disciplines, reproves, and even whips them, the author places God in the midst of their difficulty. Not as its cause—the ultimate problem is sin; this is what they are fighting against (v. 4)—but as its Sovereign. This citation resonates with Deuteronomy 32:36 LXX in Hebrews 10:30, in which the author reminds them of the Lord's judgment (the previous time "Lord" appeared in the sermon). God is not distant, simply watching the child struggle; God is in the ring with the child, allowing and shaping the blows so that they do not destroy but only strengthen. The visceral description of whipping highlights the physicality of what they are

19. Peeler, *You Are My Son*, 144–51; Peeler, "'Leading Many Sons to Glory.'"

20. Because this reading does not appear in any other extant Greek manuscript of Prov 3:11, it might be the innovation of the author. Alternatively, it is the citation of a Greek text no longer available to scholars. See Susan Docherty for an argument that advances in studies of the Greek text of Israel's Scriptures and Jewish interpretation techniques suggest that the author of Hebrews was a faithful follower of the biblical text (*Old Testament in Hebrews*). Whether he added in this pronoun or simply had it in front of him, the resonance between Heb 1:5 and 12:5 still stands.

21. See Bryan Dyer, *Suffering in the Face of Death: The Epistle to the Hebrews and Its Context of Situation*, LNTS (London: Bloomsbury, 2017). James Thompson notes that a general reading could encourage "those who are suffering in abusive relationships to endure passively" (*Hebrews*, 256).

experiencing, which stands in line with the athletic metaphors the author has used in this chapter. God is present in this lived difficulty with them and, even more important, God is sovereign over what they are experiencing. William S. Morrow comments that the issue of justice must be foregrounded in this passage. God, at times, permits what is unjust but uses it for the good of the sufferer. God's complete knowledge and trustworthiness assert that God's use of discipline will never succumb to anger or foolishness. As the author will explain in the following section, God is not like other parents, or any other authority figure for that matter, who could be misguided in the exercise of discipline.[22] God knows all things and is working them for the best.[23]

The notion that the hearers are being *reproved by him* adds another dimension. It is likely they are fighting against the sins of others, the persecution of Christ confessors, but they are also wrestling against the sins within themselves. They are not as mature as they should be (5:11–14). God may allow difficulty for reproval of sin as well as for transformation into maturity.

To reiterate, this is a very hard text and certainly has been misused. Hebrews as a whole provides an answer for every link in the progression the critics of it describe. Its Christology reveals that, as God, the Son suffers willingly as an enactment of the divine plan he created. His willing suffering need never be repeated by anyone else because it is effective once for all. His model of sonship, however, reveals that in a similar way other sons and daughters of God can rest assured in God's presence and plan in the midst of their suffering. They confess and are members of the crucified one, who knows what it is to suffer and has suffered to defeat the root cause of all suffering. When these truths keep focus on Christ and his good and costly work, the passage cannot be misapplied to any situation of suffering, especially abusive ones.

Modern interpreters should avoid doing what the author warns his congregation against, saying, *Do not devalue the discipline of the Lord*, either through ignoring the intensity of its call and the damaging interpretations that have

22. Because of the difference between God the Father and human parents, Morrow, whose essay investigates child-rearing from the perspective of indigenous Christians, concludes that Heb 12 cannot be used as support for corporal punishment in child-rearing. William S. Morrow, "What to Do with Proverbs?," in *Decolonizing Discipline: Children, Corporal Punishment, Christian Theologies, and Reconciliation*, ed. Valerie E. Michealson and Joan E. Durrant (Winnipeg: University of Manitoba Press, 2020), 102.

23. Paul's statements in Rom 8:28–29 serve as a beneficial co-text.

arisen against it or dismissing it as an ancient and ill-informed perspective that society has now advanced beyond. Neither should contemporary readers *grow weary when you are reproved by him*. Whatever difficulties readers experience, they can trust that God allows them, and so those difficulties are not cause for giving up. Hence, the necessity of divine and communal support continues. This divine support appears in the only explicit articulation of God's love for humanity in the sermon. The author is clear that the discipline of God is evidence that *the Lord loves* and *receives*.

I suggest this citation of Proverbs 3 is resonant with Psalm 88 LXX, a psalm many believe the author evokes with his mention of the *firstborn* in Hebrews 1:6. In that text, the king of Israel calls out to God as his Father (Ps 88:27 LXX), and God promises to establish the covenant with him and his throne forever. Then the psalm states:

> If his sons leave my law
> and in my judgments do not go,
> if my righteous judgments they will desecrate
> and my commandments they do not keep,
> I will look upon their lawless acts with a rod,
> and with scourges [*mastix*, "whip," another form of the word in Heb 12:6] their sins,
> but my mercy I will never break from him
> nor will I be unjust in my truth,
> nor will I desecrate my covenant
> and the things that go out through my lips I will not set aside.
> (Ps 88:31–35 LXX)

Because the author has cast the community of Hebrews as the children of Jesus the eternal King (2:13), this psalm applies to them. By virtue of their relationship with Jesus, God is kind enough to teach them, discipline, and even scourge their sin, as a demonstration of God's merciful covenant.

Right after the citation of the proverb, the author urges his congregants to *endure*. Either this is a statement of what they are already doing (indicative verb) or a command (imperative verb), but the outcome of either is the same. Since endurance is, by nature, continual, he is asking them to persevere in this action. Previously, he commended them for having endured in the past: "But remember the earlier days in which, having been enlightened, you endured a great contest of sufferings" (10:32), and in the opening paragraph of the chapter he set forth Jesus's example of endurance (12:2). Knowing that Jesus has endured and that they have endured faithfully in the past is great encouragement that they can continue to endure.

The object of the command is *discipline* (in the accusative case); this would be translated "endure discipline." The text is not this simple, however. The author has inserted, and even fronted in the sentence, a preposition, *eis*, which makes *discipline* its object rather than being the object of the verb. The translation changes slightly: *Endure **as** discipline.* The reader has to supply what is to be endured and interpret that thing *as God's discipline.* As with the author's boxing metaphor, this phrase implies a change in perception. Endure the fight with sin, he says, but know that it is God who is allowing this fight with sin for your transformation. Endure the fight as God's discipline. God has let the readers into the training gym as his own children. God's allowance of their entrance into this space, into this struggle, conveys high respect. God considers these children as able to endure the fight. God does not look down at them as weaklings unable to handle the training. People are often able to rise to heights they would not imagine for themselves when they know an authority figure in their lives considers them worthy of such demands. With this mindset, it is not just possible but preferable to see the character of God not as oppressive in this passage but empowering.

The author then puts his focus more squarely on the home rather than the sports arena. *God is offering this to you as sons.* They can rest assured that this presentation of discipline comes from none other than God. For what God *does* the author uses the verb that he frequently uses for sacrifice, *prospherō.* This casts God's offering to them as both a gift and a sacrifice. The Son had to sacrifice himself to establish the familial relationship, and this offering will demand a great deal from the readers, God's children. If they accept the costly offer, it will be a blessing. For this audience who has been invited to consider God as their Father, the discipline of their present difficulty actually confirms their standing with God. They are receiving this offering *as sons.* As stated previously, I have intentionally chosen an exclusive masculine translation to highlight the invitation this offers to listeners, both men and—in an especially arresting way—women. They are considered strong enough to receive and succeed in this discipline because they are all members of Jesus the Son.

Parental discipline for the benefit of children is a constant in every time and culture, although the nature of what constitutes correct discipline changes. The author names a conviction he shares with his readers: *For what son does a father not discipline?* A lack of discipline indicates the absence of a familial relationship. He asks them, pointedly, yet with an immediate assurance: *And if you are without discipline, of which all of you have become sharers, then you are illegitimate ones and not sons.* If this community was not experiencing challenge (but the author *immediately* acknowledges that they are), that would indicate that they are not God's children but illegitimate. In earlier periods of Greek history, these children were called *skotoi*, those born in the dark. In the Roman Empire, however, many children were born "out of wedlock" because legal marriage was not always easy to attain. Illegitimacy may not have hindered relationships within or outside the family.[24] This was less true, however, the more elite one became. Illegitimate children could not carry on respected family names or inherit family property. It was in the father's best interest to invest in—and that meant discipline—the legitimate child over the illegitimate because that one would become the heir.[25] The author is drawing from the upper echelon of society as the best point of comparison with their relationship to God. Being the child of God supersedes even being the child of the emperor himself. Therefore, in that kind of elevated relationship, they should expect discipline.

In fact, he says explicitly, they have become *sharers* of God's discipline. By using a term he has employed to describe their identity as Christ confessors (3:1, 14; 6:4), he reiterates that their connection to Christ makes them children of God and therefore puts them in the realm of God's discipline. The author is cautioning them that if they want to deny their standing with Christ so that they will no longer suffer, that is an act of putting themselves outside the family and outside the inheritance, previewing a theme he will take up again later in the chapter (12:15–17). Thankfully, none to whom he is writing have taken that step yet, because they are all still experiencing God's discipline, the cost of confessing Christ, their brother.

Warning being voiced, he can now turn to a comparison with earthly fathers. *Moreover, we used to have our fathers of the flesh as discipliners, and we respected them.* He builds a grid of analysis consisting of at least three data points: attitudes

24. Sabine R. Hübner and David M. Ratzan, "Fatherless Antiquity: Perspectives on 'Fatherlessness' in the Ancient Mediterranean," in *Growing Up Fatherless in Antiquity*, ed. Sabine R. Hübner and David M. Ratzan (Cambridge: Cambridge University Press, 2009), 20.

25. Jane Gardner, *Family and* Familia *in Roman Law and Life* (Oxford: Clarendon, 1998), 252.

of the disciplined, time of the discipline, and knowledge of the disciplinarian. They all can relate with the experience of being disciplined by their fathers. That experience was likely different depending on their status: legitimate child and slave, male and female could all experience training, but not in the same degree and kind. He keeps the comparison at the level of generality. He also assumes they responded well. They were not rebellious but respected their fathers, a subtle compliment that might warm the listeners to following difficult instructions.

Before he mentions the other two realities in human families, he reinvokes God's status as father. *Should we not much more submit to the Father of spirits and live?* He refers to God here as the *Father of spirits*, in juxtaposition to the phrase *fathers of the flesh*. This is not to indicate that the divine Father cares nothing for the body. One's relationship with God is expressed through bodily life, as the final practical instructions in ch. 13 make clear (13:1–5). Instead, as indicated by the frequent references to God's spirit messengers (1:7, 14) and God's own Spirit (2:4; 3:7; 6:4; 9:8, 14; 10:15, 29), this Father is over a much grander world than that of bodily realities alone. This Father can see deeply inside the children (4:12) and bring them into a realm of the spiritual/heavenly (ultimately with their bodies, just as is true of the resurrected Son). In a comparative move, the author establishes that the divine Father cares about what human fathers care about (the flesh) *and more*. In response to this more comprehensive care, they should act not only with respect but also with submission. Respect focuses on the attitude, submission on the action. He wants them to put their lives fully under God's wise care.

This is a beneficial move because the Father of spirits is the one who truly works toward what is beneficial. If they submit to God, they will *live*—an incredibly powerful statement soon following the assertion that in this fight against sin (as allowed by God as discipline) they might shed blood (12:4). Even if they die, by being faithful to God they will live. The resurrection hope featured in ch. 11 is now being asked of them. It is no surprise that the living God (3:12; 9:14; 12:22) who communicates a living word (4:12) chiefly in the revelation of the ever-living Son of God (7:25) has opened up the righteous path of life (10:20, 38) and can grant life to them.

In v. **10** the author turns again to the comparison with human fathers.[26] *For our fathers were disciplining for a little time according to what was seemly*

26. A focus on fathers, rather than fathers *and mothers*, makes sense in light of the analogy

to them. He acknowledges that this paternal discipline was short-lived, either through the death of the parent or the maturation of the child.[27] Moreover, it was conducted with some degree of ignorance. Parents can do only what *seems* good to them, bound as they are to their own time and own experiences. If even *this* imperfect or even detrimental discipline received respect, how much more should the readers not just respect but also submit to the discipline meted out by God.

If human parents can make mistakes and wield discipline incorrectly, God cannot: *but God does so for our benefit so that we might share in God's holiness.* As Chrysostom notes concerning human parents, they discipline to fulfill "their own pleasure oftentimes and not always looking to what [is] expedient. But here that cannot be said, for the Lord does this not for any interest of the Lord's own but for you and for your benefit alone."[28] Human parents may have ulterior motives for discipline, shaped by their own sinful (and even subconscious) bent or the pressures of the cultures around them. Divine discipline is the better thing this listening community should desire because it propels the recipient toward what is truly beneficial, a share in God's holiness. If the ancient world assumed that parents had a hand in molding the character of their children, through both nature and nurture, even the best of parenting could only be as good as the parent, and no parent could attest to being fully holy. God's fully wise discipline moves the recipient to become more like God in divine holiness and divine life. God allows growth into the quality that allows entrance into God's sacred space (12:14). The difficult news is that this discipline will last longer. Not confined to the era of childish immaturity, one might need to be disciplined by God for the entirety of natural life.

The author recognizes that prospect brings heaviness. He acknowledges, *All discipline in the present does not seem to be joyful but full of grief.* He states two things about discipline, exhibiting both compassion and truth. While it is being experienced, discipline feels like a grief, a term translated in other places in the New Testament as sorrow or pain (Luke 22:45; John 16:6, 20–22; Rom

---

he is drawing with God, the Father of Jesus Christ. This is not to say that fathers are more like God than are mothers, but only that God's name, revealed in relation to the person of Jesus Christ, is Father (see Peeler, *Women and the Gender of God*, esp. 89–117). Mothers, too, can learn lessons from this passage.

27. Oecumenius, *Fragments on the Epistle to the Hebrews* 12.9 (ACCS 10:215).

28. Chrysostom, *Hebrews* 29.3 (*NPNF*[1] 14:500).

9:2; 2 Cor 2:1, 3, 7; 7:10; 9:7; Phil 2:27). It is an intense feeling in the negative realm, the opposite of joy. This is a poignant statement coming on the heels of the assertion that on the cross even Jesus experienced pain and shame (Heb 12:2). This passage acknowledges this reality about discipline and does not ask the listeners to claim with a fake smile that things are joyful when they are not. At the same time, it asserts another reality working alongside and within the grief of the present moment, that of peace. *But later* discipline *yields the peaceful fruit of righteousness for those who have been trained through it.* This grief-filled discipline is moving somewhere. The prize in this training gym is not a perishable crown. He returns to the athletic imagery with the term "training," highlighting effort and practice, present also in 5:14. This section in ch. 12 is a further encouragement in light of the frustration he voiced in ch. 5. Solid food is for those who have been trained (5:14), and because now he says that they are experiencing God's training, that means he sees them as worthy of the complex sermon he has delivered to them. Not unlike Jesus at certain times in the Gospels, he voices frustration but does not give up on his call to teach this community.

As they endure this training, the reward is the peaceful fruit of righteousness. Just as growing fruit takes hard work over a long time, so too does the discipline of enduring God's training. This discipline lasts much longer than did the training of one's natural parents, but so too is the reward much greater. They will gain not simple human maturity or a transient inheritance but the reception of the very qualities associated with God, life from the God who lives (3:12), holiness needed to be in God's presence (12:14), peace from the God of peace (13:20), and righteousness that is the gift granted to those who have faith in God (11:7).

The author's next instructions assume the listeners have received God's discipline correctly in that they are sufficiently strong for him to set a task for them. His instructions in vv. 12–13 are in line with what he said in the last paragraph: endure. Instead of succumbing to weakness, he asks them to keep fighting to gain more strength. In other words, the discipline he is communicating to them is not a rebuke but is meant for teaching and training.

Considering the training they are enduring, he tells them, *Therefore, set right the hands that are drooping and the knees that are paralyzed.* If there are hands that are drooping, they are inert and have been neglected rather than being raised and taut, ready for the fight with sin. If there are knees that are paralyzed, they are stiff rather than nimble and ready to dance around the ring or run on the path. It is the job of the community to set those body parts aright. Now is not the time to give up but the time for everyone to stay agile and alert. That the author is drawing from Isaiah 35:3 LXX confirms this stance. The prophet commands strength for "anemic hands and paralyzed knees," and can do so because God is coming to save them (Isa 35:4 LXX).[29]

The admonitions also move outside the body. Those hearing this address should take notice of and then transform the setting of their athletic performance. Instead of depending on someone else to make the course, they need to do so and to make it well: *and make straight paths for your feet*. It is their responsibility to construct a straight path. One might wonder how they can make the path when they are the ones running. They do so, actually, *through* running. As they follow the trailblazer Jesus, they, too, are plodding down the path making it smoother and more even.

It is clear that they are doing all this work, restoring bodies and making straight paths, not for themselves alone but also for those who come after them. They do this restorative work *so that the crippled may not be put out of joint but rather be healed.* This section, much like the instruction for mutual encouragement (3:14), is another indication that the author wants everyone to acknowledge and embrace the influence they have with others. If they keep running faithfully, they help make the path straight for those who follow, especially important for the lame whose bodies are not so strong. If anyone runs on these straight paths, an amazing thing will happen. Not only will they not trip or be thrown off course, but even more, they will be healed. Their bodies will grow stronger by running on the straight paths. In ethical terms, following the leadership of a solid guide not only prevents one from vice but also aids in one's growth in virtue. The author wants the audience to keep running faithfully for their own sakes as well as for the sakes of those who will come behind them. As they have benefited from the examples of the faithful of the past, so too can they be a benefit to those who will follow.

The next instruction has a communal focus as well: *Pursue peace with all.* As God is in the process of granting them peaceful fruit by allowing them to

29. See Martin C. Albl, "Hebrews and the General Epistles," in *The Bible and Disability: A Commentary*, ed. Sarah J. Melcher, Mikeal C. Parsons, and Amos Yong (Waco: Baylor University Press, 2017),

experience discipline (12:11), so too are they to pursue peace *with all*. The concern for making good paths, then, is related to establishing good relationships. Chrysostom sees clearly the issue at stake: "For nothing so especially makes persons easily vanquished and subdued in temptations as isolation."[30] The comprehensiveness of the term *all* indicates a concern not only for those in the community—the struggling as well as the strong—but also those outside the community, including even those who persecute them.[31] As much as it depends on them, they should be at peace with all (similar to Paul's instructions in Rom 12:18).

They should also pursue another thing God is granting them through the death and resurrection of the Son (Heb 2:11; 9:13; 10:10, 14, 29)—namely, *sanctification*. The author maintains a careful integration between God's action and human participation in that action. God in Christ sanctifies them (2:11; 10:10, 29; 13:12), and because of that the quality of being set apart is also something they can actively pursue. The author of Hebrews has emphasized for his community their participation in God's sanctifying work, and he makes it most explicit in this section. They do not passively receive God's holiness, but upon reception of it they are called to press in to it. The human condition is such that people flourish when much is asked of them, if all the resources are provided to fulfill the expectation. God does not infantilize the children in the household under Christ but invites them to take the arduous but ultimately beneficial path of growing into the holiness that is theirs by virtue of confessing Jesus Christ. This pathway cannot be walked alone. Because sanctification here is linked with pursuing peace with all, it demonstrates that one's relationship with God is intimately tied with how one relates to others, just as Jesus highlighted from God's law (Matt 22:37 40/Mark 12:30 31/Luke 10:27).

A succinct statement follows that calls forth the previous warnings: *without* sanctification (which God is already granting them) *no one will see the Lord*. Some in the history of Israel were afforded the chance to see the Lord in some way (Num 12:8; Isa 6; Job 42:5), but the more immediate implication for these readers lies in the future. As the faithful were looking forward to

30. Chrysostom, *Hebrews* 30.2 (*NPNF*[1] 14:503).

31. Annang Asumang draws this insight from the echoes of this passage with the Jacob-Esau narrative. See "Strive for Peace and Holiness: The Intertextual Journey of the Jacob Traditions from Genesis to Hebrews, via the Prophets," *Conspectus* 17 (March 2014): 29.

seeing God's promises (Heb 11:13), they are looking forward to seeing Christ's return (9:28). Those who are pursuing sanctification are the same people who are eagerly awaiting the full salvation the Messiah is bringing. Holiness is requisite for a vision of the holy God. This call to pursue indicates that for this author there is no standing still in faith. If they are not moving forward, they are in danger of slipping back and missing out on this revelation. This twin admonition toward peace and sanctification has resonance with Jesus's Beatitudes in Matthew 5:8–9: "Blessed are the pure in heart, for they will see God. Blessed are the peacemakers, for they will be called children of God." Divine vision, holiness, peacemaking, and being in the family of God are all points of connection. The author closely resonates with the gospel of the Lord he has heard from others (Heb 2:3).

The communal focus continues as everyone is asked to *watch out* for their fellow believers. Here the author utilizes the term that appears as the name for a leader who oversees members of the church (*episkopos*, Acts 20:28; Phil 1:1; 1 Tim 3:2; Titus 1:7). *Watch out lest someone come short of the grace of God.* This kind of watchfulness is necessary to prevent anyone coming short of God's grace, a phrase in line with the athletic goal-oriented themes of the whole chapter. It is not as if, however, grace is reserved as the reward at the end of the race. They already are experiencing God's grace, given in the death of Jesus on their behalf (2:9), granted from the throne whenever they need it (4:16), and provided by the Spirit (10:29). Someone can, however, fail to keep receiving it, with the result that they fail to receive its end goal. The author does not want anyone to give up before they reach the end, and it takes a community to prevent that from happening.

Such a failure will have damaging implications for the whole community around this person. To elucidate his admonition the author evokes Deuteronomy 29:18 LXX: *lest a certain bitter root that springs up cause trouble and through it many are defiled.*[32] The context of Deuteronomy shows that this bitter root is not someone who simply grows weary in faith but someone who turns to other gods. Idolatry and apostasy are the issues at stake here. That person who turns away from the true and only God runs the risk of defiling others, tempting them to turn away as well.

32. Greek texts say the bitter root is springing up "with gall," *en cholē*, whereas Hebrews has made these two into one word, the present active subjunctive of *enochleō*, "to cause trouble."

The next warning is that they should also watch out *lest there be a certain fornicator and unholy person as Esau.* The idea of unfaithfulness is closely linked with the concept of idolatry. To worship other gods is to be unfaithful (Judg 2:17; 1 Chr 5:25; Ps 72:27 LXX; 105:39 LXX). The reference to a fornicator introduces the example of an unholy person, embodied in Esau.[33] Although Genesis never says that Esau is ungodly, in traditions about him (Jub. 25:1; b. Megillah 6a) he is a wicked one who is imagined to be both promiscuous and profane, preferring foreign wives over the daughters of Israel (Gen 26:34) and a meal over his birthright (Gen 25:31–34).[34] Particularly in the instance of the meal, he serves as an example of someone who prefers the readily available common over the patience-procured holy. The audience might be tempted in similar ways by the comfort of honorable society rather than the shame of confessing a criminal Messiah. In other words, Esau did not go off to serve other gods, but as a parable of that act, he was one *who for the sake of one meal gave up his own birthright as the firstborn.* He chose the temporary pleasure of one meal over the immense and long-lasting blessings of his standing in the family. This gives a picture of how utterly ridiculous it would be for anyone in this community to leave their confession of Christ for something else, as senseless as trading one's entire inheritance for a dinner.

The author skips over some important details about Jacob to continue to use Esau as a negative example. *For you know that even afterward when he wanted to inherit the blessing, he was rejected; for he did not find a place for repentance even though he sought for it with tears.* Once he had given up his standing in his family, when he wanted to inherit the blessing, he was rejected. Because the author draws together these two vignettes in his life, he makes a point about Esau that emphasizes his wrong actions: he cannot have the blessing of the firstborn because he had given up the status of the firstborn. Esau's displays of emotion through crying—the same that Jesus himself displayed (5:7), which is

33. Readers of Hebrews must also be mindful of the later history of Esau's people, the kingdom of Edom, who are portrayed as not helping Israel (Num 20:14–21) nor standing with Judah during the Babylonian siege (Obad 10–14; Ezek 35:1–5; Ps 137:7). Therefore, they are often excoriated in the prophetic literature (Isa 34; Ezek 35; Obad; Mal 1:1–5). The pejorative terms the author of Hebrews uses for him in ch. 12 fits within this stream of the tradition.

34. In a commentary on Ezekiel, Rashi saw in Esau's spurning of his birthright a rejection of the worship of God. Malachi Haim Hacohen, *Jacob and Esau: Jewish European History between Nation and Empire* (Cambridge: Cambridge University Press, 2019), 97.

also evocative of Peter's tears after denial of Christ (Matt 26:75)—did not lead to Isaac changing his mind concerning the blessing that Isaac had already given to Jacob. Esau did not get the blessing even though he cried for it. The author leaves out the deception of Rachel and Jacob in this story, but the echo of it could indicate that giving up one's confession of Christ—one's association with the firstborn—will make the apostate vulnerable to deception. The author's primary focus remains on the fact of Esau's foolish choice to give up his status in the first place. If any of the listeners were contemplating a turn away from the family of God, he is warning them against it in the strongest terms.

Several interpreters from the tradition have seen Esau's inability to secure the blessing as pointing to a failure in the *type* of repentance he offered.[35] He may have been crying, but he was not truly repentant for what he had done. He was sad about what had been done to him. His focus was on the trickery of his brother. He even carried murder against Jacob in his heart (Gen 27:41). This interpretive trajectory will often also suggest that Esau's problem was a failure of *timing* as well. Had he acknowledged his flippancy earlier, maybe Isaac could have done something to repair the act, but when he came later, *afterward*, it was too late. The blessing given to his brother could not be revoked. Following this line of interpretation suggests that the author of Hebrews puts forth this story to emphasize to his readers that if any of them chooses to walk away from Christ, time may run out. If they approach the God who is the judge of all (12:23) at the time when those who are eagerly awaiting the Son (9:28) receive the inheritance of salvation (1:14), and if they approach as people who have been in active rejection of Christ, then it would *not* be fitting for God, at that time and in those circumstances, to give them the blessing. At that moment, they may wish to inherit the blessing, but their decision would have already been made, and God would respect it. Readers outside of that original community must keep in mind that this is, after all, a *warning*, issued to those who had *not* walked away. It is a powerfully developed hypothetical that has *not* occurred. This passage does not address those who may return to Christ in true repentance *before* the full and final inheritance of the unshakable kingdom is given, but it does warn them in no uncertain terms not to take the temptation of that departure lightly.

35. Chrysostom, *Hebrews* 31.4 (*NPNF*[1] 14:507); Thomas Aquinas, *Hebrews* 12.3.694, p. 282; Calvin, *Hebrews*, 198.

A canonical reading of the entire Esau narrative in Genesis offers an alternative interpretation of Hebrews. This brief mention of the blessing on Esau in 11:20 evokes the Pentateuchal narrative, which ends Esau's story on a positive note. Not only does he have abundance, but he is even restored to his brother, participates in the burial of his father (Gen 35:29), and receives a territory that God instructs the Israelites to leave untouched (Deut 2:4). An alternative reading in light of this positive conclusion in the Torah is that the author of Hebrews mentions his name twice to point both to the consequences of his actions (12:15–17) and to the restorative blessings that God gives when one is reconciled to the community or family (11:20). What Esau misses out on is the blessing of the firstborn, but he does receive some kind of blessing, and he is *not* kicked out of the family. Isaac remains his father. If this story exerts influence in Hebrews, then possibly the author is indicating that incredible *benefits* are not accessible for as long as a person treats Christ flippantly, but the cost is not immediate and permanent removal from the family. This could be a reading that brings healing in a situation in which someone desires to return to the family of faith after a time in which the person had rejected faith.

The brief and particular way Esau is invoked, however, pushes against this reading of *Hebrews'* treatment of Esau. What he gives up is his *prōtotokia*, his status as the firstborn, and in Hebrews that status is not a collection of nice benefits but is the association with the firstborn himself (1:6) and the honor that comes to all who confess him (12:23). Moreover, Esau's desire is to *inherit* the *blessing*. Inheritance is that which is given at the end when the sons and daughters of God receive what God has prepared for them—namely, eternal salvation (Heb 1:14; 6:12, 17; 9:15). The blessing is that which is given to the faithful people of God (6:7; Abraham serves as example, 6:14; 7:1, 6, 7). If blessing and family are related but distinct in the Genesis Esau narrative, this is no longer true in the Christian community: the blessing is in and only in the family attached to the firstborn, Jesus the eternal Son. Hebrews' succinct retelling of this story joins Esau's willful and ridiculous choice with his failure to inherit the blessing of the firstborn. There might have been leftover blessings for Esau in the past (as recounted in Genesis), but now that God's firstborn has come, the only eternally salvific blessing is attached to the firstborn alone. Esau serves as an example of Hebrews 6:4–6, where the author states that repentance is not possible. If someone departs from Christ, there is no other blessing to be found, no matter how pitifully one may cry for it. Through the abbreviated story of Esau, the author says to his audience, "If you walk away from Christ the firstborn, you cannot come back to God, even if you want to, even if you express that return through heartfelt tears, for there is no other way to be in God's family except in Christ." There are no salvific blessings outside the family of Christ confessors. God has more power than Isaac, of course, and so again even this intense warning does not speak to a situation in which a person desires to return to Christ the firstborn. This is not the author of Hebrews' situation. Other texts in the New Testament, however, indicate that God readily welcomes repentance, a desire to return to the family, even when a person has denied the Son and their status of sonship (Luke 15:11–32; Mark 14:53–65/Matt 26:57–68/Luke 22:54–71; John 18:13–27; 21:1–14).

With nods to two portions of Israel's Scriptures—Deuteronomy and Genesis—the author has issued an intense and sober warning about the importance of faithfulness in community. No one should depart from God and stay in the community, thereby serving as a bitter root who damages others, but neither should anyone depart from God and remove oneself from the blessings possible only in the community of the firstborn. The primary admonition here, as it has been throughout the letter, is not to depart from God. The best way to ensure that faithfulness is to adhere to the community, allowing oneself to be open to accountability, for it is there in the community that weariness and doubts can be healed rather than fester into bitterness or rejection.

12:18–29 · CHANGED AND REFINED

18 For you have not come to that which may be touched and that which has been burned with fire, to darkness and gloom and windstorm, 19 to the burst of a trumpet and to the sound of words, and those who heard them begged that no word should be added to them, 20 for they found it hard to bear the command that if even a beast should touch the mountain, it would be stoned. 21 And so fearful was the sight that Moses said, "I am afraid, even trembling."

22 But you have come to Mount Zion and the city of the living God, to the heavenly Jerusalem, and to myriads of angels, to a celebration, 23 and to an assembly of the firstborn ones who have been inscribed in the heavens, and to the Judge, God of all, and to the spirits of the righteous who have been made perfect, 24 and to the mediator of the new covenant, Jesus, and to the sprinkled blood that speaks better than that of Abel.

[25]Watch out lest you resist the one who is speaking. For if those did not escape when they resisted the one who warned them on earth, how much less will we escape, those who turn away from the one who speaks from heaven, [26]whose voice shook the earth then, and now he has promised, saying, "Still once more I will shake not only the earth but also the heaven."

[27]And the "still once more" makes clear the change of the shaken things—that is, things that have been made—in order that the things which are not shaken might remain. [28]Therefore, because we are receiving an unshakable kingdom, let us have gratitude, through which we worship God pleasingly with reverence and fear. [29]For indeed our God is a consuming fire.

Verse **18** begins a new paragraph, yet it continues the idea of forward movement. If they are in the process of running, the author first tells them where they have *not* arrived: *For you have not come to that which may be touched and that which has been burned with fire, to darkness and gloom and windstorm, to the burst of a trumpet and to the sound of words.* They have not arrived at an entity[36] burning with fire, in darkness and gloom, engulfed in a tempest with trumpets and a booming voice sounding from it. In the minds of some readers, this description evokes a chaotic scene where sirens and a muffled voice of a loudspeaker issue warnings. To have *not* approached this overwhelming scene must be good news.

Connections within the sermon itself confirm this negative portrayal. The author has associated fire with God's judgment against enemies (10:27). God's voice is that which warns future generations against past generations' mistakes (3:7, 15; 4:7). The darkness, gloom, and windstorm appear nowhere else in Hebrews, but other New Testament authors name darkness as the place of God's judgment (2 Pet 2:4, 17; Jude 6, 13). Similarly, outside Hebrews the sounding of the trumpet is a common feature that heralds God's judgment as well (Matt 24:31; 1 Cor 15:52; 1 Thess 4:16; Rev 8:2, 6–8, 10, 12; 9:1, 13–14; 10:7; 11:15). The author of Hebrews, however, is drawing from those ominous ideas of judgment to portray the scene of the wilderness generation before Mount Sinai (Exod 19–20; Deut 4).

36. The language of these verses comes very clearly from Exod 19–20's and Deut 4's descriptions of Sinai, so later manuscripts supply the word for the thing to which they have not come—namely, a mountain.

At that time, the people who heard these things *begged that no word should be added to them.* They could not handle even one more statement. Not because of its ear-splitting quality but because they knew from whom the voice came. The presence of a holy God was an awesome thing. They had good reason to fear because of the instruction that came from the mountain. *For they found it hard to bear the command that if even a beast should touch the mountain, it would be stoned.* The first thing the author says about the mountain is that it is "touchable," emphasizing that it brings a particular danger. The people had heard from God that even if an animal were to inadvertently come too close to the mountain and transgress its boundary, it would need to die (Exod 19:12–13). The threat of mortality if one got too close to a holy God was more than they could bear.

The people were being faithful to God's command to respect the boundaries between God's holiness and their own (imperfect) humanity, but similar to Eve's misstatement of God's command (Gen 3:3), they added to the command. In addition to not touching God's mountain, they did not want to hear God's voice but instead wanted to hear the more palatable voice of Moses (Exod 20:19). It could be said that they resisted the one who was speaking to them (Heb 12:25). Moses notes that in so doing they did not endure the test God had for them, graciously given so that they would not sin (Exod 20:20). It could also be said, then, that they were resisting God's discipline (Heb 12:4–11). Michael Kibbe suggests that the author presents "their fearful withdrawal from the Sinai theophany as a rejection of God that must not be imitated."[37]

Gareth Cockerill argues that the author's descriptions portray "the terror of the disobedient when approaching God."[38] Fear related to disobedience continues as a theme in the next description as well. *And so fearful was the sight that Moses said, "I am afraid, even trembling."* The one who did not fear the king (11:27) feared the revelation of God's presence, and, the author adds, he trembled. This statement points to the consequences of disobedience because when the Sinai event is recounted in Deuteronomy 4, from which the author has been drawing, there is no statement of Moses's fear. That appears later, in Deuteronomy 9, when Moses

37. Michael Kibbe, "Requesting and Rejecting: Παραιτέομαι in Heb 12,18–29," *Biblica* 96.2 (2015): 282–86, here 286.

38. Gareth Lee Cockerill, "Hebrews 12:18–24: Apocalyptic Typology or Platonic Dualism?," *Tyndale Bulletin* 69.2 (2018): 231.

is not afraid of the pyrotechnics of the mountain but more seriously afraid of the wrath of God against the disobedience of the people who created the golden calf to worship instead of worshiping the true God who had delivered them (Deut 9:19 or Exodus either). The author emphasizes this fear by noting Moses's trembling, a point not present in Deuteronomy 9:19 or Exodus either. This invites a consideration of the connection between Moses's fear for his people and the author's great fear of what would happen if his listeners also turned away from God.

The transition in v. **22** is a sharp one. *But you have come to Mount Zion and the city of the living God, to the heavenly Jerusalem.* With the strong adversative *alla*, "but," the author asserts that the readers' journey has led them to the point of arriving at a different mountain, Mount Zion. As the only time the author of Hebrews evokes this name, he aligns with the tradition of Israel where Zion, another way of referring to Jerusalem, calls forth associations with the place and people of God (other New Testament authors refer to it as well; see Matt 21:5; John 12:15; Rom 9:33; 11:26; 1 Pet 2:6; Rev 14:1). Here his listeners will have a very different experience of the presence of God. In many ways it is the opposite of what he has described previously in vv. 18–21. This is the city of the ***living*** *God* (Heb 3:12; 9:14; 10:31), where the living High Priest (7:16, 25) opened up the living way (10:20). This is a place abundantly free of the fear of death. It is the *heavenly Jerusalem*, the location from which God's calling (3:1) and gift (6:4) come. Now it becomes clear that this is the city to which Abraham and his family were looking forward (11:10, 16) as well as the city that the congregation addressed by the sermon is still anticipating (13:14). It must be the locale where the heavenly sanctuary is located as well (8:5; 9:23). As is fitting for such a location, it is filled with *myriads of angels*, beings of *light*, not darkness (Acts 12:7; 2 Cor 11:14). Those who are, at times, on earth serving God's inheritors (Heb 1:14; 13:2) are now depicted in God's realm. It is a place of *celebration*, conjuring up images of feasts and festivals, joy and mirth (Hos 2:11; 9:5; Amos 5:21; Ezek 46:11).[39] The author is painting a very different picture than a frightful storm.

In his study of temple imagery, Philip Church suggests that this heavenly Jerusalem "symbolizes the relationship between God and his people under

39. Often the words of these prophets express frustration with these festivals since they are practiced at the same time that disobedience occurs in Israel, but that dissonance would not be true in God's realm.

the new covenant."[40] That portrayal fits well with the next elements of the description. Humans are there as well, and they are not killed for coming close. The author describes the people present in two ways: *an assembly of the firstborn ones* and *the spirits of the righteous who have been made perfect*. First, the striking paradox in the way the author describes the assembly should not be missed. They are made up of firstborn ones (*prōtotokōn*). One might expect a singular noun here. Christologically, there are many who identify with Jesus the Messiah, but he is the singular firstborn Son of God (1:6). Practically, as well, the plural is odd because in a family only one child gets the privilege of being "first born." With the employment of the plural, however, though it might be counterintuitive, the author is asserting that this reality is exactly how the Christology works. They are *all* firstborn ones, sharing in the benefits that come to the singular Son. This language is incredibly comforting after the warning that appealed to the story of Esau, who gave up his blessings of *prōtotokia*, the blessing of the firstborn (12:16). Since his readers and the faithful in the past have not done what Esau did in giving up their connection to God's family, they look forward to the participation in these firstborn blessings. The author also says that these firstborn ones *have been inscribed in the heavens*, appealing to a common apocalyptic image of heavenly writings, a canonical echo of the Lamb's book of life in Revelation (Rev 13:8; 21:27). Being inscribed in God's heavenly realm is closely connected to having God's law inscribed in their hearts (Heb 8:10; 10:16). With care and with a desire for endurability, God has written the good laws on the hearts of the covenant people and has written their names in the heavens.

Second, the author paints the humans gathered on Mount Zion as *spirits*. This term connects them with God, who is not a natural father but the Father of spirits (12:9). Because they are dwelling with God, it is fitting to describe them as *righteous* and as those who have been *made perfect*. They have reached the end of their struggle with sin. They have endured the training that took place during their lives and are now mature (5:14) and are enjoying the peaceful fruit of righteousness (12:11). Put differently, because of their faith, they are now living with God (10:38). They are experiencing the perfection the law could not bring, but that is now possible because of Christ, the perfect one.

40. Philip Church, *Hebrews and the Temple: Attitudes to the Temple in Second Temple Judaism and in Hebrews*, NovTSup 171 (Leiden: Brill, 2017), 348.

The choice of this term also allows for the development of an intermediary eschatology. They do not have resurrected bodies yet,[41] but exist as spirits. These phrases are the author of Hebrews' way of describing the reality Paul articulates as "being absent from the body is to be present [more woodenly, to be at home] with the Lord" (2 Cor 5:8).

Amid the humans stands God. That the author describes God as *Judge* shows the amazing grace of humanity's dwelling on the heavenly mountain. The author has appealed to God's judgment several times throughout the sermon to emphasize the fittingness of God's actions against disobedience (Heb 9:27; 10:27, 30; 13:4). In fact, in every other instance in the sermon, God's status as Judge is meant to provoke awe, reverence, and obedience. It is a somber reality. By including that description here, the author asserts that God has not ignored the imperfections and sins of those who are gathered—God the Judge sees and is sovereign over all (4:12–13)—but somehow those gathered have passed through this judgment. This provides hopes for the readers who stand before this mountain that they can do the same.

The final phrases of the mountain's description explain why. On this mountain dwells *the mediator of the new covenant*. The author uses a different term here for *new* than he did earlier; it is one that indicates being more recent or younger (Matt 9:17; Luke 15:12). This is the "newer" covenant established by God's word that made the first "older" (Heb 8:13). This new covenant, as articulated through the words of Jeremiah in Hebrews 8:8–12 and 10:16–17, is that which has forgiven their sins, put God's law inside them, and renewed their standing as God's people. It is a covenant effected with *sprinkled blood*, and this blood *speaks better than that of Abel*. The mention of Abel puts a bookend to this entire section, going back to the beginning of ch. 11 (11:4). This mention also invites multiple comparisons. Jesus's blood is superior to Abel's because it is living and not dead. It does not cry out (metaphorically) spilt on the ground but intercedes at the right hand of God (7:28) because Jesus is not separated from his blood but united with it in his resurrected body. Moreover, his is not a cry for justice for himself but a plea for mercy for all his siblings, precisely what humans need to stand in the presence of a holy God.[42] Finally, his vocal

41. DeSilva mentions 1 En. 22:9, which also has the phrase "the spirits of the righteous" as a description of "the departed souls of righteous human beings" (*Hebrews*, 467n57).

42. Athanasius, *Festal Letter* 1.9.

blood is in line with the fidelity he shows to God throughout his life, as captured by the Son's instances of speaking in Hebrews (2:12–13; 10:5–8). He, with his living blood, is faithful to intercede at God's right hand (7:25). In many and various ways, then, his blood is better even than that of Abel, who was viewed by Jewish interpreters of the time as a prime example of faithfulness.[43]

The proclamation that *you have come to Mount Zion* affirms their close proximity to the joyous divine, practically manifest in the access they have to God's throne now (4:16). At the same time, their arrival at Mount Zion serves as an affirmation of what is left to come. It seems to me that the author portrays them at the bottom of the mountain, not on top of it.[44] They have not yet finished their race (12:1–2). They have not yet become fully mature and perfect (5:11–14). Hence, they have not yet ascended, and cannot do so until they finish their struggle with sin (12:4) and dwell in God's presence as the faithful of previous generations do now and as all generations will do after the general resurrection. Being close to the presence of God on the mountain, an awesome presence to which they are invited to come nearer, gives them great encouragement but also healthy challenge to keep going.

If they cannot be with God on top of the mountain in the present, they can hear the divine voice. The author grabs their attention again with the imperative: *Watch out*—pay attention—*lest you resist the one who is speaking*! In the context of the author's appeal to the Sinai narrative in the previous verses (12:18–21), it is God who speaks from the mountain and *warned them on earth*. As Israel heard the voice of the Lord booming from Mount Sinai and backed away from it, now this community hears the voice of God from heaven. He does not want them to take the same steps in backing away. Even weightier, a superior location means a more intense warning. Utilizing a word that does not appear in any of the Sinai narratives in Israel's Scriptures, the author describes the wilderness generation not only as those who requested that they not hear God's voice (*aiteō* as in Deut 18:16) but also as those who *resisted* (*paraiteomai*)

43. Kevin B. McCruden, "The Eloquent Blood of Jesus: The Neglected Theme of the Fidelity of Jesus in Hebrews 12:24," *CBQ* 75 (July 2013): 504–20.

44. Christopher Holmes argues that the indicative mood of *proerchomai* (you have come) emphasizes the location to which the listeners have come and creates in them a healthy sense of seriousness in responding to their placement at this location. See *The Function of Sublime Rhetoric in Hebrews: A Study in Hebrews 12:18–29*, WUNT II.465 (Tübingen: Mohr Siebeck, 2018), 125.

the one who warned them. It is an act of God's grace to warn the people about dangers on the horizon, as God did with Noah (Heb 11:7). God's warning in this context at Mount Sinai is the giving of the law, which laid out the consequences if they rejected it. They experienced these consequences when they constructed the golden idol (Exod 32). The participants in that rebellion had to drink a concoction of water mixed with the dust of their idol (Exod 32:20), and three thousand were killed (Exod 32:28). Moreover, the Lord sent a plague to the people (Exod 32:35). To know the risks beforehand was for their protection.

The author of Hebrews warns his community to pay attention lest they, too, resist the God who is speaking to them. If the audience of Hebrews *[turns] away from* the one who is speaking to them from *heaven*, the consequences will be even greater. The chance of their *escape* is *much less*. The author returns to the language of escape that he utilized in his first warning when he also appealed to the generation who heard God's law from the mountain (2:3). He leaves those consequences from which they could not escape unspoken here, but this language evokes all the previous warnings (6:4–6; 10:26–31; 12:15–17). To pay attention to and accept the words of the speaking God is of utmost importance.

It is the same God who is speaking to them as was speaking to the people of Israel before Mount Sinai, yet now they know the identity of this God with more clarity. It is the same God who now has spoken *in the Son* (1:2). The blood of Jesus is the last thing that had done any speaking in the sermon (12:24); the same verb *laleō* appears in v. 24 and v. 25. The booming voice of God *they* hear is not the cacophony of something like trumpets or thunder (12:19), but the distinct yet resonant chord of the voice of the Father, of the Son, and of the Spirit.[45] The author is showing them how damning it would be to turn away from such a clear message.

It is this divine voice that *shook the earth then*. The author might be aware of the Hebrew of Exodus 19:18 in which the *mountain* in particular is shaking, but this phrase is not carried over into the Greek translation. On the other hand, God's voice shaking the earth is an incredibly frequent theme throughout Israel's Scriptures, especially in the Psalms.

45. See Madison Peirce's superb treatment of the speaking of the persons of God in Hebrews, *Divine Discourse in the Epistle to the Hebrews*. Several of the Reformers suggested the distinction was between Moses, who communicated God's law, and Jesus, who speaks to this community (RCS 13:185).

The author's primary interest, nevertheless, is not what happened in the past but what will happen in the future. God has made a *promise* in the prophecy of Haggai (who remains unnamed in Hebrews), saying, *Still once more I will shake* not only *the earth* but *also the heaven.* All the realms attendant to God's voice will be shaken. In the prophecy of Haggai, the joining of heavens and earth along with sea and dry land communicates the comprehensive power that God has over creation.

The text of the prophet is an attractive one to our author. In that setting, the Lord is speaking to the tribe of Judah and, in particular, to Joshua the great priest (in Greek, *Iēsous*, the same name as Jesus; Hag 1:12), urging them to be strong and endure because God's shaking will not bring complete destruction but will instead create a greater splendor for the house of God than had been true in the past. This shaking is not something they should fear but something they should anticipate.

When God spoke from earth at Sinai only the earth was shaken, but now that God, the Father, through the Son and the Spirit, speaks from heaven, everything will be shaken. The author adds *not only . . . but also* to the citation of Haggai 2:6 to emphasize even further the comprehensiveness of the shaking. Given the way the author has presented heaven, this shaking includes not just the land and the sky but God's realm as well.

That heaven itself will be shaken finds confirmation when the author reflects more on the phrase "*still once more*": *And the "still once more" makes clear the change of the shaken things—that is, things that have been made—in order that the things which are not shaken might remain.* For him, the phrase "*once more*" *makes clear* that a change is still coming. That which was in the future for the prophet Haggai remains in the future for the author of Hebrews. This event has not already happened, although the defining reality that will determine the shape of that event has already happened in Christ.[46] With his coming the last days have arrived (1:2). When this cataclysmic event occurs there will be a *change of the shaken things*. The author clarifies that these are *things that have been made*, which, as Hebrews 1:10 (a citation of Ps 101:26 LXX) notes, include both the earth and the heavens. Theologically, since there is nothing outside God that is eternal, that means that the heavens, even the dwelling place of the presence of God, are not coeternal with God.[47] The author has made clear

46. Attridge, *Hebrews*, 382.

47. Stephen Wuthrow, Wheaton PhD graduate, aided my comprehension of this idea.

that God's heavenly realm includes a tabernacle not made by hands (8:2, 5; 9:1), but it is still *made*, only by God. As indicated by the fact that the blood of Christ cleanses the heavenly realm (9:23), this realm is affected by materiality, a confirmation that it has some form of a having-been-made quality.

Some interpreters have argued that this change is a *removal* of the created things, based on a possible translation of the word *metatithesis*, but two factors tip my interpretation in the direction of "change" rather than "removal." First, this is not a contrast between the realm of God and the realm of humanity, heaven and earth, because *both* are shaken. Second, and most important, Christ's body remains though it is something that God created. That indicates that other created things can remain too. This discourages any interpretation that would assert the endurance of only spiritual/nonmaterial realities. As Christ's body changed through resurrection, so will all creation be changed.[48] There will be some kind of change, even of God's heavenly realm, possibly to prepare it to receive all God's embodied people forever—or as the Revelation of John might say, the heavenly Jerusalem will be fittingly prepared, like a bride for her husband, when the city descends to the new earth to welcome in God's people (Rev 21:2–3).

The great final shaking is also commensurate with the psalmic proclamation that all things will be put under Christ's feet (Heb 1:13). This shaking is not the elimination of all things but the setting right of all things. For an audience enduring the hardship of persecution, the author is pointing to the things they experience on earth as well as the powers that make those things happen. Those will be shaken and changed. This is an encouraging word: if things look bad, it will not always be that way. In sum, the future divine shaking of the heavens will include both an elimination of the powers and principalities that have reigned unjustly over creation and a preparation of God's realm, making it ready for God's people.

The author further reiterates the desirability of this cataclysmic event. God shakes created things *in order that the things which are not shaken might remain.* Once this final shaking happens and things are changed, there will be no more shaking necessary because the transformation will be accomplished. The tumultuous unsettledness of human life on earth as it now is will not be

48. For an argument in support of a renewed-creation reading of this text, see Jihye Lee, "The Unshakable Kingdom through the Shaking of Heaven and Earth in Heb 12:26–29," *Novum Testamentum* 62 (2020): 257–72.

true forever. This statement indicates that things exist now which are unshakable and will remain. In the thought world of Hebrews, these must be things connected to the God who endures (1:11–12; 13:8), the Father, incarnate Son, and Holy Spirit. The audience is already in relationship with the one who can never be shaken and will dwell in God's heavenly Jerusalem that will last forever (13:14).

In fact, they are already getting a taste of the steadiness that is to come. The author says to them, *We are receiving an unshakable kingdom*. While this shaking is future, they are in the process of receiving that enduring kingdom right now. They are the recipients of this kingdom because they are connected to its King (1:8). As confessors of Christ, they can see him who will invite humanity to reign justly in their God-ordained place of glory and honor (2:6–9). That inbreaking of a future hope should determine their stance before God, expressed in gratitude. The author draws a connection: *therefore, because* they are receiving this kingdom, he urges: *let us have gratitude*. The word here is *charis*, often translated as "grace," but the focus here is what they offer to God. Because God is gracious (4:16) and has been gracious toward them, preeminently in Christ (2:9), they can be thankful in return. This gratitude is that *through which we worship God pleasingly with reverence and fear*. The posture of thanksgiving allows them to worship God by serving God in a pleasing way with respect and awe, as did Jesus (5:7). This is the worship they can perform because Jesus has purified their consciences (9:14). The word for *worship* reflects general praise of and service to God (Matt 4:10/Luke 4:8; Luke 2:37), but in the context of a sermon often focused on the sacrificial cult, this statement of the author portrays the congregation doing the kind of service that the priests do in God's tabernacle (Heb 8:5; 9:9; 10:2; 13:10), a ministerial participation under their High Priest. Their faith in Christ will allow them to please God (11:5), to worship and serve God in a pleasing way. Thankfully, it is God who empowers their ability to do this pleasing work. Given their situatedness in a setting that heaps disdain on their Lord (12:3), this pleasing work will be hard, and also, therefore, it will be rewarding work, which God graciously gives to them to do (13:21). They are to worship God through the Son and serve God with ethical living, as the next chapter will discuss in detail.[49]

49. Joshua Caleb Hutchens, "Christian Worship in Hebrews 12:28 as Ethical and Exclusive," *Journal of the Evangelical Theological Society* 59 (September 2016): 507–22.

The author's support for their gratefulness is the assertion that *our God is a consuming fire*. On its own this text may seem to elicit terror rather than gratitude, but in the context of the previous passage from Haggai, it becomes clear that God's consumption, just like God's shaking, is for human benefit. God consumes what prevents humans from full flourishing in relationship with God and others. Origen notes that to be close to the fiery God is to be fervent in faith; to be far away is "to have cooled in their affection for God and to have become cold."[50] In Deuteronomy 9 God's consuming fire comes against Israel's enemies, assuring the entrance into the land God has promised them. This phrase also appears in Deuteronomy 4, where God is the jealous God who will consume the idols and those who worship them, so that the temptation to find fulfillment in another deity will be removed. If there is a bitter stump springing up in their community (12:15), it will be a good thing if God removes that person's temptation toward unfaithfulness. Considering God's intense and good judgment, this community should serve God with *reverence and fear*. They should conduct themselves with respect for God's holiness. The sobriety of this closing assertion of ch. 12 is not that different from the theme near the beginning of the chapter that God is a disciplining God. It is God's promise to burn up the powers and principalities of sin, internal and external, so that only the refined, the unshakable, remains. This promise and the inbreaking of it through the kingdom of Christ should elicit great thanksgiving and active ministry. To the shape of that ministry in their lives the author now turns.

50. Origen, *On First Principles* 2.8.3 (*ANF* 4:287–88).

HEBREWS 13:1–25

LIVING FAITHFULLY

The author has cast a vision for his community. They are on a long and arduous race (12:1–14), which puts them at the base of the mountain of God (12:22–24). As they exist in that space, he is calling them to stay attentive to God's voice and to worshipfully serve God with gratitude (12:25–28). It is certainly God's voice he wants them to hear, but he has been the one God has chosen to facilitate divine communication to this community, passing it on with his creative and compelling authorial shaping. God is the one who is speaking (12:25), but they hear God through this author's sermon.

The first section of this closing chapter (vv. 1–6) provides recommendations of specific actions to live out what they've heard. Much like his calls for continued communal gathering and relational investment (10:25; 3:13), in this closing section the author calls attention to their relationships: with insiders, outsiders, and possessions.

When he discusses their relationship with their leadership (vv. 7–17), he returns to the imagery of sacrifice so prominent throughout the sermon. They are all cast in a priestly role as those who offer the right kinds of sacrifices, patterning off the worshipful attitude of the believers who have preceded them.

The final section (vv. 18–25) reminds readers that this work is a sermon but that it had to be sent as a letter. It includes many of the common features of epistles: a prayer wish and travel plans (vv. 18–19, 23), a benediction (v. 20–21), greetings (v. 24), and a final wish (v. 25). Here the author names this work as a "word of exhortation," with which he asks them to bear (v. 22). His admission suggests that he realizes that his sermon will take fortitude—endurance to listen and even more commitment to follow what listeners hear. If they are willing to make the investment, they will receive the blessing.

The beginning and end of this work called Hebrews are rhetorically imbalanced. What began with a bang ends with a whimper. There are good reasons for this disparity. First, the epistolary ending is added simply because this author cannot be present to deliver the sermon to the community about whom he cares so deeply (vv. 18–19). Second, the practical and yet deeply theological last chapter leaves the reader not gaping in awe at the rhetoric of this talented writer, but instead empowered to go out and live faithfully. They are left with grace so that they can continue to follow their priestly pioneer on the way to God (v. 25).

13:1–6 · PRACTICAL INSTRUCTIONS FOR OUTSIDERS

[1]*Let love for siblings continue.* [2]*Do not forget love of the stranger; through this practice some, while welcoming angels as guests, did so unaware.* [3]*Remember prisoners as fellow prisoners and those who have suffered evil as also you yourselves are in a body.* [4]*Marriage is to be honorable among all of you, and the marriage bed is to be undefiled, for the fornicator and the adulterer God will judge.* [5]*Your conduct of life is to be free from the love of money; be ones who are content with your possessions. For he himself has said, "Never will I leave you; neither will I ever abandon you,"* [6]*with the result that we can say boldly, "The Lord is a helper to me. I will not fear. What can a person do to me?"*

As God consumes the unseemly things for those who are receiving the unshakable kingdom, that which is left is an ethic of pleasing worship, manifest in serving God and serving others (12:28–29). The rapid-fire admonitions at the beginning of ch. 13 provide some specifics of that ethic at work. Moreover, they give shape to the ethic of faithfulness proclaimed from Habakkuk—in short, that faith is lived-out righteousness that endures (Heb 10:38). Each of the instructions in vv. 1–5 offer pearls of wisdom on their own, but as a unit that culminates in a dialogue between God and the believer (v. 6), they advocate most clearly for faithful living in a time of threat.

Multiple times the author of this sermon has lifted up the necessity of community for the Christian life—from ch. 3, where they can fight even the sin of apostasy by encouraging one another (3:12–13), to ch. 10, where he explicitly prohibits them from not gathering together (10:25), to chs. 11 and 12, where he unites this beleaguered congregation with the honored faithful of Israel's past as one family near the presence of God.

Here at the close, he commands them concerning community once more. *Let love for siblings continue. Continue* (from *menō*, "remain/abide") is an imperative verb, employed so that they will maintain kindred love (*philanthrōpia*).[1] As their High Priest abides (7:3, 24) and their inheritance will last (10:34; 12:27), he urges them to remain steadfast in their commitment to each other. As Chrysostom perceptively noted, they had been doing so, so the author encouragingly reminds them to continue: "See how he enjoins them to persevere what they had. He does not add other things. He does not say 'be loving' . . . but 'let love continue.'"[2] The members of this community who originally received this sermon were not all of the same blood family (how much more so now that the sermon's audience has embraced all parts of the world), but now as Jesus has called them siblings (2:10), they can address each other as such (3:1) and also live for each other in the same intimate and supportive way. Hebrews provides no examples of infighting in the community, but being a human provides enough evidence that this command is not always easy to keep. The addressees have not been left without aid, however. Jesus's fraternal embrace (2:11–12) provides both the example and the holy space in which real love between Christian siblings can happen. The most tangible manifestation of this love in Hebrews is encouragement. It is what the author offers to them in his sermon (13:22), and in so doing, he clarifies that the encouragement he has in mind is not simple niceties but involves honest, carefully crafted words and faithful actions that promote the continuation of learning about God so that everyone can more maturely live as God's loving people. The power of this admonition is well captured in petitions written by enslaved Africans in America. In a time in which both master and slave could claim to be Christians, they asked how "brotherly love" could "coexist with the wretched practice of slavery." Hebrews' call for love and the practice of injustice, these enslaved Africans contended, were simply incommensurate with each other.[3] The author of Hebrews' admonition for the continuation of sibling love is not a platitude

1. Kevin B. McCruden traces the prominence of *philanthropia* in the ancient world in *Solidarity Perfected: Beneficent Christology in the Epistle to the Hebrews* (New York: de Gruyter, 2008), 70–97.

2. Chrysostom, *Hebrews* 33.1 (*NPNF*[1] 14:514).

3. Bowens, *African American Readings of Paul*, 26.

but a statement that demands action, often action that will be considered radical given the deep brokenness of our world.

With similar language and equal verve, the author immediately urges them to love those outside their circles as well: *Do not forget love of the stranger.* Instead of the language of what they should do, namely abide/continue, in this instruction he approaches the topic from the negative: Don't forget! It is vital to see, yet again, that his anthropological admonition has already been firmly grounded in his theological affirmation: God will not forget them (6:10), and they should not forget God's encouragement to them (12:5). God's faithfulness yet again provides the bulwark for their own. It serves also as a balance. It might be easy for all readers of Hebrews, initially and throughout time, to become so busy loving one's family (nuclear or ecclesial) that it becomes tempting to forget the stranger. God's love, however, which Christians should emulate, is both internal and external, exchanged between the divine persons and also sent out to creation. While humans cannot perfectly imitate the Triune love, we can, as the body of Christ, stay on mission to make sure we are both inward- and outward-facing.

Their posture of love toward the stranger is born out of empathy because membership in this family means viewing oneself as a stranger on the earth (11:13) moving toward a heavenly country (12:22–24). Every Christian, really, lives as a stranger, and so loving someone you do not know is made easier by the reminder that you share the same mode of existence on earth. For early Christians, this would have looked like welcoming traveling teachers or displaced believers. Early on instructions developed for them to discern friend from foe (3 John; Didache 6, 11, 12), but whether a person was welcomed in or kept outside (because they bore false teaching), the motivation was love. For contemporary Christians, the realities are no less complex. Discernment and costly compassion are necessary. Welcoming the stranger will often be a political act with attendant difficulty.[4]

In the second phrase of v. 2, the author offers another motivation for stranger love: *through this practice some, while welcoming angels as guests, did so unaware.* Some who have not forgotten to love the unfamiliar have, without realizing it, entertained angels. The author has several plays on words here.

4. Alfred R. Brunson and Christopher Magezi, "Fostering Embracement, Inclusion and Integration of Migrants in Complex Migration Situations: A Perspective from Matthew 25:31–46 and Hebrews 13:1–2," *Hervormde teologiese studies* 76 (2020): 1–10.

Both "guest" and "welcome" come from *xenos*, the term for foreigner, and "do not forget" at the beginning of v. 2 is echoed by what the King James puts eloquently as "unawares" at the end of v. 2, as both words are built on the same verb (*lanthanō*). Because the author believes that angels are sent by God to minister to the saints, who are journeying on their way to their inheritance (1:14), it is certainly possible that he imagines an angelic visitor could come to them. This is familiar territory for readers of Israel's Scriptures (Gen 18) and is reported as an occurrence for people in the New Testament era as well (Matt 1; Luke 1). Readers can also hear this statement as evidence of the glorious reality of all humans, who someday, having been redeemed, as Jesus promised, will be like the angels (Matt 22:30). C. S. Lewis notes we might be tempted to worship humans if we could see what each of us will become.[5] Thinking about the stranger in that way results in the increased motivation to welcome them.

Empathy again provides the posture from which to respond in v. **3** when the author encourages action for those who are in prison and those who are being ill-treated. *Remember prisoners as fellow prisoners and those who have suffered evil as also you yourselves are in a body.* He applies the golden rule, "Do to others . . ." (Luke 6:31), by urging them to respond to those who are in prison, imagining what it would be like to be in prison and also imagining what bodily suffering would feel like. It is possible such a situation is not outside the limits of their imagination; they might simply need to recall their past. His statements affirm what he spoke about in ch. 10, that some difficult days of the community lie behind them; they previously suffered with those in prison and had their belongings taken (10:34). It is also true that difficult days may lie ahead of them; they may face death (12:4). In the current time, instead of growing weary (5:11–13), they should continue to serve the suffering among their group. The author's short statement about the body focuses on actual bodily suffering but also allows a canonical connection with Paul's use of the body metaphor (Rom 12; 1 Cor 12). As they are united by the self-offering of Jesus's body (Heb 10:5, 10), they are all members of him and connected to one another.

5. "It is a serious thing to live in a society of possible gods and goddesses, to remember that the dullest and most uninteresting person you can talk to may one day be a creature which, if you saw it now, you would be strongly tempted to worship, or else a horror and a corruption such as you now meet, if at all, only in a nightmare." C. S. Lewis, *The Weight of Glory: And Other Addresses* (New York: HarperCollins, 2000), 45.

It is much harder to remember those who are suffering when you are not. It takes the jolt of a reminder, and the sermon provides this to more comfortable readers. The call to remember the prisoners and the suffering is a reminder to practice compassion consistently. Frederick Douglass saw the power of this statement when he used it to call Christians to be in solidarity with slaves.[6] Because slavery, unjust mass incarceration, persecution, and bodily oppression still exist, faithful readers of Hebrews do well to partner with other believers who have made following this admonition their vocation.[7]

If the first three admonitions pull readers' hearts toward compassion, the next stokes family values. With brevity and unmistakable clarity, the author affirms the sanctity of marriage. *Marriage is to be honorable among all of you, and the marriage bed is to be undefiled.* Among the readers of Hebrews, this bond should be honorable and undefiled. If this community, like some other early Christians (1 Cor 7:1; 1 Tim 4:3), have ascetics in their midst, they hear from the author an affirmation of marriage. To be married is an honor. It is not a command for all but a gift for some (1 Cor 7:7), and in its expression among Christians it is worthy of valuing (Eph 5:21–31). Coitus (the word used for *marriage bed* here, a cognate directly from the Greek) is not a defiling act. At the same time, the author's statements rein in those who enjoy the benefits of marriage outside its safe bounds. The following admonition supports this: If anyone fornicates or commits adultery, *God will judge* that person. As the author appealed to the tradition that Esau was a fornicator and warned against following his example (12:16), here faithfulness to God is manifest in faithfulness to one's spouse.

Not unlike the clear-cut verse about the necessity of gathering with Christians, this verse offers a clear starting place for those wondering about the Scripture's teachings on sex. It has not been common to champion adultery, to transgress a promise already made, so that instruction from Hebrews meets little confusion or disagreement. The differentiation of *moichous* (adultery) from *porneai* (general fornication) indicates that the author has other transgressions in view as well. It seems that any sex outside the marriage covenant is worthy of

6. See Bowens, *African American Readings of Paul*, 116.

7. For example, International Justice Mission seeks to free people from modern-day slavery and sex trafficking. "Trafficking and Slavery," IJM, accessed April 30, 2023, https://www.ijm.org/our-work/trafficking-slavery.

divine judgment. God forgives and restores in powerful and miraculous ways because of what Christ has done to defeat the damaging power of sin, but the author makes this statement so that his readers know that it would be better to avoid the negative consequences in the first place. This is not because God is a killjoy but because marriage is a valuable thing, and sex within marriage is one of the blessings from God. Christian communities are ideal places to form members who carry the assurance of their inherent inestimable value as image bearers of God and children in God's household (3:6). Knowing that value of self and others can result in a healthy view of humans as sexual beings and a celebratory vision of human sexuality expressed in the covenant of marriage, is one of the high callings for Christ confessors, the other high calling being that of celibacy (see 1 Cor 7:1–7). It would be a misapplication of this verse to honor marriage to the detriment of the call to celibacy or to inordinately shame those who have not honored the marriage bed. This is one among many possible transgressions and, through the effective work of Christ, is a candidate for God's forgiveness and healing like any other transgression. Hebrews' simple statement affirms the good of marriage and the good of fidelity, before and during marriage.

The final instruction in the paragraph concerns a similarly personal and potentially uncomfortable topic: money. *Your conduct of life is to be free from the love of money.* This is not only a freedom from greed but also a call to be free from the love of comfort. For the first community, their confession of Christ would have put them into economic danger. Readers of Hebrews who do not exist in situations of crisis are called to consider unshackling themselves from systems that sell comfort as "convenience." As Paul says in 1 Timothy 6:10, the love of money results in a wandering from the faith. Hebrews invites those living in communities where persecution of Christians is not prominent and subsistence living is not a reality to consider the structures of society that are "normal," and whether it is fitting as a follower of Christ to participate in them. Benefiting from the exploitation of God's creation, children, or the poor is to love money more than being faithful.[8]

Comfort, like power, adores a vacuum, so in the place of its absence the author recommends that they fill themselves with contentment: *be ones who*

8. Emily Hunter McGowin, "The End of the Christian Family: Repentance, Renewal, and Resistance" (presentation, Center for Pastor Theologians Conference, "Reconstructing Evangelicalism," Oak Park, IL, October 24–26, 2022).

are content with your possessions. They should be people who are content with whatever God allows them to have. The author of Hebrews affirms the value of simplicity here, but not for its aesthetic. Instead, the kind of simplicity for which he advocates demonstrates dependence on God. All readers should be content with whatever they have been given because their greatest "possession" is God. Christian contentment is born out of the divine proclamation: *For he himself has said, "Never will I leave you; neither will I ever abandon you."*

These words appear as a promise spoken by Moses to the people of Israel and to Joshua specifically (Deut 31:6) and by David to his son Solomon (1 Chr 28:20). In both instances the speaker keeps the statement in the third person about God. In Hebrews' citation, however, the author presents the verbs so that God is speaking directly to the audience, much like God spoke similar words directly to Joshua (Josh 1:5). The written word has become living speech to this listening community. Whatever they have or do not have pales in comparison to the unending and eternal promise of God's presence. The eternality of it reminds them of the priest who is always living to intercede for them (Heb 7:25) until they finish the race (12:1). He is ahead of them, but with them as well. This opens up the potential for multivalence in the precise divine person speaking the text, be it the Father, Son, or Spirit.[9] Because God is with them, even if everything they have is taken, they will truly lack for nothing. For readers whose choice is between necessities and faithfulness, as it was for the original audience of Hebrews, this portion of the sermon offers a direct encouragement.

For those readers who do not face such a difficult choice, the admonition still offers a direct challenge. Loving the comfort gained through sufficient funds is a temptation. The siren song of wealth is tantalizing in times of ease for those who already have enough, to puff themselves up through greed, but wealth also calls to those who have little, fanning the flames of their bitterness as well as their jealousy. Being free from this dependence on wealth, and instead being utterly dependent on God, should characterize confessors' lives in all times and places. Augustine commented beautifully on this verse, "So keep a moderate amount of money for temporal uses; treat it as journey

9. As interpreted by Madison Pierce as well. Heb 13:5 is part of a section where the author employs a "more unified discussion of God," where "Father, Son, and Spirit—all those identified as 'God' in the discourse—speak. . . . The author takes a designation that could refer to all three and portrays them speaking with one voice." Pierce, *Divine Discourse*, 195–96.

money."[10] Money is a thing that gets a person from point A to point B in this race of faith, a comparably very temporary form of existence. If someone has more than they need, then the earlier admonitions supply the answer: give to the sibling, the stranger, and the suffering. The challenge, especially for Christ followers in affluent areas, is to discern correctly what one actually needs.

Then for the first time in the sermon, the audience gets a chance to voice the scriptural spoken word. God's statement of continual presence leads to the *result that we can say boldly, "The Lord is a helper to me. I will not fear. What can a person do to me?"* Knowing that God is with them, the author and his listeners can now speak with boldness. He has not used this word (*tharreō*) or any of its cognates yet, but the theme of boldness has flowed throughout the letter, inviting them to hold their place in God's family with confidence and proceed sure-footedly into God's presence (3:6; 4:16; 10:19, 35). Now with that emotion, they speak Psalm 117:6 LXX. An apt psalm for a persecuted people celebrating God's deliverance from enemies, it may have been familiar to the author because it appears in the Christian narrative of Jesus's triumphal entry. The people shout the phrase "Blessed is he who comes in the name of the Lord" from Psalm 117:26 LXX. It also appears in several Christian authors (Luke 20:17; Acts 4:11; 1 Pet 2:4, 7) to speak of the rejected stone becoming the cornerstone (Ps 117:22 LXX). It begins and ends with the refrain "His mercy endures forever."

What an interesting nuance has taken place in this author's portrayal of God. To be close to the Lord is no longer a cause for fear, as was the case at Sinai (Heb 12:18–21), but instead the reason for its amelioration. Not that God has changed, but the people in relationship with him have, just as their experience of God before Mount Zion (12:22–24) is different from the experience of God before Sinai (12:18–21). The theological foundation of the sermon has been to strengthen their trust in God's faithfulness (as made explicit in 10:23). The author now gives them words to voice their trust in God's trustworthiness. Someone running away displays a horror for God, but someone tethered to God not only has no reason to be afraid of God but also has no reason to fear anyone. Conversely, if someone runs away from God, not only will God be just to punish sin, but God also offers no sovereign protection from one's enemies. Denying an unpopular God may decrease human foes, but the powerful and popular often prove to be fickle friends. It is infinitely better to

10. Augustine, *Sermons* 177.3 (ACCS 10:231).

maintain a costly confession in the unchanging (13:8), completely sovereign and good God.

The five admonitions listed here concerning in-group love, out-of-group hospitality, care for the imprisoned and suffering, marriage, and, finally, money and possessions may seem like disconnected ethical admonitions, but in the setting of this community, they each make sense in light of a situation of persecution, even if it is not as pressing as it once was in the past or might be in the future for them. With a threat in view, they would especially need the support of each other. They might need to welcome in previously unknown Christians who are fleeing from persecution in their own areas. Remembering the imprisoned and oppressed makes complete sense in this setting, as does the encouragement to be satisfied with their possessions, particularly if some of them had been taken away. The elevation of marriage is the most difficult to fit into the schema, but since some religious practices of the day involved sexually promiscuous activities, their refusal to participate in those any longer could result in some of the opposition against them from their neighbors.

For contemporary readers not impacted by persecution directly, the string that might tie them together becomes less taut, but we can hear the admonitions more or less loudly depending on the particular nature of our own temptations. That is not to say the admonitions in this section are presented as a buffet, leaving us free to take some and ignore the others. We are always called to love everyone, care in heart and deed, as well as keep ourselves pure from lust and greed. An ethic so comprehensive could not operate from a place of fear but could only arise from a robust sense of trust in God's ample provision and abiding presence.

13:7–19 · FOLLOWING THE LEADER

7 Remember your leaders who spoke the word of God to you; as you consider the
outcome of their life, imitate their faith. 8 Jesus the Messiah is the same yesterday and
today and forever. 9 Do not be transported by various, even strange, teachings, for it
is good for the heart to be strengthened by grace, not foods, which offer no benefit to
those who live by them. 10 We have an altar from which those who serve in the tent
do not have authority to eat. 11 For the blood from animals is brought into the holy
place for sin through [the action of] the high priest; the bodies of those are consumed

outside the camp. [12]*Therefore, also Jesus, in order that he might sanctify the people through his own blood, suffered outside the gate.* [13]*Therefore, let us go out to him outside the camp, bearing his shame.* [14]*For we do not have here an abiding city, but we are seeking that which is to come.* [15]*Therefore, through him, let us offer up a sacrifice of praise to God through all things—that is, fruit of lips confessing his name.* [16]*And do not forget good deeds and sharing, for with these sacrifices God is pleased.* [17]*Trust your leaders and yield to them, for they keep watch over your souls as those who will give an account, so that they may do this with joy and not groaning, for this is not to your advantage.*

[18]*Pray for us, for we are convinced that we have a good conscience, wanting to live in all things well.* [19]*But I encourage you even more to do this, in order that I might be restored to you quickly.*

This portion of the final chapter of Hebrews begins and ends with comments on leaders (including the author himself in vv. 18–19). In the center, the author lifts up Jesus as the leader par excellence. He alone is constant. Moreover, he does not ask his followers, those entrusted with the care of others and those who are being cared for, to do anything he has not already done; instead, he leads by example. He is present with them in the hardship of whatever they face. Moreover, he has guaranteed their victorious completion of the race of faith because he is there too at the end of their wilderness journey. If their human leaders fail them, they have an unchanging leader who never will.

Although the admonition in v. 7 continues practical instructions for how to listen to God's voice and respond faithfully, it does makes sense as the start of a new paragraph. It is the first entry of a chiasm whose match appears in v. 17. Both statements focus on leaders. At the same time, v. 7 builds on what comes before it; it is another admonition and like the second and third (vv. 2 and 3) it uses the modality of memory. This time the author urges his listeners to *remember their leaders*. He uses the same term for leaders in vv. 7, 17, and 24. This is a different way of speaking of leadership than that which appears in the letters of Timothy and Titus, where the leaders are described as overseers, elders, and deacons (Titus 1; 1 Tim 3, 5). For Hebrews, to describe those entrusted with the care of the community as those who lead (the word he uses is related to the verb *agō*) connects to Jesus, who is their chief leader (*archēgos* 2:10; 12:2). Following their human leaders is made all the easier when they know that those people are also following Jesus. And although they have these human leaders to follow and respect, they also have direct access to Jesus himself.

The fitting way to remember them is to *consider the outcome of their life*, to pay close attention to the arc of these leaders' lives, up to the very end. The author's admonition to *consider* has a visual component: they can look at or examine their lives because they knew them. It is clear that these are leaders who have passed away, underlining the fact that this community has been in existence for some time (5:12). The goal of remembering and contemplating the lives of their former leaders is action. They should reflect so that they can *imitate their faith*. The leaders ended their race successfully, without growing weary or falling away (12:3). They show that completion of the race of faith is possible by offering a memorable example, with whom they were acquainted in the flesh. Although they serve as an example of those the author had encouraged his listeners to imitate, people who inherited God's promises through faith and patience like Abraham (6:12), these leaders whom the community members knew personally grant a more intimate connection than the faithful of Israel's ancient past.

These people are designated as leaders by the author because they *spoke the word of God*. Like the author of this sermon, they have facilitated the word of God being communicated directly to the people (12:25). Since the speech of God for this author has come only as the words of the Scriptures of Israel, it seems most consistent to believe that these leaders also would have used Israel's Scripture as the foundation of their speaking. Surely, they did more than read written texts, however. Much like this author, they likely also reflected on the texts in light of their confession of Jesus as the Son of God and communicated lessons that met the needs of the congregation at that time. Because God is now speaking in the Son (1:2), those who speak the word of God speak of the Son. They proclaim God's faithfulness in the Son as made evident by God's promises through the prophets. They have participated in the revelation of the Son by facilitating others' ability to hear God speaking. What an amazing task fell to these leaders. It is the same high calling and immense blessing that falls on all those who proclaim God's word to others throughout time.

The transitory nature of their leaders, who, not unlike priests, are prevented from remaining by death (7:23), contrasts with *Jesus the Messiah* who *is the same yesterday and today and forever.* Jesus spoke to and through these leaders, helped them reach the end, and will do the same for those who remain behind. The simplicity and breadth of this statement make it easy for it to become a phrase that stands on its own. Contemporary readers may be quite familiar with this sentence even if they would struggle to identify its context. The lifting up of this sentence alone goes all the way back to the manuscript tradition. Uncial D, which has a tendency toward expansion, adds a concluding "amen" after this sentence, indicating that some had come to view it as a phrase worthy of use in a liturgical setting. For a letter that emphasizes Jesus's eternality, existing before creation and after its shaking (Heb 1:3, 11–12), this sentence summarizes in brief much of the christological work of the letter. To affirm that Jesus the Messiah is the same today and will be forever makes good sense. Once resurrected, he will reign forever with God (1:8), for God has proclaimed him to be priest forever (5:6; 6:20; 7:17, 21, 24, 28).

The mention of the past with the inclusion of the term *yesterday* provides the more challenging affirmation. The Son would not have taken on the name of Jesus until he took on flesh and blood from Mary (2:14) and did not complete his actions to become the reigning Messiah until his death, resurrection, and ascension. The inclusion of *yesterday* discloses that the powerful phrase demands a nuanced interpretation. For early interpreters of this text, the statement affirmed that he does not experience "any change in his divinity by reason of his incarnation, but remain[s] what he was and will always be."[11] Christ's eternal consistency affirmed that God's ability to work wonders endures.[12] The work of the Son is always *pro nobis*, for the sake of humanity. Hence it is fitting that Reformation interpreter Johannes Oecolampadius sees this statement as an affirmation of God's mercy: "Surely if [God's] kindness were to cease, he would stop being God."[13] This author was able to affirm those changes of incarnation, death, resurrection, and ascension for the Son alongside his unchangeability. This community now knows that the Messiah is the same one who is the eternal radiance of God (1:3). It seems fair to say that the author of Hebrews' affirmation of Jesus the Messiah's pretemporal consistency affirms that the plan for the Son to become human was ever a part of God's plan (fruitful co-texts include Eph 1:4; Rom 8:29).[14]

The faithful consistency of both Jesus and the community's deceased leaders transitions to an admonition that they should be consistent with regard to

11. Cyril of Alexandria, *Easter Homily* 1.6 (ACCS 10:233).

12. Chrysostom, *Hebrews*, 33.6 (*NPNF*[1] 14:517).

13. Explanation of Heb 13:8 in RCS 13:191.

14. For a discussion of "incarnation anyway," that the Son would have become human even without the fall into sin, see Cortez, *ReSourcing Theological Anthropology*, 85–97.

the teachings they entertain. The author urges them, *Do not be transported by various, even strange, teachings.* "Various" can simply indicate different kinds (Matt 4:24; Mark 1:34; Luke 4:40; Heb 2:4), but it can also take on a negative connotation of a dizzying array of options, the opposite of the singularity and simplicity of truth (2 Tim 3:6; Titus 3:3). While just a few verses earlier the author urged the welcoming of strangers, now he urges the rejection of strange teachings. They have heard and experienced the truth from this author and those who spoke the word of God to them until these leaders had finished their lives well. Now, the community should not welcome anything that is not consistent with what they have already heard and confessed about God's revelation of promises kept in Christ. If they entertain any inconsistent teachings, they might be carried away or *transported* off by them. This passive verb conveys the sense that ideas with which someone might imagine they can safely dabble sometimes become the master, taking the person to places they never intended to go.

Readers outside this original community do not stay in the dark about the nature of these teachings; the next statement indicates that they involve food, as so many disturbances in the early church did (Gal 2:11–13; 1 Cor 8–10; Rom 14–15). When he reminds them that *it is good for the heart to be strengthened by grace, not foods, which offer no benefit to those who live by them*, he reaffirms his ongoing concern for the internal, not unlike the statements of Jesus and Paul, who elevate heart and healthy community over precise forms of consumption (Mark 7:15/Matt 15:11; Gal 2:11–13; 1 Cor 6:13; 8:8; 1 Tim 4:3). The author is building on his concern for the heart raised in Psalm 94 LXX and Jeremiah 38 LXX (Heb 3:8, 10, 12, 15; 4:7, 12; 8:10; 10:16, 22) as well as his calls for strengthening of the heart (3:14; 6:19). They find this grace as they approach God through Jesus their Messiah and High Priest (4:16). His critique against the efficacy of foods is reminiscent of his statement about the Levitical priesthood, which deals with the external and was meant to be temporary (9:10).

In contrast with food that offers no benefit, the author claims, *We have an altar from which those who serve in the tent do not have authority to eat.* In such a food-focused section, one might imagine that the author is contrasting different people's ability to consume certain foods. They have an altar from which they can eat, as the priests ate the food that was sacrificed to God, and there are others who serve the tent who cannot eat that food.

For several reasons, actual food seems not to be in view here. First, in the New Testament the altar is either the altar in the temple or the altar in heaven.

Paul knows of the altars of the gods of the gentiles (1 Cor 9:13), and while this more localized idea of an altar could lend support to a eucharistic interpretation, that does not seem to be a connection made by Christians (altar and Lord's Supper) until later eras.[15] The author had just stated that hearts should be strengthened by grace, not by food, and because the Eucharist can have an immaterial impact of strengthening, that is another reason that the meal commanded by the Lord (1 Cor 11:23–26) does not seem to be in view. Moreover, in the next verses—linked to this statement by a connecting *therefore*—the author talks about a sacrifice that has no meat consumption, the Yom Kippur sin offering. It seems most likely that in v. 10 he is referring to food in a metaphorical or spiritual way. Those who serve the tent cannot eat from this altar because *no one* can actually eat from this altar. Food is not procured here, but inner strengthening is. The faithful of this community do not receive food from this altar, but they receive something no less real.

What kind of spiritual food they receive becomes clearer as the author moves to a comparison between Jesus and the Day of Atonement ritual. *For the blood from animals is brought into the holy place for sin through [the action of] the high priest; the bodies of those are consumed outside the camp.* The author explains some of what happens on the Day of Atonement in this verse. The blood of the bull and the goat is brought into the holy place by the high priest for himself and for the people of Israel. Then the bodies of these animals are totally consumed by fire outside the camp (Lev 16, esp. vv. 15, 27). There is no part of the sacrifice for the priests to eat. Then the author draws the comparison with Jesus: *Therefore, also Jesus, in order that he might sanctify the people through his own blood, suffered outside the gate.* Jesus is similar to the Yom Kippur offering in that his blood purifies sins and thereby sanctifies the people (2:11; 10:10, 14, 29). In addition, he, too, is removed to an "outside" place, in his shameful death on the cross (12:2).

The comparison is similar but not exact. The author imagines Jesus, like the priests, doing actions both outside and inside God's holy space. Moreover, his action in both locations involves blood, which is procured through death. On the other hand, his body is not burned like the animals but crucified, and this takes place for him outside the city gates, not outside the camp. Another

15. Koester notes that the association between Eucharist and altars does not arise until the second century (*Hebrews*, 569).

difference is that while the priest offers the blood of the animal first and then burns the body outside the camp, Jesus suffers bodily outside the gate first and then offers his blood before God's throne.[16] The comparison is a loose one rather than forced into a one-to-one correspondence. The sacrificial system provided the template to interpret what God would do through the messianic High Priest, Jesus. He fulfilled those previews in a way that made sense in the time and way in which he came.

From this comparison with the ritual, the author's admonition to his readers is this: *Therefore, let us go out to him outside the camp, bearing his shame.* This admonition for movement fits perfectly with his frequent calls to proceed toward God's rest (4:1–11), God's throne (4:16), God (7:25), the holy place (10:22), and Mount Zion (12:22). This final call is a reminder that to move toward God is often to move into shame. Jesus is no longer outside the city walls, as he is seated at the right hand of God (Ps 109:1 LXX in Heb 1:3, 13; 8:1; 10:12; 12:2), but just as Moses bore the shame of Christ before his coming (11:25), this audience is called to do so after his ascension. The author returns to the language of the Yom Kippur ritual, *outside the camp*. As the bodies of the animals were burned outside the camp, this is a call for Jesus's followers to be willing to sacrifice everything, to have God consume all that needs to be consumed of their lives (12:29) so that they are left solid and pure. Moses, who was willing to embrace the shame of Christ (11:26), met the presence of God in this space outside the camp (Exod 33:1–7).[17] The readers of Hebrews can expect to do the same, the difference being they will no longer hear the voice of God in the burning bush but will see the Son of God reigning and crowned.

The call to bear the shame would have immense weight in a society built on honor and shame.[18] They are called to be faithful to Christ even if that costs them standing and success in their families and communities. Christians throughout time have known this call could result in martyrdom, and knew that those who were gathered on God's mountain (12:23) included those witnesses (*martyres* in Greek) who had been martyred (see also Rev 6:9–11). All readers can hear this as a call to be willing to die if necessary, especially pertinent in areas where persecu-

16. Chrysostom states, "[He suffered] without, but His Blood was borne up into Heaven." *Hebrews* 33.7 (*NPNF*[1] 14:517).

17. DeSilva, *Perseverance in Gratitude*, 501–2.

18. For a discussion of this theme, see David A. deSilva, *Honor, Patronage, Kinship, and Purity: Unlocking New Testament Culture*, 2nd ed. (Downers Grove, IL: IVP Academic, 2022).

tion is still a reality.[19] Jennifer Kaalund also suggests that this motif is generative for later communities who have to find meaning in their status as outsiders: "Placing bodies outside the camp imbues them with meaning. Outside the gates, bodies are purified and perfect, and it is there that they can await entry into the new city prepared for them by God. Jesus' body provides the example."[20]

Given the themes with which the author is working in vv. 11–13, it seems that their altar named in v. 10 does not offer the benefit of food, be that priestly meals or even eucharistic bread and wine. More likely their altar offers the benefit of grace given to the heart while suffering for the sake of Christ. The altar that strengthens their hearts is the suffering of their Lord and their inclusion in it. Those who serve the tent, whomever the author has in mind, be it those associated with the Jewish cult in the past or his present or non-Jewish governmental leaders who are oppressing them,[21] do not have authority to eat from this altar. Whereas such groups had authority in the past and in the present, around this altar that authority is inconsequential. The author points to the reality that such leaders may not be willing to bear the reproach of following Christ outside the camp and therefore receive the strengthening that comes from the one whose body and blood, whose whole self, is completely given on the heavenly altar. Conversely, those who are willing to embrace the shame of Christ will be able to "eat" from this altar to their heart's content.

The embrace of societal disdain encourages the audience to maintain a loose hold on their current residence. *For we do not have here an abiding city, but we are seeking that which is to come.* Wherever *here* might be for the author and his addressees, he asserts that the world as they currently know it does not offer an abiding city for them. Scholars have made different suggestions for the specific city the author has in view, with Rome and Jerusalem as plausible options.[22] The readers have learned through experi-

19. Mi Sun Kim, "What Is the Meaning of the Book of Hebrews' Call to 'Suffer Outside the Camp' Both Then and Now?," *Journal of Korean Christian Theology* 97 (2015): 127–45.

20. Jennifer Kaalund, *Reading Hebrews and 1 Peter with the African American Great Migration* (London: T&T Clark, 2019), 104.

21. Koester explains this reading: "Hebrews identifies the tent not so much with the Law as with the 'camp,' that is, the earthly 'city' in which Jesus' followers are denounced (13:13–14)" (*Hebrews*, 569–70).

22. Jason A. Whitlark, "'Here We Do Not Have a City That Remains': A Figured Critique of Roman Imperial Propaganda in Hebrews 13:14," *JBL* 131.1 (2012): 161–79.

ence (10:34) and the teaching of the author (12:27) that many things around them do not last. Given that impermanence, wherever they might be now, they should have their eyes on that which they are seeking, the coming city. The futurity of this city connects to the coming world, of which the author spoke in 2:5, and the age to come, from where the power of God derives (6:5). The author does not say they *should* seek the coming city but that they already are. This might be a way of positively encouraging them, seeing the best in their actions, even if they also have shortfalls. The author has seen, however, tangible evidence of their faith (6:9–10; 10:25, 32–34; 13:1), and so he is right to claim that they are doing the faithful action of seeking this city. Just like their forebears, they are aliens and strangers looking forward to God's city (11:14). There, instead of being shamed and killed on the outskirts of the city, Christ reigns supreme in the midst of it. The promise of arriving at that city in the future gives them hope that helps them endure the suffering they are presently experiencing.

In the next verse, the author's focus pivots. Instead of their receiving something from the altar, here he instructs them to offer something up. *Therefore, through him, let us offer up a sacrifice of praise to God through all things—that is, fruit of lips confessing his name.* They present this offering through him, the same one who suffered outside the gate is now the one sitting at God's right hand. With the language of *offer up* and *sacrifice* the author casts them all as the priests who take the offering, serving under the leadership of the High Priest. Because he was willing to sacrifice himself, they are fit to present a sacrifice to God. In a particularly moving moment in the Eucharistic Prayer B in the *Book of Common Prayer* service, the priest prayerfully proclaims for the congregation that God in Christ has "delivered us from evil, and made us worthy to stand before you." In line with other Scriptures of Israel and other Jewish interpreters, Hebrews democratizes the acts of the priesthood to embrace all.[23] For any who had not been invited to represent the people, anyone who was not a Levitical Jewish male, this is a deeply meaningful invitation.

That which they all offer is a sacrifice *of praise*; the *fruit* is *lips confessing his name*. The author is asking for a vocal answer from them in response to a God who speaks. This statement unites with the author's frequent assertions concerning the importance of confession. This confession is that to which

23. Peeler, "'Leading Many Sons to Glory,'" 844.

thea should hold fast (4:14). It is a confession of Jesus as the one sent from God who represents them before God as their High Priest (3:1). The focus of their confession is the chief demonstration of God's faithfulness (10:23). As they confess his name, the name of Jesus, the Messiah, the Son of God, this is praise to God, a praise they join in with the faithful of the past (11:13). This could be the confession of lips in praise in the assembly or the confession of lips boldly and with risk proclaiming the name of Jesus in the marketplace. Chrysostom notes that this praise is always fitting; it should happen in times of poverty, sickness, false accusation, and affliction.[24] Confessing his name is to claim the status of "outsider" in their current setting (11:13).

To the act of uttering words, the author adds deeds. *And do not forget good deeds and sharing.* He uses the same admonition against forgetfulness that he did in 13:2. Moreover, good deeds and sharing remind readers of those instructions at the beginning of the chapter. He is saying again to keep in mind how they treat others, both inside and outside the Christian family, by responding to those who have need. *For with these sacrifices*, not directly to God, but to God through others, *God is pleased.* The author stated earlier that it is impossible to please God without faith (11:6). Here it becomes clear that the kind of faith he speaks about results in actions—actions of worship, proclamation, and service.

As a bookend to this section, the author returns to the subject of the leaders (v. 7, and now at v. **17**), but now the focus is on the leaders that are still living, whose course of life has not reached its end. The author admonishes his readers to *trust your leaders and yield to them.* This is the kind of trust he has in the community (6:9) and the posture the Son takes before God (2:13). He also urges them to submit themselves to their leaders, utilizing a word found nowhere else in the New Testament that conveys the sense of "giving way." If there is a conflict of wills, it would be in the best interest of the community to defer to the leaders, those who are following Jesus.

This is not an easy instruction, because, of course, leaders can be at best imperfect and at worst predatory. If there is someone in leadership who does not care how he or she will answer to God and, therefore, does not care too much about those under care, that person is not worthy of trust and submission and should be removed. This is necessary for their good and the good of

24. Chrysostom, *Hebrews* 33.8 (*NPNF*[1] 14:517).

the congregation. A bad leader is "a far worse evil than anarchy. It is better to be led by no one than to be led by one who is evil."[25] Verse 17 is not a blanket statement to accept whatever a leader imposes, but this instruction assumes that these leaders are worthy of trust and have good in mind for the people they are leading. The author does have a sense that these leaders, as imperfect as they may be, are still worthy of the position of leadership because they care deeply for the congregation. He describes them as those who *keep watch over your souls as those who will give an account.* He is voicing a fact of which the leaders themselves need to be aware. They will be called to give back a word to God. This is reminiscent of 4:13, where everyone is exposed and without defense before the piercing eye of the word of God. The leaders have to answer not only for themselves but also for those under their charge. In view of that end, they *keep watch* over the souls of the congregation. Literally, the term suggests they lose sleep over the souls under their care. Such a leader, who cares so much that he or she loses sleep, is worthy of trust and deference. The charge to the leaders is to care deeply and to take the responsibility of leadership with utmost seriousness. The seriousness is necessary to accept the task fittingly, with sobriety. This should not happen to the degree that it results in lack of self-care, for you can only lose sleep for so long before you become a horribly ineffective leader. With the wreckage of bad leadership strewn all over the church, from the past to the present, if one finds oneself under a faithful leader, this is a gift to celebrate.

In response to such faithful leaders, the author urges the congregation to live in such a way that the leaders can carry out their responsibilities *with joy and not groaning*, an echo of Moses's constant bewailing of the Israelites in his care. It is joy that should characterize this community (10:34; 12:11), following Jesus's lead (12:2), and that includes those who have the responsibility of congregational leadership. If the congregation makes the job of the leaders grievous, this will reflect poorly not on the leaders but on the congregation members themselves. If the members of the community are antagonistic or recalcitrant toward faithful leaders, *this is not to your advantage*, the author says. It frays the community and exposes one to correction before God. Hence, for the congregation as well, accountability to God shapes how one is to live (4:13). The charge to the congregation is to live in harmony with the leaders

25. Chrysostom, *Hebrews* 34.1 (*NPNF*[1] 14:237).

who care about them so much. The dynamic between the two—leaders and led—should be a system of support in which all contribute their gifts for the advantage of the other and the glory of God.

This mysterious author, who not only provides no introduction of his own name at the beginning of the letter but also draws so very little attention to himself throughout the sermon, again places himself after others. Verse **18** does not really begin a new section; the theme of leadership continues. As one who has brought this powerful word of God to them (v. 7), he is one of their leaders. It is noticeable, however, that only when he has urged support for the others does he ask for prayer for himself and his team. *Pray for us, for we are convinced that we have a good conscience, wanting to live in all things well.*

The author and those with him want to live like the previous leaders who spoke the word of God (v. 7), having a course of life that is good and, even more, that is deemed *well*, a term that could aptly be translated as "beautiful." This author and those with him want to have an exemplary life. Their conviction of a good conscience raises the question of an interlocutor: Did someone say that they should not have a clean conscience? Is he countering negative statements about him and his team? If so, the reference is so subtle and undeveloped in the rest of the letter that it indicates that controversy and contention against him were not major problems for this author. Instead, his assertion of a good conscience demonstrates that he is living into what Christ has procured for his followers (9:14; 10:22). The author's will has been so energized by his incorporation into the new covenant that he wants his entire life to be pleasing before God.

The author's assurance of good desires and clean conscience makes the request for prayer even more notable. He, too, is on the race with his readers and knows he needs their support to continue on the straight path. Augustine reflects, "If the apostles used to ask for prayers on their own behalf, how much more does it behoove me to do so?"[26] Later, Christians can add that if Augustine did so, we should follow suit.

The author's most ardent hope is that the straight path leads straight to this community. *But I encourage you even more to do this, in order that I might be restored to you quickly.* They can practice what he instructed concerning trusting deference to their leaders in v. 17 right away. They can show obedience to

26. Augustine, *Sermons* 305A.10 (ACCS 10:238).

this leader by praying for him as an application of his first instruction in this chapter, to show Christian love (13:1). He especially wants them to pray that he might be restored to them. He has switched here from a plural (pray for *us*; *we* are convinced; *we* have a good conscience) to a singular. He personally wants to return. For all the concerns he has expressed to this community, this comment helps readers view those through the lens of his deep love for this congregation. Not unlike Paul often does in his letters (Rom 15:24, 32; 2 Cor 13:1), likely this early leader wishes he could say things in person. The world's experience of the Covid-19 pandemic makes this desire even more relatable and palpable. Many have learned through that experience that there is no exchange for embodied presence. When that is not possible, it is fitting to pray for it and invite others to do the same.

13:20–25 · BLESSING

20And may the God of peace who led up from the dead the great shepherd of the sheep
with the blood of the eternal covenant, even our Lord Jesus, 21restore you all in every
good thing so that you might do his will, accomplishing among us what is pleasing be-
fore him through Jesus the Messiah, to whom be the glory forever and ever. Amen.
22I entreat you, brothers and sisters, to bear with the word of exhortation, for indeed I
wrote to you briefly. 23Know that our brother Timothy has been released. If he comes
quickly, he will be with me when I see you. 24Greet all your leaders and all the saints.
Those from Italy greet you. 25Grace be with you all.

In the last few sentences, the author of Hebrews leaves his community with parting words that keep their focus on God. In so doing he provides one of the most beautiful benedictions in all the New Testament (vv. 20–21). Some Christians have seen it as so powerful that they have used it as the final word of peace in the service commemorating a deceased person to God's care.[27] The author certainly has more he would like to share when he is restored to them in person, but he has said all he can with this brief word of encouragement to ensure that the community stays rooted in God's grace, which is never delayed.

27. This is the final blessing at the committal. *BCP* (1979), 486.

The rich benediction is a work of beauty and rhetorical power as it collects so many of the themes of the sermon and communicates them succinctly with fresh language. In this benediction, the author appeals to God as the *God of peace*. He invokes God's peace most clearly in the pedagogical section of ch. 12. Those who endure God's training will receive the *peaceful* fruit of righteousness (12:11). This peace is a gift from their Father God. When they put it to work in their own lives in their relationship with others, this virtue is one that will ultimately allow them to see God (12:14). This puts them into the same kingdom of peace over which the elusive Melchizedek reigned (7:2). As they dwell there, they follow the faithful example of another "outsider," Rahab who received the spies in peace (11:31). The genitive here in v. 20, *of peace*, could convey either that God is a God who is peaceful or that God reigns over a place that is peaceful. The latter lines up with what the author has displayed for them about God's rest and God's heavenly city. The character of God, on the other hand, is not necessarily peaceful, if that means that God only allows a relaxed life now. Peace is what is to come, but God has to allow some uncomfortable discipline now so that they can arrive there in the future.

Ultimate peace is guaranteed, however, because of what this God has done, named in the next way the author describes God as one *who led up from the dead the great shepherd of the sheep with the blood of the eternal covenant, even our Lord Jesus*. Their God is the one who has led someone out from death. This description of God puts this author into alignment with the Pauline corpus, which frequently describes God the Father as the one who raised Jesus from the dead (Rom 4:17, 24; 6:4; 8:11; 10:9; 1 Cor 15:15; 2 Cor 1:9; Gal 1:1; Eph 1:20; Col 2:12; 1 Thess 1:10; 2 Tim 2:8). The author of Hebrews uses a term distinct to his own sermon, however. He does not employ Paul's typical term for raising, *egeirō*, but instead uses *anagō*, resonating with the image of God and Jesus leading the many sons and daughters (2:10; 12:2). A clear reference to the resurrection, v. 20 provides the tether for those who argue that this surfacing of the concept gives evidence of its presence in the substructure of the sermon.[28] No one could say this author does not affirm resurrection even as he frequently discusses Jesus's exaltation.

The author's description of Jesus here adds fresh material to the extensive reflections on him as Son and High Priest: *the great shepherd of the sheep.*

28. As argued throughout Moffitt, *Atonement*.

Nowhere earlier has the author described Jesus as the shepherd nor the people of God as the flock. This imagery resonates, however, with the person of David, and because the author cited royal psalms in application to the Son in the first chapter (1:5, 8–9), that resonance is now, at the end, explicit. Jesus is a shepherd like his ancestor David (7:14). This image also associates him with Moses, who in Isaiah 63:11–14 is compared to a shepherd, caring for the people as he followed the leading of God.[29] Although this concept of Jesus as a shepherd is singularly expressed here in Hebrews, it sets this sermon into agreement with many other authors in the New Testament who cast Jesus in this way and God's people as the flock (Matt 2:6; 9:36; 25:32; 26:31; Mark 6:34; 14:27; Luke 12:32; John 10; 21:16; Acts 20:28–29; 1 Cor 9:7; Eph 4:11; 1 Pet 2:25; 5:2–3; Rev 7:17). Because Jesus is cast as the leader of the people (*archēgos*, 2:10 and 12:2), a shepherding image affirms that same leadership reality from a different perspective. It contributes a sense of Jesus's intimacy and care with the people who confess his name.

The ambiguity inherent in the preposition of the next phrase of the benediction invites a variety of interpretations: *with the blood of the eternal covenant, even our Lord Jesus.* Blood has certainly been a strikingly present feature in Hebrews, appearing twenty times in the letter, its importance captured succinctly with the statement "apart from the shedding of blood there is not release" (9:22). Consequently, it is no surprise to find blood here at the end. The same is true with covenant, as that concept captured the attention of the letter from its central section (first in 7:22) until the end. While the author has not (until this point) explicitly called the covenant *eternal*, the idea of God's enduring faithfulness and eternality has been very prominent, extending to the offer of eternal salvation, redemption, and inheritance (5:9; 9:12, 15). These now familiar concepts take their particular meaning in this sentence as they are joined with the preposition *en*. Regarding this flexible word, scholars have noted a variety of nuanced interpretations that largely fall into two categories. The first is that God led Jesus up from the dead *through* the blood of the eternal covenant. This translation indicates "God's vindication of Jesus and the acceptance of his sacrifice as the basis of the eternal covenant."[30] This aligns with the idea stated in 5:7 that God heard him and rescued him out of death

29. Witherington, *Letters and Homilies*, 366.
30. Harris, *Hebrews*, 424.

because of his reverent obedience, an obedience that led to his death. Alternatively, the blood of the eternal covenant could be read as what Jesus takes with him. When he is raised with a new body, which would include, in some way, resurrected blood in his body, he presents that to God in the heavenly temple, thus inaugurating the eternal covenant. Since the options find validation in the previous sections of the letter and do not cancel each other out, preachers are allowed to draw out these meanings and in so doing show the multifaceted beauty and power of the new and everlasting covenant.

The great shepherd of the sheep is, in fact, *our Lord Jesus*. While the author has, throughout the sermon, mentioned the name of Jesus and frequently referred to the Lord, this is the only time in which he joins the terms. By saying *Jesus* he confirms that the one who has been led out of the dead is the same one who took on flesh and blood by coming through the tribe of Judah (7:14). Jesus the Jewish man is at the right hand of God. By saying *Lord* the author aligns the resurrected Jesus with the Lord God. It is not clear throughout the letter whether the author has in mind God the Father or God the Son when he speaks of the Lord, and as the tradition concluded, this fruitful ambiguity confirms the shared will, glory, and activity of both as God. His place of exaltation does not mean that the Lord Jesus who now reigns with God is removed from the audience. Instead, he is *their* Lord, and as their Lord he advocates for (7:25); under Christ's advocacy the author now prays for them.

The author asks that God *restore you all in every good thing so that you might do his will . . . through Jesus the Messiah.* "Restore" is one possible translation. *Katartizō* speaks of bringing something into existence, as it is used in 11:3 where God, through speech, prepared/created the worlds, or in 10:5 where God prepared a body for the Son. Inauguration is not the right fit in this context, however, because this community has already confessed Christ and has already done good things. The sense of "restore" fittingly expresses the wish that he wants them to move back to their former days of faithful flourishing and past their current immaturity (5:11–14). Alternatively, the translation of "strengthen" captures the same sense of increasing what they have already possessed.

This improvement will, if God answers, play itself out in good things happening in the community. The author's prayer is rather comprehensive, that God restore them in ***every** good thing*. With this comprehensive term it is clear that his is not hope for an improvement that affects only some aspects of life but one that affects all of them. It is understandable that such stretching breadth was circumscribed by several scribes who specified every good thing as every good *work*.[31] If it is correct that the author intended this more fulsomely, as every good *thing*, he is praying that God give them what they need to live out all good, be it outward observable work or inward hidden demeanor. Imagining both seems correct because this author has cared a great deal about both matters of the heart (3:12; 4:12; 8:10; 10:16) and faithful actions (3:13; 10:25; 13:1–5). When they live in *all good*, they are doing God's will, as Jesus did (10:7, 9).

Importantly, the author proclaims again that they are not doing God's will on their own. In a sermon very focused on strong faith, it is ultimately God who provides the strength for that faith. *God* is at work in this community to accomplish that which pleases the divine will. That includes belief, because without faith it is impossible to please God (11:6), and that belief pours forth in worship (12:28) and service (13:16). In light of the sufficient work of God, what is left to the readers is not the exhortation to work harder but simply the reminder not to resist the God who is already at work in and among them. Heinrich Bullinger wisely noted, "For only the things that are done through Christ are acceptable to God. . . . Solely those things that are exclusively from God are truly good works."[32] Any works outside God's support are futile. God accomplishes this pleasurable life in the community through *Jesus Christ*. Every good thing is possible only through him. Because of what he has done, a faithful heart-motivated, right-action life is theirs to accept and enact.

The benediction closes with a doxology: *to whom be the glory forever and ever. Amen.* Jesus the Messiah, just mentioned, is certainly worthy of glory for eternity, as he will reign at God's right hand forever (1:13; 2:9). The attribution is just as applicable, however, to the God of peace—namely, his Father God. Because the eternal Spirit facilitated the offering that secured the eternal covenant (9:14), the Spirit is present in this glory as well. At the end of this benediction, the shared glory of the Father and Son and Holy Spirit appears in this multifaceted attribution of the doxology.

As is often the case in ancient letters, after this stirring benediction, the author includes a few personal details. *I entreat you, brothers and sisters, to bear with the word of exhortation, for indeed I wrote to you briefly.*

31. C D^{2} K P, etc. (NA^{28}, 684).

32. Bullinger, *Commentary on Hebrews*, 13:20–21 137v (RCS 13:197).

First, he exhorts (*parakaleō*) them to bear up with *the word of exhortation* (*paraklēsis*) he has written to them (this phrase is used to describe a speech in a religious setting in Acts 13:15). Six times in the letter he employs the topic of exhortation/encouragement. God offers this (6:18; 12:5), the author does (13:19, 22), and so too should they offer encouragement to one another (3:13; 10:25). These references show that for the author of Hebrews Christian encouragement protects from sin, allows endurance of difficulty, works for healthy relationship, and grants hope. It is a positive thing, but not in the sense of a shallow positivity that keeps one smiling no matter how horrid things might be. They are members of the same family (this is the fourth and final vocative of the term for sibling), and so they can, in the safety of that kind of relationship, receive this challenging but ultimately "for their good" word from their brother. He asks them to bear up with it, even as he asked them to endure God's discipline (12:5–11). He might see his letter as a form of discipline, causing grief when they realize they are far behind where they should be (5:11–14), but it is a grief meant to drive them toward improvement. As intense as the sermon is at times, his final description indicates that he does not wish anything he said to destroy his readers, but only to build them up. This seems an especially important reminder for the sections in which he describes the consequences of turning away from God's action in Christ. Any interpretation that gives no hope to someone who desires relationship with God does not fit the author's self-description of his work as that which is meant to encourage.

He indicates that his encouragement is written *briefly*. This phrase might be an indication that he envisions this letter as brief. In comparison with most of Paul's letters, it is not, but standing next to Jewish and Christian writings like 2 Maccabees and Barnabas, it is.[33] The term is a relative one, and he might have made this comment in line with epistolary convention. Reformation pastor Lucas Osiander wisely observed what many a pastor and author might need to hear: "The ministers of the church . . . should also earnestly strive for brevity as much as possible in teaching and exhorting, for long discourses rarely edify much, just as long writings also are either laid aside or rapidly read."[34]

The phrase could also be an indication that the author wrote to them with time constraints. The complexity of Hebrews' logic gives evidence of a bril-

33. Koester, *Hebrews*, 580.

34. RCS 13:197.

liant mind, but as with all authors, it is possible he felt that he could have used more time to make his exhortation even more clear and persuasive. The Spirit deemed what he might have viewed as an imperfect communication as the perfect word of God. Would this author be surprised that his hasty or short letter has become precisely what he considered to be true of Israel's Scriptures—namely, living and active (4:12)? Without access to the incarnate Christ in the flesh, or to those who were his eyewitnesses, no one now will be writing Scripture, but an encouragement lies in this for modern-day writers and preachers. The Spirit can use even those products we would view as imperfect as a vehicle for the audience to have a divine meeting.

The next few verses give some of the very few specific historical data points in the letter but fail to definitively establish the setting of the document. In v. **23** the author says, *Know that our brother Timothy has been released. If he comes quickly, he will be with me when I see you.* Readers of the New Testament immediately think of the friend of Paul mentioned frequently as a vital ministry partner (Acts 16:1; 17:14–15; 18:5; 19:22; 20:4; Rom 16:21; 1 Cor 4:17; 16:10; 2 Cor 1:1, 19; Phil 1:1; 2:19; Col 1:1; 1 Thess 1:1; 3:2, 6; 2 Thess 1:1; 1 Tim 1:2, 18; 6:20; 2 Tim 1:2; Phlm 1). The mention of his name provides one of the supports for the suggestion that this chapter was added later to make Hebrews appear more Pauline.[35]

If this is the same Timothy, and this chapter is original to Hebrews, then Timothy's association with the author and this community tethers the letter to the apostolic time period. This community is not siloed away but part of the vibrant fabric of believers united by frequent communication. The recipients of this letter could be in relationship with those communities to whom Paul writes. Even though the author did not encounter Jesus directly (2:3), he would have relationships with those who did. The mention of Timothy's name supports the possibility of those wide connections. This verse also confirms that the author is so anxious to get to them that he is not planning to wait for Timothy. If Timothy comes quickly, they can travel together; if not, the author will already be gone.

Having discussed the leaders several times in this chapter, the author closes the letter by instructing, *Greet all your leaders and all the saints.* This might indicate that the leaders are not reading this correspondence, for he gave instructions

35. Rothschild, *Hebrews as Psuedepigraphon*, 79, 160.

of how to think about and respond to leaders (13:7, 17) but no explicit instructions for *how* to lead. This might be an indication that he wrote to the leaders separately. In this sentence he also asks that they greet all of the saints. Possibly he is writing to a subset of a congregation or one congregation among many that meet in the same city. In this time period, he is certainly writing to a group of believers who gather in a house church. Imagining the possibilities of their network of connections puts flesh on these mystery people, even if our imaginations must entertain several scenarios. They were real people with relationships that stretched across the constraints of limited space and geographic location.

Finally, he says, *Those from Italy greet you*. This statement could indicate that the author is in Italy writing to another location. It is also possible that fellow expats send back their greetings to their home. This latter possibility aligns with Hebrews' first mentions from believers in the church in Rome in the writing of Clement.

This comprehensiveness (all the leaders, all the saints) continues in the parting word. *Grace be with you all*. He wishes on all of them grace. This final sentence offers a fitting lens through which to view the letter as a whole. He asks a great deal of them but believes that God will supply what they need to accomplish it all. Until he can join them again, he wants them to live neither in laziness nor in anxiety but in the unmerited favor of God revealed in the Son through the Spirit. He wants them to rest in grace.

At the end of a service, a pastor offers a benediction. This is a verbal proclamation of God's blessing on the community. It is ideal if this blessing catches up elements of the service—themes of the Scriptures and sermon of the day, lines of the songs, or echoes of the prayers. Hebrews 13 is benedictory in that way. It draws together many of the threads of the sermon—God's trustworthiness, Jesus's sacrifice, and faithful living—as it proclaims God's blessing of peace and grace on all those who hear God speaking through it.

I, too, proclaim this blessing for the reader of this commentary: May grace be with you all.

Conclusion

The week after I turned in the full manuscript of this commentary, I taught a theological study day on Hebrews. At a point at which one might imagine that I had "mastered" this ancient sermon, two experiences confirmed that this can never be the case. First, when the participants shared their insights and questions, they put the pieces together in ways that I had never considered. After years of teaching the Bible, this was not a surprise. The Scriptures are so infinitely vast and deep in the riches they hold that every Spirit-inspired believer has the potential to discover treasure previously unearthed, or at least call attention to treasure recently forgotten. Second, to some of the questions posed the only answer I could provide was "I'm not sure." This was a surprise to me, and an encouraging one at that. For any single interpreter, there will always be new vistas and new depths of greater understanding to explore. This final section might be titled a "conclusion," but for the study of biblical books there really never is an end. This truth is amply demonstrated in the rich conversation about Hebrews throughout history in both the church and, once it developed as a separate institution, the academy.

Instead of offering the final word, the conclusion of a commentary provides the reader who has read the whole commentary the chance to revisit key themes and imagine possibilities for further exploration. For the reader who might begin at the end, the conclusion reveals the interpretive lenses of the commentator in a more summative way than does the introduction. I present both the retrospective and the avenues for future research in the form of ten questions. Study groups could utilize these as a framework for group discussion or personal reflection, while for students they can serve as a catalyst for research and writing. May they be a launching pad for new questions and new discoveries for every lifelong student of Hebrews.

1. WHAT IS THE THEOLOGICAL FOUNDATION OF HEBREWS?

In the time in which all readers of Hebrews live, in the "days of the end" (1:1) existing after the revelation of the Son, all of God's speech is telescoped into and then refracted through him (1:2). The revelation of the Son is the theological foundation of Hebrews. The God proclaimed in the sermon is not simple, but I am convinced that any who listen to its message, from the greatest to the least (8:11), will hear its clarion call: the God who promised is faithful (10:23; 11:11). For Hebrews, God is first and foremost the communicative God, the one who spoke to create and then has been speaking to creation (1:1–3). The prophets served as the vehicle in the past (1:1) and do so in the present. Their words preserved in Scripture convey God's voice again and again, as long as it is today (3:7–4:13). The author's dependence on them is evident through his citations and allusions through this sermon. Since he and every other author of the New Testament include their words and because early Christians were adamant that Israel's Scriptures are an indispensable part of the Christian canon, their speech continues as God's word throughout the generations.

For this author, however, those words of God are rightly understood through this personal word of God.[1] It is the Son who demonstrates God's consistency and trustworthiness by fulfilling the promises of the past. Retaining appropriate focus on the christological center of the letter, that Jesus the Judahite, the crucified and risen one, is the hoped-for Messiah of Israel, prevents an inappropriate supersessionist reading of Hebrews, a real danger as the history of interpretation demonstrates. Israel cannot be dismissed if Jesus is from Israel (7:14) and for Israel (2:16). He brings the covenant the prophet Jeremiah hoped for to the same people with whom God made the first covenant (ch. 8). His work of atonement would not make sense if the author had not

1. Israel's Scriptures have vital lessons to teach about God, and in every instance it is necessary to hear those lessons without immediately jumping to the christological interpretation. On the other hand, even when they are understood in their context and teach their truths, the christological telos of the whole remains.

learned from the sacrificial system God graciously gave to the covenant people. It is the case that Hebrews, and subsequently Christian theology, affirms that Jesus is the Messiah, and therefore it is necessary to come under his lordship for salvation. There is an exclusivism that should not be denied. Hence Hebrews, in my interpretation, aligns with Paul's hope that all Israel will be saved by faith that integrates them into the Messiah (Rom 11:17–32). This exclusive proclamation of Christ is in debt to the people and texts of Israel even as it is for the people of Israel. Any notion that God's promises to Abraham could be revoked would be anathema to the author of this sermon called Hebrews.

God's revelation in the Son also stands as the guarantee of the promises that will be fulfilled in the future. Although circumstances may tempt readers to believe that God is absent, if the author can help them tune their ears to God's voice in the Son, they will be able to see the world rightly under God's control (2:9). If God can be trusted, then the message of Hebrews can be obeyed.

2. WHAT IS THE POSTURE OF FAITHFULNESS DEPICTED IN HEBREWS?

Obedience begins by listening. The first act of faithfulness, according to Hebrews, is to attune one's ears to God's speech (1:1–2; 2:1; 12:25). Because this community has heard the good news of salvation that began with the Lord (2:3), they can now hear afresh all of God's communication in the Scriptures as well as in the world around them. Voices of fear, guilt, and comfort will seek to drown out God's voice, and so, in order to keep listening faithfully, disciples need to do two things. First, they not only need to confess their own sin that created a barrier of impurity blocking relationship with a holy God (1:3); they also need to confess the one who eliminated that barrier, Christ Jesus (3:1; 4:14; 10:23; 13:15). The kind of listening Hebrews is interested in is not a passive and nonchalant observation but an agreement, an articulation of the same thing God said. God spoke in the Son, and now his followers agree with what God said in and through him. This kind of listening acknowledges the message and responds with agreement. To confess is not a one-time event but a perpetual and intentional holding fast to that which was confessed. Faithfulness in Hebrews is first an act of steadiness.

At the same time, this faithfulness is not the same as stagnation. The second action Hebrews commands for the faithful is forward movement. This step follows immediately upon initial confession and is henceforth practiced simultaneously. The community of Hebrews can hear the voice of God with immediacy, and yet God's voice is always addressing them from a location beyond them. Hence, they need to be moving toward it, toward rest (4:11), toward their anchor (6:18–20), toward the holy place (10:19), toward the end of the race (12:1). God's majestic address to the Christian community who hears Hebrews is so grand that the author can depict it as a presence on a mountain (12:22–29). Even though they are not fully with God yet, God can so completely fill their vision and their hearing that they can respond to God's transformative voice by holding on to what they hear and moving ever closer toward it.

In practical terms, holding fast to the confession is manifest for the individual in the act of prayer. Going to God with confident trust because of the revelation of the Son, the supplicant can name whatever is needed at that moment (4:16). Prayer is a confession, an agreement of what is true about God and what God already knows to be true about the one praying (4:12–13). In addition to manifesting in prayer, journeying forward is a metaphor that aptly describes the corporate act of worship, proclaiming the name and goodness of God, which Jesus (2:12) and the Holy Spirit (3:7; 10:15) revealed, with others who are grateful to be on the same pathway of salvation (12:1–14). Faithfulness, according to Hebrews, must be multisensory; it includes listening, speaking, and acting as one member of the responsive community before the Triune God.

3. WHAT KIND OF FAITH DOES HEBREWS INVITE?

If the *posture* of faithfulness is to listen well and respond, the *kind* of faith that listens and responds is one that believes God has the power of life even and especially in the face of death. This is not to say that faith is only a response to the crisis of death. Faithfulness to God means responding in each and every situation, no matter what the incisive word of God exposes (4:12–13). That being said, I also think it is true that in Hebrews (and truly in all of human life) death hangs over human existence (2:15) even if people are not always consciously aware of its presence. Moreover, when the author of Hebrews invokes the necessity of faith, it is often in a conversation aware of the realities of death and life in Christ.

The emphasis on life begins with the Son who was with his Father God eternally and participated with the Father in the creation of life (1:3). As the one who purified for sins, he will live and reign forever (1:8–13). These assertions are built on his unending life as the eternal God and as the resurrected human. Then in ch. 2, as the one who will reign over all things in the world to come (2:8–9), he shares his life so that he can redeem others from their imprisonment to the fear of death (2:14–15) so that they can reign with him as God planned for humanity (Ps 8/Heb 2:8). For those who follow him, in contrast to what was true for the faithless in the wilderness, death will not be the end of their story (3:7–4:13); they will experience restful life with God forever (4:1–11). They follow one who cried out to God his Father as the one who could rescue him on the other side of death (5:7). Melchizedek's story mimics his (7:3), as the one who has the power of indestructible life (7:16). The faithful who came before were looking forward to this one who would defeat death by trusting that their God could fulfill promises even on the other side of death. This thread runs throughout the stories of the faithful in ch. 11, from faith in the God who brought life out of nothing (11:3) to Abraham who trusted in God who could raise the dead (11:19) to the women who received their dead back and all who looked forward to the better resurrection (11:35). Even though the first recipients had lost their leaders to death (13:7), they trust they will be united with them and all the others made righteous on God's mountain (12:23). For Hebrews, faith can face all things because if even death has no power before God, then God can be fully trusted to aid the followers of the Son who defeated death in all things. This kind of faith allows them to listen to God and respond faithfully no matter the situation.

4. WHAT IS THE UNIQUE CONTRIBUTION OF HEBREWS TO THE WRITINGS OF THE NEW TESTAMENT?

If readers could know only one thing about this early Christian document, it should be the faithfully creative contribution that interprets the person and work of Christ as a priestly vocation. The author signals his theme in the first sentence by affirming that Christ has brought purification for sins (1:3); previously this had been a persistent result of the sacrificial system, as attested often in Israel's Scriptures. Now the Son of God has achieved this end once and for all. In the next chapter, the eternal Son's humanity serves the type of priesthood he embraces, that which is faithful to God and merciful to the covenant community (2:17). He partakes of the human condition so that he can represent them before God (2:14). He suffers death and defeats death as a way of atoning for sins (2:17). The author can conclude that the one sent from God is their High Priest (3:1). The theme continues when the author reminds the readers of their vulnerable condition before God, completely exposed (4:13). Their need for such a priest becomes clear (4:14), not because a wrathful and sadistic God needs to be placated, but because sin has created a barrier between people and God that must be eliminated.

The author draws deeply from the well of Israel's understanding of their priests and sacrifices to portray Jesus as a priest. In a way no other early Christian does, with detail and emphasis, he interprets Jesus's life mission not only to reign as King but also to serve as High Priest. His human life allows him to grow in obedience and empathy (5:7–10). This life prepares him to trust God even at the point of death on a cross (5:7; 12:2–3). This is where he is slaughtered, as he willingly gives his body, his blood, his entire self to be the sacrifice (7:27; 9:12, 14; 10:10; 12:24; 13:12). Then, when Jesus, who trusted in God his Father's living power, defeated death (2:14–15; 13:20), he ascends to the right hand of God to take his seat of power (1:13; 8:1; 10:12; 12:2). In so doing, he presents himself, his living body and blood, to God as the completely sufficient and therefore final sacrifice (9:12; 10:10). There at God's right hand he serves as the continual reminder of the sacrifice he presented that dealt with sin. Moreover, he actively prays for those who are following him on their way to dwell with God forever (7:25, 28).

This distinct contribution to the Christology of the New Testament—Jesus as High Priest leading his people into God's sacred space—became a model for interpreting the Christian life. All can think of themselves as priests, as some Christian authors say explicitly (1 Pet 2:5, 9; Rev 1:6; 5:10; 20:6), echoing God's promise to the people of Israel (Exod 19:6). The author of Hebrews demonstrates this by noting that his readers' actions can be viewed through priestly imagery, like drawing near to God's holy presence (4:16; 6:19–20; 10:19–20) and serving God (12:28) by offering sacrifices (13:16). They serve God as a member of the priesthood of all believers because they serve as members of the sovereign and eternal High Priest.

Christ's priesthood also became a template for leaders who are called to watch over the souls of the congregation in addition to their own, not unlike how the priests of Israel were called to care for others in addition to themselves (13:17; 9:7). In this way, Hebrews provides a grounding for the development of the ordained priesthood in Christianity. All follow in the footsteps of Jesus, who used his role not to serve himself but to bring glory to God as he gave everything to serve others. Christian leadership is not for self-advancement but for the building of the kingdom.

5. WHAT IS THE STATUS OF THE SHARER IN CHRIST?

Those who are served by Jesus's priesthood are not only designated his congregation, but as was true in Israel in the relationship between the Levites and their siblings, the followers of Jesus are also proclaimed as the family of Jesus. Those who confess Jesus as Son of God and Messiah become his siblings (2:11–12), even though he is Lord of all. It is a great encouragement to them that he is not ashamed to be related to them in such an intimate way. In a first-century context, and in many other times and places as well, the eldest brother bore an extra responsibility to care for his younger siblings.[2] God the Son cares for them as a brother cares for his own blood.

Because of his embrace of them as kin, God his Father has claimed them as children (2:10, 13; 12:5–11). They are given the same privileges of divine attention that Jesus receives, privileges of education (5:7–9, 11–14; 12:5–11) and inheritance (1:14; 6:12; 9:15; 12:23). They can look to Jesus as their example of how God will interact with them. If he experienced suffering for the sake of the perfection of his vocation (2:8–10; 5:7–10), so too will they. If he will inherit all things, they will participate in the stewardship of their elder brother (2:5–10; 12:28). If they leave this group, it is as serious as leaving their family (12:15–17), and so God's desire to retain them is as strong as a parent's desire to stay in relationship with a child. Consequently, God has provided everything for the relationship between them to be established and endure.

6. WHAT IS THE SHAPE OF THE LIFE OF THE COMMUNITY?

If individuals have this magnitude of encouragement by virtue of relating to God as Father and Jesus as brother, they also have the wide chain of encouragement from their brothers and sisters in the Christ-confessing community. As

2. For a full discussion, see Patrick Gray, "Brotherly Love and the High Priest Christology of Hebrews," *JBL* 122 (2003): 335–51.

interpreters have debated the ethnic makeup of the community, it is possible that the recipients would not have all been related by their family history, and it is certainly true that subsequent readers of Hebrews are not. Now, however, all those who confess Christ are related by blood, not their own but the blood that Christ shed for them to put them into the familial relationship with God. Consequently, they can and should relate to one another as they would relate to their own siblings. Since this is the family of God and not the family of a human father, the standards are even higher. Relationship between them includes honesty with one another, pointing out bitterness that might be hiding in one's heart (3:12–13; 12:15). This sibling relationship also includes care in the form of emotional encouragement as well as physical and economic provision (13:1–5). This support is very important as the group is journeying in the wilderness toward God's rest and as they are running the race to reach Jesus seated at the end (12:1–2). The path is an arduous one, and they cannot make it on their own, so thankfully God has supplied the support of each other.

The previous questions orient one to the major themes of the sermon; the last four look forward, inviting reflection on how to live after studying this sermon.

7. HOW SHOULD INTERPRETERS PASTORALLY HANDLE THE WARNING PASSAGES?

Hebrews raises many questions, but none are experienced as more existentially pressing than those prompted by the warning passages. Whether a person is worried that they have fallen into that irreparable category of sin, is concerned for a loved one who has given signs that they have done so, or should be concerned about skirting close to the edge of that dangerous territory, anyone studying Hebrews should be equipped with ways to respond to the issues these passages raise. This is especially true for leaders who have oversight for the souls of others (13:17).

The most important thing to emphasize is the sole and magnificent sufficiency of salvation offered in Christ. God chose not to leave creation in its corruption due to sin but elected to redeem and reconcile it through the person and work of the Son. This gracious and completed act offers profound assurance. Christ is victorious over all sin (1:3; 2:17; 7:27; 8:12; 9:26, 28; 10:12,

17–18). Although one of the warnings mentions willful sins (10:26), so many sins are committed in some kind of ignorance—the ignorance of being within one's culture, the ignorance of one's self-deception, or the ignorance that arises out of a false belief about God. Christ has atoned for them all, past and future. In addition to these many sins committed in ignorance, there is no sin for which the one who comes to him will not find atonement. Christ's full victory is guaranteed. Directing the concerned (or dangerously unconcerned) to him is the most important act.

This is the primary goal of the author in crafting these warning passages. He makes it clear that the denial of Christ has *not* happened among his community members. He is crafting a case study for them of the alternative reality if they turned away from the one in whom they've found their redemption and enduring life. The morbid picture he paints serves to push them away from such a reality and push them even more deeply toward Jesus the only effective Messiah.

Directing vision to Christ assuages the worries of the spiritually sensitive. If they are concerned that some sin has separated them from Christ, who they still believe is the only way of salvation, then they can be comforted that Christ has done everything necessary to bridge any gap between them and God. The sin described in these passages is incommensurate with their desire to be connected to Christ.

Often, though, the concern these passages create is for someone else who has walked away from Christianity. The worry is heavier in these instances because it appears as though the person has turned away from Christ. When such situations are considered in detail, the fine-grained nuances give evidence of various reasons why people have turned away. They might have rejected a false view of God and hopefully will find their way to a true one. Even if they have turned away from a trustworthy picture of Christ, Hebrews does not prohibit a return to Christ, but only states that it is impossible to receive a blessing apart from Christ. What is impossible is that God would provide a way of forgiveness and life in addition to the one already available through Jesus Christ.

On the other hand, these passages should not be ignored nor their intensity decreased. Those who are lured out of the cost of Christianity into comfort need to be warned in no uncertain terms that salvation does not exist outside of Christ. Even if one plans to walk away for a time and then return at one's leisure, the end may come in the interim, either one's personal end and subsequent judgment (9:27) or the corporate end when Christ returns for salvation (9:28). If a reader is not in an intense setting of persecution as the original readers were, there are always tempting reasons to reject the shame associated with Christ (13:13). These passages can act as a sobering call for any who need the alert, as was true for those who first heard this sermon.

8. HOW SHOULD READERS LIVE OUT THE PRACTICAL INSTRUCTIONS?

At the close of the sermon, the author gets very practical with his string of instructions (13:1–5). When those are joined with the sermon as a whole, two broad categories can encompass all of them. First, the author is intent on the development of healthy relationships within the community. Readers can follow these instructions by practicing regular and honest Christian friendship and meaningful worship. When the community is healthy, they are poised to let that encouragement flow out to others. Hence, second, following Hebrews results in care for the imprisoned, the persecuted brothers and sisters, as well as anyone who is a stranger. As they resist the love of money, the community will have resources to share with any in need. The ethics of Hebrews is focused both inwardly and outwardly.

It is a sermon written to encourage discipleship, but it also demonstrates the work of spreading the good news. In other words, although Hebrews is a sermon written to those who have already confessed Christ, like all parts of Scripture it can and should be used to share the good news of salvation with those who have not yet heard. Abeneazer G. Urga notes how Hebrews itself talks about the spread of the story: "The task of evangelism—according to Hebrews—is successive. Note here that God is still the one carrying out the dissemination or attestation of the salvific gospel through human intermediaries."[3] God ensures the message of salvation is available but has chosen that those who have heard the Lord speaking will share with others. Delivering

3. Abeneazer G. Urga, Edward L. Smither, and Linda P. Saunders, *Reading Hebrews Missiologically: The Missionary Motive, Message, and Methods of Hebrews* (Littleton, CO: William Carey, 2023), 309–10.

the good news of Christ serves others by enabling them to hear God speaking through the Son so that they, too, can celebrate on God's holy mountain.

9. HOW DOES HEBREWS DEMONSTRATE THE PRODUCTIVE DISCOMFORT OF LIMINALITY?

The author of Hebrews encourages his community of readers to go outside the camp and join Jesus in his shame (13:13). While the focus of this admonition rests on their willingness to endure persecution because of their confession of Christ, it also speaks to the sermon as a whole, which sits in uncomfortable places that straddle extremes. It holds together cultural and theological paradox, without fully entering into one side by leaving the other. This positioning of its form and content calls readers to follow that model and dwell in the in-between.

Unwilling to play into the false dichotomy that Jewish and Hellenistic cultures were separate in the first-century world, Hebrews exemplifies the overlapping space between them. An author adept at rhetoric in the Jewish Scriptures, the architect of this sermon provides a case study for first-century Hellenized Judaism. His visions of faith appeal to the Israelite wandering in the wilderness (3:7–4:13) as well as Greco-Roman athletics (12:1–13). Without arguing that he is directly dependent on any particular source, interpreters can see points of connection between this writing and Greek and Roman rhetoric and philosophy as well as various Second Temple Jewish authors. Clearly, this early Christ follower serves the God of Israel and draws prolifically from Israel's Scriptures, but the medium of his presentation would have been familiar to those who lived throughout the Roman Empire.

He employs his alacrity in communication to embrace seemingly disparate theological truths. He begins with the equally bold proclamations of the Son of God's divinity and Jesus's humanity, twin truths that inhere in one person, the Messiah of Israel. He is the eternal one (1:2, 8–12) who died (2:14), the sovereign (1:13) who was below the angels (2:9), the radiance of God (1:3) who took on flesh (2:14). Because of who he is, his actions dealt with the barriers that separated humanity from the holy and living God—namely, sin and death (1:3; 2:14–15). He put humanity into relationship with God his Father as their Father (2:10–13). This relationship of intimacy and care does not remove the truth that God continues to be the holy Judge of all (10:30; 12:23), even for those who are children in the divine family (12:23). Consequently, the author encourages his readers to hold the tension of boldly fearing God (10:19, 31) or, put differently, reverently running toward God (4:16; 12:1).

Hebrews is not unique in such a broad embrace; most other documents of the New Testament provide examples of the beauty and mystery of Christian paradox. Hebrews does so, however, in a liminal place in the canon, even among the Epistles. It is not explicitly Pauline, although it seems to be in conversation with the Jewish apostle to the gentiles. It affirms the solely sufficient salvation of Jesus the Messiah as fulfillment of the promises to Abraham and his descendants (2:16; 6:13–20; 8:1–13) and from that shared point narrows the focus on his work as interpreted in light of the sacrificial cult. In this salvific argument, the author draws from some of the same passages and scriptural themes as Paul (such as Jesus's session at God's right hand from Ps 109 LXX and the connection between righteousness and faith from Hab 2) and utilizes some of the same inspirational metaphors, such as athletics (1 Cor 9:24–27; Heb 12:1–13), and object lessons, as with the wilderness generation (1 Cor 10:1–22; Heb 3:7–4:13). On the other side of Hebrews' canonical location, this missive is not as broad as many of the so-called General Epistles. The author seems to have one community in mind, yet this sermon shares many of the same concerns for faithfulness during the difficulty of suffering that the documents by the named followers of Jesus do (1 Pet 1:6, 11; 2:20–24; 3:13–17; 4:1, 12–19; 5:7–11; Jas 1:2–4; Heb 10:32–39; 12:3–11). Hebrews, like John, encourages readers by proclaiming the ascended intercession of Jesus (Heb 7:25; 1 John 2:1–2) and, like Peter and the Apocalypse of John, has an interest in the priestly faithfulness of Jesus's followers (1 Pet 2:5, 9; Rev 1:6; 5:10; 20:6; Heb 10:19; 12:28; 13:16).

Hebrews is "liminal" in its call to countercultural faithfulness, and it begins that call by stretching readers' intellectual capacity to take in more of the God who transgresses simple categorization. Readers from the first audience until now live in the time of the last days, when Jesus has inaugurated but not yet completed the end. In this in-between time, Hebrews does not call its audience to retreat from the cultures in which they live, but neither does it allow them to relax the scandal of their confession of and faith in Christ. They are positioned, like the God they follow, to straddle the twin commitments of conviction and grace. They are called to proclaim, without apology, the sole sufficiency of salvation in Jesus the Messiah, the Son of God, and to live out the compassionate and peaceful service to all (12:11; 13:1–7) so that others might desire to confess him too. The christological paradoxes of Hebrews are at the center of the letter's exegetical conundrums and its theological potential.

10. HOW SHOULD ONE PREPARE TO TEACH HEBREWS?

The first response to a great discovery should be to share that discovery with others. It is one delight to read Hebrews, but it is another joy to share its riches with friends. The history of interpreting Hebrews in both the church, where it played such a vital role in the early formation of Christology, and the academy, where it has witnessed a revival of interest, reminds all students of this book that there will be no end to interpreting it, until we all rest from our works and enter God's rest (4:10). That might feel daunting, but it is exciting too. There are treasures yet to be unearthed.

To prepare to do this work of discovery, one needs to engage with more than just Hebrews. Most important is to become familiar with the narratives of Israel from which the author draws. These include the story of Abraham (Gen 12–25), the people's redemption from Egypt and time in the wilderness (Exodus), the giving of the law and its specifications (Exod 19–40), especially for the sacrificial system (Leviticus), and the entry of the spies and the failure of the faith of the people (Num 13–14). A study of the Psalms also aids interpretation of Hebrews, not only the psalms the author quotes, which are primarily royal psalms focused on God's gracious treatment of the king of Israel, but also the psalms that exemplify the dynamics of honest praise demonstrated in Jesus's prayers to God, which the followers of Jesus replicate as they cry out to God. Finally, Jeremiah's prophecy of the new covenant (Jer 31:31–34) is situated within the Book of Consolation (Jer 30–33), and the prophet's desire for God's justice and mercy shows the need answered by the new covenant. Although these texts are most prominent in Hebrews, any study of Israel's Scriptures benefits the interpretation of this sermon that is so richly interwoven with God's promises to Israel.

This step is important for both the teaching and the preaching of Hebrews, but more tailored preparation is necessary depending on which trajectory one is following in any given instance. For teaching, after study of these Scriptures, another important step is to decide on an organizational structure for instruction. One may choose to study Hebrews thematically, grouping the first mention of ideas and then their development into categories, which could include topics such as creation, family, death, priesthood, covenant, and faith. Following the logic of the argument as presented in order is another option, noting the subtle developments even within the repetitions. One approach is to trace the comparisons in Hebrews in which Jesus is superior to the prophets (1:1–2), angels (1:4–14), Moses (3:1–6), Joshua (3:6–4:13), the priests (4:14–5:10; chs. 9–10), Melchizedek (ch. 7), the old covenant (8:1–10:18), and Mount Sinai (12:18–29). It is important that in all these comparisons Jesus's superiority stands in contrast not to something bad but to something good through which God worked. These people and processes helped those of Jesus's time to understand his identity and mission.

Another organizational option is to follow the alternating pattern between exposition and exhortation, the pattern in which the author invites his community to hear God speaking Scripture and then speaks to them directly with instructions for how they should respond. A study group could give attention to each one of these pairs.[4]

God's Speaking through Scripture	*Instructions for Living*
The excellency of Jesus (ch. 1)	The need to pay attention (2:1–4)
Jesus's humanity (2:5–18)	Being God's house (3:1–6)
Psalm 95 (3:7–19)	Going into God's rest (4:1–16)
Their High Priest (4:14–5:10)	Being mature like Abraham (5:11–6:20)
Melchizedek's order and the new covenant fulfilled by Christ (7:1–10:18)	Trusting the High Priest with faith (10:19–11:40)
The discipline of the Father (12:1–17)	Approaching the speaking God on Mount Zion (12:18–13:25)

4. These organizations are simply suggestions for study. To trace out the excellent theories for the complex organization of Hebrews, see George Guthrie, *The Structure of Hebrews: A Text-Linguistic Analysis* (Grand Rapids: Baker, 1998); Cynthia Westfall, *Discourse Analysis of the Letter to the Hebrews: The Relationship between Form and Meaning*, LNTS 297 (New York: T&T Clark, 2006); Jason A. Whitlark and Michael Wade Martin, *Inventing Hebrews: Design and Purpose in Ancient Rhetoric*, SNTSMS 171 (Cambridge: Cambridge University Press, 2018).

If a group does not have time for six sessions of study, the letter can also be partitioned into three sections divided by the similarly climactic paragraphs in 4:14–16 and 10:19–25 in which the author urges approach to God through Jesus the Messiah. This division keeps the focus on priesthood and covenant in the center of the sermon, with Jesus's faithfulness standing in contrast to the faithlessness of the wilderness generation at the beginning and then, at the end, the call to faithfulness from Jesus's life as well as others in Israel's past. Preparing by giving attention to Israel's Scriptures and deciding on a structure equips the teacher and their students to experience Hebrews in all its richness.

For preaching, one might also need to consider how Hebrews is situated within the liturgy, the time of the church year in which it is appointed as well as its points of connection with other texts of the day. For example, it appears in the Revised Common Lectionary, used by many Christian denominations, on both of the major Christian feasts, Christmas and Easter. On Christmas Day, congregants hear of the majesty of the Son from Hebrews 1. The Holy Week readings feature the priestly work of Christ mediating the new covenant (9:11–14) and the necessity of looking to him and the other faithful as believers run the race of faith (12:1–3). The Epistle reading for Good Friday is one of the major summative paragraphs of Hebrews, encouraging approach to God because of what God has done in the work of the Son (4:14–16/5:7–9, or 10:16–25). Finally, preachers have the option to focus on Hebrews in the latter weeks of Ordinary Time in Year B, where for seven weeks congregants hear portions of Hebrews 1–10, and during the mid-weeks of Ordinary Time in Year C, where chs. 11–13 appear. Hebrews is a superb text for this season in which the ongoing struggles and joys of the Christian life are presented to encourage deeper discipleship.

For those who have ears to hear, Hebrews appears frequently in the words of the liturgy. Rarely a week goes by when some line of a hymn does not strike me as reminiscent of Hebrews. Few are more densely evocative than William Chatterton Dix's "Allelulia! Sing to Jesus!" The fourth stanza proclaims:

> Alleluia! King eternal, thee the Lord of lords we own:
> Alleluia! Born of Mary, earth thy footstool, heaven thy throne:
> thou within the veil hast entered, robed in flesh, our great High
> Priest:
> thou on earth both Priest and Victim in the eucharistic feast.

It captures Hebrews' affirmation of the eternal Son's humanity, his session at God's right hand, and his priestly entrance before God to serve as High Priest, where he is both the one doing the offering and the one offered. The author could not have composed such powerful poetry without Hebrews.

In the readings as well, echoes of Hebrews frequently sound. For example, prayers for the baptism of the Lord are composed of portions of the Psalms cited in Hebrews 1. The Saturday daily prayers appeal to Hebrews' discussion of Sabbath. The ordination service reflects on Jesus's priesthood. Both the Compline service and the funeral service close with a benediction naming Jesus as the great shepherd of the sheep (13:20), so that at the end of a day and at the end of a life, souls are entrusted to his care. Any Christian preacher attentive to the theology of the Christian church will need to integrate proclamation of Hebrews into their homiletic ministry, and study of this sermon will prepare the preacher to do so confidently and fruitfully.

Hebrews exemplifies the promise it contains: God's word is living and active (4:12). As long as it is called "today" (3:15), this portion of God's inspired word will encourage and exhort, challenge and comfort, all those who are sharers in Christ on their way to dwelling with God forever. Although the close of this project represents the close of a significant chapter of my scholarly life, I look forward to sojourning with this sermon forever, learning from students, discovering new insights through preaching, and being shaped by its call to faithfulness. My hope is that any who devote energy to studying it will, in a sense, never put it down but allow its beautiful words to resonate in their souls for eternity as we join the celebration of the holy God and the righteous people through the eternally effective blood of Jesus, Son of God, Messiah, and High Priest.

SELECTED BIBLIOGRAPHY

Attridge, Harold W. *The Epistle to the Hebrews: A Commentary on the Epistle to the Hebrews*. Edited by Helmut Koester. Hermeneia. Philadelphia: Fortress, 1989.

Bauckham, Richard, Daniel R. Driver, Trevor A. Hart, and Nathan MacDonald, eds. *The Epistle to the Hebrews and Christian Theology*. Grand Rapids: Eerdmans, 2009.

———. *Jesus and the God of Israel: "God Crucified" and Other Studies on the New Testament's Christology of Divine Identity*. Grand Rapids: Eerdmans, 2009.

Beavis, Mary Ann, and HyeRan Kim-Cragg. *Hebrews*. Edited by Linda M. Maloney and Barbara E. Reid. Wisdom Commentary 54. Collegeville, MN: Liturgical Press, 2015.

Bowens, Lisa. *African American Readings of Paul: Reception, Resistance, and Transformation*. Grand Rapids: Eerdmans, 2020.

Brown, Raymond. *The Message of Hebrews: Christ above All*. The Bible Speaks Today. Downers Grove, IL: InterVarsity Press, 1984.

Bruce, F. F. *The Epistle to the Hebrews*. Rev. ed. NICNT. Grand Rapids: Eerdmans, 1990.

Calvin, John. *The Epistle of Paul the Apostle to the Hebrews; and the First and Second Epistles of St. Peter*. Translated by William B. Johnston. Edited by David W. Torrance and Thomas F. Torrance. Calvin's New Testament Commentaries 12. Grand Rapids: Eerdmans, 1963.

Charles, Elizabeth Rundle. *Within the Veil: Studies in the Epistle to the Hebrews*. London: SPCK, 1888.

Cockerill, Gareth Lee. *The Epistle to the Hebrews*. NICNT. Grand Rapids: Eerdmans, 2012.

deSilva, David A. *Perseverance in Gratitude: A Socio-rhetorical Commentary on the Epistle "to the Hebrews."* Grand Rapids: Eerdmans, 2000.

Docherty, Susan E. *The Use of the Old Testament in Hebrews: A Case Study in Early Jewish Bible Interpretation*. WUNT II.260. Tübingen: Mohr Siebeck, 2009.

Ellingworth, Paul. *The Epistle to the Hebrews: A Commentary on the Greek Text*. New International Greek Testament Commentary. Grand Rapids: Eerdmans, 1993.

Griffiths, Jonathan I. *Hebrews and Divine Speech*. LNTS 507. London: Bloomsbury, 2014.

Harris, Dana M. *Hebrews*. Exegetical Guide to the Greek New Testament. Nashville: B&H Academic, 2019.

Healy, Mary. *Hebrews*. Catholic Commentary on Sacred Scripture. Grand Rapids: Baker Academic, 2016.

Heen, Erik M., and Philip D. W. Krey, eds. *Hebrews*. Ancient Christian Commentary on Scripture, New Testament 10. Downers Grove, IL: InterVarsity Press, 2005.

Jamieson, R. B. *The Paradox of Sonship: Christology in the Epistle to the Hebrews*. Studies in Christian Doctrine and Scripture. Downers Grove, IL: IVP Academic, 2021.

John Chrysostom. *Saint Chrysostom: Homilies on the Gospel of St. John and the Epistle to the Hebrews*. Vol. 14 of *The Nicene and Post-Nicene Fathers*, Series 1. Edited by Philip Schaff. 14 vols. New York: The Christian Literature Company, 1886–1889.

Jobes, Karen H. *Letters to the Church: A Survey of Hebrews and the General Epistles*. Grand Rapids: Zondervan, 2011.

Johnson, Luke Timothy. *Hebrews: A Commentary*. New Testament Library. Louisville: Westminster John Knox, 2006.

Kleinig, John. *Hebrews*. Concordia Commentary. Saint Louis: Concordia, 2017.

Koester, Craig R. *Hebrews: A New Translation with Introduction and Commentary*. AB 36. New York: Doubleday, 2001.

Laansma, Jon. *The Letter to the Hebrews: A Commentary for Preaching, Teaching, and Bible Study*. Eugene, OR: Cascade, 2017.

Laansma, Jon, George H. Guthrie, and Cynthia Long Westfall, eds. *So Great a Salvation: A Dialogue on the Atonement in Hebrews*. LNTS 516. London: T&T Clark, 2019.

Lane, William L. *Hebrews 1–8*. WBC 47A. Dallas: Word, 1991.

———. *Hebrews 9–13*. WBC 47B. Dallas: Word, 1991.

Long, D. Stephen. *Hebrews*. Belief: A Theological Commentary on the Bible. Louisville: Westminster John Knox, 2011.

Mason, Eric F., and Kevin B. McCruden, eds. *Reading the Epistle to the Hebrews: A Resource for Students*. RBS 66. Atlanta: Society of Biblical Literature, 2011.

Moffitt, David M. *Atonement and the Logic of Resurrection in the Epistle to the Hebrews*. NovTSup 141. Boston: Brill, 2011.

Peeler, Amy. "'Leading Many Sons to Glory': Historical Implications of Exclusive Language in the Epistle to the Hebrews." *Religions* 12 (2021): 844–57.

———. *You Are My Son: The Family of God in the Epistle to the Hebrews*. LNTS 486. London: Bloomsbury T&T Clark, 2014.

Perrin, Nicholas. *Jesus the Priest*. Grand Rapids: Baker Academic, 2018.

Pierce, Madison N. *Divine Discourse in the Epistle to the Hebrews: The Recontextualization of Spoken Quotations in Scripture*. SNTSMS 178. Cambridge: Cambridge University Press, 2020.

Regev, Eyal. *The Temple in Early Christianity: Experiencing the Sacred*. New Haven: Yale University Press, 2019.

Rittgers, Ronald K., ed. *Hebrews, James*. Reformation Commentary on Scripture, New Testament 13. Downers Grove, IL: IVP Academic, 2017.

Rothschild, Clare K. *Hebrews as Pseudepigraphon: The History and Significance of the Pauline Attribution of Hebrews*. WUNT 235. Tübingen: Mohr Siebeck, 2009.

Schenck, Kenneth L. *Cosmology and Eschatology in Hebrews: The Settings of the Sacrifice*. SNTSMS 143. Cambridge: Cambridge University Press, 2008.

———. *Explanatory Notes on the Sermon of Hebrews*. Eugene, OR: Cascade, 2023.

———. *A New Perspective on Hebrews: Rethinking the Parting of the Ways*. Lanham, MD: Lexington Books/Fortress Academic, 2019.

———. *Understanding the Book of Hebrews: The Story Behind the Sermon*. Louisville: Westminster John Knox, 2003.

Schreiner, Thomas R. *Hebrews*. Evangelical Biblical Theology Commentary. Bellingham, WA: Lexham Academic, 2020.

Thomas Aquinas. *Commentary on the Letter of Saint Paul to the Hebrews*. Edited by John Mortensen and Enrique Alarcón. Translated by Fabian R. Larcher. Latin/English Edition of the Works of St. Thomas Aquinas 41. Lander, WY: Aquinas Institute for the Study of Sacred Doctrine, 2012.

Thompson, James W. *Hebrews*. Paideia. Grand Rapids: Baker Academic, 2008.

Urga, Abeneazer G., Edward L. Smither, and Linda P. Saunders. *Reading Hebrews Missiologically: The Missionary Motive, Message, and Methods of Hebrews*. Littleton, CO: William Carey, 2023.

Walton, John D., and D. Brent Sandy. *The Lost World of Scripture: Ancient Literary Culture and Biblical Authority*. Downers Grove, IL: IVP Academic, 2013.

Witherington, Ben, III. *Letters and Homilies for Jewish Christians: A Socio-rhetorical Commentary on Hebrews, James and Jude*. Downers Grove, IL: IVP Academic, 2007.

INDEX OF SUBJECTS

INDEX OF AUTHORS

INDEX OF SCRIPTURE AND OTHER ANCIENT SOURCES

Old Testament

Genesis

Proverbs

Ecclesiastes

Isaiah

Greco-Roman Writings